# SOCIOLOGY
## The Points of the Compass

# SOCIOLOGY
## The Points of the Compass

**Robert J. Brym**
University of Toronto

**John Lie**
University of California, Berkeley

NELSON EDUCATION

NELSON EDUCATION

Sociology: The Points of the Compass

by Robert J. Brym and John Lie

**Associate Vice President, Editorial Director:**
Evelyn Veitch

**Editor-in-Chief:**
Anne Williams

**Executive Editor:**
Laura Macleod

**Senior Acquisitions Editor:**
Scott Couling

**Marketing Manager:**
Heather Leach

**Developmental Editor:**
Sandy Matos

**Photo Researcher and Permissions Coordinator:**
Melody Tolson

**Senior Content Production Manager:**
Natalia Denesiuk Harris

**Copy Editor:**
Dawn Hunter

**Proofreader:**
Wayne Herrington

**Indexer:**
Jin Tan

**Manufacturing Coordinator:**
Loretta Lee

**Design Director:**
Ken Phipps

**Managing Designer:**
Katherine Strain

**Interior Design:**
Iris Glaser

**Cover Design:**
Dianna Little

**Cover Image:**
Visual Language Royalty Free Photograph/Fotosearch

**Compositor:**
ICC Macmillan Inc.

**Printer:**
Quebecor World



Printed and bound in the United States
1 2 3 4 11 10 09 08

For more information contact Nelson Education Ltd., 1120 Birchmount Road, Toronto, Ontario, M1K 5G4. Or you can visit our Internet site at http://www.nelson.com



**Library and Archives Canada Cataloguing in Publication Data**

Brym, Robert J., 1951–
Sociology: the points of the compass / Robert J. Brym and John Lie.

Includes bibliographical references and index.
ISBN 978-0-17-644239-2

1. Sociology—Textbooks. I. Lie, John II. Title.

HM586.B792 2008 301
C2008-900168-0

ISBN-13: 978-0-17-644239-2
ISBN-10: 0-17-644239-1

For Rhonda, Shira, Talia, and Ariella, with thanks and love.

**Robert Brym**

For Charis Thompson, Thomas Cussions, Jessica Cussins, and Charlotte Lie, with thanks and love.

**John Lie**

**Robert J. Brym** (pronounced "brim") studied in Canada and Israel and received his Ph.D. from the University of Toronto, where he is now on faculty and especially enjoys teaching introductory sociology to 1400 students every year. He has served as the editor of several scholarly journals, and he has won numerous awards for his teaching and scholarly work, which has been translated into half a dozen languages. His main areas of research are in political sociology, race and ethnic relations, and the sociology of culture. His major books include *Intellectuals and Politics* (London and Boston: Allen & Unwin, 1980); *From Culture to Power* (Toronto: Oxford University Press, 1989), with Bonnie Fox; *The Jews of Moscow, Kiev, and Minsk* (New York: New York University Press, 1994), with Rozalina Ryvkina; and *Sociology as a Life or Death Issue* (Toronto: Nelson, 2008). He currently heads a funded research project on suicide bombers in the Middle East.

**John Lie** (pronounced "lee") was born in South Korea, grew up in Japan and Hawaii, and attended Harvard University. Currently, he is Class of 1959 Professor and Dean of International and Area Studies at the University of California at Berkeley. He has also taught at the University of Michigan, the University of Illinois at Urbana-Champaign, the University of Hawaii at Manoa, the University of Oregon, Harvard University, and universities in Japan, South Korea, Taiwan, and New Zealand. His primary research interests are comparative macrosociology and social theory. His major publications include *Blue Dreams: Korean Americans and the Los Angeles Riots* (Cambridge, MA: Harvard University Press, 1995), *Han Unbound: The Political Economy of South Korea* (Stanford, CA: Stanford University Press, 1998), *Multiethnic Japan* (Cambridge, MA: Harvard University Press, 2001), and *Modern Peoplehood* (Cambridge, MA: Harvard University Press, 2004). He has taught introductory sociology classes ranging in size from 3 to more than 700 students in several countries and hopes that this book will stimulate your sociological imagination.

# brief table of CONTENTS

# PART 1 Foundations 1

## 1 A Sociological Compass 2



# PART 2 Basic Social Processes 39

## 2 Culture 40

## 3 Socialization 68

## 4 From Social Interaction to Social Organizations 96

## 5 Deviance and Crime 132

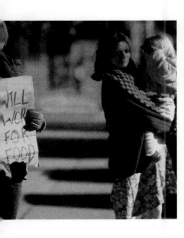

## 7 Race and Ethnicity 198

## 8 Sexuality and Gender 229

## PART 4 Institutions 265

### 9 Families 266

### 10 Religion and Education 300

# list of BOXES

## Sociology at the Movies



## Social Policy: What Do You Think?



## Mass Media and Society



## You and the Social World

# The Points of the Compass

*It was the best of times, it was the worst of times, it was the age of wisdom, it was the age of foolishness, it was the epoch of belief, it was the epoch of incredulity, it was the season of Light, it was the season of Darkness, it was the spring of hope, it was the winter of despair, we had everything before us, we had nothing before us, we were all going direct to Heaven, we were all going direct the other way—in short, the period was so far like the present period, that some of its noisiest authorities insisted on its being received, for good or for evil, in the superlative degree of comparison only.*

— Charles Dickens, *A Tale of Two Cities* (2004 [1859])

Dickens refers to the end of the eighteenth century, yet he offers a prophetic description of the times in which we live. We, too, set sail at the dawn of a new millennium, an age of superlatives, an age of uncertainty.

The Soviet Union was formally dissolved on 21 December 1991. On that day we learned that even a seemingly vast superpower can collapse and splinter almost overnight. One of the world's leading historians wrote that the twentieth century ended with the fall of the USSR, ushering in a new century of mounting indeterminacy (Hobsbawm, 1994). As if to prove the point, scientists announced on 26 June 2000 that they had finished sequencing the human genome, beginning a new era of scientific breakthroughs. Yet shortly after, the United Nations forecast that 85 million people will die of AIDS by 2020, convincing us (if we had not already been convinced) that, despite remarkable medical advances, the plague is still with us. Then, on 11 September 2001, terrorists attacked the World Trade Center and the Pentagon, killing about 3000 people. We saw the world's mood and its political and economic outlook buoyant one day, uncertain the next.

The world is an unpredictable place. It is especially disorienting for students just entering adulthood. We wrote this book to show undergraduates that sociology can nonetheless help them make sense of their lives, however uncertain they may appear to be. We hope it will serve as their sociological compass. Moreover, we show that sociology can be a liberating practical activity, not just an abstract intellectual exercise. By revealing the opportunities and constraints we face, sociology can help us navigate our lives, teaching us who we are and what we can become in this particular social and historical context. We cannot know what the future will bring, but we can at least know what choices we have and the likely consequences of our actions. Sociology can help us create the best possible future. That has always been sociology's principal justification, and so it should be today.

# From the Publisher

The editorial, marketing, and sales teams at Nelson Education Ltd. have worked alongside our authors to publish a sociology text that meets the specific needs of both students and instructors in Canadian colleges.

We began this project by inviting a group of Canadian college sociology instructors to participate in an interior design focus group. Led by our editorial and design teams, we discussed the importance of design layout and readability, and the need to maintain appropriate content. The panel's findings were clear: (1) students have difficulty relating to traditional-looking textbooks, and (2) students' engagement with the content can be dramatically enhanced when the material is presented in a dynamic and accessible manner. With the panel's findings to guide us, we have created a text in *Sociology: The Points of the Compass* that both students and instructors will find visually appealing, accessible, and engaging. Nelson Education Ltd. and the authors would like to thank the following participants for their time and expertise:

» Brenda Bennett, *George Brown College*
» Deb Boutilier, *Niagara College*
» Daniele Cerri, *Sheridan College*
» John Elias, *Humber College*
» Allison M. Jones, *Mohawk College*
» Maureen Murphy-Fricker, *Conestoga College*

Although design was a major focus with *Sociology: The Points of the Compass*, so too was content. In the fall of 2006, Nelson Education Ltd. invited college instructors teaching sociology from across Canada to participate in an open online survey. Through this survey we wanted to better understand the unique challenges faced by college sociology instructors and how we at Nelson, along with our author team, could create a book that met the specific content needs of a one-semester college introduction to sociology course. The table of contents in *Sociology: The Points of the Compass* reflects the overwhelming responses we received from this survey. Nelson Education Ltd. and our authors would like to thank the following college professors and instructors for their feedback:

» Kate Anderson, *Humber College*
» Cynthia Booth, M.A., *Cambrian College*
» Anne C. Charles, B.A., M.Sc., *Conestoga College*
» Patricia Corcoran, *George Brown College*
» Linda Frank, *Mohawk College*
» Tom Groulx, *St. Clair College*
» Kelly Henley, *St. Clair College of Applied Arts and Technology*
» Sue Honsberger, *Algonquin College*
» Mark Ihnat, *Humber College*
» Georgina King, B.A., M.Ed., *Seneca College*
» John Patterson, *Canadore College*
» Oliver R. Stoetzer, *Fanshawe College*
» William Larry Upper, *Algonquin College*
» Neil Jamieson-Williams, *Mohawk College*
» Carolyne Willoughby, *Durham College*
» Amanda Zavitz-Gocan, Ph.D., *Fanshawe College*

Our lead author, Robert Brym, is well known for his ability to effectively introduce the concepts of sociology to students who are new to the discipline. His approach creates an open learning environment for students to discover and conceptualize sociology in today's society. Robert has given *Sociology: The Points of the Compass* a fresh voice, building on a foundation laid in previous works by Robert, John Lie, and Steve Rytina. This book strongly represents a sociologist's passion for his work and enthusiasm for educating new sociologists.

Nelson Education Ltd. takes great pride in the publication of *Sociology: The Points of the Compass*. With the combined efforts of the Nelson higher education team, our authors, and the feedback of college professors and instructors, this text is sure to be one that students and instructors alike will use and enjoy.

# Unique Features

We have tried to keep sociology's main purpose and relevance front and centre in this book. As a result, this book differs from other major introductory sociology textbooks in four important ways:

1. ***Connections between people and the social world:*** *To varying degrees, all introductory sociology textbooks try to show students how their personal experiences are connected to the larger social world. However, we employ two devices to make these connections clearer than in other textbooks. First, we illustrate key sociological ideas by using examples from popular culture that resonate with students' interests and experiences. For example, to show how radical subcultures often become commercialized, we analyze hip-hop and the Osbournes. To demonstrate how functionalists study religion, we discuss the Stanley Cup Finals. We think these and many other examples speak directly to today's students about important sociological ideas in terms they understand, thus making the connection between self and society clear.*

   *We also developed several boxed pedagogical features to draw the connection between students' experiences and the larger social world.* ***Social Policy: What Do You Think?*** *sets out public policy alternatives on a range of pressing social issues. It teaches students that sociology can be a matter of the most urgent practical importance. Students also learn they can have a say in the development of public policy.* ***Sociology at the Movies*** *takes a universal and popular element of contemporary culture and renders it sociologically relevant. We provide brief reviews of movies, most of them recent releases, and highlight the sociological insights they contain.* ***Mass Media and Society*** *relates sociological problems that we discuss in the book to issues involving the Internet, TV, and other mass media. In* ***You and the Social World*** *we repeatedly challenge students to consider how and why their own lives conform to, or deviate from, various patterns of social relations and actions. These pedagogical aids include critical thinking questions and research exercises that instructors will find helpful in generating classroom discussion and assigning work outside of class. Finally, each chapter ends with a brief section called* ***The Points of the Compass*** *that relates the chapter's material to the book's overall theme.*

2. ***What to think versus how to think:*** *All textbooks teach students both* what *to think about a subject and* how *to think about it from a particular disciplinary perspective. In our judgment, however, introductory sociology textbooks usually place too much stress on the "what" and not enough on the "how." As a result, they sometimes read more like encyclopedias than invitations to look at the world in a new way. We have tipped the balance in the other direction. Of course, this book contains definitions and literature reviews. It features standard pedagogical aids, such as a list of Learning Outcomes at the beginning of each chapter, and a Chapter Summary, a Key Terms list, a list of Recommended Web Sites, and a set of Questions to Consider at the end of each chapter. However, we devote more space than other textbooks to showing how sociologists think. We often relate a personal anecdote to highlight an issue's importance, present contending interpretations of the issue, and then adduce data to show the merits of the various interpretations. When evidence warrants, we reject theories and endorse others. Thus, many sections of the book read more like a simplified journal article than an encyclopedia. If this sounds just like what sociologists do professionally, then we have achieved our aim: to present a less antiseptic, more realistic, and therefore intrinsically exciting account of how sociologists practise their*

**Social Policy: What Do You Think?** encourages students to become aware of social policy in Canada and shows them that they, too, can have a say in the development of public policy.

5.2

of violence" (quoted in Grange, 2000). He has a point. Hockey glorifies violence. A Web site even exists where you can find videos of every fight in professional hockey (neatly indexed by year, team, and player), comment on the fight, and vote on who won it. Cumulative voting results are conveniently displayed in bar graphs (see http://www.hockeyfights.com/).

## SOCIAL POLICY: WHAT DO YOU THINK?

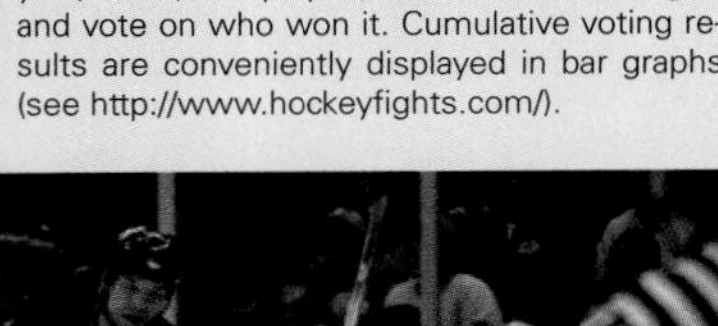

**Should We Define Hockey Violence as Criminal, Deviant, or Normal?**

On 8 March 2007, Chris
wielded his hockey stick
blow to the head of N
Hollweg. Miraculously, I
injury. Simon received a
weeks preceding the in
Chris Neil had delivered
a concussion but resulte
while New Jersey De
delivered a high body bl
that resulted in no penal
The NHL is inconsis
hockey violence, perhaps
public are divided over v
considered deviant or no
be criminal. Seldom do
charges being laid, and pl
acquitted or given only m
Vancouver Canucks' Todd

Students will be intrigued by **Sociology at the Movies**—a look at sociological insights that can be gleaned from current films demonstrates sociology's vitality and relevance to their own lives.

3.2

## SOCIOLOGY AT THE MOVIES

Owen Wilson and Vince Vaughan in a scene from *The Wedding Crashers*

***The Wedding Crashers*** **(2005)**

John Beckwith (Owen Wilson) and Jeremy Gray (Vince Vaughn) are 30-something partners in a divorce mediation firm. Neither is married because of their belief that, as Jeremy says during one particularly heated mediation, "the real enemy here is the institution of marriage. It's not realistic. It's crazy."

So what do these handsome, single, professional men do for excitement come spring? They crash wed-

retirement savings), they represent a growing category of young adults who are often a big worry to their elders.

Between 1981 and 2001, the percentage of Canadians between the ages of 25 and 34 living with their parents doubled—rising from 12 percent to 24 percent for the 25–29 age cohort and from 5 percent to 11 percent for the 30–34 age cohort (Beaupré, Turcotte, and Milan, 2007). One reason for this phenomenon is economic. In the first few decades after World War II, housing and education costs were low, and the number of years a person had to spend in school to get a steady, well-paying job was

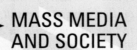

11.4

**Mass Media and Society** integrates the ideas and theories presented in the text with those in the media that students interact with everyday.

## MASS MEDIA AND SOCIETY

Subcomandante Marcos

**The First Postmodern Revolution**

An example of a social movement using modern technology to go global involves the peasants of Chiapas, a southern Mexican province. They participated in the 1910 Mexican Revolution and in a more globalized uprising against the Mexican government in 1994. Oppressed by Europeans and their descendants for nearly 500 years, the poor, indigenous people of southern Mexico were now facing a government edict preventing them from gaining access to farmland. They wanted the land for subsistence agriculture. But the government wanted to make sure the land stayed in the hands of large, Hispanic ranchers and farmers, who could earn foreign revenue by exporting goods to the United States and Canada under the terms of the new North American Free Trade Agreement. The peasants seized a large number of ranches and farms. A mysterious masked man known simply as Subcomandante Marcos was their leader. Effectively using the Internet and the international mass media as his secret weapon against the Mexican government, Marcos led what the *New York Times* called "the first postmodern revolution," combining a peasant uprising with the World Wide Web, short-wave radio, and photo spreads in *Marie Claire*. Ingeniously keeping the movement in the international public eye by using modern technologies of communication, Marcos mobilized support abroad and limited the retaliatory actions of the Mexican government (*A Place Called Chiapas*, 1998; Jones, 1999).

**You and the Social World** challenges students to think about how patterns of social relations and actions are connected to their own lives.

9.2

# YOU AND THE SOCIAL WORLD

### The Abortion Issue

Many shades of opinion and ambiguities exist in people's attitudes toward the abortion issue. At the extremes, however, we can distinguish between right-to-life and pro-choice advocates. Right-to-life advocates argue that life begins at conception. Therefore, they say, abortion destroys human life and is morally indefensible. They advocate adoption instead of abortion. In their opinion, the pro-choice option is selfish, expressing greater concern for career advancement and sexual pleasure than moral responsibility. In contrast, pro-choice advocates argue that every woman has the right to choose what happens to her own body and that bearing an unwanted child can harm not only a woman's career but the child too. For example, unwanted children are more likely to be neglected or abused. They are more likely to get in trouble with the law because of inadequate adult supervision and discipline. Furthermore, according to pro-choice advocates, religious doctrines claiming that life begins at conception are arbitrary. In any case, they point out, such ideas have no place in law because they violate the principle of separation of church and state.

**WRITING ASSIGNMENT**

- *What are your views on abortion? To what degree are your views influenced by your social characteristics (family income, education, religiosity, etc.)? How do your views compare with those of people with social characteristics similar to yours? Table 9.3 shows some results from one survey on the abortion issue. Why do certain social characteristics influence public opinion on abortion in more or less predictable ways? What variables other than those listed in Table 9.3 might influence public opinion on the abortion issue? Answer these questions in about 500 words.*

Each chapter's ideas are summed up in **The Points of the Compass.**

## The Points of the Compass

The founders of sociology developed their ideas to help solve the great sociological puzzle of their time—the causes and consequences of the Industrial Revolution. This raises two interesting questions: What are the great sociological puzzles of *our* time? How are today's sociologists responding to the challenges presented by the social settings in which *we* live? We devote the rest of this book to answering these questions in depth.

It would be wrong to suggest that the research of tens of thousands of sociologists around the world is animated by just a few key issues. Viewed up close, sociology today is a heterogeneous enterprise enlivened by hundreds of theoretical debates, some focused on small issues relevant to particular fields and geographical areas, others focused on big issues that seek to characterize the entire historical era for humanity as a whole. Among the big issues, two stand out. Perhaps the greatest sociological puzzles of our time are the causes and consequences of the Postindustrial Revolution and globalization.

The **Postindustrial Revolution** is the technology-driven shift from employment in factories to employment in offices, and the consequences of that shift for nearly all human activities (Bell, 1973; Toffler, 1990). For example, as a result of the Postindustrial Revolution, non-manual occupations now outnumber manual occupations, and women have been drawn into the system of higher education and the paid labour force in large numbers. This shift has transformed the way we work and study, our standard of living, the way we form families, and much else. **Globalization** is the process by which formerly separate economies, nation-states, and cultures are becoming tied together and people are becoming increasingly aware of their growing interdependence (Giddens, 1990: 64; Guillén, 2001). Especially in recent decades, rapid increases in the volume of international trade, travel, and communication have broken down the isolation and independence of most countries and people. Also contributing to globalization is the growth of many institutions that bind corporations, companies, and cultures together. These processes have caused people to depend more than ever on people in other countries for products, services, ideas, and even a sense of identity.

The text features standard **pedagogical aids**—but more importantly, it shows how sociologists actually go about the business of solving sociological puzzles.

## Key Terms

bureaucracy (p. 116)
competition (p. 111)
conflict theories of social interaction (p. 110)
crude death rate (p. 100)
domination (p. 111)
dramaturgical analysis (p. 104)
dyad (p. 120)
emotion labour (p. 100)
emotion management (p. 99)
ethnomethodology (p. 106)
exchange theory (p. 103)
formal organizations (p. 125)
groupthink (p. 122)
in-group (p. 123)
mesostructures (p. 111)
out-group (p. 123)
power (p. 110)
primary groups (p. 120)
rational choice theory (p. 103)
reference group (p. 124)
role distancing (p. 104)
role set (p. 98)
secondary groups (p. 120)
social category (p. 120)
social group (p. 120)
social interaction (p. 97)
social network (p. 117)
status cues (p. 108)
status set (p. 98)
stereotypes (p. 108)
triad (p. 120)

## Questions to Consider

1. Write a list of your current and former girlfriends or boyfriends. Indicate the race, religion, age, and height of each person on the list. How similar or different are you from the people with whom you have chosen to be intimate? What does this list tell you about the social distribution of intimacy? Is love blind? What criteria other than race, religion, age, and height might affect the social distribution of intimacy?
2. In what sense (if any) is it reasonable to claim that all of social life consists of role-playing and that people have no "true selves," just ensembles of roles?
3. Would you have acted any differently from ordinary Germans if you were living in Nazi Germany? Why or why not? What if you were a member of a Nazi police battalion? Would you have been a traitor to your group? Why or why not?

## Web Resources

Companion Web Site for This Book
http://www.pointsofthecompass.nelson.com

*craft. Said differently, one of the strengths of this book is that it does not present sociology as a set of immutable truths. Instead, it shows how sociologists actually go about the business of solving sociological puzzles.*

3. ***Objectivity versus subjectivity:*** *Sociologists since Max Weber have understood that sociologists—indeed, all scientists—are members of society whose thinking and research are influenced by the social and historical context in which they work. Yet introductory sociology textbooks tend to present a stylized and not very sociological view of the research process. They emphasize sociology's objectivity and the hypothetico-deductive method of reasoning, for the most part ignoring the more subjective factors that go into the research mix (Lynch and Bogen, 1997). We think this emphasis is a pedagogical error. In our own teaching, we have found that drawing the connection between objectivity and subjectivity in sociological research makes the discipline more appealing to students. It shows how research issues are connected to the lives of real people and how sociology is related to students' existential concerns. Accordingly, in most chapters of* Sociology: The Points of the Compass, *we feature a* **Personal Anecdote** *that explains how certain sociological issues first arose in our own minds. We often adopt a narrative style because stories let students understand ideas on an emotional as well as an intellectual level, and when we form an emotional attachment to ideas, they stay with us more effectively than if our attachment is solely intellectual. We also place the ideas of important sociological figures in social and historical context. We show how sociological methodologies serve as a reality check, but we also make it clear that socially grounded personal concerns often lead sociologists to decide which aspects of reality are worth checking on in the first place. We believe* Sociology: The Points of the Compass *is unique in presenting a realistic and balanced account of the role of objectivity and subjectivity in the research process.*

**Personal Anecdotes** show how sociological issues first arose in the minds of the authors.

In 1941, the large stone and glass train station was one of the proudest structures in Smolensk, a provincial capital of about 100 000 people on Russia's western border. Always bustling, it was especially busy on the morning of June 28. Besides the usual passengers and well-wishers, hundreds of Soviet Red Army soldiers were nervously talking, smoking, writing hurried letters to their loved ones, and sleeping fitfully on the station floor while waiting for their train. Nazi troops had invaded the nearby city of Minsk in Belarus a couple of days before. The Soviet soldiers were being positioned to defend Russia against the inevitable German onslaught.

Robert Brym's father, then in his 20s, had been standing in line for nearly two hours to buy food when he noticed flares arching over the station. Within seconds, Stuka bombers, the pride of the German air force, swept down, releasing their bombs just before pulling out of their dive. Inside the station, shards of glass, blocks of stone, and mounds of earth fell indiscriminately on sleeping soldiers and nursing mothers alike. Everyone panicked. People trampled over one another to get out. In minutes, the train station was rubble.

4. ***Diversity and a global perspective:*** *It is gratifying to see how much less parochial introductory sociology textbooks are today than they were just 20 years ago. Contemporary textbooks highlight gender and race issues. They broaden students' understanding of the world by comparing Canada with other societies. They show how global processes affect local issues and how local issues affect global processes. Sociology: The Points of the Compass is no different in this regard. We, too, have made diversity and globalization prominent themes of this book. We make frequent and effective use of cross-national comparisons. And we remain sensitive to gender and race issues throughout. This has been easy for us because we are members of racial and ethnic minority groups. We are multilingual. We have lived in other countries for extended periods. And we have published widely on countries other than Canada. As you will see in the following pages, our backgrounds have enabled us to bring greater depth to issues of diversity and globalization than do other textbooks.*

# Supplements

At Nelson Education Ltd., we believe a textbook is only one resource available for learning and teaching. A full range of high-quality ancillaries has been prepared to help instructors and students get the most out of *Sociology: The Points of the Compass.*

## *Supplements for Instructors*

### Instructor's Manual (ISBN 978-0-17-647354-9)

The Instructor's Manual contains lecture outlines, supplemental lecture material, suggested activities for students, and Internet and InfoTrac® College Edition exercises. It is available in paper, online on the password-protected Instructor's Web site at **http://www.pointsofthecompass.nelson.com**, and electronically on the Instructor's Resource CD-ROM.

### Test Bank (ISBN 978-0-17-647353-2)

The Test Bank consists of multiple-choice questions and true/false questions for each chapter, all with rejoinders and page references. This supplement also includes short answer and extended essay questions. The electronic version of the Test Bank is available on the Instructor's Resource CD-ROM. The print version of the Test Bank is available from your Nelson Education Ltd. sales representative.

## Instructor's Resource CD-ROM (ISBN 978-0-17-647355-6)

Your complete teaching tool to supplement *Sociology: The Points of the Compass*, the Instructor's Resource CD-ROM contains a suite of teaching resources. Microsoft® PowerPoint® lecture slides, the Instructor's Manual, and the *ExamView* Computerized Test Bank are all contained for convenience on one CD-ROM.

## InfoTrac® College Edition

**http://www.infotrac-college.com**

Ignite discussions or augment your lectures with the latest developments in sociology and societal change. Create your own course reader by selecting articles or by using the search keywords provided at the end of each chapter. *InfoTrac® College Edition* gives you and your students four months of free access to an easy-to-use online database of reliable, full-length articles (not abstracts) from hundreds of top academic journals and popular sources. Among the journals available 24 hours a day, seven days a week are the *Canadian Review of Sociology and Anthropology*, the *Canadian Journal of Sociology, Canadian Ethnic Studies, Public Policy*, the *American Journal of Sociology*, *Social Forces*, *Social Research*, and *Sociology*. Contact your Nelson Education Ltd. representative for more information. *InfoTrac® College Edition* is available only to North American college and university students. Journals are subject to change.

## *Think Outside the Book:* Nelson Videos for Introductory Sociology

This six-volume set of 44 video segments, each 5 to 30 minutes in length, was created to stimulate discussions of topics raised in sociology. This newly released DVD set contains current and relevant footage that can easily be used in your classroom. Robert J. Brym chose the selections based on his years of experience as a teacher and researcher. Produced in conjunction with Face to Face Media, the selections have been edited to optimize their impact in the classroom. Many of the selections are taken from films that have won national and international awards. Six of the selections are from the celebrated work of Gwynne Dyer, one of Canada's leading media intellectuals. Videos and an accompanying Video Guide and Instructor's Manual are available from your local Nelson Education Ltd. sales and editorial representative. Visit **http://www.thinkoutsidethebook.nelson.com** for more information.

Newly released! *Think Outside the Book* covers current sociological topics that will highlight the discussions in your course.

## JoinIn™ on TurningPoint®

Book-specific JoinIn™ content from *Sociology: The Points of the Compass* for classroom response systems allows you to transform your classroom and assess your students' progress with instant in-class quizzes and polls. Our exclusive agreement to offer TurningPoint® software lets you pose book-specific questions and display students' answers seamlessly within the Microsoft® PowerPoint® slides of your own lecture, in conjunction with the "clicker" hardware of your choice. Enhance how your students interact with you, your lecture, and one another. For college and university adopters only. Contact your local Nelson Education Ltd. representative to learn more.

## Supplements for Students

### InfoTrac® College Edition

Included free with every new text, InfoTrac® is a world-class online university library that offers the full text of articles from more than 5000 scholarly and popular publications—updated daily and going back as far as 20 years. InfoTrac is a great research tool and the included password allows unlimited access for four months. Visit InfoTrac® Online at **http://www.infotrac-college.com**.

### Companion Book Web Site

**http://www.pointsofthecompass.nelson.com**

The book's Web site contains an unusually rich collection of materials that are appropriate for review and further exploration. From chapter-specific quizzes and Weblinks that will help students clarify concepts and review for tests, to materials on studying sociology, this free resource is an important component of the learning package. This Web site also includes an interactive glossary, flashcards, and crossword puzzles. The Lecture Hall provides access to more than 20 sociologically relevant lectures, interviews, and discussions of varying length by professors from leading universities in Canada, the United States, and the United Kingdom. Now included in this set are several lectures from Robert J. Brym. Transcripts of Brym's lectures are also available in Microsoft® Word for downloading. Instructors can download the Instructor's Manual and the Microsoft® PowerPoint® series directly from the site.

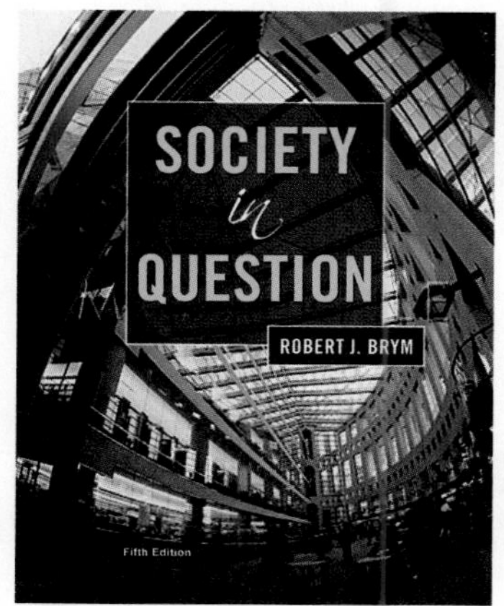

*Society in Question,* fifth edition

## Additional Resources

### *Society in Question,* Fifth Edition

*Society in Question,* fifth edition, by Robert J. Brym, is an introductory sociology reader that combines Canadian and international readings. This reader provides balanced coverage of the approaches and methods in current sociology as well as unique and surprising perspectives on many major sociological topics. All readings have been chosen for their ability to speak directly to contemporary Canadian students about how sociology can enable them to make sense of their lives in a rapidly changing world. (ISBN 978-0-17-610281-4)

ROBERT J. BRYM

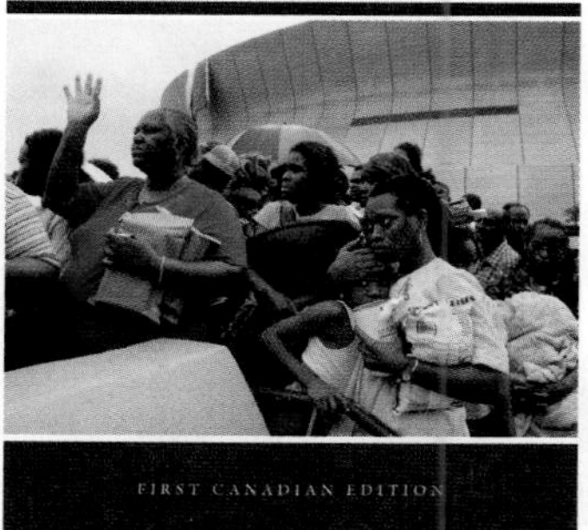


### *Sociology as a Life or Death Issue*

In a series of beautifully written essays on hip hop culture, Palestinian suicide bombers, and the plight of victims of hurricanes in the Caribbean region and on the coast of the Gulf of Mexico, Robert Brym introduces sociology by analyzing the social causes of death. In doing so he reveals the powerful social forces that help to determine who lives and who dies, and demonstrates the promise of a well-informed sociological understanding of the world. Reviewers have said that *Sociology as a Life or Death Issue* is the most accessible book for undergraduates since Becker's *Outsiders* and that it accomplishes what Mills's *The Sociological Imagination* did for an earlier generation. This brief and inexpensive volume is an eye-opener, an inspiration, and a guide for students of sociology and for anyone with an inquiring mind and hopes for a better world for future generations. (ISBN 978-0-17-650041-2)

## *Controversies in Canadian Sociology*

*Controversies in Canadian Sociology*, by M. Reza Nakhaie, explores theoretical, conceptual, and empirical contacts and debates on key sociological issues, with three main objectives. The first is to introduce key sociological concepts and theories through detailed introductions, examples, and evidence. The second objective is to introduce 12 sociological debates and controversies that are relevant to an understanding of concepts, theories, and research in sociology so that undergraduate students can grasp how sociologists view the work of colleagues. The third objective is to teach critical thinking by studying sociologists as they debate each other. The debate format will encourage students to re-examine their preconceptions and submit their views to critical reasoning. (ISBN 978-0-17-610468-9)

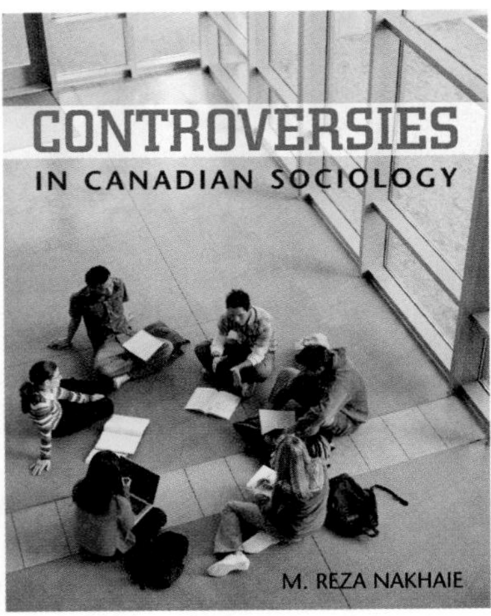

*Controversies in Canadian Sociology*

## *The Pleasure of Inquiry: Readings in Sociology*

*The Pleasure of Inquiry: Readings in Sociology*, by Ed Ksenych and David Liu, is an innovative, lively, but rigorous introduction to sociological inquiry that uses original readings aimed at exciting students about sociology as a meaningful perspective in their lives and as a practice they can develop. (ISBN 978-0-17-610474-0)

*The Pleasure of Inquiry: Readings in Sociology*

## *Thomson Nelson Guide to Success in Social Science: Writing Papers and Exams*

*Thomson Nelson Guide to Success in Social Science: Writing Papers and Exams*, by Diane Symbaluk, is an indispensable resource for any social science student. *Thomson Nelson Guide to Success in Social Science* is a roadmap to the often unfamiliar terrain of university and college academia. Leveraging best practices of master students, author Diane Symbaluk has created a book that will help students achieve excellence in writing and research. (ISBN 978-0-17-625182-6)

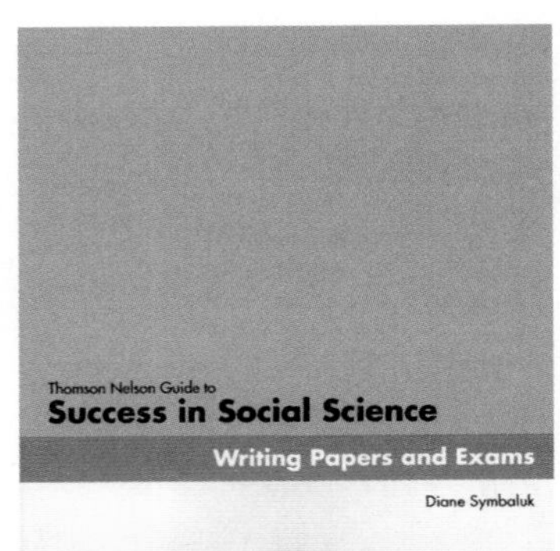

*Thomson Nelson Guide to Success in Social Science: Writing Papers and Exams*

## *Thomson Nelson Canadian Dictionary for the Social Sciences*

*Thomson Nelson Canadian Dictionary for the Social Sciences*, by Gary Parkinson and Robert Drislane, has more than 1400 entries covering the fields of anthropology, sociology, and political science. This dictionary is designed for undergraduate students and covers the main concepts, names, and events in social sciences in Canada. Each entry is designed to provide sufficient information to grasp the basic content of a concept, how the term is used, and its connection to other concepts. (ISBN 978-0-17-625237-3)

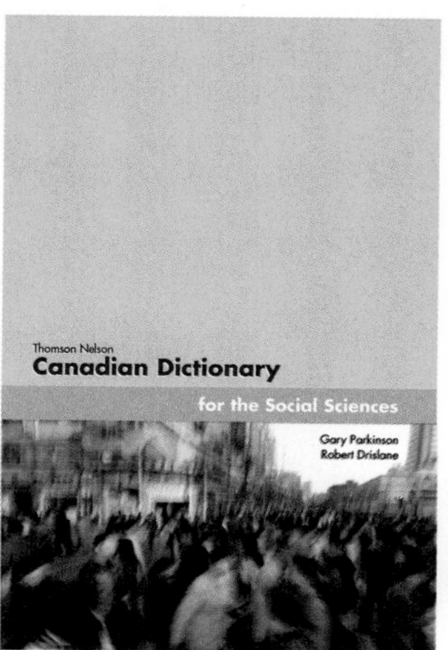


*Thomson Nelson Canadian Dictionary for the Social Sciences*

# Acknowledgments from the Authors

Anyone who has gone sailing knows that when you embark on a long voyage you need more than a compass. Among other things, you need a helm operator blessed with a strong sense of direction and an intimate knowledge of likely dangers. You need crew members who know all the ropes and can use them to keep things intact and in their proper place. And you need sturdy hands to raise and lower the sails. On the voyage to complete this book, the crew demonstrated all these skills. We are especially grateful to our senior acquisitions editor, Scott Couling, who saw this book's promise from the outset, understood clearly the direction we had to take to develop its potential, and on several occasions steered us clear of threatening shoals. We are also deeply indebted to the following crew members: Sandy Matos, developmental editor; Cara Yarzab, executive editor; Lesley Mann, senior developmental editor; Natalia Denesiuk Harris, senior content production manager; Heather Leach, marketing manager; Dawn Hunter, copy editor; Wayne Herrington, proofreader; and Melody Tolson, permissions and photo researcher.

We also want to thank the following colleagues who kindly took part in a textbook review and provided a wealth of helpful suggestions:

» Elizabeth Dennis, *University College of the Fraser Valley*
» Lidia O. Dorosz, *St. Lawrence College*
» Dr. Laurie Forbes, *Lakehead University*
» Kelly Henley, *St. Clair College of Applied Arts and Technology*
» Camille Hernandez-Ramdwar, *Ryerson University*
» Lisa Kowalchuk, *University of Guelph*
» Elizabeth Lange, *Concordia University College of Alberta*
» Lori Lockey, *Durham College*
» Helmut-Harry Loewen, *University of Winnipeg*
» Nan McBlane, *Thompson Rivers University*
» Brian R. McMillan, *Lakehead University*
» William Larry Upper, *Algonquin College*
» Carolyne Willoughby, *Durham College*
» Amanda Zavitz-Gocan, Ph.D., *Fanshawe College*

# PART 1 FOUNDATIONS

## chapter 1

a sociological compass

# chapter 1

## a sociological compass



**In this chapter, you will learn that**

→ The causes of human behaviour lie partly in the patterns of social relations that surround us and permeate our lives.

→ **Sociology** is the systematic study of human behaviour in social context.

→ Sociologists are often motivated to do research by the desire to improve people's lives. At the same time, sociologists adopt scientific methods to test their ideas.

→ Sociologists have developed a variety of theories to explain human behaviour. They assess the validity of these theories by seeing how well they correspond to data collected during research.

→ In the nineteenth and early twentieth centuries, the founders of sociology examined the massive social transformations caused by the Industrial Revolution and suggested ways of overcoming the social problems those transformations created. The Postindustrial Revolution and the process of globalization similarly challenge sociologists today.

# Introduction

## *Why You Need a Compass for a New World*

"When I was a child, a cleaning lady came to our house twice a month," Robert Brym recalls. "Her name was Lena White, and she was what we then called an 'Indian.' I was fond of Lena because she possessed two apparently magical powers. First, she could let the ash at the end of her cigarette grow 5 centimetres before it fell off. I sometimes used to play where Lena was working just to see how long she could scrub, vacuum, climb the stepladder, and chatter before the ash made its inevitable descent to the floor. Second, Lena could tell stories. My mother would serve us lunch at the kitchen table. During dessert, as we sipped tea with milk, Lena would spin tales about Gluskap, the creator of the world.

"I liked Gluskap because he was mischievous and enormously powerful. He fought giants, drove away monsters, taught people how to hunt and farm, and named the stars. But he also got into trouble and learned from his mistakes. For example, one day the wind was blowing so hard that Gluskap couldn't paddle his canoe into the bay to hunt ducks. So he found the source of the wind: the flapping wings of the Wind Eagle. He then tricked the Wind Eagle into getting stuck in a crevice where he could flap no more. Now Gluskap could go hunting. However, the air soon grew so hot that Gluskap found it difficult to breathe. The water became dirty and began to smell. It had so much foam on it that Gluskap found it hard to paddle. When he complained to his grandmother, she explained that the wind was needed to cool the air, wash the earth, and move the waters to keep them clean. And so, Gluskap freed the Wind Eagle and the winds returned to the earth. Gluskap decided it was better to wait for good weather and *then* go duck hunting rather than to conquer the winds.

Source: Lisa M. Ripperton

"Like the tale of the Wind Eagle, many of the Gluskap stories Lena told me were about the need for harmony among humans and between humans and nature. You can imagine my surprise, therefore, when I got to school and learned about the European exploration of what was called the New World. My teachers taught me all about the glories of the *conquest* of nature—and of other people. I learned that in the New World a Native population perhaps a hundredth as large as Europe's occupied a territory more than four times larger. I was taught that the New World was unimaginably rich in resources. European rulers saw that by controlling it they could increase their power and importance. Christians recognized new possibilities for spreading their religion. Explorers discerned fresh opportunities for rewarding adventures. A wave of excitement swelled as word spread of the New World's vast potential and challenges. I, too, became excited as I heard stories of conquest quite unlike the tales of Gluskap. Of course, I learned little about the violence required to conquer the New World.

"Forty years ago I was caught between thrilling stories of conquest and reflective stories that questioned the wisdom of conquest. Today, I think many people are in a similar position. On the one hand, we feel like the European explorers because we, too, have reached the frontiers of a New World. Like them, we are full of anticipation. Our New World is one of virtually instant long-distance communication, global economies and cultures, weakening nation-states, and technological advances that often make the daily news seem like reports from a distant planet. In a fundamental way, the world is not the same place it was just 50 years ago. Orbiting telescopes now peer to the fringes of the universe; the human genetic code has been laid bare, like a road map; fibre optic cable carries a trillion bits of information per second; spacecraft transport robots to Mars. They all help make this a New World.

"However, we understand that not all is hope and bright horizons; our anticipation is mixed with dread. Gluskap stories make more sense than ever. Scientific breakthroughs are announced almost daily, but the global environment has never been in worse shape and HIV/AIDS is now the leading cause of death in Africa. Marriages and nations unexpectedly break up and then reconstitute themselves in new and unanticipated forms. We celebrate the advances made by women and racial minorities only to find that some people oppose their progress, sometimes violently. Waves of people migrate between continents, establishing both cooperation and conflict between previously separated groups. New technologies make work more interesting and creative for some, offering unprecedented opportunities to make money, but they also make work more routine for many others. The standard of living goes up for many people but stagnates for many more.

"Amid all this contradictory news, uncertainty about the future prevails. That is why John Lie and I wrote this book: we set out to show undergraduates that sociology can help them to make sense of their lives, however uncertain they may appear to be. Five hundred years ago, the early European explorers of North and South America set themselves the preliminary task of mapping the contours of the New World. We set ourselves a similar task here. Their frontiers were physical; ours are social. Their maps were geographical; ours are sociological. But in terms of functionality, our maps are much like theirs: all maps allow us to find our place in the world and see ourselves in the context of larger forces. *Sociological* maps, as the famous American sociologist C. Wright Mills (1916–62) wrote, allow us to 'grasp the interplay of [people] and society, of biography and history' (Mills, 1959: 4). This book, then, shows you how to draw sociological maps so that you can figure out how to navigate your world, find your place in it, and perhaps discover how to improve it. It is your sociological compass."

In this chapter we aim to achieve four goals:

1. *Because **sociology** is the systematic study of human behaviour in social context, we first illustrate the power of sociology to dispel foggy assumptions and to help us see the operation of the social world more clearly. To that end, we examine a phenomenon that at first glance appears to be solely the outcome of breakdowns in individual functioning: suicide. We show that, in fact, social relations powerfully influence suicide rates. This exercise introduces you to what is unique about the sociological perspective.*
2. *We then show that, from its origins, sociological research has been motivated by a desire to improve the social world. Thus, sociology is not just a dry, academic exercise but also a means of charting a better course for society. We illustrate this by briefly analyzing the work of the discipline's founders.*

3. *We go on to review the main methods of collecting sociological data and assess their strengths and weaknesses. Although much of sociology is motivated by the desire to improve the social world, sociologists use scientific methods to test their ideas, thus increasing their validity.*

4. *Finally, we suggest that sociology can help you come to grips with your century, just as it helped the founders of sociology deal with theirs. Today, we are witnessing massive and disorienting social changes. As was the case in the nineteenth century, sociologists today try to understand social phenomena and suggest credible ways to improve society. By promising to make sociology relevant to you, this chapter is an open invitation to participate in sociology's challenge.*

Before showing how sociology can help you to understand and improve your world, we look briefly at the problem of suicide. This examination will help to illustrate how the sociological perspective can clarify and sometimes overturn common-sense beliefs.

# The Sociological Perspective

By analyzing suicide sociologically, you can test the claim that sociology offers a unique, surprising, and enlightening perspective on social events. After all, suicide appears to be the supreme antisocial and non-social act. First, it is condemned by nearly everyone in society. Second, it is typically committed in private, far from the public's intrusive glare. Third, it is comparatively rare: in recent years, about 13 suicides have occurred annually for every 100 000 Canadians. (Canada's suicide rate places us in about the middle of the countries that publish suicide statistics; see Figure 1.1.) And, finally, when you think about why people commit such an act, you are likely to focus on their individual states of

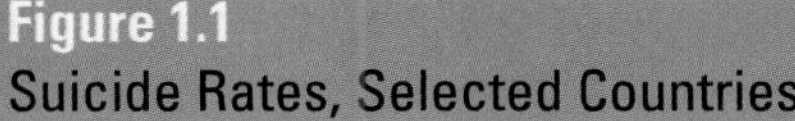
**Figure 1.1**
Suicide Rates, Selected Countries

■ Source: From World Health Organization (2002a). Reprinted with permission.

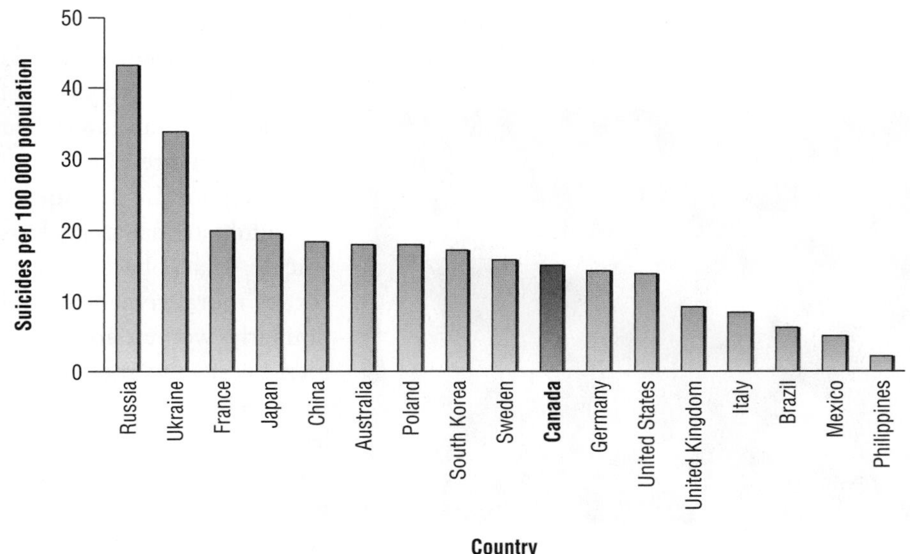

*Pacific.* Alex Colville, 1967

mind rather than on the state of society. In other words, we are usually interested in the aspects of specific individuals' lives that caused them to become depressed or angry enough to commit suicide. We do not usually think about the patterns of social relations that might encourage or inhibit such actions in general. If sociology can reveal the hidden social causes of such an apparently non-social and antisocial phenomenon, there must be something to it!

### *The Sociological Explanation of Suicide*

At the end of the nineteenth century, French sociologist Émile Durkheim, one of the pioneers of the discipline, demonstrated that suicide is more than just an individual act of desperation that results from psychological disorder, as was commonly believed at the time. Suicide rates, Durkheim showed, are strongly influenced by social forces (Durkheim, 1951 [1897]).

Durkheim made his case by first examining the association between rates of suicide and rates of psychological disorder for different groups. The idea that psychological disorder causes suicide is supported, he reasoned, only if the suicide rate tends to be high where the rate of psychological disorder is high, and low where the rate of psychological disorder is low. But his analysis of European government statistics, hospital records, and other sources revealed nothing of the kind. He discovered that slightly more women than men were in insane asylums but that four male suicides occurred for every female suicide. Jews had the highest rate of psychological disorder among the major religious groups in France, but they also had the lowest suicide rate. Psychological disorders occurred most frequently when a person reached maturity, but suicide rates increased steadily with advancing age.

Clearly, suicide rates and rates of psychological disorder did not vary directly. In fact, they often appeared to vary inversely. Why? Durkheim argued that the suicide rates varied as a result of differences in the degree of **social solidarity** in different categories of the population. According to Durkheim, the more a group's members share beliefs and values, and the more frequently and intensely they interact, the more social solidarity exists within the group. (**Values** are ideas about what is good and bad, right and wrong.)

In turn, the more social solidarity a group has, the more firmly anchored its individuals are to the social world and the less likely they are to take their own lives. In other words, Durkheim expected high-solidarity groups to have lower suicide rates than low-solidarity groups—at least up to a point (see Figure 1.2).

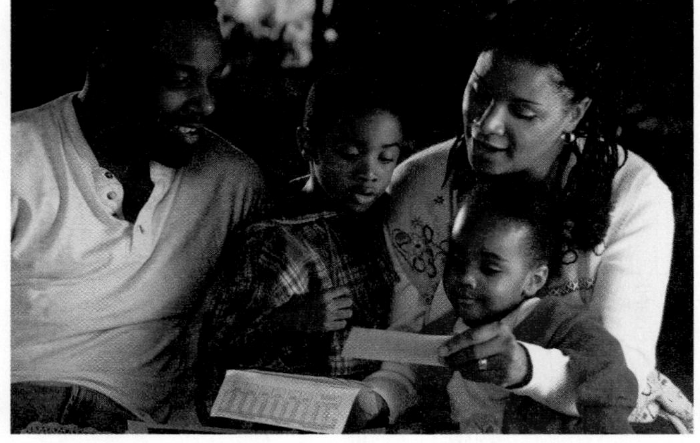

Strong social bonds decrease the probability that a person will commit suicide.

To support his argument, Durkheim showed that married adults are half as likely as unmarried adults to commit suicide. That is because marriage creates social ties and a sort of moral cement that bind the individual to society. Similarly, women are less likely to commit suicide than men because women are more involved in the intimate social relations of family life. Jews, Durkheim wrote, are less likely to commit suicide than Christians because centuries of persecution have turned them into a group that is more defensive and tightly knit. And seniors are more prone than the young and the middle-aged to taking their

## Figure 1.2
## Durkheim's Theory of Suicide

Durkheim's **theory** of suicide states that the suicide rate declines and then rises as social solidarity increases. Durkheim called suicides that occur in high-solidarity settings altruistic. **Altruistic suicide** occurs when norms tightly govern behaviour. Soldiers who knowingly give up their lives to protect comrades commit altruistic suicide out of a deep sense of patriotism and comradeship. In contrast, suicide in low-solidarity settings may be egoistic or anomic. **Egoistic suicide** results from the poor integration of people into society because of weak social ties to others. Someone who is unemployed and unmarried is thus more likely to commit suicide than is someone who is employed and married. **Anomic suicide** occurs when vague norms govern behaviour. The rate of anomic suicide is likely to be high among people living in a society that lacks a widely shared code of morality.

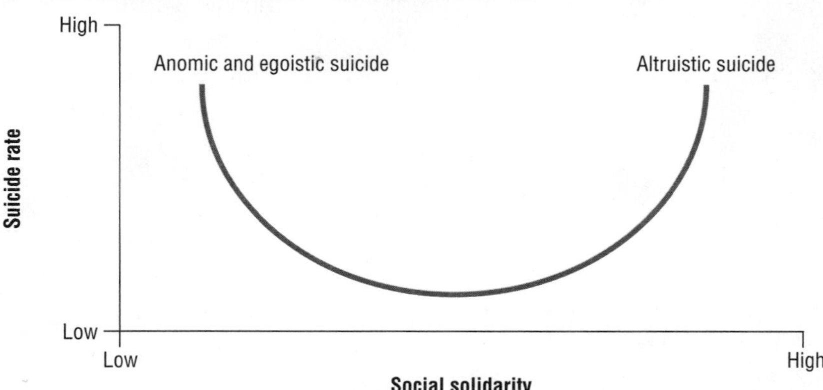


own lives because they are most likely to live alone, to have lost a spouse, and to lack a job and a wide network of friends. In general, Durkheim wrote, "suicide varies with the degree of integration of the social groups of which the individual forms a part" (Durkheim, 1951 [1897]: 209). Of course, his generalization tells us nothing about why any particular individual may take his or her own life. That issue is the province of psychology. But it does tell us that a person's likelihood of committing suicide decreases as the degree to which he or she is anchored in society increases. It says something surprising and uniquely sociological about how and why the suicide rate varies across groups (see Figure 1.3 and Box 1.1).

## Figure 1.3
## Suicide by Age and Sex, Canada, 2003

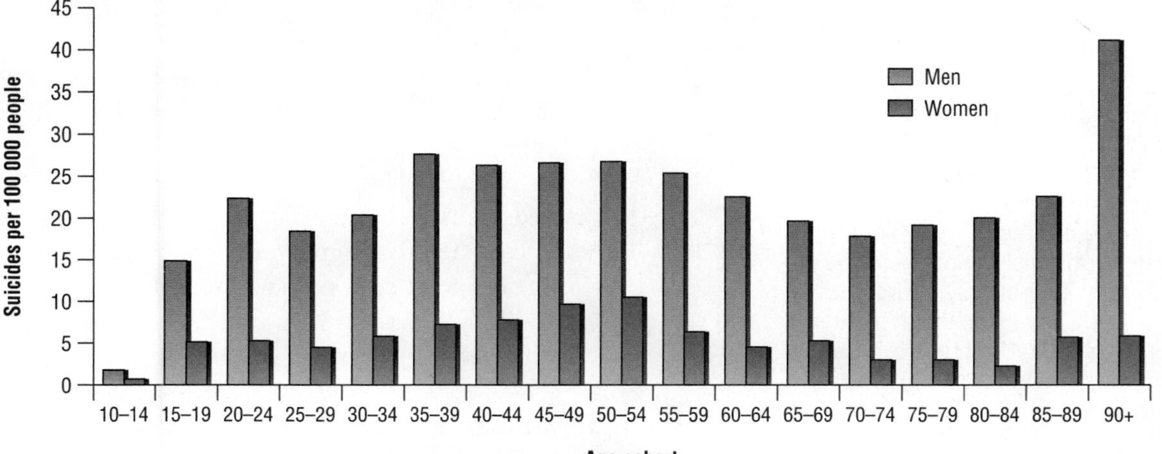


As in Durkheim's France, men in Canada today are about four times as likely to commit suicide as are women. However, youth suicide is much more common in Canada today than in nineteenth-century France.

■ Source: Statistics Canada (2006a, 2006b).

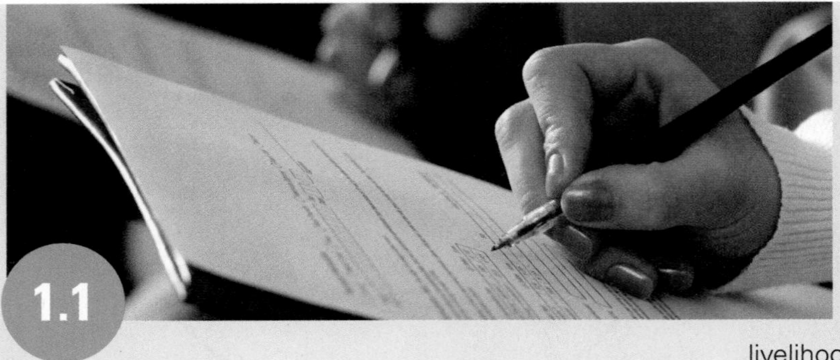

1.1

# SOCIAL POLICY: WHAT DO YOU THINK?

## Suicide and the Innu of Labrador

The Canadians with the highest suicide rate are Aboriginal peoples. For instance, the suicide rate among registered Indians is four times as high as the rate for the Canadian population as a whole (Health Canada, 1999a: 24). Among Canada's Aboriginal peoples, the 2000 Innu of Labrador have the highest suicide rate. They are one of the most suicide-prone people on earth, with a suicide rate that is nearly 13 times as high as the rate for all Canadians (Rogan, 2001; Samson, Wilson, and Mazower, 1999).

Durkheim's theory of suicide helps to explain the Innu people's tragic propensity to commit suicide. Over the past half-century, the Innu's traditional norms and values have been destroyed. Moreover, the Innu have been prevented from participating in stable and meaningful patterns of social interaction. Social solidarity among the Innu has been reduced to an abysmally low level.

How did this state of affairs come about? Historically, the Innu were a nomadic people who relied on hunting and trapping for their livelihood. In the mid-1950s, however, shortly after Newfoundland and Labrador became part of Canada, the provincial and federal governments were eager to gain control of traditional Innu land and encourage economic development. Government officials wanted new roads, mines, lumber operations, hydroelectric projects, and low-level flight training facilities for NATO air forces to be built, and wanted the Innu to be concentrated in stable settlements and learn the practical and cultural skills associated with a modern industrial society. Accordingly, governments put tremendous pressure on the Innu to give up their traditional way of life and to settle in such places as Davis Inlet and Sheshatsui.

In these new communities, Canadian laws, schools, and churches discouraged the Innu from hunting, practising their religion, and raising their children in the traditional way. Hunting regulations limited Innu access to their age-old livelihood. Some priests beat children who missed church or school to go hunting, thus introducing interpersonal violence into a culture that formerly knew none. Teachers transmitted North American and European skills and culture, often denigrating Innu practices in the process. At the same time, few alternative jobs existed in the new communities. Most Innu wound up living on welfare. In the absence of work, and lacking the stabilizing influence of their traditional culture, a people long known for their peacefulness and cooperative spirit became victims of widespread family breakdown, sexual abuse, and alcohol-related problems. Today in Sheshatsui, at least 20 percent of the children regularly get high by sniffing gasoline. In Davis Inlet, the figure is nearly 60 percent.

A study conducted in 1984 showed that a movement among the Innu to return to the land and to their traditional hunting practices for up to seven months of the year led to a dramatic improvement in their health. They lived a vigorous outdoor life. Alcohol abuse stopped. Diet improved. Their emotional and social environment stabilized and became meaningful. Suicide was unknown (Samson et al., 1999: 25).

Unfortunately, a big political obstacle stands in the way of the Innu returning to their traditional lifestyle on a wide scale. The governments of Canada and Newfoundland and Labrador will not allow it. A widespread Innu return to the land conflicts with government and private economic development plans. For instance, the Lower Churchill Falls hydroelectric project (the second-biggest hydroelectric project in the world) and the Voisey's Bay nickel mine (working the world's biggest deposit of nickel) are located in the middle of traditional Innu hunting and burial grounds. The Innu are vigorously attempting to regain control of their land. They also want to be able to decide *on their own* when and how to use Canadian health services, training facilities, and the like.

**CRITICAL THINKING QUESTIONS**

- *Do you think that the interests of the Innu necessarily exclude or contradict the interests of the federal and provincial governments? Or can the interests of the conflicting parties be reconciled? If so, how? Imagine that you have been asked to help resolve the conflict between the Innu and the governments of Canada and Newfoundland and Labrador. What sorts of policies would you recommend that could satisfy the interests of all parties?*

## *Suicide in Canada Today*

Although the rate of suicide among youth and young adults was low in Durkheim's France, his theory of social solidarity helps us to understand why it is high in Canada today. In brief, shared moral principles and strong social ties have eroded since the early 1960s, especially for Canada's youth. Consider the following facts:

» Church, synagogue, mosque, and temple attendance is down. More than half of all Canadians attended weekly religious services in the 1960s, but in 2005 the figure was just 25 percent (Bibby, 2007: 351). It is likely that this decline is particularly significant for young people, who are in the process of forming moral principles.

» Unemployment is up, especially for youth. The unemployment rate remained near 3 percent for most of the 1960s. It rose steadily and stayed near 10 percent for most of the 1990s. As of February 2007, the unemployment rate was 6.1 percent; however, the unemployment rate is about twice as high for Canadians under the age of 24 as it is for older Canadians (Statistics Canada, 2007a).

» The rate of divorce has increased sixfold since the early 1960s. Births outside marriage are also much more common than they used to be. As a result, children are more often brought up in single-parent families than in the past. This fact suggests that they enjoy less frequent and intimate social interaction with parents and less adult supervision.

In sum, the figures cited above suggest that the level of social solidarity is now lower than it was just a few decades ago, especially for young people. Less firmly rooted in society, and less likely to share moral standards, young people in Canada today are more likely than young people were half a century ago to take their own lives if they happen to find themselves in a deep personal crisis (see also Box 1.1).

## *The Sociological Imagination*

You have known for a long time that you live in a society. Yet until now, you may not have fully appreciated that society also lives in you. That is, patterns of social relations, such as the level of social solidarity, affect your innermost thoughts and feelings, influence your actions, and thus help to shape who you are. Sociologists call relatively stable patterns of social relations **social structures.**

Half a century ago, Mills (1959) called the ability to see these connections the **sociological imagination.** He argued that one of the sociologist's main tasks is to identify and explain the connection between people's personal troubles and the social structures in which people are embedded. An important step in broadening our awareness involves recognizing that three levels of social structure surround and permeate us. Think of these structures as concentric circles radiating out from you:

1. ***Microstructures*** *are patterns of intimate social relations formed during face-to-face interaction. Families, friendship circles, and work associations are all examples of microstructures.*
2. ***Macrostructures*** *are patterns of social relations that lie outside and above your circle of intimates and acquaintances. One important macrostructure is* ***patriarchy,*** *the traditional system of economic and political inequality between women and men in most societies. Other macrostructures include religious institutions and social classes.*
3. ***Global structures*** *are the third level of social structure. International organizations, patterns of worldwide travel and communication, and economic relations among countries are examples of global structures. Global structures are increasingly important, because inexpensive travel and communication allow all parts of the world to become interconnected culturally, economically, and politically.*[1]

Personal problems are connected to social structures at the micro, macro, and global levels. Whether the personal problem involves finding a job, keeping a marriage intact, or figuring out a way to act justly to end world poverty, social-structural considerations broaden our understanding of the problem and suggest appropriate courses of action (see Box 1.2).

## *Origins of the Sociological Imagination*

The sociological imagination is only a few hundred years old. Although in ancient times some philosophers wrote about society, their thinking was not sociological. They believed that God and nature controlled society. These philosophers spent much of their time sketching blueprints for the ideal society and urging people to follow those blueprints. They relied on speculation rather than evidence to reach conclusions about how the world worked. The sociological imagination was born when three modern revolutions pushed people to think about society in an entirely new way.

### The Scientific Revolution

The Scientific Revolution began about 1550. It encouraged the view that sound conclusions about the workings of society must be based on solid evidence, not just speculation.

People often link the Scientific Revolution to specific ideas, such as Newton's laws of motion and Copernicus's theory that the earth revolves around the sun. However, science is less a collection of ideas than a method of inquiry. For instance, in 1609 Galileo pointed his newly invented telescope at the sky, made some careful observations, and showed that his observations fit Copernicus's theory. This is the core of the scientific method: using evidence to make a case for a particular point of view. By the

1.2

# SOCIOLOGY AT THE MOVIES

Tom Cruise and Samantha Morton in *Minority Report*

## *Minority Report* (2002)

The year is 2054 and the place is Washington, D.C. John Anderton (played by Tom Cruise) is a police officer who uses the latest technologies to apprehend murderers *before* they commit their crimes. This remarkable feat is possible because scientists have nearly perfected the use of "Pre-Cogs"—or so it seems. The Pre-Cog system consists of three psychics whose brains are wired together and who are kept sedated so they can develop a collective vision about future murders. Together with powerful computers, the Pre-Cogs are apparently helping to create a crime-free society.

All is well until one psychic's visions show Anderton himself murdering a stranger in less than 36 hours. Suddenly, Anderton is on the run from his own men. Desperate to figure out whether the Pre-Cog system is somehow mistaken, he breaks into it, unwires one of the psychics, and discovers that the psychics do not always agree about the future. Sometimes there is a "minority report," and sometimes the minority report is correct. People are arrested even though they would never have broken the law. The authorities have concealed this system flaw and allowed the arrest of innocent people in their zeal to create a crime-free world.

And so Anderton comes to realize that not everything is predetermined—that, in his words, "it's not the future if you stop it." And stop it he does. Along the way Steven Spielberg dazzles us with armies of spider-like robots that track down criminals, automated cars that speed up and down 16-kilometre-tall skyscrapers at 160 kilometres an hour, and miniature jets that police officers strap to their backs, allowing them to race to the scene of a predicted crime.

The special effects should not, however, detract from the important sociological lesson of *Minority Report*. Many people believe two contradictory ideas with equal conviction. First, they believe that they are perfectly free to do whatever they want. Second, they believe that the "system" (or "society") is so big and powerful they are unable to do anything to change it. Neither idea is accurate. Some aspects of society exert powerful influences on our behaviour; we are not perfectly free. Nonetheless, it is possible to change many aspects of society; we are not wholly predetermined either. Changing society is possible under certain specifiable circumstances, with the aid of specialized knowledge and often through great individual and collective effort.

Understanding the social constraints and the possibilities for freedom that envelop us requires an active sociological imagination. The sociological imagination urges us to connect our biography with history and with social structure—to make sense of our lives against a larger historical and social background and to act in light of our understanding.

### CRITICAL THINKING QUESTIONS

- *Have you ever tried to put events in your own life in the context of history and social structure? Did the exercise help you make sense of your life? Did it lead to a life more worth living?*

mid-seventeenth century, some philosophers were calling for a science of society. When sociology emerged as a distinct discipline in the nineteenth century, commitment to the scientific method was one firm pillar of the sociological imagination.

### The Democratic Revolution

The Democratic Revolution began about 1750. It suggested that people are responsible for organizing society and that human intervention can therefore solve social problems. Before the Democratic Revolution, most people thought otherwise. They believed that God ordained the social order. The American Revolution (1775–83) and the French Revolution (1789–99) helped undermine that idea. These democratic political upheavals showed that society could experience massive change in a short period. They proved that people could replace unsatisfactory rulers. They suggested that *people* control society. The implications for social thought were profound, for if it was possible to change society through human intervention, a science of society could play a big role. The new science could help people find ways of overcoming social problems, improving the welfare of citizens, and effectively reaching goals. Much of the justification for sociology as a science arose out of the democratic revolutions that shook Europe and North America.

### The Industrial Revolution

The **Industrial Revolution** began about 1775. It created a host of new and serious social problems that attracted the attention of social thinkers. As a result of the growth of industry, masses of people moved from countryside to city, worked agonizingly long hours in crowded and dangerous mines and factories, lost faith in their religions, confronted faceless bureaucracies, and reacted to the filth and poverty of their existence by means of strikes, crime, revolutions, and wars. Scholars had never seen a sociological laboratory like this. The Scientific Revolution suggested that a science of society was possible. The Democratic Revolution suggested that people could intervene to improve society. The Industrial Revolution now presented social thinkers with a host of pressing social problems crying out for solution. They responded by creating the sociological imagination.

### Auguste Comte and the Tension between Science and Values

French social thinker Auguste Comte (1798–1857) coined the term *sociology* in 1838 (Comte, 1975). Comte tried to place the study of society on scientific foundations. He said he wanted to understand the social world as it was, not as he or anyone else imagined it should be. Yet there was a tension in his work: although Comte was eager to adopt the scientific method in the study of society, he was a conservative thinker, motivated by strong opposition to rapid change in French society, as is evident in his writings. When he moved from his small, conservative hometown to Paris, Comte witnessed the democratic forces unleashed by the French Revolution, the early industrialization of society, and the rapid growth of cities. What he saw shocked and saddened him. Rapid social change was destroying much of what he valued, especially respect for traditional authority. He therefore urged slow change and the preservation of all that was traditional in social life.

To varying degrees, we see the same tension in the work of the three giants in the early history of sociology: Karl Marx (1818–83), Émile Durkheim (1858–1917), and Max Weber (pronounced VAY-ber; 1864–1920). The lives of these three men

*Liberty Leading the People.* Eugene Delacroix, July 28, 1830. The democratic forces unleashed by the French Revolution suggested that people are responsible for organizing society and that human intervention can therefore solve social problems. As such, democracy was a foundation stone of sociology.

spanned just more than a century. They witnessed various phases of Europe's wrenching transition to industrial capitalism. They wanted to explain the great transformation of Europe and suggest ways to improve people's lives. Like Comte, they were committed to the scientific method of research. However, the ideas they developed are not just diagnostic tools from which we can still learn, but, like many sociological ideas, they are also prescriptions for combating social ills.

Durkheim, Marx, and Weber stood close to the origins of the major theoretical traditions in sociology: functionalism, conflict theory, and symbolic interactionism. A fourth theoretical tradition, feminism, has arisen in recent decades to correct some deficiencies in the three long-established traditions. It will become clear as you read this book that many more theories exist in addition to these four. However, because these four traditions have been especially influential in the development of sociology, we present a thumbnail sketch of each.

# Sociological Theory and Theorists

## *Functionalism*

### Émile Durkheim

Durkheim's theory of suicide is an early example of what sociologists now call **functionalism.** Functionalist theories incorporate four features:

1. *Functionalist theories stress that human behaviour is governed by stable patterns of social relations, or social structures. For example, Durkheim emphasized how patterns of social solidarity influence suicide rates. The social structures typically analyzed by functionalists are macrostructures.*
2. *Functionalist theories show how social structures maintain or undermine social stability. This is why functionalists are sometimes called structural functionalists; they analyze how the parts of society (structures) fit together and how each part contributes to the stability of the whole (its function). Thus, Durkheim argued that high social solidarity contributes to the maintenance of social order. However, the growth of industries and cities in nineteenth-century Europe lowered the level of social solidarity and contributed to social instability. One aspect of instability, wrote Durkheim, is a higher suicide rate. Another is frequent strikes by workers.*

Émile Durkheim (1858–1917) was the first professor of sociology in France and is often considered to be the first modern sociologist. In *The Rules of Sociological Method* (1938 [1895]) and *Suicide* (1951 [1897]), he argued that human behaviour is shaped by "social facts," or the social context in which people are embedded. In Durkheim's view, social facts define the constraints and opportunities within which people must act. Durkheim was also keenly interested in the conditions that promote social order in "primitive" and modern societies, and he explored this problem in depth in such works as *The Division of Labor in Society* (1997 [1893]) and *The Elementary Forms of the Religious Life* (1976 [1915/1912]).

Robert Merton (1910–2003) made functionalism a more flexible theory from the late 1930s to the 1950s. In *Social Theory and Social Structure* (1968 [1949]), he proposed that social structures are not always functional; they may be dysfunctional for some people. Moreover, not all functions are manifest; some are latent. Merton also made major contributions to the sociology of science, notably in *On the Shoulders of Giants* (1985 [1956]), a study of creativity, tradition, plagiarism, the transmission of knowledge, and the concept of progress.

3. *Functionalist theories emphasize that social structures are based mainly on shared values. Thus, when Durkheim wrote about social solidarity, he sometimes meant the frequency and intensity of social interaction, but more often he thought of social solidarity as a kind of moral cement that binds people together.*
4. *Functionalism suggests that re-establishing equilibrium can best solve most social problems. Durkheim said that social stability could be restored in late-nineteenth-century Europe by creating new associations of employers and workers that would lower workers' expectations about what they should hope for in life. If more people could agree on wanting less, Durkheim wrote, social solidarity would rise, fewer strikes would occur, and suicide rates would drop. Functionalism, then, was a conservative response to widespread social unrest. A more liberal or radical response would have been to argue that if people were expressing discontent because they were getting less out of life than they expected, discontent could be lowered by finding ways for them to get more out of life.*

### Talcott Parsons and Robert Merton

Although functionalist thinking influenced American sociology at the end of the nineteenth century, it was only during the Great Depression of 1929–39 that it took deep root (Russett, 1966). With about 30 percent of the labour force unemployed and labour unrest reaching unprecedented levels by 1934, sociologists with a conservative frame of mind were attracted to a theory that focused on how social equilibrium could be restored. Functionalist theory remained popular in North America for approximately 30 years.

Sociologist Talcott Parsons (1902–79) was a leading American proponent of functionalism. He is best known for identifying how various institutions must work to ensure the smooth operation of society as a whole. He argued that society is well integrated and in equilibrium when the family successfully raises new generations, the military successfully defends society against external threats, schools are able to teach students the skills and values they need to function as productive adults, and religions create a shared moral code among people (Parsons, 1951).

Parsons was criticized for exaggerating the degree to which members of society share common values and social institutions contribute to social harmony. This criticism led Robert Merton (1910–2003), the other leading functionalist in the United States, to propose that social structures may have different consequences for different groups. Merton noted that some of those consequences may be disruptive or **dysfunctional** (Merton, 1968 [1949]). Moreover, said Merton, while some functions are **manifest** (intended and easily observed), others are **latent** (unintended and less obvious). For instance, a manifest function of schools is to transmit skills from one generation to the next. A latent function of schools is to encourage the development of a separate youth culture that often conflicts with parents' values (Coleman, 1961; Hersch, 1998).

## *Conflict Theory*

The second major theoretical tradition in sociology emphasizes the centrality of conflict in social life. It incorporates the following four features:

1. ***Conflict theory** generally focuses on large, macrolevel structures, such as class relations or patterns of domination, submission, and struggle between people of high and low standing.*

Karl Marx (1818–83) was a revolutionary thinker whose ideas affected not just the growth of sociology but also the course of world history. He held that major sociohistorical changes are the result of conflict between society's main social classes. In his major work, *Capital* (1967 [1867–94]), Marx argued that capitalism would produce such misery and collective strength among workers that they would eventually take state power and create a classless society in which production would be based on human need rather than profit.

Max Weber (1864–1920), Germany's greatest sociologist, profoundly influenced the development of the discipline worldwide. Engaged in a lifelong "debate with Marx's ghost," Weber held that economic circumstances alone do not explain the rise of capitalism. As he showed in *The Protestant Ethic and the Spirit of Capitalism* (1958 [1904–05]), independent developments in the religious realm had unintended, beneficial consequences for capitalist development in some parts of Europe. He also argued that capitalism would not necessarily give way to socialism. Instead, he regarded the growth of bureaucracy and the overall "rationalization" of life as the defining characteristics of the modern age. These themes were developed in *Economy and Society* (1968 [1914]).

2. *Conflict theory shows how major patterns of inequality in society produce social stability in some circumstances and social change in others.*
3. *Conflict theory stresses how members of privileged groups try to maintain their advantages while subordinate groups struggle to acquire theirs. From this point of view, social conditions at a given time are the expression of an ongoing power struggle between privileged and subordinate groups.*
4. *Conflict theory typically leads to the suggestion that lessening privilege will lower the level of conflict and increase human welfare.*

## Karl Marx

Conflict theory originated in the work of the German social thinker Karl Marx. A generation before Durkheim, Marx observed the destitution and discontent produced by the Industrial Revolution and proposed a sweeping theory about the ways societies develop (Marx, 1904 [1859]; Marx and Engels, 1972 [1848]). Marx's theory differs radically from Durkheim's. **Class conflict,** the struggle between classes to resist and overcome the opposition of other classes, lies at the centre of his ideas.

Marx argued that owners of industry are eager to improve the way work is organized and to adopt new tools, machines, and production methods. These innovations allow them to produce more efficiently, earn higher profits, and drive inefficient competitors out of business. However, the drive for profits also causes capitalists to concentrate workers in larger and larger establishments, keep wages as low as possible, and invest as little as possible in improving working conditions. Thus, wrote Marx, a large and growing class of poor workers opposes a small and shrinking class of wealthy owners.

Marx believed that workers would ultimately become aware of belonging to the same exploited class. He called this awareness **class consciousness.** He believed that working-class consciousness would encourage the growth of trade unions and labour parties. According to Marx, these organizations would eventually try to put an end to private ownership of property and replace it with a communist society, defined as system in which everyone shares property and wealth according to their needs, and no private property exists.

## Max Weber

Although some of Marx's ideas have been usefully adapted to the study of contemporary society, his predictions about the inevitable collapse of capitalism have been questioned. Max Weber, a German sociologist who wrote his major works a generation after Marx, was among the first to point out some of the flaws in Marx's argument (Weber, 1946). Weber noted the rapid growth of the so-called service sector of the economy, with its many non-manual (or white-collar) workers and professionals. He argued that many members of these occupational groups would stabilize society because they enjoyed more prestige and income than manual (or blue-collar) workers in the manufacturing sector. Weber also showed that class conflict is not the only driving force of history. In his view, politics and religion are also important sources of historical change. Other writers pointed out that Marx did not appreciate how investment in technology would make it possible for workers to toil fewer hours under less oppressive conditions. Nor did Marx foresee that higher wages, better working conditions, and welfare-state benefits would pacify manual workers. Thus, many of the particulars of Marx's theory were called into question by Weber and other sociologists.

John Porter (1921–79) was Canada's leading sociologist in the 1960s and 1970s.

### John Porter

Nevertheless, Marx's insights about the fundamental importance of conflict in social life are still highly influential in modern sociology. Conflict theory became especially popular in North America in the 1960s and 1970s, decades that were rocked by major labour unrest, peace demonstrations on university campuses, the rise of the black power movement, and the emergence of contemporary feminism. Strikes, demonstrations, and riots were almost daily occurrences in the 1960s and 1970s, and it seemed evident to many sociologists of that generation that conflict among classes, nations, races, and generations was the very essence of social life. For example, John Porter (1921–79) was Canada's premier sociologist in the 1960s and 1970s. Born in Vancouver, he received his Ph.D. from the London School of Economics. He spent his academic career at Carleton University in Ottawa, where he served as chair of the Department of Sociology and Anthropology, dean of Arts and Science, and vice president. His major work, *The Vertical Mosaic* (1965), is a study of class and power in Canada. Firmly rooted in conflict theory, it influenced a generation of Canadian sociologists in their studies on social inequality, elite groups, French–English relations, and Canadian–American relations.

## *Symbolic Interactionism*

### Weber and the Protestant Ethic

We noted earlier that Weber criticized Marx's interpretation of the development of capitalism. Among other things, Weber argued that early capitalist development was not caused by favourable *economic* circumstances alone. In addition, he said, certain *religious* beliefs encouraged robust capitalist growth. In particular, sixteenth- and seventeenth-century Protestants believed their religious doubts could be reduced, and a state of grace assured, if they worked diligently and lived modestly. Weber called this belief the **Protestant ethic.** He believed it had an unintended effect: people who adhered to the Protestant ethic saved and invested more than others. Thus, according to Weber, capitalism developed most robustly where the Protestant ethic took hold. He concluded that capitalism did not develop because of the operation of economic forces alone, as Marx argued. Instead, it depended partly on the religious *meaning* individuals attached to their work (Weber, 1958 [1904–05]). In much of his research, Weber emphasized the importance of empathically understanding people's motives and the meanings they attach to things to gain a clear sense of the significance of their actions. He called this aspect of his approach to sociological research the method of *Verstehen* ("understanding" in German).

The idea that subjective meanings and motives must be analyzed in any complete sociological analysis was only one of Weber's contributions to early sociological theory. Weber was also an important conflict theorist, as you will learn in later chapters. At present, however, it is enough to note that his emphasis on subjective meanings found rich soil in North America in the late nineteenth and early twentieth centuries, because his ideas resonated deeply with the individualism of North American culture. A century ago, people widely believed that individual talent and initiative could achieve just about anything. Much of early North American sociology therefore focused on the individual or, more precisely, the connection between the individual and the larger society.

George Herbert Mead (1863–1931)

## George Herbert Mead

The connection between the individual and the larger society was certainly a focus of sociologists at the University of Chicago, which was the most influential Department of Sociology in North America before World War II. For example, George Herbert Mead (1863–1931) was the driving force behind the study of how the individual's sense of self is formed through interaction with other people. We discuss his contribution in Chapter 3, Socialization. Here, we note only that the work of Mead and his colleagues produced symbolic interactionism, a distinctively North American theoretical tradition that continues to be a major force in sociology today.

Functionalist and conflict theories assume that people's group memberships—whether they are rich or poor, male or female, black or white—help shape their behaviour. This can sometimes make people seem like balls on a pool table that get knocked around and cannot choose their own destinations. We know from our everyday experience, however, that people often make choices, sometimes difficult ones. Sometimes, they change their minds. Moreover, two people with similar group memberships may react differently to similar social circumstances because they interpret those circumstances differently.

Erving Goffman (1922–82)

## Erving Goffman

Recognizing these issues, some sociologists focus on the subjective side of social life. They work in **symbolic interactionism,** a school of thought that was given its name by sociologist Herbert Blumer (1900–86), who was Mead's student at the University of Chicago. This tradition incorporates four features:

1. *Symbolic interactionism focuses on interpersonal communication in microlevel social settings, distinguishing it from both functionalist and conflict theories.*
2. *Symbolic interactionism emphasizes that social life is possible only because people attach meanings to things. It follows that an adequate explanation of social behaviour requires understanding the subjective meanings that people associate with their social circumstances.*
3. *Symbolic interactionism stresses that people help create their social circumstances and do not merely react to them. For example, Erving Goffman (1922–82) was one of the most influential symbolic interactionists of the twentieth century. Born in Mannville, Alberta, he studied sociology and anthropology as an undergraduate at the University of Toronto, completed his Ph.D. at the University of Chicago, and pursued his academic career at the University of California, Berkeley, and the University of Pennsylvania. Goffman developed an international reputation for his "dramaturgical" approach to symbolic interactionism. This approach highlights the way people present themselves to others, managing their identities in order to create desired impressions on their "audience," in much the same way as actors do. For Goffman, social interaction is like a play, complete with stage, backstage, defined roles, and props. In this play, a person's age, gender, race, and other characteristics may help shape his or her actions, but there is much room for individual creativity as well (Goffman, 1959).*
4. *By focusing on the subjective meanings people create in small social settings, symbolic interactionists sometimes validate unpopular and unofficial viewpoints. This increases our understanding and tolerance of people who may be different from us.*

## Feminism

Few women figured prominently in the early history of sociology. The strict demands placed on them by the nineteenth-century family and the lack of opportunity for women in the larger society prevented most of them from attaining a higher education and making major contributions to the discipline. The women who did make their mark on the discipline in its early years tended to have unusual biographies. For example, Harriet Martineau (1802–76) is often called the first female sociologist (Martineau, 1985). Born in England in 1802 to a prosperous family, she never married. Martineau translated Comte into English and wrote one of the first books on sociological research methods. She undertook critical studies of slavery, factory laws, and gender inequality. She was also a leading advocate of voting rights and higher education for women, as well as of gender equality in the family. As such, Martineau was one of the first feminists. Exceptional women like Martineau introduced gender issues that were largely ignored by Marx, Durkheim, Weber, Mead, and other early sociologists. Appreciation for the sociological contribution of these pioneer women has grown as concern with gender issues has come to form a substantial part of the modern sociological enterprise.

### Modern Feminism

Despite its encouraging beginnings, feminist thinking had little impact on sociology until the mid-1960s, when the rise of the modern feminist movement drew attention to the many remaining inequalities between women and men. Because of **feminist theory**'s major influence on sociology today, it may fairly be regarded as sociology's fourth major theoretical tradition. Modern feminism has several variants (see Chapter 8, Sexuality and Gender). However, the various strands of feminist theory share the following features:

Margrit Eichler (1942– ) was born in Berlin, Germany. She took her Ph.D. at Duke University in the United States before beginning her academic career in Canada. She served as chair of the Department of Sociology at the Ontario Institute for Studies in Education and was the first director of the Institute for Women's Studies and Gender Studies (IWSGS) at the University of Toronto. Eichler is internationally known for her work on feminist methodology (Eichler, 1987). Her work on family policy in Canada has influenced students, professional sociologists, and policymakers for nearly two decades (Eichler, 1988).

1. *Feminist theory focuses on various aspects of patriarchy, the system of male domination in society. Patriarchy, feminists contend, is as important as class inequality, if not more so, in determining a person's opportunities in life.*
2. *Feminist theory holds that male domination and female subordination are determined not by biological necessity but by structures of social power and social convention. From this point of view, women are subordinate to men only because men enjoy more legal, economic, political, and cultural rights.*
3. *Feminist theory examines how patriarchy operates in both micro and macro settings.*
4. *Feminist theory contends that existing patterns of gender inequality can and should be changed for the benefit of all members of society. The main sources of gender inequality include differences in the way boys and girls are brought up; barriers to equal opportunity in education, paid work, and politics; and the unequal division of domestic responsibilities between women and men.*

Table 1.1 summarizes feminist theory, symbolic interactionism, conflict theory, and functionalism (see also Figure 1.4). As you will see in the following chapters, sociologists have applied these theoretical traditions to all of the discipline's branches and have elaborated and refined each of them. To give you a taste of things to come, we now illustrate how sociologists apply all four theoretical traditions by analyzing the problem of fashion.

**Table 1.1**
Four Theoretical Traditions in Society

| Theoretical Tradition | Main Levels of Analysis | Main Focus | Main Question |
|---|---|---|---|
| Functionalist | Macro | Values | How do the institutions of society contribute to social stability and instability? |
| Conflict | Macro | Inequality | How do privileged groups seek to maintain their advantages and subordinate groups seek to increase theirs, often causing social change in the process? |
| Symbolic interactionist | Micro | Meaning | How do individuals communicate to make their social settings meaningful? |
| Feminist | Macro and mirco | Patriarchy | Which social structures and interaction processes maintain male dominance and female subordination? |

## *Applying the Four Theoretical Perspectives: The Problem of Fashion*

*"Oh. Two weeks ago I saw Cameron Diaz at Fred Siegel and I talked her out of buying this truly heinous angora sweater. Whoever said orange is the new pink is seriously disturbed."*

—Elle Woods (Reese Witherspoon) in *Legally Blonde* (2001)

In 2002, the *Wall Street Journal* announced that grunge might be back (Tkacik, 2002). Since 1998, one of the main fashion trends among white, middle-class, preteen and young teenage girls had been the Britney Spears look: bare midriffs, highlighted hair,

**Figure 1.4**
A Sociological Timeline of Some Major Figures in the Development of Sociological Theory, 1820–1965

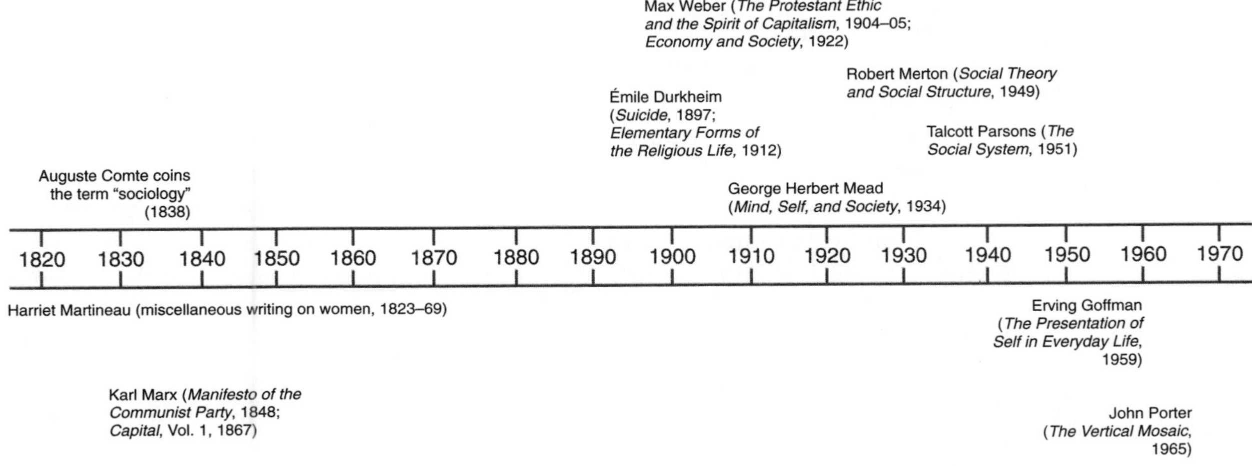

wide belts, glitter purses, big wedge shoes, and Skechers "energy" sneakers. But in 2002 a new star, Avril Lavigne, was rising in the pop charts. Nominated for a 2003 Grammy Award in the "Best New Artist" category, the 17-year-old skater-punk from Napanee in eastern Ontario affected a shaggy, unkempt look. She sported worn-out T-shirts, 1970s-style plaid Western shirts with snaps, low-rise blue jeans, baggy pants, undershirts, ties, backpacks, chain wallets, and, for shoes, Converse Chuck Taylors. The style was similar to the grunge look of the early 1990s, when Nirvana and Pearl Jam were the big stars on MTV and Kurt Cobain was king of the music world.

Why were the glamorous trends of the pop era possibly giving way in one market segment to "neo-grunge"? Why, in general, do fashion shifts take place? Sociological theory has interesting things to say on this subject (Davis, 1992).

Until the 1960s, the standard sociological approach to explaining the ebb and flow of fashion trends was *functionalist*. In the functionalist view, fashion trends worked like this: every season, exclusive fashion houses in Paris, Milan, New York, and London would show new styles. Some of the new styles would catch on among the exclusive clientele of big-name designers. The main appeal of wearing expensive, new fashions was that wealthy clients could distinguish themselves from people who were less well off. Thus, fashion performed an important social function. By allowing people of different rank to distinguish themselves from one another, fashion helped to preserve the ordered layering of society into classes. But by the twentieth century, thanks to technological advances in clothes manufacturing, it didn't take long for inexpensive knockoffs to reach the market and trickle down to lower classes. New styles then had to be introduced frequently so that fashion could continue to perform its function of helping to maintain an orderly class system. Hence the ebb and flow of fashion.

The functionalist theory was a fairly accurate account of the way fashion trends worked until the 1960s. Then, fashion became more democratic. Paris, Milan, New York, and London are still important fashion centres today. However, new fashion trends are increasingly initiated by lower classes, minority racial and ethnic groups, and people who spurn high fashion altogether. Napanee is, after all, pretty far from Paris, and today big-name designers are more likely to be influenced by the inner-city styles of hip-hop than vice versa. New fashions no longer just trickle down from upper classes and a few high-fashion centres. Upper classes are nearly as likely to adopt lower-class fashion trends that emanate from just about anywhere. As a result, the functionalist theory no longer provides a satisfying explanation of fashion cycles.

Some sociologists have turned to *conflict theory* as an alternative view of the fashion world. Conflict theorists typically view fashion cycles as a means by which industry owners make big profits. Owners introduce new styles and render old styles unfashionable because they make more money when many people are encouraged to buy new clothes often. At the same time, conflict theorists think fashion keeps people distracted from the many social, economic, and political problems that might otherwise incite them to express dissatisfaction with the existing social order and even rebel against it. Conflict theorists, like functionalists, thus believe that fashion helps to maintain social stability. Unlike functionalists, however, they argue that social stability bestows advantages on industrial owners at the expense of non-owners.

Conflict theorists have a point. Fashion *is* a big and profitable business. Owners *do* introduce new styles to make more money. They have, for example, created The Color Marketing Group (known to insiders as the "Color Mafia"), a committee that meets regularly to help change the palette of colour preferences for consumer products. According to one committee member, the Color Mafia makes sure that "the mass media, . . . fashion magazines and catalogs, home shopping shows, and big clothing chains all present the same options" (Mundell, 1993).

Yet the Color Mafia and other influential elements of the fashion industry are not all-powerful. Remember what Elle Woods said after she convinced Cameron Diaz not to buy that heinous angora sweater: "Whoever said orange is the new pink is seriously disturbed." Like many consumers, Elle Woods *rejected* the advice of the fashion industry. And, in fact, some of the fashion trends initiated by industry owners flop, one of the biggest being the introduction of the midi-dress (with a hemline midway between knee and ankle) in the mid-1970s. Despite a huge ad campaign, most women simply would not buy it.

This analysis points to one of the main problems with the conflict interpretation: it incorrectly makes it seem as if fashion decisions are dictated from above. Reality is more complicated. Fashion decisions are made partly by consumers. This idea can best be understood by thinking of clothing as a form of *symbolic interaction*, a sort of wordless "language" that allows us to tell others who we are and learn who they are.

If clothes speak, sociologist Fred Davis has perhaps done the most in recent years to help us see how we can decipher what they say (Davis, 1992). According to Davis, a person's identity is always a work in progress. True, we develop a sense of self as we mature. We come to think of ourselves as members of one or more families, occupations, communities, classes, ethnic and racial groups, and countries. We develop patterns of behaviour and belief associated with each of these social categories. Nonetheless, social categories change over time, and so do we as we age and move through them. As a result, our identities are always in flux. We often become anxious or insecure about who we are. Clothes help us express our shifting identities. For example, clothes can convey whether you are sexually available, athletic, conservative, and much else, thus telling others how you want them to see you and the kinds of people with whom you want to associate. At some point you may become less conservative, sexually available, and so on. Your clothing style is likely to change accordingly. (Of course, the messages you try to send are subject to interpretation and may be misunderstood.) For its part, the fashion industry feeds on the ambiguities within us, investing much effort in trying to discern which new styles might capture current needs for self-expression.

For example, capitalizing on the need for self-expression among many young girls in the late 1990s, Britney Spears hit a chord. Feminist interpretations of the meaning and significance of Britney Spears are especially interesting in this respect because they focus on the gender aspects of fashion.

Traditionally, feminists thought of fashion as a form of patriarchy, a means by which male dominance was maintained. They argued that fashion was mainly a female preoccupation. It takes a lot of time and money to choose, buy, and clean clothes. Fashionable clothing is often impractical and uncomfortable, and some of it is even unhealthy. Modern fashion's focus on youth, slenderness, and eroticism diminishes women by turning them into sexual objects, say some feminists. Britney Spears was of interest to traditional feminists because she supposedly helped to lower the age at which girls fell under male domination.

In recent years, this traditional feminist view has given way to a feminist interpretation that is more compatible with symbolic interactionism ("Why Britney Spears Matters," 2001). Some feminists now applaud the "girl power" movement that crystallized in 1996 with the release of the Spice Girls' hit single "Wannabe." They regard Britney Spears as part of that movement. In their judgment, Spears's music, dance routines, and dress style expressed a self-assuredness and assertiveness that resonated with the less submissive

Britney Spears versus Avril Lavigne

and more independent role that girls were carving out for themselves. With her kicks, her shadow boxing, and songs like the 2000 single "Stronger," Spears spoke for the *empowerment* of young women. Quite apart from her musical and dancing talent, then, some feminists think many young girls were wild about Britney Spears because she helped them express their own social and sexual power. Of course, not all young girls agree. Some, like Avril Lavigne, found Spears "phony" and too much of a "showgirl." They wanted "more authentic" ways of asserting their identity through fashion (Pascual, 2002). Still, the symbolic interactionist and feminist interpretations of fashion help us see more clearly the ambiguities of identity that underlie the rise of new fashion trends.

Our analysis of fashion shows that each of the four theoretical perspectives—functionalism, conflict theory, symbolic interactionism, and feminism—can clarify different aspects of a sociological problem. This does not mean that each perspective always has equal validity. Often, the interpretations that derive from different theoretical perspectives are incompatible. They offer *competing* interpretations of the same social reality. It is then necessary to do research to determine which perspective works best for the case at hand.

# Conducting Research

Theorizing without research is like painting a portrait without paint. You might have a spectacular idea for the portrait, but you can never be sure it's going to work out until you get your hands dirty and commit the idea to canvas. Similarly, sociologists conduct research to see how well their theories fit the real world. We devote the second half of this chapter to outlining the research process, given its importance to the sociological enterprise as a whole.

Social conditions often colour theoretical speculation. Think of the influence of the Great Depression on the functionalists and the influence of the radical 1960s on the conflict theorists. The personal values of individual theorists also come into play when they formulate theories. Remember how the biases of theorists since Comte have helped shape theories. Should we conclude that theories are merely speculative and totally subjective? Not at all. Sociologists have a powerful means of controlling bias and assessing the validity of theories: conducting **research.**

Before we do research, we rarely see things as they are. We see them as *we* are. Then, in the research process, a sort of waltz begins. Subjectivity leads, objectivity follows. When the dance is finished, we see things more accurately. As many advances in sociological thinking show, subjective experiences often enhance objective sociological knowledge, leading to the discovery of new problems and new solutions to old problems. Acknowledging that our experiences inspire us to ask particular questions about the social world is not the same as saying that those questions, or the answers we eventually uncover, are biased. Bias arises only when we remain unaware of our subjectivity. It is the purpose of research to help us become aware of our biases and to test theories against systematic observations of the social world that other researchers can repeat to check up on us. On the basis of research, we reject some theories, modify others, and are forced to invent new ones. Having outlined the main theoretical approaches in sociology, it is now time to discuss the research process.

## *The Research Cycle*

Ideally, sociological research is a cyclical process that involves six steps (Figure 1.5). The sociologist's first step is to *formulate a research question.* A research question must be stated so that it can be answered by systematically collecting and analyzing sociological data.

Sociological research cannot determine whether God exists or what the best political system is. Answers to such questions require faith more than evidence. However, sociological research can determine why some people are more religious than others and which political system creates most opportunities for higher education. Answers to such questions require evidence more than faith.

The second step involves a *review of the existing research literature.* Researchers must elaborate their research questions in the clear light of what other sociologists have already debated and discovered. Why? Because reading the relevant sociological literature stimulates researchers' sociological imaginations, allows them to refine their initial questions, and prevents duplication of effort.

**Figure 1.5**
**The Research Cycle**

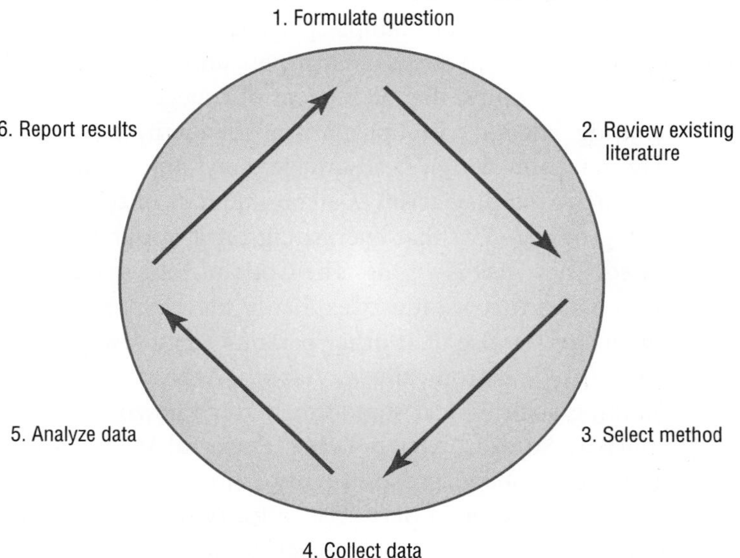

*Selecting a research method* is the third step in the research cycle. As we will see in detail later in this chapter, each data collection method has strengths and weaknesses. Each method is therefore best suited to studying a different kind of problem. When choosing a method, researchers must keep these strengths and weaknesses in mind.

In the fourth stage of the research cycle, researchers *collect data* by observing subjects, interviewing them, reading documents produced by or about them, and so forth. Many researchers think this is the most exciting stage of the research cycle because it brings them face to face with the puzzling sociological reality that so fascinates them.

Other researchers find the fifth step of the research cycle, when they *analyze the data*, the most challenging. During data analysis you can learn things that nobody knew before. At this stage, data confirm some of your expectations and confound others, requiring you to think creatively about familiar issues, reconsider the relevant theoretical and research literature, and abandon pet ideas.

Research is not useful for the sociological community, the subjects of the research, or the wider society if researchers do not complete the sixth step—*publish the results* in a report, a scientific journal, or a book. Publication serves another important function, too: it allows other sociologists to scrutinize and criticize the research. On that basis, errors can be corrected and new and more sophisticated research questions can be formulated for the next round of research. Science is a social activity governed by rules defined and enforced by the scientific community.

## *Ethics in Sociological Research*

Researchers must be mindful of the need to respect their subjects' rights throughout the research cycle. This means, first, that researchers must do their subjects no harm. This is the right to *safety*. Second, research subjects must have the right to decide whether their attitudes and behaviours may be revealed to the public and, if so, in what way. This is the right to *privacy*. Third, researchers cannot use data in a way that allows them to be traced to a particular subject. This is the subject's right to *confidentiality*. Fourth, subjects must be told how the information they supply will be used. They must also be allowed to judge the degree of personal risk involved in answering questions so that they can decide whether they will be studied and, if so, in what way. This is the right to *informed consent*.

Ethical issues arise not only in the treatment of subjects but also in the treatment of research results. For example, plagiarism is a concern in academic life, especially among students, who write research papers and submit them to professors for evaluation. A 2003 study found that 38 percent of college and university students admitted to committing "cut and paste" plagiarism when writing essays, up from just 10 percent in 2000 (Edmundson, 2003). Ready-made essays are also widely available for purchase.

Increased plagiarism is a consequence of the spread of the World Wide Web and the growing view that everything on it is public and therefore does not have to be cited. That view is wrong. The Code of Ethics of the American Sociological Association states that we must "explicitly identify, credit, and reference the author" when we make any use of another person's written work, "whether it is published, unpublished, or electronically available" (American Sociological Association, 1999: 16). Making such ethical standards better known can help remedy the problem of plagiarism. So can better policing. Powerful Web-based applications are now available that help college and university instructors determine whether essays are plagiarized in whole or in part (visit http://www.turnitin.com). Perhaps the most effective remedy, however, is for instructors to ensure that what they teach really matters to their students. If they do, students won't be as inclined to plagiarize because they will regard essay writing as a process of personal discovery. You can't cut and paste or buy enlightenment (Edmundson, 2003).

Bearing in mind our thumbnail sketch of the research cycle, we devote the next part of this chapter to exploring its fourth and fifth stages—gathering and analyzing evidence. We will now describe each of sociology's major research methods: experiments, surveys, field research, and the examination of existing documents and official statistics.

# The Main Sociological Research Methods

## *Experiments*

In the mid-1960s, the first generation of North American children exposed to high levels of TV violence virtually from birth reached their mid-teens. At the same time, the rate of violent crime began to increase. Some commentators said that TV violence made violence in the real world seem normal and acceptable. As a result, they concluded, North American teenagers in the 1960s and subsequent decades were more likely than pre-1960s teens to commit violent acts. The increasing prevalence of violence in movies, video games, and popular music seemed to add weight to their conclusion.

Social scientists soon started investigating the connection between media and real-world violence by using experimental methods. An **experiment** is a carefully controlled artificial situation that allows researchers to isolate presumed causes and measure their effects precisely (Campbell and Stanley, 1963) by manipulating a **variable,** a concept that can take on more than one value.

Aggressive behaviour among children is common, from siblings fighting to bullying in the schoolyard. Since the inception of home TV in the 1950s, social scientists have sought to find strong research designs capable of examining the causal effects, if any, of viewing violence on television.

Experiments use a procedure called **randomization** to create two similar groups. Randomization involves assigning individuals to one of the two groups by chance processes. For example, researchers may ask 50 children to draw a number from 1 to 50 from a covered box. The researchers assign children who draw odd numbers to one group and those who draw even numbers to the other group. By assigning subjects to the two groups by using a chance process, researchers ensure that each group has about the same proportion of boys and girls, members of different races, children highly motivated to participate in the study, and so forth, if the experiment is performed many times.

After subjects have been randomly assigned to the two groups, the researchers may put the groups in separate rooms and give them toys to play with. They observe the children through one-way mirrors, rating each child in terms of the aggressiveness of his or her play. This is the child's initial score on the dependent variable, which is aggressive behaviour. The **dependent variable** is the effect in any cause-and-effect relationship.

Then the researchers introduce the hypothesized cause to one group—now called the **experimental group.** They may show children in the experimental group an hour-long TV program in which many violent acts take place. They do not show the program to children in the other group, now called the **control group.** In this case, the violent TV show is the independent variable. The **independent variable** is the presumed cause in any cause-and-effect relationship.

Immediately after the children see the TV show, the researchers again observe the children in both groups at play. Each child's play is given a second aggressiveness score. By comparing the aggressiveness scores of the two groups before and after only one of the groups has been exposed to the presumed cause, an experiment can determine whether the presumed cause (watching violent TV) has the predicted effect (increasing violent behaviour).

Many experiments show that exposure to media violence has a short-term effect on violent behaviour in young children, especially boys. However, the results of experiments are mixed when it comes to assessing longer-term effects, especially on older children and teenagers (Anderson and Bushman, 2002; Browne and Hamilton-Giachritsis, 2005; Freedman, 2002).

Experiments allow researchers to isolate the single cause of theoretical interest and measure its effect with high **reliability,** that is, consistently from one experiment to the next. Yet many sociologists argue that experiments are highly artificial situations. They believe that removing people from their natural social settings lowers the **validity** of experimental results, that is, the degree to which they measure what they are actually supposed to measure.

To understand why experiments on the effects of media violence may lack validity, consider that, in the real world, violent behaviour usually means attempting to harm another person physically. Shouting or kicking a toy is not the same thing. In fact, such acts may enable children to relieve frustrations, lowering their chance of acting violently in the real world. Moreover, in a laboratory situation, aggressive behaviour may be encouraged because it is legitimized. Simply showing a violent TV program may suggest to subjects how the experimenter expects them to behave. That aggressive behaviour is not punished or controlled in the laboratory setting as it is in the real world. If a boy watching a violent TV show stands up and delivers a karate kick to his brother, a parent or other caregiver is likely to take action to prevent a recurrence. This usually teaches the boy not to engage in aggressive behaviour. In the lab, the lack of disciplinary control may facilitate unrealistically high levels of aggression (Felson, 1996).

## *Surveys*

Surveys are the most widely used sociological research method, and they have also been used to measure the effects of media violence on behaviour. Overall, the results of surveys show a weaker relationship between exposure to violent mass media and violent behaviour than do experiments, and some surveys show no relationship at all between these two variables (Anderson and Bushman, 2002; Huesmann, Moise-Titus, Podolski, and Eron, 2003; Johnson, Cohen, Smailes, Kasen, and Brook, 2002; see Table 1.2).

In a **survey,** people are asked questions about their knowledge, attitudes, or behaviour. All survey researchers aim to study part of a group—a **sample**—to learn about the whole group of interest—the **population.** To safely generalize about the population on the basis of findings from a sample, researchers must be sure that the characteristics of the people in the sample match those of the population. To draw a sample from which they can safely generalize, researchers must choose **respondents** (people who answer the survey questions) at random, and an individual's chance of being chosen must be known and greater than zero. A sample with these characteristics is known as a **probability sample.**

To draw a probability sample you first need a **sampling frame,** a list of all the people in the population of interest. You also need a randomizing method, a way of ensuring that every person in the sampling frame has a known and nonzero chance of being selected. A frequently used sampling frame is the telephone directory, which is now available for the entire country on CD-ROM. Researchers program computers

**Table 1.2**
Watching TV and Approval of Violence (in percentage)

| TV Viewing | 0–2 Hours/Day | 3+ Hours/Day | Total |
|---|---|---|---|
| Punching approval | | | |
| Yes | 69 | 65 | 67 |
| No | 31 | 35 | 33 |
| Total | 100 | 100 | 100 |
| *n* | 5 188 | 5 022 | 10 210 |

This table comes from one of the most respected surveys in the United States, the General Social Survey, conducted most years since 1972. The survey regularly asks people how many hours of TV they watch every day. Until 1994, it also asked respondents if they ever approve of a man punching an adult male. This table shows the results for these two questions, combining responses from 1972 to 1994.

An **association** between two variables exists if the value of one variable changes with the value of the other. For example, if the percentage of people who approve of a man punching an adult male is *higher* among those who watch 3 or more hours of TV a day, a *positive* association exists between the two variables. If the percentage of people who approve of a man punching an adult male is *lower* among those who watch 3 or more hours of TV a day, a *negative* association exists between the two variables. The greater the percentage difference between frequent and infrequent TV viewers, the stronger the association. This table shows that 69 percent of respondents who watched TV 0–2 hours a day approved punching compared with 65 percent of respondents who watched TV 3 or more hours. Is this a positive or a negative association?

To interpret tables, you must pay careful attention to what adds up to 100 percent. The table says that 69 percent *of people who watched TV 0–2 hours a day* approved of a man punching an adult male. It does *not* say that 69 percent of all people who approved of a man punching an adult male watched TV 0–2 hours a day. We know this because each category of the "TV viewing" variable equals 100 percent.

To test your understanding, calculate the number of respondents represented by the following percentages in the table: 69%, 65%, 31%, and 35%. Answers are given below.

Answers
69% = (69/100) × 5188 = 3580 respondents
65% = (65/100) × 5022 = 3264 respondents
31% = (31/100) × 5188 = 1608 respondents
35% = (35/100) × 5022 = 1758 respondents

Source: National Opinion Research Center (2006).

Researchers collect information through surveys by asking people in a representative sample an identical set of questions. People interviewed on a downtown street corner do not constitute a representative sample of Canadian adults, because the sample does not include people who live outside the urban core, it underestimates the number of older people and people with disabilities, it does not take into account regional diversity, and so forth.

to dial residential phone numbers at random, thus allowing them to create samples based on all households with phones—roughly 99 percent of Canadian households.

When sociologists conduct a survey, they may mail a form containing questions to respondents. Respondents then mail the completed questionnaire back to the researcher. Alternatively, sociologists may conduct face-to-face interviews in which questions are presented to the respondent by the interviewer during a meeting. Sociologists can also conduct surveys by means of telephone interviews.

Questionnaires can contain two types of questions. A **closed-ended question** provides the respondent with a list of permitted answers. Each answer is given a numerical code so the data can later be easily input into a computer for statistical analysis. Often, the numerical results of surveys are arranged in tables like Table 1.2. An **open-ended question** allows respondents to answer in their own words. Open-ended questions are particularly useful when researchers don't have enough knowledge to create a meaningful and complete list of possible answers.

To ensure that survey questions elicit valid responses, researchers must guard against four dangers:

1. *The exclusion of part of the population from the sampling frame*
2. *The refusal of some people to participate in the survey*
3. *The unwillingness of some respondents to answer questions frankly*
4. *The asking of confusing, leading, or inflammatory questions or questions that refer to several, unimportant or non-current events*

Much of the art and science of survey research involves overcoming these threats to validity (Converse and Presser, 1986; Ornstein, 1998). Recall that surveys tend to show a weaker relationship than do experiments between exposure to violent mass media and violent behaviour. That may be because survey researchers have developed more valid measures of violent behaviour.

## Field Research

The method that comes closest to people's natural social settings is **field research**. Field research involves systematically observing people wherever they meet, from the ethnic slum to the alternative hard rock scene to the public school classroom (Schippers, 2002; Whyte, 1981).

When they go into the field, researchers go prepared with strategies to ensure their observations are accurate. One such strategy is **detached observation,** which involves classifying and counting the behaviour of interest according to a predetermined scheme. Although useful for some purposes, two main problems confound direct observation. First, the presence of the researcher may cause **reactivity;** the observed people may conceal certain things or act artificially to impress the researcher (Webb, Campbell, Schwartz, and Sechrest, 1966). Second, the meaning of the observed behaviour may remain obscure to the researcher. A wink may be an involuntary muscle contraction, an indication of a secret being kept, a sexual come-on, and so on. We can't know what a wink means just by observing it.

To avoid reactivity and understand the meaning of behaviour, we must be able to see it in its social context and from the point of view of the people we are observing. To do that, researchers must immerse themselves in their subjects' world by learning their language and their culture in depth. When sociologists observe a social setting systematically *and* take part in the activities of the people they are studying, they are engaging in **participant observation** research (Lofland and Lofland, 1995).

Participant observation research helps us better understand how media violence may influence youth violence. For example, sociologists have spent time in schools where shooting rampages have taken place. They have developed a deep appreciation of the social and cultural context of school shootings by living in the neighbourhoods where they occur; interviewing students, teachers, neighbourhood residents, and shooters' family members; and studying police and psychological reports, the shooters' own writings, and other relevant materials (Harding, Fox, and Mehta, 2002; Sullivan, 2002). They have tentatively concluded that only a small number of young people—those who are weakly connected to family, school, community, and peers—seem to be susceptible to translating media violence into violent behaviour. A lack of social support allows their personal problems to become greatly magnified, and if guns are readily available, these youth are prone to using violent media messages as models for their own behaviour. In contrast, for the overwhelming majority of young people, violence in the mass media is just a source of entertainment and a fantasy outlet for emotional issues, not a template for action (Anderson, 2003).

Like other research methods, participant observation has strengths and weaknesses. On the plus side, it allows researchers to develop a deep and sympathetic understanding of the way people see the world. It is especially useful in the "exploratory" stage of research, when investigators have only a vague sense of what they are looking for and little sense of what they will discover. On the minus side, because participant observation research usually involves just one researcher in one social setting, it is difficult to know whether other researchers would measure things in the same way (this is the problem of reliability) and it is difficult to know how broadly findings can be generalized to other settings.

### *Analysis of Existing Documents and Official Statistics*

The fourth important sociological research method involves the **analysis of existing documents and official statistics.** What do existing documents and official statistics have in common? They are created by people other than the researcher for purposes other than sociological research.

Three types of existing documents that sociologists have mined most deeply are diaries, newspapers, and published historical works. Census data, police crime reports, and records of key life events are perhaps the most frequently used sources of official statistics. The modern census tallies the number of Canadian residents and classifies them by place of residence, race, ethnic origin, occupation, age, and hundreds of other variables. Statistics Canada publishes an annual *Uniform Crime Reporting Survey* that reports the number of crimes in Canada and classifies them by the location and type of crime, the age and sex of offenders and victims, and other variables. Statistics Canada also publishes an *Annual Compendium of Vital Statistics* that reports births, deaths, marriages, and divorces by sex, age, and so forth.

Census and crime data put into perspective the limited effect of media violence on violent behaviour. For example, researchers have discovered big differences in violent behaviour when they compare Canada and the United States. The homicide rate (the number of murders per 100 000 people) has historically been about four times as high in the United States. Yet TV programming, movies, and video games are nearly identical in the two countries, so exposure to media violence can't account for the difference. Researchers instead attribute the difference in homicide rates to the higher level of economic and social inequality and the wider availability of handguns in the United States (Government of Canada, 2002; Lenton, 1989; National Rifle Association, 2005).

Existing documents and official statistics have several advantages over other types of data. They can save the researcher time and money because they are usually available at no cost in libraries or on the World Wide Web. Official statistics usually cover entire populations and are collected by using rigorous and uniform methods, thus yielding highly reliable data. Existing documents and official statistics are especially useful for historical analysis. Finally, since the analysis of existing documents and official statistics does not require live subjects, reactivity is not a problem. The researcher's presence does not influence the subjects' behaviour.

Existing documents and official statistics also share one big disadvantage, however. They are not created with the researcher's needs in mind. In a sense, the researcher starts at stage 4 of the research cycle (data collection; see Figure 1.5) and then works within the limitations imposed by available data, including biases that reflect the interests of the individuals and organizations that created them.

For example, the census undercounts Aboriginal and homeless people. Moreover, it renders certain *characteristics* of individuals invisible and denies the existence of certain groups. For example, until recently the census let people say they were from Jamaica or China but it did not allow them to identify themselves as members of a "visible minority." Similarly, the 1981 census was the first to ask people if they were living common law, and the 2001 census was the first to recognize that some Canadians live in same-sex common-law relationships. So some categories of people have been ignored by the Canadian census until recently, and some people still are. This neglect matters because government programs and government funding are based on census counts. It also matters to researchers who use census data. Researchers must always bear in mind the biases of the census and other official statistics.

By now, you should have a pretty good idea of the basic methodological issues that confront any sociological research project. You should also know the strengths and weaknesses of some of the most widely used data collection techniques (see Table 1.3). In the remainder of this chapter, we outline what you can expect to learn from this book.

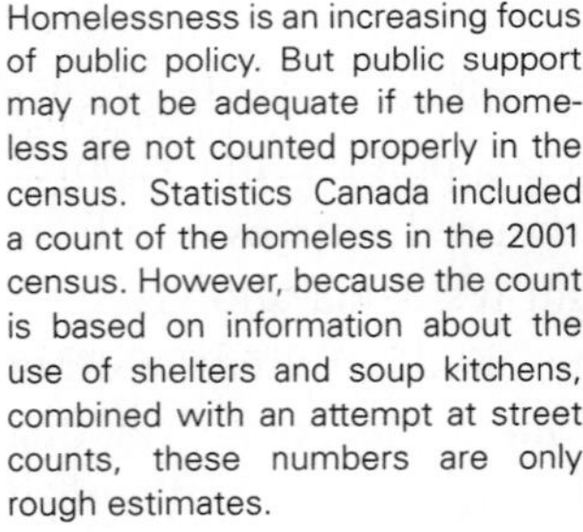

Homelessness is an increasing focus of public policy. But public support may not be adequate if the homeless are not counted properly in the census. Statistics Canada included a count of the homeless in the 2001 census. However, because the count is based on information about the use of shelters and soup kitchens, combined with an attempt at street counts, these numbers are only rough estimates.

**Table 1.3**
Strengths and Weaknesses of Four Research Methods

| Method | Strengths | Weaknesses |
|---|---|---|
| Experiment | High reliability; excellent for establishing cause-and-effect relationships | Low validity for many sociological problems because of the unnaturalness of the experimental setting |
| Survey | Good reliability; useful for establishing cause-and-effect relationships | Validity problems exist unless researchers make strong efforts to deal with them |
| Participant observation | Allows researchers to develop a deep and sympathetic understanding of the way people see the world; especially useful in exploratory research | Low reliability and generalizability |
| Analysis of existing documents and official statistics | Often inexpensive and easy to obtain; provides good coverage; useful for historical analysis; non-reactive | Often contains biases reflecting the interests of their creators and not the interests of the researcher |

## The Points of the Compass

The founders of sociology developed their ideas to help solve the great sociological puzzle of their time—the causes and consequences of the Industrial Revolution. This raises two interesting questions: What are the great sociological puzzles of *our* time? How are today's sociologists responding to the challenges presented by the social settings in which *we* live? We devote the rest of this book to answering these questions in depth.

It would be wrong to suggest that the research of tens of thousands of sociologists around the world is animated by just a few key issues. Viewed up close, sociology today is a heterogeneous enterprise enlivened by hundreds of theoretical debates, some focused on small issues relevant to particular fields and geographical areas, others focused on big issues that seek to characterize the entire historical era for humanity as a whole. Among the big issues, two stand out. Perhaps the greatest sociological puzzles of our time are the causes and consequences of the Postindustrial Revolution and globalization.

The **Postindustrial Revolution** is the technology-driven shift from employment in factories to employment in offices, and the consequences of that shift for nearly all human activities (Bell, 1973; Toffler, 1990). For example, as a result of the Postindustrial Revolution, non-manual occupations now outnumber manual occupations, and women have been drawn into the system of higher education and the paid labour force in large numbers. This shift has transformed the way we work and study, our standard of living, the way we form families, and much else. **Globalization** is the process by which formerly separate economies, nation-states, and cultures are becoming tied together and people are becoming increasingly aware of their growing interdependence (Giddens, 1990: 64; Guillén, 2001). Especially in recent decades, rapid increases in the volume of international trade, travel, and communication have broken down the isolation and independence of most countries and people. Also contributing to globalization is the growth of many institutions that bind corporations, companies, and cultures together. These processes have caused people to depend more than ever on people in other countries for products, services, ideas, and even a sense of identity.

**Figure 1.6**
**A Sociological Compass**

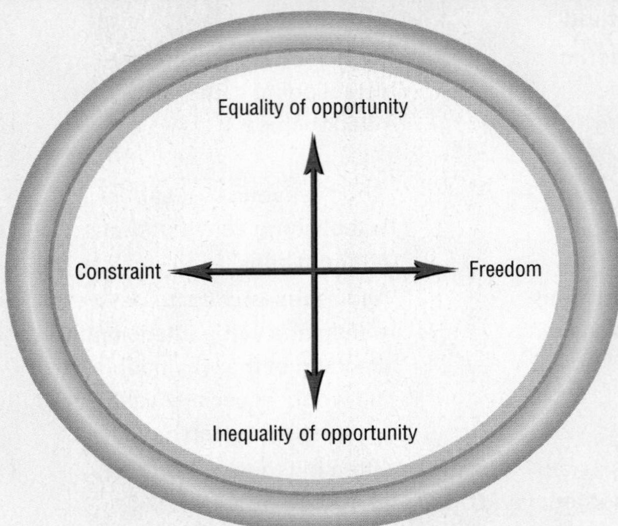


Sociologists agree that globalization and postindustrialism promise many exciting opportunities to enhance our quality of life and increase human freedom. However, they also see many social-structural barriers to the realization of that promise. We can summarize both the promise and the barriers by drawing a compass—a sociological compass (Figure 1.6). Each axis of the compass contrasts a promise with the barriers to its realization. The vertical axis contrasts the promise of equality of opportunity with the barrier of inequality of opportunity. The horizontal axis contrasts the promise of individual freedom with the barrier of constraint on that freedom. Let us consider these axes in more detail because much of our discussion in the following chapters turns on them.

## Equality versus Inequality of Opportunity

Optimists forecast that postindustrialism will provide more opportunities for people to find creative, interesting, challenging, and rewarding work. In addition, the postindustrial era will generate more equality of opportunity, that is, better chances for *all* people to get an education, influence government policy, and find good jobs.

You will find evidence to support these claims in the following pages. For example, we show that the average standard of living and the number of good jobs are increasing in postindustrial societies, such as Canada. Women are making rapid strides in the economy, the education system, and other institutions. Postindustrial societies, like Canada, are characterized by a decline in discrimination against members of ethnic and racial minorities, while democracy is spreading throughout the world. The desperately poor form a declining percentage of the world's population. Yet, as you read this book, it will also become clear that all of these seemingly happy stories have a dark underside. For example, it turns out that the number of routine jobs with low pay and few benefits is growing faster than the number of creative, high-paying jobs. Inequality between the wealthiest and poorest Canadians has grown in recent decades. An enormous opportunity gulf still separates women from men. Racism and discrimination are still a big part of our world. The absolute number of desperately poor people in the world continues to grow, as does the gap between rich and poor nations. Many people attribute the world's most serious problems to globalization. They have formed organizations and

movements—some of them violent—to oppose it. In short, equality of opportunity is an undeniably attractive ideal, but it is unclear whether it is the inevitable outcome of a globalized, postindustrial society.

## Individual Freedom versus Individual Constraint

We can say the same about the ideal of freedom. In an earlier era, most people retained their religious, ethnic, racial, and sexual identities for a lifetime, even if they were not particularly comfortable with them. They often remained in social relationships that made them unhappy. One of the major themes of this book is that many people are now freer to construct their identities and form social relationships in ways that suit them. To a greater degree than ever before, it is possible to *choose* who you want to be, with whom you want to associate, and how you want to associate with them. The postindustrial and global era frees people from traditional constraints by encouraging virtually instant global communication, international migration, greater acceptance of sexual diversity and a variety of family forms, the growth of ethnically and racially diverse cities, and so forth. For instance, in the past people often stayed in marriages even if they were dissatisfied with them. Families often involved a father working in the paid labour force and a mother keeping house and raising children without pay. Today, people are freer to end unhappy marriages and create family structures that are more suited to their individual needs.

Again, however, we must face the less rosy aspects of postindustrialism and globalization. In many of the following chapters, we point out how increased freedom is experienced only within certain limits and how social diversity is limited by a strong push to conformity in some spheres of life. For example, we can choose from a far wider variety of consumer products than ever before, but consumerism itself increasingly seems a compulsory way of life. Moreover, it is a way of life that threatens the natural environment. Large, impersonal bureaucracies and standardized products and services dehumanize both staff and customers. The tastes and the profit motive of vast media conglomerates, most of them U.S. owned, govern most of our diverse cultural consumption and arguably threaten the survival of distinctive national cultures. Powerful interests are trying to shore up the traditional nuclear family even though it does not suit some people. As these examples show, the push to uniformity counters the trend toward growing social diversity.

Postindustrialism and globalization may make us freer in some ways, but they also place new constraints on us.

## Where Do You Fit In?

Our overview of themes in this book drives home the fact that we live in an era "suspended between extraordinary opportunity . . . and global catastrophe" (Giddens, 1987: 166). A whole range of environmental issues; profound inequalities in the wealth of nations and of classes; religious, racial, and ethnic violence; and unsolved problems in the relations between women and men continue to stare us in the face and profoundly affect the quality of our everyday lives.

Giving in to despair and apathy is one possible response to these complex issues, but it is not a response that humans often favour. If it were our nature to give up hope, we would still be sitting around half-naked in the mud outside a cave. People are more inclined to look for ways of improving their lives, and this period of human history is full of opportunities to do so. We have, for example, advanced to the point at which for the first time we have the means to feed and educate everyone in the world. Similarly, it now seems possible to erode some of the inequalities that have always been the major source of human conflict.

Sociology offers useful advice on how to achieve these goals—for sociology is more than just an intellectual exercise; it is also an applied science with practical, everyday uses. Sociologists teach at all levels, from high school to graduate school. They conduct research for local, provincial or territorial, and federal governments; colleges and universities; corporations; the criminal justice system; public opinion firms; management consulting firms; trade unions; social service agencies; international non-governmental organizations; and private research and testing firms. They are often involved in the formulation of public policy, the creation of laws and regulations by organizations and governments. This is because sociologists are trained not just to see what is but also to see what is possible.

So please consider this book an invitation to explore your society's, and your own, possibilities. We don't provide easy answers. However, we are sure that if you grapple with the questions we raise, you will find that sociology can help you figure out where you fit into society and how you can make society fit you.

# Summary


1. *What does the sociological study of suicide tell us about society and about sociology?*

Durkheim noted that suicide is apparently a non-social and antisocial action that people often but unsuccessfully try to explain psychologically. In contrast, he showed that suicide rates are influenced by the level of social solidarity of the groups to which people belong. This argument suggests that a distinctively *social* realm influences all human behaviour.

2. *What is the sociological perspective?*

The sociological perspective analyzes the connection between personal troubles and three levels of social structure: microstructures, macrostructures, and global structures.

3. *What are the major theoretical traditions in sociology?*

Sociology has four major theoretical traditions. *Functionalism* analyzes how social order is supported by macrostructures. The *conflict approach* analyzes how social inequality is maintained and challenged. *Symbolic interactionism* analyzes how meaning is created when people communicate in microlevel settings. *Feminism* focuses on the social sources of patriarchy in both macrolevel and microlevel settings.

4. *What were the main influences on the rise of sociology?*

The rise of sociology was stimulated by the Scientific, Democratic, and Industrial Revolutions. The Scientific Revolution encouraged the view that sound conclusions about the workings of society must be based on solid evidence, not just speculation. The Democratic Revolution suggested that people are responsible for organizing society and that human intervention can therefore solve social problems. The Industrial Revolution created a host of new and serious social problems that attracted the attention of many social thinkers.

5. *Does sociological research have a subjective side?*

It does. The subjective side of the research enterprise is no less important than the objective side. Creativity and the motivation to study new problems from new perspectives arise from individual passions and interests.

6. *What methodological issues must be addressed in any research project?*

To maximize the scientific value of a research project, researchers must address issues of reliability (consistency in measurement) and validity (precision in measurement).

7. *What is participant observation?*

Participant observation is one of the main sociological methods. It involves carefully observing people's face-to-face interactions and participating in their lives over a long period. Participant observation is particularly useful for conducting exploratory research.

Issues of reliability and generalizability make participant observation less useful for other research purposes.

8. *What is an experiment?*

An experiment is a carefully controlled artificial situation that allows researchers to isolate hypothesized causes and measure their effects by randomizing the allocation of subjects to experimental and control groups and exposing only the experimental group to an independent variable. Experiments get high marks for reliability and analysis of causality, but issues of validity and generalizability make them less than ideal for many research purposes.

9. *What is a survey?*

In a survey, people are asked questions about their knowledge, attitudes, or behaviour, in a face-to-face interview, a telephone interview, or a paper-and-pencil format. Surveys rank high on reliability and validity as long as researchers phrase questions carefully and take measures to ensure high response rates.

10. *What are the advantages and disadvantages of using official documents and official statistics as sources of sociological data?*

Existing documents and official statistics are inexpensive and convenient sources of high-quality data. However, they must be used cautiously because they often reflect the biases of the individuals and organizations that created them rather than the interests of the researcher.

11. *What are the main influences on, and concerns of, sociology today?*

The Postindustrial Revolution is the technology-driven shift from manufacturing to service industries. Globalization is the process by which formerly separate economies, nation-states, and cultures are becoming tied together and people are becoming increasingly aware of their growing interdependence. The causes and consequences of postindustrialism and globalization form the great sociological puzzles of our time. The tensions between equality and inequality of opportunity, and between freedom and constraint, are among the chief interests of sociology today.

# Key Terms

**altruistic suicide (p. 7)**
**analysis of existing documents and official statistics (p. 29)**
**anomic suicide (p. 7)**
**association (p. 27)**
**class conflict (p. 15)**
**class consciousness (p. 15)**
**closed-ended question (p. 28)**
**conflict theory (p. 14)**
**control group (p. 26)**
**dependent variable (p. 26)**
**detached observation (p. 28)**
**dysfunctions (p. 14)**
**egoistic suicide (p. 7)**
**experiment (p. 25)**
**experimental group (p. 26)**
**feminist theory (p. 18)**
**field research (p. 28)**
**functionalism (p. 13)**
**global structures (p. 10)**
**globalization (p. 31)**
**independent variable (p. 26)**
**Industrial Revolution (p. 12)**
**latent functions (p. 14)**
**macrostructures (p. 10)**
**manifest functions (p. 14)**
**microstructures (p. 10)**
**open-ended question (p. 28)**
**participant observation (p. 29)**
**patriarchy (p. 10)**
**population (p. 27)**
**Postindustrial Revolution (p. 31)**
**probability sample (p. 27)**
**Protestant ethic (p. 16)**
**randomization (p. 26)**
**reactivity (p. 28)**
**reliability (p. 26)**
**research (p. 22)**
**respondent (p. 27)**
**sample (p. 27)**
**sampling frame (p. 27)**
**social solidarity (p. 6)**
**social structures (p. 10)**

**sociological imagination (p. 10)**
**sociology (p. 2)**
**survey (p. 27)**
**symbolic interactionism (p. 17)**
**theory (p. 7)**
**validity (p. 26)**
**values (p. 6)**
**variable (p. 25)**

## Questions to Consider

1. In this chapter, you learned how variations in the level of social solidarity affect the suicide rate. How do you think variations in social solidarity might affect other areas of social life, such as criminal behaviour and political protest?
2. Is a science of society possible? If you agree that such a science is possible, what are its advantages over common sense? What are its limitations?
3. What is the connection between objectivity and subjectivity in sociological research?
4. What are the methodological strengths and weaknesses of various methods of data collection?
5. Do you think the promises of freedom and equality will be realized in this century? Why or why not?

## Web Resources

### Companion Web Site for This Book

http://www.pointsofthecompass.nelson.com

Begin by clicking on the Student Resources section of the Web site. Next, select the chapter you are currently studying from the pull-down menu. From the Student Resources page you will have easy access to InfoTrac® College Edition, MicroCase online exercises, and additional Weblinks. The Web site also has many useful tips to aid you in your study of sociology, including practice tests for each chapter.

### InfoTrac® Search Terms

These search terms are provided to assist you in beginning to conduct research on this topic by visiting **http://www.infotrac-college.com**:

**conflict theory**
**feminism**
**functionalism**
**historical sociology**
**participant observation**
**social structure**
**sociological survey**
**symbolic interactionism**

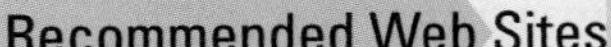

### Recommended Web Sites

For an inspiring essay on the practice of the sociological craft by one of North America's leading sociologists, see Gary T. Marx, "Of Methods and Manners for Aspiring Sociologists: 37 Moral Imperatives," on the World Wide Web at **http://www.colorado.edu/Sociology/gimenez/gary/aspiring_sociologists.html**.

SocioWeb is a comprehensive guide to sociological resources on the World Wide Web at **http://www.socioweb.com/~markbl/socioweb**.

The Canadian Sociology Association (CSAA) is the professional organization of Canadian sociologists. Visit the CSAA Web site at **http://www.csaa.ca**.

Canada's two sociology journals are the *Canadian Journal of Sociology* (**http://www.cjsonline.ca**) and the *Canadian Review of Sociology* (**http://www.csaa.ca/CRSA/BookReview/ReviewsList.htm**).

## Note

1. Some sociologists also distinguish "mesostructures," social relations that link microstructures and macrostructures (see Chapter 4, From Social Interaction to Social Organizations).

# PART 2 BASIC SOCIAL PROCESSES

# chapter 2

## culture



**In this chapter, you will learn that**

→ **Culture** is the sum of shared ideas, practices, and material objects that people create to adapt to, and thrive in, their environments.

→ Humans have thrived in their environments because of their unique ability to think abstractly, cooperate with one another, and make tools.

→ In some respects, the development of culture makes people freer. For example, culture has become more diversified and consensus has declined in many areas of life, allowing people more choice in how they live.

→ In other respects, the development of culture puts limits on who we can become. For example, the culture of buying consumer goods has become a virtually compulsory pastime. Increasingly, therefore, people define themselves by the goods they purchase.

# Culture as Problem Solving

If you follow or participate in sports, you probably know that many athletes perform little rituals before each game. For instance, Canadian hockey legend Wayne Gretzky never got his hair cut while playing on the road because the last time he did, his team lost. He always put his equipment on in the same order: left shin pad, left stocking, right shin pad, right stocking, pants, left skate, right skate, shoulder pads, left elbow pad, right elbow pad, and, finally, jersey—with the right side tucked into his pants. During warm-up, he would always shoot his first puck far to the right of the goal. When he went back to the dressing room, he would drink a Diet Coke, a glass of ice water, a Gatorade, and another Diet Coke—in that order. Former NHL goalie Patrick Roy juggled a puck between periods and bounced it on the ground. "Then I put it in a special place where no one will find it and make off with it, otherwise . . . so the legend goes, bad luck could befall the culprit and he would suddenly turn into an alligator" ("Mad about Hockey," 2002). Former NHL forward Bruce Gardiner dipped his hockey stick in a toilet before taking to the ice (Arace, 2000).

Like soldiers going off to battle, undergraduate students about to write final exams, and other people in high-stress situations, athletes invent practices to help them stop worrying and focus on the job at hand. Some wear a lucky piece of jewellery or item of clothing. Others say special words or a quick prayer. Still others cross themselves. And then there are those who engage in more elaborate rituals. For example, two sociologists interviewed 300 university students about their superstitious practices before final exams. One student felt she would do well only if she ate a sausage and two eggs sunny-side up on the morning of each exam. She had to place the sausage vertically on the left side of her plate and the eggs to the right of the sausage so they formed the "100" percent she was aiming for (Albas and Albas, 1989). Of course, the ritual had a more direct influence on her cholesterol level than on her grades. Yet indirectly it may have had the desired effect: if it helped to relieve her anxiety and relax her, she may have done better on her exams.

Culture can solve practical problems. Although some sports rituals are undoubtedly stranger than others, athletes (like Wayne Gretzky, shown here) often create a little culture to help them manage stress.

When some people say *culture,* they mean opera, ballet, art, and fine literature. For sociologists, however, this definition is too narrow. Sociologists call opera, ballet, art, and similar activities, **high culture** to distinguish it from **popular culture** or **mass culture.** Whereas high culture is consumed mainly by upper classes, popular or mass culture is consumed by all classes. Sociologists define **culture** in the general sense broadly as all the ideas, practices, and material objects that people create to deal with real-life problems. For example, when the university student invented the ritual of preparing for exams by eating sausage and eggs arranged just so, she was creating culture in the sociological sense. This practice helped the student deal with the real-life problem of anxiety. Similarly, tools help people solve the problem of how to plant crops and build houses. Religion helps people come to terms with death and gives meaning to life. Tools and religion are also elements of culture because they, too, help people solve real-life problems. Note, however, that religion, technology, and many other elements of culture differ from the superstitions of athletes in an important way: superstitions may be unique to the individuals who create them. Religion and technology are widely shared. They are even passed on from one generation to the next. How does cultural sharing take place? By means of communication and learning. Thus, shared culture is socially transmitted. It requires a society to persist. (In turn, a **society** is a number of people who interact, usually in a defined territory, and share a culture.) We conclude that culture is composed of the *socially transmitted* ideas, practices, and material objects that enable people to adapt to, and thrive in, their environments.

# The Origins and Components of Culture

You can appreciate the importance of culture for human survival by considering the predicament of early humans about 100 000 years ago. They lived in harsh natural environments. They had poor physical endowments, being slower runners and weaker fighters than many other animals. Yet, despite these disadvantages, they survived. More than that, they prospered and came to dominate nature. Domination was possible largely because humans were the smartest creatures around. Their sophisticated brains enabled them to create cultural survival kits of enormous complexity and flexibility. These cultural survival kits contained three main tools. Each tool was a uniquely human talent, and each gave rise to a different element of culture.

## *Symbols, Norms, and Values*

The first tool in the human cultural survival kit was **abstraction,** the capacity to create general ideas or ways of thinking that are not linked to particular instances. **Symbols,** for example, are one important type of idea. Symbols are things that carry particular meanings. Alphabets, mathematical notations, and signs are all sets of symbols. Symbols allow us to classify experience and generalize from it. For example, we recognize that we can sit on many objects but that only some of those objects have four legs, a back, and space for one person. We distinguish the latter from other objects by giving them a name: chairs. By the time babies reach the end of their first year, they have heard that word repeatedly and understand that it refers to a certain class of objects.

**Cooperation** is the second main tool in the human cultural survival kit. It is the capacity to create a complex social life. This feat is accomplished by establishing **norms,** or generally accepted ways of doing things. When we raise children and build schools, we are cooperating to reproduce and advance the human race. When we create communities and industries, we are cooperating by pooling resources and encouraging people to acquire specialized skills. Cooperation enables people to accomplish things that no one person could possibly do on his or her own. As people cooperate, they generally come to accept certain common *values*, or ideas about what is right and wrong, good and bad, beautiful and ugly. By analyzing people's values, we can learn much about what distinguishes one culture from another.

**Production** is the third main tool in the human cultural survival kit. It involves making and using tools and techniques that improve our ability to take what we want from nature. Such tools and techniques are known as **material culture** because they are tangible, whereas the symbols, norms, values, and other elements of **non-material culture**

By acquiring specialized skills, people are able to accomplish things that no person could possibly do alone.

are intangible. All animals take from nature to subsist, and an ape may sometimes use a rock to break another object. But only humans are sufficiently intelligent and dexterous to *make* tools and use them to produce everything from food to computers. Understood in this sense, production is a uniquely human activity.

Table 2.1 illustrates each of the basic human capacities and their cultural offshoots with respect to three types of human activity: medicine, law, and religion.

### *Sanctions, Taboos, Mores, and Folkways*

People are usually rewarded when they follow cultural guidelines and punished when they do not. These rewards and punishments, aimed at ensuring conformity, are known as **sanctions.** Taken together these sanctions are called the system of **social control.** Rewards (or positive sanctions) include everything from praise and encouragement to money and power. Punishments (or negative sanctions) range from avoidance and contempt to arrest, physical violence, and banishment.

**Table 2.1**
The Building Blocks of Culture

| **Human Capacities** | | | |
|---|---|---|---|
| | **Abstraction** | **Cooperation** | **Production** |
| | ↓ | ↓ | ↓ |
| **Elements of Culture** | **Ideas** | **Norms** | **Material Culture** |
| | | **Cultural Activities** | |
| Medicine | Theories | Experiments | Treatments |
| Law | Values | Laws | Courts, jails |
| Religion | Religious folklore | Religious customs | Church art, architecture |

Source: Adapted from Bierstedt (1963).

Note also that norms may be weak or strong. **Taboos** are among the strongest norms. When someone violates a taboo, it causes revulsion in the community and punishment is severe. Incest is one of the most widespread taboos. Breaking other core norms does not cause revulsion, but most people still believe such norms are essential for the survival of their group or their society. Sociologist William Graham Sumner (1940 [1907]) called such core norms **mores** (the Latin word for "customs," pronounced MORE-ays). Sumner called the least important norms **folkways.** They evoke the least severe punishment. If a man walks down the street wearing nothing on the top half of his body, he is violating a folkway. If he walks down the street wearing nothing on the bottom half of his body, he is violating a more.

Despite efforts to control them, people often reject elements of existing culture and create new elements of culture. Reasons for this rejection are discussed below and in Chapter 5, Deviance and Crime. Here, it is enough to say that just as social control is needed to ensure stable patterns of interaction, so resistance to social control is needed to ensure cultural innovation and social renewal. Stable but vibrant societies are able to find a balance between social control and cultural innovation.

## *Language and the Sapir-Whorf Thesis*

Language is one of the most important parts of any culture—some would say *the* most important part. A **language** is a system of symbols strung together to communicate thought. Equipped with language, we can share understandings, pass experience and knowledge from one generation to the next, and make plans for the future. In short, language allows culture to develop. Consequently, sociologists commonly think of language as a cultural invention that distinguishes humans from other animals.

In the 1930s, Edward Sapir and Benjamin Lee Whorf proposed an influential argument about the connection between experience, thought, and language. It came to be known as the **Sapir-Whorf thesis.** The Sapir-Whorf thesis holds that we experience certain things in our environment and form concepts about those things (path 1 → 2 in Figure 2.1). We then develop language to express our concepts (path 2 → 3). Finally, language itself influences how we see the world (path 3 → 1).

Whorf saw speech patterns as "interpretations of experience" (Whorf, 1956: 137), and this view seems uncontroversial. The Garo of Burma, a rice-growing people, distinguish many types of rice. Nomadic Arabs have more than 20 different words for

**Figure 2.1**
The Sapir-Whorf Thesis

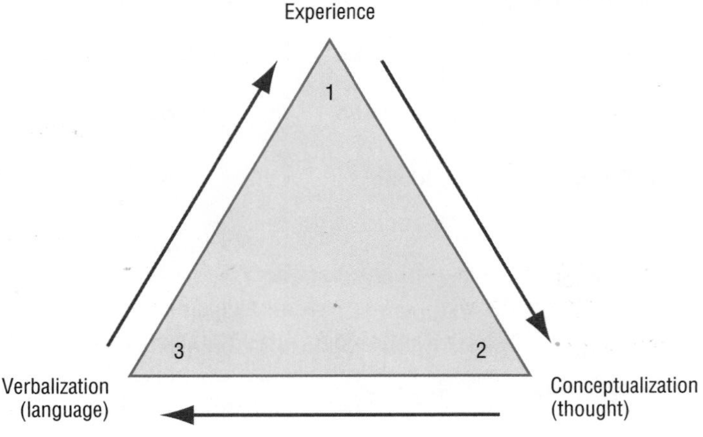

*camel* (Sternberg, 1998: 305). Verbal distinctions among types of rice and camels are necessary for different groups of people because these objects are important in their environment. As a matter of necessity, they distinguish among many different types of what we may regard as "the same" object. Similarly, terms that apparently refer to the same things or people may change to reflect a changing reality. For example, a committee used to be headed by a "chairman." When women entered the paid labour force in large numbers in the 1960s and some of them became committee heads, the term changed to "chairperson" or simply "chair." In such cases, we see clearly how the environment or our experience influences language.

The controversial part of the Sapir-Whorf thesis is path 3 → 1. In what sense does language *in and of itself* influence the way we experience the world? In the first wave of studies based on the Sapir-Whorf thesis, researchers focused on whether speakers of different languages perceive colour in different ways. By the 1970s, researchers had concluded that they do not. People who speak different languages may have a different number of basic colour terms, but everyone with normal vision is able to see the full visible spectrum. The Russian language has two words for *blue,* whereas the English language has only one. This does not mean that English speakers are handicapped in their ability to distinguish shades of blue.

In the 1980s and 1990s, researchers found that language itself can affect perception. For example, the German word for *key* is masculine, whereas the Spanish word for *key* is feminine. When German and Spanish speakers are asked to describe keys, German speakers tend to use words like *hard, heavy,* and *jagged,* whereas Spanish speakers use words such as *lovely, shiny,* and *shaped.* Apparently, the gender of the noun in and of itself influences how people see the thing to which the noun refers (Minkel, 2002). Still, the degree to which language itself influences thought is a matter of controversy. Some men use terms like *fox, babe, bitch, ho,* and *doll* to refer to women. These terms are deeply offensive to many people. They certainly reflect underlying inequalities between women and men. Some people assert that these terms *in and of themselves* influence people to think of women simply as sexual objects, but social scientists have yet to demonstrate the degree to which words influence people.

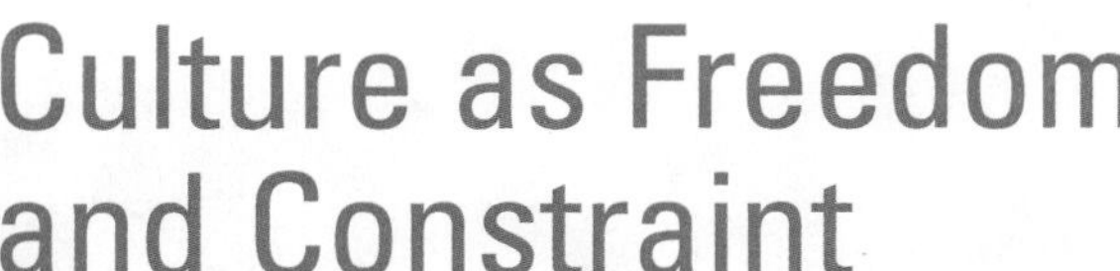

# Culture as Freedom and Constraint

### *Culture and Ethnocentrism: A Functionalist Analysis of Culture*

Despite its central importance in human life, culture is often invisible. That is, people tend to take their own culture for granted. It usually seems so sensible and natural they rarely think about it. In contrast, people are often startled when confronted by cultures other than their own. The ideas, norms, values, and techniques of other cultures frequently seem odd, irrational, and even inferior.

Judging another culture exclusively by the standards of our own is known as **ethnocentrism** (Box 2.1). Ethnocentrism impairs sociological analysis. This can be illustrated by Marvin Harris's (1974) functionalist analysis of a practice that seems bizarre to many Westerners: cow worship among Hindu peasants in India.

2.1

# SOCIOLOGY AT THE MOVIES

***Borat: Cultural Learnings of America for Make Benefit Glorious Nation of Kazakhstan* (2006)**

Borat is a journalist from Kazakhstan who visits the United States so he can learn about American culture and return home with useful lessons. The movie's humour turns on the apparent differences between Borat's culture and that of his audience and the people he meets. His values, beliefs, and norms seem deeply offensive to the Americans he encounters on his travels. Because Borat is capable of seeing the world only from his own cultural viewpoint, the movie at one level is a story of ethnocentrism gone mad.

The joke is apparent from the get-go. Many DVDs let you choose to hear the dialogue in English, French, or Spanish. The *Borat* DVD appears to give you the additional options of hearing the dialogue in Russian or Hebrew. However, when you select "Hebrew," you hear the repeated warning, "Jew in vocinity, Jew in vocinity," while the screen flashes the following messages: "You have been trapped Jew!" "Keep your claws where they can be seen." "Do not attempt shift your shape."

We soon discover that Kazakhs are not just anti-Semites; they are racists, homophobes, and sexists, too. At its Toronto Film Festival debut, Borat (played by Sasha Baron Cohen) sat with a horse in a cart, while four women dressed as peasants pulled the cart. As Borat explained in an interview, in Kazakhstan the highest being is God. Next comes man, followed by the horse, the snake, "the little crawly thing," and, finally, woman.

Borat directs many of our biggest laughs against Americans. At one point he secures the agreement of a rodeo organizer in Salem, Virginia, to let him sing the national anthem before the show begins. Borat first makes a little speech: "My name Borat, I come from Kazakhstan. Can I say first, we support your war of terror. [applause and cheers] May we show our support to our boys in Iraq. [applause and cheers] May U.S. and A kill every single terrorist! [applause and cheers] May George Bush drink the blood of every single man, woman, and child of Iraq! [applause and cheers] May you destroy their country so that for the next 1000 years not even a single lizard will survive in their desert! [applause and cheers]." After thus demonstrating the inhumanity of his audience, Borat sings his version of the Kazakh national anthem in English, to the tune of the United States national anthem:

> Kazakhstan is the greatest country in the world.
> All other countries are run by little girls.
> Kazakhstan is number one exporter of potassium.
> Other Central Asian countries have inferior potassium.
> Kazakhstan is the greatest country in the world.
> All other countries is the home of the gays.

To the suggestion that another country exceeds the United States in glory, the audience responds with jeers and boos that grow so loud, viewers fear for Borat's life. In this and other scenes, the movie forces us to conclude that American culture is as biased in its own way as Kazakh culture allegedly is.

Is *Borat* just one long prejudicial rant against Jews, Americans, Kazakhs, blacks, gays, women, and so on? Some people think so. But that opinion is not credible for two reasons. First, it is inconsistent with who Sasha Baron Cohen is. He is a well-educated liberal who completed a degree in history at Cambridge and wrote his thesis on

Borat Sagdiyev (Sasha Baron Cohen) in *Borat*

the civil rights movement in the United States. And he is a Jew who strongly identifies with his ethnic heritage. (One of the movie's biggest and largely unappreciated jokes is that Borat speaks mostly Hebrew to his producer, Azamat Bagatov [Ken Davitian]).

*Borat* certainly is one long and very funny rant, but the real objects of its satire are the world's racists, sexists, anti-Semites, and homophobes, regardless of their race, creed, or national origin. The deeper message of *Borat* is universal, not ethnocentric: respect for human dignity is a value that rises above all cultures, and people who think otherwise deserve to be laughed at.

**CRITICAL THINKING QUESTIONS**

- *Does* Borat *help you see the prejudices of other people more clearly?*
- *Does* Borat *help you see your own prejudices more clearly?*
- *Borat talks and acts like a bigot from the opening title to the closing credits. Do you think that the expression of bigotry is inherently offensive and should always be avoided? Or do you believe that the satirical expression of bigotry can usefully reveal hidden prejudices?*

Hindu peasants refuse to slaughter cattle and eat beef because, for them, the cow is a religious symbol of life. Pinup calendars throughout rural India portray beautiful women with the bodies of fat, white cows, milk jetting out of each teat. Cows are permitted to wander the streets, defecate on the sidewalks, and stop to chew their cud in busy intersections or on railroad tracks, forcing traffic to a complete halt. In Madras, police stations maintain fields where stray cows that have fallen ill can graze and be nursed back to health. The government even runs old-age homes for cows, where dry and decrepit cattle are kept free of charge. All this special care seems mysterious to most Westerners, for it takes place amid poverty and hunger that could presumably be alleviated if only the peasants would slaughter their "useless" cattle for food instead of squandering scarce resources to feed and protect these animals.

According to Harris (1974: 3–32), however, ethnocentrism misleads many Western observers. Cow worship, it turns out, is an economically rational practice in rural India. For one thing, Indian peasants can't afford tractors, so cows are needed to give birth to oxen, which are in high demand for plowing. For another, the cows produce hundreds of millions of pounds of recoverable manure, about half of which is used as fertilizer and half as a cooking fuel. With oil, coal, and wood in short supply, and with the peasants unable to afford chemical fertilizers, cow dung is, well, a godsend. What is more, cows in India don't cost much to maintain because they eat mostly food that is not fit for human consumption. And they represent an important source of protein as well as a livelihood for members of low-ranking castes, who have the right to dispose of the bodies of dead cattle. These "untouchables" eat beef and form the workforce of India's large leather craft industry. The protection of cows by means of cow worship is thus a perfectly sensible and highly efficient economic practice. It seems irrational only when judged by the standards of Western agribusiness.

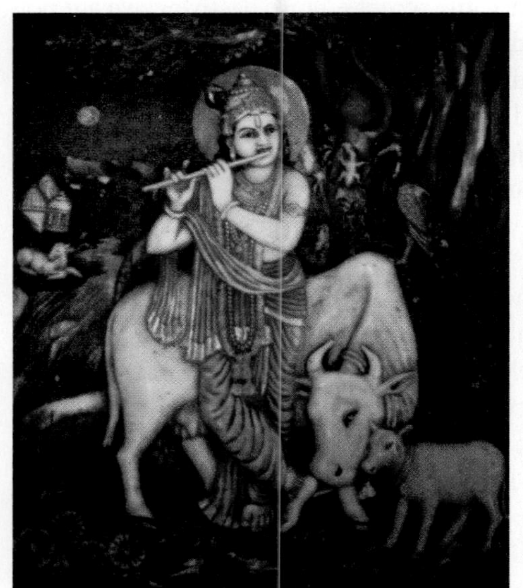

Many Westerners find the Indian practice of cow worship bizarre. However, cow worship performs several useful economic functions and is, in that sense, entirely rational. By viewing cow worship exclusively as an outsider (or, for that matter, exclusively as an insider), we fail to see its rational core.

Harris's (1974) analysis of cow worship in rural India is interesting for two reasons. First, it illustrates how functionalist theory can illuminate otherwise mysterious social practices. Harris uncovers a range of latent functions performed by cow worship, thus showing how a particular social practice has unintended consequences that make social order possible. Second, we can draw an important lesson about ethnocentrism from Harris's analysis: if you refrain from judging other societies by the standards of your own, you will have taken an important first step toward developing a sociological understanding of culture.

# Culture as Freedom

Culture has two faces. First, culture provides us with an opportunity to exercise our *freedom*. We create elements of culture in our everyday life to solve practical problems and express our needs, hopes, joys, and fears.

However, creating culture is just like any other act of construction in that we need raw materials to get the job done. The raw materials for the culture we create consist of cultural elements that either existed before we were born or that other people have created since our birth. We may put these elements together in ways that produce something genuinely new. But we have no other well to drink from, so existing culture puts limits on what we can think and do. In that sense, culture *constrains* us. This is culture's second face. In the rest of this chapter, we take a close look at both faces of culture.

## Cultural Production and Symbolic Interactionism

Until the 1960s, many sociologists argued that culture is a "reflection" of society. Using the language introduced in Chapter 1, we can say that they regarded culture as a dependent variable. Harris's (1974) analysis of rural Indians certainly fits that mould. In Harris's view, the social necessity of protecting cows caused the cultural belief that cows are holy.

In recent decades, the symbolic interactionist tradition we discussed in Chapter 1 has influenced many sociologists of culture. Symbolic interactionists regard culture as an *independent* variable. In their view, people do not just accept culture passively; we are not empty vessels into which society pours a defined assortment of beliefs, symbols, and values. Instead, we produce and interpret culture, creatively fashioning it to suit our diverse needs.

The idea that people creatively produce and interpret culture implies that, to a degree, we are at liberty to choose how culture influences us. Let us linger a moment on the question of why we enjoy more cultural freedom than ever before.

## Cultural Diversity

One reason we are increasingly able to choose how culture influences us is that Canadian society has diversified. Historically, Europe provided the great bulk of Canadian immigrants, but that started to change in the 1960s. Today, Europe and the United States supply only about 20 percent of Canadian immigrants while Asia and Africa supply nearly 70 percent. The four top source countries for immigrants are China, India, the Philippines, and Pakistan (Citizenship and Immigration Canada, 2005: 24). As a result, Canada is now a more heterogeneous society, racially and ethnically, than it has ever been. Members of visible minorities composed 4 percent of Canada's population in 1981 and 13 percent in 2001, and are projected to compose 19 percent in 2016 (Statistics Canada, 1998a: 75, 2003a).

The cultural diversification of Canadian society is evident in all aspects of life, from the growing popularity of Latino and Brazilian music, through the increasing influence of Asian design in clothing and architecture, to the ever-broadening international assortment of foods consumed by most Canadians. Marriage between people of different ethnic groups is widespread, and interracial marriage is increasingly accepted. At the political level, however, cultural diversity has become a source of conflict. This is nowhere more evident than in the debates that have surfaced recently concerning curricula in the Canadian educational system.

### *Multiculturalism*

Although each province and territory in Canada holds jurisdiction over education, it was common until recent decades for schools across Canada to stress the common elements of our culture, history, and society. Students learned the historical importance of the "charter groups"—the English and the French—in Canada's history. School curricula typically neglected the contributions of non-white, non-French, and non-English people to Canada's historical, literary, artistic, and scientific development. Moreover, students learned little about the less savoury aspects of Canadian history, including Canada's racist immigration policies that sought to preserve Canada's "English stock" by restricting or denying entry to certain groups (see Chapter 7, Race and Ethnicity). In general, history books were written from the perspective of the victors, not the vanquished.

For the past few decades, advocates of **multiculturalism** have argued that school, college, and university curricula should present a more balanced picture of Canadian history, culture, and society—one that better reflects the country's ethnic and racial diversity in the past and its growing ethnic and racial diversity today (Henry, Tator, Mattis, and Rees, 2001; James, 2003). In the words of one group of experts, "The purpose of schooling must be to 'empower' [minority groups] . . . , to give them the ability to participate fully in struggles, large and small, to gain respect, dignity, and power" (Gaskell, McLaren, and Novogrodsky, 1995: 105). Advocates of multiculturalism suggest that we must bring our educational system in line with Canada's status as the world's first officially multicultural society. They point out that, in launching its multiculturalism policy in 1971, the government declared that Canada, although officially bilingual, has no "official" culture—that is, none of the distinguishable cultures in Canada take precedence over the others. Moreover, with the passage of the Canadian Multiculturalism Act in 1988, the government confirmed its commitment to recognizing all Canadians "as full and equal participants in Canadian society." Multiculturalists conclude that to the extent that school curricula are culturally biased, they fail to provide students with the type of education a country devoted to multiculturalism must demand.

Most critics of multiculturalism do not argue against teaching cultural diversity. What they fear is that multicultural education is being taken too far (Fekete, 1994). Specifically, they say multiculturalism has three negative consequences:

1. *Critics believe that multicultural education hurts minority students by forcing them to spend too much time on non-core subjects. To get ahead in the world, they say, students need to be skilled in English, French, science, and math. By taking time away from these subjects, multicultural education impedes the success of minority group members in the work world. (Multiculturalists counter that minority students develop pride and self-esteem from a curriculum that stresses cultural diversity. They argue that this helps minority students get ahead in the work world.)*
2. *Critics also believe that multicultural education causes political disunity and results in more interethnic and interracial conflict. Therefore, they want school and postsecondary curricula to stress the common elements of the national experience*

Canada continues to diversify culturally.

*and highlight Europe's contribution to our culture. (Multiculturalists reply that political unity and interethnic and interracial harmony simply maintain inequality in Canadian society. Conflict, they say, although unfortunate, is often necessary to achieve equality between majority and minority groups.)*

3. *Finally, critics of multiculturalism complain that it encourages the growth of* ***cultural relativism.*** *Cultural relativism is the opposite of ethnocentrism. It is the belief that all cultures and all cultural practices have equal value. The trouble with this view is that some cultures oppose the most deeply held values of most Canadians. Other cultures promote practices that most Canadians consider inhumane (Box 2.2). Critics argue that to the degree it promotes cultural relativism, a truly multicultural system of education might encourage respect for practices that are abhorrent to most Canadians. (Multiculturalists reply that cultural relativism need not be taken to such an extreme.* Moderate *cultural relativism encourages tolerance, and it should be promoted.)*

### *The Rights Revolution: A Conflict Analysis of Culture*

What are the social roots of cultural diversity and multiculturalism? Conflict theory suggests where we can look for an answer. Recall from Chapter 1 the central argument of conflict theory: social life is an ongoing struggle between more and less advantaged groups. Privileged groups try to maintain their advantages while subordinate groups struggle to increase theirs. And sure enough, if we probe beneath cultural diversification and multiculturalism, we find what has been called the **rights revolution,** the process by which socially excluded groups have struggled to win equal rights under the law and in practice.

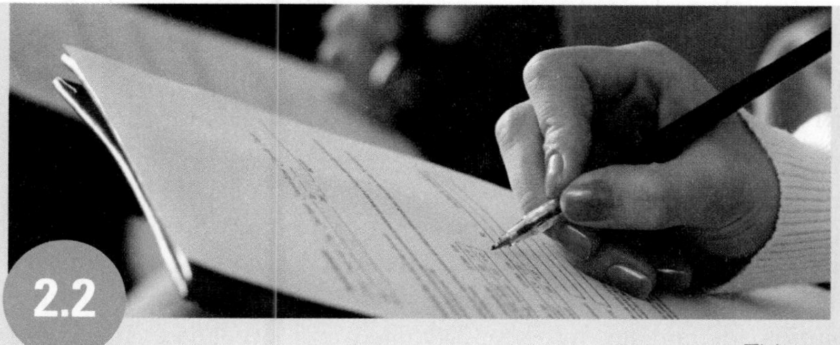

2.2

# SOCIAL POLICY: WHAT DO YOU THINK?

## Female Genital Mutilation: Cultural Relativism or Ethnocentrism?

The World Health Organization (WHO) defines female genital mutilation as "all procedures involving partial or total removal of the external female genitalia or other injury to the female genital organs whether for cultural or other nontherapeutic reasons" (World Health Organization, 2001). Elderly women who lack medical training usually perform these procedures.

Female genital mutilation results in pain, humiliation, psychological trauma, and loss of sexual pleasure. In the short term it is associated with infection, shock, injury to neighbouring organs, and severe bleeding. Long-term effects include infertility, chronic infections in the urinary tract and reproductive system, and increased susceptibility to hepatitis B and HIV/AIDS.

Although frequently associated with Islam, female genital mutilation is rare in many predominantly Muslim countries. It is a social custom, not a religious practice. It is nearly universal in parts of Africa, and about 2 million girls, mainly between the ages of 4 and 14, are at risk of undergoing it every year (Ahmad, 2000; World Health Organization, 2001).

In some cultures, people think female genital mutilation enhances female fertility. Furthermore, they assume that women are naturally "unclean" and "masculine" inasmuch as they possess a remnant of a "male" sex organ, the clitoris. From this point of view, women who have not experienced genital mutilation are more likely to demonstrate masculine levels of sexual interest and activity. They are less likely to remain virgins before marriage and faithful within marriage. Accordingly, these people think female genital mutilation lessens or eradicates sexual arousal in women.

One reaction to female genital mutilation is from a human rights perspective. In this view, the practice is simply one manifestation of gender-based oppression and the violence that women experience in societies worldwide. Adopting this perspective, the United Nations has defined female genital mutilation as a form of violence against women. This perspective is also reflected in a growing number of international, regional, and national agreements that commit governments (including Canada's) to preventing female genital mutilation, assisting women at risk of undergoing it, and punishing people who commit it.

Proponents of a second perspective on female genital mutilation are cultural relativists. They regard the human rights perspective as ethnocentric. Cultural relativists view interventions that interfere with the practice as little more than attacks on African cultures. From their point of view, all talk of universal human rights denies cultural sovereignty to less powerful peoples. Moreover, opposition to female genital mutilation undermines tolerance and multiculturalism while reinforcing racist attitudes. Accordingly, cultural relativists argue that we should affirm the right of other cultures to practise female genital mutilation even if we regard it as destructive, senseless, oppressive, and abhorrent. We should respect the fact that other cultures regard female genital mutilation as meaningful and as serving useful functions.

### CRITICAL THINKING QUESTIONS

- *Which of these perspectives do you find more compelling?*
- *Do you believe that certain principles of human decency transcend the particulars of any specific culture? If so, what are those principles?*
- *If you do not believe in the existence of any universal principles of human decency, then does anything go?*
- *Would you agree that, say, genocide is acceptable if most people in a society favour it? Or are there limits to your cultural relativism?*
- *In a world where supposedly universal principles often clash with the principles of particular cultures, where do you draw the line?*

After the outburst of nationalism, racism, and genocidal behaviour among the combatants in World War II, the United Nations proclaimed the Universal Declaration of Human Rights in 1948. It recognized the "inherent dignity" and "equal and inalienable rights of all members of the human family" and held that "every organ of society" should "strive by teaching and education to promote respect for these rights and freedoms and by progressive measures, national and international, to secure their universal and effective recognition and observance" (United Nations, 1998a). Fanned by such sentiment, the rights revolution was in full swing by the 1960s. Today, women's rights, minority rights, gay and lesbian rights, the rights of people with special needs, constitutional rights, and language rights are all part of our political discourse. Because of the rights revolution, democracy has been widened and deepened. The rights revolution is by no means finished. Many categories of people are still discriminated against socially, politically, and economically. However, in much of the world, all categories of people now participate more fully than ever before in the life of their societies (Ignatieff, 2000).

The rights revolution raises some difficult issues. For example, some members of groups that have suffered extraordinarily high levels of discrimination historically, such as Aboriginal Canadians, Chinese Canadians, and others, have demanded reparations in the form of money, symbolic gestures, land, and political autonomy (see Chapter 7, Race and Ethnicity). Much controversy surrounds the extent to which today's citizens are obligated to compensate past injustices.

Such problems notwithstanding, the rights revolution is here to stay and it affects our culture profoundly. Specifically, the rights revolution fragments Canadian culture by (1) legitimizing the grievances of groups that were formerly excluded from full social participation and (2) renewing their pride in their identity and heritage. Our history books, our literature, our music, our use of languages, and our very sense of what it means to be Canadian have diversified culturally. White, male, heterosexual property owners of northern European origin are still disproportionately influential in Canada, but our culture is no longer dominated by them in the way that it was just half a century ago.

### *From Diversity to Globalization*

The cultural diversification we witness today is not evident in preliterate or tribal societies. In such societies, cultural beliefs and practices are virtually the same for all group members. For example, many tribal societies organize **rites of passage.** These cultural ceremonies mark the transition from one stage of life to another (e.g., from childhood to adulthood) or from life to death (e.g., funerals). They involve elaborate procedures, such as body painting and carefully orchestrated chants and movements. They are conducted in public, and no variation from prescribed practice is allowed. Culture is homogeneous (Durkheim, 1976 [1915]).

In contrast, pre-industrial Western Europe and North America were rocked by artistic, religious, scientific, and political forces that fragmented culture. The Renaissance, the Protestant Reformation, the Scientific Revolution, the French and American revolutions—between the fourteenth and eighteenth centuries, all these movements involved people questioning old ways of seeing and doing things. Science placed skepticism about established authority at the very heart of its method. Political revolution proved nothing was ordained about who should rule and how they should

The idea of globalization first gained prominence in marketing strategies in the 1970s. In the 1980s, such companies as Coca-Cola and McDonald's expanded into non-Western countries to find new markets. Today, Kellogg's markets products in more than 160 countries. Basmati Flakes cereal was first produced by the Kellogg's plant in Tajola, India, in 1992.

do so. Religious dissent ensured that the Catholic Church would no longer be the supreme interpreter of God's will in the eyes of all Christians. Authority and truth became divided as never before.

Cultural fragmentation picked up steam during industrialization, as the variety of occupational roles grew and new political and intellectual movements crystallized. Its pace is quickening again today as a result of globalization. *Globalization,* as defined in Chapter 1, is the process by which formerly separate economies, nation-states, and cultures are becoming tied together and people are becoming increasingly aware of their growing interdependence.

One of the most important roots of globalization is the expansion of international trade and investment. Even the most patriotic of Canadians has probably dined at McDonald's—and even a business as "American" as McDonald's now reaps most of its profits from outside the United States; its international operations are growing at four times the rate of its U.S. outlets (Commins, 1997). At the same time, members of different ethnic and racial groups are migrating and coming into sustained contact with one another. Influential transnational organizations, such as the International Monetary Fund, the World Bank, the European Union, Greenpeace, and Amnesty International, are increasing in number. Relatively inexpensive international travel and communication make contact among people from diverse cultures routine. The mass media make Tom Cruise and *The Apprentice* nearly as well known in Warsaw as in Winnipeg. MTV brings music to the world via MTV Canada, MTV Latino, MTV Brazil, MTV Europe, MTV Asia, MTV Japan, MTV Mandarin, and MTV India (Hanke, 1998). In short, globalization destroys political, economic, and cultural isolation, bringing people together in what Canadian media analyst Marshall McLuhan (1964) first called a "global village" (Box 2.3). Because of globalization, people are less obliged to accept the culture into which they are born and freer to combine elements of culture from a wide variety of historical periods and geographical settings. Globalization is a schoolboy in Bombay, India, listening to Avril Lavigne on his MP3 player as he rushes to pull on his Levis, wolf down a bowl of Kellogg's Basmati Flakes, and say goodbye to his parents in Hindi because he's late for his English-language school.

2.3

# MASS MEDIA AND SOCIETY

## English, Globalization, and the Internet

A good indicator of the influence and extent of globalization is the spread of English. In 1600, English was the mother tongue of between 4 million and 7 million people. Not even all people in England spoke it. Today, about 1.5 billion people speak English worldwide, more than half as a second language (McCrum, Cran, and MacNeil, 1992; Peritz, 2006) (Figure 2.2). Most of the world's technical and scientific periodicals are written in English. English is the official language of the Olympics, of the Miss Universe contest, of navigation in the air and on the seas, and of the World Council of Churches.

English is dominant because Britain and the United States have been the world's most powerful and influential countries—economically, militarily, and culturally—for more than 200 years. (Someone once defined *language* as a dialect backed up by an army.) In recent decades, the global spread of capitalism, the popularity of Hollywood movies and American TV shows, and the widespread access to instant communication via telephone and the Internet have increased the reach of the English language. There are now more speakers of excellent English in India than in Britain, and when a construction company jointly owned by German, French, and Italian interests undertakes a building project in Spain, the language of business is English.

Because of the rise of English (as well as the influence of French, Spanish, and the languages of a few other colonizing nations), several thousand languages around the world are in the process of being eliminated. These endangered languages are spoken by the tribes of Papua, New Guinea; the Native peoples of the Americas; the national and tribal minorities of Asia, Africa, and Oceania; and marginalized European peoples, such as the Irish and the Basques. It is estimated that the 5000 to 6000 languages spoken in the world today will be reduced to 1000 to 3000 in a century. Much of

**Figure 2.2**
**English as Official of Majority Language**

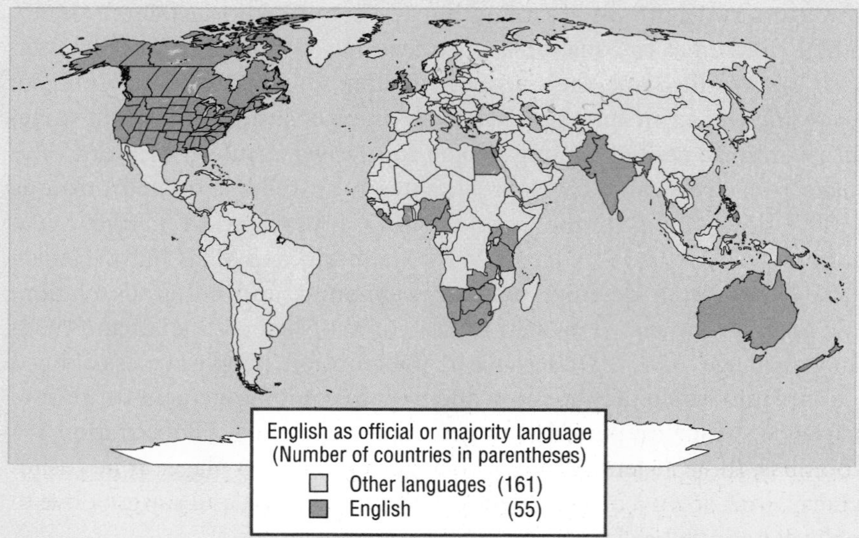


Sources: Central Intelligence Agency (2002); United Nations Educational, Scientific, and Cultural Organization ([UNESCO], 2001).

**Figure 2.3**
Internet Usage by Language Group, June 2001 and September 2004

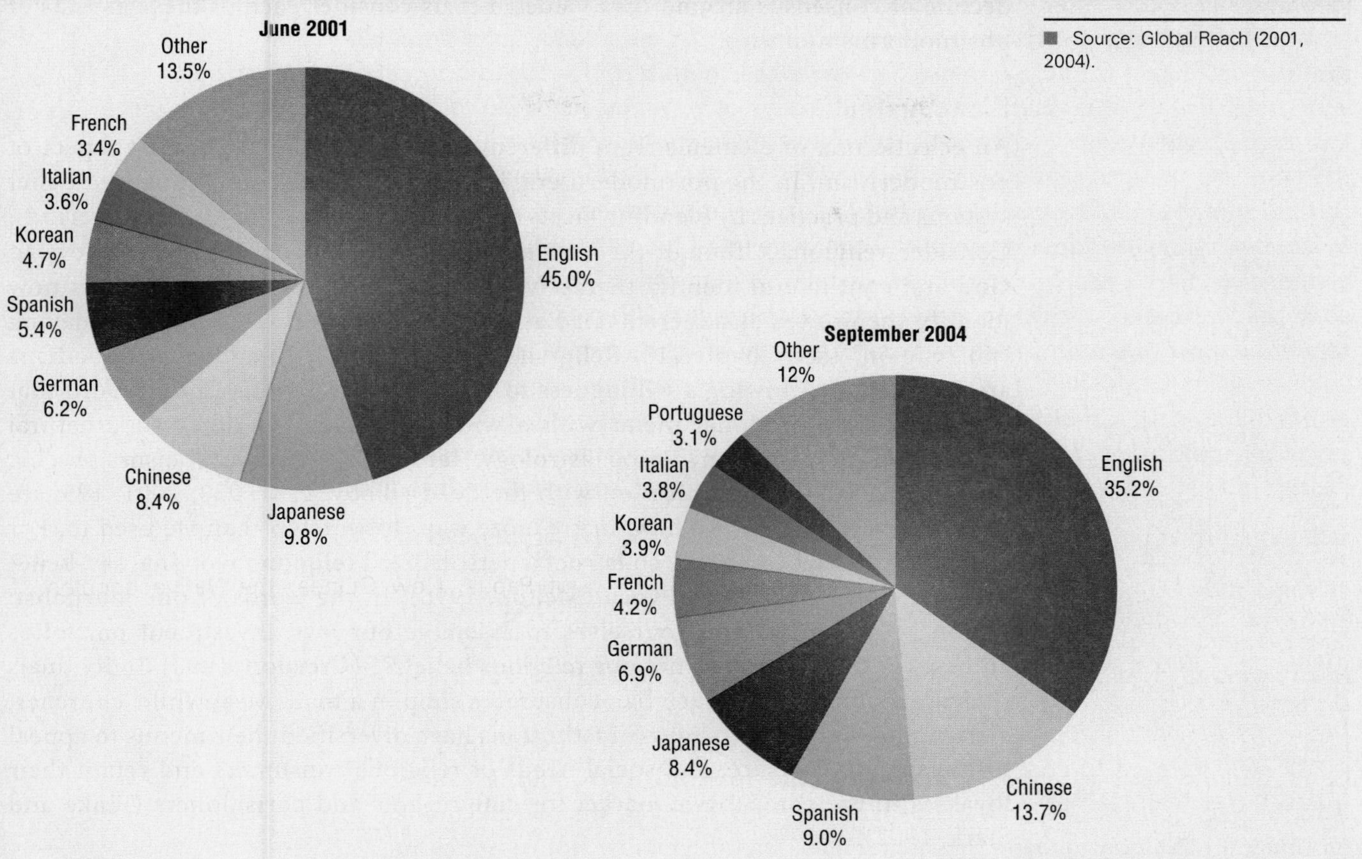


■ Source: Global Reach (2001, 2004).

the culture of a people—its prayers, humour, conversational styles, technical vocabulary, myths, and so on—is expressed through language. Therefore, the loss of language amounts to the disappearance of tradition and perhaps even identity. These are often replaced by the traditions and identity of the colonial power, with television playing an important role in the transformation (Woodbury, 2003).

Still, major languages other than English are holding their own and even pushing back the English onslaught in some areas, such as the Internet. Consider the pie charts in Figure 2.3, which show how language use on the Internet changed from June 2001 to September 2004. In 39 months, English usage dropped nearly 10 percent, while Chinese usage jumped more than 5 percent, Spanish usage grew nearly 4 percent, and the usage of other languages, such as Portuguese, increased more than 3 percent. This suggests that globalization does not necessarily involve the homogenization of culture.

## *Aspects of Postmodernism*

Some sociologists think that so much cultural fragmentation and reconfiguration has taken place in the last few decades that a new term is needed to characterize the culture of our times: **postmodernism.** Scholars often characterize the last half of the nineteenth century and the first half of the twentieth century as the era of modernity. During this hundred-year period, belief in the inevitability of progress, respect for authority, and consensus around core values characterized much of Western culture. In contrast, postmodern culture involves an eclectic mix of elements from different times and places, the erosion of authority, and the decline of consensus around core values. Let us consider each of these aspects of postmodernism in turn.

### Blending Culture

An eclectic mix of elements from different times and places is the first aspect of postmodernism. In the postmodern era, it is easier to create individualized belief systems and practices by blending facets of different cultures and historical periods. Consider religion. Although the vast majority of Canadians say they believe in God and continue to identify themselves as Christians, increasing numbers now identify themselves as adherents of Eastern non-Christian religions or as having "no religion" (see Chapter 10, Religion and Education). In addition, Canadians are increasingly showing a willingness to feast from a religious smorgasbord that combines a conventional menu with a wide assortment of other supernatural beliefs and practices, including astrology, tarot, New Age mysticism, psychic phenomena, and communication with the dead (Bibby, 1987: 233, 2001: 195; see Table 2.2). Simply put, we have many more ways to worship than we used to. For example, a person can easily construct a personalized religion involving, say, belief in the divinity of Jesus *and* yoga (Melton, 1996). In the words of one journalist: "In an age when we trust ourselves to assemble our own investment portfolios and cancer therapies, why not our religious beliefs?" (Creedon, 1998). Individuals thus draw on religions much like consumers shop in a mall. Meanwhile, churches, synagogues, and other religious institutions have diversified their menus to appeal to the spiritual, leisure, and social needs of religious consumers and retain their loyalties in the competitive market for congregants and parishioners (Finke and Stark, 1992).

A hallmark of postmodernism is the combining of cultural elements from different times and places. Architect I. M. Pei unleashed a storm of protest when his 22-metre glass pyramid became an entrance to the Louvre in Paris. It created a postmodern nightmare in the eyes of some critics.

**Table 2.2**
Beliefs across Generations, Canada, 2000

| "I believe . . ." | Grandparents (%) | Parents (%) | Younger Adults (%) |
|---|---|---|---|
| **Conventional** | | | |
| God exists | 85 | 81 | 78 |
| God or a higher power cares about you | 77 | 72 | 71 |
| Jesus was the Divine Son of God | 77 | 71 | 68 |
| In life after death | 64 | 69 | 72 |
| Have felt the presence God/higher power | 51 | 47 | 42 |
| **Less Conventional** | | | |
| In near-death experiences | 57 | 71 | 76 |
| In ESP | 59 | 70 | 67 |
| Personally have experienced precognition | 46 | 61 | 68 |
| Can have contact with the spirit world | 30 | 48 | 57 |
| In astrology | 31 | 34 | 36 |

Source: Bibby (2001: 252).

## Erosion of Authority

The erosion of authority is the second aspect of postmodernism. Half a century ago, Canadians were more likely than they are today to defer to authority in the family, schools, politics, medicine, and so forth. As the social bases of authority and truth have multiplied, however, we have become more likely to challenge authority. Authorities once widely respected, including parents, physicians, and politicians, are now held in lower regard by many people. In the 1950s, Robert Young played the firm, wise, and always-present father in the TV hit *Father Knows Best.* Fifty years later, Homer Simpson plays a fool in *The Simpsons.* Compared with Canadian teenagers in the first decade of the twenty-first century, Canadian teenagers in the 1980s—merely two decades ago—were more likely to express confidence in our police, our politicians, our court systems, and the leaders of religious organizations (Bibby, 2001: 193). Today, both young and old Canadians are likely to be critical of social institutions, such as religious organizations, that previously enjoyed special veneration. The rise of Homer Simpson and the decline of confidence in government both reflect the society-wide erosion of traditional authority (Nevitte, 1996).

## Instability of Core Values

The decline of consensus around core values is the third aspect of postmodernism. Half a century ago, people's values remained quite stable during their adult lives and many values were widely accepted. Today, value shifts are more rapid and consensus has broken down on many issues. For example, in the middle of the twentieth century, most adults remained loyal to one political party from one election to the next. However, specific issues and personalities have increasingly eclipsed party loyalty as the driving forces of Canadian politics (Clarke, Jenson, LeDuc, and Pammett, 1996). Today, people are more likely to vote for different political parties in succeeding elections than they were in 1950.

**Figure 2.4**
Percentage Who Believe That Scientific Advances Will Help Humanity, 2000

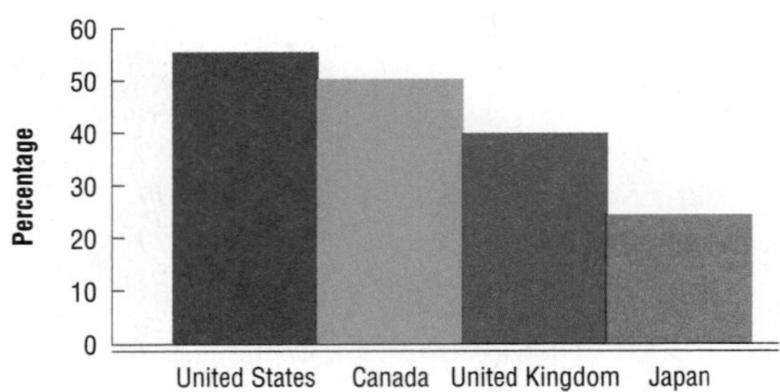


Source: *World Values Survey* (2000).

The decline of consensus can also be illustrated by considering the fate of "big historical projects." For most of the past 200 years, consensus throughout the world was built around big historical projects. Various political and social movements convinced people they could take history into their own hands and create a glorious future just by signing up. German Nazism was a big historical project. Its followers expected the Reich to enjoy 1000 years of power. Communism was an even bigger big historical project, mobilizing hundreds of millions of people for a future that promised to end inequality and injustice for all time. However, the biggest and most successful big historical project was not so much a social movement as a powerful idea—the belief that progress is inevitable and that life will always improve, mainly because of the spread of democracy and scientific innovation.

The twentieth century was unkind to big historical projects. Russian communism lasted 74 years. German Nazism endured a mere 12. The idea of progress fell on hard times as 100 million soldiers and civilians died in wars; the forward march of democracy took wrong turns into fascism, communism, and regimes based on religious fanaticism; and pollution from urbanization and industrialization threatened the planet. In the postmodern era, people increasingly recognize that apparent progress, including scientific advances, often have negative consequences (Scott, 1998; see Figure 2.4). As the poet E. E. Cummings once wrote, "nothing recedes like progress."

## *Is Canada the First Postmodern Country?*

Until the mid-1960s, the image of Canadians among most sociologists was that of a stodgy people: peaceful, conservative, respectful of authority, and therefore quite unlike our American cousins.

According to conventional wisdom, the United States was born in open rebellion against the British motherland. Its Western frontier was lawless. Vast opportunities for striking it rich bred a spirit of individualism. Thus, American culture became an anti-authoritarian culture.

Canada developed differently according to this conventional view. It became an independent country not through a revolutionary upheaval but in a gradual, evolutionary manner. The North-West Mounted Police and two hierarchical churches (Roman Catholic and Anglican) established themselves on the Western frontier *before* the era of mass settlement, allowing for the creation of an orderly society rather than a

"Wild West." Beginning with the Hudson's Bay Company, large corporations quickly came to dominate the Canadian economy, hampering individualism and the entrepreneurial spirit. Thus, Canadian culture became a culture of deference to authority. That, at least, was the common view until the 1960s (Lipset, 1963).

Although the contrast between deferential Canadian culture and anti-authoritarian American culture had validity 40 years ago, it is inaccurate today (Adams, 1997: 62–95). As we have seen, the questioning of authority spread throughout the Western world beginning in the 1960s. Nowhere, however, did it spread as quickly and thoroughly as in Canada. Canadians used to express more confidence in big business than Americans did, but surveys now show the opposite. Canadians used to be more religious than Americans, but that is no longer the case. Fewer Canadians (in percentage terms) say they believe in God and fewer attend weekly religious services. Confidence in government has eroded more quickly in Canada than in the United States. Americans are more patriotic than Canadians, according more respect to the state. Finally, Americans are more likely than Canadians to regard the traditional nuclear family as the ideal family form and to think of deviations from tradition—same-sex couples, single-parent families, cohabitation without marriage—as the source of a whole range of social problems. Thus, whether sociologists examine attitudes toward the family, the state, government, religion, or big business, they now find that Americans are more deferential to traditional institutional authority than Canadians are.

Because Canadians are less deferential to traditional institutional authority than Americans are, some commentators say that Canadians lack a distinct culture. For example, American patriotism sparks awareness of great national accomplishments in art, war, sports, science, and, indeed, all fields of human endeavour. Anthems, rituals, myths, and festivities celebrate these accomplishments and give Americans a keen sense of who they are and how they differ from non-Americans. Not surprisingly, therefore, a larger percentage of Americans than of Canadians think of themselves in unhyphenated terms—as "Americans" plain and simple rather than, say, Italian Americans. In Canada, a larger percentage of the population thinks of itself in hyphenated terms; compared with the Americans, our identity is qualified, even tentative.

Does this mean that Canadians lack a distinct national culture? Hardly. It means that although American culture is characterized by a relatively high degree of deference to dominant institutions, Canadian culture is characterized by a relatively high degree of tolerance and respect for diversity. We are more likely than Americans to favour gender equality, accept gay and lesbian relationships, encourage bilingualism and multiculturalism, and accept the right of Aboriginals to political autonomy. Characteristically, a large international survey by a condom manufacturer found that Americans have sex more often than anyone else, but Canadians are most likely to say that the pleasure of their partner is very important. As public opinion pollster Michael Adams writes:

> *Twenty-five years of public-opinion polling in Canada has taught me a seemingly paradoxical truth. Canadians feel* strongly *about their* weak *attachments to Canada, its political institutions and their fellow citizens. In other words, they feel strongly about the right to live in a society that allows its citizens to be detached from ideology and critical of organizations, and not to feel obliged to be jingoistic or sentimentally patriotic. Canadians* lack *of nationalism is, in many ways, a distinguishing feature of the country. (1997: 171)*

In short, Canadian culture *is* distinctive, and its chief distinction may be that it qualifies us as the first thoroughly postmodern society.

# Culture as Constraint

We noted above that culture has two faces. One we labelled *freedom*, the other *constraint*. Diversity, globalization, and postmodernism are all aspects of the new freedoms that culture allows us today. We now turn to an examination of two contemporary aspects of culture that act as constraining forces on our lives: rationalization and consumerism.

## *Rationalization*

In fourteenth-century Europe, an upsurge in demand for textiles caused loom owners to look for ways of increasing productivity. To that end, they imposed longer hours on loom workers. They also turned to a new technology for assistance: the mechanical clock. They installed public clocks in town squares. The clocks, known as *Werkglocken* (work clocks) in German, signalled the beginning of the workday, the timing of meals, and quitting time.

Workers were accustomed to enjoying many holidays and a flexible and vague work schedule regulated only approximately by the seasons and the rising and setting of the sun. The regimentation imposed by the work clocks made life more difficult. So the workers staged uprisings to silence the clocks—but to no avail. City officials sided with the employers and imposed fines for ignoring the work clocks. Harsher penalties, including death, were imposed on anyone trying to use the clocks' bells to signal a revolt (Thompson, 1967).

Today, 700 years later, many people are, in effect, slaves of the work clock. This is especially true of big-city North American couples who are employed full-time in the paid labour force and have preteen children. For them, life often seems an endless round of waking up at 6:30 a.m., getting everyone washed and dressed, preparing the kids' lunches, getting them out the door in time for the school bus or the car pool, driving to work through rush-hour traffic, facing the increased pace of work that resulted from the recent downsizing, driving back home through rush-hour traffic, preparing dinner, taking the kids to their soccer game, returning home to clean up the dishes and help with homework, getting the kids washed, brushed, and into bed, and (if you haven't brought some office work home) grabbing an hour of TV before collapsing, exhausted, for 6.5 hours of sleep before the story repeats itself. Life is less hectic for residents of small towns, unmarried people, couples without small children, retirees, and the unemployed. But the lives of most people are so packed with activities that time must be carefully regulated, each moment precisely parcelled out so that we may tick off item after item from an ever-growing list of tasks that need to be completed on schedule (Schor, 1992).

Have we come to depend too heavily on the *Werkglock*? Harold Lloyd in *Safety Last* (1923).

After centuries of conditioning, it is unusual for people to rebel against the clock in the town square anymore. In fact, we now wear a watch on our wrist without giving it a second thought, signifying that we have accepted and internalized the regime of the work clock. Allowing clocks to precisely regulate our activities seems the most natural thing in the world—which is a pretty good sign that the internalized work clock is, in fact, a product of culture.

The precise regulation of time is a rational means of ensuring efficiency. Minding the clock maximizes how much work you get done in a day. The regulation of time makes it possible for trains to run on schedule and university classes to begin punctually. But is minding the clock rational as an end in itself? For many people, it is not. They complain that the precise regulation of time has made life too hectic for them to enjoy. How rational is it that a restaurant in Japan has installed a punch-clock for its customers? The restaurant offers all you can eat for 35 yen per minute. As a result, "the diners rush in, punch the clock, load their trays from the buffet table, and concentrate intensely on efficient chewing and swallowing, trying not to waste time talking to their companions before rushing back to punch out" (Gleick, 2000: 244). Meanwhile, in New York and Los Angeles some upscale restaurants have gotten in on the act. An increasingly large number of business clients are so pressed for time, they pack in *two* half-hour lunches with successive guests. The restaurants oblige, making the resetting of tables "resemble the pit-stop activity at the Indianapolis 500" (Gleick, 2000: 155). Arguably, as these examples illustrate, a *rational means* (the use of the work clock) has been applied to a *given goal* (maximizing work) but has led to an *irrational end* (a too-hectic life).

This, briefly, is Max Weber's thesis about the rationalization process. **Rationalization,** in Weber's usage, means (1) the application of the most efficient means to achieve given goals, and (2) the unintended, negative consequences of doing so. Weber claimed that rationality of means has crept into all spheres of life, leading to unintended consequences that dehumanize and constrain us (see Figure 2.5). As our analysis of the way we use time shows, rationalization enables us to do just about everything more efficiently, but at a steep cost. In Weber's view, rationalization is one of the most constraining aspects of contemporary culture; it makes life in the modern world akin to living inside an "iron cage," wrote Weber (1958 [1904–05]: 181).

Sociologist George Ritzer develops this theme. He argues that just as the modern bureaucracy epitomized the rationalization process for Weber at the turn of the twentieth century, the McDonald's restaurant is the epitome of rationalization today (Ritzer, 1993, 1996). Instead of adapting institutions to the needs of people, says Ritzer, people must increasingly adapt to the needs of "McDonaldization." We are dehumanized in the process (Leidner, 1993; Reiter, 1991).

**Figure 2.5**
**The Rationalization of Chinese Script**

Reprinted here are the Chinese characters for "listening" (*t'ing*) in traditional Chinese script (left) and simplified, modern script (right). Each character is composed of several word-symbols. In traditional script, listening is depicted as a process involving the eyes, the ears, and the heart. It implies that listening demands the utmost empathy and involves the whole person. In contrast, modern script depicts listening as something that involves merely one person speaking and the other "weighing" speech. Modern Chinese script has been rationalized. Has empathy been lost in the process?

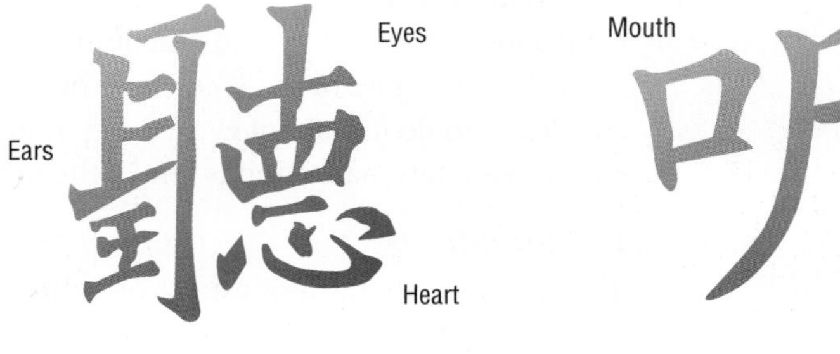

"McDonaldization" is a global phenomenon, as this busy McDonald's restaurant in Beijing, China, suggests.

As Ritzer shows, McDonald's has lunch down to a science. The meat and vegetables used to prepare your meal must meet minimum standards of quality and freshness. Each food item contains identical ingredients. Each portion is carefully weighed and cooked according to a uniform and precisely timed process. McDonald's executives have carefully thought through every aspect of your lunch. They have turned its preparation into a model of rationality. With the goal of making profits, they have optimized food preparation to make it as fast and as cheap as possible.

Unfortunately, however, the rationalization of lunch dehumanizes both staff and customers. For instance, meals are prepared by nonunionized, uniformed workers who receive minimum wage. They must execute their tasks within specific time limits. To boost sales, they must smile as they recite fixed scripts ("Would you like fries with your burger?"). Nearly half of all McDonald's employees are so dissatisfied with their work they quit after a year or less. To deal with this problem, McDonald's is now field-testing vending machines that will be used to replace staff and boost sales. Meanwhile, customers are expected to spend as little time as possible eating the food—hence the drive-through window, chairs designed to be comfortable for only about 20 minutes, and small express outlets in subways and department stores where customers eat standing up or on the run.

Nonetheless, powerful forces make the Big Mac popular. On the demand side, fast food fits the rushed lifestyle of many individuals and families in the more affluent countries of the world and the growing middle class in developing countries. On the supply side, big profits can be made by turning meal preparation into a mass production industry. Motivated by these forces, rationality of means (turning lunch into a science) results in irrationality of ends (dehumanizing staff and customers).

As the examples of the *Werkglock,* bureaucracy, and McDonald's show, rationalization enables us to do just about everything more efficiently but at a steep cost. Because it is so widespread, rationalization is one of the most constraining aspects of culture today.

### Consumerism

The second constraining aspect of culture we will examine is **consumerism,** the tendency to define ourselves in terms of the goods and services we purchase.

2.4

## YOU AND THE SOCIAL WORLD

### Ads "R" Us

Because advertising stimulates sales, businesses tend to spend more on advertising over time. Because advertising is widespread, most people unquestioningly accept it as part of their lives. In fact, many people have *become* ads. When your father was a child and quickly threw on a shirt, allowing the label to hang out, your grandmother might have told him to "tuck in that label." Today, many people proudly display consumer labels as marks of status and identity. Advertisers teach us to associate the words "Gucci" and "Nike" with different kinds of people, and when people display these labels on their clothes, they are telling us something about the kind of people they are. Advertising becomes us.

Record all labels displayed on the clothes worn by your three closest friends over a week. During the same week, record all labels displayed on the clothes worn by three classmates who seem as if they could never be your friends. Finally, record all labels displayed on the clothes you wear over the week.

**WRITING ASSIGNMENT**

In about 500 words, write an essay addressing the following questions: Do your labels resemble those of your friends or non-friends? What do the labels worn by your friends and non-friends tell you about who they are? On the basis of your observations, do you think it is reasonable to conclude that clothing labels are cultural artifacts that increase the solidarity of social groups and segregate them from other groups? (Note: If you, your friends, or your non-friends don't display clothing labels, what does this tell you?)

The rationalization process, when applied to the production of goods and services, enables us to produce more efficiently and to have more of just about everything than our parents did. But it is consumerism that ensures all the goods we produce will be bought. Of course, we have many choices. We can select from dozens of styles of running shoes, cars, toothpaste, and all the rest. We can also choose to buy items that help define us as members of a particular **subculture,** adherents of a set of distinctive values, norms, and practices within a larger culture (Box 2.4).

Regardless of individual tastes and inclinations, nearly all of us have one thing in common: we tend to be good consumers. We are motivated by advertising, which is based on the accurate insight that people will tend to be considered cultural outcasts if they fail to conform to stylish trends. By creating those trends, advertisers push us to buy, even if doing so requires that we work more and incur large debts (Schor, 1999). That is why the "shop-till-you-drop" lifestyle of many North Americans prompted French sociologist Jean Baudrillard to remark pointedly that even what is best in America is compulsory (Baudrillard, 1988 [1986]). And it is why we say that consumerism, like rationalization, acts as a powerful constraint on our lives.

### *From Counterculture to Subculture*

In concluding our discussion of culture as a constraining force, we note that consumerism is remarkably effective in taming countercultures. **Countercultures** are subversive subcultures. They oppose dominant values and seek to replace them. The hippies of the 1960s formed a counterculture and so do environmentalists today. Countercultures rarely pose a serious threat to social stability. Most often, the system of social control, of rewards and punishments, keeps countercultures at bay. In our society, consumerism acts as a social control mechanism that normally prevents countercultures from disrupting the social order. It does that by transforming deviations from mainstream culture into means of making money and by enticing rebels to become entrepreneurs (Frank and Weiland, 1997). Two examples from popular music help illustrate the point:

1. *Ozzy Osbourne was an important figure in the counterculture that grew up around heavy metal music beginning in the late 1960s. He and his band, Black Sabbath, inspired Metallica, Marilyn Manson, and others to play loud, nihilistic music; reject conventional morality; embrace death and violence; and spark youthful rebellion and parental panic. In the early 1980s, Tipper Gore, wife of future presidential candidate Al Gore, formed the Parents Music Resource Center to fight against violence and sex in the lyrics of popular music. Osbourne was one of the committee's principal targets. The "Prince of Darkness," as he was often called, was about as rebellious a figure as one could imagine in 1982.*

   *Flash forward 20 years. In 2002, Osbourne, at 55, had the sixth-most-popular show on American television among 18- to 34-year-olds, just behind* Survivor *in the ratings. MTV placed a dozen cameras throughout his Beverly Hills mansion, and every Tuesday night viewers saw everything going on in the Osbourne household for half an hour. According to* USA Today, *Osbourne is "a lot like anyone's adorable dad. Shuffles a bit. Forgets things. Worries about the garbage. Snores on the couch while the TV blares. Walks the dog" (Gundersen, Keveney, and Oldenburg, 2002: 1A). Rosie O'Donnell says to Ozzy's wife, Sharon, "What I love most about [your show] is not only the relationship you have with Ozzy—and you obviously adore each other—but the honesty with which you relate to your children. The love is so evident between all of you. It's heartwarming" (Gundersen et al., 2002: 2A). Sharon and Ozzy were invited to dinner at the White House in 2002.* The Osbournes, *it turns out, was a comfort to many people. The show*

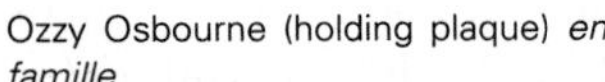
Ozzy Osbourne (holding plaque) *en famille*

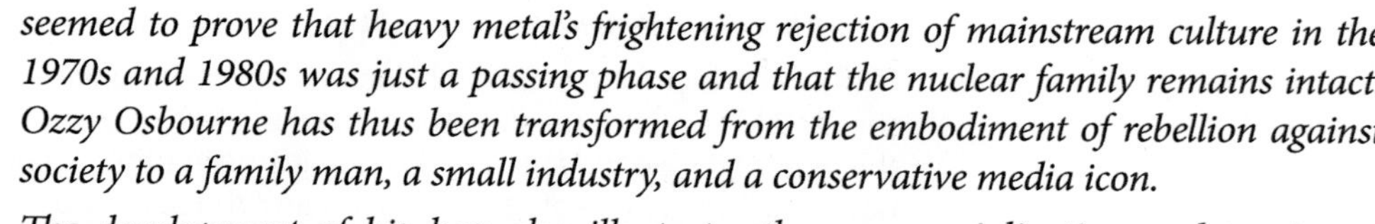

*seemed to prove that heavy metal's frightening rejection of mainstream culture in the 1970s and 1980s was just a passing phase and that the nuclear family remains intact. Ozzy Osbourne has thus been transformed from the embodiment of rebellion against society to a family man, a small industry, and a conservative media icon.*

Sean "Diddy" Combs in his Sunday best

2. *The development of hip-hop also illustrates the commercialization and taming of rebellion (Brym, 2007a). Originating in the squalor of inner-city American ghettos in the 1970s, hip-hop gave rise to a highly politicized counterculture. Early hip-hop artists glorified the mean streets of the inner city and held the police, the mass media, and other pillars of white society in contempt, blaming them for arbitrary arrests, the political suppression of black activists, and the spreading of lies about blacks. However, by the late 1980s, MTV had aired its first regular program devoted to the genre, and much of hip-hop's audience was composed of white, middle-class youth. Hip-hop artists were quick to see the potential of commercialization. Soon Wu-Tang Clan had its own line of clothes, while Gianni Versace was marketing clothing influenced by ghetto styles. Puff Daddy (Sean Combs, now known as Diddy) reminded his audience in his 1999 CD* Forever: *"N——get money, that's simply the plan." By 2002 he was, according to* Forbes *magazine, one of the forty richest men under 40; by 2005, he had his own line of clothing, Sean John. Like heavy metal, hip-hop's radicalism gave way to the lures of commerce.*

The fate of heavy metal and hip-hop is testimony to the capacity of consumerism to change countercultures into mere subcultures, thus constraining dissent and rebellion.

## The Points of the Compass

In this chapter, we have focused on the freedom-versus-constraint points of the sociological compass that we introduced in Chapter 1 (see Figure 1.6).

Today's culture grants people more freedom to explore and fulfill their individual and collective aspirations than at any time in human history. Although much distance remains to be covered, previously marginalized groups, such as women, gays and lesbians, and members of racial minorities, are closer than ever to equality with majority groups. They have the rights revolution to thank for that. At the same time, multiculturalism, globalization, and postmodernism give people more freedom than they enjoyed in the past to choose their religion, ethnicity, nationality, and sexuality—in short, their very identity.

We would develop a distorted picture of social reality, however, if we ignored the opposite point of the compass. Today's culture also constrains us, putting limits on what we can become. The constraints became evident when we examined the growth of rationalization and the spread of consumerism. Rationalization limits us by focusing our attention on how we can do things more efficiently while diverting our attention from the ultimate goals of our actions. Consumerism acts as a constraint too, driving us to want more things while simultaneously acting as a form of social control. Some freedoms, it emerges, are also straitjackets.

## Summary

1. *What are the main components of culture, and what is culture's main function?*

Culture comprises various types of ideas (e.g., symbols, language, values, beliefs), norms of behaviour, and human-made material objects. The ability to create symbols, cooperate, and make tools has enabled humans to thrive in their environments.

2. *What does it mean to say that culture has two faces?*

First, culture provides us with increasing opportunities to exercise our freedom in some respects. The rights revolution, multiculturalism, globalization, and postmodernism all reflect this tendency. Second, culture constrains us in other respects, putting limits on what we can become. The growth of rationalization and the spread of consumerism reflect this tendency.

3. *What is the multiculturalism debate?*

Advocates of multiculturalism want school, college, and university curricula to reflect the country's growing ethnic and racial diversity. They also want curricula to stress that all cultures have equal value. They believe that multicultural education will promote self-esteem and economic success among members of racial minorities. Critics fear that multiculturalism results in declining educational standards. They believe that multicultural education causes political disunity and interethnic and interracial conflict, promoting an extreme form of cultural relativism.

4. *What is the rights revolution?*

The rights revolution is the process by which socially excluded groups have struggled to win equal rights under the law and in practice. In full swing by the 1960s, the rights revolution involves the promotion of women's rights, minority rights, gay and lesbian rights, the rights of people with special needs, constitutional rights, and language rights. The rights revolution fragments North American culture by legitimizing the grievances of groups that were formerly excluded from full social participation and renewing their pride in their identity and heritage.

5. *What causes the globalization of culture?*

The globalization of culture has resulted from the growth of international trade and investment, ethnic and racial migration, influential transnational organizations, and inexpensive travel and communication.

6. *What is postmodernism?*

Postmodernism involves an eclectic mixing of elements from different times and places, the decline of authority, and the erosion of consensus around core values.

7. *What is rationalization?*

Rationalization involves the application of the most efficient means to achieve given goals and the unintended, negative consequences of doing so. Rationalization is evident in the increasingly regulated use of time and in many other areas of social life.

8. *What is consumerism?*

Consumerism is the tendency to define ourselves in terms of the goods we purchase. Excessive consumption limits who we can become, constrains our capacity to dissent from mainstream culture, and degrades the natural environment.

## Key Terms

**abstraction (p. 42)**
**consumerism (p. 62)**
**cooperation (p. 42)**
**counterculture (p. 63)**
**cultural relativism (p. 50)**
**culture (p. 40)**
**ethnocentrism (p. 45)**
**folkways (p. 44)**
**high culture (p. 41)**
**language (p. 44)**
**mass culture (p. 41)**
**material culture (p. 42)**
**mores (p. 44)**
**multiculturalism (p. 49)**
**non-material culture (p. 42)**
**norms (p. 42)**
**popular culture (p. 41)**
**postmodernism (p. 55)**

**production (p. 42)**
**rationalization (p. 61)**
**rights revolution (p. 50)**
**rites of passage (p. 52)**
**sanctions (p. 43)**
**Sapir-Whorf thesis (p. 44)**
**social control (p. 43)**
**society (p. 42)**
**subculture (p. 63)**
**symbol (p. 42)**
**taboos (p. 44)**

# Questions to Consider

1. To what extent do we shape our culture and to what extent does it shape us?
2. Select a subcultural practice that seems odd, inexplicable, or irrational to you. By interviewing members of the subcultural group and reading about them, explain how the practice that you chose to research makes sense to members of the subcultural group.
3. Do you think the freedoms afforded by postmodern culture outweigh the constraints it places on us? Why or why not?

# Web Resources

## Companion Web Site for This Book

http://www.pointsofthecompass.nelson.com

Begin by clicking on the Student Resources section of the Web site. Next, select the chapter you are currently studying from the pull-down menu. From the Student Resources page you will have easy access to InfoTrac® College Edition, MicroCase online exercises, and additional Weblinks. The Web site also has many useful tips to aid you in your study of sociology, including practice tests for each chapter.

## InfoTrac® Search Terms

These search terms are provided to assist you in beginning to conduct research on this topic by visiting **http://www.infotrac-college.com**:

**consumerism**
**culture**
**globalization**
**multiculturalism**
**postmodernism**
**rationalization**

## Recommended Web Sites

Benjamin Barber, "Jihad vs. McWorld," on the World Wide Web at **http://www.theatlantic.com/doc/199203/barber** is a brief, masterful analysis of the forces that are simultaneously making world culture more homogeneous and more heterogeneous. The article was originally published in *The Atlantic Monthly* (March 1992).

Adbusters is a Vancouver-based organization devoted to analyzing and criticizing consumer culture. Its provocative Web site is at **http://adbusters.org/home/**.

CultureWeb is the resource centre for the Sociology of Culture section of the American Sociological Association at **http://www.ibiblio.org/culture/**.

The Resource Center for Cyberculture Studies is an organization devoted to studying emerging cultures on the World Wide Web. Its Web site is at **http://www.com.washington.edu/rccs/**.

# chapter 3
## socialization



### In this chapter, you will learn that

→ The view that social interaction unleashes human abilities is supported by studies showing that children raised in isolation do not develop normal language and other social skills.

→ Although the socializing influence of the family decreased in the twentieth century, the influence of schools, peer groups, and the mass media increased.

→ People's identities change faster, more often, and more completely than they did just a couple of decades ago; the self has become more plastic.

→ The main socializing institutions often teach children and adolescents contradictory lessons, making socialization a more confusing and stressful process than it used to be.

→ Declining parental supervision and guidance, increasing assumption of adult responsibilities by youth, and declining participation in extracurricular activities are transforming the character of childhood and adolescence today.

# Social Isolation and Socialization

One day in 1800, a 10- or 11-year-old boy walked out of the woods in southern France. He was filthy, naked, and unable to speak, and he had not been toilet trained. After being taken by the police to a local orphanage, he repeatedly tried to escape and refused to wear clothes. No parent ever claimed him. He became known as "the wild boy of Aveyron." A thorough medical examination found no major abnormalities of either a physical or a mental nature. Why, then, did the boy seem more animal than human? Because, until he walked out of the woods, he had been raised in isolation from other human beings (Shattuck, 1980).

Similar horrifying reports lead to the same conclusion. Occasionally a child is found locked in an attic or a cellar, where he or she saw another person for only short periods each day to receive food. Like the wild boy of Aveyron, such children rarely develop normally. Typically, they remain disinterested in games. They cannot form intimate social relationships with other people. They develop only the most basic language skills.

Some of these children may suffer from congenitally low intelligence. The amount and type of social contact they had before they were discovered is unknown. Some may have been abused. Therefore, their condition may not be due to social isolation alone. However, these examples do at least suggest that the ability to learn culture and become human is only a potential. To be actualized, **socialization** must unleash this human potential. Socialization is the process by which people learn their culture. They do so by (1) entering into and disengaging from a succession of roles and (2) becoming aware of themselves as they interact with others. A **role** is the behaviour expected of a person occupying a particular position in society.

Convincing evidence of the importance of socialization in unleashing human potential comes from a study conducted by René Spitz (1945, 1962). Spitz compared children who were being raised in an orphanage with children who were being raised in a nursing home attached to a women's prison. Both institutions were hygienic and provided good food and medical care. However, the children's mothers cared for the babies in the nursing home, whereas just six nurses cared for the 45 babies in the orphanage. The orphans therefore had much less contact with other people. Moreover, from their cribs, the nursing home infants could see a slice of society. They saw other babies playing and receiving care. They saw mothers, doctors, and nurses talking, cleaning, serving food, and providing medical treatment. In contrast, the caregivers in the orphanage would hang sheets from the cribs to prevent the infants from seeing the activities of the institution. Depriving the infants of social stimuli for most of the day apparently made them less demanding.

Social deprivation had other effects too. Because of the different patterns of child care just described, by the age of 9 to 12 months the orphans were more susceptible to infections and had a higher death rate than the babies in the nursing home. By the time

In the 1960s, researchers Harry and Margaret Harlow placed baby rhesus monkeys in various conditions of isolation to study the animals' reactions. Among other things, they discovered that baby monkeys raised with an artificial mother made of wire mesh, a wooden head, and the nipple of a feeding tube for a breast were later unable to interact normally with other monkeys. However, when the artificial mother was covered with a soft terry cloth, the infant monkeys clung to it in comfort and later revealed less emotional distress. Infant monkeys preferred the cloth mother even when it had less milk than the wire mother. The Harlows concluded that emotional development requires affectionate cradling.

they were two to three years old, all the children from the nursing home were walking and talking, compared with fewer than 8 percent of the orphans. Normal children begin to play with their own genitals by the end of their first year. Spitz found that the orphans began this sort of play only in their fourth year. He took this as a sign that they might have an impaired sexual life when they reached maturity. This outcome has been observed in rhesus monkeys raised in isolation. Spitz's natural experiment thus amounts to quite compelling evidence for the importance of childhood socialization in making us fully human. Without childhood socialization, most of our human potential remains undeveloped.

## *The Crystallization of Self-Identity*

The formation of a sense of self continues in adolescence. Adolescence is a particularly turbulent period of rapid self-development. Consequently, many people can remember experiences from their youth that helped crystallize their self-identity. Do you? Robert Brym clearly recalls one such defining moment (Brym, 2006).

"I can date precisely the pivot of my adolescence," says Robert. "I was in grade 10. It was December 16. At 4 p.m. I was a nobody, and I knew it. Half an hour later, I was walking home from school, delighting in the slight sting of snowflakes melting on my upturned face, knowing I had been swept up in a sea of change.

"About 200 students had sat impatiently in the auditorium that last day of school before the winter vacation. We were waiting for Mr. Garrod, the English teacher who headed the school's drama program, to announce the cast of *West Side Story*. I was hoping for a small speaking part and was not surprised when Mr. Garrod failed to read my name as a chorus member. However, as the list of remaining characters grew shorter, I became despondent. Soon only the leads remained. I knew that an unknown kid in grade 10 couldn't possibly be asked to play Tony, the male lead. Leads were usually reserved for more experienced grade 12 students.

"Then came the thunderclap. 'Tony,' said Mr. Garrod, 'will be played by Robert Brym.'

"'Who's Robert Brym?' whispered a girl sitting two rows ahead of me. Her friend merely shrugged in reply. If she had asked *me* that question, I might have responded similarly. Like nearly all 15-year-olds, I was deeply involved in the process of figuring out exactly who I was. I had little idea of what I was good at. I was insecure about my social status. I wasn't sure what I believed in. In short, I was a typical teenager. I had only a vaguely defined sense of self.

"A sociologist once wrote that 'the central growth process in adolescence is to define the self through the clarification of experience and to establish self-esteem' (Friedenberg, 1959: 190). From this point of view, playing Tony in *West Side Story* turned out to be the first section of a bridge that led me from adolescence to adulthood. Playing Tony raised my social status in the eyes of my classmates, made me more self-confident, taught me I could be good at something, helped me to begin discovering parts of myself I hadn't known before, and showed me that I could act rather than merely be acted upon. In short, it was through my involvement in the play (and, subsequently, in many other plays throughout high school) that I began to develop a clear sense of who I am."

The crystallization of self-identity during adolescence is just one episode in a lifelong process of socialization. Socialization is by no means the only social process that influences human behaviour (see Box 3.1); but it is a fundamentally important influence. To paint a picture of the socialization process in its entirety, we first review the main theories of how a sense of self develops during early childhood. We then discuss the operation and relative influence of society's main socializing institutions or "agents of socialization": families, schools, peer groups, and the mass media. In these settings, we learn, among other things, how to control our impulses, think of ourselves as members of different groups, value certain ideals, and perform various roles. You will see that these institutions do not always work hand in hand to produce happy, well-adjusted adults. They often give mixed messages and are often at odds with one another. That is, they teach children and adolescents different and even contradictory lessons. You will also see that although recent developments give us more freedom to decide who we are, they can make socialization more disorienting than ever before. Finally, in the concluding section of this chapter, we examine how decreasing supervision and guidance by adult family members, increasing assumption of adult responsibilities by youths, and declining participation in extracurricular activities by youths are changing the nature of childhood and adolescence today. Some analysts even say that childhood and adolescence are vanishing before our eyes. Thus, the main theme of this chapter is that the development of self-identity is often a difficult and stressful process—and it is becoming more so.

It is during childhood that the contours of the self are first formed. We therefore begin by discussing the most important social-scientific theories of how the self originates in the first years of life.

Students from W. R. Myers High School in Taber, Alberta, console each other following a memorial service for slain student Jason Lang. Are acts of violence that are committed by teenagers best understood as the result of faulty socialization, inadequate controls on firearms, or some combination of both?

3.1

# SOCIAL POLICY: WHAT DO YOU THINK?

## Socialization versus Gun Control

On April 29, 1999, Columbine High School in Littleton, Colorado, was the scene of a mass shooting by two students. The shooters, Dylan Klebold and Eric Harris, murdered 13 people (12 fellow students and 1 teacher) and then turned their guns on themselves.

After the massacre at Columbine High School, newspapers, magazines, Internet chat rooms, and radio and television talk shows were abuzz with the problem of teenage violence. "What is to be done?" people asked. One solution that seems obvious to many Canadians is to limit the availability of firearms. Their reasoning is simple: all advanced industrial societies except the United States restrict gun ownership, and only the United States has a serious problem with teenagers shooting one another. Other countries have problems with teenage violence. For example, just eight days after the shooting rampage at Columbine, a 15-year-old boy in Taber, Alberta, gunned down one teen and wounded another in a school hallway. Exactly one year after the Columbine massacre, a teenager in an Ottawa-area high school stabbed four students and one staff member before his principal convinced him to surrender ("Echoes of the Columbine Massacre," 2000: 20). However, in countries where guns are less readily available, such as Canada, Australia, Britain, and Japan, teenage violence does not generally lead to mass killings. According to a Canadian government report, the rate of homicide using firearms per 100 000 people is 2.2 in Canada, 1.8 in Australia, 1.3 in Britain, 1.2 in Japan, and 9.3 in the United States (Department of Justice, Canada, 1995; see Figure 3.1).

**Figure 3.1**
**Gunshot Death Rate by Percentage of Households with Guns**

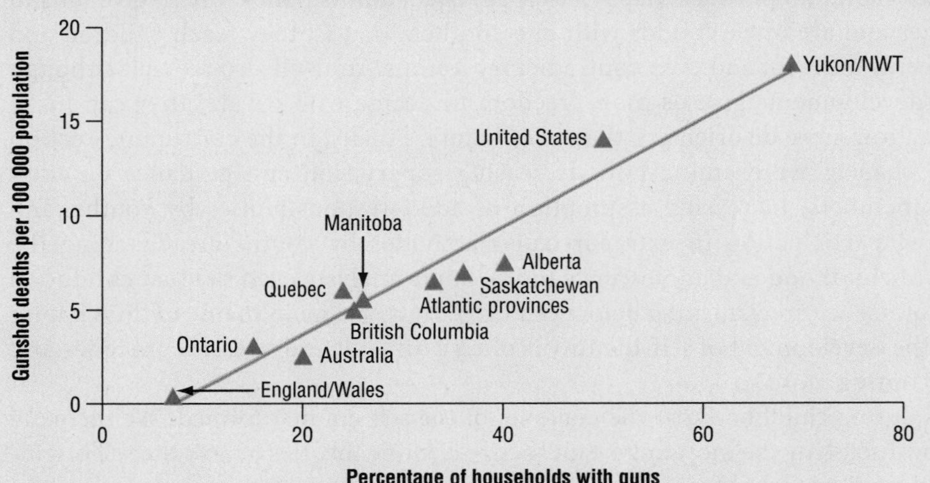


Source: Miller and Cohen (1997: 339).

In a series of bills passed from the 1960s to the 1990s, the Canadian government attempted to restrict the availability of firearms. Some firearms are now prohibited, others restricted. Criminals and those of "unsound mind" are forbidden from possessing a firearm. Would-be gun owners must be screened and wait 28 days before obtaining a Firearm Acquisition Certificate. Firearm owners and users must obtain a firearm licence and register their weapons.

In the United States, however, most political discussions about teenage violence focus on the problem of socialization, not gun control. Soon after the Columbine tragedy, for example, the U.S. House of Representatives passed a "juvenile crime bill." It cast blame on the entertainment industry, especially Hollywood movies, and the decline of "family values." Henry Hyde, an Illinois Republican, complained: "People were misled and disinclined to oppose the powerful entertainment industry" (quoted in Lazare, 1999: 57). Tom DeLay, a Republican congressional representative from Texas, worried: "We place our children in daycare centers where they learn their socialization skills . . . under the law of the jungle" (quoted in Lazare: 58). In other words, according to these American politicians, teenage massacres result from poor childhood socialization, the corrupting influence of Hollywood movies, and declining family values.

Some American politicians want to re-introduce Christianity in public schools to help overcome this presumed decay. DeLay thus reported an e-mail message he received. It read: "'Dear God, why didn't you stop the shootings at Columbine?' And God writes, 'Dear student, I would have, but I wasn't allowed in school'" (quoted in Lazare, 1999, pp. 57–58). One consequence of the Littleton massacre was not a gun control bill, but a bill to display the Ten Commandments in public schools.

**CRITICAL THINKING QUESTIONS**

- *Is the problem of students shooting each other a problem of socialization, lack of gun control, another factor, or a combination of factors? In answering this question, think about the situation in Canada as well as other countries and refer back to the discussion of media influence in Chapter 1, A Sociological Compass.*

# Theories of Childhood Socialization

Socialization begins soon after birth. Infants cry, driven by elemental needs, and are gratified by food, comfort, or affection. Because their needs are usually satisfied immediately, they do not at first seem able to distinguish themselves from their main caregivers, usually their mothers. However, social interaction soon enables infants to begin developing a self-image or sense of **self**—a set of ideas and attitudes about who they are as independent beings.

## *Freud*

Sigmund Freud proposed the first social-scientific interpretation of the process by which the self emerges (Freud, 1962 [1930], 1973 [1915–17]). Freud referred to the part of the self that demands immediate gratification as the **id.** According to Freud, a self-image begins to emerge as soon as the id's demands are denied. For example, at a certain point, parents usually decide not to feed and comfort a baby every time it wakes up in the middle of the night. The parents' refusal at first incites howls of protest.

Sigmund Freud (1856–1939)

Eventually, however, the baby learns certain practical lessons from the experience: to eat more before going to bed, to sleep for longer periods, and to go back to sleep if it wakes up. Equally important, the baby begins to sense that its needs differ from those of its parents, it has an existence independent of others, and it must somehow balance its needs with the realities of life.

Because of many such lessons in self-control, including toilet training, the child eventually develops a sense of what constitutes appropriate behaviour and a moral sense of right and wrong. Soon a personal conscience, or to use Freud's term, a **superego,** crystallizes. The superego is a repository of cultural standards. In addition, the child develops a third component of the self, the **ego.** According to Freud, the ego is a psychological mechanism that, in well-adjusted individuals, balances the conflicting needs of the pleasure-seeking id and the restraining superego.

In Freud's view, the emergence of the superego is a painful and frustrating process. In fact, said Freud, to get on with our daily lives we have to repress memories of denying the id immediate gratification. Repression involves storing traumatic memories in a part of the self that we are not normally aware of: the **unconscious.**

Repressed memories influence emotions and actions even after they are stored away. Particularly painful instances of childhood repression can cause various types of psychological problems later in life that require therapy to correct. However, some repression is the price we pay for civilization. As Freud said, we cannot live in an orderly society unless we deny the id (Freud, 1962 [1930]).

## Criticisms of Freud's Analysis

Researchers have called into question many of the specifics of Freud's argument. Three criticisms stand out:

1. The connections between early childhood development and adult personality are more complex than Freud assumed. *Freud wrote that when the ego fails to balance the needs of the id and the superego, individuals develop personality disorders. Typically, he said, this occurs if a young child is raised in an overly repressive atmosphere. To avoid later psychiatric problems, Freud and his followers recommended that young children should be raised in a relaxed and permissive environment. Such an environment is characterized by prolonged breast-feeding, nursing on demand, gradual weaning, lenient and late bladder and bowel training, frequent mothering, freedom from restraint and punishment, and so forth. However, sociological research reveals no connection between these aspects of early childhood training and the development of well-adjusted adults (Sewell, 1958).*
2. Many sociologists criticize Freud for gender bias in his analysis of male and female sexuality. *Freud argued that psychologically normal women are immature and dependent on men because they envy the male sexual organ. Women who are mature and independent he classified as abnormal. The historical bias of Freud's argument is evident: in today's society, mature and independent women are considered perfectly normal. Note also that Freudians have not collected any experimental or survey data showing that boys become more independent than girls because of their emotional reactions to the discovery of their sex organs.*
3. Sociologists often criticize Freud for neglecting socialization after childhood. *Freud believed that the human personality is fixed by about the age of five. However, sociologists have shown that socialization continues throughout the life course. We devote much of this chapter to exploring socialization after early childhood.*

Despite these shortcomings, the sociological implications of Freud's theory are profound. His main sociological contribution was his insistence that the self emerges during early social interaction and that early childhood experience exerts a lasting impact on personality development. As we will now see, later sociologists and social psychologists took these ideas in a still more sociological direction.

### *Cooley's Symbolic Interactionism*

More than a century ago, the American sociologist Charles Horton Cooley (1902) introduced the idea of the **"looking-glass self,"** making him a founder of the symbolic interactionist tradition and an early contributor to the sociological study of socialization.

Cooley observed that when we interact with others, they gesture and react to us. This allows us to imagine how we appear to them. We then judge how others evaluate us. Finally, from these judgments we develop a self-concept or a set of feelings and ideas about who we are. In other words, our feelings about who we are depend largely on how we see ourselves evaluated by others. Just as we see our physical body reflected in a mirror, so we see our social selves reflected in people's gestures and reactions to us (Cooley, 1902). When teachers evaluate students negatively, for example, students may develop a negative self-concept that causes them to do poorly in school. Poor performance may have as much to do with teachers' negative evaluations as with students' innate abilities (Hamachek, 1995; see Chapter 10, Religion and Education). Here, succinctly put, we have the hallmarks of what came to be known as symbolic interactionism—the idea that in the course of face-to-face communication, people engage in a creative process of attaching meaning to things.

### *Mead*

George Herbert Mead (1934) took up and developed Cooley's idea of the looking-glass self. Like Freud, Mead noted that a subjective and impulsive aspect of the self is present from birth. Mead called it simply the **I.** Again like Freud, Mead argued that a repository of culturally approved standards emerges as part of the self during social interaction. Mead called this objective, social component of the self the **me.** However, whereas Freud focused on the denial of the id's impulses as the mechanism that generates the self's objective side, Mead drew attention to the unique human capacity to "take the role of the other" as the source of the me.

Mead understood that human communication involves seeing yourself from other people's points of view. How, for example, do you interpret your mother's smile? Does it mean "I love you," "I find you humorous," or something else entirely? According to Mead, you can find the answer by using your imagination to take your mother's point of view for a moment and see yourself as she sees you. In other words, you must see yourself objectively as a "me" to understand your mother's communicative act. All human communication depends on being able to take the role of the other, wrote Mead. The self thus emerges from people using symbols, such as words and gestures, to communicate. It follows that the "me" is not present from birth. It emerges only gradually during social interaction.

Much socialization takes place informally, with the participants unaware they are being socialized. These girls are learning gender roles as they get ready to go to the mall dressed like Paris Hilton.

### Mead's Four Stages of Development: Role-Taking

Unlike Freud, Mead did not view the emergence of the self as a trauma. On the contrary, he thought it was fun. Mead saw the self as developing in four stages of role-taking. At first, children learn to use language and other symbols by *imitating* important people in their lives, such as their mother and father. Mead called such people **significant others.** Second, children pretend to *be* other people. That is, they use their imaginations to role-play in games, such as "house," "school," and "doctor." Third, about the time they reach the age of seven, children learn to play complex games that require them to simultaneously take the role of *several* other people. In baseball, for example, the infielders have to be aware of the expectations of everyone in the infield. A shortstop may catch a line drive. If she wants to make a double play, she must almost instantly be aware that a runner is trying to reach second base and that the person playing second base expects her to throw there. If she hesitates, she probably cannot execute the double play. Once a child can think in this complex way, he or she can begin the fourth stage in the development of the self, which involves taking the role of what Mead called the **generalized other.** Years of experience may teach an individual that other people, employing the cultural standards of their society, usually regard him or her as funny or temperamental or intelligent. A person's image of these cultural standards and how they are applied to him or her is what Mead meant by the generalized other.

Since Mead, some psychologists interested in the problem of childhood socialization have analyzed how the style, complexity, and abstractness of thinking (or "cognitive skills") develop in distinct stages from infancy to the late teenage years (Piaget and Inhelder, 1969). Other psychologists have analyzed how the ability to think in abstract moral terms develops in stages (Kohlberg, 1981). From a sociological point of view, however, it is important to recognize that the development of cognitive and moral skills is more than just the unfolding of a person's innate characteristics. That development is also shaped by the structure of a person's society and his or her position in it.

By emphasizing that moral development is socially differentiated and does not follow universal rules, researcher Carol Gilligan made a major sociological contribution to our understanding of childhood development.

### *Gilligan and Gender Differences*

One of the best-known examples of how social position affects socialization comes from the research of Carol Gilligan. Gilligan demonstrated that sociological factors help explain differences in the sense of self that boys and girls usually develop, because parents and teachers tend to pass on different cultural standards to each sex. Such adult authorities usually define the ideal woman as eager to please and therefore not assertive. Most girls learn this lesson as they mature. The fact that girls usually encounter more male and fewer female teachers and other authority figures as they grow up reinforces the lesson. Consequently, much research shows that girls tend to develop lower self-esteem than boys, although it seems doubtful that teenage girls in general experience the decline in self-esteem that Gilligan detected in her early work (Brown and Gilligan, 1992; Kling, Hyde, Showers, and Buswell, 1999).

### *Civilization Differences*

In a like manner, sociological factors help explain the development of different ways of thinking or cognitive styles of different civilizations (Cole, 1995; Vygotsky, 1987).

Consider, for example, the contrast between ancient China and ancient Greece. In part because of complex irrigation needs, the rice agriculture of ancient southern China required substantial cooperation among neighbours. It had to be centrally organized in an elaborate hierarchy within a large state. Harmony and social order were therefore central to ancient Chinese life. Ancient Chinese thinking, in turn, tended to stress the importance of mutual social obligation and consensus rather than debate. Ancient Chinese philosophy focused on the way in which whole systems, not analytical categories, cause processes and events.

In contrast, the hills and seashores of ancient Greece were suited to small-scale herding and fishing rather than large-scale, centrally organized agriculture. Ancient Greece was less socially complex than ancient China. It was more politically decentralized, and it gave its citizens more personal freedom. As a result, philosophies tended to be analytical, which means, among other things, that processes and events were viewed as the result of discrete categories rather than whole systems. Markedly different civilizations grew up on these different cognitive foundations; ways of thinking depended less on people's innate characteristics than on the structure of society (Nisbett, Peng, Choi, and Norenzayan, 2001).

We thus see that society plays a major role in shaping the way we think and the way we think of ourselves. It does so through various "agents of socialization," including families, schools, peer groups, and, in modern times, the mass media. Let us now consider in detail how these institutions socialize us.

# Agents of Socialization

## *Families*

The family is the most important agent of **primary socialization,** the process of mastering the basic skills required to function in society during childhood. The family is well suited to providing the kind of careful, intimate attention required for primary socialization: it is a small group, its members are in frequent face-to-face contact, and most parents love their children and are therefore highly motivated to care for them. These characteristics make most families ideal for teaching small children everything from language to their place in the world.

The socialization function of the family was more pronounced a century ago, partly because adult family members were more readily available for child care than they are today. As industry grew across Canada, families left farming for city work in factories and offices. Especially after the 1950s, many women had to work outside the home for a wage to maintain an adequate standard of living for their families. Fathers partly compensated by spending somewhat more time with their children. But because divorce rates have increased and many fathers have less contact with their children after divorce, children probably see less of their fathers on average now than they did a century ago. In some countries, such as Sweden and France, the creation of state-funded child-care facilities compensated for these developments by helping teach, supervise, and discipline children (see Chapter 9, Families). In Canada, however, child care—and therefore childhood socialization—became a big social problem, leading in some cases to child neglect and abuse.

The family is still an important agent of socialization, although its importance has declined since the nineteenth century.

### Schools

For children over the age of five, the child-care problem was partly resolved by the growth of the public school system, which became increasingly responsible for **secondary socialization,** or socialization outside the family after childhood. Industry needed better trained and better educated employees. Therefore, by the early twentieth century, every province had established a compulsory education rule, which prescribed the minimum and maximum ages between which a child had to attend school. Today, two-thirds of Canadians over the age of 15 have completed high school and more than half have postsecondary qualifications (Statistics Canada, 2003b). This makes Canadians among the most highly educated people in the world.

Although schools help prepare students for the job market, they do not necessarily give students an accurate picture of what the job market requires. In 1992, for example, a nationwide U.S. survey highlighted the mismatch between the ambitions of American high school students and the projected needs of the American economy in 2005 (Schneider and Stevenson, 1999: 77–78; see Figure 3.2). The number of high school students wanting to become lawyers and judges was five times the projected number needed. The number who wanted to become writers, artists, entertainers, and athletes was 14 times higher than the expected openings in 2005. At the other extreme, in 2005 there were expected to be five times as many administrative and clerical jobs as students interested in such work. And there were expected to be seven times as many service jobs as teenagers wanting them. High school students, it seems safe to say, often have unrealistically high expectations about the kinds of jobs they are likely to get when they finish their education.

We see no reason to believe that Canadians are any different from Americans in this regard. In 2000, a national survey of Canadians teenagers found that the great majority had very high expectations for their future careers. Regardless of whether they expected to graduate from university, teens believed that they would be able to pursue a career, obtain the job they wanted after graduation, and stay with the same career for life (Bibby, 2001: 139). Few Canadian and American students realistically anticipate underemployment, let alone unemployment (Livingstone, 1999).

**Figure 3.2**

**Adolescent Job Preferences and Projected Jobs in Paid Labour Force, United States, 2005 (in percent)**

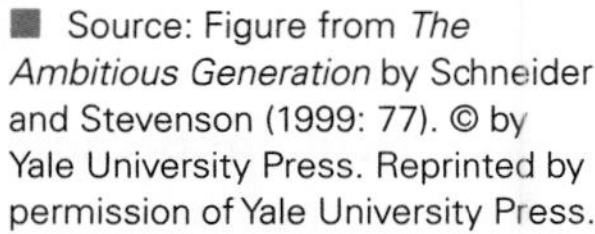

■ Source: Figure from *The Ambitious Generation* by Schneider and Stevenson (1999: 77). © by Yale University Press. Reprinted by permission of Yale University Press.

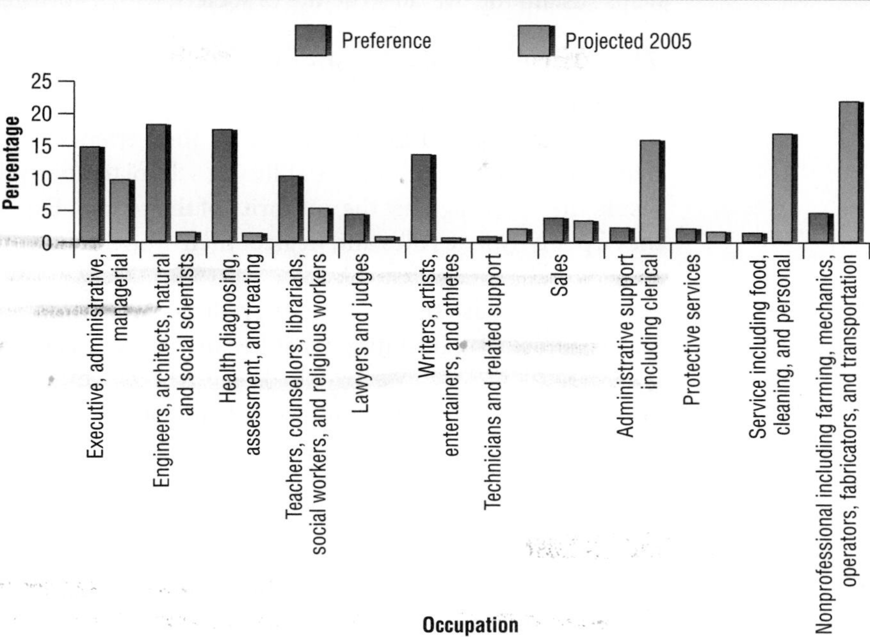


## *Class, Race, and Conflict Theory*

Instructing students in academic and vocational subjects, however, is just one part of the school's job. In addition, a **hidden curriculum** teaches students what will be expected of them in the larger society once they graduate. The hidden curriculum teaches them how to be conventionally "good citizens." Most parents approve of this instruction. According to one survey conducted in several highly industrialized countries, the capacity of schools to socialize students is more important to the public than all academic subjects except mathematics (Galper, 1998).

What is the content of the hidden curriculum? In the family, children tend to be evaluated on the basis of personal and emotional criteria. As students, however, they are led to believe that they are evaluated solely on the basis of their performance on impersonal, standardized tests. They are told that similar criteria will be used to evaluate them in the work world. The lesson is, of course, only partly true. As you will see in Chapter 7 (Race and Ethnicity), Chapter 8 (Sexuality and Gender), and Chapter 10 (Religion and Education), it is not just performance but also class, gender, sexual orientation, and racial criteria that help to determine success in school and in the work world. But the accuracy of the lesson is not the issue here; the important point is that the hidden curriculum has done its job if it convinces students that they are judged on the basis of performance alone. Similarly, a successful hidden curriculum teaches students punctuality, respect for authority, the importance of competition in leading to excellent performance, and other conformist behaviours and beliefs that are expected of good citizens, conventionally defined.

The idea of the hidden curriculum was first proposed by conflict theorists, who, you will recall, see an ongoing struggle between privileged and disadvantaged groups whenever they probe beneath the surface of social life (Willis, 1984). From the point of view of conflict theory, some poor and racial-minority students accept the hidden curriculum, thereby learning to act like conventionally good citizens. Other such students reject the hidden curriculum, consequently doing poorly in school and eventually entering the work world near the bottom of the socioeconomic hierarchy. In either case, the hidden curriculum helps sustain the overall structure of society, with its privileges and disadvantages.

### *The Self-Fulfilling Prophecy*

Why do some poor and racial-minority students reject the hidden curriculum? Because their experience and the experience of their friends, peers, and family members may make them skeptical about the ability of school to open job opportunities for them. As a result, they rebel against the authority of the school. Expected to be polite and studious, they openly violate rules and neglect their work. Believing that education does not lead to economic success can become a **self-fulfilling prophecy,** which is an expectation that helps to cause the situation it predicts. W. I. Thomas and Dorothy Swaine Thomas had a similar idea in stating what became known as the **Thomas theorem:** "Situations we define as real become real in their consequences" (Thomas, 1966 [1931]: 301). For example, believing that school won't help you get ahead may cause you to do poorly in school, and you are more likely to wind up near the bottom of the class structure if you perform poorly in school (Willis, 1984).

Teachers, for their part, can also develop expectations that turn into self-fulfilling prophecies. In one famous study, two researchers informed the teachers in a primary school that they were going to administer a special test to the pupils to predict intellectual "blooming." In fact, the test was just a standard IQ test. After the test, they told teachers which students they could expect to become high achievers and which students they could expect to become low achievers. In fact, the researchers assigned pupils to the two groups at random. At the end of the year, the researchers repeated the IQ test. They found that the students singled out as high achievers scored significantly higher than those singled out as low achievers. Because the only difference between the two groups of students was that teachers expected one group to do well and the other to do poorly, the researchers concluded that teachers' expectations alone influenced students' performance (Rosenthal and Jacobson, 1968). The clear implication of this research is that if a teacher believes that poor or minority group children are likely to do poorly in school, chances are they will. That is because students who are members of groups that are widely expected to perform poorly *internalize* social expectations; they feel anxiety about their performance and the anxiety lowers their performance level (Steele, 1997).

Learning disciplined work habits is an important part of the socialization that takes place in schools.

## *Peer Groups*

A second socialization agent whose importance increased in the twentieth century is the **peer group.** Peer groups consist of individuals who are not necessarily friends but who are about the same age and of similar status. (**Status** refers to a recognized social position an individual can occupy.) Peer groups help children and adolescents to separate from their families and to develop independent sources of identity. They particularly influence such lifestyle issues as appearance, social activities, and dating. In fact, from middle childhood through adolescence, the peer group is often the dominant socializing agent.

As you probably learned from your own life experience, conflict often exists between the values promoted by the family and those promoted by the adolescent peer group. Families are controlled by parents; they represent the values of childhood. Under these circumstances, such issues as tobacco, drug, and alcohol use; hair and dress styles; political views; music; and curfew times are likely to become points of conflict between the generations. In contrast, adolescent peer groups are controlled by youth, and through them young people begin to develop their own identities. They do this by rejecting some parental values, experimenting with new elements of culture, and engaging in various forms of rebellious behaviour. For example, according to a Canadian survey, 12- and 13-year-old Canadians who identified themselves as belonging to a group that did "risky" things were up to seven times as likely as others to report smoking, disorderly conduct, skipping school at least once, and attaching low importance to marks. They were also much more likely to report at least three instances of stealing and fighting (Figure 3.3). Peer influence also appears to play a significant role in the smoking habits of young adolescents. Eight-four percent of 12- and 13-year-olds who smoked reported having three or more friends who also smoked, while only 26 percent of their nonsmoking counterparts claimed that three or more of their friends smoked (Figure 3.4). Although parents' smoking behaviour—especially that of mothers—was linked to a youth's decision to smoke, the influence of peers was far greater (Statistics Canada, 1999a).

We should not, however, overstate the significance of adolescent–parent conflict. For one thing, the conflict is usually temporary. Once adolescents mature, the family exerts a more enduring influence on many important issues. Research shows that families have more influence than peer groups over the educational aspirations and the political,

**Figure 3.3**
**Risk Behaviour among 12- and 13-Year-Olds, by Membership/Non-membership in a Risk-Taking Group**

Respondents were asked 29 questions to assess their involvement in several generally unacceptable activities (e.g., staying out all night without permission, running away from home, being questioned by the police, stealing, fighting, vandalizing property, carrying a knife, using drugs, and committing arson). Respondents were then asked whether they had been part of a group that had done "bad" or risky things within the past year.

■ Source: Adapted from Statistics Canada (1999a).

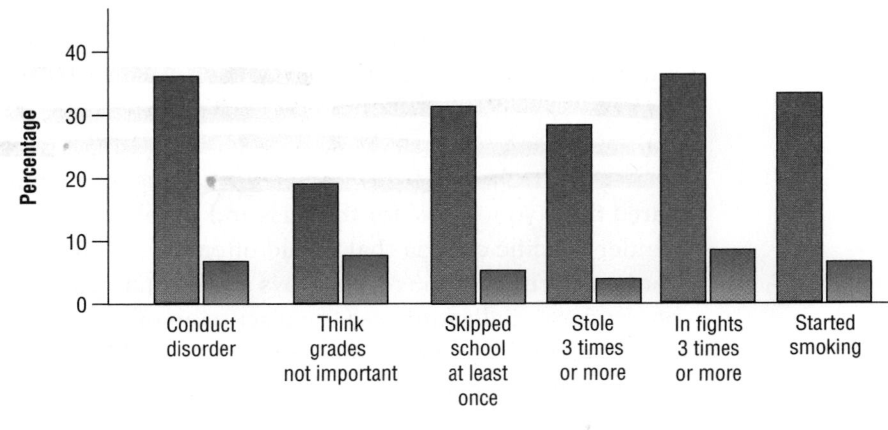

**Figure 3.4**
**Current Smoking Status of Youths, Aged 12 and 13, by Number of Their Friends Who Smoke**

■ Source: Adapted from Statistics Canada (1999a).

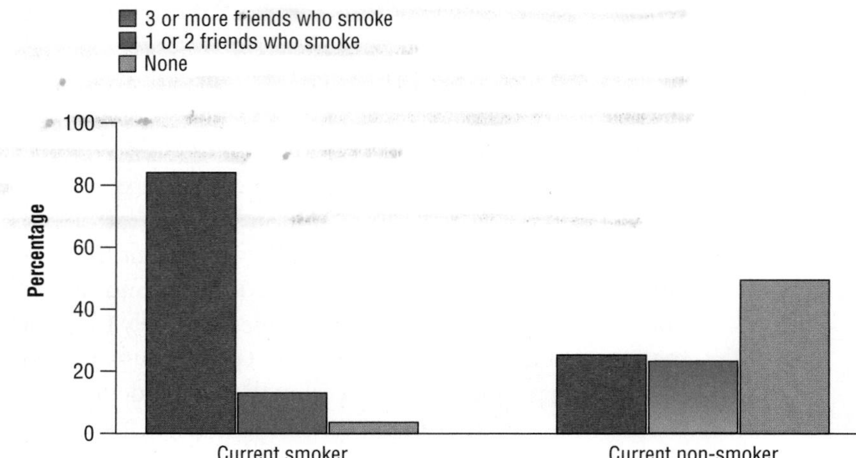


social, and religious preferences of adolescents and university students (Davies and Kandel, 1981; Milem, 1998). A survey of 3500 Canadian high school students found that 91 percent said that how they live their lives has been influenced by the way they were brought up, and a clear majority felt that their parents, and especially their mothers, continued to have an effect on how they live their daily lives (Bibby, 2001: 55).

A second reason that we should not exaggerate the extent of adolescent–parent discord is that peer groups are not just sources of conflict; they also help integrate young people into the larger society. A study of pre-adolescent children in a small North American city illustrates the point. Over eight years, sociologists Patricia and Peter Adler conducted in-depth interviews at schools with children between the ages of 8 and 11. They lived in a well-to-do community comprising about 80 000 whites and 10 000 racial minority group members (Adler and Adler, 1998). In each school they visited, they found a system of cliques arranged in a strict hierarchy, much like the arrangement of classes and racial groups in adult society. In schools with a substantial number of visible minority students, cliques were divided by race. Visible minority cliques were usually less popular than white cliques. In all schools, the most popular boys were highly successful in competitive and aggressive achievement-oriented activities, especially athletics. The most popular girls came from well-to-do and permissive families. One important basis of the students' popularity was that they had the means and the opportunity to participate in the most interesting social activities, ranging from skiing to late-night parties. Physical attractiveness was also an important basis of girls' popularity. Thus, elementary-school peer groups prepared these youngsters for the class and racial inequalities of the adult world and the gender-specific criteria that would often be used to evaluate them as adults, such as competitiveness in the case of boys and attractiveness in the case of girls. (For more on gender socialization, see the discussion of the mass media below and Chapter 8, Sexuality and Gender.) What we learn from this research is that peer groups function not only to help adolescents form an independent identity by separating them from their families but also to teach them how to adapt to the ways of the larger society.

Peer groups are strong socializing agents during adolescence.

## *The Mass Media*

Like the school and the peer group, the mass media have also become increasingly important socializing agents in the twenty-first century. The mass media include television, radio, movies, videos, CDs, audiotapes, the Internet, newspapers, magazines, and books.

The fastest-growing mass medium is the Internet. Worldwide, the number of Internet users jumped from 40 million in 1995 to almost 1 billion by 2005 (see Figure 3.5). However, TV viewing consumes more of the average Canadian's free time than any other mass medium. Ninety-nine percent of Canadians own at least one colour television set (Statistics Canada, 2001a). In 2003, Canadians spent an average of 21.7 hours per week watching television, down from a record high of 23.5 hours in 1988 (Statistics Canada, 2001a, 2005a). Low-income Canadians watch more TV than high-income

**Figure 3.5**
Number of Internet Users, 1996–2005

Sources: "Face of the Web" (2000); "Internet Growth" (2000).

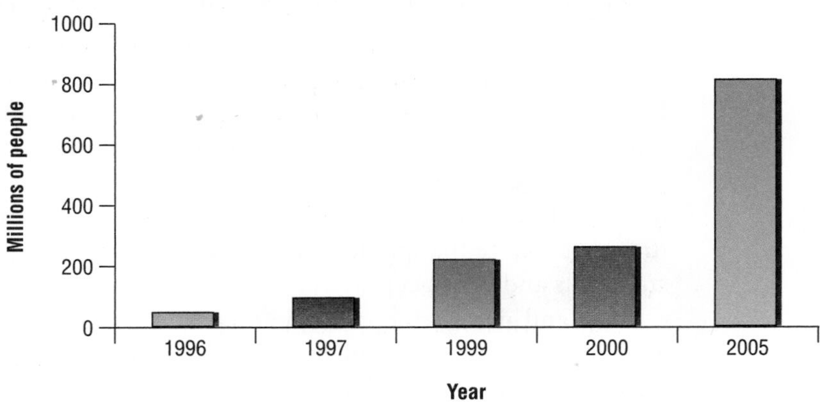

Canadians, women watch more than men, people over the age of 59 watch more than younger Canadians, and Quebecers watch more than people in any other province or territory (Statistics Canada, 2005; Williams, 2002: 10).

### *Self-Socialization*

Children and adolescents use the mass media for entertainment and stimulation. The mass media also help young people cope with anger, anxiety, and unhappiness, and the cultural materials provided by the mass media help young people to construct their identities—for example, by emulating the appearance and behaviour of appealing movie stars, music idols, and sports heroes. In performing these functions, the mass media offer youth much choice: many Canadians have access to scores of radio stations and TV channels, hundreds of magazines, thousands of CD titles, hundreds of thousands of books, and millions of Web sites. Most of us can gain access to hip-hop, heavy metal, or Haydn with equal ease. Thus, although adolescents have little choice over how they are socialized by their family and their school, the very proliferation of the mass media gives them more say over which media messages will influence them. To a degree, the mass media allow adolescents to engage in what sociologist Jeffrey Jensen Arnett (1995) calls **self-socialization,** or the ability to choose socialization influences from the wide variety of mass media offerings.

### *Gender Roles, the Mass Media, and the Feminist Approach to Socialization*

Although people are to some extent free to choose socialization influences from the mass media, they choose some influences more often than others. Specifically, they tend to choose influences that are more pervasive, that fit existing cultural standards, and that are made especially appealing by those who control the mass media. We can illustrate this point by considering how we learn gender roles from the mass media. **Gender roles** are widely shared expectations about how males and females are supposed to act.

The learning of gender roles by the mass media begins when small children learn that only a kiss from Snow White's Prince Charming will save her from eternal sleep. It continues in magazines, romance novels, television, advertisements, and music, and on the Internet. It is big business. For example, Toronto's Harlequin Enterprises, the world's largest publisher of romance fiction, sells more than 130 million books a year in 25 languages in 94 international markets. About one in every six mass-market paperbacks sold in North America is a Harlequin romance. The average romance reader spends $800 a year on the genre. Most readers of Harlequin romances consume between 3 and 20 books a month. A central theme in these romances is the transformation of women's bodies into objects for men's pleasure. In the typical Harlequin romance, the men are expected to be the sexual aggressors. They are typically more experienced and promiscuous than the women. Women are expected to desire love before sexual intimacy. They are assumed to be sexually passive, giving only subtle cues to indicate their interest in male overtures. Supposedly lacking the urgent sex drive that preoccupies men, women are often held accountable for moral standards and contraception.

Boys and girls do not passively accept such messages about appropriate gender roles. They often interpret them in unique ways and sometimes resist them. For the most part, however, children try to develop skills that will help them to perform gender roles in a conventional way (Eagley and Wood, 1999: 412–13). Of course, conventions change. It is important to note in this regard that what children learn about femininity and masculinity today is less sexist than what they learned just a few generations ago. For example, comparing *Cinderella* and *Snow White* with *Mulan,* we see immediately that children going to Disney movies today are sometimes presented with more assertive and heroic female role models than the passive heroines of the 1930s and 1940s. However, the amount of change in gender socialization should not be exaggerated. *Cinderella* and *Snow White* are still popular movies. Moreover, for every *Mulan* there is a *Little Mermaid,* a movie that simply modernizes old themes about female passivity and male conquest.

As the learning of gender roles through the mass media suggests, then, not all media influences are created equal. We may be free to choose which media messages influence us, but most people are inclined to choose the messages that are most widespread, that are most closely aligned with existing cultural standards, and that are made most enticing by the mass media. In the case of gender roles, these messages are those that support conventional expectations about how males and females are supposed to act.

### *Resocialization and Total Institutions*

In concluding our discussion of socialization agents, we must underline the importance of resocialization in the lifelong process of social learning. **Resocialization** takes place when powerful socializing agents deliberately cause rapid change in people's values, roles, and self-conception, sometimes against their will.

You can see resocialization at work in the ceremonies staged when someone joins a fraternity, a sorority, the Canadian Armed Forces, or a religious order. Such a ceremony, or **initiation rite,** signifies the transition of the individual from one group to another and ensures his or her loyalty to the new group. Initiation rites require new recruits to abandon old self-perceptions and assume new identities. Often the rites comprise three stages: (1) separation from the person's old status and identity (ritual rejection), (2) degradation, disorientation, and stress (ritual death), and (3) acceptance of the new group culture and status (ritual rebirth).

Not all initiation rites or rites of passage involve resocialization; some rites of passage are normal parts of primary and secondary socialization and merely signify the transition from one status to another. Here, an Italian family celebrates the first communion of a young girl.

Much resocialization takes place in what Erving Goffman (1961) called **total institutions.** Total institutions are settings in which people are isolated from the larger society and under the strict control and constant supervision of a specialized staff. Asylums and prisons are examples of total institutions. Because of the pressure-cooker atmosphere in such institutions, resocialization in total institutions is often rapid and thorough, even in the absence of initiation rites.

A famous failed experiment illustrates the immense resocializing capacity of total institutions (Haney, Banks, and Zimbardo, 1973; Zimbardo, 1972). In the early 1970s, a group of researchers created their own mock prison. They paid about 24 male volunteers to act as guards and inmates. The volunteers were mature, emotionally stable, intelligent, university students from middle-class American and Canadian homes. None had a criminal record. By the flip of a coin, half the volunteers were designated prisoners, the other half guards. The guards made up their own rules for maintaining law and order in the mock prison. The prisoners were picked up by city police officers in a squad car, searched, handcuffed, fingerprinted, booked at the police station, and taken blindfolded to the mock prison. At the mock prison, each prisoner was stripped, deloused, put into a uniform, given a number, and placed in a cell with two other inmates.

To better understand what it means to be a prisoner or a prison guard, the researchers wanted to observe and record social interaction in the mock prison for two weeks. However, they were forced to end the experiment abruptly after only six days because what they witnessed frightened them. In less than a week, the prisoners and prison guards could no longer tell the difference between the roles they were playing and their "real" selves. Much of the socialization these young men had undergone over a period of about 20 years was quickly suspended.

About a third of the guards began to treat the prisoners like despicable animals, taking pleasure in cruelty. Even the guards who were regarded by the prisoners as tough but fair stopped short of interfering in the tyrannical and arbitrary use of power by the most sadistic guards.

All the prisoners became servile and dehumanized, thinking only about survival, escape, and their growing hatred of the guards. Had they been thinking as university students, they could have walked out of the experiment at any time. Some of the prisoners did, in fact, beg for parole. However, by the fifth day of the experiment they were so programmed to think of themselves as prisoners that they returned docilely to their cells when their request for parole was denied.

The Palo Alto experiment suggests that your sense of self and the roles you play are not as fixed as you may think. Radically alter your social setting and, like the university students in the experiment, your self-conception and patterned behaviour are also likely to change. Such change is most evident among people undergoing resocialization in total institutions. However, the sociological eye is able to observe the flexibility of the self in all social settings—a task made easier by the fact that the self has become more flexible over time. We now turn to an examination of the growing flexibility of the self.

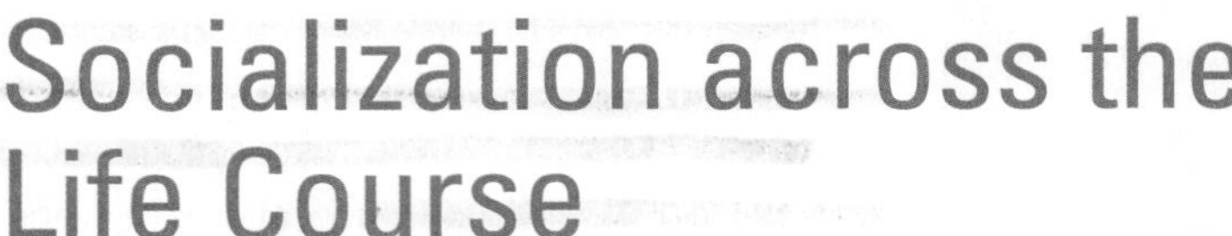

# Socialization across the Life Course

## *Adult Socialization and the Flexible Self*

The development of the self is a lifelong process (Mortimer and Simmons, 1978). When young adults enter a profession or get married, they must learn new occupational and family roles. Retirement and old age present an entirely new set of challenges. Giving up a job, seeing children leave home and start their own families, losing a spouse and close friends—all these changes later in life require people to think of themselves in new ways and to redefine who they are. Many new roles are predictable. To help us learn them we often engage in **anticipatory socialization,** which involves beginning to take on the norms and behaviours of the roles to which we aspire. (Think of 15-year-old fans of the TV show *Friends* learning from the show what it might mean to be a young adult.) Other new roles are unpredictable. You might unexpectedly fall in love and marry someone from a different ethnic, racial, or religious group. You might experience a sudden and difficult transition from peace to war. If so, you will have to learn new roles and adopt new cultural values or at least modify old ones. Even in adulthood, then, the self remains flexible.

Today, people's identities change faster, more often, and more completely than they did just a couple of decades ago. One important factor contributing to the growing flexibility of the self is globalization. As we saw in Chapter 2, Culture, people are now less obliged to accept the culture into which they are born. Because of globalization, they are freer to combine elements of culture from a wide variety of historical periods and geographical settings.

A second factor increasing our freedom to design our selves is our growing ability to fashion new bodies from old. People have always defined themselves partly in terms of their bodies; your self-conception is influenced by whether you're a man or a woman, tall or short, healthy or ill, conventionally attractive or plain. But our bodies used to be fixed by nature. People could do nothing to change the fact that they were born with certain features and grew older at a certain rate.

Now, however, you can change your body, and therefore your self-conception, radically and virtually at will—if, that is, you can afford it. Some examples of such changes include the following:

» Bodybuilding, aerobic exercise, and weight-reduction regimens are more popular than ever.
» Sex-change operations, although infrequent, are no longer a rarity.
» Plastic surgery and other cosmetic procedures allow people to buy new breasts, noses, lips, eyelids, and hair—and to remove unwanted fat, skin, and hair from various parts of their body. In North America, plastic surgery procedures were up more than tenfold—from 1.5 million to 16.2 million—between 1992 and 2006. In 2006, two-thirds of plastic surgery procedures were cosmetic, and about 90 percent of them were performed on women. The top five surgical procedures for women: breast augmentation, nose reshaping, liposuction, eyelid surgery, and tummy tuck (American Society of Plastic Surgeons, 2007).

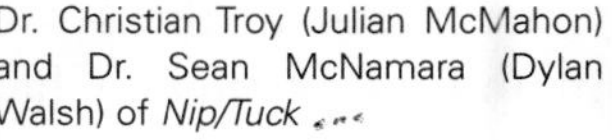

Dr. Christian Troy (Julian McMahon) and Dr. Sean McNamara (Dylan Walsh) of *Nip/Tuck*

Given the appeal and influence of such TV shows as *Extreme Makeover, The Swan,* and *Nip/Tuck,* it seems likely that cosmetic procedures will become still more popular.

- Organ transplants are routine. At any given time about 55 000 North Americans are waiting for a replacement organ. Brisk, illegal international trade in human hearts, lungs, kidneys, livers, and eyes enables well-to-do people to enhance and extend their lives (Rothman, 1998).
- In 2002, Kevin Warwick, a professor of cybernetics at Reading University in the United Kingdom, became the first cyborg (part man, part computer) when he had a computer chip implanted in his wrist and connected to about 100 neurons. A wire now runs under the skin up his arm to a point just below his elbow, where a junction box allows data from his neurons to be transmitted wirelessly to a computer. He plans to implant a similar device in his wife. Through an Internet connection, they will each be able to feel what the other feels in his or her arm. Warwick predicts that before 2020 more sophisticated implants will allow a primitive form of telepathy (Akin, 2002).

As these examples illustrate, many new opportunities for changing our self-conception have been introduced in recent decades.

### *Self-Identity and the Internet*

Further complicating the process of identity formation today is the growth of the Internet and its audiovisual component, the World Wide Web. In the 1980s and early 1990s, most observers believed that social interaction by means of computer would involve only the exchange of information between individuals. They were wrong. Computer-assisted social interaction profoundly affects how people think of themselves (Brym and Lenton, 2001; Haythornwaite and Wellman, 2002).

Internet users interact socially by exchanging text, images, and sound via e-mail, instant messaging (such as MSN Messenger), Internet phone, video conferences, computer-assisted work groups, and online dating services. In the process, they form virtual communities. **Virtual communities** are associations of people, scattered across the city or around the world, who communicate via computer and modem about subjects of common interest.

Some virtual communities are short-lived and loosely structured in the sense that they have few formal rules and people quickly drift in and out of them. Chat groups are typical of this genre. Other virtual communities are more enduring and structured. For example, discussion groups cater to people's interest in specialized subjects, such as French culture or white-water canoeing. Still other virtual communities are highly structured, with many formal rules and relatively stable membership. For example, MUDs (multiple-user dimensions) are computer programs that allow people to role-play and engage in a sort of collective fantasy. These programs define the aims and rules of the virtual community and the objects and spaces it contains. Users around the world log on to the MUD from their computers and define their character—their identity—any way they want. They interact with other users by exchanging text messages or by having their avatars (graphical representations) act and speak for them.

Because virtual communities allow interaction by using concealed identities, people are free to assume new identities and are encouraged to discover parts of themselves they were formerly unaware of. In virtual communities, shy people can become bold, normally assertive people can become voyeurs, old people can become young, straight people can become gay, and women can become men (Turkle, 1995). Experience on the Internet thus reinforces our main point: in recent decades, the self has become increasingly flexible, and people are freer than ever to shape their selves as they choose.

However, this freedom comes at a cost, particularly for young people. In concluding this chapter, we consider some of the socialization challenges Canadian youth faces today.

## *Dilemmas of Childhood and Adolescent Socialization*

In pre-industrial societies, children are considered small adults. From a young age, they are expected to conform as much as possible to the norms of the adult world. That is largely because children are put to work as soon as they can contribute to the welfare of their families. Often, this contribution means doing chores by the age of 5 and working full-time by the age of 10 or 12. Marriage, and thus the achievement of full adulthood, is common by the age of 15 or 16.

Children in Europe and North America fit this pattern until the late seventeenth century, when the idea of childhood as a distinct stage of life emerged. At that time, the feeling grew among well-to-do Europeans and North Americans that boys should be permitted to play games and receive an education that would allow them to develop the emotional, physical, and intellectual skills they would need as adults. Girls continued to be treated as "little women" (the title of Louisa May Alcott's 1869 novel) until the nineteenth century. Most working-class boys did not enjoy much of a childhood until the twentieth century. Thus, it is only in the past century that the idea of childhood as a distinct and prolonged period of life became universal in the West (Ariès, 1962).

## *The Emergence of Childhood and Adolescence*

The idea of childhood emerged when and where it did because of social necessity and social possibility. Prolonged childhood was *necessary* in societies that required better educated adults to do increasingly complex work, because childhood gave young people a chance to prepare for adult life. Prolonged childhood was *possible* in societies where improved hygiene and nutrition allowed most people to live more than 35 years, the average life span in Europe in the early seventeenth century. In other words, before the late seventeenth century, most people did not live long enough to permit the luxury of childhood. Moreover, young people had no social need for a period of extended training and development before the comparatively simple demands of adulthood were thrust on them.

In general, wealthier and more complex societies whose populations enjoy a long average life expectancy stretch out the pre-adult period of life. For example, we saw that in Europe in the seventeenth century, most people reached mature adulthood by the age of about 16. In contrast, in such countries as Canada today, most people are considered to reach mature adulthood only around the age of 30, by which time they have completed their formal education, possibly gotten married, and "settled down." Once teenagers were relieved of adult responsibilities, a new term had to be coined to describe the teenage years: *adolescence*. Subsequently, the term *young adulthood* entered popular usage as an increasingly large number of people in their late teens, 20s, and early 30s delayed marriage to attend university (see Box 3.2).

3.2

# SOCIOLOGY AT THE MOVIES

Owen Wilson and Vince Vaughan in a scene from *The Wedding Crashers*

*The Wedding Crashers* (2005)

John Beckwith (Owen Wilson) and Jeremy Gray (Vince Vaughn) are 30-something partners in a divorce mediation firm. Neither is married because of their belief that, as Jeremy says during one particularly heated mediation, "the real enemy here is the institution of marriage. It's not realistic. It's crazy."

So what do these handsome, single, professional men do for excitement come spring? They crash weddings, party till dawn, and bed the unsuspecting beauties who fall for their fast talk and scripted charm.

Early in the movie, John expresses misgivings:

| | |
|---|---|
| John: | **You ever think we're being a little—I don't want to say sleazy, because that's not the right word—but a little irresponsible? I mean . . .** |
| Jeremy: | **No. One day you'll look back on all this and laugh, and say we were young and stupid. Coupla dumb kids, runnin' around . . .** |
| John: | **We're not *that* young.** |

Indeed they're not, which is why John's reflective moment raises an important sociological issue posed by a host of recent movies. *The Wedding Crashers*, *The 40-Year-Old Virgin* (2005), *Failure to Launch* (2006), and *Clerks II* (2006) all ask the question of how it came about that people old enough to be considered adults just a couple of generations ago now seem stuck between adolescence and adulthood. They aren't married. Some of them live with their parents. They may still be in school. And some of them lack steady, well-paying, full-time jobs. Sometimes called "kippers" (kids in parents' pockets, eroding retirement savings), they represent a growing category of young adults who are often a big worry to their elders.

Between 1981 and 2001, the percentage of Canadians between the ages of 25 and 34 living with their parents doubled—rising from 12 percent to 24 percent for the 25–29 age cohort and from 5 percent to 11 percent for the 30–34 age cohort (Beaupré, Turcotte, and Milan, 2007). One reason for this phenomenon is economic. In the first few decades after World War II, housing and education costs were low, and the number of years a person had to spend in school to get a steady, well-paying job was modest. Today, housing and education costs are high, and young people must typically spend more years in school before starting their careers. As a result, many young people continue to live in their parents' home into their 20s and 30s as a matter of economic necessity.

Such economic factors undoubtedly affect working-class and middle-class families more than upper-middle-class families. For the latter, a change in child-rearing practices seems to account in part for the reluctance of some young adults to leave home. Many well-educated and well-to-do parents seem to be raising children who are simply too dependent. They are reluctant to insist that their children get part-time jobs when they are in their mid-teens, and they neglect to teach them the importance of saving money by always giving them as much money as they want. They provide too much assistance with schoolwork (either by themselves or by hiring tutors), and they organize too many extracurricular activities for their children, thus not giving them enough space to figure out their interests for themselves.

In *The Wedding Crashers*, John and Jeremy finally seem able to break the mould when Jeremy marries Gloria Cleary (Isla Fisher) and John commits to her sister, Claire (Canadian Rachel McAdams). But as the happy foursome drive away, they get the bright idea of posing as a folk singing quartet from Utah and crashing a wedding for the great Japanese food that is bound to be served. It seems that their parents' worries are far from over.

Although these new terms describing the stages of life were firmly entrenched in North America by the middle of the twentieth century, some of the categories of the population they were meant to describe began to change dramatically. Somewhat excitedly, some analysts began to write about the "disappearance" of childhood and adolescence altogether (Friedenberg, 1959; Postman, 1982). Although undoubtedly overstating their case, these social scientists did identify some of the social forces responsible for the changing character of childhood and adolescence in recent decades. We examine these social forces in the concluding section of this chapter.

## *Problems of Childhood and Adolescent Socialization Today*

Declining adult supervision and guidance, increasing mass media and peer group influence, and increasing assumption of substantial adult responsibilities to the neglect of extracurricular activities have done much to change the socialization patterns of North American youth over the past 40 or 50 years (see Box 3.3). Let us consider each of these developments in turn.

### Declining Adult Supervision and Guidance

In a six-year, in-depth study of adolescence, Patricia Hersch wrote that "in all societies since the beginning of time, adolescents have learned to become adults by observing, imitating and interacting with grown-ups around them" (Hersch, 1998: 20). However, in contemporary North America, adults are increasingly absent from the lives of adolescents. Why? According to Hersch, "society has left its children behind as the cost of progress in the workplace" (1998: 19). What she means is that more adults are working longer hours than ever before. In Canada in 2005, adults in the paid labour force living

3.3

## YOU AND THE SOCIAL WORLD

### Your Adolescent Socialization

When you were between the ages of 10 and 17, how often were you at home or with friends but without adult supervision? How often did you have to prepare your own meals or take care of a younger sibling while your parent or parents were at work? How many hours a week did you spend cleaning house? How many hours a week did you have to work at a part-time job to earn spending money and save for college or university? How many hours a week did you spend on extracurricular activities associated with your school? How many hours a week did you watch TV and spend on other mass media use? If you were like most Canadian preteens and teenagers, many of your waking hours outside of school were spent without adult supervision and assuming substantial adult responsibilities such as those just listed. You are unlikely to have spent much time on extracurricular activities associated with your school but quite a lot of time viewing TV and using other mass media.

**CRITICAL THINKING QUESTIONS**

- *How did your childhood socialization affect who you are today? Would you try to socialize your children differently from the way you were socialized? If so, how? What factors influence your ideals about child rearing and socialization?*

with a spouse or a child spent nearly 20 percent less time in activities with family members during a typical workday than they did in 1986. The main reason? They are required to spend more time at work (Turcotte, 2007). Because adults have less time to spend with their children than they used to, young people are increasingly left alone to socialize themselves and build their own community.

This community sometimes revolves around high-risk behaviour. It is therefore not coincidental that the peak hours for juvenile crime are between 3 p.m. and 6 p.m. on weekdays—that is, after school and before most parents return home from work (Hersch, 1998: 362). Girls are less likely to engage in juvenile crime than boys, partly because parents tend to supervise and socialize their sons and daughters differently (Hagan, Simpson, and Gillis, 1987). These research findings suggest that many of the teenage behaviours commonly regarded as problematic result from declining adult guidance and supervision.

### Increasing Media Influence

Declining adult supervision and guidance also leave North American youth more susceptible to the influence of the mass media and peer groups. As one parent put it, "When they hit the teen years, it is as if they can't be children anymore. The outside world has invaded the school environment" (quoted in Hersch, 1998: 111). In an earlier era, family, school, church, and community usually taught young people more or less consistent beliefs and values. Now, however, the mass media and peer groups often pull young people in different directions from the school and the family, leaving them uncertain about what constitutes appropriate behaviour and making the job of growing up more stressful than it used to be (Arnett, 1995).

### Declining Extracurricular Activities and Increasing Adult Responsibilities

As the chapter's opening anecdote about Robert Brym's involvement in high school drama illustrates, extracurricular activities are important for adolescent personality development. These activities provide opportunities for students to develop concrete skills and thereby make sense of the world and their place in it. In schools today, academic subjects are too often presented as disconnected bits of knowledge that lack relevance to the student's life. Drama, music, and athletics programs are often better at giving students a framework within which they can develop a strong sense of self, because they are concrete activities with clearly defined rules. By training and playing hard on a hockey team, mastering an instrument, or acting in plays, students can learn something about their physical, emotional, and social capabilities and limitations, about what they are made of, and about what they can and cannot do. These are just the sorts of activities adolescents require for healthy self-development.

If you're like most young Canadians today, you spent fewer hours per week on extracurricular activities associated with school than your parents did when they went to school. Educators estimate that only about a quarter of today's high school students take part in sports, drama, music, and so forth (Hersch, 1998). Many of them are simply too busy with homework, household chores, child-care responsibilities, and part-time jobs to enjoy the benefits of school activities outside the classroom. Half of Canadian teenagers work at jobs averaging 15 hours a week (Bibby, 2001: 35).

### "The Vanishing Adolescent"

Some analysts wonder whether the assumption of so many adult responsibilities, the lack of extracurricular activities, the declining adult supervision and guidance, and the increasing mass media and peer group influence are causing childhood and adolescence to disappear. As early as 1959, one sociologist spoke of "the vanishing adolescent" in North American society (Friedenberg, 1959). More recently, another commentator remarked: "I think that we who were small in the early sixties were perhaps the last generation who actually had a childhood, in the . . . sense of . . . a space distinct in roles and customs from the world of adults, oriented around children's own needs and culture rather than around the needs and culture of adults" (Wolf, 1997: 13). Childhood and adolescence became universal categories of social thought and experience in the twentieth century. Under the impact of the social forces discussed above, however, the experience and meaning of childhood and adolescence now seem to be changing radically.

## The Points of the Compass

In this chapter, we have again drawn attention to the freedom-versus-constraint points of the sociological compass, but this time we have done so at two levels of analysis.

First, we focused on the *individual.* Beginning in the early twentieth century, social scientists established the existence of a tension between an impulsive, freedom-seeking part of the self (Freud's id and Mead's I) and a constraining part that helps to impose the norms of society on the individual (Freud's superego and Mead's me). From the point of view of Freud, Mead, and other leading scholars of socialization, people cannot develop normally unless they interact socially; only social interaction allows the socializing and constraining part of the self to temper the impulsive, freedom-seeking part. Our identity emerges out of this interaction. Tension between the desire to satisfy our impulses and the imposition of social constraint forges our sense of who we are and how we should act in the world.

We also analyzed the interplay between freedom and constraint at the level of *social institutions.* The family, the peer group, the school, and the mass media are powerful socializing agents. Within their constraints, people learn and relearn society's values, beliefs, and norms. For three reasons, however, institutions allow people varying degrees of freedom to choose socializing influences. First, the influence of the most powerful socializing agent, the family, has weakened in the past century or so. Second, institutions do not act as a monolithic and coordinated socializing force. Instead, they promote patterns of socialization that are often at odds with one another. Third, technological innovation and globalization have created new opportunities for socialization. Institutional weakening and competition, and the proliferation of socialization opportunities, increase people's freedom to select the socializing influences that best suit them.

In the next two chapters, we elaborate the idea that freedom and constraint are two points of the sociological compass at various levels of analysis.

## Summary

1. *Why is social interaction necessary?*

Studies show that children raised in isolation do not develop normally. This finding corroborates the view that social interaction unleashes human potential.

2. *What are the major theories of childhood socialization?*

Freud called the part of the self that demands immediate gratification the *id.* He argued that a self-image begins to emerge when the id's demands are denied. Because of many lessons in self-control, a child eventually develops a sense of what constitutes appropriate behaviour, a moral sense of right and wrong, and a personal conscience or superego. The *superego* is a repository of cultural standards. A third component of the self, the *ego,* develops to balance the demands of the id and superego. Like Freud, Mead noted that an impulsive aspect of the self is present from birth. He called it the *I.* Developing Cooley's idea of the *looking-glass self,* Mead also argued that a repository of culturally approved standards emerges as part of the self during social interaction. Mead called it the *me.* However, Mead drew attention to the unique human capacity to take the role of the other as the source of the *me.* People develop, he wrote, by first imitating and pretending to be their significant others, then learning to play complex games that require understanding several roles simultaneously, and finally developing a sense of cultural standards and how they apply. Since the early twentieth century, psychologists have contributed to our understanding of cognitive and moral socialization, but sociologists have done more to underline the social conditions that account for variations in cognitive and moral development. Specifically, their work suggests that gender and economic and political structures shape socialization patterns.

3. ***How has the influence of various agents of socialization changed over the past century?***

Over the past century, the increasing socializing influence of schools, peer groups, and the mass media has been matched by the decreasing socializing influence of the family.

4. ***In what sense is the self more flexible than it used to be?***

People's self-conceptions are subject to more flux now than they were even a few decades ago. Cultural globalization, medical advances, and computer-assisted communication are among the factors that have made the self more plastic.

5. ***What social forces have caused changes in the character and experience of childhood and adolescence?***

Childhood as a distinct stage of life emerged for well-to-do boys in the late seventeenth century, when life expectancy started to increase and boys had to be trained for more complex work tasks. Girls were treated as "little women" until the nineteenth century, and most working-class boys first experienced childhood only in the twentieth century. Once teenagers were relieved of adult responsibilities, the term *adolescence* was coined to describe the teenage years. Subsequently, the term *young adulthood* entered popular usage as an increasingly large number of people in their late teens and 20s delayed marriage to attend college or university.

Today, decreasing parental supervision and guidance, the increasing assumption of substantial adult responsibilities by children and adolescents, the declining participation in extracurricular activities, and increased mass media and peer group influence are causing changes in the character and experience of childhood and adolescence. According to some analysts, childhood and adolescence as they were known in the first half of the twentieth century are disappearing.

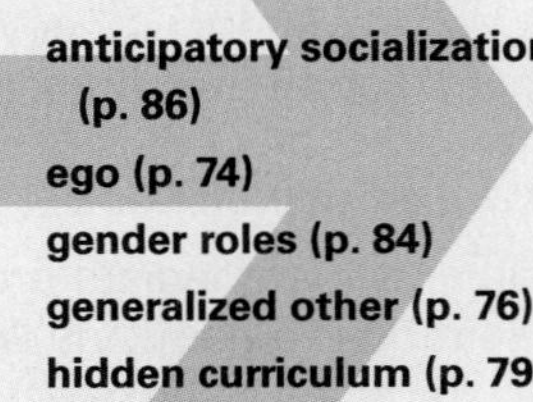

# Key Terms

**anticipatory socialization (p. 86)**
**ego (p. 74)**
**gender roles (p. 84)**
**generalized other (p. 76)**
**hidden curriculum (p. 79)**
**I (p. 75)**
**id (p. 73)**
**initiation rite (p. 85)**
**looking-glass self (p. 75)**
**me (p. 75)**
**peer group (p. 81)**
**primary socialization (p. 77)**
**resocialization (p. 85)**
**role (p. 69)**
**secondary socialization (p. 78)**
**self (p. 73)**

self-fulfilling prophecy (p. 80)
self-socialization (p. 84)
significant others (p. 76)
socialization (p. 69)
status (p. 81)
superego (p. 74)
Thomas theorem (p. 80)
total institutions (p. 85)
unconscious (p. 74)
virtual community (p. 88)

# Questions to Consider

1. Do you think of yourself in a fundamentally different way from the way your parents (or other close relatives or friends at least 20 years older than you) thought of themselves when they were your age? Interview your parents, relatives, or friends to find out. Pay particular attention to the way in which the forces of globalization may have altered self-conceptions over time.
2. Watch an hour of prime-time TV. How are gender, racial, ethnic, class, age, and disability roles portrayed? Are stereotypes used to characterize different types of people? What impact might such portrayals have on children watching TV?
3. Have you ever participated in an initiation rite on a sports team, in university, in the military, or in a religious organization? If so, describe the ritual rejection, ritual death, and ritual rebirth that made up the rite. Do you think the rite increased your identification with the group you were joining? Did it increase the sense of solidarity—the "we-feeling"—of group members?

# Web Resources

## Companion Web Site for This Book

http://www.pointsofthecompass.nelson.com

Begin by clicking on the Student Resources section of the Web site. Next, select the chapter you are currently studying from the pull-down menu. From the Student Resources page you will have easy access to InfoTrac® College Edition, MicroCase online exercises, and additional Weblinks. The Web site also has many useful tips to aid you in your study of sociology, including practice tests for each chapter.

## InfoTrac® Search Terms

These search terms are provided to assist you in beginning to conduct research on this topic by visiting **http://www.infotrac-college.com:**

**hidden curriculum**
**initiation rite**
**peer group**
**primary socialization**
**secondary socialization**

## Recommended Web Sites

For the socialization experiences that characterize different generations, go to a major search engine on the Web, such as Yahoo at **http://www.yahoo.ca**, and search for "teenagers," "generation X," "baby boomers," "the elderly," and so on.

Initiation rites (or rites of passage) are conveniently summarized in the online version of the *Encarta* encyclopaedia. Go to the Encarta search engine at **http://encarta.msn.com** and search for "rites of passage."

Do parents influence the personality development of their children? For a provocative reassessment of this view, read the article by Judith Rich Harris at **http://home.att.net/~xchar/tna/devpsyjh.htm**.

# chapter 4

## from social interaction to social organizations



### In this chapter, you will learn that

→ Social interaction involves people communicating face to face, acting and reacting in relation to one another. The character of every social interaction depends on people's distinct positions in the interaction (statuses), their standards of conduct (norms), and their sets of expected behaviours (roles).

→ Nonverbal means of communication, including facial expressions, gestures, body language, and status cues, are as important as language in social interaction.

→ Sociological theories of social interaction focus on the way (1) people exchange valued resources; (2) people maximize gains and minimize losses; (3) people interpret, negotiate, and modify norms, roles, and statuses; (4) people manage the impressions they give to others; (5) pre-existing norms influence social interaction; and (6) status hierarchies influence social interaction.

→ We commonly explain the way people act in terms of their interests and emotions. However, sometimes people act against their interests and suppress their emotions because groups, networks, and social organizations influence what people do.

→ The patterns of social ties through which emotional and material resources flow form social networks. Among other things, information and social support typically spread through social networks.

→ People who are bound together by interaction and a common identity form social groups. Groups impose conformity on members and draw boundaries between those who belong and those who do not.

# Humour and the Building Blocks of Social Interaction

Some years ago, a researcher and his assistants eavesdropped on 1200 conversations of people laughing in public places, such as shopping malls (Provine, 2000). When they heard someone laughing, they recorded who laughed (the speaker, the listener, or both) and the gender of the speaker and the listener. To simplify things, they eavesdropped only on two-person groups.

They found that women laugh more than men do in everyday conversations. The biggest discrepancy in laughing occurs when the speaker is a woman and the listener is a man. In such cases, women laugh more than twice as often as men do (88.1 percent versus 38.9 percent). But even when a man speaks and a woman listens, the woman is more likely to laugh than the man (71 percent versus 66 percent).

A sociologist would notice that the gender distribution of laughter fits a pattern. If *status* is defined as a recognized social position, it is generally the case that people with higher status (in this case, men) get more laughs, while people with lower status (in this case, women) laugh more. That is perhaps why class clowns are nearly always boys. It is also why a classic sociological study of laughter among staff members in a psychiatric hospital discovered "downward humour" (Coser, 1960). At a series of staff meetings, psychiatrists averaged 7.5 witticisms, medical students doing their residency averaged 5.5, and paramedics averaged just 0.7. Moreover, the psychiatrists most often made the residents the target of their humour, whereas the residents and the paramedics targeted the patients or themselves. Laughter in everyday life, it turns out, is not as spontaneous as you may think. It is often a signal of dominance or subservience; social structure influences our laughter.

Whenever people communicate, acting and reacting in relation to one another, they are engaging in **social interaction.** Much social interaction takes place among status equals—among members of the same national or racial group, for example. If status equals enjoy a privileged position in the larger society, they often direct their humour at perceived social inferiors. Canadians tell "Newfie" jokes. The English laugh about the Irish and, more recently, the Welsh. The French howl at the Belgians. And the Russians make jokes about the impoverished and oppressed Chukchi people of northern Siberia ("When a Chukchi man comes back from hunting he first wants his supper on the table. Then he wants to make love to his wife. Then he wants to take off his skis"). Similarly, when people point out that the only good thing about having Alzheimer's disease is that you can hide your own Easter eggs, they are making a joke about a socially marginal and powerless group. It has the effect of excluding outsiders, making the teller of the joke feel superior, and reinforcing the status hierarchy itself.

Laughter in everyday life is often a signal of dominance or subservience.

Social statuses are just one of the three building blocks that structure all social interactions. The other building blocks are roles and norms. A *role* is a set of expected behaviours. Whereas people *occupy* a status, they *perform* a role. Students may learn to expect that when things get dull, the class clown will brighten their day. The class clown will rise to the occasion, knowing that his fellow students expect him to do so. A *norm* is a generally accepted way of doing things. Classroom norms are imposed by instructors, who routinely punish class clowns for distracting their classmates from the task at hand (see Figure 4.1).

**Figure 4.1**
**Roles and Statuses**

**Role set and status set**

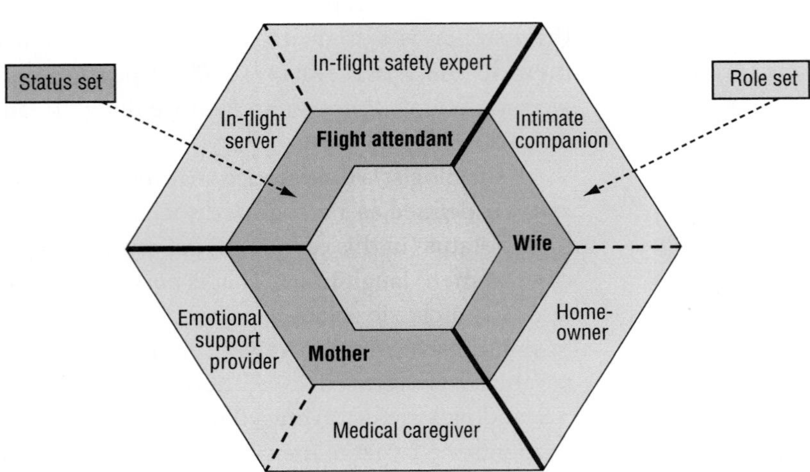


Each person occupies many statuses. For instance, an individual can be a flight attendant, a wife, and a mother at the same time. Sociologists call the entire ensemble of statuses occupied by an individual a **status set**. A **role set** is a cluster of roles attached to a single status. For example, someone occupying the status of flight attendant can play the roles of in-flight safety expert and server.

**Role conflict**

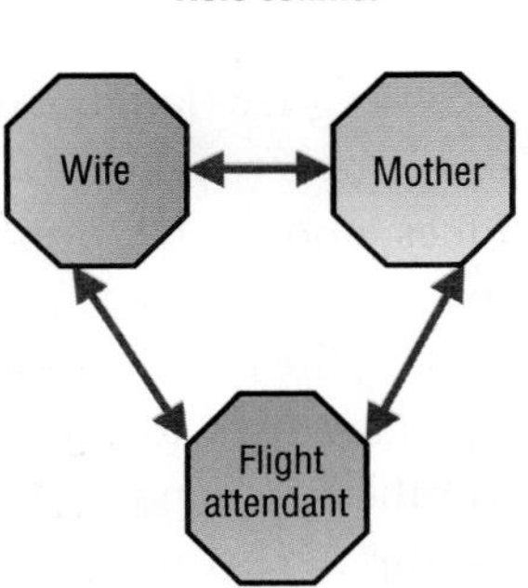


Role conflict takes place when different role demands are placed on a person by two or more statuses held at the same time. How might a flight attendant experience role conflict because of the contradictory demands of the statuses diagrammed above?

**Role strain**

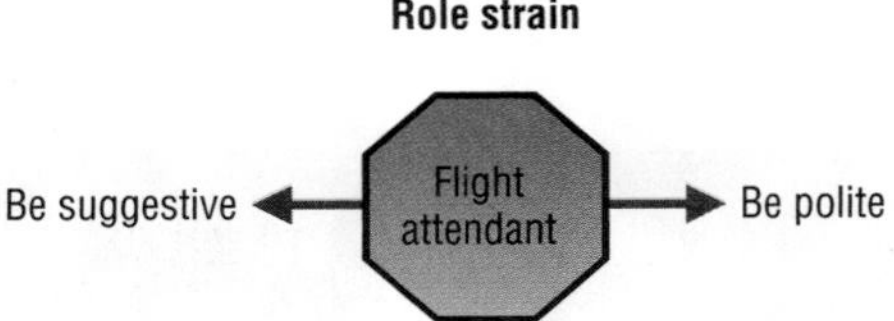


Role strain occurs when incompatible role demands are placed on a person in a single status. For instance, in the 1960s, when most air travellers were businessmen, flight attendants (or *stewardesses* as they were called at the time) were required by their employers to be slim and single and to appear to be "available." This requirement maximized role strain; flight attendants had to constantly be suggestive while also politely warding off unwanted, impolite, and crude overtures.

Figure 4.2
How People Get Emotional

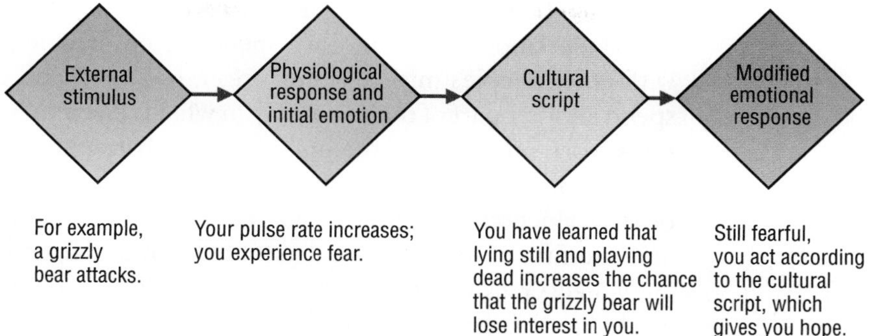
External stimulus
Physiological response and initial emotion
Cultural script
Modified emotional response
For example, a grizzly bear attacks.
Your pulse rate increases; you experience fear.
You have learned that lying still and playing dead increases the chance that the grizzly bear will lose interest in you.
Still fearful, you act according to the cultural script, which gives you hope.

## *Emotion Management*

Some scholars think that emotions are like the common cold. In both cases, an external disturbance causes a reaction that people presumably experience involuntarily. The external disturbance, for example, could be a grizzly bear attack that causes us to experience fear or exposure to a virus that causes us to catch cold. In either case, we can't control our body's patterned response. Emotions, like colds, just happen to us (Thoits, 1989: 319).

The trouble with this argument is that we often *do* control our emotions. Emotions don't just happen to us; we manage them. If a grizzly bear attacks you in the woods, you can run as fast as possible or calm yourself, lie down, play dead, and silently pray for the best. You are more likely to survive the grizzly bear attack if you control your emotions and follow the second strategy. You will also temper your fear with a new emotion: hope (see Figure 4.2).

When people manage their emotions, they usually follow certain cultural "scripts," like the culturally transmitted knowledge that lying down and playing dead gives you a better chance of surviving a grizzly bear attack. That is, individuals usually know the culturally designated emotional response to a particular external stimulus and try to respond appropriately. If they don't succeed in achieving the culturally appropriate emotional response, they are likely to feel guilt, disappointment, or (as in the case of the grizzly bear attack) something much worse.

Sociologist Arlie Russell Hochschild is a leading figure in the study of **emotion management.** In fact, she coined the term. She argues that emotion management involves people obeying "feeling rules" and responding appropriately to the situations in which they find themselves (Hochschild, 1979, 1983). So, for example, people talk about the "right" to feel angry and they acknowledge that they "should" have mourned a relative's death more deeply. People have conventional expectations not only about what they should feel but also about how much they should feel, how long they should feel it, and with whom they should share those feelings. For example, we are expected to mourn the end of a love relationship. Shedding tears is regarded as completely natural today among Canadians, though if you shot yourself—as was the fad among some European Romantics in the early nineteenth century—then you would be regarded as deranged. If you go on a date minutes after you break up with your long-time love, then most people will regard you as callous. Norms and rules govern our emotional life.

## *Emotion Labour*

Hochschild distinguishes emotion management (which everyone does in their everyday life) from **emotion labour** (which many people do as part of their job and for which they are paid). Teachers, sales clerks, nurses, and flight attendants must be experts in emotion labour. They spend a considerable part of their workday dealing with other people's misbehaviour, anger, rudeness, and unreasonable demands. They spend another part of their workday in what is essentially promotional and public relations work on behalf of the organizations that employ them. In all these tasks, they carefully manage their own emotions while trying to render their clientele happy and orderly. Hochschild estimates that in the United States, nearly half the jobs women do and one-fifth of the jobs men do involve substantial amounts of emotion labour.

Moreover, as the focus of the economy shifts from the production of goods to the production of services, the market for emotion labour grows. More and more people are selected, trained, and paid for their skill in emotion labour. Hence, employers look for people with not just high IQs but also "emotional intelligence." Emotion labour becomes a commodity that employers buy in much the same way as a furniture manufacturer buys fabric to upholster chairs. The emotional life of workers—or at least the way they openly express their feelings—is increasingly governed by the organizations for which they work and is therefore less and less spontaneous and authentic.

## *Emotions in Historical Perspective*

We can glean additional evidence of the impact of society on our emotional life from historical studies. Feeling rules take different forms under different social conditions, which vary historically. Two examples from the social history of emotions help illustrate the point:

1. Grief. *Among other factors, the* ***crude death rate*** *(the annual number of deaths per 1000 people in a population) helps determine our experience of grief (Lofland, 1985). In Europe as late as 1600, life expectancy was only 35 years. Many infants died at birth or in their first year of life. Infectious diseases decimated entire populations. The medical profession was in its infancy. The risk of losing family members, especially babies, was thus much greater than today. As a result, people invested less emotionally in their children than they typically do today. As health conditions improved and the infant mortality rate fell over the years, emotional investment in children increased. It intensified especially in the nineteenth century, when women started having fewer babies on average as a result of industrialization. As emotional investment in children increased, grief response to child deaths intensified and lasted longer. To put it crudely, in Europe and North America in 1600 it was normal to lose a few children. Today, in contrast, every child's death is a major tragedy.*

2. Disgust. *Manners in Europe in the Middle Ages were disgusting by our standards. Even the most refined aristocrats spat in public and belched shamelessly during banquets (with the king in attendance, no less). Members of high society didn't flinch*

Manners in Europe during the Middle Ages were disgusting by today's standards.

*at scratching themselves and passing gas at the dinner table, where they ate with their hands and speared food with knives. What was acceptable then causes revulsion now because feeling rules have changed. Specifically, manners began to change with the emergence of the modern political state, especially after 1700. The modern political state raised armies and collected taxes, imposed languages, and required loyalty. All this coordination of effort necessitated more self-control on the part of the citizenry. Changes in standards of public conduct—signalled by the introduction of the fork, the nightdress, the handkerchief, the spittoon, and the chamber pot—accompanied the rise of the modern state. Good manners also served to define who had power and who lacked it. For example, there is nothing inherently well mannered about a father sitting at the head of the table carving the turkey and children waiting to speak until they are spoken to. These rules about the difference between good manners and improper or disgusting behaviour were created to signify the distribution of power in the family by age and gender (Elias, 1994 [1939]).*

Thus, although emotions form an important part of all social interactions, they are neither universal nor constant. They have histories and deep sociological underpinnings in statuses, roles, and norms. In turn, big social structures and social changes—industrialization, the rise of the state, improvements in health conditions, and so forth—shape statuses, roles, and norms.

These observations fly in the face of common sense. We typically think of our interactions as outcomes of our emotional states. We interact differently with people depending on whether they love us, make us angry, or make us laugh. We usually think our emotions are evoked involuntarily and result in uncontrollable action. But as you have just seen, emotions are not as unique, involuntary, and uncontrollable as people often believe. Underlying the turbulence of emotional life is a measure of order and predictability governed by sociological principles.

Just as building blocks need cement to hold them together, so norms, roles, and statuses require a sort of "social cement" to prevent them from falling apart and to turn them into a durable social structure. What is the nature of the cement that holds the building blocks of social life together? Asked differently, exactly how is social interaction maintained? This is the most fundamental sociological question anyone can ask, for it is really a question about how social structures, and society as a whole, are possible. There are three main ways of maintaining social interaction and thereby cementing social structures and society as a whole: competition, domination, and cooperation. In the next sections, we investigate each of these modes of interaction in detail.

# Modes of Social Interaction

## *Interaction as Competition and Exchange*

Have you ever been in a conversation where you can't get a word in edgewise? If you are like most people, this situation is bound to happen from time to time. The longer a one-sided conversation persists, the more neglected you feel. You may make increasingly less subtle attempts to turn the conversation your way. But if you fail, you may decide to end the interaction altogether. If this experience repeats itself—if the person you're talking to consistently monopolizes conversations—you're likely to want to avoid getting into conversations with him or her in the future. Maintaining interaction (and maintaining a relationship) requires that both parties' need for attention is met.

Most people don't consistently try to monopolize conversations. If they did, there wouldn't be much talk in the world. In fact, taking turns is one of the basic norms that govern conversations; people literally take turns talking to make conversation possible. Nonetheless, a remarkably large part of all conversations involves a subtle competition for attention. Consider the following snippet of dinner conversation:

John: "I'm feeling really starved."
Mary: "Oh, I just ate."
John: "Well, I'm feeling really starved."
Mary: "When was the last time you ate?"

Sociologist Charles Derber recorded this conversation (Derber, 1979: 24). John starts by saying how hungry he is. The attention is on him. Mary replies that she's not hungry, and the attention shifts to her. John insists he's hungry, shifting attention back to him. Mary finally allows the conversation to focus on John by asking him when he last ate. John thus "wins" the competition for attention (Box 4.1).

Derber (1979) recorded 1500 conversations in family homes, workplaces, restaurants, classrooms, dormitories, and therapy groups. He concluded that North Americans usually try to turn conversations toward themselves. They usually do so in ways that go unnoticed. Nonetheless, says Derber, the typical conversation is a covert competition for attention. Derber is careful to point out that conversations are not winner-take-all competitions. Unless both people in a two-person conversation receive some attention, the interaction is likely to cease. Therefore, conversation typically involves the exchange of attention.

4.1

## YOU AND THE SOCIAL WORLD

### Competing for Attention

Observe the competition for attention yourself. Record a couple of minutes of conversation in your university or college residence, home, or workplace. Then play it back.

**WRITING ASSIGNMENT**

Write a 500-word essay evaluating each statement in the conversation. Does the statement try to change who is the subject of the conversation? Or does it say something about the *other* conversationalist(s) or ask them about what *they* said? How does not responding, or merely saying "uh-huh" in response, operate to shift attention? Are other conversational techniques especially effective in shifting attention? Who "wins" the conversation? What is the winner's gender, race, and class position? Is the winner popular or unpopular? Do you think a connection exists between the person's status in the group and his or her ability to win? What other factors might account for winning?

### *Exchange and Rational Choice Theories*

The idea that social interaction involves trade in attention and other valued resources is the central insight of **exchange theory** (Blau, 1964; Homans, 1961). Exchange theorists believe, as did the Beatles, that "in the end, the love you take is equal to the love you make." But not just love: social exchange theorists argue that *all* social relationships involve a literal give and take. From this point of view, when people interact, they exchange valued resources, including attention, pleasure, approval, prestige, information, and money. With payoffs, relationships endure and can give rise to various organizational forms. Without payoffs, relationships end.

A variant of this approach is **rational choice theory** (Coleman, 1990; Hechter, 1987). Rational choice theory focuses less on the resources being exchanged than on the way interacting people weigh the benefits and costs of interaction. According to rational choice theory, interacting people always try to maximize benefits and minimize costs. Businesspeople want to keep their expenses to a minimum so that they can keep their profits as high as possible. Similarly, everyone wants to gain the most from their interactions—socially, emotionally, and economically—while paying the least.

Undoubtedly, we can explain many types of social interaction in terms of exchange and rational choice theories—but not all. For example, people get little or nothing of value out of some relationships, yet the relationships persist. Slaves remain slaves not because they are well paid or because they enjoy the work but because they are forced to do it. Some people remain in abusive relationships because their abusive partner keeps them socially isolated and psychologically dependent. They lack the resources needed to get out of the abusive relationship.

At the other extreme, people often act in ways they consider fair or just, even if this does not maximize their personal gain (Frank, 1988; Gamson, Fireman, and Rytina, 1982). Some people even engage in altruistic or heroic acts from which they gain nothing. Heroes respond to cries for help based on emotion (which, physiologists tell us, takes 1/125th of a second to register in the brain), not rational calculation (which takes seconds or even minutes). When people behave fairly or altruistically, they are interacting with others based on *norms* they have learned—norms that say they should act justly and help people in need, even if substantial costs are attached. Such norms are, for the most part, ignored by exchange and rational choice theorists. Exchange and rational choice theorists think that you do for others what they do for you because if you don't, then others will stop doing things for you (Homans, 1950). But social life is richer than this narrow view suggests. Interaction is not all selfishness. One researcher found that freshman sociology and economics majors were equally selfish, but by the time they graduated, the economics majors were much more likely than the sociology majors to consider selfish actions natural and normal (Frank, 1988). Clearly, what we learn has an impact on our norms and expectations regarding social interaction.

Moreover, we cannot *assume* what people want, because norms (as well as roles and statuses) are not presented to us fully formed, nor do we accept them mechanically. Instead, we constantly negotiate and modify norms—as well as roles and statuses—as we interact with others. We will now explore this theme by considering the ingenious ways in which people manage the impressions they give to others during social interaction.

### *Symbolic Interaction*

Soon after they enter medical school, students become adept at managing the impression they make on other people. As sociologists Jack Haas and William Shaffir (1987) show in their study of professional socialization, medical students adopt a new medical vocabulary and wear a white lab coat to set themselves apart from patients. They try to model their behaviour after the doctors who have authority over them. They may ask questions they know the answer to so that they can impress their teachers. When dealing with patients, they may hide their ignorance under medical jargon to maintain their authority. By engaging in these and related practices, medical students reduce the distance between their pre-medical-school selves and the role of doctor. By the time they finish medical school, they have reduced the distance so much that they no longer see any difference between the two. They come to take for granted a fact they once had to socially construct—the fact that they are doctors.

Haas and Shaffir's study is an application of symbolic interactionism, a theoretical approach introduced in Chapter 1. Symbolic interactionists regard people as active, creative, and self-reflective. Whereas exchange theorists *assume* what people want, symbolic interactionists argue that people create meanings and desires in the course of social interaction (Blumer, 1969; Berger and Luckmann, 1966; Strauss, 1993).

### Dramaturgical Analysis

Although several distinct approaches to symbolic interactionism exist (Denzin, 1992), probably the most widely applied approach is **dramaturgical analysis.** As first developed by Erving Goffman (1959), and briefly discussed in Chapter 1, A Sociological Compass, dramaturgical analysis takes literally Shakespeare's line from *As You Like It:* "All the world's a stage and all the men and women merely players."

From Goffman's point of view, people are constantly engaged in role-playing. This fact is most evident when we are "front stage" in public settings. Just as being front stage in a play requires the use of props, set gestures, and memorized lines, so does acting in public space. A server in a restaurant, for example, must dress in a uniform, smile, and recite fixed lines ("How are you? My name is Sam and I'm your server today. May I get you a drink before you order your meal?"). When the server goes "backstage," he or she can relax from the front-stage performance and discuss it with fellow actors ("Those kids at table six are driving me nuts!"). Thus, we often distinguish between our public roles and our "true" selves. Note, however, that even backstage we engage in role-playing and impression management; it's just that we are less likely to be aware of it. For instance, in the kitchen, a server may try to present herself in the best possible light to impress another server so that she can eventually ask him out for a date. Thus, the implication of dramaturgical analysis is that there is no single self, just the ensemble of roles we play in various social contexts (Box 4.2). Servers in restaurants play many roles off the job. They play on basketball teams, sing in church choirs, and hang out with friends at shopping malls. Each role is governed by norms about what kinds of clothes to wear, what kind of conversation to engage in, and so on. Everyone plays on many front stages in everyday life.

They do not always do so enthusiastically. If a role is stressful, people may engage in role distancing. **Role distancing** involves giving the impression of just "going through the motions" but lacking serious commitment to a role. Thus, when people think a role they are playing is embarrassing or beneath them, they typically want to give their peers the impression that the role is not their "true" self. My parents force me to sing in the church choir; I'm working at McDonald's just to earn a few extra dollars, but I'm going back to college next semester; this old car I'm driving is just a loaner. These are the kinds of rationalizations individuals offer when distancing themselves from a role.

Sandra Bullock and William Shatner in a scene from *Miss Congeniality* (2000)

4.2

# SOCIOLOGY AT THE MOVIES

*Miss Congeniality* (2000)

Scene: A New Jersey schoolyard in 1982. An eight-year-old schoolyard bully is picking a fight with another, smaller boy. Unexpectedly, a girl comes to the rescue, telling the bully to back off. The following dialogue ensues:

**Bully:** **"If you weren't a girl, I'd beat your face off."**

**Girl:** **"If *you* weren't a girl I'd beat *your* face off."**

**Bully:** **"You calling me a girl?"**

**Girl:** **"You called *me* one."**

Whereupon the bully takes a swing at the girl, which she neatly evades, and she proceeds to deck him. She then approaches the other boy, and says sweetly: "Forget those guys. They're just jealous. You're funny. You're smart. Girls like that."

**Other boy:** **"Well I don't like you. Now everyone thinks I need a girl to fight for me. You are a dork brain." Girl punches other boy in nose. End of scene.**

Almost predictably, the girl grows up to become a tough-talking and tomboyish undercover agent (played by Sandra Bullock) without a boyfriend. The plot thickens when Bullock is forced to take an undercover assignment as a contestant in a beauty pageant. Someone is plotting a terrorist act during the pageant and she has to find out who it is. First, however, she has to undergo a role change, something far deeper than a mere makeover. A beauty consultant (played by Michael Caine) teaches her how to walk like a stereotypical woman, wear makeup, and dress to kill. In her interaction with the other contestants, she begins to learn how to behave in a conventionally feminine way. She even becomes a finalist in the beauty pageant. In the end, she gets the bad guy, captures the heart of the handsome FBI agent (played by Benjamin Bratt), and wins the pageant's "Miss Congeniality" award. Her true self emerges, and everyone goes home happy.

This movie's theme is at least as old as *Cinderella*. In Hollywood, as in fairy tales, the emergence of one's "true self" is often the resolution of the conflict that animates the story. Yet life rarely comes in such neat packages. The sociological study of social interaction shows how we balance different selves in centre stage and backstage performances, play many roles simultaneously, are pulled in different directions by role strain and role conflict, and distance ourselves from some of our roles. To make matters even more complex and dynamic, sociology underlines how we continuously enter new stages, roles, conflicts, strains, and distancing manoeuvres as we mature. This social complexity makes our "true self" not a thing we discover once and for all but a work in progress. The resolution of every conflict that animates our lives is temporary. *Miss Congeniality* is an entertaining escape from reality's messiness, but it is a poor guide to life as we actually live it. For that we need sociology.

### CRITICAL THINKING QUESTIONS

- *Do you have a "true self" or are you just a bundle of roles that you perform?*
- *When do we act and when do we stop acting?*

### Ethnomethodology

By emphasizing how people construct social reality in the course of interaction, symbolic interactionists downplay the importance of the norms and understandings that *precede* any given interaction. **Ethnomethodology** tries to correct that shortcoming. Ethnomethodology is the study of the methods ordinary people use, often unconsciously, to make sense of what others do and say. Ethnomethodologists stress that everyday interactions could not take place without *pre-existing* shared norms and understandings.

To illustrate the importance of pre-existing shared norms and understandings, Harold Garfinkel conducted a series of experiments. In one such experiment he asked one of his students to interpret a casual greeting in an unexpected way (Garfinkel, 1967: 44):

Acquaintance: [waving cheerily] How are you?
Student: How am I in regard to what? My health, my finances, my schoolwork, my peace of mind, my . . . ?
Acquaintance: [red in the face and suddenly out of control] Look! I was just trying to be polite. Frankly, I don't give a damn how you are.

As this example shows, social interaction requires tacit agreement between the actors about what is normal and expected. Without shared norms and understandings, no sustained interaction can occur. People are likely to get upset and end an interaction when one person violates the assumptions underlying the stability and meaning of daily life.

Assuming the existence of shared norms and understandings, let us now inquire briefly into the way people communicate in face-to-face interaction. Having a conversation is actually a wonder of intricate complexity; even today's most advanced supercomputer cannot conduct a natural-sounding conversation with a person (Kurzweil, 1999: 61, 91).

## *Verbal and Nonverbal Communication*

Fifty years ago an article appeared in the British newspaper *News Chronicle,* trumpeting the invention of an electronic translating device at the University of London. According to the article, "As fast as [a user] could type the words in, say, French, the equivalent in Hungarian or Russian would issue forth on the tape" (quoted in Silberman, 2000: 225). The report was an exaggeration, to put it mildly. It soon became a standing joke that if you asked a computer to translate "The spirit is willing, but the flesh is weak" into Russian, the output would read, "The vodka is good, but the steak is lousy." Today we are closer to high-quality machine translation than we were in the 1950s; however, a practical universal translator exists only on *Star Trek.*

### The Social Context of Language

Why are human beings much better translators than computers are? Because computer programs find it difficult to make sense of the *social and cultural context* in which language is used. The same words can mean different things in different settings, so computers, lacking contextual cues, routinely botch translations. Machine translation works best when applications are restricted to a single social context—say, weather forecasting or oil exploration. In such cases, specialized vocabularies and meanings specific to the context of interest can be built into the program. Ambiguity is thus reduced and computers can "understand" the meaning of words well enough to translate them with reasonable accuracy. Similarly, humans must be able to reduce ambiguity and make sense of words to become good translators. They do so by learning the nuances of meaning in different cultural and social contexts over an extended time. They are greatly assisted in that task by *nonverbal* cues.

### Facial Expressions, Gestures, and Body Language

A few years ago, *Cosmopolitan* magazine featured an article advising female readers on "how to reduce otherwise evolved men to drooling, panting fools." Basing his analysis on the work of several psychologists, the author of the article first urges readers to "delete the old-school seductress image (smoky eyes, red lips, brazen stare) from your consciousness." Then, he writes, you must "upload a new inner temptress who's equal parts good girl and wild child." The article recommends invading a man's personal space and entering his "intimate zone" by finding an excuse to touch him. Picking a piece of lint off his jacket ought to do the trick. Then you can tell him how much you like his cologne (Willardt, 2000). If things progress, another article in the same issue of *Cosmopolitan* explains how you can read his body language to tell whether he's lying (Dutton, 2000).

Whatever we may think of the soundness of *Cosmopolitan*'s advice or the images of women and men it tries to reinforce, this example drives home the point that social interaction typically involves a complex mix of verbal and nonverbal messages. The face alone is capable of more than 1000 distinct expressions, reflecting the whole range of human emotion. Arm movements, hand gestures, posture, and other aspects of body language send many more messages to a person's audience (Wood, 1999).

Despite the wide variety of facial expressions in the human repertoire, most researchers believed until recently that the facial expressions of six emotions are similar across cultures. These six emotions are happiness, sadness, anger, disgust, fear, and surprise (Ekman, 1978). Especially since the mid-1990s, however, some researchers have questioned whether a universally recognized set of facial expressions reflects basic human emotions. Among other things, critics have argued that "facial expressions are not the readout of emotions but displays that serve social motives and are mostly determined by the presence of an audience" (Fernandez-Dols, Sanchez, Carrera, and Ruiz-Belda, 1997: 163). From this point of view, a smile will reflect pleasure if it serves a person's interest to present a smiling face to his or her audience. Conversely, a person may be motivated to conceal anxiety by smiling or to conceal pleasure by suppressing a smile.

At times, different cultural expectations can lead to colossal misunderstanding. Until recently, it was considered rude among educated Japanese to say "no." Disagreement was instead conveyed by discreetly changing the subject and smiling politely. Consequently, it was common for visiting North Americans to think that their Japanese hosts were saying "yes" because of the politeness, the smile, and the absence of a "no" when in fact they were saying "no."

No gestures or body postures mean the same thing in all societies and all cultures. In our society, people point with an outstretched hand and an extended finger. However, people raised in other cultures tip their head or use their chin or eyes to point out something. We nod our heads "yes" and shake "no," but others nod "no" and shake "yes."

Finally, we must note that in all societies people communicate by manipulating the space that separates them from others (Hall, 1959, 1966). This point is well illustrated in our *Cosmopolitan* example. Sociologists commonly distinguish four zones that surround us. The size of these zones varies from one society to the next. In North America, an intimate zone extends about 0.5 metres from the body. It is restricted to people with whom we want sustained, intimate physical contact. A personal zone extends from about 0.5 metres to 1.5 metres away. It is reserved for friends and acquaintances. We tolerate only

Among other things, body language communicates the degree to which people conform to gender roles, or widely shared expectations about how males and females are supposed to act. In these photos, which postures suggest power and aggressiveness? Which suggest pleasant compliance? Which are "appropriate" to the sex of the person?

a little physical intimacy from such people. The social zone is situated in the area roughly 1.5 metres to 3.5 metres away from us. Apart from a handshake, no physical contact is permitted from people we restrict to that zone. The public zone starts around 3.5 metres from our bodies. It is used to distinguish a performer or a speaker from an audience.

### Status Cues

Aside from facial expressions, gestures, and body language, nonverbal communication takes place by means of **status cues,** or visual indicators of other people's social position. Goffman (1959) observed that when individuals come into contact, they typically try to acquire information that will help them define the situation and make interaction easier. That goal is accomplished in part by attending to status cues.

Although status cues can be useful in helping people define the situation and thus greasing the wheels of social interaction, they also pose a social danger; status cues can quickly degenerate into **stereotypes,** or rigid views of how members of various groups act, regardless of whether individual group members really behave that way. Stereotypes create social barriers that impair interaction or prevent it altogether. For instance, police officers in some places routinely stop young black male drivers without cause to check for proper licensing, possession of illegal goods, and other similar violations (see Figure 4.3). In this case, a social cue has become a stereotype that guides police policy. Young black males, the great majority of whom never commit an illegal act, view this police practice as harassment. Racial stereotyping therefore helps perpetuate the sometimes poor relations between young black men and law enforcement officials.

As these examples show, face-to-face interaction may at first glance appear to be straightforward and unproblematic. Most of the time, it is. However, underlying the surface of human communication is a wide range of cultural assumptions, unconscious understandings, and nonverbal cues that make interaction possible.

**Figure 4.3**
**Probability of Being Stopped by Police, Toronto, by Race, Sex, and Age**

Black male drivers are more likely to be stopped by the police than any other race–sex group. White and Asian female drivers are least likely to be stopped. Black males with higher education are more likely to be stopped than black males with lower education. How does stereotyping influence the chance of being stopped by the police?

■ Source: Wortley et al. (1996).

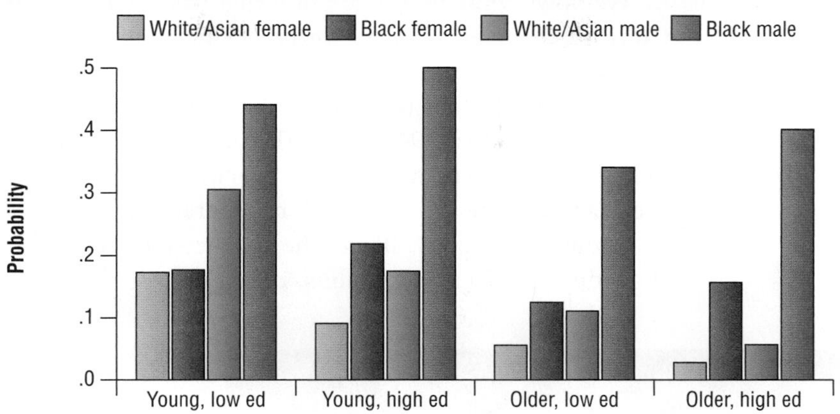


## *Power and Conflict Theories of Social Interaction*

In our discussion of the social cement that binds statuses, roles, and norms together, we have made four main points (see Table 4.1):

1. *One of the most important forces that cements social interaction is the competitive exchange of valued resources. People communicate to the degree they get something valuable out of the interaction. Simultaneously, however, they must engage in a careful balancing act. If they compete too avidly and prevent others from getting much out of the social interaction, communication will break down. This is exchange and rational choice theory in a nutshell.*
2. *Nobody hands values, norms, roles, and statuses to us fully formed, nor do we accept them mechanically. We mould them to suit us as we interact with others. For example, we constantly engage in impression management so that others will see the roles we perform in the best possible light. This is a major argument of symbolic interactionism and its most popular variant, dramaturgical analysis.*
3. *Norms do not emerge entirely spontaneously during social interaction, either. In general form, they exist before any given interaction takes place. Indeed, sustained interaction would be impossible without pre-existing shared understandings. This is the core argument of ethnomethodology.*

**Table 4.1**
Theories of Social Interaction

| Theory | Focus |
|---|---|
| Exchange theory | Exchange of valued resources |
| Rational choice theory | Maximization of gains and minimization of losses |
| Symbolic interactionism | Interpretation, negotiation, and modification of norms, roles, and statuses |
| Dramaturgical analysis | Impression management |
| Ethnomethodology | Influence of pre-existing norms |
| Conflict theory | Influence of status hierarchies |

4. *Nonverbal mechanisms of communication greatly facilitate social interaction. These mechanisms include facial expressions, hand gestures, body language, and status cues.*

We now highlight a final point that has been in the background of our discussion. **Conflict theories of social interaction** emphasize that when people interact, their statuses are often arranged in a hierarchy. People on top enjoy more **power** than those on the bottom—that is, they are "in a position to carry out [their] own will despite resistance" (Weber, 1947: 152). This disparity in power is well illustrated by the mass media, where the conversation is overwhelmingly one-sided; in most cases, the media speak and we listen (Box 4.3). More generally, in face-to-face communication the degree of inequality strongly affects the character of social interaction between the parties (Bourdieu, 1977 [1972]; Collins, 1982).

4.3

# MASS MEDIA AND SOCIETY

## The Problem of Domination

The mass media include print, radio, television, and other communication technologies. The word *mass* implies that the media reach many people. The word *media* signifies that communication does not take place directly through face-to-face interaction. Instead, technology intervenes or mediates in transmitting messages from senders to receivers.

Communication via the mass media is usually one way, or at least one-sided: there are few senders (or producers) and many receivers (or audience members). Ordinary people may appear on the *Oprah Winfrey Show,* compete in *Canadian Idol,* or even delight in a slice of fame on *Survivor*. However, producers choose the guests and create the content for these programs.

Usually, then, members of the audience cannot exert much influence on the mass media. They can choose only to tune in or tune out. And even tuning out is difficult because it excludes one from the styles, news, gossip, and entertainment most people depend on to grease the wheels of social interaction. Few people want to be cultural misfits.

This does not mean that people are always passive consumers of the mass media. For one thing, we can filter, interpret, and resist what we see and hear if it contradicts our experience and beliefs. For another, at least one mass medium, the Internet, allows consumers to become producers with relative ease. Many millions of Internet users participate in discussion groups, chat groups, and role-playing communities; create their own Web sites; and develop and use free music-sharing programs, such as Napster and Kazaa. True, the original Napster was shut down, and a group of recording companies tried to close Kazaa by taking it to an American court for copyright infringement. However, the companies discovered that the distributor of Kazaa software is incorporated in the South Pacific island of Vanuatu. Kazaa is managed from Australia, its servers are in Denmark, its source code is stored in Estonia, its developers live in the Netherlands, and it has 60 million users in 150 countries. It is therefore highly doubtful that a decision on behalf of the recording companies could be enforced ("Digital Dilemmas," 2003). It seems that as soon as one illegal music-sharing service is shut down, another pops up. Nonetheless, the Internet is a partial exception to the general rule. In the interaction between audiences and all other media sources, the media sources dominate.

### CRITICAL THINKING QUESTIONS

- *To what degree do you think the mass media shape your life?*
- *To what degree do you think you shape the mass media?*
- *Is your relationship (and the relationship of your peers) to the mass media acceptable or would you like to see it change in some way? If so, how?*
- *How might such change be accomplished?*

We can see how the distribution of power affects interaction by examining male–female interaction. Women are typically socialized to assume subordinate positions, whereas men are typically socialized to assume superordinate positions. This distribution of power is evident in the way men usually learn to be aggressive and competitive, and women learn to be cooperative and supportive (see Chapter 3, Socialization, and Chapter 8, Sexuality and Gender). Because of this learning, men often dominate conversations. Thus, conversation analyses conducted by Deborah Tannen show that men are more likely than women to engage in long monologues and interrupt when others are talking (1994a, 1994b). Men are also less likely to ask for help or directions because doing so would imply a reduction in their authority. Many male–female conflicts result from these differences. A stereotypical case is the lost male driver and the helpful female passenger. The female passenger, seeing that the male driver is lost, suggests that they stop and ask for directions. The male driver doesn't want to ask for directions because he thinks that would make him look incompetent. If both parties remain firm in their positions, an argument is bound to result.

### Modes of Interaction

In sum, **domination** represents one type of interaction. In social interaction based on domination, nearly all power is concentrated in the hands of people of similar status, whereas people of different status enjoy almost no power. In extreme cases of domination, subordinates live in a state of near-constant fear.

The opposite form of interaction is based on *cooperation*. Here, power is more or less equally distributed among people of different statuses. Cooperative interaction is based on feelings of trust.

Between the two extremes of interaction based on domination and interaction based on cooperation is interaction based on **competition.** In this mode of interaction, power is unequally distributed, but the degree of inequality is less than in systems of domination. Most of the social interactions analyzed by exchange and rational choice theorists are of this type. Envy is an important emotion in most competitive interactions (see Table 4.2).

Note that people are least free in systems of domination and freest in systems of cooperation. Even in systems of cooperation, however, social constraint exists. People creatively modify and negotiate the microstructures in which they find themselves, but norms, roles, and statuses always influence their behaviour. Moreover, microstructures are nested inside higher-level structures, such as groups, networks, and organizations, which also shape human behaviour. These **mesostructures** or mid-level structures are the subject of the rest of this chapter (see Figure 4.4).

**Table 4.2**
Main Modes of Interaction

| | Mode of Interaction | | |
|---|---|---|---|
| | **Domination** | **Competition** | **Cooperation** |
| Level of inequality | High | Medium | Low |
| Characteristic emotion | Fear | Envy | Trust |
| Efficacy | Low | Medium | High |

## Figure 4.4
## Big Structures, Small Processes

Society fits together like a set of nested dolls, with face-to-face interaction constituting the smallest doll in the set. Norms, roles, and statuses are the building blocks of social life. They form the *microstructures* within which face-to-face interaction takes place. Sustained microlevel interaction is shaped by *mesostructures* or mid-level structures, such as groups, networks, and organizations. Still larger *macrostructures,* including classes, states, and systems of patriarchy, constrain the functioning of networks, groups, and organizations. Finally, international trade, global communication, state relations, and organizations that span many countries form the overarching *global structures* that limit the freedom of the smaller structures operating within them (we'll look at macrostructures and global structures in Chapters 6 to 11). Social structures thus constrain our actions at various levels of analysis.

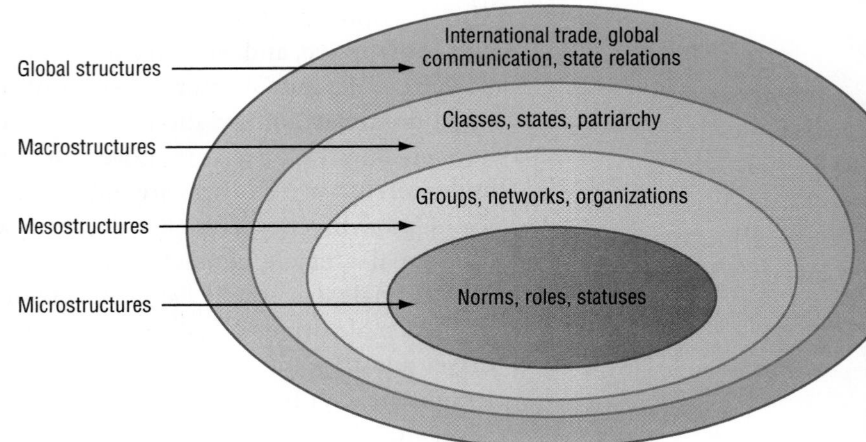


# Networks, Groups, and Organizations
## *The Holocaust*

In 1941, the large stone and glass train station was one of the proudest structures in Smolensk, a provincial capital of about 100 000 people on Russia's western border. Always bustling, it was especially busy on the morning of June 28. Besides the usual passengers and well-wishers, hundreds of Soviet Red Army soldiers were nervously talking, smoking, writing hurried letters to their loved ones, and sleeping fitfully on the station floor while waiting for their train. Nazi troops had invaded the nearby city of Minsk in Belarus a couple of days before. The Soviet soldiers were being positioned to defend Russia against the inevitable German onslaught.

Robert Brym's father, then in his 20s, had been standing in line for nearly two hours to buy food when he noticed flares arching over the station. Within seconds, Stuka bombers, the pride of the German air force, swept down, releasing their bombs just before pulling out of their dive. Inside the station, shards of glass, blocks of stone, and mounds of earth fell indiscriminately on sleeping soldiers and nursing mothers alike. Everyone panicked. People trampled over one another to get out. In minutes, the train station was rubble.

Nearly two years earlier, Robert's father had managed to escape Poland when the Nazis invaded his hometown near Warsaw. Now he was on the run again. By the time the Nazis occupied Smolensk a few weeks after their dive-bombers destroyed its train station, Robert's father was deep in the Russian interior serving in a workers' battalion attached to the Soviet Red Army.

"My father was one of 300 000 Polish Jews who fled eastward into Russia before the Nazi genocide machine could reach them," says Robert. "The remaining 3 million Polish Jews were killed in various ways. Some died in battle. Many more, like my father's mother and younger siblings, were rounded up like diseased cattle and shot. However, most of Poland's Jews wound up in the concentration camps. Those deemed unfit were shipped to the gas chambers. Those declared able to work were turned into slaves until they could work no more. Then they, too, met their fate. A mere 9 percent of Poland's 3.3 million Jews survived World War II. The Nazi regime was responsible for the death of 6 million Jews in Europe.

"One question that always perplexed my father about the war was this: How was it possible for many thousands of ordinary Germans—products of what he regarded as the most advanced civilization on earth—to systematically murder millions of defenceless and innocent Jews, Roma, homosexuals, and people with mental disabilities in the death camps?" To answer this question adequately, we must borrow ideas from the sociological study of networks, groups, and bureaucracies.

## *How Social Groups Shape Our Actions*

How could ordinary German citizens commit the crime of the twentieth century? The conventional, non-sociological answer is that many Nazis were evil, sadistic, or deluded enough to think that Jews and other undesirables threatened the existence of the German people. Therefore, in the Nazi mind, the innocents had to be killed. This answer is given in the 1993 movie *Schindler's List* and in many other accounts. Yet it is far from the whole story. Sociologists emphasize three other factors:

1. Norms of solidarity demand conformity. *When we form relationships with friends, lovers, spouses, teammates, and comrades-in-arms, we develop shared ideas, or* norms of solidarity, *about how we should behave toward them to sustain the relationships. Because these relationships are emotionally important to us, we sometimes pay more attention to norms of solidarity than to the morality of our actions. For example, a study of the Nazis who roamed the Polish countryside to shoot and kill Jews and other "enemies" of Nazi Germany found that the soldiers often did not hate the people they systematically slaughtered, but they did not have many qualms about their actions (Browning, 1992). They simply developed deep loyalty to one another. They felt they had to get their assigned job done or face letting down their comrades. Thus, they committed atrocities partly because they just wanted to maintain group morale, solidarity, and loyalty. They committed evil deeds not because they were extraordinarily bad but because they were quite ordinary—ordinary in the sense that they acted to sustain their friendship ties and to serve their group, just like most people.*

   *The case of the Nazi regime may seem extreme, but other instances of going along with criminal behaviour uncover a similar dynamic at work. Why do people rarely report crimes committed by corporations? Employees may worry about being reprimanded or fired if they become whistleblowers, but they also worry about letting down their coworkers. Why do gang members engage in criminal acts? They may seek financial gain, but they also regard crime as a way of maintaining a close social bond with their fellow gang members (see Box 4.4).*

The movie *Schindler's List* turns the history of Nazism into a morality play, a struggle between good and evil forces. It does not probe into the sociological roots of good and evil.

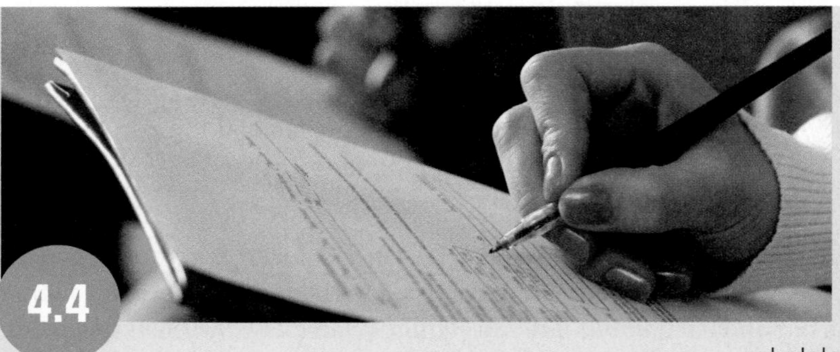

4.4

# SOCIAL POLICY: WHAT DO YOU THINK?

## Group Loyalty or Betrayal?

Group cohesion led Nazi soldiers to commit genocide. Group loyalty led many ordinary German citizens to support them. Although the Nazis are an extreme case, ordinary people often face a stark choice between group loyalty and group betrayal.

Glen Ridge, New Jersey, is an affluent white suburb. It was also the site of a terrible rape case in 1989. A group of 13 teenage boys lured a sweet-natured young woman with the mental age of an eight-year-old into a basement. There, four of them raped her while three others looked on; six left when they realized what was going to happen. The rapists used a baseball bat and a broomstick.

The boys were the most popular students in the local high school. They had everything going for them. And the young woman was not a stranger to them. Some of them had known her since she was five years old, when they convinced her to lick the point of a ballpoint pen that had been coated in dog feces.

What possessed these boys to gang rape a helpless young woman? And how can we explain the subsequent actions of many of the leading citizens of Glen Ridge? It was weeks before anyone reported the rape to the police and years before the boys went to trial. At the trial, many members of the community rallied behind the boys, blaming and ostracizing the rape victim. The courts eventually handed out only light sentences. Why did members of the community refuse to believe the clear-cut evidence? What made them defend the rapists? Why were these boys let off so easily?

Bernard Lefkowitz (1997a) interviewed 250 key players and observers in the Glen Ridge rape case. Ultimately, he indicted the *community* for the rape. He concluded that "[the rapists] adhered to a code of behavior that mimicked, distorted, and exaggerated the values of the adult world around them," while "the citizens supported the boys because they didn't want to taint the town they treasured" (Lefkowitz, 1997a: 493). What were some of the community values the elders upheld and the boys aped?

- The subordination of women. *All of the boys had grown up in families where men were the dominant personalities. Only one of them had a sister. Not a single woman occupied a position of authority in Glen Ridge High School. The boys classified their female classmates either as "little mothers" who fawned over them or "bad girls" who were simply sexual objects.*
- Lack of compassion for the weak. *According to the minister of Glen Ridge Congregational Church, "Achievement was honored and respected almost to the point of pathology, whether it was the achievements of high school athletes or the achievements of corporate world conquerors." Adds Lefkowitz: "Compassion for the weak wasn't part of the curriculum" (Lefkowitz, 1997a: 130).*
- Tolerance of male misconduct. *The boys routinely engaged in delinquent acts. However, their parents always paid damages, covered up the misdeeds, and rationalized them with phrases like "boys will be boys." Especially because they were town football heroes, many people felt the boys could do no wrong.*
- Intense group loyalty. *"The guys prized their intimacy with each other far above what could be achieved with a girl," writes Lefkowitz (1997a: 146). The boys formed a tight clique, and team sports reinforced group solidarity. Under such circumstances, the probability of someone "ratting" on his friends was very low.*

In the end, of course, there was a "rat." His name was Charles Figueroa. He did not participate in the rape, but he was an athlete, part of the jock clique, and therefore aware of what had happened. Significantly, he was one of the few black boys in the school, tolerated because of his athletic ability but never trusted because of his race and often called a n—— by his teammates behind his back. This young man's family was highly intelligent and morally sensitive. He was the only one to have the courage to betray the group (Lefkowitz, 1997a, 1997b).

Lefkowitz raises the important question of where we ought to draw the line between group loyalty and group betrayal. You may have to choose between them on more than one occasion, so thinking about this line—and clearly understanding the values for which your group stands—will help you make a more informed choice.

**CRITICAL THINKING QUESTIONS**

- *Considering your own group loyalties, are there times when you regret not having spoken up?*
- *Are there times when you regret not having been more loyal?*
- *What is the difference between these two types of situations?*
- *Can you specify criteria for deciding when loyalty is required and when betrayal is the right thing?*

*A study of the small number of Polish Christians who helped save Jews during World War II helps clarify why some people violate group norms (Tec, 1986). The heroism of these Polish Christians was not correlated with their educational attainment, political orientation, religious background, or even attitudes toward Jews. In fact, some Polish Christians who helped save Jews were quite anti-Semitic. Instead, these Christian heroes were for one reason or another estranged or cut off from mainstream norms. Because they were poorly socialized into the norms of their society, they were freer not to conform and instead act in ways they believed were right. We could tell a roughly similar story about corporate whistleblowers or people who turn in their fellow gang members. They are disloyal from an insider's point of view but heroic from an outsider's point of view, often because they have been poorly socialized into the group's norms.*

2. Structures of authority tend to render people obedient. *Most people find it difficult to disobey authorities because they fear ridicule, ostracism, and punishment. This was strikingly demonstrated in an experiment conducted by social psychologist Stanley Milgram (1974). Milgram informed his experimental subjects that they were taking part in a study on punishment and learning. He brought each subject to a room*

*where a man was strapped to a chair. An electrode was attached to the man's wrist. The experimental subject sat in front of a console. It contained 30 switches with labels ranging from "15 volts" to "450 volts" in 15-volt increments. Labels ranging from "slight shock" to "danger: severe shock" were pasted below the switches. The experimental subjects were told to administer a 15-volt shock for the man's first wrong answer and then increase the voltage each time he made an error. The man strapped in the chair was, in fact, an actor. He did not actually receive a shock. As the experimental subject increased the current, however, the actor began to writhe, shouting for mercy and begging to be released. If the experimental subjects grew reluctant to administer more current, Milgram assured them the man strapped in the chair would be fine and insisted that the success of the experiment depended on the subject's obedience. The subjects were, however, free to abort the experiment at any time.*

*Remarkably, 71 percent of experimental subjects were prepared to administer shocks of 285 volts or more, even though the switches at that level were labelled "intense shock," "extreme intensity shock," and "danger: severe shock" and despite the fact that the actor appeared to be in great distress at this level of current (see Figure 4.5).*

*Milgram's experiment teaches us that as soon as we are introduced to a structure of authority, we are inclined to obey those in power. This is the case even if the authority structure is new and highly artificial, even if we are free to walk away from it with no penalty, and even if we think that by remaining in its grip we are inflicting terrible pain on another human being. In this context, the actions and inactions of German citizens in World War II become more understandable if no more forgivable.*

3. Bureaucracies are highly effective structures of authority. *The Nazi genocide machine was also so effective because it was bureaucratically organized. As Max Weber (1968 [1914]) defined the term, a* **bureaucracy** *is a large, impersonal organization comprising many clearly defined positions arranged in a hierarchy. A bureaucracy has a permanent, salaried staff of qualified experts and written goals, rules, and procedures. Staff members always try to find ways of running their organization more efficiently.* Efficiency *means achieving the bureaucracy's goals at the least cost. The goal of the Nazi genocide machine was to kill Jews and other undesirables. To achieve that goal with maximum efficiency, the job was broken into many small tasks. Most officials performed only one function, such as checking train schedules,*

**Figure 4.5**
**Obedience to Authority Increases with Separation from the Negative Effects of the Actions**

Milgram's experiment supports the view that separating people from the negative effects of their actions increases the likelihood of compliance.

■ Source: Bar graph based on information in Chapter 4, "Closeness of the Victim," in *Obedience to Authority*, by Stanley Milgram. Copyright © 1974 by Stanley Milgram.

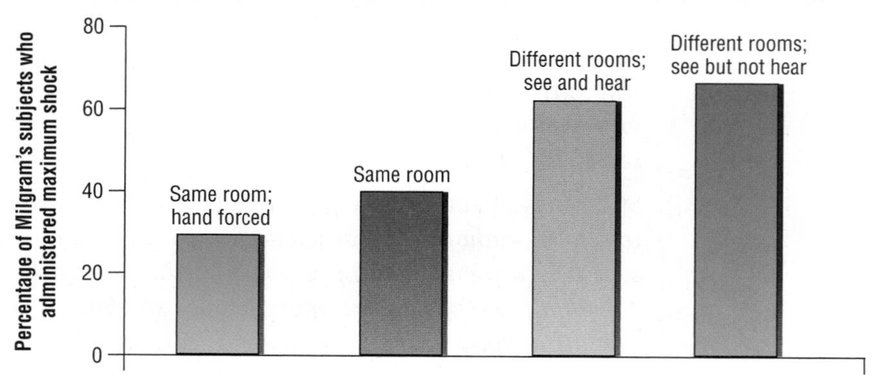

*organizing entertainment for camp guards, maintaining supplies of Zyklon B gas, and removing ashes from the crematoria. The full horror of what was happening eluded many officials or at least could be conveniently ignored as they concentrated on their jobs, most of them far removed from the gas chambers and death camps in occupied Poland. Many factors account for variations in Jewish victimization rates across Europe during World War II. One factor was bureaucratic organization. Not coincidentally, the proportion of Jews killed was highest not in the Nazi-controlled countries where the hatred of Jews was most intense (e.g., Romania), but in countries where the Nazi bureaucracy was best organized (e.g., Holland) (Bauman, 1989; Sofsky, 1997 [1993]).*

In short, the sociological reply to the question posed by Robert's father is that it was not just blind hatred but also the nature of groups and bureaucracies that made it possible for the Nazis to kill innocent people so ruthlessly.

People commonly think that *individual* motives prompt their actions. And for good reason: as you saw in the first half of this chapter, people often make rational calculations to maximize gains and minimize losses. In addition, deeply held emotions partly govern behaviour. However, this chapter asks you to make a conceptual leap beyond the individual motives that prompt people to act in certain ways; it asks you to consider the way three kinds of social *collectivities* shape people's actions: networks, groups, and organizations. The limitations of an analysis based exclusively on individual motives should be clear from the discussion of the social roots of evil. The advantages of considering how social collectivities affect us will become clear below. We begin by considering the nature and effects of social networks.

# Social Networks

Suppose someone asked you to deliver a letter to a complete stranger on the other side of the country by using only acquaintances to pass the letter along. You give the letter to an acquaintance, who can give the letter to one of his or her acquaintances, and so forth. Research shows that, on average, it would take no more than about six acquaintances to get the letter to the stranger. This fact suggests that in a fundamental sociological sense, we live in a small world: just a few social ties separate us from everyone else.

Our world is small because we are enmeshed in overlapping sets of social relations, or social networks. Although any particular individual may know a small number of people, his or her family members, friends, coworkers, and others know many more people who extend far beyond that individual's personal network. So, for example, the authors of this textbook are likely to be complete strangers to you. Yet your professor may know one of us or at least know someone who knows one of us. Probably no more than two links separate us from you. Put differently, although our personal networks are small, they lead quickly to much larger networks. We live in a small world because our social networks connect us to the larger world.

Sociologists define a **social network** as a bounded set of units (individuals, organizations, countries, etc.) linked by the exchange of material or emotional resources, everything from money to friendship. The patterns of exchange determine the boundaries of the network. Network members exchange resources more frequently with each other than with non-members. Individuals in a network think of themselves as network members. Social networks may be formal (i.e., defined in writing) or informal (i.e., defined only in practice). The people you know personally form the boundaries of your personal network. However, each of your network members is linked to other people. This is what connects you to people you have never met, creating a "small world" that extends far beyond your personal network.

## The Value of Network Analysis

The study of social networks is not restricted to ties among individuals (Wasserman and Faust, 1994; Wellman and Berkowitz, 1997). The units of analysis (or *nodes*) in a network can be individuals, groups, organizations, and even countries. Thus, social network analysts have examined everything from intimate relationships between lovers to diplomatic relations among nations.

Unlike organizations, most networks lack names and offices. There is a Boy Scouts of Canada but no North American Trading Bloc. In a sense, networks lie beneath the more visible collectivities of social life, but that makes them no less real or important. Some analysts claim that we can gain only a partial sense of why certain things happen in the social world by focusing on highly visible collectivities. From their point of view, the whole story requires probing below the surface and examining the network level. The study of social networks clarifies a wide range of social phenomena, including how people find jobs and form communities.

### Finding a Job

Many people learn about important events, ideas, and opportunities from their social networks. Friends and acquaintances often introduce you to everything from an interesting college course or a great restaurant to a satisfying occupation or a future spouse. Social networks aren't the only source of information, but they are highly significant.

Consider how people find jobs. Do you look in the Help Wanted section of your local newspaper, scan the Internet, or walk around certain areas of town looking for "Employee Wanted" signs? Although these strategies are common, people often learn about employment opportunities from other people.

What kind of people? According to sociologist Mark Granovetter (1973), you may have strong or weak ties to another person. You have strong ties to people who are close to you, such as family members and friends. You have weak ties to mere acquaintances, such as people you meet at parties and friends of friends. In his research, Granovetter found that weak ties are more important than strong ties in finding a job, which is contrary to common sense. You might reasonably assume that a mere acquaintance wouldn't do much to help you find a job, whereas a close friend or relative would make a lot more effort in this regard. However, by focusing on the flow of information in personal networks, Granovetter found something different. Mere acquaintances are more likely to provide useful information about employment opportunities than friends or family members because people who are close to you typically share overlapping networks. Therefore, the information they can provide about job opportunities is often redundant.

Parents can help their graduating children find jobs by getting them "plugged into" the right social networks. Here, in the 1968 movie *The Graduate,* a friend of the family advises Dustin Hoffman that the future lies in the plastics industry.

In contrast, mere acquaintances are likely to be connected to *diverse* networks. They can therefore provide information about many different job openings and make introductions to many different potential employers. Moreover, because people typically have more weak ties than strong ties, the sum of weak ties holds more information about job opportunities than the sum of strong ties. These features of personal networks allowed Granovetter to conclude that the "strength of weak ties" lies in their diversity and abundance.

### *Urban Networks*

We rely on social networks for a lot more than job information. Consider everyday life in the big city. We often think of big cities as cold and alienating places where few people know one another. In this view, urban acquaintanceships tend to be few and functionally specific; we know someone fleetingly as a bank teller or a server in a restaurant but not as a whole person. Even dating can involve a series of brief encounters. In contrast, people often think of small towns as friendly, comfortable places where everyone knows everyone else (and everyone else's business). Indeed, some of the founders of sociology emphasized just this distinction. Notably, German sociologist Ferdinand Tönnies (1988 [1887]) contrasted *community* with *society.* According to Tönnies, a community is marked by intimate and emotionally intense social ties, whereas a society is marked by impersonal relationships held together largely by self-interest. A big city is a prime example of a society in Tönnies's judgment.

Tönnies's view prevailed until network analysts started studying big-city life in the 1970s. Where Tönnies saw only sparse, functionally specific ties, network analysts found elaborate social networks, some functionally specific and some not. For example, Barry Wellman and his colleagues studied personal networks in Toronto (Wellman, Carrington, and Hall, 1997). They found that each Torontonian had an average of about 400 social ties, including immediate and extended kin, neighbours, friends, and coworkers. These ties provided everything from emotional aid (e.g., visits after a personal tragedy) and financial support (e.g., small loans) to minor services (e.g., fixing a car) and information of the kind Granovetter studied.

Strong ties that last a long time are typically restricted to immediate family members, a few close relatives and friends, and a close coworker or two. Beyond that, however, people rely on a wide array of ties for different purposes at different times. Downtown residents sitting on their front stoops on a summer evening, sipping soda, and chatting with neighbours as the kids play stickball or road hockey may be less common than they were 50 years ago. However, the automobile, public transportation, the telephone, and the Internet help people stay in close touch with a wide range of contacts for a variety of purposes (Haythornwaite and Wellman, 2002). Far from living in an impersonal and alienating world, the lives of today's city dwellers are network rich.

## Groups

Intensity and intimacy characterize many two-person relationships (see Figure 4.6). However, outside forces can often destroy them. For instance, the star-crossed lovers in *Romeo and Juliet* are torn between their love for each other and their loyalty to the feuding Montague and Capulet families. In the end, Romeo and Juliet die, victims of the feud.

## Figure 4.6
### Dyad and Triad

The most elementary network form is the **dyad,** a social relationship between two nodes or social units (e.g., people, firms, organizations, countries). A **triad** is a social relationship among three nodes. The difference between a dyad and a triad may seem small; however, the social dynamics of these two elementary network forms are fundamentally different, as sociologist Georg Simmel (1950) showed early in the twentieth century.

**Characteristics of the dyad**

- Both partners are intensely absorbed in the relationship.
- The dyad needs both partners to live but only one to die.
- No free riders are possible.
- Neither partner can deny responsibility by shifting it to a larger collectivity.

A

C B

**Characteristics of the triad**

- Intensity and intimacy are reduced.
- The triad restricts individuality by allowing a partner to be constrained for the collective good. A partner can be outvoted by a majority, for example.
- Coalitions are possible.
- Third-party mediation of conflict between two partners is possible.
- Third-party exploitation of rivalry between two partners is possible.
- A third-party divide-and-conquer strategy is possible.
- Free riders are possible.
- It is possible to shift responsibility to the larger collectivity.

Love thwarted by conflicting group loyalty is the stuff of many tragic plays, novels, and movies. Most audiences have no problem grasping the fact that group loyalty is often more powerful than romantic love. However, why group loyalty holds such power over us is unclear. The sociological study of groups provides some useful answers.

**Social groups** are composed of one or more networks of people who identify with one another, routinely interact, and adhere to defined norms, roles, and statuses. We usually distinguish social groups from **social categories,** people who share similar status but do not routinely interact or identify with one another. Coffee drinkers form a social category. They do not normally share norms, routinely interact, and identify with one another. In contrast, members of a family, sports team, or college are aware of shared membership. They think of themselves as members of a collectivity and routinely interact. They form groups.

The family is the most important primary group.

### *Primary and Secondary Groups*

Many kinds of social groups exist. However, sociologists make a basic distinction between primary and secondary groups. In **primary groups,** norms, roles, and statuses are agreed on but are not put in writing. Social interaction creates strong emotional ties, extends over a long period, and involves a wide range of activities. It results in group members knowing one another well. The family is the most important primary group.

**Secondary groups** are larger and more impersonal than primary groups. Compared with primary groups, social interaction in secondary groups creates weaker emotional ties. It extends over a shorter period and involves a narrow range of activities. It results in most group members having at most a passing acquaintance with one another. Your sociology class is an example of a secondary group. Bearing these distinctions in mind, we can begin to explore the power of groups to ensure conformity.

## *Group Conformity*

Television's first reality TV show was *Candid Camera.* In an early episode, an unsuspecting man waits for an elevator. When the elevator door opens, he finds four people, all confederates of the show, facing the elevator's back wall. Seeing the four people with their backs to him, the man at first hesitates. He then tentatively enters the elevator. However, rather than turning around so he faces the door, he remains facing the back wall, just like the others. The scene is repeated several times. Men and women, black and white, all behave the same. Confronting unanimously bizarre behaviour, they all chose conformity over common sense.

Conformity is an integral part of group life, and primary groups generate more pressure to conform than secondary groups. Strong social ties create emotional intimacy. They also ensure that primary group members share similar attitudes, beliefs, and information. Beyond the family, friendship groups (or cliques) and gangs demonstrate these features. Group members tend to dress and act alike, speak the same lingo, share the same likes and dislikes, and demand loyalty, especially in the face of external threat. Conformity ensures group cohesion.

### The Asch Experiment

A famous experiment conducted by social psychologist Solomon Asch half a century ago demonstrates how group pressure creates conformity (Asch, 1955). Asch gathered seven men, one of whom was the experimental subject. The other six were Asch's confederates. Asch showed the seven men a card with a line drawn on it. He then showed them a second card with three lines of varying length drawn on it (see Figure 4.7). One by one, he asked the confederates to judge which line on card 2 was the same length as the line on card 1. The answer was obvious. One line on card 2 was much shorter than the line on card 1. One line was much longer. One was exactly the same length. Yet, as instructed by Asch, all six confederates said that either the shorter or the longer line was the same length as the line on card 1. When it came time for the experimental subject to make his judgment, he typically overruled his own perception and agreed with the majority. Only 25 percent of Asch's experimental subjects consistently gave the right answer. Asch thus demonstrated how easily group pressure can overturn individual conviction and result in conformity.

### Factors Affecting Conformity

Asch's work and subsequent research show that several factors affect the likelihood of conformity (Sternberg, 1998: 499–500). First, the likelihood of conformity increases as *group size* increases to three or four members. For groups larger than four, the likelihood

**Figure 4.7**
**The Asch Experiment**

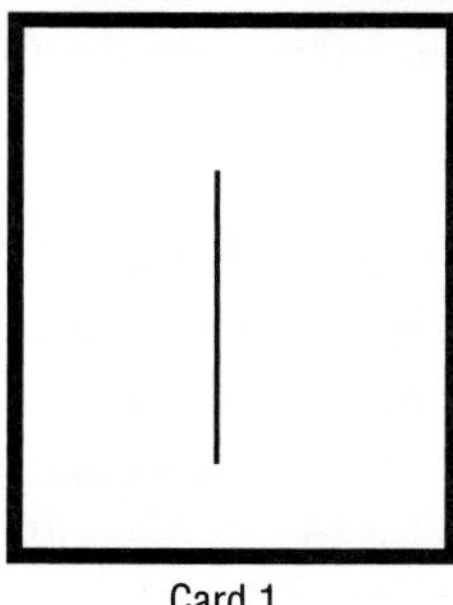

Card 1

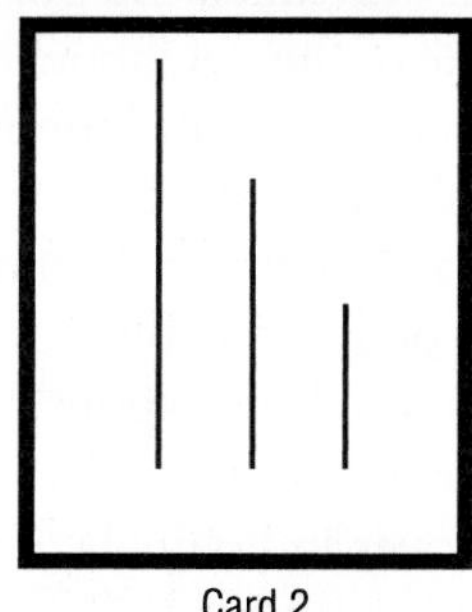

Card 2

of conformity generally does not increase. Second, as *group cohesiveness* increases, so does the likelihood of conformity. Where greater intimacy and sharing of values occur, group members are less likely to express dissent. Third, *social status* affects the likelihood of conformity. People with low status in a group (e.g., because of their gender or race) are less likely to dissent than people with high status. Fourth, *culture matters.* People in individualistic societies, like Canada, tend to conform less than people in collectivist societies, like China. Fifth, the *appearance of unanimity* affects the likelihood of conformity. Even one dissenting voice greatly increases the chance that others will dissent.

### Groupthink

The power of groups to ensure conformity is often a valuable asset. Sports teams could not excel without the willingness of players to undergo personal sacrifice for the good of the group, and armies could not function. In fact, as sociologists have demonstrated and as high-ranking military officers have observed, group cohesion—not patriotism or bravery—is the main factor motivating soldiers to engage in combat (Stouffer et al., 1949; Marshall, 1947: 160–61). As one soldier says in the 2001 movie *Black Hawk Down*: "When I go home people will ask me: 'Hey, Hoot, why do you do it, man? Why? Are you some kinda war junkie?' I won't say a goddamn word. Why? They won't understand. They won't understand why we do it. They won't understand it's about the men next to you. And that's it. That's all it is."

However, being a "good team player" can have a downside, because the consensus of a group can sometimes be misguided or dangerous. Dissent might save the group from making mistakes, but the pressure to conform despite individual misgivings—sometimes called **groupthink** (Janis, 1972)—can lead to disaster. Groupthink was at work in high-level meetings preceding the space shuttle *Columbia* disaster in 2003. Transcripts of those meetings at the National Aeronautics and Space Administration (NASA) show that the official who ran shuttle management meetings, a non-engineer, believed from the outset that foam insulation debris could not damage the spacecraft. She dismissed the issue and cut off discussion when an engineer expressed his concerns. The others present quickly fell into line with the non-engineer running the meeting (Wald and Schwartz, 2003). A few days later, damage caused by foam insulation debris caused *Columbia* to break apart on re-entry into the earth's atmosphere. Seven astronauts died.

A famous example of how the lack of a single dissenting voice can result in tragedy comes from a homicide case that grabbed the world's attention. In 1964 in Queens, New York, 28-year-old Kitty Genovese parked her car after returning home from work. When she got out, a man grabbed and stabbed her. She screamed for help. For 35 minutes, at least 38 middle-class, law-abiding neighbours watched from darkened windows as the man repeatedly attacked Genovese and stabbed her 17 times. Finally, one neighbour called the police, but only after he had called a friend and asked what to do. Some of the neighbours later pleaded ignorance. Others said they thought it was just a lovers' quarrel or "some kids having fun." Still others admitted they didn't want to get involved (Gado, 2003).

This case illustrates "bystander apathy." As the number of bystanders increases, the likelihood of any one bystander helping decreases, because the greater the number of bystanders, the less responsibility any one individual feels. This behaviour shows that people usually take their cues for action from others and again demonstrates the power of groups over individuals. If no one else in a large collectivity responds, most people figure nothing is wrong. This is in part what made the Holocaust possible.

Natural or artificial boundaries—rivers, mountains, highways, railway tracks—typically separate groups or communities.

## *Inclusion and Exclusion: In-Groups and Out-Groups*

If a group exists, it follows that some people must not belong to it. Accordingly, sociologists distinguish in-group members (i.e., those who belong) from out-group members (i.e., those who do not). Members of an **in-group** typically draw a boundary separating themselves from members of the **out-group,** and they try to keep out-group members from crossing the line. Anyone who has gone to high school knows all about in-groups and out-groups. They have seen firsthand how race, class, athletic ability, academic talent, and physical attractiveness act as boundaries separating groups.

### Group Boundaries: Competition and Self-Esteem

Why do group boundaries crystallize? One theory is that group boundaries emerge when people compete for scarce resources. For example, old immigrants may greet new immigrants with hostility if the latter are seen as competitors for scarce jobs (Levine and Campbell, 1972). Another theory is that group boundaries emerge when people are motivated to protect their self-esteem. From this point of view, drawing group boundaries allows people to increase their self-esteem by believing that out-groups have low status (Tajfel, 1981).

Both theories are supported by a classic experiment on prejudice, the Robber's Cave Study (Sherif, Harvey, White, Hood, and Sherif, 1988). Researchers brought two groups of 11-year-old boys to a summer camp at Robber's Cave State Park in Oklahoma in 1954. The boys were strangers to one another, and for about a week the two groups were kept apart. They swam, camped, and hiked. Each group chose a name for itself, and the boys printed their group's name on their caps and T-shirts. Then the two groups met. A series of athletic competitions were set up between them. Soon, each group became highly antagonistic toward the other. Each group came to hold the other in low esteem. The boys ransacked cabins, started food fights, and stole various items from members of the other group. Thus, under competitive conditions, the boys quickly drew sharp group boundaries.

The investigators next stopped the athletic competitions and created several apparent emergencies whose solution required cooperation between the two groups. One such emergency involved a leak in the pipe supplying water to the camp. The researchers assigned the boys to teams comprising members of *both* groups. Their job was to inspect the pipe and fix the leak. After engaging in several such cooperative ventures, the boys started playing together without fighting. Once cooperation replaced competition and the groups ceased to hold each other in low esteem, group boundaries melted away as quickly as they had formed. Significantly, the two groups were of equal status—the boys were all white, middle-class, and 11 years old—and their contact involved face-to-face interaction in a setting where norms established by the investigators promoted a reduction of group prejudice. Social scientists today recognize that all these conditions must be in place before the boundaries between an in-group and an out-group fade away (Sternberg, 1998: 512).

### Dominant Groups

The boundaries separating groups often seem unchangeable and even natural. In general, however, dominant groups construct group boundaries in particular circumstances to further their goals (Barth, 1969; Tajfel, 1981). Consider Germans and Jews. By the early twentieth century, Jews were well integrated into German society. They were economically successful, culturally innovative, and politically influential, and many of them considered themselves more German than Jewish. In 1933, the year Hitler seized power, 44 percent of marriages involving at least one German Jew were to a non-Jew. In addition, some German Jews converted before marrying non-Jewish Germans (Gordon, 1984). Yet, although the boundary separating Germans from Jews was quite weak, the Nazis chose to redraw and reinforce it. Defining a Jew as anyone who had at least one Jewish grandparent, they passed a whole series of anti-Jewish laws and, in the end, systematically slaughtered the Jews of Europe. The division between Germans and Jews was not "natural." It came into existence because of its perceived usefulness to a dominant group.

## *Groups and Social Imagination*

So far, we have focused almost exclusively on face-to-face interaction in groups. However, people also interact with other group members in their imagination. Take reference groups, for example. A **reference group** is composed of people against whom an individual evaluates his or her situation or conduct. Put differently, members of a reference group function as "role models." Reference groups may influence us even though they represent a largely imaginary ideal. For instance, the advertising industry promotes certain body ideals that many people try to emulate, although we know that hardly anyone looks like a runway model or a Barbie doll.

We have to exercise our imaginations vigorously to participate in the group life of a large, complex society like ours because much social life involves belonging to secondary groups without knowing or interacting with most group members. For an individual to interact with any more than a small fraction of the 33 million people living in this country is impossible. Nonetheless, most Canadians feel a strong emotional bond to their fellow citizens. Similarly, think about the employees and students at your college or university. They know they belong to the same secondary group, and many of them are probably loyal to it. Yet, how many people at your school have you met? Probably no more than a small fraction of the total. One way to make sense of the paradox of intimacy despite distance is to think of your school or Canada as an "imagined community." It is imagined because you cannot possibly meet most members of the group and can only speculate about what they must be like. It is nonetheless a community because people believe strongly in its existence and importance (Anderson, 1991).

Many secondary groups are **formal organizations,** or secondary groups designed to achieve explicit objectives. In complex societies like ours, the most common and influential formal organizations are bureaucracies. We now turn to an examination of these often frustrating but necessary organizational forms.

# Bureaucracy

Earlier in this chapter, we noted that Weber regarded bureaucracies as the most efficient type of secondary group. This runs against the grain of common knowledge. In everyday speech, when someone says "bureaucracy," people commonly think of bored clerks sitting in small cubicles spinning out endless trails of "red tape" that create needless waste and frustrate the goals of clients. The idea that bureaucracies are efficient may seem very odd.

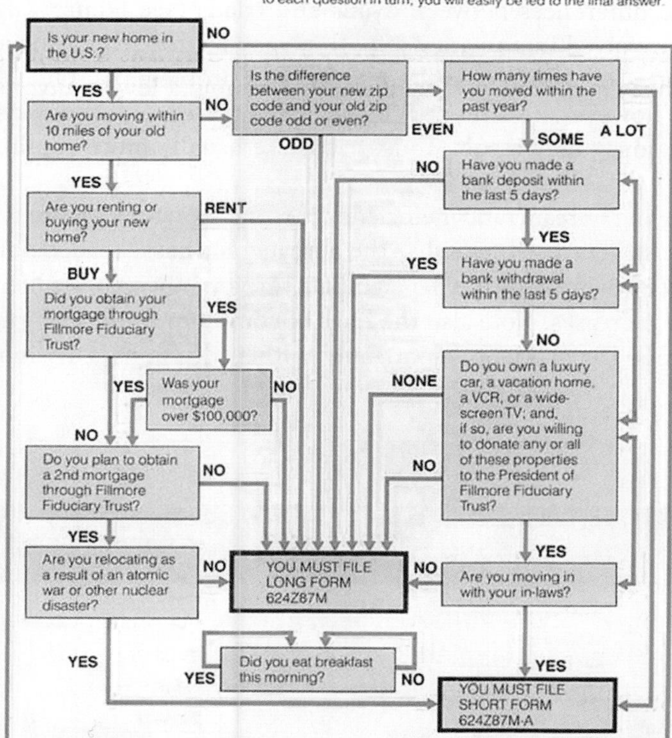


The 1980s Infocom game Bureaucracy satirized the conventional view of bureaucratic red tape.

Source: Infocom (2003). "Bureaucracy." On the World Wide Web at http://infocom.elsewhere.org/gallery/bureaucracy.bureaucracy.html (14 March 2003).

How can we square the reality of bureaucratic inefficiencies—even tragedies—with Weber's view that bureaucracies are the most efficient type of secondary group? The answer is twofold. First, we must recognize that when Weber wrote about the efficiency of bureaucracy, he was comparing it with older organizational forms. These had operated on the basis of either traditional practice ("We do it this way because we've always done it this way") or the charisma of their leaders ("We do it this way because our chief inspires us to do it this way"). Compared with such "traditional" and "charismatic" organizations, bureaucracies are generally more efficient. Second, we must recognize that Weber thought bureaucracies could operate efficiently only in the ideal case. He wrote extensively about some of bureaucracy's less admirable aspects in the real world. In other words, he understood that reality is often messier than the ideal case. In reality, bureaucracies vary in efficiency. Therefore, rather than proclaiming bureaucracy efficient or inefficient, we need to find out what makes bureaucracies work well or poorly.

**Figure 4.8**
**Number of Possible Dyadic Relationships by Number of People in Group**

Note: The number of dyadic relationships = $n^2 - n/2$, where $n$ is the number of people.

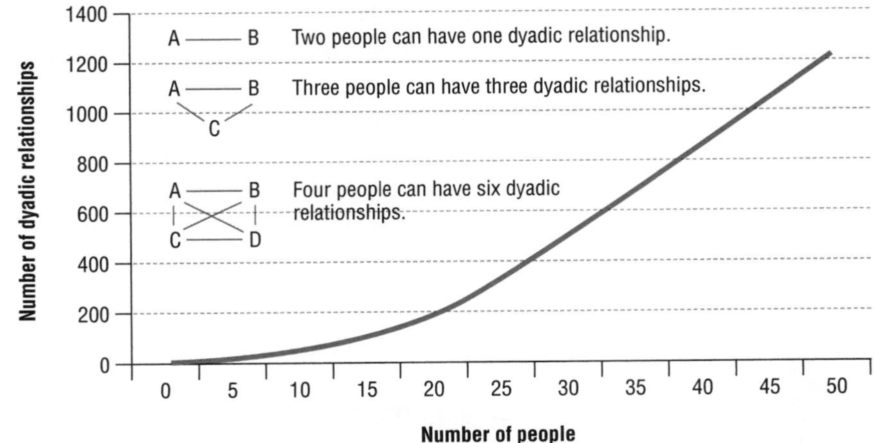


Two main factors underlie bureaucratic inefficiency: size and social structure. Consider size first. Something can be said for the view that bigger is almost inevitably more problematic. Some of the problems caused by size are evident even when you remember some of the differences between dyads and triads (see Figure 4.8). When only two people are involved in a relationship, they may form a strong social bond. If they do, communication is direct and sometimes unproblematic. Once a third person is introduced, however, a secret may be kept, a coalition of two against one may crystallize, and jealousy may result. Thus, triads are usually more conflict ridden than dyads.

The second factor underlying bureaucratic inefficiency is social structure. Figure 4.9 shows a typical bureaucratic structure: a hierarchy. The bureaucracy has a head, below which are three divisions, below which are six departments. As you move up the hierarchy, the power of the staff increases. Note also the lines of communication that join the various bureaucratic units. Departments report only to their divisions. Divisions report only to the head.

**Figure 4.9**
**Bureaucratic Structure**

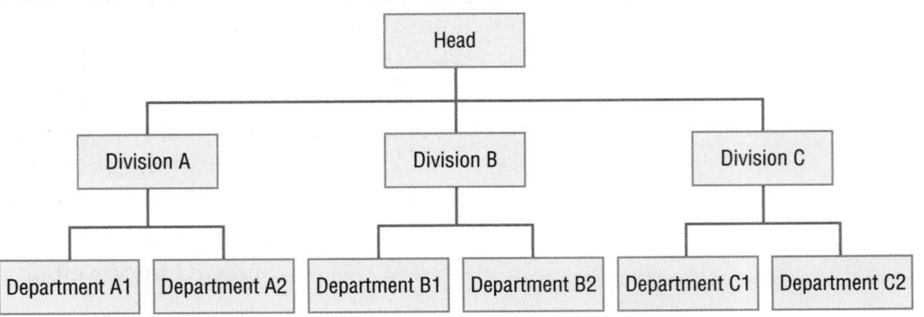

Figure 4.10
Network Structure

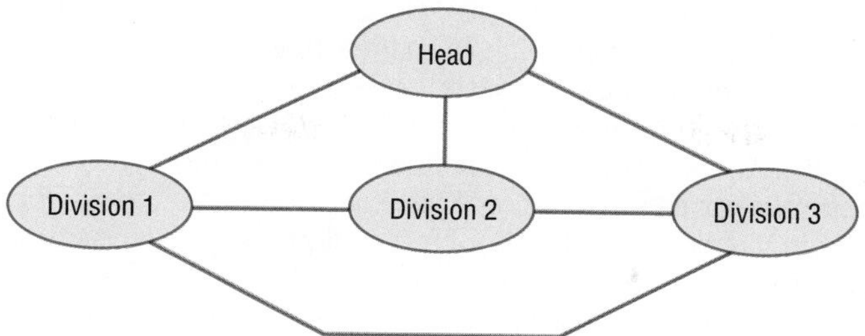


Usually, the more levels in a bureaucratic structure, the more difficult communication becomes, because people have to communicate indirectly, through department and division heads, rather than directly with each other. Information may be lost, blocked, reinterpreted, or distorted as it moves up the hierarchy, or an excess of information may cause top levels to become engulfed in a paperwork blizzard that prevents them from clearly seeing the needs of the organization and its clients. Bureaucratic heads may have only a vague and imprecise idea of what is happening "on the ground" (Wilensky, 1967).

Consider also what happens when the lines of communication directly joining departments or divisions are weak or nonexistent. As the lines joining units in Figure 4.9 suggest, department A1 may have information that could help department B1 do its job better, but A1 may have to communicate that information indirectly through the division level. At the division level, the information may be lost, blocked, reinterpreted, or distorted. Thus, just as people who have authority may lack information, people who have information may lack the authority to act on it directly (Crozier, 1964).

In the business world, large bureaucratic organizations are sometimes unable to compete against smaller, innovative firms, particularly in industries that are changing quickly (Burns and Stalker, 1961). This situation occurs partly because innovative firms tend to have flatter and more democratic organizational structures, such as the network illustrated in Figure 4.10. Compare the flat network structure in Figure 4.10 with the traditional bureaucratic structure in Figure 4.9. Note that the network structure has fewer levels than the traditional bureaucratic structure. Moreover, in the network structure, lines of communication link all units. In the traditional bureaucratic structure, information flows only upward.

Much evidence suggests that flatter bureaucracies with decentralized decision making and multiple lines of communication produce more satisfied workers, happier clients, and bigger profits (Kanter, 1989). Some of this evidence comes from Sweden and Japan. Beginning in the early 1970s, such corporations as Volvo and Toyota were at the forefront of bureaucratic innovation in those countries. They began eliminating middle-management positions. They allowed worker participation in a variety of tasks related to their main functions. They delegated authority to autonomous teams of a dozen or so workers that were allowed to make many decisions themselves. They formed "quality circles" of workers to monitor and correct defects in products and services. As a result, product quality, worker morale, and profitability improved. Today, these ideas have spread well beyond the Swedish and Japanese automobile industries and are evident in many large North American companies, both in the manufacturing and in the service sectors.

## The Points of the Compass

Throughout this chapter, we have emphasized the capacity of networks, groups, and bureaucracies to constrain human behaviour. As we have seen, such social collectivities can even encourage dangerously high levels of conformity, compel people to act against their better judgment, and dominate people in a vice of organizational rigidity.

We stressed the constraining aspect of social collectivities because we wanted to counter the common-sense view that motives alone determine the way people act. In conclusion, however, we should remember that people are often free to exercise two options other than bowing to the will of their social collectivities: "exit" and "voice" (Hirschman, 1970). In some circumstances, they can leave the social collectivities to which they belong (exit). In other circumstances, they can struggle against the constraints their social collectivities seek to impose on them (voice). After all, it is always possible to say no, even to the worst tyrant. Less dramatically but no less importantly, knowledge, including sociological knowledge, can increase the ability of people to resist the constraints imposed on them. Recall the Milgram experiment we discussed earlier in this chapter, in which subjects administered what they thought were painful shocks to people just because the experimenters told them to. When the experiment was replicated years later, many of the subjects refused to go along with the demands of the experimenters. Some invoked the example of the Nazis to justify their refusal to comply. Others mentioned Milgram's original experiment. Their knowledge, some of it perhaps gained in sociology courses, enabled them to resist unreasonable demands (Gamson, Fireman, and Rytina, 1982).

Paradoxically, to succeed in challenging social collectivities, people must sometimes form a new social collectivity themselves. Half a century ago, sociologists Seymour Martin Lipset, Martin A. Trow, and James S. Coleman (1956) conducted a classic sociological study that made just this point. They investigated the remarkable case of the International Typographical Union (ITU)—remarkable because in the 1950s it was the outstanding exception to the tendency of trade union bureaucracies to turn into hierarchical organizations run by the few. The ITU remained democratic because the nature of printing as an occupation and an industry made the resources for democratic politics more widely available than is typical in trade unions. Strong local unions that valued their autonomy had founded the international union. The local and regional markets typical of the printing industry at the time strengthened their autonomy. At the same time, strong competing factions in the union prevented any one faction from becoming dominant. Finally, strong social networks on the shop floor enabled ordinary printers to fight for their rights and resist the slide into rule by the few and dull obedience. This case illustrates how people can exercise their freedom to form social collectivities that counteract other social collectivities. Embedded in social relations, we can use them for good or evil.

## Summary

1. *What is social interaction?*

Social interaction involves verbal and nonverbal communication between people acting and reacting to one another. It is ordered by norms, roles, and statuses.

2. *Don't emotions govern all social interaction? Aren't emotions natural, spontaneous, and largely uncontrollable?*

Emotions do form an important part of all social interactions, but they are less spontaneous and uncontrollable than people commonly believe.

3. *In what sense is social interaction based on competition?*

When people interact socially they exchange valued resources—everything from attention and pleasure to prestige and money. However, because people typically try to maximize

their rewards and minimize their losses, social interaction may be seen as a competition for scarce resources.

### 4. *Is competition the only basis of social interaction?*

No. People may interact cooperatively and altruistically because they have been socialized to do so. They may also maintain interaction based on domination.

### 5. *How do symbolic interactionists analyze social interaction?*

Symbolic interactionists focus on how people create meaning in the course of social interaction and on how they negotiate and modify roles, statuses, and norms. Symbolic interactionism has several variants. For example, dramaturgical analysis is based on the idea that people play roles in their daily lives in much the same way as actors on stage. Ethnomethodology analyzes the methods people use to make sense of what others do and say. It insists on the importance of pre-existing shared norms and understandings in making everyday interaction possible.

### 6. *Is all social interaction based on language?*

No. Nonverbal communication, including socially defined facial expressions, gestures, body language, and status cues, is as important as verbal communication in conveying meaning.

### 7. *Do people act the way they do only because of their interests and emotions?*

People's motives are important determinants of their actions, but social collectivities also influence the way we behave. Because of the power of social collectivities, people sometimes act against their interests, values, and emotions.

### 8. *What is network analysis?*

Social networks are bounded sets of units (individuals, organizations, countries, etc.) linked by the exchange of material or emotional resources, everything from money to friendship. Network analysis involves studying how the structure of networks affects a wide variety of social processes.

### 9. *What are groups?*

Groups are clusters of people who identify with one another. Groups impose conformity on members and seek to exclude non-members.

### 10. *Is bureaucracy just "red tape"? Is it possible to overcome bureaucratic inefficiency?*

Although bureaucracies often suffer from various forms of inefficiency, they are generally efficient compared with other organizational forms. Bureaucratic inefficiency increases with size and degree of hierarchy. By flattening bureaucratic structures, decentralizing decision-making authority, and opening lines of communication between bureaucratic units, efficiency can often be improved.

### 11. *What does the sociological analysis of networks, groups, and bureaucracies tell us about the possibility of human freedom?*

Networks, groups, and bureaucracies influence and constrain everyone. However, people also use these social collectivities to increase their freedom from other social collectivities. In this sense, social collectivities are a source of both constraint and freedom.

# Key Terms

bureaucracy (p. 116)
competition (p. 111)
conflict theories of social interaction (p. 110)
crude death rate (p. 100)
domination (p. 111)
dramaturgical analysis (p. 104)
dyad (p. 120)
emotion labour (p. 100)
emotion management (p. 99)
ethnomethodology (p. 106)
exchange theory (p. 103)
formal organizations (p. 125)
groupthink (p. 122)
in-group (p. 123)
mesostructures (p. 111)
out-group (p. 123)
power (p. 110)
primary groups (p. 120)
rational choice theory (p. 103)
reference group (p. 124)
role distancing (p. 104)
role set (p. 98)
secondary groups (p. 120)
social category (p. 120)
social group (p. 120)
social interaction (p. 97)
social network (p. 117)
status cues (p. 108)
status set (p. 98)
stereotypes (p. 108)
triad (p. 120)

# Questions to Consider

1. Write a list of your current and former girlfriends or boyfriends. Indicate the race, religion, age, and height of each person on the list. How similar or different are you from the people with whom you have chosen to be intimate? What does this list tell you about the social distribution of intimacy? Is love blind? What criteria other than race, religion, age, and height might affect the social distribution of intimacy?
2. In what sense (if any) is it reasonable to claim that all of social life consists of role-playing and that people have no "true selves," just ensembles of roles?
3. Would you have acted any differently from ordinary Germans if you were living in Nazi Germany? Why or why not? What if you were a member of a Nazi police battalion? Would you have been a traitor to your group? Why or why not?

# Web Resources

## Companion Web Site for This Book

http://www.pointsofthecompass.nelson.com

Begin by clicking on the Student Resources section of the Web site. Next, select the chapter you are currently studying from the pull-down menu. From the Student Resources page you will have easy access to InfoTrac® College Edition, MicroCase online exercises, and additional Weblinks. The Web site also has many useful tips to aid you in your study of sociology, including practice tests for each chapter.

## InfoTrac® Search Terms

These search terms are provided to assist you in beginning to conduct research on this topic by visiting http://www.infotrac-college.com:

**bureaucracy**
**dramaturgical analysis**
**exchange theory**
**rational choice theory**
**social network**

## Recommended Web Sites

If you need convincing that social interaction on the Internet can have deep emotional and sociological implications, read Julian Dibbell's "A Rape in Cyberspace," on the World Wide Web at **http://www.juliandibbell.com/texts/bungle_vv.html**. This compelling article is especially valuable for showing how social structure emerges in virtual communities. Originally published in *The Village Voice* (1993, 21 December, 36–42).

For social interaction on the World Wide Web, visit The MUD Connector at **http://www.mudconnect.com**.

The Society for the Study of Symbolic Interaction is a professional organization of sociologists "interested in qualitative, especially interactionist, research." Visit their Web site at **http://www.espach.salford.ac.uk/sssi/index.php**.

Sociologists at Columbia University have organized "The Small World Project." They are trying to extend Stanley Milgram's ideas to the entire wired world. To participate in this study, visit **http://smallworld.columbia.edu**.

A key excerpt from Max Weber's classic essay on bureaucracy is available at **http://www2.pfeiffer.edu/~lridener/DSS/Weber/BUREAU.HTML**.

Yahoo! sponsors many sociology discussion groups. To join, visit **http://dir.groups.yahoo.com/dir/Science/Social_Sciences/Sociology**.

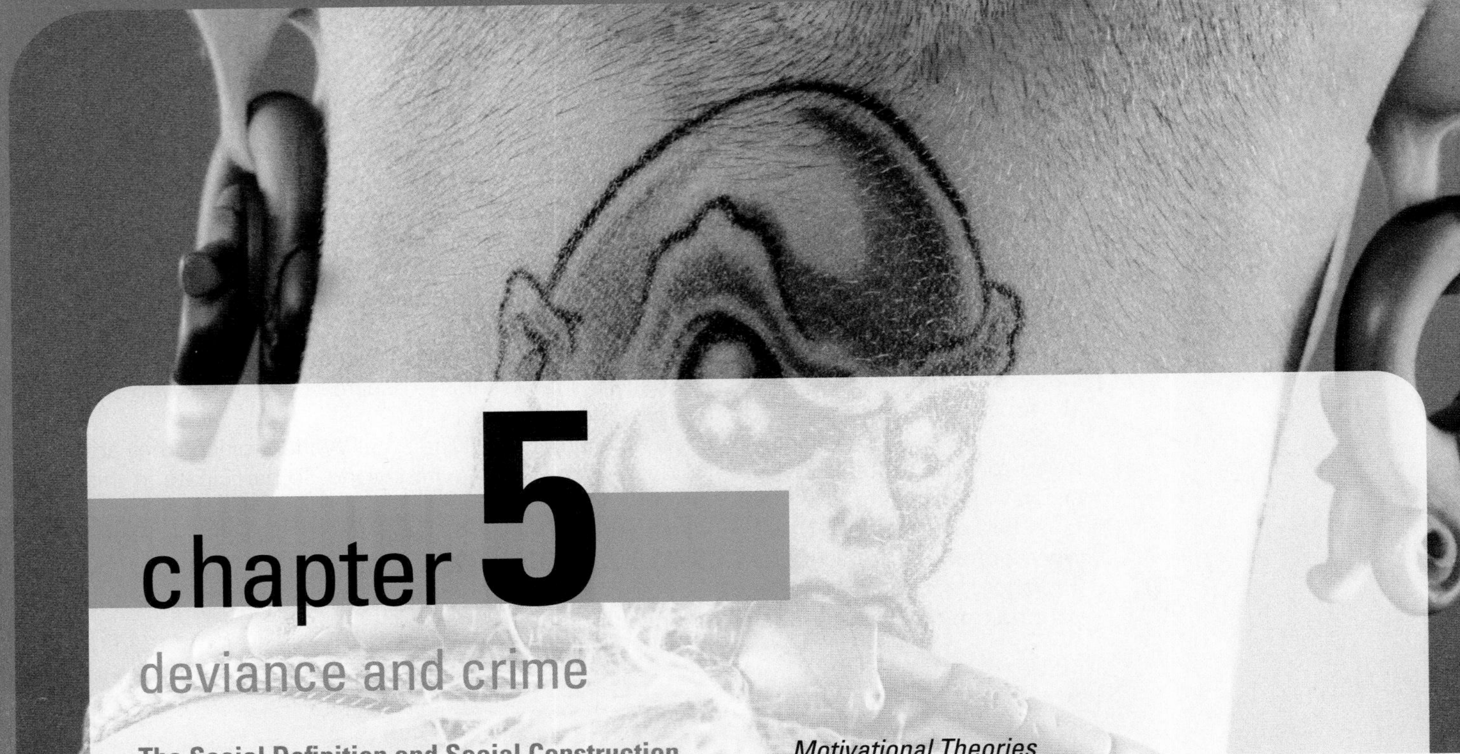

# chapter 5

## deviance and crime



### In this chapter, you will learn that

→ Deviance and crime vary among cultures, across history, and from one social context to another.

→ Rather than being inherent in the characteristics of individuals or actions, deviance and crime are socially defined and constructed. The distribution of power is especially important in the social construction of deviance and crime.

→ Many theories exist regarding deviance and crime. Each theory illuminates a different aspect of the process by which people break rules and are defined as deviants and criminals.

→ As with deviance and crime, conceptions of appropriate punishment vary culturally and historically.

→ Imprisonment is one of the main forms of punishment in industrial societies.

→ Fear of crime may be subject to manipulation by commercial and political groups that benefit from it.

→ There are cost-effective and workable alternatives to current methods of punishment.

# The Social Definition and Social Construction of Deviance

If you happen to come across members of the Tukano tribe in northern Brazil, don't be surprised if they greet you with a cheery "Have you bathed today?" You would probably find the question insulting, but think how you would feel if you were greeted by the Yanomamö people in Brazil's central highlands. A French anthropologist reports that when he first encountered the Yanomamö, they rubbed mucus and tobacco juice into their palms, then inspected him by running their filthy hands over his body (Chagnon, 1992). He must have been relieved to return to urban Brazil and be greeted with a simple kiss on the cheek.

Rules for greeting people vary widely from one country to the next and among different cultural groups within one country. That is why a marketing company recently created an animated Web site showing business travellers how to greet their hosts in the 15 countries where the firm does business ("The Business of Touch," 2006). After all, violating local norms can cause great offence and result in the loss of a contract, a fact that one visitor to South Korea found out too late. He beckoned his host with an index finger, after which the host grew quiet. He discovered after he lost the deal that Koreans beckon only cats and dogs with an index finger. If you want to beckon someone politely in South Korea, you should do so with all four fingers facing down, much like Canadians wave goodbye.

Because norms vary widely, deviance is relative. What some people consider normal, others consider deviant, and vice versa. No act is deviant in and of itself. People commit deviant acts only when they break a norm and cause others to react negatively. From a sociological point of view, *everyone* is a deviant in one social context or another.

## *The Difference between Deviance and Crime*

**Deviance** involves breaking a norm and evoking a negative reaction from others. Societies establish some norms as laws. **Crime** is deviance that breaks a **law,** which is a norm stipulated and enforced by government bodies.

Nelson Mandela spent decades imprisoned in South Africa for activities designed to end apartheid. Today Mandela is hailed as a hero. He was awarded the Nobel Peace Prize and served as the first democratically elected president of South Africa from 1994 to 1999.

Just as deviance is relative, so is crime. Consider that a list of famous people who have been labelled criminals would include Socrates, Jesus, Martin Luther, Louis Riel, Mahatma Ghandi, Martin Luther King, Jr., and Nelson Mandela. For many people today, these historical figures are heroes. In contrast, those who planned and participated in the extermination of Jews, Romani, and homosexuals in Nazi Germany were acting in a way that was defined, at the time in Germany, as law-abiding. You would probably consider the actions taken by the Nazis in Germany, rather than the actions of Jesus or Martin Luther, to be deviant or criminal. That is because norms and laws have changed dramatically. Today, anyone who advocates or promotes genocide commits a crime under Canadian law. We conclude that what is considered a crime in some times and places is considered perfectly normal in other times and places (see Box 5.1).

# SOCIOLOGY AT THE MOVIES

*Paradise Now* (2005)

Of all the social types who populate today's world, perhaps none is more difficult to understand than the suicide attacker. Many people in the West wonder who in their right mind would fly a plane into a building. What kind of person do you have to be to blow yourself up in a bus full of ordinary people or a mosque full of worshippers? Somehow, the terms *deviant* and *criminal* seem inadequate to describe such people; they are widely seen by people in the West as crazy fanatics who lack all conscience and humanity.

*Paradise Now,* nominated for an Oscar as best foreign-language film of 2005, demonstrates that the common Western view is ethnocentric. It sketches the social circumstances that shaped the lives of two suicide bombers, showing that they are a lot like us and that if we found ourselves in similar circumstances, we might turn out to be a lot like them. The film is critical of suicide bombing, but it helps us understand what makes suicide bombers tick, thereby enlightening us sociologically and politically.

Said (Kais Nashef) and Khaled (Ali Suliman) are ordinary twenty-something garage mechanics and best friends. They live in the Palestinian city of Nablus, which, like the rest of the West Bank and the Gaza Strip, has been under Israeli military occupation their whole lives. As a result of the occupation, Said and Khaled have never been able to travel outside of the West Bank, they enjoy limited economic opportunities, they are bored stiff, and, most importantly, they have been robbed of their dignity. Like all Palestinians, they want the Israelis out so they can establish an independent country of their own. But their demonstrations, their rock throwing, and their armed attacks have had no effect on the powerful Israeli military. Consequently, some time before the film begins, Said and Khaled volunteered to serve as weapons of last resort: suicide bombers.

A study of all 462 suicide bombers who attacked targets worldwide between 1980 and 2003 found not a single case of depression, psychosis, past suicide attempts, or other such mental health issues among them. The bombers were rarely poor, came most often from working- or middle-class families, and were better educated than the populations from which they were recruited. Many of them were religious, but most of them, like Said and Khaled, were not. What they had in common was an ardent desire to liberate territory from what they regarded as foreign occupation or control (Pape, 2005). Said and Khaled are, then, quite typical suicide bombers: they are convinced by their powerlessness and their experience that they have no weapon other than suicide bombing that might help them achieve their aim of national liberation.

As *Paradise Now* opens, the two friends are informed that they have been selected for a suicide attack in 48 hours. Their mundane preparations are peppered with humour, errors, and everyday trivia that make Said and Khaled seem like very ordinary people. For example, in the middle of recording his "martyrdom tape" for TV broadcast, Khaled incongruously remembers to tell his mother, whom he knows will watch the tape, that he saw a bargain on water filters at a local merchant's store. But underlying such humanizing events is a tension that gives the movie its force. Said and Khaled are ambivalent about their mission, not just because they have misgivings about dying but also because they feel guilty about its inhumanity to civilians and are unsure of its ultimate political utility.

In the end, only Said manages to go through with the attack, but not before we get the full story about his ambivalence. Suha (Lubna Azabal), the woman he loves, is the daughter of a famous martyr for the Palestinian cause, but she strongly opposes suicide bombing. Said listens

Ali Suliman and Kais Nashef in *Paradise Now*

intently when she argues that suicide bombing is contrary to the spirit of Islam, it kills innocent victims, and it accomplishes nothing because it invites retaliation in a never-ending cycle of violence. But more compelling are the forces pushing Said to carry out the attack. Thousands of Palestinians are paid, threatened, and blackmailed to serve as informants for the Israelis. Said's father was one of them. When he was caught, he was executed by Palestinian militants. Said has been deeply ashamed of his father's actions his whole life and angry with the Israelis for forcing his father to serve as a collaborator. His ultimate motivation for becoming a suicide bomber is retaliation against Israel for turning his father into an informant. Like most suicide bombers in the country, he is driven by the desire for revenge (Brym, 2007b; Brym and Araj, 2006).

**CRITICAL THINKING QUESTIONS**

- *From whose point of view are suicide bombers deviant and criminal?*
- *From whose point of view are suicide bombers normal?*
- *Must you agree with the actions of suicide bombers to understand them?*
- *What would you do if you were in Said's position?*

### *Sanctions*

Many otherwise deviant acts go unnoticed or are considered too trivial to warrant negative *sanctions,* which are actions indicating disapproval of deviance. People who are observed committing more serious acts of deviance are typically punished, either informally or formally. **Informal punishment** is mild. It may involve raised eyebrows, a harsh stare, an ironic smile, gossip, ostracism, "shaming," or stigmatization (Braithwaite, 1989). When people are **stigmatized,** they are negatively evaluated because of a marker that distinguishes them from others (Goffman, 1963b). For example, until recently people with physical or mental disabilities were often treated with scorn or as a source of amusement. Pope Leo X (1475–1521) is said to have retained several mentally retarded dwarves as a form of entertainment! **Formal punishment** results from people breaking laws. For example, criminals can be formally punished by having to serve time in prison or perform community service.

Types of deviance and crime vary in terms of the *severity of the social response,* which ranges from mild disapproval to capital punishment (Hagan, 1994). They vary also in terms of the *perceived harmfulness* of the deviant or criminal act. Note that actual harmfulness is not the only issue here—*perceived* harmfulness is involved too. Coca-Cola got its name because, in the early part of the last century, it contained a derivative of cocaine. Now cocaine is an illegal drug because people's perceptions of its harmfulness changed. Finally, deviance and crime vary in terms of the *degree of public agreement* about whether an act should be considered deviant. Even the social definition of murder varies over time and across cultures and societies. Thus, at the beginning of the twentieth century, Inuit communities sometimes allowed newborns to freeze to death. Life in the far north was precarious. Killing newborns was not considered a punishable offence if community members agreed that investing scarce resources in keeping the newborn alive could endanger everyone's well-being. Similarly, whether we classify the death of a miner as accidental or a case of manslaughter depends on the kind of worker safety legislation in existence. Some societies have more stringent worker safety rules than others, and deaths considered accidental in some societies are classified as criminal offences in others

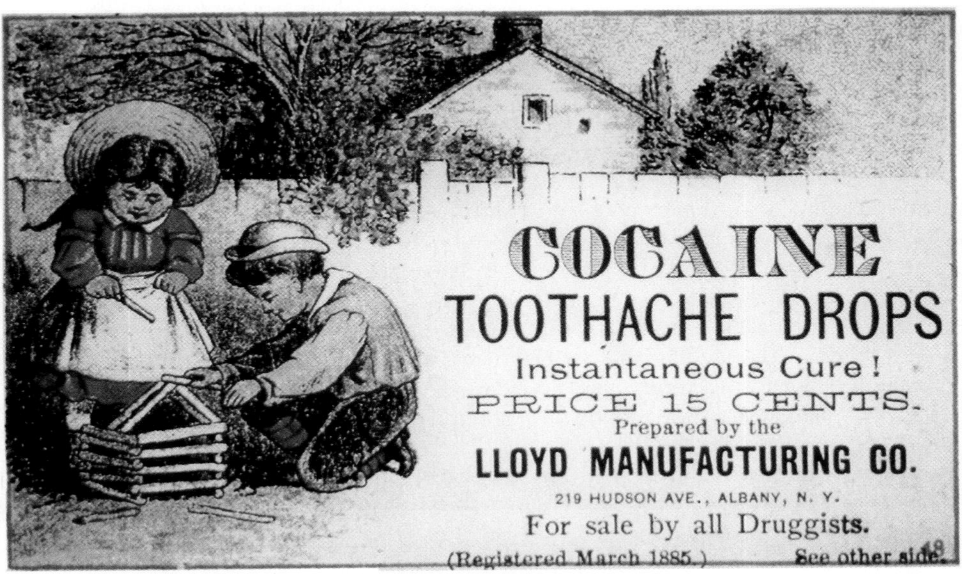


One of the determinants of the seriousness of a deviant act is its perceived harmfulness. Perceptions vary historically, however. For instance, until the early part of the twentieth century, cocaine was considered a medicine. It was an ingredient of cold formulas and toothache drops, and in these forms it was commonly given to children.

(McCormick, 1999). So we see that, even when it comes to serious crimes, social definitions are variable (see Box 5.2).

## *Power and the Social Construction of Crime and Deviance*

To truly understand deviance and crime, you have to study how people socially construct norms and laws. Social problems, including crime, are not inherent in certain actions themselves. Instead, some people are in a position to create norms and pass laws that stigmatize other people. Therefore, we must study how norms and laws are constructed to understand why particular actions are defined as deviant or criminal in the first place. Relatively powerful groups are generally able to create norms and laws that suit their interests. Relatively powerless groups are usually unable to do so. The powerless, however, often struggle against stigmatization. If their power increases, they may succeed in their struggle. We now illustrate the importance of power in the social construction of deviance and crime by analyzing crimes against women and white-collar crime.

### Crimes against Women

Until recently, many types of crimes against women were largely ignored in Canada and most other parts of the world. This was true even when the crime involved non-consensual sexual intercourse, an act that was defined under Canadian criminal law as "rape" before 1983 and is now considered a form of "sexual assault." Admittedly, rapes involving strangers were sometimes severely punished. But so-called date rapes or acquaintance rapes involving a friend or an acquaintance were rarely prosecuted. And until 1983, Canadian law viewed marital rape as a contradiction in terms, as if it were logically impossible for a married woman to be raped by her spouse. In her research, Susan Estrich (1987) found that law professors, judges, police officers, rapists, and even victims did not think date rape was "real rape." Similarly, judges, lawyers, and social scientists rarely discussed physical violence against women and sexual harassment until the 1970s. Governments did not collect data on the topic and few social scientists showed any interest in what has now become a large and important area of study.

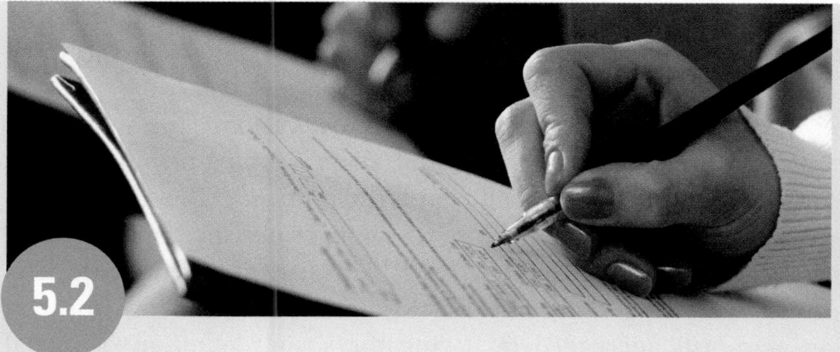

5.2

# SOCIAL POLICY: WHAT DO YOU THINK?

**Should We Define Hockey Violence as Criminal, Deviant, or Normal?**

On 8 March 2007, Chris Simon of the New York Islanders wielded his hockey stick like an axe, delivering a punishing blow to the head of New York Rangers forward Ryan Hollweg. Miraculously, Hollweg escaped without serious injury. Simon received a 25-game suspension. In the three weeks preceding the incident, Ottawa Senators forward Chris Neil had delivered a blindside head shot that caused a concussion but resulted in no penalty and no suspension, while New Jersey Devils enforcer Cam Janssen had delivered a high body blow, causing a serious head injury that resulted in no penalty and a three-game suspension.

The NHL is inconsistent in meting out penalties for hockey violence, perhaps because officials, players, and the public are divided over whether hockey violence should be considered deviant or normal. Few Canadians think it should be criminal. Seldom do on-ice incidents result in criminal charges being laid, and players who face charges are usually acquitted or given only mild sanctions. Cases like that of the Vancouver Canucks' Todd Bertuzzi are rare. In 2004, Bertuzzi was fined half a million dollars and suspended for the rest of the season for stalking, punching, and breaking the neck of Steve Moore of the Colorado Avalanche.

Bill McMurtry, a lawyer who wrote a report on amateur hockey, observed: "Hockey is the only sport in the history of sport anywhere in the world that not only tolerates fighting, but rewards it. . . . It breeds a culture of violence" (quoted in Grange, 2000). He has a point. Hockey glorifies violence. A Web site even exists where you can find videos of every fight in professional hockey (neatly indexed by year, team, and player), comment on the fight, and vote on who won it. Cumulative voting results are conveniently displayed in bar graphs (see http://www.hockeyfights.com/).

Chris Simon after he hit Ryan Hollweg in the face with a hockey stick, 8 March 2007

**CRITICAL THINKING QUESTIONS**

- *Is violence just part of the game? Should athletes involved in hockey and other contact sports be exempt from criminal laws prohibiting assault?*
- *If so, would you extend this exemption to cases that result in severe injury to—or the death of—another player?*
- *If not, do you think we should crack down on violence in sports? Should we charge more athletes? impose harsher penalties?*

Today, the situation has improved. To be sure, sexual assault is still associated with a low rate of prosecution (Scully, 1990). Rapists often hold women in contempt and do not regard sexual assault as a real crime. Yet a series of changes to criminal law in Canada emphasizes that non-consensual sexual acts are crimes. These new laws have helped raise people's awareness of date, acquaintance, and marital rape. Sexual assault is more often prosecuted now than it used to be. The same is true for other forms of violence against women, such as wife battery, sexual harassment, and criminal harassment ("stalking").

Why the change? In part because women's position in the economy, the family, and other social institutions has improved over the past 35 years. Women now have more autonomy in the family, earn more, and enjoy more political influence. They also created a movement for women's rights that heightened concern about crimes disproportionately affecting them. For instance, until recently, male sexual harassment of female workers was considered normal. Following Catharine MacKinnon's path-breaking work on the subject, however, feminists succeeded in having the social definition of sexual harassment transformed (MacKinnon, 1979). Sexual harassment is now considered a social deviation and, in some circumstances, a crime. Increased public awareness of the extent of sexual harassment has probably made it less common. We thus see how social definitions of crimes against women have changed with a shift in the distribution of power between women and men.

### White-Collar Crime

**White-collar crime** refers to illegal acts "committed by a person of respectability and high social status in the course of his [or her] occupation" (Sutherland, 1949: 9). Such crimes include embezzlement, false advertising, tax evasion, insider stock trading, fraud, unfair labour practices, copyright infringement, and conspiracy to fix prices and restrain trade. Sociologists often contrast white-collar crimes with **street crimes.** The latter include arson, breaking and entering, robbery, and assault. Although street crimes are committed disproportionately by people from lower classes, white-collar crime is committed disproportionately by people from middle and upper classes.

Many sociologists think white-collar crime is more costly to society than street crime. Tax evasion alone has been estimated to cost Canadians approximately $30 billion a year (Gabor, 1994). In the 1990s, Canada's Bre-X stock fraud, reputedly one of the world's largest, cost investors $6 billion. In this case, the Calgary-based company's geologist had sought to make worthless mines seem valuable by adding gold to core samples. After he was exposed, Bre-X stock collapsed (Hagan, 2000).

Although white-collar crime costs society more than street crime, white-collar criminals, including corporations, are infrequently prosecuted (Geis, 1994). They are convicted even less often. This is true even in extreme cases, when white-collar crimes result in environmental degradation or death because of, for example, the illegal relaxation of safety standards. Typically, the report of an official inquiry into the 1992 explosion at the Westray coal mine in Pictou County, Nova Scotia, which instantly killed 26 miners, noted that the managers at Westray had displayed a "disdain for safety and appeared to regard safety-conscious workers as the wimps in the organization" (Hagan, 2000: 463). There were no convictions.

White-collar crime results in few prosecutions and still fewer convictions for two main reasons. First, much white-collar crime takes place in private and is therefore difficult to detect. For example, corporations may illegally decide to fix prices and divide markets, but executives make these decisions in boardrooms and private clubs that are not generally subject to police surveillance. Second, corporations can afford legal experts, public relations firms, and advertising agencies that advise their clients on how to bend laws, build up their corporate image in the public mind, and influence lawmakers to pass laws without teeth. Moreover, even when prosecutions are successful, the punishment is usually light (Snider, 1999).

Governments, too, commit serious crimes. However, it is difficult to punish political leaders (Chambliss, 1989). Authoritarian governments may call their opponents terrorists and even torture people who are fighting for democracy, but such governments rarely have to account for their deeds (Herman and O'Sullivan, 1989). Even the United States government, with its democratic ideals, sometimes behaves criminally. In the late 1980s, for example, while the United States was engaged in a war on drugs, the CIA participated in the drug trade to help arm the right-wing Contra military forces in Nicaragua (Scott and Marshall, 1991). When called to account for such behaviour, a common claim made is that the end justifies the means. That is, good motives excuse bad behaviour.

In sum, white-collar crime is underdetected, underprosecuted, and underconvicted because it is the crime of the powerful and the well-to-do. The social construction of crimes against women has changed over the past 30 years, partly because women have become more powerful. In contrast, the social construction of white-collar crime has changed very little since 1970 because upper classes are no less powerful now than they were then.

## *Measuring Crime*

Some crimes are more common than others, and rates of crime vary over place and time and among different social groups. We now describe some of these variations. Then we review the main sociological explanations of crime and deviance.

First, a word about crime statistics. Information on crime collected by the police is our main source of crime statistics. Since 1962, Canada has used a system called the Canadian Uniform Crime Reports (UCR). Under this system, information is collected from more than 400 municipal police departments across Canada on 91 detailed categories of crime. Annually, the government publishes data on types of offences and characteristics of offenders.

These statistics have two main shortcomings. First, much crime is not reported to the police. This is particularly true of so-called **victimless crimes,** which involve violations of the law in which no victim steps forward and is identified. Communicating for the purposes of prostitution, illegal gambling, and the use of illegal drugs are all victimless crimes. In addition, many common or "level 1" assaults go unreported because the assailant is a friend or relative of the victim. Many victims of sexual assault are also reluctant to report the crime because they are afraid they will be humiliated or not believed and stigmatized by making it public. The second main shortcoming of official crime statistics is that authorities and the wider public decide which criminal acts to report and which to ignore. If, for instance, the authorities decide to crack down on drugs, more drug-related crimes will be counted, not because more drug-related crimes are committed, but because more drug criminals are apprehended. Changes in legislation, which either create new offences or amend existing offences, will also influence the number of recorded offences. Recognizing these difficulties, students of crime often supplement official crime statistics with other sources of information.

**Self-report surveys** are especially useful. In such surveys, respondents are asked to report their involvement in criminal activities, either as perpetrators or as victims. Self-report data compensate for many of the problems associated with official statistics. In general, self-report surveys report approximately the same rate of serious crime as official statistics but find two or three times the rate of less serious crimes.

Self-report surveys are useful because they tell us that a majority of Canadians have engaged in some type of criminal activity and that about a quarter of the population in any given year believe that they have been the victim of crime. These large proportions

**Figure 5.1**
**The Canadian Crime Funnel**

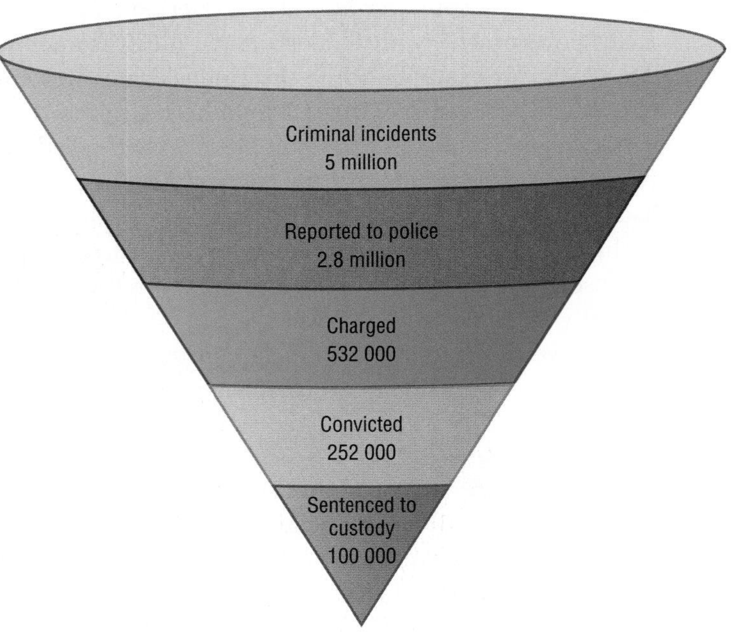


An offence is considered "actual" when a police investigation confirms that a criminal offence has occurred. An offence is "cleared" when police are satisfied that they have identified an offender. However, it may not be possible to lay a charge against an offender because he or she is dead, under age 12, is a youth (aged 12 to 17) whom police feel is better dealt with in another manner, has diplomatic immunity, is already in prison, and so on. If police lay a charge against an offender, the offence is "cleared by charge."

■ Sources: Adapted from Grimes (1997); Hendrick (1997); Kong (1997).

remind us that committing an act in violation of the law does not automatically result in being officially labelled a criminal. The process of criminal labelling can be likened to a funnel, wide at one end and narrow at the other (see Figure 5.1). To be officially identified as a criminal, an individual's law-violating behaviour must first be observed and felt to justify action. The behaviour must be reported to the police who, in turn, must respond to the incident, decide that it warrants further investigation, file a report, and make an arrest. Next, the accused person must appear at a preliminary hearing, an arraignment, and a trial. If the person does not plead guilty, the possibility always exists that he or she will not be convicted because guilt has not been proven "beyond a reasonable doubt."

In **victimization surveys,** people are asked whether they have been victims of crime. Although these types of surveys date back to the mid-1960s in the United States, no national victimization survey was conducted in Canada until 1988 (Fattah, 1991). The International Crime Victim Survey (ICVS) collected victimization data by using the same questionnaire in many countries, including Canada, in 1989, 1992, 1996–97, and 2000 (Besserer, 2002). It examined householders' experience with crime, policing, crime prevention, and feelings of being unsafe. This survey found that, on average, 55 percent of victimization incidents are reported to police, with property crimes more likely to be reported than crimes against persons. In part, this reflects the general requirement by insurance companies that individuals seeking compensation for property stolen or damaged as the result of a criminal act file a police report. Although victimization surveys provide detailed information about crime victims, they provide less reliable data about offenders.

Bearing these caveats in mind, what does the official record show? Most Canadians would be understandably alarmed to hear that, in 2005, 2.5 million Criminal Code incidents (excluding traffic and drug incidents) were reported to Canadian police agencies.

**Figure 5.2**
Crime Rate, Canada, 1962–2005

■ Sources: Wallace (2004); Statistics Canada (2006c).

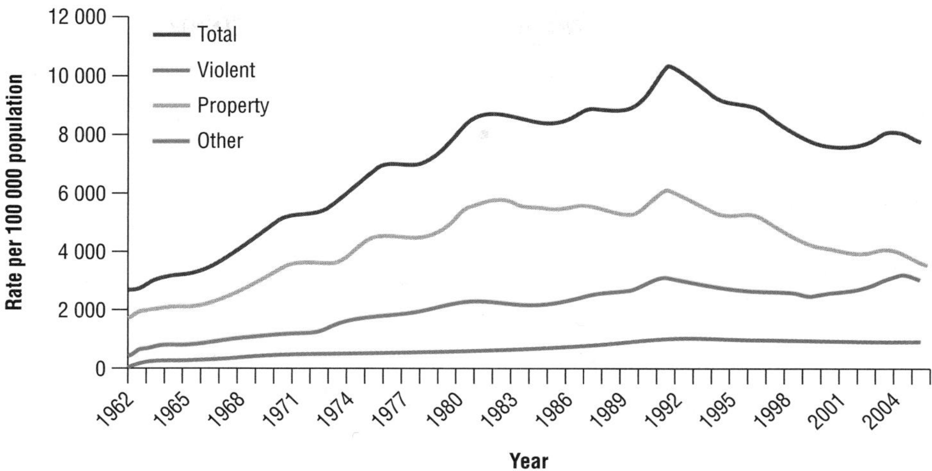


They might assume that each of these incidents was interchangeable with the violent, dramatic, and lurid offences that are brought to our attention daily by media reports of crime. But that is hardly the case. In 2005, 48 percent of Criminal Code incidents involved property crimes, 12 percent involved violent crimes, and 40 percent involved other Criminal Code offences, primarily mischief and disturbing the peace (see Figure 5.2). The bad news is that in 2005 the Canadian crime rate was 180 percent higher than in 1962. The good news is that the long crime wave that began its upswing in Canada in the early 1960s peaked and then fell in the 1990s. In 2000, the total crime rate began to rise slightly, but the violent crime rate remained quite stable. To put this in perspective, although there were 658 homicides in Canada in 2005, this is less than one-third the American rate (see Table 5.1). The good news, then, is evident. How do we explain it?

First, the "war against crime" is increasingly being fought by large numbers of well-trained troops: "Veritable armies of law enforcement and correctional officers have grown phenomenally since the 1960s, not only in manpower but in programs and technical sophistication" (Mohr and Spencer, 1999: 588). Recent declines in Canada's crime rate may reflect the introduction of community policing initiatives, enforcement efforts that target specific types of crime, the refinement of case management methods, improvements in the field of forensics, and efforts directed toward crime prevention (Logan, 2001: 3).

Second, young men are most prone to street crime, but Canada is aging and the number of young people in the population has declined (see Figure 5.3). Men between the ages of 15 and 24 have the highest risk of offending, but this age cohort has decreased in size by 6 percent since 1991 (Logan, 2001: 3).

**Table 5.1**
Homicide Rates for Selected Countries, 2001

| Country | Homicide rate per 100 000 population |
|---|---|
| Russia | 21.13 |
| United States | 5.64 |
| Finland | 2.98 |
| Hungary | 2.48 |
| Austria | 1.93 |
| Sweden | 1.87 |
| France | 1.78 |
| **Canada** | **1.78** |
| England and Wales | 1.66 |
| Ireland | 1.60 |
| Germany | 1.05 |
| Norway | 0.81 |

Source: Adapted from Dauvergne (2002: 3).

**Figure 5.3**
**Crime Rate and Population Aged 15–24, Canada, 1962–2003**

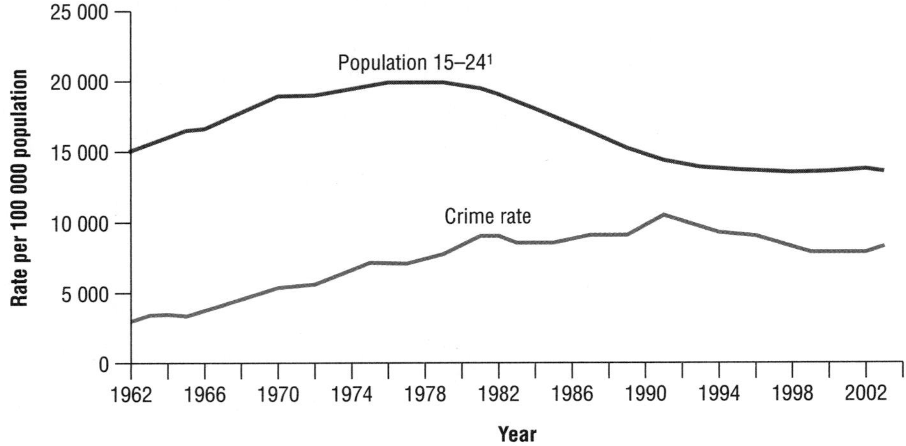


*1. This line represents the number of 15- to 24-year-olds expressed as a rate per 100 000 population and not the crime rate of this age group.*

■ Source: Adapted from Wallace (2004).

Third, following a steep recession in 1990–91, the economy boomed in the 1990s and has grown every year since 1993 with the exception of 2001. Economic conditions, then, may have favoured a decrease in crime. The variable most strongly correlated with the crime rate is the male unemployment rate (John Howard Society, 1999b: 3).

Finally, and more controversially, some American researchers argue that declining crime rates may be linked to the legalization of abortion (Donahue and Levitt, 2001). They observe that, in the United States, the crime rate started to decline 19 years after abortion was legalized. They suggest that the decline occurred because, with the legalization of abortion, proportionately fewer unwanted children were in the population. They argue that unwanted children are more prone to criminal behaviour than wanted children, because they tend to receive less parental supervision and guidance. In Canada, no comparable research has been conducted to date.

Note that we have not claimed that putting more people in prison and imposing tougher penalties for crime help to account for lower crime rates. We will explain why these actions generally do not result in lower crime rates when we discuss *social control* (methods of ensuring conformity) and punishment. We will also probe one of the most fascinating questions raised by official statistics: if crime rates fell in the 1990s, what accounts for our increased enthusiasm for get-tough policies, our increasing prison population, and our widespread and growing fear of crime?

## *Criminal Profiles*

### Age and Sex

In 83 percent of Canadian adult criminal court cases, the accused is a man. Women account for a significant percentage of offenders in only a few types of crimes: nearly half of offences involving prostitution, and nearly three out of ten cases of fraud and theft (including shoplifting) (Thomas, 2004: 3). This pattern repeats itself for cases processed in youth courts. Men account for nearly eight of ten youth court cases. In

2000–01, males accounted for 77 percent of youth charged with a Criminal Code offence and eight in ten youth court cases. However, with every passing year women compose a slightly bigger percentage of arrests (Hartnagel, 2000). This change is partly due to the fact that, in the course of socialization, traditional social controls and definitions of femininity are less often being imposed on women (see Chapter 8, Sexuality and Gender).

Most crime is committed by people who have not reached middle age. The 15- to 24-year-old age cohort is the most prone to criminal behaviour. Although this age cohort represented just 14 percent of the Canadian population in 2001, it accounted for 46 percent of those charged with a property crime and 31 percent of those charged with a violent crime (Savoie, 2002: 3).

## Race

Analysis of official statistics also reveals that race is a factor in who is arrested. For instance, although Aboriginal peoples represent 2 percent of the adult population in Canada, they are overrepresented as a proportion of those incarcerated in both federal (17 percent) and provincial or territorial institutions (19 percent; Hendrick and Farmer, 2002: 10; see Figure 5.4). For the past two decades, Aboriginal peoples have consistently accounted for 15 percent to 19 percent of admissions to both provincial or territorial and federal sentenced custody (Hendrick and Farmer, 2002: 11). Canada has a high incarceration rate among developed countries, and the rate of incarceration for Aboriginal adults is more than eight times the national rate. The overrepresentation of Aboriginal peoples in Canada's prisons is particularly marked in the Prairie provinces. Although Aboriginal peoples represent 10 percent of Saskatchewan's population, they accounted for 78 percent of the adults sentenced to custody in 2002–03. In Alberta, where Aboriginal peoples make up 4 percent of the population, they accounted for 34 percent of custodial sentences in 2002–03. Aboriginal peoples were a majority among those sentenced to custody in 2002–03 in Nunavut, the Northwest Territories, Yukon, Saskatchewan, and Manitoba (Johnson, 2004).

**Figure 5.4**
**Representation of Aboriginal People in Provincial and Territorial Custody, 1993–1994 to 2001–2002**

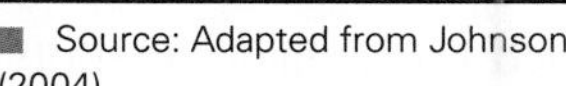

■ Source: Adapted from Johnson (2004).

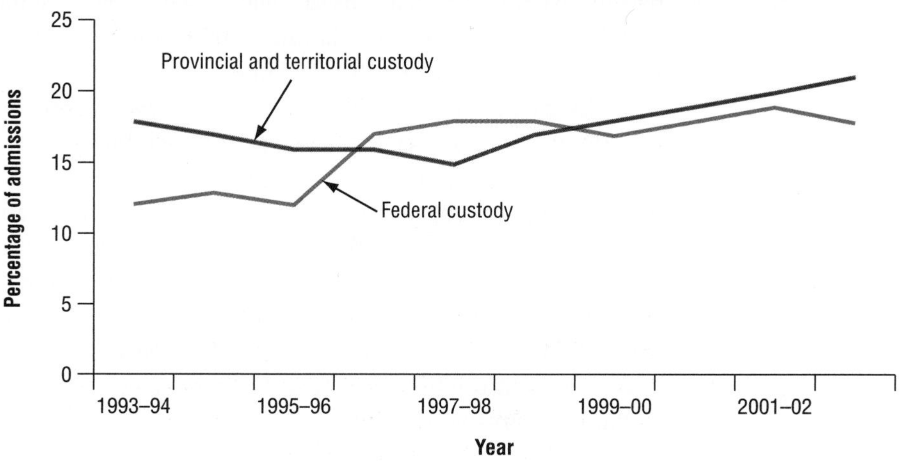

Several explanations for the overrepresentation of Aboriginal peoples in Canada's prisons exist (Hartnagel, 2000). First, a disproportionately large number of Aboriginal peoples are poor. Although the great majority of poor people are law abiding, poverty and its handicaps are associated with elevated crime rates. Second, Aboriginal peoples commit crimes that are more detectable than those committed by non-Aboriginal people. For example, as we have seen, street crimes are generally more detectable than white-collar crimes, and they more often lead to prosecution and conviction. Third, the police, the courts, and other institutions may discriminate against Aboriginal peoples. As a result, Aboriginal peoples may be more likely to be apprehended, prosecuted, and convicted. Fourth, contact with Western culture has disrupted social life in many Aboriginal communities (see Chapter 7, Race and Ethnicity). This disruption has led to a weakening of social control over community members. Some people think that certain "races" are *inherently* more law abiding than others, but they are able to hold such an opinion only by ignoring the powerful *social* forces that cause so many Aboriginal peoples to be incarcerated in Canada (Roberts and Gabor, 1990).

# Explaining Deviance and Crime

*Lep: "I remember your li'l ass used to ride dirt bikes and skateboards, actin' crazy an' shit. Now you want to be a gangster, huh? You wanna hang with real muthaf— and tear shit up, huh? Stand up, get your li'l ass up. How old is you now anyway?"*

*Kody: "Eleven, but I'll be twelve in November."*

—Sanyika Shakur (1993: 8)

"Monster" Kody Scott eagerly joined the notorious gang the Crips in South Central Los Angeles in 1975 when he was in grade 6. He was released from Folsom Prison on parole in 1988, at the age of 24. Until about three years before his release, he was one of the most ruthless gang leaders in Los Angeles and the California prison system. In 1985, however, he decided to reform. He adopted the name Sanyika Shakur, became a black nationalist, and began a crusade against gangs. Few people in his position have chosen that path. In Scott's heyday, about 30 000 gang members roamed Los Angeles County. Today there are an estimated 150 000.

What makes engaging in crime an attractive prospect to so many people? In general, why do deviance and crime occur at all? Sociologists have proposed dozens of explanations. However, we can group them into two basic types. **Motivational theories** identify the social factors that *drive* people to commit deviance and crime. **Constraint theories** identify the social factors that *impose* deviance and crime (or conventional behaviour) on people. Later we examine three examples of each type of theory. Before doing so, however, we want to stress that becoming a *habitual* deviant or criminal is a learning process that occurs in a social context. Motive and lack of constraint may ignite a single deviant or criminal act, but repeatedly engaging in that act requires the learning of a deviant or criminal role.

### *Becoming Deviant: The Case of Marijuana Users*

Howard S. Becker, a giant in the sociological study of deviance, analyzed this learning process in a classic study of marijuana users (Becker, 1963: 41–58). In 1948 and 1949, Becker financed his Ph.D. studies at the University of Chicago by playing piano in local jazz bands. He used the opportunity to do participant-observation research, carefully observing his fellow musicians, informally interviewing them in depth, and writing up detailed field notes after performances. Becker observed and interviewed 50 jazz musicians who smoked marijuana.

Becker found that his fellow musicians had to pass through a three-stage learning process before becoming regular marijuana users. Failure to pass a stage meant failure to learn the deviant role and become a regular user. These are the three stages:

1. Learning to smoke the drug in a way that produces real effects. *First-time marijuana smokers do not ordinarily get high. To do so, they must learn how to smoke the drug in a way that ensures a sufficient dosage to produce intoxicating effects (taking deep drags and holding their breath for a long time). This process takes practice, and some first-time users give up, typically claiming that marijuana has no effect on them or that people who claim otherwise are just fooling themselves. Others are more strongly encouraged by their peers to keep trying. If they persist, they are ready to go to stage two.*
2. Learning to recognize the effects and connect them with drug use. *Those who learn the proper smoking technique may not recognize that they are high or they may not connect the symptoms of being high with smoking the drug. They may get very hungry, laugh uncontrollably, play the same song for hours on end, and yet still fail to realize that these are symptoms of intoxication. If so, they will stop using the drug. Becker found, however, that his fellow musicians typically asked experienced users how they knew whether they were high. Experienced users identified the symptoms of marijuana use and helped novices make the connection between what they were experiencing and smoking the drug. Once they made that connection, novices were ready to advance to stage three.*
3. Learning to enjoy the perceived sensations. *Smoking marijuana is not inherently pleasurable. Some users experience a frightening loss of self-control (paranoia). Others feel dizzy, uncomfortably thirsty, itchy, forgetful, or dangerously impaired in their ability to judge time and distance. If these negative sensations persist, marijuana use will cease. However, Becker found that experienced users typically helped novices redefine negative sensations as pleasurable. They taught novices to laugh at their impaired judgment, take special pleasure in quenching their deep thirst, and find deeper meaning in familiar music. If and only if novices learned to define the effects of smoking as pleasurable did they become habitual marijuana smokers.*

So we see that becoming a regular marijuana user involves more than just motive and opportunity. In fact, learning *any* deviant or criminal role requires a social context like the one Becker describes. Experienced deviants or criminals must teach novices the "tricks of the trade." Bearing this fact in mind, we now examine the two main types of theories that seek to explain deviance and crime—those that ask what motivates people to break rules and those that ask how social constraints sometimes fail to prevent rules from getting broken.

## *Motivational Theories*

### Strain Theory

You will recall Durkheim's idea that the absence of clear norms can result in elevated rates of suicide and other forms of deviant behaviour (see Chapter 1, A Sociological Compass). Robert Merton's **strain theory** extends Durkheim's insight (Merton, 1938). Merton argued that cultures often teach people to value material success. Just as often, however, societies do not provide enough legitimate opportunities for everyone to succeed. As a result, some people experience strain. Most of them will force themselves to adhere to social norms despite the strain. The rest adapt in one of four ways. They may drop out of conventional society. They may reject the goals of conventional society but continue to follow its rules. They may protest against convention and support alternative values. Or they may find alternative and illegitimate means of achieving their society's goals—that is, they become criminals. The value of material success starkly contradicts the lack of opportunity available to poor youths. As a result, poor youths sometimes engage in illegal means of attaining socially approved goals.

### Subcultural Theory

A second type of motivational theory, **subcultural theory,** emphasizes the importance of social groups. It suggests that deviant and criminal acts, including the formation of criminal gangs, are a *collective* adaptation to social conditions. This collective adaptation involves the formation of a subculture with distinct norms and values. Members of this subculture reject the legitimate world that, they feel, has rejected them (Cohen, 1955).

In some areas, delinquent youths are recruited by organized crime, such as the Mafia. In areas that lack organized crime networks, delinquent youths are more likely to create violent gangs. Thus, the relative availability of different subcultures influences the type of criminal activity to which a person turns (Cloward and Ohlin, 1960).

The members of criminal subcultures typically spin a whole series of rationalizations for their criminal activities. These justifications make their illegal activities appear morally acceptable and normal, at least to the members of the subculture. Typically, criminals deny personal responsibility for their actions ("It wasn't my fault!") or deny the wrongfulness of the act ("I was just borrowing it."). They condemn those who pass judgment on them ("The cops are bigger crooks than anyone!"). They claim their victims get what they deserve ("She had it coming to her."). And they appeal to higher loyalties, particularly to friends and family ("I had to do it because he dissed my gang."). The creation of such justifications and rationalizations enables criminals to clear their consciences and get on with the job. Sociologists call such rationalizations **techniques of neutralization** (Sykes and Matza, 1957).

Although deviants may depart from mainstream culture in many ways, they are strict conformists when it comes to the norms of their own subculture. They tend to share the same beliefs, dress alike, eat similar food, and adopt the same mannerisms and speech patterns. Deviance is strongly discouraged *within* the subculture.

Strain and subcultural theories exaggerate the connection between crime and lower-class origins. Many self-report surveys find, at most, a weak tendency for criminals to come disproportionately from lower classes. Some self-report surveys report no such tendency at all, especially among young people and for less serious types of crime (Weis, 1987). A stronger correlation exists between *serious street*

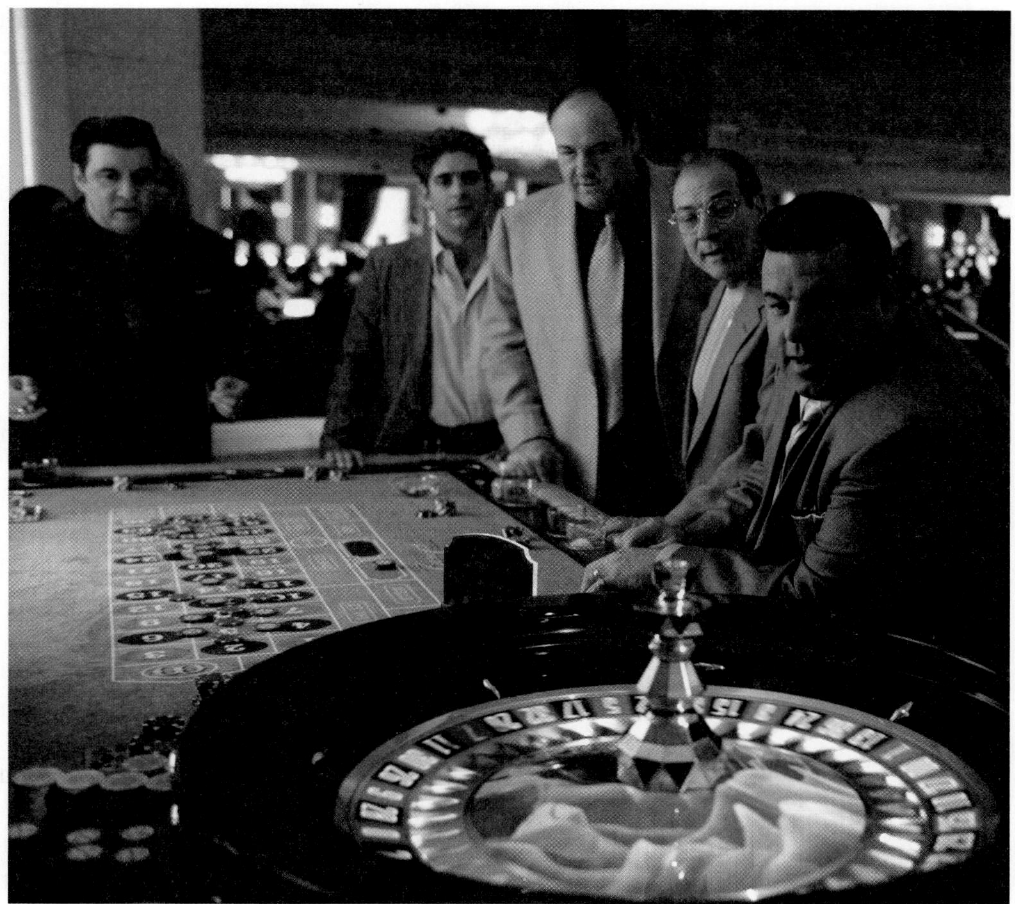

According to Edwin Sutherland's theory of differential association, people who are exposed to more deviant than non-deviant experiences as they grow up are likely to become deviants. As in *The Sopranos,* having family members and friends in the Mafia predisposes a person to Mafia involvement.

*crimes* and class. Armed robbery and assault, for instance, are more common among people from lower classes. A stronger correlation also exists between *white-collar* crime and class. Middle- and upper-class people are most likely to commit white-collar crimes. Thus, generalizations about the relationship between class and crime must be qualified by taking into account the severity and type of crime (Braithwaite, 1981). Note also that official statistics usually exaggerate class differences because they are more accurate barometers of street crime than suite crime. It is obvious that generally more police surveillance occurs in lower-class neighbourhoods than in upper-class boardrooms.

### Learning Theory

Apart from exaggerating the association between class and crime, strain and subcultural theories are problematic because they tell us little about *why* some people who experience strain choose a life of crime, while others (the great majority) do not. Edwin Sutherland (1939) addressed both the class and the choice problems 70 years ago by proposing a third motivational theory, which he called the theory of **differential association.** In Sutherland's view, a person learns to favour one adaptation over another because of his or her life experiences or socialization. Specifically, everyone is exposed to both deviant and non-deviant values and behaviours as they grow up. If you happen to be exposed to more deviant than non-deviant experiences, chances are you will learn to become a deviant yourself. You will come to value a particular deviant lifestyle and consider it normal. Everything depends, then, on the exact mix of deviant and conformist influences a person faces.

Significantly, the theory of differential association holds for people in all class positions. For instance, Sutherland applied the theory of differential association in his path-breaking research on white-collar crime. He noted that white-collar criminals, like their counterparts on the street, learn their skills from associates and share a culture that rewards rule breaking and expresses contempt for the law (Sutherland, 1949).

## *Constraint Theories*

Motivational theories ask how some people are driven to break norms and laws. Constraint theories, in contrast, pay less attention to people's motivations. How are deviant and criminal labels imposed on some people? How do various forms of social control fail to impose conformity on them? How does the distribution of power in society shape deviance and crime? These are the kinds of questions posed by constraint theorists.

### Labelling Theory

In 1995 in Saskatchewan, after a night of heavy drinking, two 20-year-old university students, Alex Ternowetsky and Steven Kummerfield, both white and middle class, picked up Pamela George, an Aboriginal single mother who occasionally worked as a prostitute, in downtown Regina. They drove the 28-year-old woman outside the city limits, demanded that she perform oral sex on them without pay, and then savagely beat her to death. Although originally charged with first-degree murder, a jury later found them guilty of the lesser charge of manslaughter. In a controversial move, Justice Ted Malone of the Saskatchewan Court of Queen's Bench instructed the jurors to consider that the two men had been drinking and that George was "indeed a prostitute." Members of the victim's family were appalled, Native leaders outraged. Tone Cote of the Yorkton Tribal Council said the sentence would send the message that "it's all right for little white boys to go out on the streets, get drunk and use that for an excuse to start hunting down our people."

A central insight of **labelling theory** is that deviance results not just from the actions of the deviant but also from the responses of others, who define some actions as deviant and other actions as normal. As the above example suggests, terms like *deviant* or *criminal* are not applied automatically when a person engages in rule-violating behaviour. Some individuals escape being labelled as deviants despite having engaged in deviant behaviour. Others, like Ternowetsky and Kummerfield, are labelled deviant but found to be guilty of a lesser charge than would typically be the case. Still others, such as Pamela George, who do not engage in deviant acts at all or are the victims of such acts, may find themselves labelled as deviant (Matsueda, 1988, 1992).

That labelling plays an important part in who is caught and who is charged with crime was demonstrated 40 years ago by Aaron Cicourel (1968). Cicourel examined the tendency to label rule-breaking adolescents as juvenile delinquents if they came from families in which the parents were divorced. He found that police officers tended to use their discretionary powers to arrest adolescents from divorced families more often than adolescents from intact families who committed similar delinquent acts. Judges, in turn, tended to give more severe sentences to adolescents from divorced families than to adolescents from intact families who were charged with similar delinquent acts. Sociologists and criminologists then collected data on the social characteristics of adolescents who were charged as juvenile delinquents, "proving" that children from divorced families were more likely to become juvenile delinquents. Their finding reinforced the beliefs of police officers and judges. Thus, the labelling process acted as a self-fulfilling prophecy.

### Control Theory

All motivational theories assume that people are good and require special circumstances to make them bad. A popular type of constraint theory assumes that people are bad and require special circumstances to make them good. According to **control theory,** the rewards of deviance and crime are many. Proponents of this approach argue that nearly everyone wants fun, pleasure, excitement, and profit. Moreover, they say, if we could get away with it, most of us would commit deviant and criminal acts to acquire more of these valued things. For control theorists, the reason most of us do not engage in deviance and crime is that we are prevented from doing so. The reason deviants and criminals break norms and laws is that social controls are insufficient to ensure their conformity.

Travis Hirschi developed the control theory of crime (Hirschi, 1969; Gottfredson and Hirschi, 1990). He argued that adolescents are more prone to deviance and crime than adults because they are incompletely socialized and therefore lack self-control. Adults and adolescents may both experience the impulse to break norms and laws, but adolescents are less likely to control that impulse. Hirschi went on to show that the adolescents who are most prone to delinquency are likely to lack four types of social control. They tend to have few social *attachments* to parents, teachers, and other respectable role models; few legitimate *opportunities* for education and a good job; few *involvements* in conventional institutions; and weak *beliefs* in traditional values and morality. Because of the lack of control stemming from these sources, these adolescents are relatively free to act on their deviant impulses. For similar reasons, boys are more likely to engage in juvenile delinquency than girls, and people who experience job and marital instability are more likely than others to engage in crime (Hagan et al., 1987; Peters, 1994; Sampson and Laub, 1993).

Labelling and control theories have little to say about why people regard certain kinds of activities as deviant or criminal in the first place. For the answer to that question, we must turn to conflict theory, a third type of constraint theory.

### Conflict Theory

The day after Christmas in 1996 JonBenet Ramsey was found strangled to death in the basement of her parents' US$800 000 home in Boulder, Colorado. The police found no footprints in the snow surrounding the house and no sign of forced entry. The investigators concluded that nobody had entered the house during the night when, according to the coroner, the murder had taken place. The police did find a ransom note saying that the child had been kidnapped. A linguistics expert later compared the note with writing samples by the child's mother. The expert concluded that the child's mother was the author of the ransom note. It was also determined that all the materials used in the crime had been purchased by the mother. Finally, it was discovered that JonBenet had been sexually abused. Although by no means an open-and-shut case, enough evidence was available to cast a veil of suspicion over the parents.

Yet, apparently because of the lofty position of the Ramsey family in their community, the police treated them in an extraordinary way. On the first day of the investigation, the commander of the Boulder police detective division designated the Ramseys an "influential family" and ordered that they be treated as victims, not suspects (Oates, 1999: 32). The father was allowed to participate in the search for the child. In the process, he may have contaminated crucial evidence. The police also let him leave the house unescorted for about an hour. This led to speculation that he might have disposed of incriminating evidence. Because the Ramseys are millionaires, they were able to hire accomplished lawyers who prevented the Boulder police from interviewing them for four months and a public relations team that reinforced the idea that the Ramseys were victims. A grand jury decided on 13 October 1999 that nobody would be charged with the murder of JonBenet Ramsey.

Regardless of the Ramseys' innocence or guilt, the way their case was handled adds to the view that the law applies differently to rich and poor. That is the perspective of *conflict theory*. In brief, conflict theorists maintain that the rich and the powerful impose deviant and criminal labels on the less powerful members of society, particularly those who challenge the existing social order. Meanwhile, the powerful are usually able to use their money and influence to escape punishment for their own misdeeds.

Steven Spitzer (1980) conveniently summarizes this school of thought. He notes that capitalist societies are based on private ownership of property. Moreover, their smooth functioning depends on the availability of productive labour and respect for authority. When thieves steal, they challenge private property. Theft is therefore a crime. When so-called bag ladies and drug addicts drop out of conventional society, they are defined as deviant because their refusal to engage in productive labour undermines a pillar of capitalism. When young, politically volatile students or militant trade unionists strike or otherwise protest against authority, they, too, represent a threat to the social order and are defined as deviant or criminal.

Of course, says Spitzer, the rich and the powerful engage in deviant and criminal acts too. But, he adds, they tend to be dealt with more leniently. Industries can grievously harm people by damaging the environment, yet serious charges are rarely brought against the owners of industry. White-collar crimes are less severely punished than street crimes, regardless of the relative harm they cause. Compare the crime of break and enter with fraud, for example. Fraud almost certainly costs society more than break and enter. But breaking and entering is a street crime committed mainly by lower-class people, while fraud is a white-collar crime committed mainly by middle- and upper-class people. Not surprisingly, therefore, in Canada in 2000–01, 61 percent of convicted break and enter cases but just 35 percent of convicted fraud cases resulted in a prison sentence (Thomas, 2002: 9). Laws and norms may change with shifts in the distribution of power in society; however, according to conflict theorists, definitions of deviance and crime, and also punishments for misdeeds, are always influenced by who's on top.

Many theories contribute to our understanding of the social causes of deviance and crime. Some forms of deviance and crime are better explained by one theory than by another. Different theories illuminate different aspects of the process by which people are motivated to break rules and be defined as rule breakers. Our overview should make it clear that no one theory is best. Instead, taking many theories into account allows us to develop a fully rounded appreciation of the complex processes surrounding the social construction of deviance and crime (see Table 5.2 for a summary).

**Table 5.2**
The Main Theories of Deviance and Crime Theory

| Theory | Summary |
|---|---|
| MOTIVATIONAL THEORIES | They identify the social factors that drive people to deviance and crime. |
| 1. Strain theory | Societies do not provide enough legitimate opportunities for everyone to succeed, resulting in strain, one reaction to which is to find alternative and illegitimate means of achieving society's goals. |
| 2. Subcultural theory | It emphasizes the collective adaptations to strain, such as the formation of gangs and organized crime, and the degree to which these collective adaptations have distinct norms and values that reject the non-deviant or non-criminal world. |
| 3. Learning theory | People become deviants or criminals—or fail to do so—because of differential association; that is, they are exposed to, and therefore learn, deviant and criminal values to varying degrees. |
| CONSTRAINT THEORIES | They identify the social factors that impose deviance and crime (or conventional behaviour) on people. |
| 1. Labelling theory | Deviance and crime result not just from the actions of the deviant or criminal but also from the responses of others, who define some actions as deviant and other actions as normal. |
| 2. Control theory | Deviants and criminals tend to be people with few social attachments to parents, teachers, and other respectable role models, few legitimate opportunities for education and a good job, few involvements in conventional institutions, and weak beliefs in traditional values and morality; the lack of control from these sources leaves them relatively free to act on their deviant impulses. |
| 3. Conflict theory | The rich and the powerful impose deviant and criminal labels on the less powerful members of society, particularly on those who challenge the existing social order; meanwhile, the powerful are usually able to use their money and influence to escape punishment for their own misdeeds. |

# Punishment

All societies seek to ensure that their members obey norms and laws. All societies impose sanctions on rule breakers. However, the *degree* of social control varies over time and place. *Forms* of punishment also vary.

In many respects people are freer today than ever. We elect leaders, choose consumer products, change religions, and so forth. In other respects, however, social control has intensified over time. Much of the regimentation of modern life is tied to the growth of capitalism and the state. Factories require strict labour regimes, with workers arriving and leaving at a fixed time and, while there, performing fixed tasks at a fixed pace. Institutions regulated by the state's armies, police forces, public schools, health care systems, and various other bureaucracies also demand strict work regimes, curricula, and procedures. These institutions existed on a much smaller scale in pre-industrial times or did not exist at all. Today, they penetrate our lives and sustain strong norms of belief and conduct (Foucault, 1977 [1975]).

Electronic technology makes it possible for authorities to exercise more effective social control than ever. With millions of cameras mounted in public places and workplaces, some sociologists say we now live in a "surveillance society" (Lyon and Zureik, 1996). Spy cameras enable observers to see deviance and crime that would otherwise go undetected and to take quick action to apprehend rule breakers. Moreover, when people are aware of the presence of spy cameras, they tend to alter their behaviour. For example, attentive shoplifters migrate to stores that lack electronic surveillance. On factory floors and in offices, workers display more conformity to management-imposed work norms. On campuses, students are inhibited from engaging in organized protests (Boal, 1998).

Recent developments in social control include the medicalization of deviance and the rise of the prison. In some societies, authorities still deal with serious crime by means of capital punishment. Let us examine each of these reactions to deviance and crime in turn.

## *The Medicalization of Deviance*

Increasingly, we deal with deviance by medicalizing it. The **medicalization of deviance** refers to the fact that "medical definitions of deviant behavior are becoming more prevalent in . . . societies like our own" (Conrad and Schneider, 1992: 28–29). In an earlier era, much deviant behaviour was labelled evil. Deviants tended to be chastised, punished, and otherwise socially controlled by members of the clergy, neighbours, family members, and the criminal justice system. Today, however, a person prone to drinking sprees is more likely to be declared an alcoholic and treated in a detoxification centre. A person predisposed to violent rages is more likely to be medicated. A person inclined to overeating is more likely to seek therapy and, in extreme cases, surgery. A heroin addict is more likely to seek the help of a methadone program. As these examples illustrate, what used to be regarded as willful deviance is now often regarded as involuntary deviance. Increasingly, what used to be defined as "badness" is defined as "sickness." As our definitions of deviance change, deviance is increasingly coming under the sway of the medical and psychiatric establishments (see Figure 5.5).

### The Spread of Mental Disorders

Many mental disorders have obvious organic causes, such as chemical imbalances in the brain. These problems can often be precisely identified and treated with drugs or other therapies. Experiments can be conducted to verify their existence and establish the effectiveness of one treatment or another. Little debate takes place over whether such ailments should be listed in the psychiatrist's "bible," the *Diagnostic and Statistical Manual of Mental Disorders* (*DSM*).

The organic basis for other ailments is unclear. In such cases, social values and political conflict can determine whether they are listed in the *DSM*. Thus, in the 1970s and 1980s, North American psychiatrists fiercely debated whether neurosis,

## Figure 5.5
## An Example of the Medicalization of Deviance

Five North American surveys conducted in the 1950s and 1960s presented respondents with the accompanying anecdote. The graph shows the percentage of respondents who considered the behaviour described in the anecdote evidence of mental illness. Notice the difference between the 1950s and the 1960s. (Nearly 100 percent of psychiatrists who evaluated the anecdote thought it illustrated "simple schizophrenia.")

■ Source: Adapted from Peter Conrad and Joseph W. Schneider, *Deviance and Medicalization: From Badness to Sickness*, p. 59. © 1992 by Temple University Press.

*"Now here's a young woman in her twenties, let's call her Betty Smith . . . she has never had a job, and she doesn't seem to want to go out and look for one. She is a very quiet girl, she doesn't talk much to anyone—even her own family, and she acts like she is afraid of people, especially young men her own age. She won't go out with anyone, and whenever someone comes to visit her family, she stays in her own room until they leave. She just stays by herself and daydreams all the time and shows no interest in anything or anybody."*

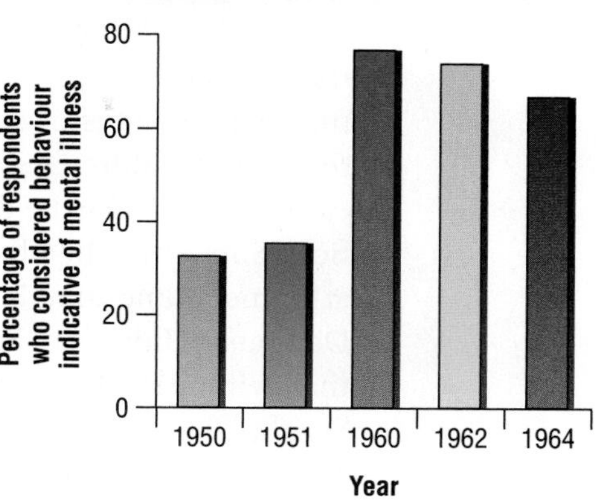


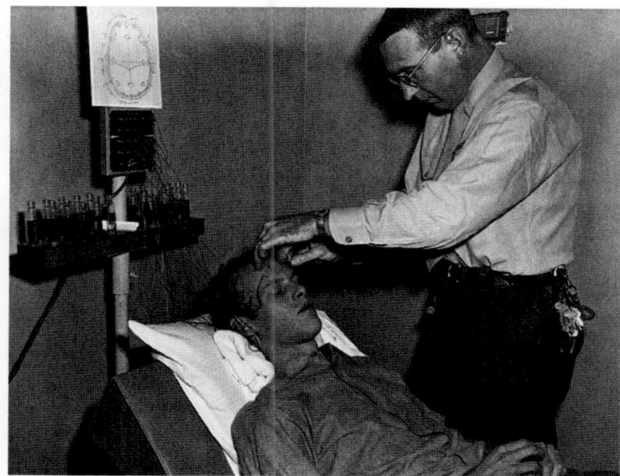

An example of the medicalization of deviance. A lobotomy is performed in Vacaville State Prison in California in 1961 to "cure" the inmate of criminality.

post-traumatic stress disorder, homosexuality, and self-defeating personality disorder were real mental disorders. In the end, homosexuality was dropped from the *DSM*, largely in response to the efforts of liberal-minded psychiatrists, as was self-defeating personality disorder, thanks to the efforts of feminists. Neurosis was retained at the insistence of Freudians. Post-traumatic stress disorder (PTSD) was added to the *DSM* after a strenuous lobbying campaign by Vietnam War veterans and their supporters (Scott, 1990). These cases illustrate that the medicalization of deviance is in part a social and political process.

In the mid-nineteenth century there was just one officially recognized mental disorder: idiocy/insanity. The current *DSM* lists 297. As the number of mental disorders has grown, so has the proportion of North Americans presumably affected by them. In the mid-nineteenth century, few people were defined as suffering from mental disorders, but one respected survey conducted in the early 1990s found that 48 percent of people will suffer from a mental disorder—very broadly defined, of course—during their lifetime (Blazer, Kessler, McGonagle, and Swartz, 1994; Shorter, 1997: 294).

The number and scope of mental disorders have grown partly because North Americans are now experiencing more stress than ever before, mainly because of the increased demands of work and a growing time crunch. At the same time, traditional institutions for dealing with mental health problems are less able to cope with them. The weakening authority of the church and the weakening grip of the family over the individual leave the treatment of mental health problems more open to the medical and psychiatric establishments.

The cultural context also stimulates inflation in the number and scope of mental disorders. North Americans are inclined to turn their problems into medical and psychological issues, sometimes without inquiring deeply into the disadvantages of doing so. For example, in 1980 the term "attention deficit disorder" (ADD) was coined to label hyperactive and inattentive schoolchildren, mainly boys. By the mid-1990s, doctors were writing 6 million prescriptions a year for Ritalin, an amphetamine-like compound that controls ADD. Evidence shows that some children diagnosed with ADD have problems absorbing glucose in the brain or suffer from imbalances in chemicals that help the brain regulate behaviour. Yet the diagnosis of ADD is typically conducted clinically, that is, by interviewing and observing children to see if they exhibit signs of serious inattention, hyperactivity, and impulsivity. This means that many children diagnosed with ADD may have no organic disorder at all. Some cases of ADD may be due to the school system failing to capture children's imagination. Some may involve children acting out because they are deprived of attention at home. Some may involve plain, old-fashioned youthful enthusiasm. (Doctors at Dalhousie University Medical School in Halifax made a plausible case a few years ago that Winnie the Pooh suffered from ADD; see Shea, Gordon, Hawkins, Kawchuk, and Smith, 2000.) However, once hyperactivity and inattentiveness in school are defined as a medical and psychiatric condition, officials routinely prescribe drugs to control the problem and tend to ignore possible social causes.

Finally, we have witnessed inflation in the number and scope of mental disorders because various professional organizations have an interest in it. Consider PTSD. There is no doubt that PTSD is a real condition and that many veterans suffer from it. However, once the disorder was officially recognized in the 1970s, some therapists trivialized the term. By the mid-1990s some therapists were talking about PTSD "in children exposed to movies like *Batman*" (Shorter, 1997: 290). Some psychiatric social workers, psychologists, and psychiatrists may magnify the incidence of such mental disorders because doing so increases their stature and their patient load. Others may do so simply because the condition becomes trendy. Whatever the motive, overdiagnosis is the result.

### *The Prison*

In October 2001, a 63-year-old man with Parkinson's disease and addicted to cocaine was arrested in Ottawa. A passer-by had noticed that the man had a shotgun in his gym bag and had notified the police. The man, who was charged with possession of a weapon, did not resist arrest. He knew what awaited him. Roger Caron, dubbed Mad Dog Caron by the press, had first been sentenced to prison at the age of 16 for breaking and entering. He had spent most of his adult life as an inept robber, going in and out of Eastern Canada's major prisons.

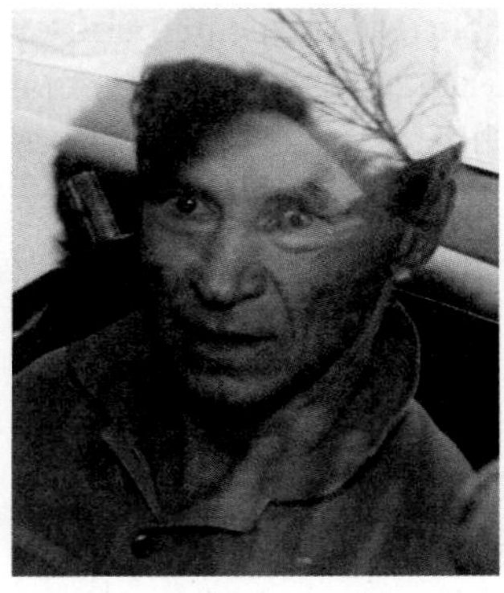

Roger Caron, who was 16 years old when he was first sentenced to prison for breaking and entering, has spent much of his life behind bars. His acclaimed book, *Go-Boy!*, provides a chilling account of his life in almost all the major prisons in Eastern Canada.

After having already spent almost 20 years in prison, Caron wrote a chilling account of his life behind bars. He was still in prison when *Go-Boy!* was published in 1978. The book describes in harrowing detail the harshness of the prison experience—the violence, the intense hatreds, the hard labour, the horrors of solitary confinement, the twisted, manipulative friendships, and the brutal use of corporal punishment. He describes the use of the "paddle": "three leather straps with wooden handles, so thick and coarse as to barely sag. Each one was perforated with hundreds of tiny holes designed to trap and rip the flesh from the buttocks." He writes that when this form of punishment was first administered to him in 1955, "white searing pain exploded throughout my being and blood gushed from my lips as I struggled to stifle a scream. It was brutal and it was horrible" (Caron, 1979: 59; see also Farrell, n.d.).

*Go-Boy!* was honoured in 1978 with the Governor General's Literary Award and, in the years that followed, Caron wrote other books. However, he was unable to leave his past life behind. Following imprisonment for another botched robbery attempt, Caron

In pre-industrial societies, criminals who committed serious crimes were put to death, often in ways that seem cruel by today's standards. One method of putting criminals to death in pre-industrial societies involved hanging them upside down, bound and alive, so that starving dogs could rip them apart.

was released from prison in 1998 and was still on parole at the time of his 2001 arrest. Regardless of the initial factors that caused Caron to turn to crime, it was his experiences in prison that turned him into a career criminal (CyberPress, 2001).

Caron's experience follows a pattern known to sociologists for a long time. Prisons are agents of socialization, and new inmates often become more serious offenders as they adapt to the culture of the most hardened, long-term prisoners (Wheeler, 1961).

## Origins of Imprisonment

Because prison often turns criminals into worse criminals, it is worth pondering the institution's origins, development, and current dilemmas. As societies industrialized, imprisonment became one of the most important forms of punishment for criminal behaviour (Garland, 1990; Morris and Rothman, 1995). In pre-industrial societies, criminals were publicly humiliated, tortured, or put to death, depending on the severity of their transgressions. In the industrial era, depriving criminals of their freedom by putting them in prison seemed less harsh, more "civilized" (Durkheim, 1973 [1899–1900]).

## Goals of Incarceration

Some people still take a benign view of prisons, even seeing in them opportunities for *rehabilitation*. They believe that prisoners, while serving time, can be taught how to be productive citizens on release. In Canada, this idea predominated from the 1950s to the early 1970s, when many prisons sought to reform criminals by offering them psychological counselling, drug therapy, skills training, education, and other programs that would help at least the less violent offenders reintegrate into society (McMahon, 1992: xvii).

Today, however, many Canadians scoff at the idea that prisons can rehabilitate criminals. We have adopted a much tougher line and politicians routinely campaign on promises of a get-tough approach to crime and to criminals. Some people see prison as a means of *deterrence*. In this view, people will be less inclined to commit crimes if they know they are likely to be caught and serve long and unpleasant prison terms. Others think of prisons as institutions of *revenge*. They believe that depriving criminals of their freedom and forcing them to live in poor conditions is fair retribution for their illegal acts. Still others see prisons as institutions of *incapacitation*. From this viewpoint, the chief function of the prison is to keep criminals out of society as long as possible to ensure they can do no more harm (Simon, 1993; Zimring and Hawkins, 1995).

No matter which of these views predominates, one thing is clear: the Canadian public has demanded that more criminals be arrested and imprisoned—and it has gotten what it wants. In 2005, 107 of every 100 000 Canadians were in prison (see Figure 5.6). Although Canada's incarceration rate is higher than that of many Western industrialized societies, it is much lower than that of the United States, which has the world's highest rate of incarceration at 737 inmates per 100 000 people. Still, the cost of incarceration is high. The adult prison system cost Canadians $2.7 billion in 2003–04 (Statistics Canada, 2006c). In 2001, the average annual cost of incarcerating an offender in a federal penitentiary was $66 381 for a male inmate and $110 473 for a female inmate (Correctional Service of Canada, 2001).

**Figure 5.6**
Number of Prisoners per 100 000 Population, Selected Countries, c. 2005

■ Source: Sentencing Project (2006).

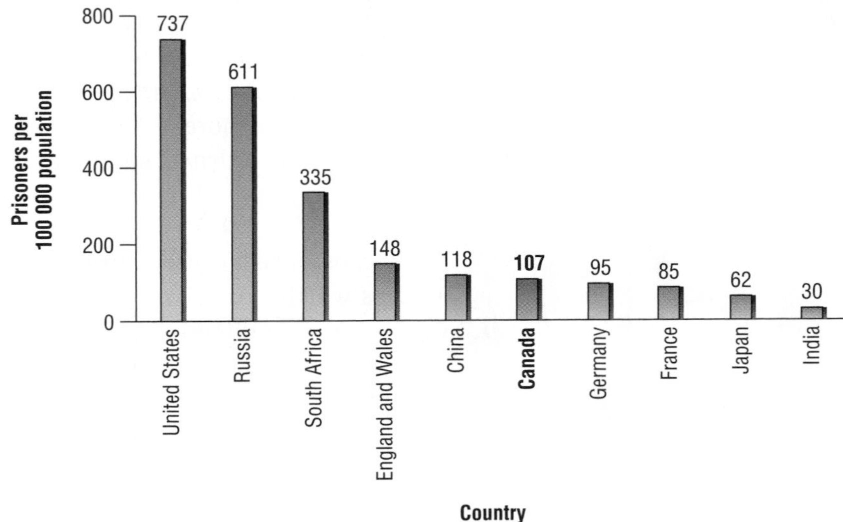

Intensive media coverage of the most notorious and violent crimes and criminals may lead to a heightened fear of crime and demands for tougher penalties. Karla Homolka, with her husband, Paul Bernardo, was responsible for the sexual assault and brutal murder of Tammy Homolka, Leslie Mahaffy, and Kristen French in the early 1990s.

## *Moral Panic*

What accounts for our increased enthusiasm for get-tough policies? In a phrase, we have been gripped by **moral panic,** a widespread fear that crime poses a grave threat to society's well-being. Partly in response to lurid headlines that direct attention to the most notorious and atypical crimes and criminals, many members of the public incorrectly conclude that all crime is violent and predatory, all criminals are dangerous, and our current crime rate signals a grave threat to our society's well-being (Cohen, 1972; Goode and Ben-Yehuda, 1994; see Box 5.3).

## *Forms of Punishment: Two Extremes*

The two most contentious issues concerning the punishment of criminals are these: (1) Should Canada reintroduce the death penalty for the most violent criminals? (2) Should we use strategies other than imprisonment for other criminals? In concluding this chapter, we briefly consider these issues.

### Capital Punishment

Although capital punishment has not been employed in Canada since 1962 and was formally abolished in 1976, most Canadians favour its re-introduction. According to one survey, 74 percent of Canadian adults and 59 percent of teenagers agreed with the statement that "the death penalty should sometimes be used to punish criminals" (Bibby, 2001: 244).

Although the death penalty ranks high as a form of revenge, it is questionable whether it is much of a deterrent. First, murder is often committed in a rage, when the perpetrator is not thinking entirely rationally. As such, the murderer is unlikely to coolly consider the costs and consequences of his or her actions. Second, the United States has capital punishment, but its homicide rate is much higher than that of Canada and Western European countries that do not practise capital punishment (Mooney, Knox, Schacht, and Nelson, 2001: 131; see Figure 5.7).

5.3

## YOU AND THE SOCIAL WORLD

### Moral Panic

The current North America–wide moral panic about crime is occurring during a period when all major crime indexes first stabilized and then decreased dramatically. Why then the panic? Who benefits from it? We mention several interested parties:

1. *The mass media benefit from moral panic because it allows them to rake in hefty profits. They publicize every major crime because crime draws big audiences, and big audiences mean more revenue from advertisers. Fictional crime programs draw tens of millions of additional viewers to their TVs.*
2. *The crime prevention and punishment industry benefits from moral panic for much the same reason. Prison construction and maintenance firms, firearms manufacturers, and so forth, are all big businesses that flourish in a climate of moral panic. Such industries want people to own more guns and imprison more people, so they lobby hard for relaxed gun laws and invigorated prison construction programs.*
3. *The criminal justice system is a huge bureaucracy with many employees. They benefit from moral panic because increased spending on crime prevention, control, and punishment secures their jobs and expands their turf.*
4. *Perhaps most important, the moral panic is useful politically. Since the early 1970s, many politicians have based entire careers on get-tough policies.*

**WRITING ASSIGNMENT**

- *Interview at least one adult member of your family about the precautions your family has taken over the past decade to protect itself from criminal activity. Has your family installed a security system, new door or window locks, or bars on basement windows? Has your family installed new lighting outside your home, a motion detector, or a closed circuit camera? Has your family purchased a gun for protection? Have any members of your family been motivated to take a course in self-defence or the martial arts to protect themselves in case of attack? Once you have drawn up a list of safety precautions your family has taken over the past decade, ask your respondent to indicate the degree to which he or she was personally victimized by crime during the past decade and during the decade before that. Answers can be given on a scale of 1 to 5, where 1 indicates no criminal victimization and 5 indicates a lot of criminal victimization. Also, ask your respondent to indicate the degree to which other family members were personally victimized by crime during the past decade and during the decade before that, again on a scale of 1 to 5.*
- *Write a report based on the results of your survey. In 250–500 words address these questions:*
- *Does the amount of criminal victimization experienced by your respondent or other family members over two decades explain the degree to which your family has taken new safety precautions over the past decade? If so, exactly how is victimization related to safety precautions? If not, how do you explain the degree to which your family has taken new safety precautions over the past decade?*

Moreover, we must remember that capital punishment, where it is actually practised, is hardly a matter of blind justice. Research conducted in the United States reveals that, other things being equal, killers of white people are more likely to receive death sentences than killers of black people, especially if the murderer is black (Culver, 1992). Social class is also a factor. A study conducted in Texas in 2000 found that people represented

## Figure 5.7
## The Death Penalty Worldwide, 2005

The most controversial punishment is the death penalty, or capital punishment. Much research shows that it is not an effective deterrent, and concern continues to rise regarding racial bias and wrongful conviction in its use. Despite the controversy, 48 percent of the world's countries allow capital punishment for at least some types of crimes.

■ Source: Infoplease (2005).

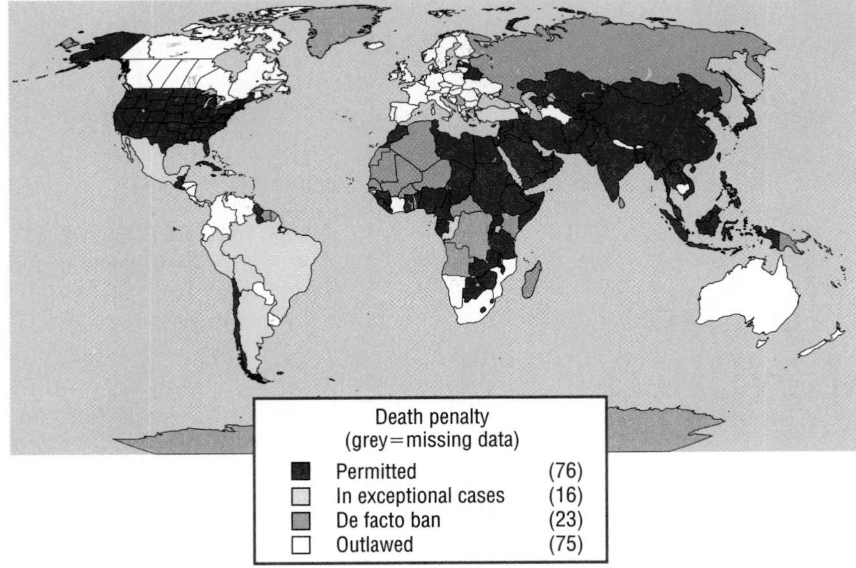


by court-appointed lawyers were 28 percent more likely to be convicted than those who could afford to hire their own lawyers and, if convicted, 44 percent more likely to be sentenced to death (Vago and Nelson, 2003: 205). As such, we cannot view the death penalty as a justly administered punishment.

Sometimes people favour capital punishment because they think it saves money. They argue that killing someone outright costs less than keeping the person alive in prison for the rest of his or her life. However, the experience of the United States suggests otherwise. In that country, where an exhaustive system of judicial review is required before anyone is executed, trials of capital cases cost more than $2.6 million each on average—enough to keep a man in prison in Canada for almost 40 years (Costanzo, 1997).

Finally, in assessing capital punishment, remember that mistakes are common. Nearly 40 percent of death sentences in the United States since 1977 have been overturned because of new evidence or mistrial (Haines, 1996). In Canada, the wrongful convictions of Donald Marshall, Guy Paul Morin, David Milgaard—and many others in recent times—for murders they did not commit should be sufficient to remind us that the wheels of justice do not always turn smoothly.

### Alternative Strategies

In recent years, analysts have suggested two main reforms to our prison regime. First, they have argued that we should reconsider rehabilitation. Advocates of rehabilitation suggest that the rate of **recidivism,** or the degree to which convicted offenders commit another crime, can be reduced through such programs as education and job training, individual and group therapy, substance abuse counselling, and behaviour modification. Second, they have argued that, whenever possible, we should attempt to reduce the number of incarcerated offenders. Proponents of this idea say that at least part of the increase in crime in the past four decades is attributable to the introduction of new and broadened definitions of criminal conduct. They believe that charging and imprisoning more and more Canadians, especially youth, is unlikely to help these individuals develop pro-social behaviour. Accordingly, they advise us to seek alternative methods that divert adults and juveniles from formal criminal justice system processing.

Although alternative procedures vary in each province and territory, their use generally arises after the police or Crown prosecutor recommends that an offender be considered suitable for "diversion." One example of an alternative measure is a victim–offender reconciliation program (VORP) in which victim and offender meet under controlled circumstances. Victims have the opportunity to describe the impact the crime has had on them, and offenders are usually required to apologize to their victims and compensate them financially. Tens of thousands of youth cases are dealt with by alternative measures programs every year. Most cases referred for diversion involve theft under $5000 (e.g., shoplifting), which is not surprising, because to be recommended for diversion, the offence must be minor. To be considered candidates for diversion, offenders must first acknowledge that they are guilty of the act they have been accused of committing. Young offenders selected for inclusion in the program are usually more than 15 years old, and they generally complete the provisions of the agreements they make (Tufts, 2000).

Similarly, the Supreme Court of Canada has urged judges to "take into account the primary importance of restorative justice principles within Aboriginal conceptions of sentencing," especially for less serious offences (Hendrick and Farmer, 2002: 11). Restorative justice deals with the harmful effects of crime "by engaging victims, offenders and the community in a process of reparation and healing" (Solicitor General, 2002a). This model of justice views crime as behaviour that violates people and relationships rather than the state and its laws. Within a restorative justice framework, each offence is considered in terms of its moral, social, economic, political, religious, and cosmic considerations (Bryant, 1999). Rather than focusing on punishment, restorative justice emphasizes individual and social healing, communication, and joint problem solving through restitution and reconciliation. Although the behaviour of the offender is condemned, the essential value of the individual is affirmed and the offender reassured that, through conformity, the stigma associated with a crime can be removed.

In like fashion, proponents of decarceration recommend that such options as fines (the most commonly used penal sanction in Canada), probation, and community service become more widely used as alternatives to imprisonment.

Not everyone views such strategies as desirable. It has been argued that the increased use of community programs does not truly reduce the numbers of people subject to formal social control. Rather, such strategies may simply "widen the net" through the creation of more intensive, intrusive, and prolonged control mechanisms (Lowman, Menzies, and Palys, 1987). Noting such objections, some analysts suggest that we go further still and lobby for legislative reform that would decriminalize certain categories of conduct currently prohibited under Canadian criminal law, such as marijuana possession. This last suggestion serves to remind us, yet again, that crime and deviance are social constructs.

## The Points of the Compass

When Robert Merton was looking for a term to denote deviants and criminals, he settled on "innovators." It was a revealing choice. As we saw, Merton's theory is based on the idea that deviants and criminals are, to a degree, the architects of their own fate. They innovate when they create alternative and illegitimate means of achieving their society's goals. Merton recognized that certain social conditions promote innovation, but his choice of terms emphasizes the freedom of choice inherent in every deviant and criminal act.

Other giants in the study of deviance and crime, especially those we have labelled motivational theorists, have learned Merton's lesson well. When they analyze the forces that drive some people to commit deviant and criminal acts, they stress that deviants and criminals do not respond mechanically to the conditions of their existence. Instead, considerable instruction, imagination, and daring are needed to break norms and laws, create deviant and criminal subcultures, avoid sanctions, and stay one step ahead of the law. Motivational theorists know that they can't sketch an accurate picture of deviance and crime if they ignore the point of the sociological compass marked "freedom."

Constraint theorists balance our appreciation of the sources of deviance and crime by stressing the opposite point of the sociological compass. They want to know things like why social control mechanisms work under some circumstances (producing conformity) and fail to work under others (producing deviance and crime). They also want to know how the distribution of power in society tends to impose deviant and criminal labels on some categories of the population but not others. By focusing on the operation or non-operation of social constraints, they add much to our understanding of how human freedom is channelled to produce particular patterns of social action, both conformist and nonconformist.

## Summary

1. *What are deviance and crime? What determines how serious a deviant or criminal act is?*

Deviance involves breaking a norm. Crime involves breaking a law. Both crime and deviance evoke societal reactions that help define the seriousness of the rule-breaking incident. The seriousness of deviant and criminal acts depends on the severity of the societal response to them, their perceived harmfulness, and the degree of public agreement about whether they should be considered deviant or criminal.

2. *Are definitions of deviance and crime the same everywhere and at all times?*

No. Definitions of deviance and crime vary historically and culturally. These definitions are socially defined and constructed. They are not inherent in actions or the characteristics of people.

3. *In what sense is power a key element in defining deviance and crime?*

Powerful groups are generally able to create norms and laws that suit their interests. Less powerful groups are usually unable to do so. For example, the increasing power of women has led to greater recognition of crimes committed against them. However, no similar increase has occurred in the prosecution of white-collar criminals because the distribution of power between classes has not changed much in recent decades.

4. *Where do crime statistics come from?*

Crime statistics come mainly from official sources and self-report surveys.

**5.** ***How has the rate of crime changed in Canada over the past four decades?***

A crime wave occurred in the 1960s and 1970s. The crime rate began to decrease substantially in the 1990s because of more policing, a smaller proportion of young men in the population, a booming economy, and perhaps also a decline in the number of unwanted children resulting from the availability of abortion.

**6.** ***Why do Aboriginal Canadians experience disproportionately high arrest, conviction, and incarceration rates?***

Aboriginal Canadians experience disproportionately high arrest, conviction, and incarceration rates because of the poverty of Aboriginal communities, racial discrimination in the criminal justice system, the social disruption that was caused when these communities came into contact with Europeans, and the fact that Aboriginal peoples commit crimes that are more detectable than those committed by non-Aboriginal people.

**7.** ***What are the main types of theories of deviance and crime?***

Theories of deviance and crime include motivational theories (i.e., strain theory, subcultural theory, and the theory of differential association) and constraint theories (i.e., labelling theory, control theory, and conflict theory). Motivational theories focus on the forces that drive people to commit deviant and criminal acts. Constraint theories focus on the forces that impose or fail to impose conformity on human behaviour. Different theories illuminate different aspects of the process by which people are motivated to break rules and become defined as rule breakers.

**8.** ***What is the medicalization of deviance?***

The medicalization of deviance refers to the fact that medical definitions of deviant behaviour are becoming more prevalent in societies like ours. Deviance formerly defined as voluntary evil is now being defined as involuntary sickness and is coming under the sway of health care professionals.

**9.** ***What kind of society uses prisons for punishment? How has the rationale for using prisons changed?***

Modern industrial societies rely on prisons as important forms of punishment. Prisons now focus less on rehabilitation than on isolating and incapacitating inmates.

**10.** ***What is a moral panic?***

A moral panic occurs when many people fervently believe that some form of deviance or crime poses a profound threat to society's well-being. For example, a moral panic about crime has engulfed North America, although crime rates have been falling recently. In all aspects of crime prevention and punishment, many North Americans have taken a "get-tough" stance. Some commercial and political groups benefit from the moral panic over crime and therefore encourage it.

**11.** ***What are some of the problems with the death penalty as a form of punishment?***

Although the death penalty ranks high as a form of revenge, its effectiveness as a deterrent is questionable. Moreover, the death penalty is administered in a racially biased manner, does not save money, and sometimes results in tragic mistakes.

**12.** ***How should Canadians respond to crime?***

The question of how we should respond to crime has resulted in many different suggestions. They range from the re-introduction of capital punishment to the suggestion that we apply restorative justice more widely and decriminalize various types of conduct currently prohibited under Canadian law.

## Key Terms

constraint theories (p. 144)
control theory (p. 149)
crime (p. 133)
deviance (p. 133)
differential association (p. 147)
formal punishment (p. 135)
informal punishment (p. 135)
labelling theory (p. 148)
law (p. 133)
medicalization of deviance (p. 152)
moral panic (p. 156)
motivational theories (p. 144)
recidivism rates (p. 158)
self-report surveys (p. 139)
stigma (p. 135)
strain theory (p. 146)
street crimes (p. 138)
subcultural theory (p. 146)
techniques of neutralization (p. 146)
victimization surveys (p. 140)
victimless crimes (p. 139)
white-collar crime (p. 138)

## Questions to Consider

1. Has this chapter changed your view of criminals and the criminal justice system? If so, how? If not, why not?
2. Do you think that different theories are useful in explaining different types of deviance and crime? Or do you think that one or two theories explain all types of deviance and crime and that other theories are not very illuminating? Justify your answer by using logic and evidence.
3. Do TV crime shows and crime movies give a different picture of crime than this chapter gives? What are the major differences? Which picture do you think is more accurate? Why?

## Web Resources

### Companion Web Site for This Book

http://www.pointsofthecompass.nelson.com

Begin by clicking on the Student Resources section of the Web site. Next, select the chapter you are currently studying from the pull-down menu. From the Student Resources page you will have easy access to InfoTrac® College Edition, MicroCase online exercises, and additional Weblinks. The Web site also has many useful tips to aid you in your study of sociology, including practice tests for each chapter.

### InfoTrac® Search Terms

These search terms are provided to assist you in beginning to conduct research on this topic by visiting **http://www.infotrac-college.com**:

**moral panic**
**prison**
**stigma**
**street crime**
**white-collar crime**

### Recommended Web Sites

For a measure of how widespread corruption is in the governments of every country in the world, visit **http://www.transparency.org/policy_research/surveys_indices/cpi/2006**.

What makes crime news? For interesting material on this subject, visit **http://www.criminology.fsu.edu/cjlinks/media2.html**.

For Canadian crime and justice statistics, visit the Statistics Canada Web site at **http://www40.statcan.ca/l01/ind01/l2_2693.htm**.

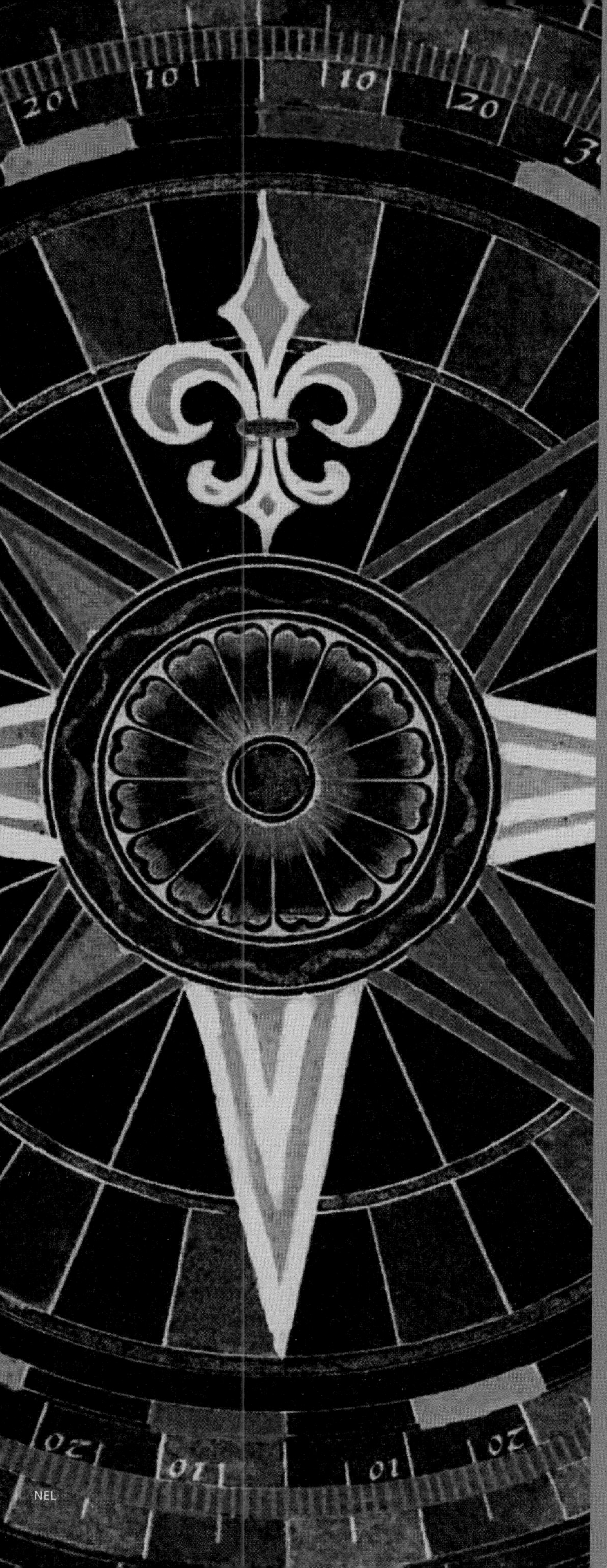

# PART 3 INEQUALITY

# chapter 6

## social stratification: canadian and global perspectives



### In this chapter, you will learn that

→ Wealth and income are unequally distributed in Canada. The government plays a small but important role in redistributing money to children and families who are poor.

→ Although some sociologists used to think that talent and hard work alone determined a person's position in the socioeconomic hierarchy, it is now clear that being a member of certain groups limits opportunities for success. In this sense, social structure shapes the distribution of inequality.

→ Most theories of social inequality focus on its economic roots. Some theories regard inequality as inevitable and others regard it as doomed to disappear, but the reality probably lies somewhere between these two extremes: inequality can be lessened under certain circumstances.

→ Prestige and power are important non-economic sources of inequality.

→ Global inequality has increased tremendously since industrialization and is still increasing in some respects today.

→ Global inequality has two competing explanations. One stresses how the deficiencies of some societies contribute to their own lack of economic growth. The other stresses how the history of social relations among countries enriched some nations at the expense of others.

→ For identifiable reasons, some non-Western countries have successfully industrialized.

# Social Stratification: Shipwrecks and Inequality

Writers and filmmakers sometimes tell stories about shipwrecks and their survivors to make a point about social inequality. They use the shipwreck as a literary device. It allows them to sweep away all traces of privilege and social convention. What remains are human beings stripped to their essentials, guinea pigs in an imaginary laboratory for the study of wealth and poverty, power and powerlessness, esteem and disrespect.

The tradition began with Daniel Defoe's *Robinson Crusoe,* first published in 1719. Defoe tells the story of an Englishman marooned on a desert island. His strong will, hard work, and inventiveness turn the poor island into a thriving colony. Defoe was one of the first writers to portray capitalism favourably. He believed that people get rich if they possess the virtues of good businesspeople—and stay poor if they don't.

The 1975 Italian movie *Swept Away* tells almost exactly the opposite story. In the movie, a beautiful woman, one of the idle rich, boards her yacht for a cruise in the Mediterranean. She treats the hardworking deck hands in a condescending and abrupt way. The deck hands do their jobs but seethe with resentment. Then comes the storm. The yacht is shipwrecked. Only the beautiful woman and one handsome deck hand remain alive, marooned on a desert island. Now equals, the two survivors soon have passionate sex and fall in love. All is well until the day of their rescue. As soon as they return to the mainland, the woman resumes her haughty ways. She turns her back on the deck hand, who is reduced again to the role of a common labourer. Thus, the movie sends the audience three harsh messages. First, it is possible to be rich without working hard, because a person can inherit wealth. Second, people can work hard without becoming rich. Third, something about the structure of society causes inequality, for inequality disappears only on the desert island, without society as we know it.

*Titanic* is a more recent movie on the shipwreck-and-inequality theme. At one level, the movie shows that class differences are important. For example, in first class, living conditions are luxurious, whereas in third class they are cramped. Indeed, on the *Titanic,* class differences spell the difference between life and death. After the *Titanic* strikes the iceberg off the coast of Newfoundland and Labrador, the ship's crew prevents second- and third-class passengers from entering the few available lifeboats. They give priority to rescuing first-class passengers. Consequently, 75 percent of third-class passengers perished, compared with 40 percent of first-class passengers.

As the tragedy of the *Titanic* unfolds, however, another contradictory theme emerges. Under some circumstances, we learn, class differences can be insignificant. In the movie, the sinking of the *Titanic* is the backdrop to a fictional love story about a wealthy young woman in first class and a working-class youth in the decks below. The sinking of the *Titanic* and the collapse of its elaborate class structure give the young lovers an opportunity to cross class lines and profess their devotion to each other. At one level, then, the movie *Titanic* is an optimistic tale that holds out hope for a society in which class differences matter little.

Kate Winslet (Rose) and Leonardo DiCaprio (Jack) in a scene from *Titanic*

*Robinson Crusoe*, *Swept Away*, and *Titanic* raise many of the issues we address in this chapter. What are the sources of social inequality? Do determination, industry, and ingenuity shape the distribution of advantages and disadvantages in society, as the tale of *Robinson Crusoe* portrays? Or is *Swept Away* more accurate? Do certain patterns of social relations underlie and shape that distribution? Is *Titanic*'s first message of social class differences still valid? Does social inequality still have big consequences for the way we live? What about *Titanic*'s second message? Can people overcome or reduce inequality in society? If so, how?

To answer these questions, we first sketch patterns of social stratification in Canada and globally. We then critically review major theories of **social stratification,** the way society is organized in layers or strata. We also analyze the movement of individuals up and down the stratification system over time. Finally, we round out our discussion by analyzing non-economic dimensions of inequality, including power and prestige.

# Patterns of Social Inequality

## *Wealth*

Your wealth is what you own. For most adults, it includes a house (minus the mortgage), a car (minus the car loan), and some appliances, furniture, and savings (minus the credit card balance). Wealth is assets minus liabilities. Owning a nice house and a good car and having a substantial sum of money invested securely enhances your sense of well-being. You know you have a cushion to fall back on in difficult times and

**Table 6.1**
Canada's Wealthiest Families, 2006

| World Rank | Surname | US$ Billion | Source | Inheritance |
|---|---|---|---|---|
| 10 | Thomson | 22.0 | Publishing | Yes |
| 93 | Weston | 7.9 | Retail food | Yes |
| 129 | Irving | 5.8 | Oil refining, etc. | Yes |
| 165 | Rogers | 4.9 | Mass media | Yes |
| 188 | Sherman | 4.4 | Pharmaceuticals | No |
| 204 | Skoll | 4.2 | Internet | No |
| 214 | Desmarais | 4.0 | Financial services, communications | No |
| 230 | Pattison | 3.8 | Advertising, etc. | No |
| 314 | Miller | 2.9 | Electronics distribution | No |
| 349 | McCain | 2.6 | Food processing | Yes |
| 390 | Bronfman | 2.4 | Liquor | Yes |
| 538 | Jarislowsky | 1.9 | Finance | No |
| 538 | Katz | 1.9 | Pharmacies | No |
| 557 | Saputo | 1.8 | Dairy | Yes |
| 557 | Schnaider | 1.8 | Steel, etc. | No |

Source: Forbes.com (2007).

you know you don't have to worry about paying for your children's postsecondary education or how you will make ends meet during retirement. Wealth can also give you more political influence. Campaign contributions to political parties and donations to favourite political causes increase the chance that policies you favour will become law. Wealth even improves your health. Because you can afford to engage in leisure pursuits, turn off stress, consume high-quality food, and employ superior medical services, you are likely to live a healthier and longer life than someone who lacks these advantages.

The Thomsons, Canada's wealthiest family, rank 10th on the list of the world's wealthiest families. Before his death in 2006, Ken Thomson handed over the reins of the Thomson publishing empire to his son, David.

We list the 15 wealthiest Canadian families in Table 6.1. Their net worth ranges from US$22.0 billion to US$1.8 billion. These sums are so big that they are hard to imagine. You can begin to grasp them by considering that it would take you three years to spend $1 million at the rate of $1000 a day. How long would it take you to spend $1 billion? If you spent $1000 a day, you couldn't spend the entire sum in a lifetime. It would take nearly 3000 years to spend $1 billion at the rate of $1000 a day—assuming you didn't invest part to earn still more money.

Unfortunately, wealth figures are sparse. However, one recent government study gives us some insight into how net worth (defined as assets minus debt) changed between 1984 and 2005 (see Figure 6.1). Dividing Canadian families into the poorest fifth (or "quintile"), the second-poorest fifth, the middle fifth, the second-richest fifth, and the richest fifth, we see that over this 21-year period the big winners were the richest families. The net worth of the richest quintile increased by more than 64 percent, taking inflation into account. Gains in wealth decrease as you

**Figure 6.1**
**Median Net Worth of Families, Canada, 1984, 1999, 2005 (in 1999 dollars)**

■ Source: Statistics Canada (2006d).

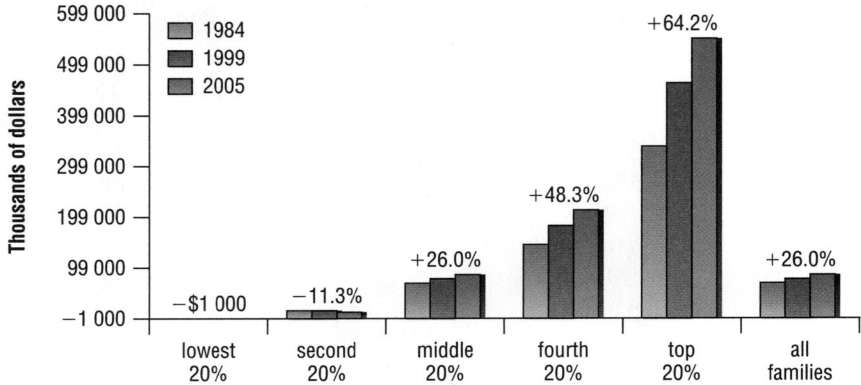


In each 20-percent category, half the cases are wealthier than the median and half are less wealthy. The following assets are not included: employer-sponsored pension plans, contents of the home, collectibles and valuables, annuities, and registered retirement income funds. If these items were included, wealth inequalities would be greater than shown.

move down the scale and turn into losses for the bottom 40 percent of families. The second quintile of families was, on average, more than 11 percent poorer in 2005 than in 1984, and the bottom quintile of families was on average $1000 poorer. This permits us to conclude that, in terms of wealth, the rich are getting richer while the poor are getting poorer.

## *Income*

Income is the amount of money earned in a given period. In 1951 the average Canadian family earned about $3500, while in 2001 it earned close to $60 000. This may be a 17-fold increase, but it is less impressive than it sounds. More than half the gain is due to inflation. After all, a soft drink that once cost a dime now costs a dollar. Moreover, the number of earners per family increased as more women entered the paid labour force. As a result, more people are now generating the income of the average family than was the case in 1951. Even so, Canadian families earn considerably more now than they did half a century ago because they are more productive. That is, the average worker is more skilled and is using more sophisticated technology to produce more goods and services.

How has the distribution of income changed over time? Is economic inequality growing or shrinking? To answer these questions, we can again divide the population into fifths, but this time by income: the top 20 percent of families and unattached individuals by income, the second 20 percent, the middle 20 percent, and so forth. We can then determine what percentage of all income earned in Canada in a year is earned by each fifth. A completely unequal distribution would exist if the top quintile earned 100 percent of the country's income. A completely equal distribution would exist if each quintile earned 20 percent of the country's income.

Figure 6.2 shows that in 2002, the bottom quintile of families and unattached individuals earned just 4.6 percent of all income, while the top quintile earned 45.0 percent. Almost half of all income was earned by the richest quintile. Moreover, the distribution of income has become more unequal since 1951. For example, in 2002 the bottom

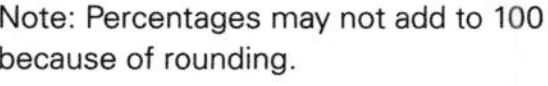

**Figure 6.2**

**The Distribution of Total Income among Families and Unattached Individuals, Canada, 1951 and 2002**

Note: Percentages may not add to 100 because of rounding.

■ Source: Adapted in part from Statistics Canada (n.d.-1).

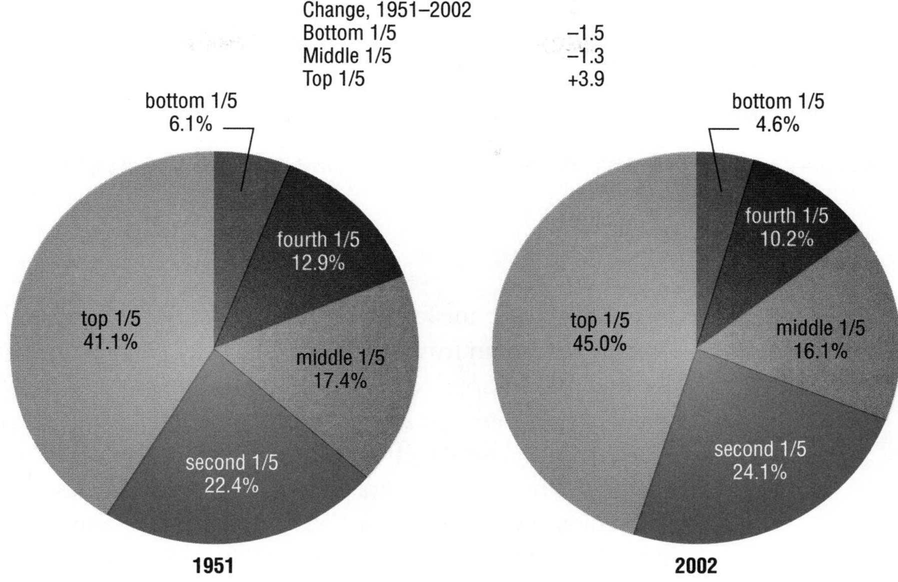


quintile received 4.6 percent of income, while in 1951 the comparable figure was 6.1 percent. At the top end, the richest quintile increased its share of income over the past 50 years from 41.1 percent of income to 45.0 percent. This pattern mirrors a trend witnessed in most rich countries: income gaps have been widening for decades (Förster and Pellizzari, 2000).

The incomes just reported represent the money that Canadians earn before paying income tax and receiving government benefits. But Canada is a welfare state that collects taxes and redistributes them in the form of welfare payments, employment insurance payments, child tax credits, GST credits, and so on. The richest fifth of Canadians lose about a fifth of their income to income tax, while the poorest fifth of Canadians see their incomes increase by nearly two-thirds as a result of government transfers.

## Explanations of Income Inequality

Why do some people fall into the highest quintile and others into the lowest? What explains the distribution of income? Obviously, a person's job has a significant influence. Bank managers are paid more than bank tellers, schoolteachers more than daycare workers. As well, people who work more earn more. But these are rather obvious factors that predict earnings. They can't be ignored, but are there more general factors that explain income inequality?

We know that some individuals earn high salaries because of their natural talent. Jarome Iginla (hockey), Karen Kain (ballet), Ben Heppner (opera), Lorie Kane (golf), Jim Carrey (acting), Shania Twain (popular music), and Mike Weir (golf) are Canadians whose success on the world stage has provided them with substantial earnings. The principal reason for their excellence is a natural endowment in dance, music, or athletics. A genetic gift sets them apart. At the other end of the economic spectrum, some people

**Figure 6.3**
Explanations for Income Inequality

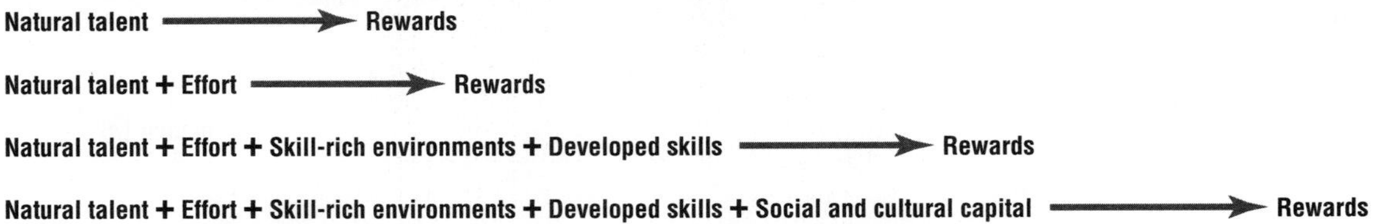


have the genetic misfortune of Down syndrome, schizophrenia, or autism, conditions that prevent them from earning big salaries. Such people, at both ends of the spectrum, are exceptions, however. Sociologists believe that for the vast majority of people, genes play only a minor role in determining income.

Even for people with a natural talent in the performing arts or athletics, effort is essential. Practice and years of dedication to the basics of a profession are common to all who enjoy success. Effort is also significant for many Canadians who spend long hours at work—whether amassing billable hours in a law practice, doing the endless chores in a small business, or working overtime at a construction site. However, although diligence and perseverance might be necessary conditions for rewards, they are not sufficient. Effort alone does not result in high income (see Figure 6.3).

Raw talent needs to be sharpened. Training, coaching, schooling—these are crucial ways in which skills are developed and nurtured. Natural talents and our efforts are important ingredients in this process, to be sure, but education matters. Indeed, the importance of education as a determinant of occupation and income continues to increase (Baer, 1999; Statistics Canada, 2003c: 9). In 2000, for example, more than 60 percent of Canadians in the top earnings category ($100 000 or more) had a university degree; more than 60 percent of those in the lowest category (under $20 000) had a high school education or less. As the Canadian occupational structure moves further away from its traditional resource-based foundation to a more mature knowledge-driven economy, the importance of education will continue to grow (see Table 6.2).

Human capital theory stresses the increasing importance of education as a factor affecting economic success. If physical capital is understood as investment in industrial plants and equipment, **human capital** is investment in education and training. Just as productivity increases by upgrading manufacturing plants and introducing new technology, productivity gains can also result from investment in the skills and abilities of people. Jobs requiring advanced skills are increasingly numerous in Canada. Better educated workers are more skilled and more productive in these jobs because they have made investments in acquiring the skills and knowledge essential to our economy (Betcherman and Lowe, 1997).

Much evidence supports a human capital interpretation of the link between schooling and incomes (Baer, 1999). However, this is not a complete explanation for why people earn what they earn. For example, in the legal profession, almost everyone makes the same human capital investment. Every lawyer acquires a law degree. Yet economic rewards vary even for people with the same experience and type of legal practice (Kay and Hagan, 1998).

**Table 6.2**
Average Hourly Earnings by Occupational Group, Canada, February 2007

| Occupational Group | Average Hourly Earnings ($) |
|---|---|
| Management occupations | 31.37 |
| Natural and applied sciences and related occupations | 28.38 |
| Occupations in social science, education, government service, and religion | 25.82 |
| Health occupations | 23.85 |
| Occupations in art, culture, recreation, and sport | 20.26 |
| Trades, transport and equipment operators, and related occupations | 20.03 |
| Occupations unique to primary industry | 18.85 |
| Occupations unique to processing, manufacturing, and utilities | 17.42 |
| Sales and service occupations | 13.46 |

Source: Statistics Canada (2007b).

Part of the reason that people with the same amount of human capital may receive different economic rewards is that they possess different amounts of social capital. **Social capital** refers to people's networks or connections. Individuals are more likely to succeed if they have strong bonds of trust, cooperation, mutual respect, and obligation with well-positioned individuals or families. Knowing the right people, and having strong links to them, helps in finding opportunities and taking advantage of them (Coleman, 1988).

A related version of this argument is captured in the notion of cultural capital (Bourdieu and Passeron, 1990). **Cultural capital** comprises the set of social skills people have: their ability to impress others, to use tasteful language and images effectively, and thus to influence and persuade people. Although the notion of social capital stresses your networks and connections with others, the idea of cultural capital emphasizes your impression management skills, your ability to influence others. In different ways, both concepts emphasize being part of the right "social club."

What the concepts of social and cultural capital also have in common is the idea that families higher in the social hierarchy enjoy more capital of all types. Connections and culture help you find a good job. The hiring of new recruits, then, depends on the talent, effort, and skills that people bring to the interview, but it also depends on the connections and culture that people have. Indeed, culture and connections often influence who gets an interview.

In summary, natural talent and effort are important, and for a few occupations very significant (e.g., opera singer, golfer). For most Canadians, level of education (or developed skill) is a critical factor in finding continuous, well-paying employment. In addition, social and cultural capital are consequential for many people in finding economic success. Explaining an individual's position in the income hierarchy depends on several factors, but the four themes outlined in Figure 6.3 are crucial.

## *Poverty*

At the bottom of the income distribution are the homeless. In recent decades the number of people with "no fixed address" has increased considerably. We do not know how many Canadians are homeless, but in cities across the country, people sleep under bridges, in back allies, behind dumpsters, and in thickets in public parks. They do so night after night, month after month.

Homelessness is one manifestation of **poverty.** Exactly how many Canadians are poor is a matter of intense debate. Poverty lacks an agreed-on definition. A first disagreement occurs around whether poverty should be defined in absolute or relative terms. An absolute definition of poverty focuses on essentials, suggesting that poor families have inadequate resources to acquire the necessities of life (food, clothing, and shelter). Agreement on "essentials" depends on values and judgments (Sarlo, 2001). What is essential varies from time to time, place to place, and group to group. Many of our ancestors lived without indoor plumbing, and some Canadians still do, but most people would define indoor plumbing as essential. A family could survive on a steady diet of cod and potatoes, but most would define such a family as poor.

A relative poverty line also has certain drawbacks. Two issues are central: relative to what, and how relative? Whether poverty ought to be defined narrowly in terms of economic measures (e.g., income) or more broadly with respect to community standards (e.g., safety of working conditions, environmental quality, housing stock) illustrates this second area of disagreement. Most definitions tend to be narrow, focusing primarily on income. But even if a relative poverty line is defined narrowly, how relative ought it to be? One-third of average income? one-half? some other fraction?

Yet another disagreement plagues any definition. Should poverty be defined on the basis of income or consumption? Because "bare essentials" is a core idea in any definition of poverty, it makes good sense to think about, and measure, poverty as the cost of purchasing bare essentials. Deprivation occurs when a family cannot acquire the essentials, not necessarily when income is too low. Income and consumption are correlated, of course, but people with high net wealth can live off their savings even with low income.

In one sense, the definition of poverty means little to a homeless person sleeping on a hot air vent. The immediate experience of poverty by families in remote coastal communities, by single parents in the urban core, and by farmers on the Prairies is unaffected by whether poverty is defined absolutely or relatively, narrowly or broadly, by income or by consumption. However, the definition of poverty is consequential for these people because social policies are enacted, or not enacted, based on levels and trends in poverty. Definitions matter.

Social policy has a profound impact on the distribution of opportunities and rewards in Canada. Politics can reshape the distribution of income and the system of inequality by changing laws governing people's right to own property. Politicians can also alter patterns of inequality by entitling people to various welfare benefits and by redistributing income through tax policies. When politicians de-emphasize poverty, legislative efforts to maintain or expand welfare benefits and redistribute income are less likely. A definition of poverty showing fewer poor Canadians implies little need for government action. Conversely, for politicians and political parties supporting the poor, a definition of poverty showing a growing proportion of poor people is beneficial to their cause.

In addition to poverty definitions having political consequences, they are important research tools for the sociologist. A democratic society depends on the full participation of all citizens—everyone has the right to vote, anyone can run for political office, and everyone's voice should influence political choices. As the National Council of Welfare (1999a: 4) argues, the proportion of Canadians who are poor is "one measure of how well our democracy is working." Can someone without a permanent home or someone in a family with bare cupboards participate fully in our national affairs?

Unlike some other countries, such as the United States, Canada does not have an official definition of poverty. Statistics Canada argues that there is no internationally accepted definition of poverty and that any definition is arbitrary. Therefore, it does not attempt to estimate the number of Canadians who are poor (Fellegi, 2000: 124). Instead, Statistics Canada reports what it calls a "low income cutoff." This cutoff conveys "the income level at which a family may be in straitened circumstances because it has to spend a greater proportion of its income on necessities than the average family of similar size" (Statistics Canada, 2000c: 122). The threshold is reported for seven different family sizes and for five sizes of community because "straitened circumstances" depend on the number of people in your family and the place you live. Most advocates for the poor interpret these thresholds, shown for 2005 in Table 6.3, as poverty lines. For example, in Canada's largest cities, a family of four with an income less than $32 556 after government transfer payments would be considered poor. In 2004, 15.5 percent of Canadians lived in poverty by this definition (CBC News, 2006).

### Myths about Poverty

The language we use to speak of the poor is often revealing. For example, referring to someone as "poor but honest" or "poor but virtuous" implicitly suggests that we view such combinations as unlikely and feel it necessary to single out those who possess both characteristics as exceptions to the rule. Popular mythology also depicts the poor—especially those who receive public assistance (i.e., welfare)—as lazy, irresponsible, and lacking in motivation, abilities, and moral values. These images are potent and contribute to stereotypes of the "deserving" and the "undeserving" poor (e.g., war

**Table 6.3**
After-Tax Low Income Cutoffs (LICOs), 2005

| | | Size of Community, by Population | | | |
|---|---|---|---|---|---|
| **Family Size** | **Rural** | **Under 30 000** | **30 000 to 99 999** | **100 000 to 499 999** | **Over 500 000** |
| 1 | $11 264 | $12 890 | $14 380 | $14 562 | $17 219 |
| 2 | $13 709 | $15 690 | $17 502 | $17 723 | $20 956 |
| 3 | $17 071 | $19 535 | $21 794 | $22 069 | $26 095 |
| 4 | $21 296 | $24 373 | $27 190 | $27 532 | $32 556 |
| 5 | $24 251 | $27 754 | $30 962 | $31 351 | $37 071 |
| 6 | $26 895 | $30 780 | $34 338 | $34 769 | $41 113 |
| 7+ | $29 539 | $33 806 | $37 713 | $38 187 | $45 155 |

Source: Statistics Canada (2006e).

veterans and children versus "welfare bums" and those "looking for a handout"). However, research conducted in the past few decades shows that many of the stereotypes about the poor are myths.

- *Myth 1: People are poor because they don't want to work.* The myth that poor people don't want to work fails to acknowledge that many poor people cannot work because of a disability or because they must take care of their young children because of inadequate child-care provisions in Canada. Moreover, it ignores that many poor people work full time, and many more work part time. But having a job is no guarantee of escaping poverty because the minimum wage set by provincial and territorial governments is so low. In September 2007, the minimum wage was $8 an hour in Ontario, Quebec, British Columbia, Alberta, and Manitoba. Even if a person living in Toronto, Montreal, Vancouver, Edmonton, or Winnipeg worked 52 weeks at 40 hours a week for $8 an hour, he or she would earn only $16 640 a year—$579 below the low-income cutoff (see Table 6.3). But it gets worse. Among Canada's ten provinces, Quebec has historically had the highest minimum wage and Newfoundland and Labrador the lowest. Figure 6.4 shows how the minimum wage changed from 1965 to 2006 in these two provinces. The numbers in Figure 6.4 take inflation into account; they are expressed in terms of the purchasing power of 1992 dollars. This means that in Quebec in 2006, the hourly minimum wage allowed a person to buy as much as $5.97 would have allowed that individual to buy in 1992. In Newfoundland and Labrador, the comparable figure was $5.39. In terms of purchasing power, the minimum wage has thus *fallen* by about 25 percent across Canada since the mid-1970s. The low minimum wage thus ensures widespread low income and poverty.
- *Myth 2: Most poor people are immigrants.* Actually, only recent immigrants experience poverty rates significantly higher than the Canadian-born; and recent immigrants are only a small fraction of all Canadian immigrants. Moreover, once they are established, immigrants have lower poverty rates than people born in Canada (National Council of Welfare, 2004).

**Figure 6.4**
**The Minimum Wage in Quebec and Newfoundland and Labrador, 1965–2006 (in 1992 dollars)**

Note: (1) Until the early 1970s, women received a lower minimum wage than men. The data reported here are for the male minimum wage. (2) The minimum wage declined from about 1973 until the mid- to late 1980s because conflict in the Middle East caused the price of oil to triple and then triple again, leading to rapid inflation, while, for part of this period, the federal government imposed wage controls. Subsequently, the real minimum wage recovered about 20 percent by 2006.

Sources: Human Resources and Social Development Canada (2006); Statistics Canada (2007c).

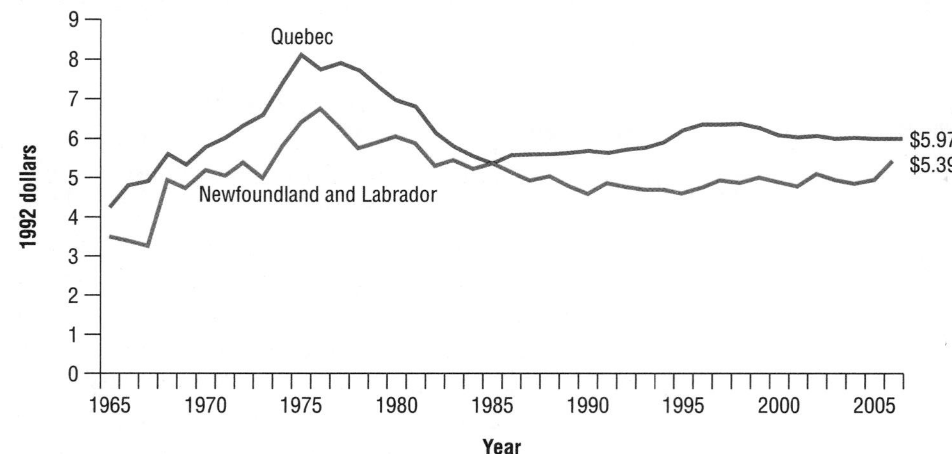

» *Myth 3: Most poor people are trapped in poverty.* One in three people with low income in 2002 escaped poverty by 2003. Of the roughly 25 percent of Canadians who had experienced one or more years of low income in 2003, only one in eight had lived in poverty for six years. On average, those who experienced low income for at least one year spent 2.8 years in poverty (Statistics Canada, 2004d: 124). We conclude that most people try to move out of difficult financial circumstances and most succeed, at least for a time.

## Explaining Poverty

Definitions aside, why are some Canadians poor? Answers to this question vary from individual-level explanations to structural explanations.

*Individual-level explanations* focus on the attributes of people who are poor, asking how these people differ from people who are not poor. This type of explanation focuses on causes that lie "within the person." Someone is poor, according to this logic, because of a personal attribute, such as low intelligence or a behaviour abnormality.

Some evidence suggests that individual attributes do explain a small amount of poverty. For example, we have noted that people with disabilities have a higher risk of living in poverty than do others. Not all people with disabilities live in poverty, however, and the vast majority of people living in poverty do not have a disability. On balance, this reminds us that poverty is, for the most part, not a consequence of individual attributes even though they are important in some cases.

A related explanation focuses more on the attitudes of individuals—not on attributes that are inherited, but on attributes or stigmas that are acquired. A social-psychological type of explanation emphasizes low self-esteem, lack of achievement motivation, and an inability to delay gratification. Poverty is perpetuated, on this logic, because poor families employ inadequate child-rearing practices, practices that enhance bad attitudes. A related version of this argument stresses a "culture of poverty," a way of thinking and acting shared by poor families. This culture reinforces and perpetuates itself through poor upbringing and ill-formed personalities.

Various objections undermine this type of explanation. First, it presents a chicken or egg problem. People who are poor may develop "bad attitudes," but these may result from poverty and not be causes of poverty. The culture of poverty might provide an adequate description for some circumstances, but it is not an adequate explanation in general. Put differently, descriptions of poverty stressing a culture of depression, lack of hope, and fatalism may be accurate, but these effects of poverty ought not to be confused with the causes of poverty. Second, many people who are poor do work, are religious, don't smoke or drink, and so on. Therefore, evidence that supports explanations founded on these personal deficits is often lacking.

Another type of explanation, one with greater currency in sociology, stresses the social organization of society, or subsystems in society, as explanations of poverty. The organization of our economy, for example, affects poverty. Capitalist economies feature cyclical booms and busts, periods of low unemployment and high profits, followed by high unemployment and low profits. During recessions, more people lose their jobs and fall into poverty. Moreover, as we have seen, people with minimum-wage jobs don't earn enough to escape poverty. The lack of good jobs is thus a major cause of poverty.

Other analysts stress social policy as a factor affecting poverty levels. For example, as noted above, if you received the minimum hourly wage while working full time, full year, you would still be poor, especially if you had children to support. In this sense, minimum wage legislation is a social policy that creates a group of working poor.

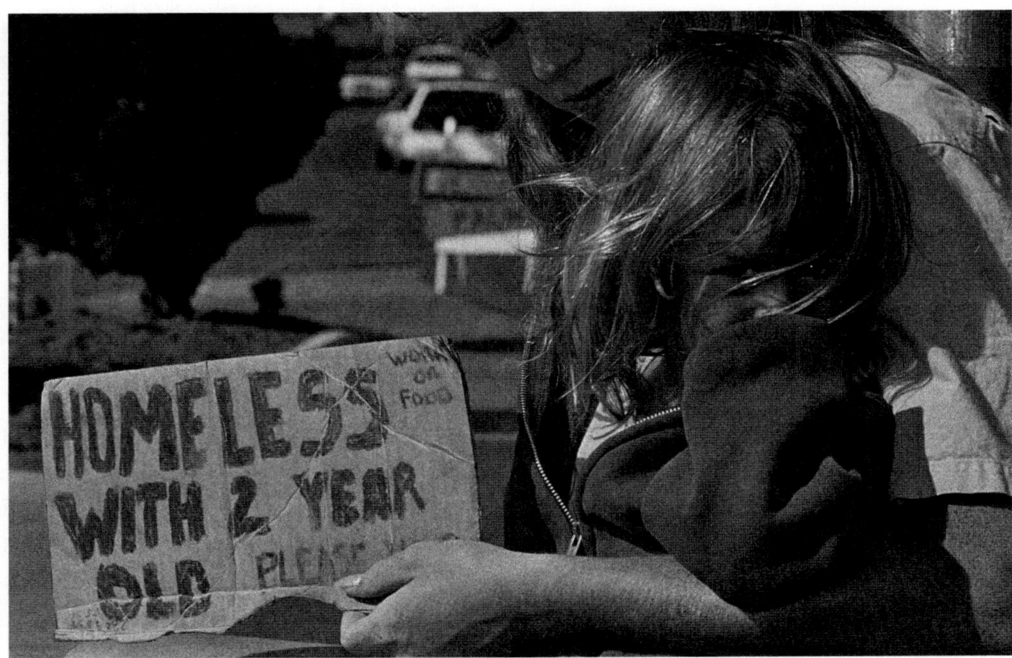


Answers to the question of why some people are poor vary from individual-level to structural explanations.

The social world is not quite so simple, of course, and if minimum wages were to rise too much or too quickly, so too might the level of unemployment because some employers might not be able to afford a sudden big jump in wages. Debate over these issues continues, but the point is that our social policies affect people's well-being, and understanding the consequences of policies is critical.

The system of tax collection and tax allocation illustrates another way that social policies affect poverty. A *progressive* tax system is one in which a greater proportion of income is paid in tax as incomes rise. For example, those who earn $100 000 pay a larger percentage of their income as tax than do those who earn $50 000. In Canada, although our income tax system is progressive, the overall tax system is relatively neutral. Most Canadian families pay about the same percentage of their total income in tax. This occurs because two interrelated factors undermine the "Robin Hood" effect of progressive income taxes. First, other taxes, such as GST and fuel taxes, are neutral. They are not based on the income of the taxpayer. Second, those who earn more are able to shelter much of their income from taxation in registered education saving plans and registered retirement savings plans, through capital gains tax exemptions, and so on. As a result, the tax system does little to erode poverty.

Finally, other sociologists stress ways of thinking, or ideological perspectives, as explanations for poverty. Negative images of various groups lead to an undervaluing of the ways of life of some people, such as Aboriginal people, recent immigrants, and members of visible minorities. Discrimination follows from this undervaluing. Discrimination causes poverty because it leads to less success in finding jobs and, when jobs are found, to more unsteady and low-paying work.

Is poverty an inevitable feature of society? It may be, at least to the extent that inequality is known to exist in all societies. However, the extent of poverty in Canada could be reduced if we chose to follow the examples of Western European nations. Many countries in Western Europe have poverty rates well below Canada's, because many European governments have established job training and child-care programs that allow poor people to take jobs with liveable wages and benefits. This is, however, clearly a political choice. Many Canadians argue that providing welfare benefits dampens the work ethic and actually perpetuates poverty (see Box 6.1). Although the Western European evidence does not support that view, the political will does not currently exist in Canada to change our social policies and alleviate poverty.

Is growing inequality inevitable? These are questions that have concerned sociologists for 150 years. We next review some classical answers to these questions in an effort to shed light on our prospects today.

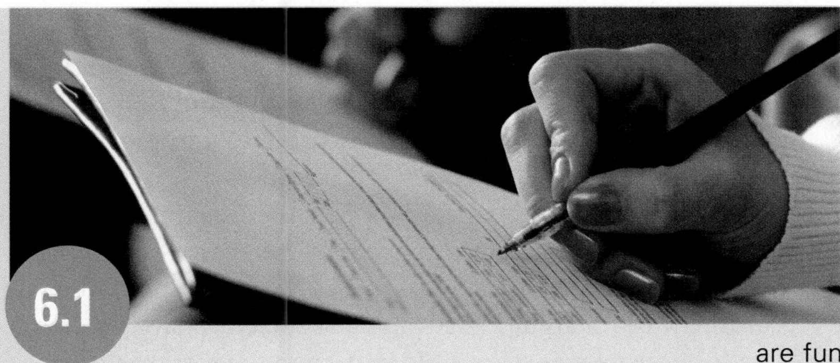

6.1

# SOCIAL POLICY: WHAT DO YOU THINK?

## Income Redistribution and Taxation

The idea of rugged individualism implies that our personal fortunes ought to rest on our own shoulders. Those who work hard, persevere, and make wise decisions supposedly deserve rewards. By implication, those who are lazy and unwise deserve less.

The contrasting idea of collective responsibility suggests that as members of a community we ought to look out for each other. In this view, those who have ought to share. The interests of the many should come before the riches of a few.

Few Canadians support either of these extreme ideas, but examples of each principle are easy to find. The unequal distribution of income in Canada and the high salaries of the presidents of large corporations are consistent with the theme of rugged individualism. Government support for postsecondary education and health care illustrates the theme of collective responsibility. Both of these themes represent contrasting social policies, one focused on the supremacy of individual rights, the other emphasizing collective responsibility and the common good.

How much tax revenue should governments collect, and should they redistribute that revenue in ways that benefit lower income groups? Should governments act like Robin Hood and transfer some tax money to the poor? Should governments support hospitals and schools with tax dollars, or should individual families pay directly for medical care and education? These are questions of social policy.

**CRITICAL THINKING QUESTIONS**

Here are some of the arguments for and against income redistribution, arguments that are fundamental to some of the major political debates in many countries in recent years. What choices would you make if you and your friends could run government for a few years? Why?

*Against Redistribution*

- *Taking from the rich and giving to the poor decreases the motivation for people in either group to work hard.*
- *Taking from one group and giving to another requires some agency first to collect money and then to allocate it. The cost of redistribution is high.*
- *Some individuals and families cheat and deceive. Some hide or misrepresent their earnings, either to pay less in tax or to receive more through welfare. Redistribution promotes both tax cheats and welfare frauds.*

*For Redistribution*

- *A society with a reasonable degree of equality is a better place to live than a society with a high level of inequality.*
- *An extra dollar to a poor family is more helpful than an extra dollar to a rich family.*
- *Improving the material well-being of a poor family through benevolence enhances the social well-being of a rich family.*
- *Aid to poorer families reduces the risk of crime and political conflict because poorer families are thereby less likely to seek illegal means of earning income or to unite in protest over living conditions.*

# Is Stratification Inevitable? Three Theories

## *Marx's Conflict Theory*

Karl Marx can fairly be regarded as the founder of conflict theory in sociology. It is ironic, therefore, that social stratification and the accompanying conflict between classes are *not* inevitable in Marx's view (Marx, 1904 [1859]; Marx and Engels, 1972 [1848]). He believed that capitalist growth would eventually produce a society without classes and therefore without class conflict.

In Marx's sense of the term, **class** is determined by a person's "relationship to the means of production" or the source of that person's income. The source of income is profit if the person owns a factory or a mine. It is a wage if he or she must work in a factory or a mine. Accordingly, Marx argued that capitalist societies have two main classes: the ownership class (or **bourgeoisie,** to use his term) and the working class (or what Marx termed the **proletariat**), distinguished from each other by whether they own productive property.

According to Marx, during the Industrial Revolution that began in Great Britain in the late eighteenth century, industrial owners were eager to adopt new tools, machines, and production methods so they could produce goods more efficiently and earn higher profits. Such innovations had unforeseen consequences, however. First, some owners were driven out of business by more efficient competitors. They were forced to become members of the working class. Together with former peasants pouring into the cities from the countryside to take factory jobs, this caused the working class to grow. Second, the drive for profits motivated owners to concentrate workers in increasingly larger factories, keep wages as low as possible, and invest as little as possible in improving working conditions. Thus, as the bourgeoisie grew richer and smaller, the proletariat grew larger and more impoverished.

As described in Chapter 1 (A Sociological Compass), Marx felt that workers would ultimately become aware of their exploitation. Their sense of *class consciousness* would, he wrote, encourage the growth of unions and workers' political parties. These organizations would eventually try to create a new "communist" society in which there would be no private wealth. Instead, under communism, everyone would share wealth, said Marx.

### Critical Evaluation of Marx's Conflict Theory

Things did not work out the way Marx had predicted. First, industrial societies did not polarize into two opposed classes engaged in bitter conflict. Instead, a large and heterogeneous middle class of white-collar workers emerged. Some of them are non-manual employees. Others are professionals. Many of them enjoy higher income and status than manual workers. With a bigger stake in capitalism than propertyless manual workers, non-manual employees and professionals have generally acted as a stabilizing force in society. Second, although Marx correctly argued that investment in technology makes it possible for capitalists to earn high profits, he did not expect investment in technology also to make it possible for workers to earn higher wages and toil fewer hours under less oppressive conditions. Yet that is just what happened. Their improved living standard tended to pacify workers, as did the availability of various welfare state benefits, such as employment insurance. Third, communism took root not where industry was most highly developed, as Marx predicted, but in semi-industrialized countries, such as Russia in 1917 and China in 1949. Moreover, instead of evolving into classless societies, new forms of privilege emerged under communism. According to a Russian quip from the 1970s, "under capitalism, one class exploits the other, but under communism it's the other way around."

## *The Functionalist Theory of Davis and Moore*

In the mid-twentieth century, American sociologists Kingsley Davis and Wilbert Moore proposed a **functional theory of stratification** that, in contrast to Marx's theory, asserts the inevitability of social stratification (Davis and Moore, 1945). Davis and Moore observed that jobs differ in importance. A judge's work, for example, contributes more to society than the work of a janitor. This presents a problem: how can people be motivated to undergo the long training they need to serve as physicians, engineers, and so forth? Higher education is expensive. You earn little money while training. Long and hard study rather than pleasure seeking is essential. Clearly, an incentive is needed to motivate the most talented people to train for the most important jobs. The incentives, said Davis and Moore, are money and prestige. More precisely, social stratification is necessary (or "functional") because the prospect of high rewards motivates people to undergo the sacrifices needed to get a higher education. Without substantial inequality, they conclude, the most talented people would have no incentive to become judges, physicians, and so forth.

### Critical Evaluation of Functionalism

Although the functional theory of stratification may at first seem plausible, we can quickly uncover one of its chief flaws by imagining a society with just two classes of people—physicians and farmers. The farmers grow food. The physicians tend the ill. Then, one day, a rare and deadly virus strikes. The virus has the odd property of attacking only physicians. Within weeks, there are no more doctors in our imaginary society. As a result, the farmers are much worse off. Cures and treatments for their ailments are no long available. Soon the average farmer lives fewer years than his or her predecessors. The society is less well off, though it survives.

Now imagine the reverse. Again we have a society comprising only physicians and farmers. Again a rare and lethal virus strikes. This time, however, the virus has the odd property of attacking only farmers. Within weeks, the physicians' stores of food are depleted. After a few more weeks, the physicians start dying of starvation. The physicians who try to become farmers catch the new virus and expire. Within months, the society has been wiped out. Who, then, does the more important work, physicians or farmers? Our thought experiment suggests that farmers do, for without them society cannot exist.

From a historical point of view, we can say that *none* of the jobs regarded by Davis and Moore as "important" would exist without the physical labour done by people in "less important" jobs. To sustain the witch doctor in a tribal society, hunters and gatherers had to produce enough for their own subsistence plus a surplus to feed, clothe, and house the witch doctor. To sustain the royal court in an agrarian society, peasants had to produce enough for their own subsistence plus a surplus to support the royal family. By using taxes, tithes, and force, government and religious authorities have taken surpluses

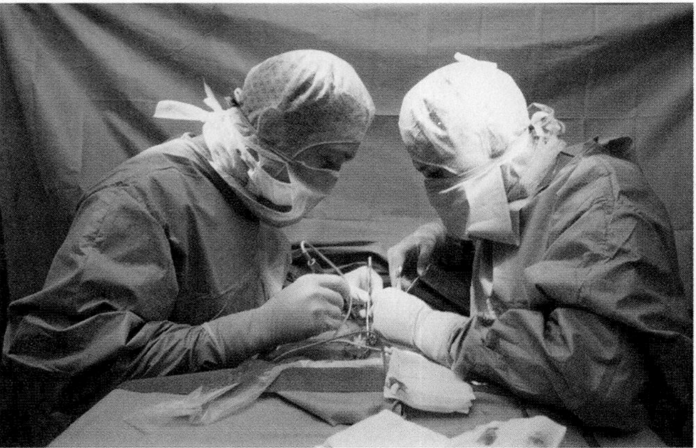

One of the problems with the functional theory of stratification is that it is difficult to establish which jobs are more important, especially when we take a historical perspective.

from ordinary working people for thousands of years. Among other things, these surpluses were used to establish the first institutions of higher learning in the thirteenth century. Out of these, modern universities developed.

Thus, the question of which occupations are most important is not clear-cut. To be sure, physicians earn a lot more money than farmers today, and they also enjoy a lot more prestige. But it is not because their work is more important in any objective sense of the word. (On the question of why physicians and other professionals earn more than nonprofessionals, see Chapter 10, Religion and Education.)

Sociologists have noted other problems with the functional theory of stratification (Tumin, 1953). First, the functional theory of stratification stresses how inequality helps society discover talent. But it ignores the pool of talent lying undiscovered because of inequality. Bright and energetic adolescents may be forced to drop out of high school to help support themselves and their families. Capable and industrious high school graduates may be forced to forgo a postsecondary education because they can't afford it. Inequality may encourage the discovery of talent but only among those who can afford to take advantage of the opportunities available to them. For the rest, inequality prevents talent from being discovered.

Second, the functional theory of stratification fails to examine how advantages are passed from generation to generation. Like *Robinson Crusoe,* the functional theory correctly emphasizes that talent and hard work often result in material rewards. However, it is also the case that inheritance allows parents to transfer wealth to children regardless of their talent. For example, glancing back at Table 6.1, we see that about half of the largest personal fortunes in Canada were inherited.

### *Weber's Compromise*

Like the functionalists, Max Weber argued that the emergence of a classless society is highly unlikely. Like Marx, however, he recognized that under some circumstances people can act to lower the level of inequality in society.

Writing in the early twentieth century, Weber held that a person's class position is determined by his or her "market situation," including the possession of goods, opportunities for income, level of education, and level of technical skill. Accordingly, in Weber's view four main classes exist in capitalist societies: large property owners, small property owners, propertyless but relatively highly educated and well-paid employees, and propertyless manual workers (Weber, 1946: 180–95).

Weber also recognized that two types of groups other than classes—status groups and parties—have a bearing on the way a society is stratified. **Status groups** differ from one another in the prestige or social honour they enjoy and in their style of life. Consider members of a minority ethnic community who have recently immigrated. They may earn relatively high income but endure relatively low prestige. The longer-established members of the majority ethnic community may look down on them as vulgar "new rich." If their cultural practices differ from those of the majority ethnic group, their style of life may become a subject of scorn. Thus, the position of the minority ethnic group in the social hierarchy does not derive just from its economic position but also from the esteem in which it is held.

In Weber's usage, **parties** are not just political groups but, more generally, organizations that seek to impose their will on others through the exercise of power (Weber, 1947: 152). Control over parties, especially large bureaucratic organizations, does not depend just on wealth. A person can head a military, scientific, political, or other bureaucracy without being rich, just as a person can be rich and still have to endure low prestige.

Weber argued that to draw an accurate picture of a society's stratification system we must analyze classes, status groups, and parties as somewhat independent bases of social inequality. Each basis of stratification influences the others. For example, one political party may want to tax the rich and distribute benefits to the poor, thus increasing opportunities for upward mobility. Another political party may want to cut taxes to the rich and decrease benefits to the poor, thus decreasing opportunities for upward mobility. The class system will be affected in different ways depending on which party comes to power. From this point of view, nothing is inevitable about the level of social stratification in society. We are neither headed inexorably toward classlessness nor are we bound to endure high levels of inequality. Instead, the level of social stratification depends on the complex interplay of class, status, and party, and their effect on **social mobility,** or movement up and down the stratification system. We devote the next section to exploring these themes.

# Social Mobility

Mordecai Richler's *The Apprenticeship of Duddy Kravitz* is one of the true classics of modern Canadian literature (Richler, 1959). Made into a 1974 film starring Richard Dreyfuss as Duddy, it is the story of a poor 18-year-old Jewish Montrealer in the mid-1940s who is desperately seeking to establish himself in the world. To that end, he waits on tables, smuggles drugs, drives a taxi, produces wedding and bar mitzvah films, and rents out pinball machines. He is an obnoxious charmer with relentless drive, a young man so fixed on making it that he is even willing to sacrifice his girlfriend and his only coworker to achieve his goals. We cannot help but admire Duddy for his ambition and his artfulness even while we are shocked by his guile and his single-mindedness.

Part of what makes *The Apprenticeship of Duddy Kravitz* universally appealing is that it could be a story about anyone. It is not just some immigrants and their children who may start out as pushy little people engaged in shady practices and unethical behaviour. As Richler reminds us repeatedly, many of the wealthiest establishment families in Canada and elsewhere started out in just this way. Duddy, then, is a universal symbol of "upward mobility"—and the compromises a person must sometimes make to achieve it (see Box 6.2).

6.2

# SOCIOLOGY AT THE MOVIES

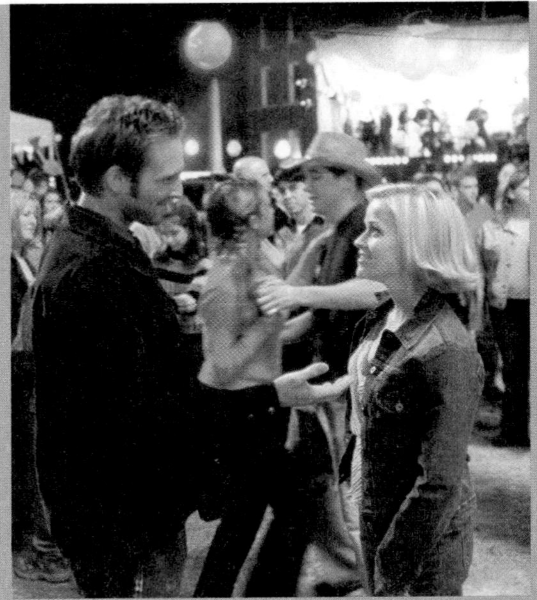

Josh Lucas and Reese Witherspoon in *Sweet Home Alabama*

***Sweet Home Alabama*** **(2002)**

*Sweet Home Alabama* is a Cinderella story with a twist: the successful heroine from humble beginnings gets the handsome prince but is not sure he is truly what she wants.

In the seven years since Melanie Carmichael (Reese Witherspoon) left her small-town Alabama home, she has achieved impressive upward social mobility. Beginning as a daughter of the working class, she has become a world-famous fashion designer in New York City. As the film begins, the mayor's son is courting Melanie. Andrew (Patrick Dempsey) proposes to her in Tiffany's. She says yes, but before she can marry him she has to clear up a not-so-minor detail: she needs a divorce from Jake (Josh Lucas), the childhood sweetheart she left behind.

Most of the story unfolds back in rural Alabama. Melanie finds herself caught between two classes and two subcultures, and the film follows her struggle to reconcile her conflicting identities. Her dilemma will require her to acknowledge and reconnect with her mother (Mary Kay Place), who lives in a trailer park, while standing up to her future mother-in-law, the mayor of New York City (Candice Bergen).

In the end, Melanie returns to Jake, while Andrew, briefly heartbroken, pleases his mother by marrying a woman of his own class. Melanie's homecoming does not, however, require that she return to life in a trailer park. She discovers that while she was in New York, Jake transformed his life. The working-class "loser" built a successful business as a glass-blower. This change allows Melanie to imagine an upwardly mobile future by Jake's side.

*Sweet Home Alabama* sends the message that people are happiest when they marry within their own subculture. That message is comforting because it helps the audience reconcile itself to two realities. First, although many people want to "marry up," most North Americans do not in fact succeed in doing so. We tend to marry within our own class—and within our own religion and ethnic and racial group (Kalmijn, 1998: 406–08). Second, marrying outside your subculture is likely to be unsettling insofar as it involves abandoning old norms, roles, and values, and learning new ones. It is, therefore, in some sense a relief to learn you're better off marrying within your own subculture, especially because you will probably wind up doing just that anyway.

There is a problem with this message, however. Staying put in your own subculture denies the dream of upward mobility. *Sweet Home Alabama* resolves the problem by holding out the promise of upward mobility without having to leave home, as it were. Melanie and Jake can enjoy the best of both worlds, moving up the social hierarchy together without forsaking the community and the subculture they cherish. *Sweet Home Alabama* achieves a happy ending by denying the often difficult process of adapting to a new subculture when experiencing social mobility.

### CRITICAL THINKING QUESTIONS

- *Does upward social mobility imply that you change your community or subculture?*
- *Does remaining in your own community or subculture diminish your chances of upward social mobility? Why or why not?*

Much of our discussion to this point has focused on how we describe inequality and how we explain its persistence. Here we take up a different, though related, set of questions. To what extent are we trapped in a disadvantaged social position or assured of maintaining an advantaged position? At birth, do all people have the same freedom to gain wealth and fame? Are the opportunities we enjoy, our "life chances," equally accessible to everyone?

Sociologists use the term *social mobility* to refer to the dynamics of the system of inequality and, in particular, to movement up and down the stratification system. If we think about inequality as either a hierarchy of more or less privileged positions or a set of higher and lower social classes, an important question is how much opportunity people have to change positions. Typically, change has been measured by using one of two benchmarks: your first position in the hierarchy (e.g., your first full-time job) and the position of your parents in the hierarchy. Comparing your first job with your current job is an examination of occupational or **intragenerational mobility.** Comparing the occupations of parents with their children's current occupation is an examination of the inheritance of social position or **intergenerational mobility.**

Whichever benchmark is used, social mobility analysts are interested in the openness or fluidity of society. Open or fluid societies have greater equality of access to all positions in the hierarchy of inequality, both the low and the high. Regardless of your social origins, in more open societies you are more likely to rise or fall to a position that reflects your capabilities. In contrast, in closed or rigid societies, your social origins have major consequences for where you are located in the hierarchy of inequality. In such societies, poverty begets poverty, wealth begets wealth. In feudal Europe or in the Indian caste system, your birth determines your fate—you are a peasant or a lord, a member of an upper caste or a lower caste, based on the position of the family to which you are born.

In modern times, societies have become more open. The circumstances of your birth do not completely determine your fate. Think about the changes in Canadian society over the past century. A mainly agrarian, resource-based economy has transformed into a modern, advanced postindustrial nation. We have experienced substantial growth in well-paying occupations in finance, marketing, management, and the professions. To what extent have people from all walks of life, from all economic backgrounds, been able to benefit from this transformation? This question introduces a second, related theme to discussions of mobility—equality of opportunity.

In the 1950s and 1960s, proponents of the functional theory of stratification and human capital theory imagined that equality of opportunity would pervade society. They argued that as more and more skilled jobs are created in the new economy, the best and the brightest must rise to the top to take those jobs and perform them diligently. We would then move from a society based on **ascription** to one based on **achievement.** In a system of inequality based on ascription, your family's station in life determines your own fortunes. In a system based on achievement, your own talents determine your lot in life. If you achieve good grades in school, your chance of acquiring a professional or managerial job rises.

Other sociologists, however, cautioned that this scenario of high individual social mobility might not follow from the transformation of the economy. They emphasized how advantaged families have long attempted to ensure that their offspring inherit their advantages (Collins, 1979).

On the world stage, Blossfeld and Shavit (1993) demonstrated that in 11 of 13 advanced industrial countries, little evidence supports the view that greater equality of opportunity exists in societies with expanding education systems (Sweden and the Netherlands are the two exceptions). In most countries, the openness of the system of inequality did not increase over the last half of the twentieth century. Richard Wanner (1999) tested these ideas by using Canadian data. He asked whether "Canada's investment in educational expansion reduced the amount of ascription in educational attainment" (Wanner, 1999: 409). In other words, has the growth of education—more high schools, colleges, and universities—benefited people from all social backgrounds equally?

If in earlier decades the chances of children from poorer families going to university were small, then these chances should have increased in more recent decades if ascription were weakening. As measures of socioeconomic background, Wanner (1999) used mother's and father's education and father's occupation. He tested his central question by using detailed information from a sample of 31 500 Canadians. Wanner found that class-based ascription still operates strongly. Despite the fact that more Canadians are acquiring more years of schooling and more degrees than ever, the long arm of family socioeconomic background continues to exert a strong hold on educational attainment. The link between family advantage and children's educational achievement has not weakened.

Explanations for how and why this occurs remain a matter of controversy (Davies, 1999). One explanation focuses on the way the school system has become increasingly differentiated. New high school programs have proliferated. These include storefront schools for at-risk students in poorer neighbourhoods, language-immers ion streams, private schools, and enriched learning tracks. These different types of schools tend to enrol students from different socioeconomic backgrounds. Students from lower socioeconomic backgrounds tend to take various routes through high school vocational programs and college diploma programs. Students from higher socioeconomic backgrounds typically continue on to university. That is how it is possible for Canadians to acquire more years of schooling and more degrees while the link between family background and educational achievement persists.

## Prestige and Taste

Weber, you will recall, said status groups differ from one another in terms of their lifestyles and the honour in which they are held. Here we may add that members of status groups signal their rank by means of material and symbolic culture. That is, they seek to distinguish themselves from others by displays of taste in fashion, food, music, literature, manners, and so forth.

The difference among good taste, common taste, and bad taste is not inherent in cultural objects themselves. Rather, cultural objects that are considered to be in the best taste are generally those that are least accessible in two senses. First, fully appreciating cultural objects that are considered to be in the best taste, such as abstract paintings or classical music, may require special education (Bourdieu, 1984 [1979]). Second, purely

The differences among good taste, common taste, and bad taste are not inherent in cultural objects themselves. Rather, cultural objects that are considered to be in the best taste are generally those that are least accessible. *Left.* Don Cherry *Right.* Karen Kain in the National Ballet of Canada's production of *Swan Lake.*

financial considerations also enter the picture. A Mercedes costs four times more than a Ford, and a two-week winter ski trip to Whistler can cost far more than a two-month summer vacation in Gimli, Manitoba. Of course, anyone can get from point A to point B quite comfortably in a Ford and have a perfectly enjoyable vacation in different places. Still, most people would prefer the Mercedes and Whistler, at least partly because they signal higher status. Access to tasteful cultural objects, then, is as much a matter of cost as of education.

Often, rich people engage in conspicuous displays of consumption, waste, and leisure not because they are necessary, useful, or pleasurable but simply to impress their peers and inferiors (Veblen, 1899). That is evident if we consider how clothing acts as a sort of language that signals status to others (Lurie, 1981).

For thousands of years, certain clothing styles have indicated rank. In ancient Egypt, only people in high positions were allowed to wear sandals. The ancient Greeks and Romans passed laws controlling the type, number, and colour of garments people could wear and the type of embroidery with which they could be trimmed. In medieval Europe, too, various aspects of dress were regulated to ensure that certain styles were specific to certain groups.

European laws governing the dress styles of different groups fell into disuse after about 1700, because a new method of control emerged as Europe became wealthier. From the eighteenth century on, the *cost* of clothing came to designate a person's rank. Expensive materials, styles that were difficult to care for, heavy jewellery, and superfluous trimmings became all the rage. It was not for comfort or utility that rich people wore elaborate powdered wigs, heavy damasked satins, the furs of rare animals, diamond tiaras, and patterned brocades and velvets. Such getups were often hot, stiff, heavy, and itchy. People could scarcely move in many of them. And that was just their point—to prove not only that the wearer could afford enormous sums for handmade finery but also that he or she did not have to work to pay for them.

Today, we have different ways of using clothes to signal status. Designer labels loudly proclaim the dollar value of garments. In addition, the language of status often takes the form of looking "cool." Consider jeans. Long regarded as a garment for cowboys and industrial workers, jeans have become wildly popular for just about everyone. In some circles, designer brands distinguish someone who is cool from someone who is not. Not wearing low-rise jeans with holes in the right places would doom a person to second-class status in many high schools.

How pervasive and important are brand names for establishing status? One indicator comes from the world of popular music. Top recording artists are much admired by young people and act as role models. The brands they popularize help to define cool, high-status commodities. In that light, consider Table 6.4, based on the top 20 songs of 2005 on the Billboard charts. The top half of Table 6.4 shows how many times the 10 most frequently mentioned brands were referred to in the top 20 songs. The bottom half lists the eight recording artists who referred to brands most frequently. The numbers tell a fascinating story. Each of the top 20 songs of 2005 mentioned brands 25.5 times on average. Assuming the average song is two and a half minutes long, that works out to one brand mentioned every six seconds. From this point of view, popular music is a lot like a commercial. Status in the world of popular music—especially the music of 50 Cent—is strongly associated with driving a Mercedes, wearing Nikes, drinking Hennessy cognac, and packing an AK-47 assault rifle.

**Table 6.4**
Brand Names in Popular Music

| **BRANDS MENTIONED IN TOP 20 SONGS** | |
|---|---|
| **Brand** | **Number of Mentions** |
| 1. Mercedes Benz automobile | 100 |
| 2. Nike sports shoes | 63 |
| 3. Cadillac automobile | 62 |
| 4. Bentley automobile | 51 |
| 5. Rolls Royce automobile | 46 |
| 6. Hennessy cognac | 44 |
| 7. Chevrolet automobile | 40 |
| 8. Louis Vuitton luggage | 35 |
| 9. Cristal champagne | 35 |
| 10. AK-47 assault rifle | 33 |
| Total | 509 |
| Mentions/song | 25.5 |
| **TOP 5 BRAND-DROPPING ARTISTS** | |
| **Singer** | **Number of Brands** |
| 1. 50 Cent | 20 brands in 7 songs |
| 2. Ludacris | 13 brands in 6 songs |
| 2. The Game | 13 brands in 2 songs |
| 4. Ciara | 10 brands in 4 songs |
| 5. Jamie Foxx | 6 brands in 1 song |
| 5. Kanye West | 6 brands in 1 song |
| 5. Lil' Jon | 6 brands in 2 songs |
| 5. Trick Daddy | 6 brands in 2 songs |
| Total | 80 brands in 25 songs |
| Brands/song | 3.2 |

Source: Agenda Inc. (2005: 4–7).

# Politics and the Perception of Class Inequality

We expect you have had some strong reactions to our review of sociological theories and research on social stratification. You may therefore find it worthwhile to reflect more systematically on your own attitudes to social inequality. Do you consider the family in which you grew up to have been lower class, working class, middle class, or upper class? Do you think the gaps between classes in Canadian society are big, moderate, or small? How strongly do you agree or disagree with the view that big gaps between classes are needed to motivate people to work hard and maintain national prosperity? How strongly do you agree or disagree with the view that inequality persists because it benefits the rich and the powerful? How strongly do you agree or disagree with the view that inequality persists because ordinary people don't join together to get rid of it?

Answering these questions will help you to clarify the way you perceive and evaluate the Canadian class structure and your place in it. If you take note of your answers, you can compare them with the responses of representative samples of Canadians, which we review below.

Surveys show that few Canadians have trouble placing themselves in the class structure when asked to do so. Most Canadians consider themselves to be middle class or working class. They also think that the gaps between classes are relatively large. But do Canadians think that these big gaps between classes are needed to motivate people to work hard, thus increasing their own wealth and the wealth of the nation? Some Canadians think so, but most do not. A survey conducted in 18 countries, including Canada, asked more than 22 000 respondents if large differences in income are necessary for national prosperity. Canadians were among the most likely to disagree with that view (Pammett, 1997: 77).

So Canadians know that they live in a class-divided society. They also tend to think that deep class divisions are not necessary for national prosperity. Why then do Canadians think inequality continues to exist? The 18-nation survey sheds light on that issue. One of the survey questions asked respondents how strongly they agree or disagree with the view that "inequality continues because it benefits the rich and powerful." Most Canadians agreed with that statement. Only about a quarter of them disagreed with it in any way. Another question asked respondents how strongly they agree or disagree with the view that "inequality continues because ordinary people don't join together to get rid of it." Again, most Canadians agreed, with less than a third disagreeing in any way (Pammett, 1997: 77–78).

Despite widespread awareness of inequality and considerable dissatisfaction with it, most Canadians are opposed to the government playing an active role in reducing inequality. Most do not want governments to provide citizens with a basic income. They tend to oppose government job-creation programs. They even resist the idea that government should reduce income differences through taxation (Pammett, 1997: 81). Most Canadians remain individualistic and self-reliant. On the whole, they persist in the belief that opportunities for mobility are abundant and that it is up to the individual to make something of those opportunities by means of talent and effort.

Significantly, however, all the attitudes summarized above vary by class position. For example, discontent with the level of inequality in Canadian society is stronger at the bottom of the stratification system than at the top. The belief that Canadian society is full of opportunities for upward mobility is stronger at the top of the class hierarchy than at the bottom. We find considerably less opposition to the idea that government should reduce inequality as we move down the stratification system. This permits us to conclude that, if Canadians allow inequality to persist, it is because the balance of attitudes—and of the power that supports those attitudes—favours continuity over change.

# Global Inequality

## *Levels and Trends in Global Inequality*

Despite the existence of considerable social stratification in Canada, we live in one of the 20 or so richest counties in the world—an elite club that also includes the United States, Japan, Australia, Germany, France, the U.K., and a dozen or so other Western

6.3

# MASS MEDIA AND SOCIETY

### The Internet and Social Stratification

Internet access mirrors social inequality. After all, the Internet requires an expensive infrastructure and people must pay for it. Consequently, access is not open to everyone. In Canada, people with a higher education and above-average income are most likely to enjoy Internet access. Globally, the United States is the overwhelming leader in getting its population connected (see Figure 6.5). In 2000 the *rate* of Internet connectivity (Internet users per 1000 people) in North America was more than 68 times higher than in the Middle East and Africa. Although more than 59 percent of Americans used the Internet in 2003, fewer than 9 percent of people outside the United States did so. These figures illustrate how international inequalities in Internet access mirror global inequalities overall.

**CRITICAL THINKING QUESTIONS**

- *Consider the relationship between Internet access and other types of social inequality. Is Internet access an independent or a dependent variable? In other words, does Internet access have an impact on other aspects of social inequality or is inequality of Internet access caused by other inequalities, such as inequality of income? Or is the relationship between Internet access and other forms of inequality reciprocal, with each type of inequality influencing the other?*

**Figure 6.5**
Top Ten Countries, Millions of Internet Users, 2003

■ Sources: "50 Largest" (2003); "Population Explosion!" (2003).

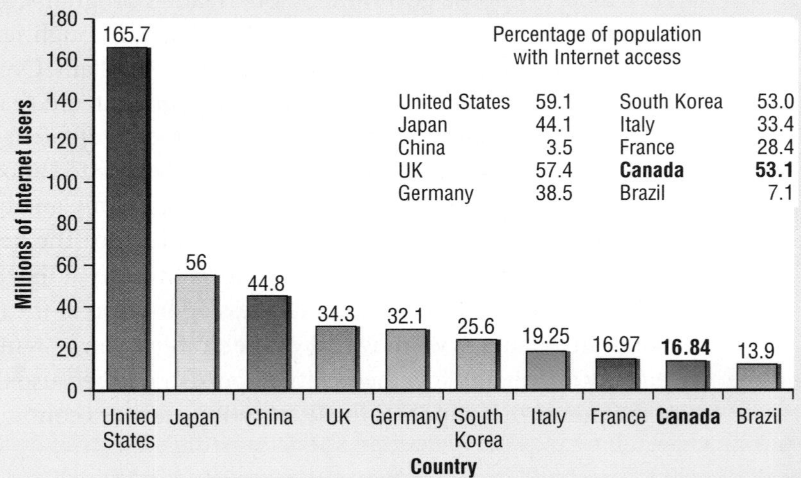


European countries. In contrast, the world's poor countries cover much of Africa, South America, and Asia (see Box 6.3). Inequality between rich and poor countries is staggering. In a Manhattan restaurant, pet owners can treat their cats to US$100-a-plate birthday parties. In Cairo (Egypt) and Manila (the Philippines), garbage dumps are home to entire families who sustain themselves by picking through the refuse.

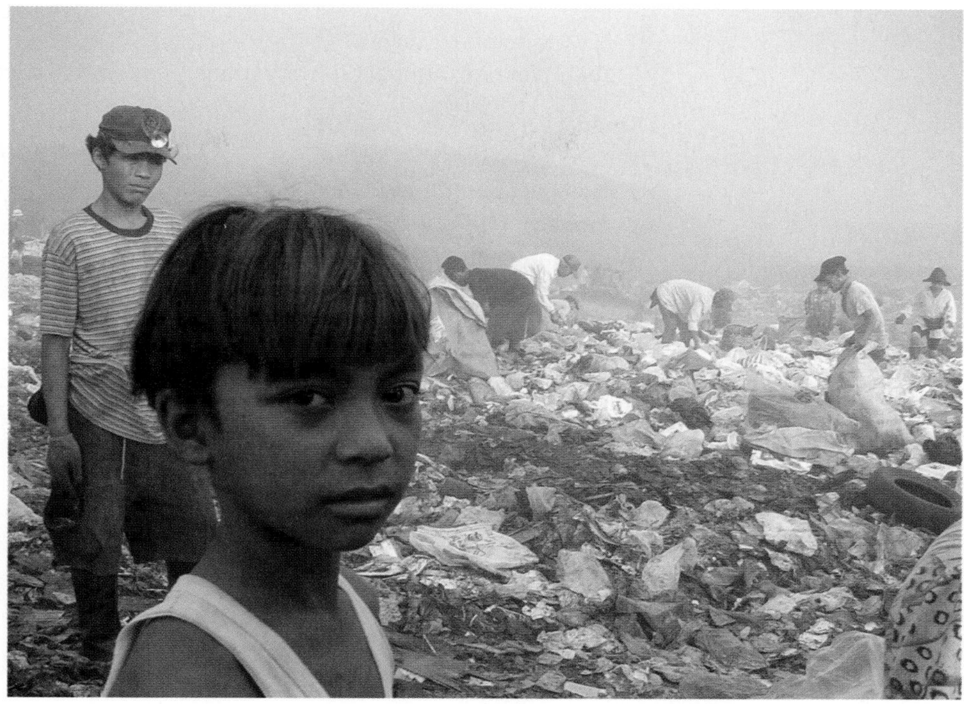

A half-hour's drive from the centre of Manila, the capital of the Philippines, an estimated 70 000 Filipinos live on a 22-hectare mountain of rotting garbage 45 metres high. It is infested with flies, rats, dogs, and disease. On a lucky day, residents can earn up to $5 retrieving scraps of metal and other valuables. On a rainy day, the mountain of garbage is especially treacherous. In July 2000 an avalanche buried 300 people alive. People who live on the mountain of garbage call it "The Promised Land."

The average income of citizens in the highly industrialized countries far outstrips that of citizens in the developing societies. Yet because poor people live in rich countries and rich people live in poor countries, averages fail to capture the extent of inequality between the richest of the rich and the poorest of the poor. Noting that the total worth of the world's 358 billionaires equals that of the world's 2.3 billion poorest people (45 percent of the world's population) is perhaps more revealing. The three richest people in the world own more than the combined gross domestic product (GDP) of the 48 least developed countries. The richest 1 percent of the world's population earns as much income as the bottom 57 percent (United Nations, 2002). According to the UN, 800 million people in the world are malnourished and 4 billion people—two-thirds of the world's population—are poor in the sense that they lack the ability to obtain adequate food, clothing, shelter, and other basic needs. The citizens of the 20 or so rich, highly industrialized countries spend more on cosmetics or alcohol or ice cream or pet food than it would take to provide basic education or water and sanitation or basic health and nutrition for everyone in the world (see Table 6.5).

Has global inequality increased or decreased over time? Between 1975 and 2000, the annual income gap between the 20 or so richest countries and the rest of the world grew enormously. The share of world income going to the top 10 percent of individuals has also been increasing, and the share of world income going to the bottom 20 percent of individuals has been falling. On the slightly brighter side, the number of people in the world living on $1 a day or less peaked in 1950 and then started to decline gradually. However, if we consider only the less developed countries, the number of people living on $1 a day or less *increased* by 20 million in the 1990s. Even by the most optimistic interpretation, these figures are little cause for joy. Nearly half of the world's population lives on $2 a day or less (Milanovic, 2005; Figure 6.6).

**Table 6.5**
Global Priorities: Annual Cost of Various Goods and Services

| Good/Service | Annual Cost (US$ billion) |
|---|---|
| Basic education for everyone in the world | 6 |
| Cosmetics in the United States | 8 |
| Water and sanitation for everyone in the world | 9 |
| Ice cream in Europe | 11 |
| Reproductive health for all women in the world | 12 |
| Perfumes in Europe and the United States | 12 |
| Basic health and nutrition for everyone in the world | 13 |
| Pet foods in Europe and the United States | 17 |
| Business entertainment in Japan | 35 |
| Cigarettes in Europe | 50 |
| Alcoholic drinks in Europe | 105 |
| Narcotic drugs in the world | 400 |
| Military spending in the world | 780 |

Source: United Nations (1998b: 37).

Statistics never speak for themselves. We need theories to explain them. Let us now outline and critically assess the two main theories that seek to explain the origins and persistence of global inequality.

## *Modernization Theory: A Functionalist Approach*

Two main sociological theories claim to explain global inequality. The first, **modernization theory,** is a variant of functionalism. According to modernization theory, global inequality results from various dysfunctional characteristics of poor societies themselves. Specifically, modernization theorists say the citizens of poor societies lack sufficient *capital* to invest in Western-style agriculture and industry. They lack rational, Western-style *business techniques* of marketing, accounting, sales, and finance. As a result, their productivity and profitability remain low. They lack stable, Western-style *governments* that could provide a secure framework for investment. Finally, they lack a Western *mentality:* values that stress the need for savings, investment, innovation, education, high achievement, and self-control in having children (Inkeles and Smith, 1976; Rostow, 1960). Societies characterized by these dysfunctions are poor. It follows that people living in rich countries can best help their poor cousins by transferring Western culture and capital to them and eliminating the dysfunctions. Only then will the poor countries be able to cap population growth, stimulate democracy, and invigorate agricultural and industrial production. Government-to-government foreign aid can accomplish some of this. Much work also needs to be done to encourage Western businesses to invest directly in poor countries and to increase trade between rich and poor countries.

## *Dependency Theory: A Conflict Approach*

Proponents of **dependency theory,** a variant of conflict theory, have been quick to point out the chief flaw in modernization theory (Baran, 1957; Cardoso and Faletto, 1979;

**Figure 6.6**
**People Living on Less Than $2 and Less Than $1 a Day**

■ Source: Poverty Mapping (2005).

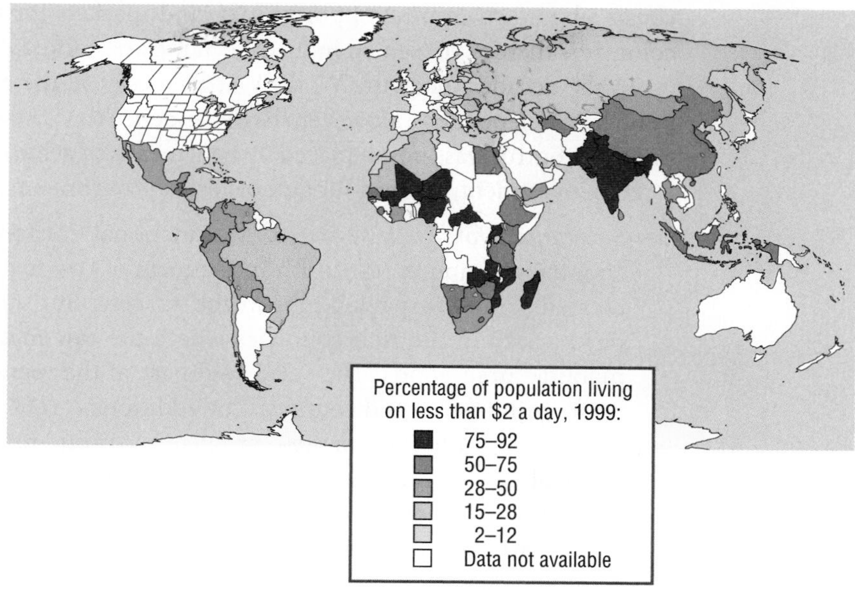


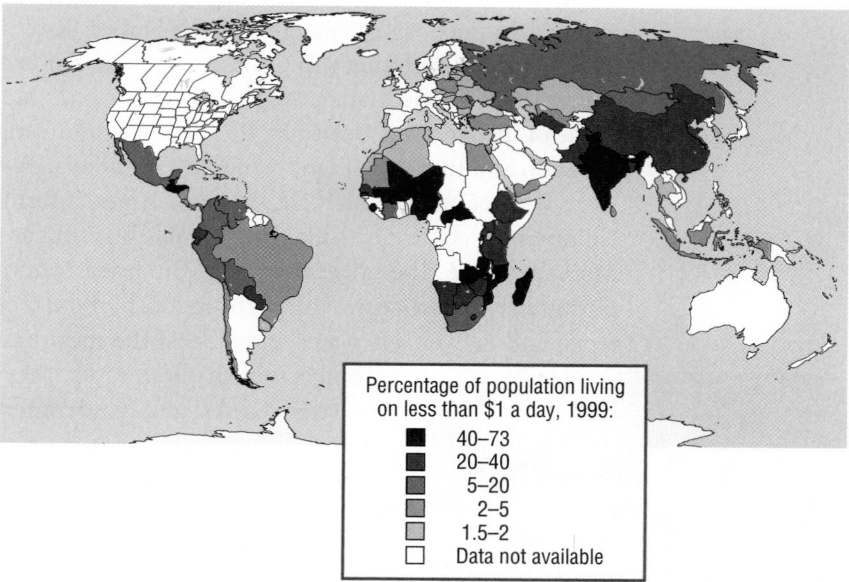


Wallerstein, 1974–89). For the past 500 years, the most powerful countries in the world have deliberately impoverished the less powerful countries. Focusing on internal characteristics blames the victim rather than the perpetrator of the crime. It follows that an adequate theory of global inequality should not focus on the internal characteristics of poor countries themselves. Instead, it should follow the principles of conflict theory and focus on patterns of domination and submission—specifically, in this case, on the relationship between rich and poor countries. That is just what dependency theory does.

According to dependency theorists, less global inequality existed in 1500 and even in 1750 than today. However, beginning around 1500, the armed forces of the world's most powerful countries subdued and then annexed or colonized most of the rest of the world.

The Industrial Revolution began around 1775. It enabled the Western European countries, Russia, Japan, and the United States to amass enormous wealth, which they used to extend their global reach. They forced their colonies to become a source of raw materials, cheap labour, investment opportunities, and markets for the conquering nations. The colonizers thereby prevented industrialization and locked the colonies into poverty.

In the decades following World War II, nearly all the colonies in the world became politically independent. However, the dependency theorists say that exploitation by direct political control was soon replaced by new means of achieving the same end: substantial foreign investment, support for authoritarian governments, and mounting debt.

- *Substantial foreign investment.* Multinational corporations invested in the poor countries to siphon off wealth in the form of raw materials and profits. True, they created some low-paying jobs in the process. But they created many more high-paying jobs in the rich countries where the raw materials were used to produce manufactured goods. They also sold part of the manufactured goods back to the poor, unindustrialized countries for additional profit.
- *Support for authoritarian governments.* According to dependency theorists, multinational corporations and rich countries continued their exploitation of the poor countries in the postcolonial period by giving economic and military support to local authoritarian governments. These governments managed to keep their populations subdued most of the time. When that was not possible, Western governments sent in troops and military advisers, engaging in what became known as "gunboat diplomacy." In the postcolonial period, the United States has been particularly active in using gunboat diplomacy in Central America. For example, in 1952 the democratic government of Guatemala began to redistribute land to impoverished peasants. Some of the land was owned by the United Fruit Company, a U.S. multinational corporation and the biggest landowner in Guatemala. Two years later, the CIA backed a right-wing coup in Guatemala, preventing land reform and allowing the United Fruit Company to continue its highly profitable business as usual (LaFeber, 1993).
- *Mounting debt.* The governments of the poor countries struggled to create transportation infrastructures (airports, roads, harbours, etc.), build their education systems, and deliver safe water and at least the most basic health care to their people. To accomplish these tasks, they had to borrow money from Western banks and governments. Some rulers also squandered money on luxuries. So it came about that debt—and the interest payments that inevitably accompany debt—grew every year. Crushing interest payments leave governments of poor countries with too little money for development tasks. Foreign aid helps, but not much. In 2002, foreign aid to the world's developing countries was only one-seventh the amount that the developing countries paid to Western banks in loan interest (United Nations, 2004: 201).

In 1893 leaders of the British mission pose before taking over what became Rhodesia and is now Zimbabwe. To raise a volunteer army, every British trooper was offered about 23 square kilometres of native land and 20 gold claims. The Matabele and Mashona peoples were subdued in a three-month war. Nine hundred farms and 10 000 gold claims were granted to the troopers and about 100 000 cattle were looted, leaving the native survivors without a livelihood. Forced labour was subsequently introduced by the British so that the natives could pay a £2 a year tax.

## Core, Periphery, and Semiperiphery

Although dependency theory provides a more realistic account of the sources of global inequality than modernization theory, it leaves a big question unanswered: how have some countries managed to escape poverty and start rapid economic development? After all, the world does not consist just of **core** capitalist countries that are major sources of capital and technology (the United States, Japan, and Germany) and **peripheral** countries that are major sources of raw materials and cheap labour (the former colonies). In addition, a middle tier of **semiperipheral** countries consists of former colonies that are making considerable headway in their attempts to become prosperous (South Korea, Taiwan, and Israel, for example) (Wallerstein, 1974–89). Comparing the poor peripheral countries with the more successful semiperipheral countries presents us with a useful natural experiment. The comparison suggests the circumstances that help some poor countries overcome the worst effects of colonialism.

The semiperipheral countries differ from the peripheral countries in four main ways, which we outline below (Kennedy, 1993: 193–227; Lie, 1998).

### Type of Colonialism

Around the turn of the twentieth century, Taiwan and Korea became colonies of Japan. They remained so until 1945. However, in contrast to the European colonizers of Africa, Latin America, and other parts of Asia, the Japanese built up the economies of their colonies. They established transportation networks and communication systems. They built steel, chemical, and hydroelectric power plants. After Japanese colonialism ended, Taiwan and South Korea were thus at an advantage compared with the former colonies of Britain and France. South Korea and Taiwan could use the Japanese-built infrastructure and Japanese-trained personnel as springboards to development.

### Geopolitical Position

Although the United States was the leading economic and military power in the world by the end of World War II, it began to feel its supremacy threatened in the late 1940s by the Soviet Union and China. Fearing that South Korea and Taiwan might fall to the communists, the United States poured unprecedented aid into both countries in the 1960s. It also gave them large, low-interest loans and opened its domestic market to Taiwanese and South Korean products. Because the United States saw Israel as a crucially important ally in the Middle East, it also received special economic assistance. Other countries with less strategic importance to the United States received less help in their drive to industrialize.

### State Policy

A third factor that accounts for the relative success of some countries in their efforts to industrialize and become prosperous concerns state policies. As a legacy of colonialism, the Taiwanese and South Korean states were developed on the Japanese model. They kept workers' wages low, restricted trade union growth, and maintained quasi-military discipline in factories. Moreover, by placing high taxes on consumer goods, limiting the import of foreign goods, and preventing their citizens from investing abroad, they encouraged their citizens to put much of their money in the bank. This situation created a large pool of capital for industrial expansion. The South Korean and Taiwanese states also gave subsidies, training grants, and tariff protection to export-based industries from the 1960s onward. (Tariffs are taxes on foreign goods.) These policies did much to stimulate industrial growth. Finally, the Taiwanese and South Korean states invested heavily in basic education, health care, roads, and other public goods. A healthy and well-educated labour force, combined with good transportation and communication systems, laid solid foundations for economic growth.

## Social Structure

Taiwan and South Korea are socially cohesive countries, which makes it easy for them to generate consensus around development policies. It also allows them to get their citizens to work hard, save a lot of money, and devote their energies to scientific education.

Social solidarity in Taiwan and South Korea is based partly on the sweeping land reform they conducted in the late 1940s and early 1950s. By redistributing land to small farmers, both countries eliminated the class of large landowners, who usually oppose industrialization. Land redistribution got rid of a major potential source of social conflict. In contrast, many countries in Latin America and Africa have not undergone land reform. The United States often intervened militarily in Latin America to prevent land reform because U.S. commercial interests profited handsomely from the existence of large plantations (LaFeber, 1993).

Another factor underlying social solidarity in Taiwan and South Korea is that neither country suffered from internal conflicts like those that wrack Africa south of the Sahara desert. British, French, and other Western European colonizers often drew the borders of African countries to keep antagonistic tribes in the same jurisdiction and often sought to stir up tribal conflict. Keeping tribal tensions alive made it possible to play one tribe against another. That made it easier for imperial powers to dominate. This policy led to much social and political conflict in postcolonial Africa. Today, the region suffers from frequent civil wars, coups, and uprisings. It is the most conflict-ridden area of the world. This high level of internal conflict acts as a barrier to economic development.

In sum, postcolonial countries that enjoy a solid industrial infrastructure, strategic geopolitical importance, strong states with strong development policies, and socially cohesive populations are in the best position to join the ranks of the rich countries in the coming

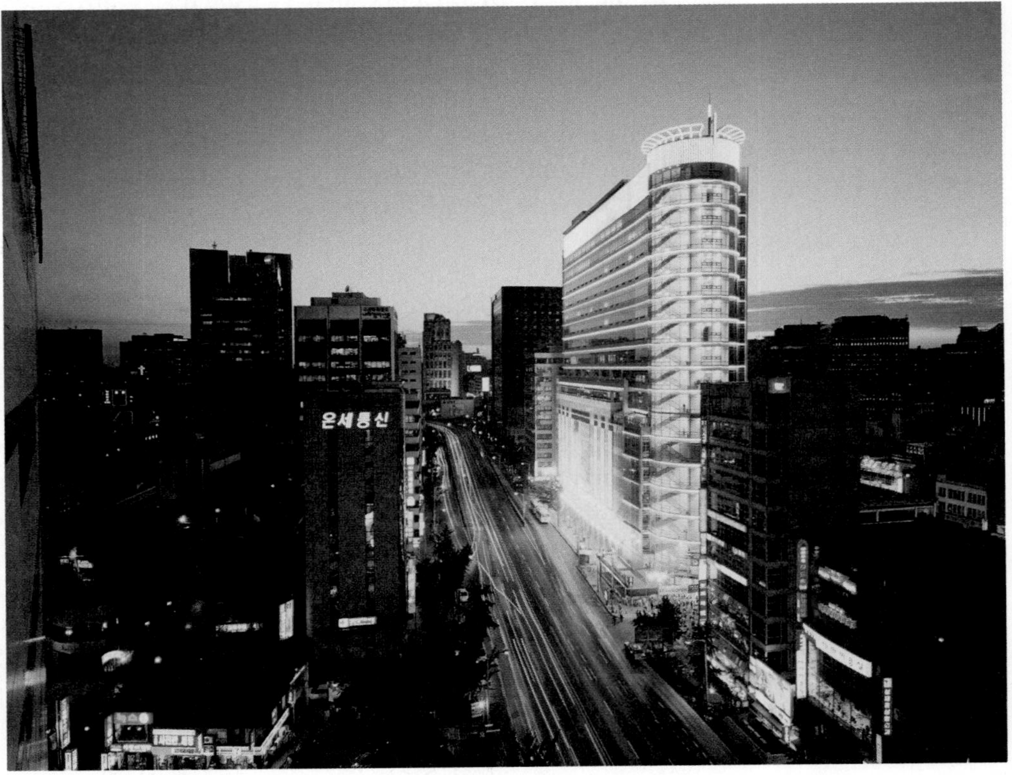


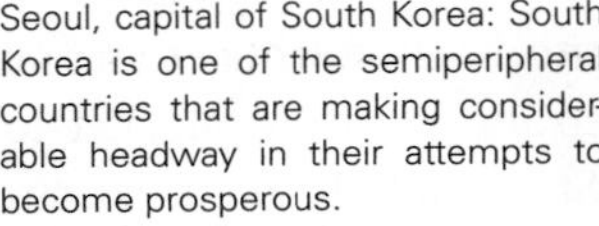
Seoul, capital of South Korea: South Korea is one of the semiperipheral countries that are making considerable headway in their attempts to become prosperous.

decades. Countries that have some of these characteristics are likely to experience economic growth and an increase in the well-being of their populations in the near future. Such countries include China, India, Chile, Thailand, Indonesia, Mexico, and Brazil. We conclude that, as is the case for social stratification within highly developed countries like Canada, the existing level of global inequality is not inevitable and can under some circumstances change for the better. We take up this theme again in the book's final chapter.

## The Points of the Compass

Stratification systems are opportunity structures that are more or less open to upward mobility. Their theoretical extremes are represented by the north and south points of our sociological compass (see Figure 1.6). At one extreme, people lack all opportunity. Their positions are fixed at birth. The class they are born into is the class in which they die. Because some people are born and remain privileged, while others are born and remain disadvantaged, we say that such a stratification system is characterized by inequality of opportunity.

At the other theoretical extreme, opportunities for upward mobility are evenly distributed throughout the stratification system. People born in the middle have no greater likelihood of reaching the top than people born at the bottom. People born at the top are as likely to fall to the bottom as people born in the middle. Merit and drive, not origins, determine a person's eventual position in the hierarchy. This is a meritocratic system, a system of equality of opportunity.

Canada is built on an image of equality of opportunity, and the reality is that Canadians enjoy more opportunity for upward mobility than Canadians of centuries past and people living in most less developed countries today. As we have seen, however, opportunities for upward mobility in Canada are still constrained by powerful social forces. Inheritance continues to play an important role in the transmission of advantage from one generation to the next. The link between family advantage and children's educational achievement has not weakened in the past several decades. Inequality of wealth and income has increased since the 1970s.

In this chapter we identified a remarkable similarity between the opportunity structure for individuals and the opportunity structure for countries. Over the past half century, a few countries have managed to rise from peripheral to semiperipheral status, and one may reasonably anticipate that a few more countries (and some very large ones at that) will make the trek over the next half century. Still, the global inequality that derives from the colonial era is still with us; the poles of the sociological compass remain useful guides to global inequality.

## Summary

### 1. *What is the difference between wealth and income? How are they distributed in Canada?*

Wealth is assets minus liabilities. Income is the amount of money earned in a given period. Substantial inequality of both wealth and income exists in Canada. Both types of inequality have increased over the past quarter of a century.

### 2. *What are the main differences between Marx's and Weber's theories of stratification?*

Marx's theory of stratification distinguishes between classes on the basis of their role in the productive process. It predicts inevitable conflict between the bourgeoisie and the proletariat and the birth of a communist system. Weber distinguished between classes on the basis of their "market relations." His model of stratification included four main classes. He argued that class consciousness may develop under some circumstances but is by no means inevitable. Weber also emphasized prestige and power as important non-economic sources of inequality.

3. *What is the functional theory of stratification?*

Davis and Moore's functional theory of stratification argues that (1) some jobs are more important than others, (2) people have to make sacrifices to train for important jobs, and (3) inequality is required to motivate people to undergo these sacrifices. In this sense, stratification is "functional."

4. *Is stratification inevitable?*

Although some level of inequality may be inevitable, much variation exists in the level of inequality from one country to the next. This suggests that, under certain conditions, people can lower the level of inequality in their society, as Weber argued.

5. *Is stratification based only on economic criteria?*

No. People often engage in conspicuous consumption, waste, and leisure to signal their position in the social hierarchy. Moreover, politics often influences the shape of stratification systems by changing the distribution of income, welfare entitlements, and property rights.

6. *How do Canadians view the class system?*

Most Canadians are aware of the existence of the class system and their place in it. They believe that large inequalities are not necessary to achieve national prosperity. Most Canadians also believe that inequality persists because it serves the interests of the most advantaged members of society and because the disadvantaged don't join together to change things. However, most Canadians disapprove of government intervention to lower the level of inequality.

7. *What are the main trends in global inequality and poverty?*

Global inequality and poverty are staggering and in some respects are getting worse. The income gap between rich and poor countries and between rich and poor individuals has grown in recent decades, and the number of desperately poor people has increased in the less developed countries.

8. *What are the main sociological theories of economic development?*

Modernization theory argues that global inequality occurs as a result of some countries lacking sufficient capital, Western values, rational business practices, and stable governments. Dependency theory counters with the claim that global inequality results from the exploitative relationship between rich and poor countries.

9. *What are the characteristics of formerly poor countries that emerged from poverty?*

The poor countries best able to emerge from poverty have a colonial past that left them with industrial infrastructures. They also enjoy a favourable geopolitical position. They implement strong, growth-oriented economic policies, and they have socially cohesive populations.

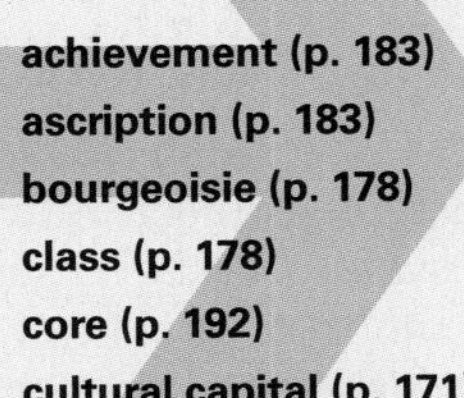

## Key Terms

**achievement (p. 183)**
**ascription (p. 183)**
**bourgeoisie (p. 178)**
**class (p. 178)**
**core (p. 192)**
**cultural capital (p. 171)**
**dependency theory (p. 190)**
**functional theory of stratification (p. 179)**
**human capital (p. 170)**
**intergenerational mobility (p. 183)**
**intragenerational mobility (p. 183)**
**modernization theory (p. 190)**
**parties (p. 181)**
**peripheral (p. 193)**
**poverty (p. 172)**

**proletariat (p. 178)**
**semiperipheral (p. 193)**
**social capital (p. 171)**
**social mobility (p. 181)**
**social stratification (p. 166)**
**status groups (p. 181)**

## Questions to Consider

1. How do you think the Canadian and global stratification systems will change over the next 25 years? Why do you think these changes will occur?
2. Why do you think most Canadians oppose more government intervention to reduce the level of inequality in society? In answering this question, think about the advantages that inequality brings to many people and the resources at their disposal for maintaining inequality.
3. Compare the number and quality of public facilities, such as playgrounds and libraries, in various parts of your community. How is the distribution of public facilities related to the socioeconomic status of neighbourhoods? Why does this relationship exist?

## Web Resources

### Companion Web Site for This Book

http://www.pointsofthecompass.nelson.com

Begin by clicking on the Student Resources section of the Web site. Next, select the chapter you are currently studying from the pull-down menu. From the Student Resources page you will have easy access to InfoTrac® College Edition, MicroCase online exercises, and additional Weblinks. The Web site also has many useful tips to aid you in your study of sociology, including practice tests for each chapter.

### InfoTrac® Search Terms

These search terms are provided to assist you in beginning to conduct research on this topic by visiting **http://www.infotrac-college.com**:

**class**
**class consciousness**
**global inequality**
**poverty**
**social mobility**

### Recommended Web Sites

For comprehensive statistics about income and wealth inequality in Canada, visit the Statistics Canada Web site at **http://www.statcan.ca**.

For information about Canada's efforts at reducing national and international poverty levels, see the Canadian International Development Agency's Web site at **http://www.acdi-cida.gc.ca/cidaweb/acdicida.nsf/En/Home**.

For research on social and economic security, visit the Canadian Council on Social Development at **http://www.ccsd.ca**.

For publications and statistics on international economic and social issues, go to the Organisation for Economic Co-operation and Development at **http://www.oecd.org**.

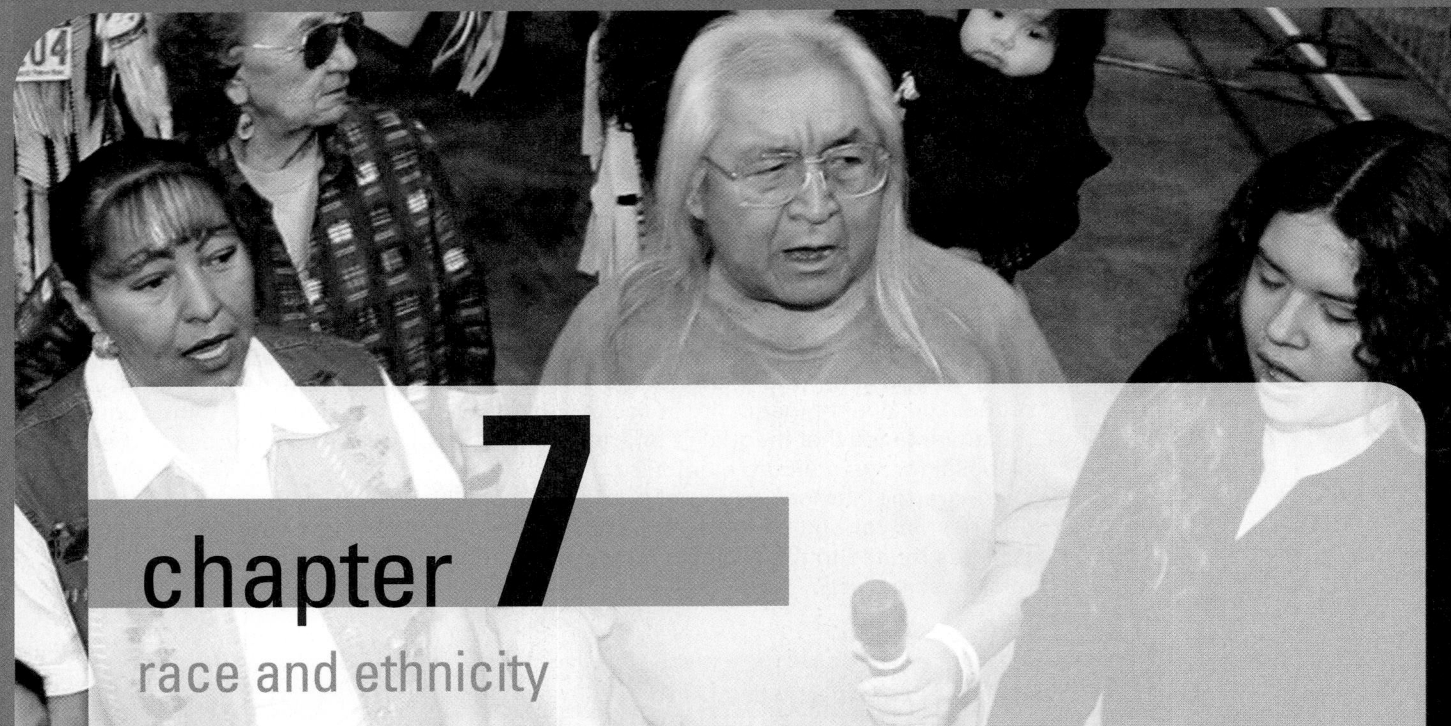

# chapter 7

## race and ethnicity



### In this chapter, you will learn that

→ Race and ethnicity are socially constructed labels. These labels, which have profound consequences for people's lives, distinguish people by perceived physical or cultural differences.

→ Racial and ethnic labels and identities change over time and place. Relations among racial and ethnic groups help to shape these labels and identities.

→ In Canada, racial, ethnic, and ancestral groups are blending over time. However, this tendency is weaker among members of highly disadvantaged groups, especially Aboriginal peoples and recent refugee immigrants.

→ Identifying with a racial or ethnic group can be economically, politically, and emotionally advantageous or disadvantageous.

→ Racial and ethnic inequality is likely to persist in Canada.

# Defining Race and Ethnicity

## *What Is Race?*

In the 1920s, Peter Sandiford, a professor in the Department of Education at the University of Toronto, administered some IQ tests and concluded that Canada must adopt a policy of selective immigration to ensure that "misfits" and "defectives" are kept out of the country. He encouraged the immigration of Britons, Germans, and Danes, and discouraged the immigration of Poles, Italians, Greeks, and Asians. The latter groups scored low on his IQ tests, and he believed that their apparent intellectual inferiority was rooted in their biological makeup (McLaren, 1990). Around the same time in the United States, Jewish immigrants were scoring below non-Jews on IQ tests. These results were used by many people as an argument against Jewish immigration. In modern times, blacks have, on average, scored below European Americans on IQ tests. Some people say this justifies slashing budgets for schools in the inner city, where many black people live. Why invest good money in inner-city schooling, such people ask, if low IQ scores are rooted in biology and therefore fixed (Herrnstein and Murray, 1994)?

The people who argued against the immigration of certain groups and better education for inner-city blacks ignored two facts. First, IQ scores are remarkably flexible. The descendants of Sandiford's low-IQ Asians are among the stars of the Canadian system of higher education today. As Jews experienced upward mobility and could afford better education, their IQ scores rose to above-average levels. Enriched educational facilities routinely boost the IQ scores and achievements of inner-city black children (Campbell and Ramey, 1994; Frank Porter Graham Child Development Center, 1999; Gould, 1996; Hancock, 1994). We are obliged to conclude that the social setting in which a person is raised and educated has a big impact on IQ. The average IQ of members of racial and ethnic groups has nothing to do with biology (Cancio, Evans, and Maume, 1996; Fischer et al., 1996).[1]

The view persists, nonetheless, that races differ biologically. For instance, we commonly hear that, for biological reasons, black people are better than whites at sports. Is there any evidence to support that belief? At first glance, the evidence might seem strong. Aren't 67 percent of NFL players and 65 percent of NBA players black? Don't blacks of West African descent hold the 200 fastest 100-metre-dash times, all under 10 seconds? Don't North and East Africans regularly win 40 percent of the top international distance-running honours yet represent only a fraction of 1 percent of the world's population (Entine, 2000; Lapchick, 2004)? Although these facts are undeniable, the argument for the genetic basis of black athletic superiority begins to falter once we consider two additional points. First, no gene linked to general athletic superiority has ever been identified. Second, black athletes do not perform unusually well in many sports, such as equestrian events, swimming, hockey, cycling, tennis, gymnastics, and soccer. The idea that black people are in general superior athletes is simply untrue.

Sociologists have identified certain *social* conditions that lead to high levels of participation in sports. These operate on all groups of people, whatever their race. Specifically, people who face widespread prejudice and discrimination often enter sports in disproportionately large numbers for lack of other ways to improve their social and economic standing. For such people, other avenues of upward mobility tend to be blocked. (**Prejudice** is an attitude that judges a person on his or her group's real or imagined characteristics. **Discrimination** is unfair treatment of people because of their group membership.) For example, it was not until the 1950s that prejudice and discrimination against North American Jews began to decline appreciably. Until then, Jews played a prominent role in some professional sports, such as boxing, baseball, and basketball. When the New York Knicks played their first game on November 1, 1946, beating the Toronto Huskies 68–66, the starting lineup for New York consisted of Ossie Schechtman, Stan Stutz, Jake Weber, Ralph Kaplowitz, and Leo "Ace" Gottlieb—an all-Jewish squad ("New York Knicks History," 2000). Similarly, Koreans in Japan today are subject to much prejudice and discrimination. They often pursue careers in sports. In contrast, Koreans in Canada face less prejudice and discrimination. Few of them become professional athletes.

The idea that black people are genetically superior to whites in athletic ability is the complement of the idea that they are genetically inferior to whites in intellectual ability. Both ideas have the effect of reinforcing black–white inequality. For although there are just a few thousand professional athletes in North America, there are millions of pharmacists, graphics designers, lawyers, systems analysts, police officers, nurses, and people in other interesting occupations that offer steady employment and good pay. By promoting only the Chris Boshes and Donovan Baileys of the world as suitable role models for youth, the idea of "natural" black athletic superiority and intellectual inferiority in effect asks blacks to bet on a high-risk proposition—that they will make it in professional sports. At the same time, it deflects attention from a much safer bet—that they can achieve upward mobility through academic excellence (Guppy and Davies, 1998; Hoberman, 1997).

Another problem undermines the argument that genes determine the behaviour of racial groups: it is impossible to neatly distinguish races based on genetic differences. A high level of genetic mixing has taken place among people throughout the world. In North America, for instance, it was not uncommon for white male slave owners to rape black female slaves, who then gave birth to children of mixed race. Many Europeans had children with Aboriginal peoples in the eighteenth and nineteenth centuries. We know from the census that ethnic and racial intermarriage has been increasing in Canada at least since 1871. In the 2001 census, more than 11.3 million Canadians (38 percent of the total population) reported multiple ethnic or racial identities (Statistics Canada, 2003d: 15). Usually, people who report multiple ethnic or racial identities have parents of different ethnic or racial origins (Kalbach and Kalbach, 1998). A growing number of North Americans are similar to Tiger Woods. Woods claims he is of "Cablinasian" ancestry—part Caucasian, part black, part Native American Indian, and part Asian. As these examples illustrate, the differences among black, white, Asian, and so forth are often anything but clear-cut.

Athletic heroes, such as Donovan Bailey, are often held up as role models for black youth, even though the chance of making it as an athlete is much less than the chance of getting a postsecondary education and succeeding as a professional. Racial stereotypes about black athletic prowess and intellectual inferiority are often reinforced through the idolization of sporting heroes.

Some respected scholars believe we all belong to one human race, which originated in Africa (Cavalli-Sforza, Menozzi, and Piazza, 1994). They argue that subsequent migration, geographical separation, and inbreeding led to the formation of more or less distinct races. However, particularly in modern times, humanity has experienced so much intermixing that race as a biological category has lost nearly all meaning. Some biologists and social scientists therefore suggest we drop the term *race* from the vocabulary of science.

Most sociologists, however, continue to use the term. They do so because *perceptions* of race continue to affect the lives of most people profoundly. Everything from your wealth to your health is influenced by whether others see you as black, white, brown, or something else. Race as a *sociological* concept is thus an invaluable analytical tool.

It is valuable, however, only to the degree that people who use the term remember that it refers to *socially significant* physical differences (e.g., skin colour) rather than to biological differences that shape behaviour patterns.

Said differently, perceptions of racial difference are socially constructed and often arbitrary. The Irish and the Jews were regarded as "blacks" by many people long ago, and today many northern Italians still think of southern Italians from Sicily and Calabria as "blacks" (Gilman, 1991; Ignatiev, 1995; Roediger, 1991). During World War II, some people made arbitrary physical distinctions between Chinese allies and Japanese enemies that helped to justify the Canadian policy of placing Japanese Canadians in internment camps. These examples show that racial distinctions are social constructs, not biological givens.

*Time* Magazine Explains How to Make Arbitrary Racial Distinctions, 1941

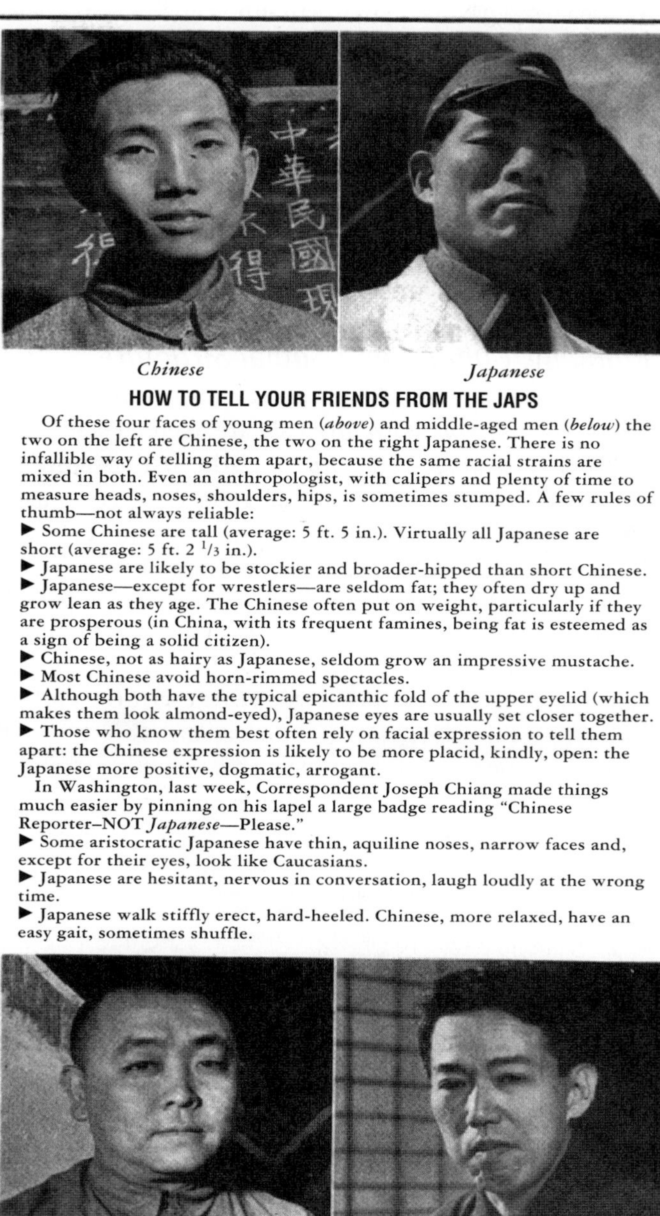

*Chinese* *Japanese*

**HOW TO TELL YOUR FRIENDS FROM THE JAPS**

Of these four faces of young men (*above*) and middle-aged men (*below*) the two on the left are Chinese, the two on the right Japanese. There is no infallible way of telling them apart, because the same racial strains are mixed in both. Even an anthropologist, with calipers and plenty of time to measure heads, noses, shoulders, hips, is sometimes stumped. A few rules of thumb—not always reliable:

▶ Some Chinese are tall (average: 5 ft. 5 in.). Virtually all Japanese are short (average: 5 ft. 2 1/3 in.).

▶ Japanese are likely to be stockier and broader-hipped than short Chinese.

▶ Japanese—except for wrestlers—are seldom fat; they often dry up and grow lean as they age. The Chinese often put on weight, particularly if they are prosperous (in China, with its frequent famines, being fat is esteemed as a sign of being a solid citizen).

▶ Chinese, not as hairy as Japanese, seldom grow an impressive mustache.

▶ Most Chinese avoid horn-rimmed spectacles.

▶ Although both have the typical epicanthic fold of the upper eyelid (which makes them look almond-eyed), Japanese eyes are usually set closer together.

▶ Those who know them best often rely on facial expression to tell them apart: the Chinese expression is likely to be more placid, kindly, open: the Japanese more positive, dogmatic, arrogant.

In Washington, last week, Correspondent Joseph Chiang made things much easier by pinning on his lapel a large badge reading "Chinese Reporter–NOT *Japanese*—Please."

▶ Some aristocratic Japanese have thin, aquiline noses, narrow faces and, except for their eyes, look like Caucasians.

▶ Japanese are hesitant, nervous in conversation, laugh loudly at the wrong time.

▶ Japanese walk stiffly erect, hard-heeled. Chinese, more relaxed, have an easy gait, sometimes shuffle.

*Chinese* *Japanese*

Carl Mydans, Black Star

Finally, then, we can define **race** as a social construct used to distinguish people in terms of one or more physical markers. However, this definition raises an interesting question. If race is merely a social construct and not a useful biological term, why are perceptions of physical difference used to distinguish groups of people in the first place? Why, in other words, does race matter? Most sociologists believe that race matters because it allows social inequality to be created and perpetuated. The English who colonized Ireland, the Americans who went to Africa looking for slaves, and the Germans who used the Jews as a scapegoat to explain their deep economic and political troubles after World War I, all created systems of racial domination. (A **scapegoat** is a disadvantaged person or category of people that others blame for their own problems.) Once colonialism, slavery, and concentration camps were established, behavioural differences developed between subordinates and their masters. For example, North American slaves and Jewish concentration camp inmates, with little motivating them to work hard except the ultimate threat of the master's whip, tended to do only the minimum work necessary to survive. Their masters noticed this and characterized their subordinates as inherently slow and unreliable workers (Collins, 1982, pp. 66–69). In this way, racial stereotypes are born. The stereotypes then embed themselves in literature, popular lore, journalism, and political debate. This reinforces racial inequalities (see Figure 7.1). We thus see that race matters to the degree that it helps create and maintain systems of social inequality.

## *Ethnicity, Culture, and Social Structure*

Race is to biology as ethnicity is to culture. A *race* is a socially defined category of people whose perceived *physical* markers are deemed significant. An **ethnic group** comprises people whose perceived *cultural* markers are deemed significant. Ethnic groups differ from one another in terms of language, religion, customs, values, ancestors, and the like. However, just as physical distinctions don't *cause* differences in the behaviour of various races, so cultural distinctions are often not by themselves the major source of

**Figure 7.1**
The Vicious Circle of Racism

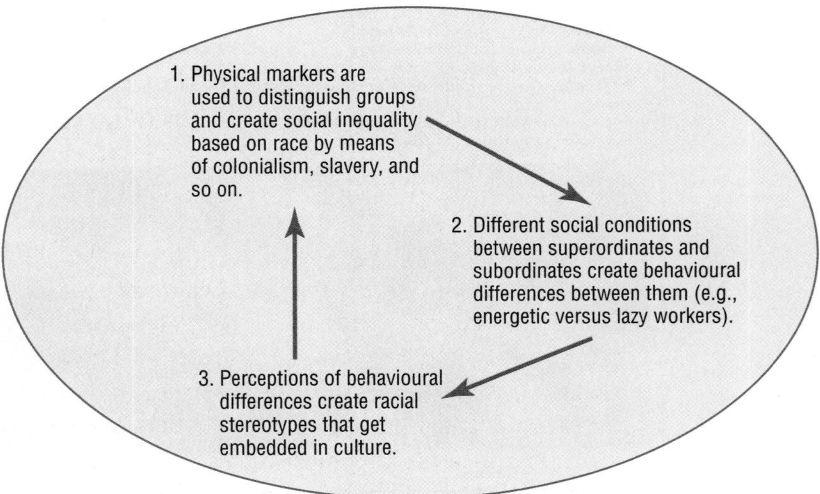
1. Physical markers are used to distinguish groups and create social inequality based on race by means of colonialism, slavery, and so on.
2. Different social conditions between superordinates and subordinates create behavioural differences between them (e.g., energetic versus lazy workers).
3. Perceptions of behavioural differences create racial stereotypes that get embedded in culture.

differences in the behaviour of various ethnic groups. In other words, ethnic values and other elements of ethnic culture have less of an effect on the way people behave than we commonly believe. That is because *social structural* differences frequently underlie cultural differences.

An example will help drive home the point. People often praise Jews, Koreans, and other economically successful groups for their cultural values, including an emphasis on education, family, and hard work. People less commonly notice, however, that Canada's immigration policy has been highly selective. For the most part, the Jews and Koreans who arrived in Canada were literate, urbanized, and skilled. Some even came with financial assets (Brym, Shaffir, and Weinfeld, 1993; Li, 1995; Wong and Ng, 1998). They certainly confronted prejudice and discrimination but far less than that reserved for the descendants of slaves or members of Canada's Aboriginal peoples. These social-structural conditions facilitated Jewish and Korean success. They gave members of these groups a firm basis on which to build and maintain a culture emphasizing education, family, and other middle-class virtues. In contrast, descendants of slaves and members of Canada's Aboriginal peoples were typically illiterate and unskilled, and they experienced more prejudice and discrimination than other ethnic or racial groups in Canada. These social-structural disadvantages—not their culture—made them less economically successful than Jews and Koreans on average.

In general, much Canadian research supports the argument that culture by itself is unimportant in determining the economic success of racial or ethnic groups. There *are* substantial differences in average annual income among some racial groups. For example, the average annual income of Aboriginal peoples is substantially below that of white Canadians. So is the average annual income of non-white immigrants below that of white Canadians. The point, however, is that these differences are due largely to such factors as how many years of education the average Aboriginal Canadian has and how many years the average non-white immigrant has been in the country. Practically no income differences exist between white Canadians and the Canadian-born children of non-white immigrants. A professor who happens to be an Aboriginal Canadian earns as much as a white professor with the same training, years of work experience, research and publication record, and so on. The problem is that there are so few Aboriginal professors because of the centuries-long discriminatory treatment of Aboriginal Canadians by the white majority (discussed later in the chapter).

### Resources and Opportunities

As we saw in our brief comparison of Koreans and Jews with Aboriginal peoples, what really matters in determining the economic success of an ethnic or racial group are the *resources* people possess, such as education, literacy, urbanity, and financial assets. We can now add that what also matters in determining economic success are the kinds of *economic opportunities* open to people. The latter point can be seen clearly if we compare Canada in the mid-twentieth century with Canada today.

Half a century ago, Canada was a society sharply stratified along ethnic and racial lines. The people with the most power and privilege were of British origin. WASPs (White Anglo-Saxon Protestants) controlled almost all the big corporations in the country and dominated politics. Immigrants who arrived later enjoyed less power and privilege. Even among them, big economic differences were evident, with European immigrants enjoying higher status than immigrants of Asian ancestry, for example.

John Porter, one of the founders of modern Canadian sociology, called mid-twentieth-century Canada an ethnically and racially stratified "vertical mosaic." He thought that the retention of ethnic and racial culture was a big problem in Canada because it hampered the upward mobility of immigrants. In his view, the "Canadian value system" encouraged the retention of ethnic culture, making Canada a low-mobility society (Porter, 1965, 1979: 91).

By the 1970s, however, many Canadian sociologists, including Porter himself, had to reject or at least qualify the view that ethnic and racial culture determines economic success or failure. Events upset their earlier assumptions. The Canadian economy grew quickly in the decades after World War II. Many members of ethnic and racial minority groups were economically successful despite ethnic and racial prejudice and discrimination. Economic differences among ethnic groups and, to a lesser degree, among racial groups, diminished. Among the wealthiest Canadians, and among politicians at all levels of government, ethnic and racial diversity increased. Such diversity became even more evident among professional groups. For the most part, visible minority status had little bearing on educational, occupational, and income attainment in Canada, especially among the Canadian-born (Guppy and Davies, 1998; Lautard and Guppy, 2008; Lian and Matthews, 1998; Pendakur and Pendakur, 1998; see Table 7.1). Aboriginal Canadians and black men (even black men born in Canada) continued to face discrimination that significantly impeded their upward mobility. But for the great majority of Canadians in the decades after World War II, ethnic and racial culture mattered less than the structure of mobility opportunities in determining a person's economic success.

True, in the 1990s, recent immigrants who were members of visible minority groups were significantly less successful economically than we would expect given their educational and other resources. However, their cultural values had little to do with that. Canada experienced an unusually high rate of unemployment in the 1990s, hovering around 10 percent until late in the decade. This situation made it more difficult than in previous decades for recently arrived visible minority immigrants to succeed economically. It has now become evident that many recent visible minority immigrants

**Table 7.1**
Percentage with Below-Average Canadian Income by Ethnic Identity and Place of Birth, Canada, 2001

| | Born Abroad (%) | Born in Canada (%) |
|---|---|---|
| British | 53 | 51 |
| French | 51 | 52 |
| Other European | 59 | 45 |
| African | 65 | 20 |
| Arab | 67 | 35 |
| Other Asian | 64 | 27 |
| Caribbean | 67 | 20 |
| Other Latin, Central, and South American | 55 | 34 |
| Aboriginal | 77 | 54 |
| Canadian | 62 | 50 |

Source: Adapted from Statistics Canada (n.d.-2).

Note: Data are for a random sample of 31 100 Canadian residents who gave a single ethnic origin in the 2001 census. Average individual annual income was $27 141. The income data were truncated at $200 000.

face a second problem limiting their upward mobility. Although they may be selected to come to Canada because they are highly educated, their credentials are often not recognized by employers here. The mechanisms for receiving accreditation for foreign credentials are poorly developed in this country and need to be improved (Reitz, 2008). But the relative lack of success of recent visible minority immigrants reinforces our point. In addition to the resources a person possesses, it is the structure of opportunities for economic advancement that determines income and occupational and educational attainment. Ethnic or racial culture by itself plays at best a minor role.

In sum, we see that racial and ethnic inequality is more deeply rooted in social structure than in biology and culture. The biological and cultural aspects of race and ethnicity are secondary to their sociological character when it comes to explaining inequality. The interesting question from a sociological point of view is why social definitions of race and ethnicity change. We now consider that issue.

# Race and Ethnic Relations

## *Labels, Identity, and Symbolic Interaction*

John Lie moved with his family from South Korea to Japan when he was a baby. He moved from Japan to Hawaii when he was 10 years old, and again from Hawaii to the American mainland when he started university. The move to Hawaii and the move to the U.S. mainland changed the way John thought of himself in ethnic terms.

In Japan, Koreans form a minority group. Before 1945, when Korea was a colony of Japan, some Koreans were brought to Japan to work as miners and unskilled labourers. The Japanese thought the Koreans who lived there were beneath and outside Japanese society (Lie, 2001). Not surprisingly, Korean children in Japan—including John—were often teased and occasionally beaten by their Japanese schoolmates. "The beatings hurt," says John, "but the psychological trauma resulting from being socially excluded by my classmates hurt more. In fact, although I initially thought I was Japanese like my classmates, my Korean identity was literally beaten into me.

"When my family immigrated to Hawaii, I was sure things would get worse. I expected Americans to be even meaner than the Japanese. (By Americans, I thought only of white European Americans.) Was I surprised when I discovered that most of my schoolmates were not white European Americans, but people of Asian and mixed ancestry! Suddenly I was a member of a numerical majority. I was no longer teased or bullied. In fact, I found that students of Asian and non-European origin often singled out white European Americans (called *haole* in Hawaiian) for abuse. We even had a 'beat up *haole* day' in school. Given my own experiences in Japan, I empathized somewhat with the white Americans. But I have to admit that I also felt a great sense of relief and an easing of the psychological trauma associated with being Korean in Japan.

"As the years passed, I finished public school in Hawaii. I then went to college in Massachusetts and got a job as a professor in Illinois and then in Michigan. I associated with, and befriended, people from various racial and ethnic groups. My Korean origin became an increasingly less important factor in the way people treated me. There was simply less prejudice and discrimination against Koreans during my adulthood in the

According to the 2001 census, the largest ethnic groups in Canada, other than Canadian, British, and French, include Canadians of German, Italian, Chinese, Ukrainian, and Aboriginal origin.

United States than in my early years in Japan. I now think of myself less as Japanese or Korean than as American. My ethnic identity has changed over time in response to the significance others have attached to my Korean origin. I now understand what the French philosopher Jean-Paul Sartre meant when he wrote that 'the anti-Semite creates the Jew'" (Sartre, 1965 [1948]: 43).

The details of John Lie's life are unique. But experiencing a shift in racial or ethnic identity is common. Social contexts, and in particular the nature of a person's relations with members of other racial and ethnic groups, shape and continuously reshape a person's racial and ethnic identity. Change your social context and your racial and ethnic self-conception eventually change, too (Miles, 1989; Omi and Winant, 1986).

Consider Italian Canadians. Around 1900, Italian immigrants thought of themselves as people who came from a particular town or perhaps a particular province, such as Sicily or Calabria. They did not usually think of themselves as Italians. Italy became a unified country only in 1861. A mere 30 years later, many Italian citizens still did not identify with their new Italian nationality. In both Canada and the United States, however, government officials and other residents identified the newcomers as Italians. The designation at first seemed odd to many of the new immigrants. However, over time it stuck. Immigrants from Italy started thinking of themselves as Italian Canadians because others defined them that way. A new ethnic identity was born (Yancey, Ericksen, and Leon, 1979).

As symbolic interactionists emphasize, the development of racial and ethnic labels, and ethnic and racial identities, is typically a process of negotiation. For example, members of a group may have a racial or an ethnic identity, but outsiders may impose a new label on them. Group members then reject, accept, or modify the label. The negotiation between outsiders and insiders eventually results in the crystallization of a new, more or less stable ethnic identity. If the social context changes again, the negotiation process begins anew.

One such case involves the labelling of the indigenous peoples of North America by European settlers. When Christopher Columbus landed in North America in 1492, he assumed he had reached India. He called the indigenous peoples "Indians" and the misnomer stuck—not only among European settlers but also among many indigenous peoples themselves. Indigenous peoples still identified themselves in tribal terms—as Mi'kmaq or Mohawk or Haida—but they typically thought of themselves collectively and *in opposition to European settlers* as Indians. A new identity was thus grafted onto tribal identities because indigenous peoples confronted a group that had the power to impose a name on them.

In time, however, an increasingly large number of indigenous people began to reject the term *Indian*. White settlers and their governments took land from the indigenous peoples, forced them onto reserves, and thus caused their resentment, anger, and solidarity to grow. Especially since the 1960s, indigenous North Americans have begun to fight back culturally and politically, asserting pride in their languages, art, and customs and making legal claims to the lands that were taken from them. One aspect of their resistance involved questioning use of the term *Indian*. In Canada, many of them preferred instead to be called Native Canadians, indigenous peoples, Aboriginal Canadians, or First Nations. These new terms, especially the last one, were all assertions of newfound pride. Today, many North Americans of European origin accept these new terms out of respect for indigenous North Americans and in recognition of their neglected rights. New, more or less stable ethnic identities have thus been negotiated as the power struggle between indigenous peoples and more recent settlers continues. As the social context changed, the negotiation of ethnic identities proceeded apace.

### *Imposition versus Choice*

The idea that race and ethnicity are socially constructed does not mean that everyone can always choose their racial or ethnic identity freely. Wide variations occur over time, between societies, and within societies in the degree to which people can exercise such freedom of choice.

The Canadians with the most freedom to choose their ethnic identity are whites whose ancestors arrived in Canada more than two generations ago. For example, identifying as an Irish Canadian no longer has negative implications it did in, say, 1900. Then, wherever a substantial number of Irish immigrants were concentrated, the English-Protestant majority typically regarded working-class Irish Catholics as often drunk, inherently lazy, and born superstitious. This strong anti-Irish sentiment, which often erupted into conflict, meant that the Irish found it difficult to escape their ethnic identity even if they wanted to. Since then, however, Irish Canadians have followed the path taken by many other white European groups: they have achieved upward mobility and blended with the majority.

As a result, Irish Canadians no longer find their identity imposed on them. Instead, they can *choose* whether to march in a St. Patrick's Day parade, enjoy the remarkable contributions of Irish authors to English-language literature and drama, and take pride in the athleticism and artistry of Riverdance. For them, ethnicity is largely a *symbolic* matter, as it is for the other white European groups that have undergone similar social processes. Herbert Gans defines **symbolic ethnicity** as "a nostalgic allegiance to the culture of the immigrant generation, or that of the old country; a love for and a pride in a tradition that can be felt without having to be incorporated in everyday behavior" (Gans, 1991: 436).

A grandfather and grandson clicking their heels in a St. Patrick's Day parade in Toronto

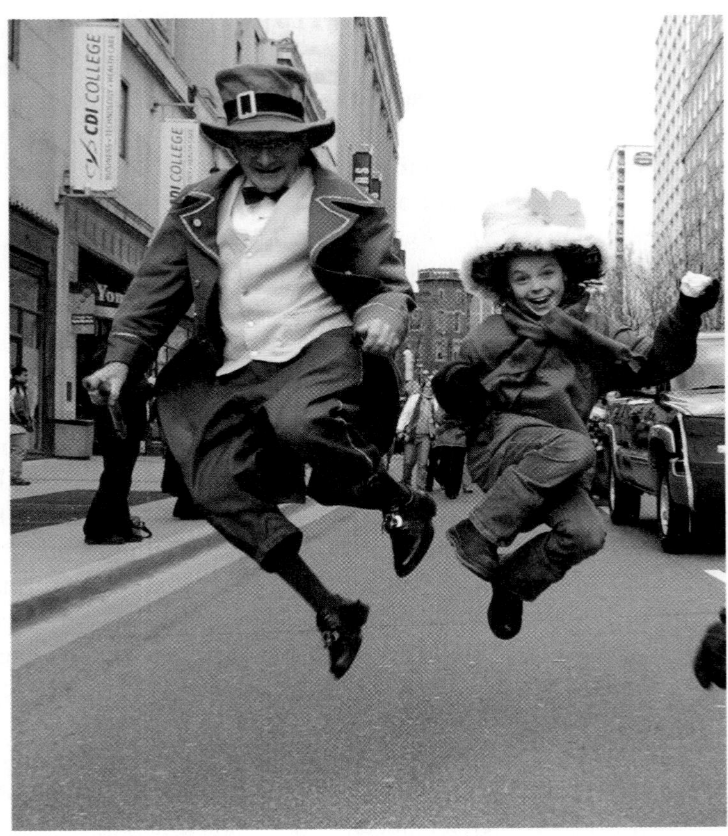

As Malcolm X noted, it doesn't matter to a racist whether a black person is a professor or a panhandler, a genius or a fool, a saint or a criminal. Where racism is common, racial identities are compulsory and at the forefront of a person's self-identity.

In contrast, most black Canadians lack the freedom to enjoy symbolic ethnicity. They may well take pride in their cultural heritage. However, their identity as black people is not optional because a considerable number of non-blacks are racists and impose it on them daily. **Racism** is the belief that a visible characteristic of a group, such as skin colour, indicates group inferiority and justifies discrimination. **Institutional racism** is bias that is inherent in social institutions and is often not noticed by members of the majority group. Recent surveys show that somewhere between 30 percent and 55 percent of Canadians (depending on the wording of the question) hold racist views (Henry et al., 2001: 147–51). In his autobiography, the black militant Malcolm X poignantly noted how racial identity can be imposed on people. He described one of his black Ph.D. professors as "one of these ultra-proper-talking Negroes" who spoke and acted snobbishly. "Do you know what white racists call black Ph.D.s?" asked Malcolm X. "He said something like, 'I believe that I happen not to be aware of that . . .' And I laid the word down on him, loud: 'Nigger!'" (X, 1965: 284). Malcolm X's point is that it doesn't matter to a racist whether a black person is a professor or a panhandler, a genius or a fool, a saint or a criminal. Where racism is common, racial identities are compulsory and at the forefront of a person's self-identity.

As the contrast between Irish Canadians and black Canadians suggests, then, relations among racial and ethnic groups can take different forms. We now discuss several theories that explain why forms of racial and ethnic relations vary over time and from place to place.

# Theories of Race and Ethnic Relations

## *Ecological Theory*

Nearly a century ago, Robert Park proposed an influential theory of how race and ethnic relations change over time (Park, 1950 [1914]). His **ecological theory** focuses on the struggle for territory. He distinguished five stages in the process by which conflict among ethnic and racial groups emerges and is resolved:

1. Invasion. *One racial or ethnic group tries to move into the territory of another. The territory may be as large as a country or as small as a city neighbourhood.*
2. Resistance. *The established group tries to defend its territory and institutions against the intruding group. It may use legal means, violence, or both.*
3. Competition. *If the established group does not drive out the newcomers, the two groups begin to compete for scarce resources. These resources include housing, jobs, public park space, and political positions.*
4. Accommodation and cooperation. *Over time, the two groups work out an understanding of what they should segregate, divide, and share.* ***Segregation*** *involves the spatial and institutional separation of racial or ethnic groups. For example, the two groups may segregate churches, heritage associations, and newspapers; divide political positions in proportion to the size of the groups; and share public parks equally.*
5. Assimilation. ***Assimilation*** *is the process by which a minority group blends into the majority population and eventually disappears as a distinct group. Park argued that assimilation is bound to occur as accommodation and cooperation allow trust and understanding to develop. Eventually, goodwill allows ethnic groups to fuse socially and culturally. Where there were formerly two or more groups, only one remains.*

Park's theory stimulated important and insightful research in the United States and Canada (Dawson, 1936; Hughes, 1943). However, it applies to some ethnic groups better than others. In North America, it applies best to whites of European origin. As Park predicted, many whites of European origin stopped thinking of themselves as Italian Canadian or Irish Canadian or German Canadian after their families were in Canada for three or four generations. Today, they think of themselves just as Canadians (Boyd, 1999; Boyd and Norris, 2001). Over time, they have achieved rough equality with members of the majority group and, in the process, began to blend in with them. The story of the Irish is fairly typical. During the first half of the twentieth century, Irish Canadians experienced upward mobility. By the middle of the century they earned about as much as others of British origin (the Scottish, the Welsh, and the English). The tapering off of working-class Irish immigration prevented the average status of the group from falling. As their status rose, Irish Canadians increasingly intermarried with members of other ethnic groups. Use of the Irish language, Gaelic, virtually disappeared. The Irish became less concentrated in particular cities and less segregated in certain neighbourhoods. Finally, conflict with most majority-group Canadians declined. With variations, a similar story can be told about Italian Canadians, German Canadians, and so on.

However, the story does not apply to all Canadians. Park's theory resonates less well with the experiences of Aboriginal peoples, Québécois, black Canadians, and Asian Canadians, in particular. For reasons we will now explore, some racial and ethnic groups seem stuck between Park's third and fourth stages (competition, and accommodation and cooperation).

### *The Theory of Internal Colonialism: A Conflict Theory of Ethnic and Race Relations*

The main weakness of Park's theory is that it pays insufficient attention to the social-structural conditions that prevent some groups from assimilating. Robert Blauner examined one such condition, which he called **internal colonialism** (Blauner, 1972; Hechter, 1974). Blauner's work is important because it stimulated the development of several theories that emphasize the social-structural (and especially class) roots of race and ethnicity, and the degree to which group conflict helps to form and sustain racial and ethnic groups.

*Colonialism* involves people from one country invading another. In the process, the invaders change or destroy the native culture. They gain virtually complete control over the native population. They develop the racist belief that the native inhabitants are inherently inferior. And they confine the natives to work considered demeaning. Internal colonialism involves much the same processes but within the boundaries of a single country. Internal colonialism prevents assimilation by segregating the colonized in terms of jobs, housing, and social contacts ranging from friendship to marriage. To varying degrees, Russia, China, France, Great Britain, Canada, Australia, the United States, and other countries have engaged in internal colonialism. In Canada, the main victims of internal colonialism are Aboriginal peoples, the Québécois, and black people.

### *Canada's Aboriginal Peoples*

The single word that best describes the treatment of Canada's Aboriginal peoples by European immigrants in the nineteenth century is *expulsion*. **Expulsion** is the forcible removal of a population from a territory claimed by another population.

Expulsion is dramatically illustrated by the plight of the Beothuk, the Aboriginal inhabitants of what is today Newfoundland and Labrador. The Beothuk were Algonkian-speaking hunter-gatherers who probably numbered fewer than a thousand people at the time of European contact. In the sixteenth century, European fishermen used Newfoundland and Labrador as a fishing port, returning to Europe each year after the fishing season. In the seventeenth century, year-round European settlement began. This caused a revolution in the life of the Beothuk because the Europeans viewed them as a nuisance. They offered incentives to Mi'kmaq Indians from Nova Scotia to kill off the Beothuk. The Beothuk population declined and gradually withdrew from European contact.

As European settlement grew in the eighteenth century, the Beothuk were squeezed into the interior. There they competed for scarce resources with fur traders. Eventually the Beothuk were reduced to a small refugee population along the Exploits River system, living off the meagre resources of the Newfoundland and Labrador interior. The expulsion of the Beothuk from their traditional territories because of European colonization led to their eventual extinction. Today, all that remains of the Beothuk aside from their tragic history and a few artifacts is a statue outside the Newfoundland and Labrador provincial legislature in St. John's.

The story of the Beothuk is an extreme case. However, *all* First Nations tribes had broadly similar experiences. In the eighteenth and nineteenth centuries, as the European settlers' fur trade gave way to the harvesting of timber, minerals, oil, and gas, Aboriginal peoples were shunted aside so that the Canadian economy could grow. At the time, Europeans thought they were "assimilating" the Aboriginal peoples. The Indian Act spoke of the need to transform a hunting-gathering people into an agricultural labour force (Menzies, 1999). Sir John A. Macdonald, Canada's first prime minister, spoke of the need "to do away with the tribal system and assimilate the Indian people in all respects with the inhabitants of the Dominion, as speedily as they are fit to change" (quoted in Montgomery, 1965: 13). In contrast, many Aboriginal peoples understood the settlers' actions—the passage of the Indian Act, the establishment of the reserve system, the creation of residential schools, and so forth—less as an attempt to assimilate them than an attempt to obliterate their heritage. It is in this sense that the government of Canada has been accused by some Aboriginal peoples of perpetuating cultural genocide (Cardinal, 1977). **Genocide** is the intentional extermination of an entire population defined as a "race" or a "people" (see Box 7.1).

Adding insult to injury, early historical writing about Canada depicted the First Nations as either irrelevant or evil. Typically, in *The History of the Dominion of Canada*, a book widely used in Canadian schools at the turn of the twentieth century, only five pages were devoted to Aboriginal peoples (Clement, 1897). They are described as "cruel,"

The Canadian policy of assimilation. In its annual report of 1904, the Department of Indian Affairs published the photographs of Thomas Moore of the Regina Industrial School, "before and after tuition." These images are "a cogent expression of what federal policy had been since Confederation and what it would remain for many decades. It was a policy of assimilation, a policy designed to move Aboriginal communities from their 'savage' state to that of 'civilization' and thus to make in Canada but one community—a non-Aboriginal one" (Milloy, 1999).

7.1

Paul Rusesabagina (played by Don Cheadle) and his wife (played by Sophie Okonedo) protect their children in *Hotel Rwanda*.

# SOCIOLOGY AT THE MOVIES

## *Hotel Rwanda* (2004)

In just a few days in 1994, the Hutus of Rwanda massacred 800 000 Tutsis—more than a tenth of Rwanda's population—with guns, machetes, hammers, and spears. Most of the world watched the attempted genocide with horror but did nothing. After all, Rwanda is in Africa, and as a United Nations peacekeeper explains to the manager of the Hotel Des Milles Collines in *Hotel Rwanda*, most of the world thinks of Africans as dung.

*Hotel Rwanda* is based on the true story of how the hotel manager, Paul Rusesabagina (Don Cheadle), used cunning and bribery to save more than 1200 Tutsis and sympathetic Hutus by protecting them in his hotel. Rusesabagina, a Hutu married to a Tutsi (Sophie Okonedo) is not the only hero of the piece. The UN peacekeeper (Nick Nolte) stands in for Romeo Dallaire, the Canadian general who led a tiny 500-man force credited with saving the lives of 20 000 Rwandans. Contemplating the horror outside the hotel gates, one of Rusesabagina's trusted employees asks: "Why are people so cruel?" Rusesabagina replies: "Hatred. Insanity. I don't know." Rusesabagina and Dallaire remind us that in an insane world, not everyone must succumb to madness.

*Hotel Rwanda* is a beautifully acted and heartbreaking movie. Because it unblinkingly shows the world its responsibility for failing to respond to genocide, it is worthwhile propaganda. But it is poor sociology because it leaves the viewer with the impression that "hatred" and "insanity" explain what the Hutus did to the Tutsis—or that we simply cannot know why people periodically kill one another in the name of ethnicity.

But we can know. Hutus and Tutsis existed as somewhat distinct ethnic groups for centuries before 1994. The Hutus were mainly farmers and the Tutsis mainly cattle herders. The Tutsis were the ruling minority yet they spoke the same language as the Hutus, shared the same religious beliefs, lived side by side, often intermarried, and never came into serious conflict with the Hutus.

When the Belgians took over Rwanda in 1916, they made ethnic divisions far more inflexible than they had been. Now one *had* to be a Tutsi to serve in an official capacity, and the Belgians started distinguishing Tutsis from Hutus by measuring the width of their noses; Tutsi noses, they arbitrarily proclaimed, are thinner. It was a preposterous policy (not least because half the population of Rwanda is of mixed Hutu-Tutsi ancestry) and it served to sharply increase animosity between the two ethnic groups (Organization of African Unity, 2000: 10).

Before the Belgians left Rwanda in 1962, they encouraged power sharing between the Tutsis and the Hutus, but by that time the damage had been done. The Tutsis objected to any loss of power and civil war broke out. Tutsi rebels fled to Uganda, and when Rwanda proclaimed independence, the Hutu majority took power. Then, in the early 1990s, descendants of the Tutsi rebels, backed by the United States and Britain, tried to overthrow the Hutu government, backed by France and Belgium. (Western interest in the region is high because it is rich in minerals; Rose, 2001.) The 1994 genocide erupted when the plane of the Hutu president was shot down, killing the president.

Belgium, the United States, Britain, and France must, then, bear responsibility for stoking the flames of ethnic conflict in Rwanda and not just for standing by when the conflict degenerated into genocide. Although Belgium and the United States have at least apologized to Rwanda for looking the other way, most people continue to believe that the Rwandans alone are responsible for what transpired in their country in 1994. Unfortunately, *Hotel Rwanda* helps to reinforce that misconception.

### CRITICAL THINKING QUESTIONS

- *Do you think hatred and insanity are sufficient explanations for instances of attempted genocide? If so, why? If not, why not?*
- *In general, what are the strengths and weaknesses of subjective and objective explanations of ethnic and racial conflict—respectively, those that focus on people's states of mind and those that focus on social forces outside the individual?*

"rude," "false," "crafty," "savages," and "ferocious villains" who plotted against the Europeans with "fiendish ingenuity." Canadian schoolbooks continued to portray Aboriginal peoples in much this way until the mid-twentieth century.

Throughout North America, the confrontation with European culture undermined the way of life of the Aboriginal peoples. Because of internal colonialism and, in particular, expulsion from their traditional lands, Canada's Aboriginal peoples were prevented from practising their traditional ways and from assimilating into the larger society. Most of them languished on reserves and, in more recent times, in urban slums. There they experienced high rates of unemployment, poverty, ill health, and violence. The history of Canada's Aboriginal peoples raises in the most distressing way possible the issue of whether and in what form white society should take responsibility for past injustices.

### *The Québécois*

A second form of internal colonialism involves not expulsion but **conquest,** the forcible capture of land and the economic and political domination of its inhabitants. For example, as part of their centuries-long struggle to control North America, the English conquered New France and its 60 000 Canadien settlers in 1759. They thereby created a system of ethnic stratification that remained in place for more than 200 years and became a major source of political conflict (McRoberts, 1988).

The British recognized that any attempt to impose their language, religion, laws, and institutions on the former French colony could result in unacceptably high levels of resistance and conflict. Therefore, they tried to accommodate farmers and the Catholic clergy by reinforcing their rights and privileges. The British believed this would win the allegiance of these two Canadien groups, who would in turn help to build loyalty to Britain among the population as a whole. In contrast, the British undermined the rights and privileges of Canadien merchants engaged mainly in the fur trade. They took over virtually all large-scale commerce. In this manner, big business became a British domain. Agriculture, religion, and politics remained the province of the French. This pattern of ethnic stratification remained intact for two centuries. True, by 1950 most farmers had been transformed into urban, industrial workers. Some Québécois had become physicians, lawyers, and members of the "new middle class" of administrators, technicians, scientists, and intellectuals. However, the upper reaches of the stratification system remained overwhelmingly populated by people of British origin. Social separation reinforced economic segregation. The French and the British tended to speak different languages, live in different towns and neighbourhoods, interact occasionally, befriend one another infrequently, and intermarry rarely. The novel that became emblematic of the social relations between French and English in Quebec is entitled *Two Solitudes* (MacLennan, 1945).

Apart from its rigid system of ethnic stratification, Quebec in the middle of the twentieth century was remarkable because of its undeveloped government services. Health, education, and welfare were largely controlled by the Catholic Church. Intervention of the government in economic matters was almost unknown. Because of this political backwardness, members of Quebec's new middle class, together with blue-collar workers, began campaigning to modernize the provincial political system in the late 1940s. They pressed for more liberal labour laws that would recognize the right of all workers to form unions and to strike. They wanted state control over education and a new curriculum that stressed the natural and social sciences rather than the classical languages and catechism. They desired a government that would supply a wide range of social services to the population. They demanded that the state provide better infrastructure for economic development and assist francophone entrepreneurs in expanding their businesses. The partial realization of these aims in the 1960s came to be known as the Quiet Revolution.

However, the modernization of the Quebec state failed to resolve four issues:

1. The potential demographic decline of the Québécois. *By 1981, Québécois women were giving birth to fewer children on average than women in any other province. In fact, they were having fewer than the 2.1 children women must bear on average to ensure that the size of the population does not decline (Romaniuc, 1984: 14–18). Noticing this trend in the 1970s, many Québécois felt they were becoming an endangered species.*
2. The assimilation of immigrants into English culture. *Fears of demographic decline were reinforced by the preference of most new immigrants to have their children educated in English-language schools. Together with the falling birth rate, this development threatened to diminish the size—and therefore, potentially, the power—of Quebec's francophone population.*
3. Persistent ethnic stratification. *The Quiet Revolution helped create many thousands of jobs for highly educated francophones—but almost exclusively in the government bureaucracy, the educational system, and new Crown corporations such as Hydro-Québec. It became apparent in the 1970s that management positions in the private sector remained the preserve of English-origin Canadians.*
4. The continued use of English as the language of private industry. *English remained the language of choice in the private sector because the largest and technologically most advanced businesses were controlled by English Canadians and Americans. This situation was felt particularly keenly when the expansion of the state sector, and therefore the upward mobility of the francophone new middle class, slowed in the 1970s.*

Because of the issues just listed, many Québécois felt that the survival and prosperity of their community required active state intervention in non-francophone institutions. For example, many Québécois came to believe that most shares of banks, trust companies, and insurance firms should be held in Quebec and that these financial institutions should be obliged to reinvest their profits in the province. They argued that the state should increase its role as economic planner and initiator of development and should forbid foreign ownership of cultural enterprises. Finally, the Québécois increasingly demanded compulsory French-language education for the children of most immigrants, obligatory use of French among private-sector managers, and French-only signs in public places. Most Québécois regarded these proposals as the only means by which their community could survive and attain equality with other groups. Moreover, because the Quebec state did not have the legal authority to enact some of the proposed changes, they felt that the province ought to negotiate broader constitutional powers with the federal government. A large minority of Québécois went a step further. They became convinced that Quebec ought to become a politically sovereign nation, albeit a nation economically associated with Canada.

The pro-independence Parti Québécois won the provincial election in 1976. In 1980, it held a referendum to see whether Quebecers favoured "sovereignty-association." Nearly 60 percent voted "no." A second referendum was held in 1995. This time, the forces opposed to sovereignty-association won by the narrowest of margins—about 1 percent. The Parti Québécois promises to hold additional referenda until it gets the result it wants. Thus, in the early twenty-first century, Canada's future is still uncertain

# TO BE SOLD,

A BLACK WOMAN, named PEGGY, aged about forty years ; and a Black boy her ſon, named JUPITER, aged about fifteen years, both of them the property of the Subſcriber.

The Woman is a tolerable Cook and waſher woman and perfectly underſtands making Soap and Candles.

The Boy is tall and ſtrong of his age, and has been employed in Country buſineſs, but brought up principally as a Houſe Servant—They are each of them Servants for life. The Price for the Woman is one hundred and fifty Dollars—for the Boy two hundred Dollars, payable in three years with Intereſt from the day of Sale and to be properly ſecured by Bond &c.—But one fourth leſs will be taken in ready Money.

PETER RUSSELL.

York, Feb. 10th 1806.

Black Slave for Sale: Many distinguished persons were slave owners, including Peter Russell, who held positions in the executive and legislative councils and became administrator of Upper Canada.

because of the economic, social, and cultural segregation of the Québécois from English Canada that is a legacy of the conquest.

## *Black Canadians*

We have seen that internal colonialism, whether accomplished by expulsion or conquest, creates big barriers to assimilation than can endure for centuries. A third form of internal colonialism—slavery—creates similar barriers. **Slavery** is the ownership and control of people.

By about 1800, 24 million Africans had been captured and placed on slave ships headed to North, Central, and South America. Because of violence, disease, and shipwreck, fewer than half survived the passage. Black slaves were bought and sold in Canada at least until the 1820s. Only in 1833, when the British government banned slavery throughout the British Empire, did the practice become illegal in all of what is now Canada. Slavery was abolished in the United States 30 years later.

It is true that the extent of slavery in Canada paled in comparison with its widespread use in the United States, where tobacco and cotton production depended entirely on the work of dirt-cheap black labour. It is also true that for decades Canada served as the terminus of the "underground railway," a network that smuggled escaped slaves out of the United States to freedom in Canada. As Martin Luther King, leader of the American civil rights movement in the 1960s, said in 1967:

> *Deep in our history of struggle for freedom Canada was the North Star. The Negro slave knew that far to the north a land existed where a fugitive slave, if he survived the horrors of the journey, could find freedom. The legendary underground railroad started in the south and ended in Canada. Our spirituals, now so widely admired around the world, were often codes. We sang of "heaven" that awaited us, and the slave masters listened in innocence, not realizing that we were not speaking of the hereafter. Heaven was the word for Canada and the Negro sang of the hope that his escape on the underground railroad would carry him there. One of our spirituals, "Follow the Drinking Gourd," in its disguised lyrics contained directions for escape. The gourd was the big dipper, and the North Star to which its handle pointed gave the celestial map that directed the flight to the Canadian border. (King, 1967: 1)*

*The Migration of the Negro, Panel No. 57*. Jacob Lawrence, 1940–1941. Jacob Lawrence's *The Great Migration* series of paintings illustrates the mass exodus of black Americans from the South to the North in search of a better life. Many former slaves came to Canada by using the "underground railway," a network of blacks and whites who opposed slavery, and settled mainly in southern Ontario, after Lieutenant Governor John Graves Simcoe signed the Upper Canadian Act Against Slavery in 1793.

What King neglected to mention is that after the American Civil War (1861–65) the practice of encouraging black settlement in Canada was reversed. Government policy required the rejection of most immigration applications by black people. This policy reflected a deeply felt prejudice on the part of the Canadian population that persisted throughout the twentieth century (Sissing, 1996). Moreover, social relations between black Canadians and the white European majority were anything but intimate and based on

**Table 7.2**
Immigrants by Immigrant Category, Canada, 2005

| Immigration Category | Number | Percentage |
|---|---|---|
| Economic class | 156 310 | 59.61 |
| Family class | 63 352 | 24.16 |
| Refugees | 35 768 | 13.64 |
| Other | 6 806 | 2.60 |
| Total | 262 236 | 100.0 |

Source: Citizenship and Immigration Canada (2006).

equality. Until the mid-twentieth century, blacks tended to do unskilled labour and be residentially and socially segregated—for example, in the Halifax community of Africville, established around 1850 by runaway American slaves (Clairmont and Magill, 1999).

Canadian immigration policy was liberalized in the 1960s. Racial and ethnic restrictions were removed. Immigrants were now admitted on the basis of their potential economic contribution to Canada, their close family ties with Canadians, or their refugee status (see Table 7.2). As a result, Canada became a much more racially and ethnically diverse society (see Figure 7.2). Today, about three-quarters of Canadian immigrants are members of visible minority groups, about the same proportion who arrive from Africa, Asia, and South and Central America. According to the 2001 census, Canada is the home of 622 000 blacks, up 15 percent from 1996. They form Canada's third-largest visible minority (after Chinese and

**Figure 7.2**
Immigrants by Source Area, Canada, pre-1961 and 2005

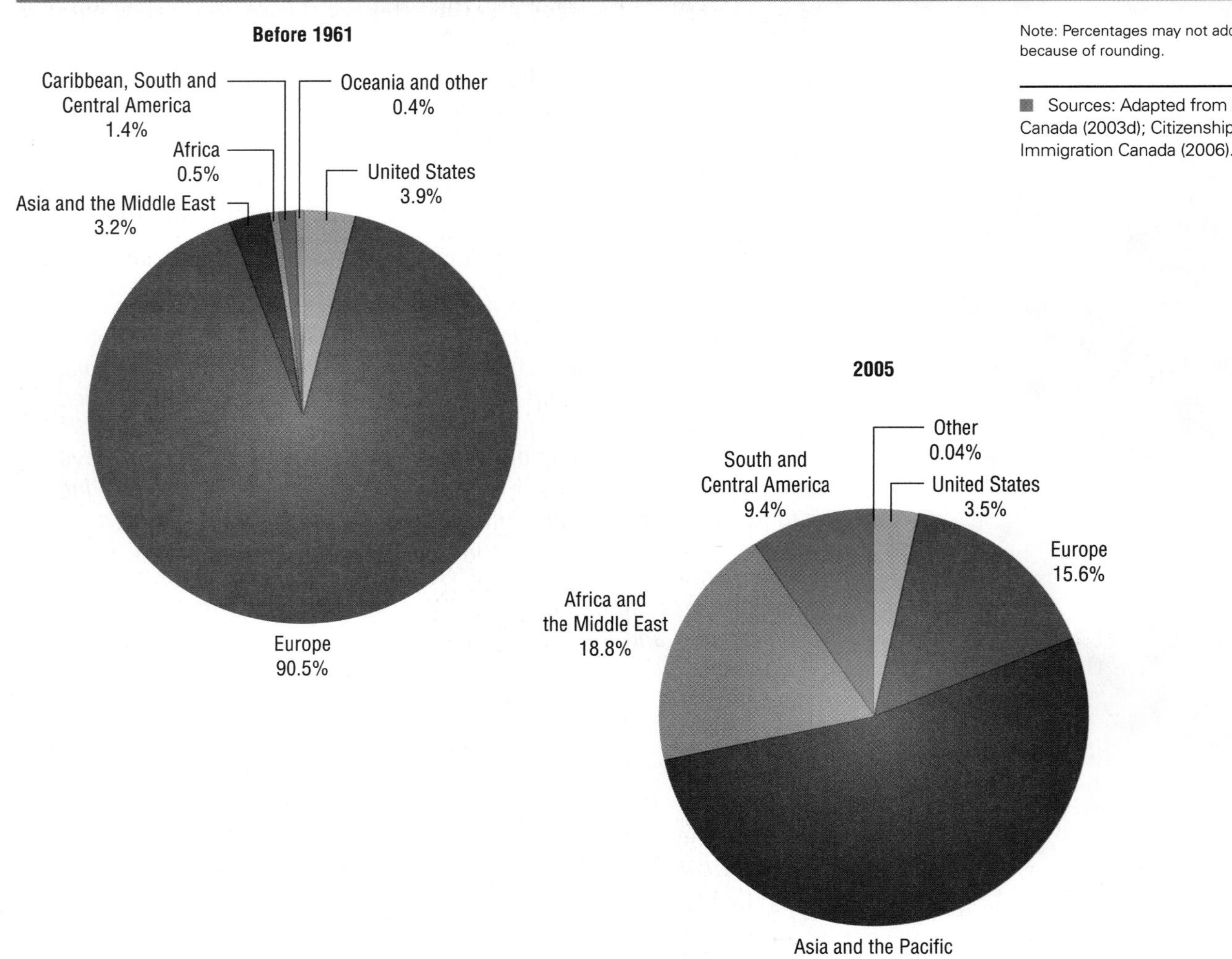


Note: Percentages may not add to 100 because of rounding.

Sources: Adapted from Statistics Canada (2003d); Citizenship and Immigration Canada (2006).

Indians), representing 2.2 percent of the population and 17 percent of the visible minority population (Statistics Canada, 2003d; Citizenship and Immigration Canada, 2006).

With the influx of new immigrants in recent decades, the social standing of Canada's black community has improved significantly. Many new immigrants had completed postsecondary education before their arrival. Others attended colleges and universities in Canada. Nonetheless, black Canadians still tend to interact little with white Canadians of European descent, especially in their intimate relations, and they still tend to live in different neighbourhoods. Like the aftermath of expulsion and conquest, the aftermath of slavery—prejudice, discrimination, disadvantage, and segregation—continues to act as a barrier to assimilation (Box 7.2).

### *Another Conflict Theory: Split Labour Markets and the Case of Asian Canadians*

We have seen how the theory of internal colonialism explains the persistence of inequality and segregation among racial and ethnic groups. A second theory that focuses on the social-structural barriers to assimilation is the theory of the **split labour market,** first proposed by sociologist Edna Bonacich (1972). Bonacich's theory explains why racial identities are reinforced by certain labour market conditions. In brief, she argues that where low-wage workers of one race and high-wage workers of another

7.2

## YOU AND THE SOCIAL WORLD

**Your Ethnic and Racial Barriers**

You can easily judge for yourself the strength of social barriers between Canadians of different ethnic and racial backgrounds. You can also determine how this barrier has changed over time. Draw up a list of your five closest friends and note the ethnic or racial background of each one. Now ask one of your parents (or someone of their generation) to do the same for *their* five closest friends. Finally, ask one of your grandparents (or someone of their generation) to draw up a similar list.

Now, instead of focusing on friends, perform the same exercise for your cousins and the cousins of your parent and grandparent.

**CRITICAL THINKING QUESTIONS**

- *How racially and ethnically diverse is your friendship network? How do you explain its racial and ethnic diversity or lack of diversity? How racially and ethnically diverse is your friendship network compared with the friendship network of your parent and grandparent? How do you explain differences among generations?*
- *How racially and ethnically diverse is your kinship network? How diverse it is compared with the kinship network of your parent and grandparent? How do you explain differences among generations?*
- *Compare the racial and ethnic diversity of friendship and kinship networks. For each generation (yours, your parent's, and your grandparent's), is the kinship or the friendship network more racially and ethnically diverse? Why? Where do you and your family fit into the web of racial and ethnic diversity that composes Canadian society?*

race compete for the same jobs, high-wage workers are likely to resent the presence of low-wage competitors and conflict is bound to result. Consequently, racist attitudes develop or are reinforced.

That resentment is certainly what happened during the early years of Asian immigration in Canada. Chinese, then Japanese, and later Sikhs were allowed into Canada from about the 1850s to the early 1920s for one reason: to provide scarce services and cheap labour in the booming West. Chinese-owned restaurants, grocery stores, laundries, and import businesses dotted the West and especially British Columbia by the early twentieth century (Li, 1998; Whitaker, 1987). Numerically more important, however, were the Asian labourers who worked in lumbering, mining, and railway construction. For example, 15 000 Chinese men were allowed into Canada to complete construction of the final and most difficult section of the Canadian Pacific Railway (CPR), which involved blasting tunnels and laying rail along dangerous Rocky Mountain passes. The Chinese were paid half the wages of white workers. It is said that they "worked like horses." It is also said that they "dropped like flies" because of exposure, disease, malnutrition, and explosions. Three Chinese workers died for every kilometre of track laid.

Asian immigration in general was widely viewed as a threat to cherished British values and institutions, an evil to be endured only as long as absolutely necessary. Therefore, once the CPR was completed in 1885, the Chinese were no longer welcome in British Columbia. A prohibitively expensive "head tax" equal to two months' wages was placed on each Chinese immigrant. The tax was increased tenfold in 1903. In 1923, Chinese immigration was banned altogether. During the Great Depression, more than 28 000 Chinese were deported because of high unemployment. Asian immigration did not resume on a large scale until the 1960s, when racial criteria were finally removed from Canadian immigration regulations.

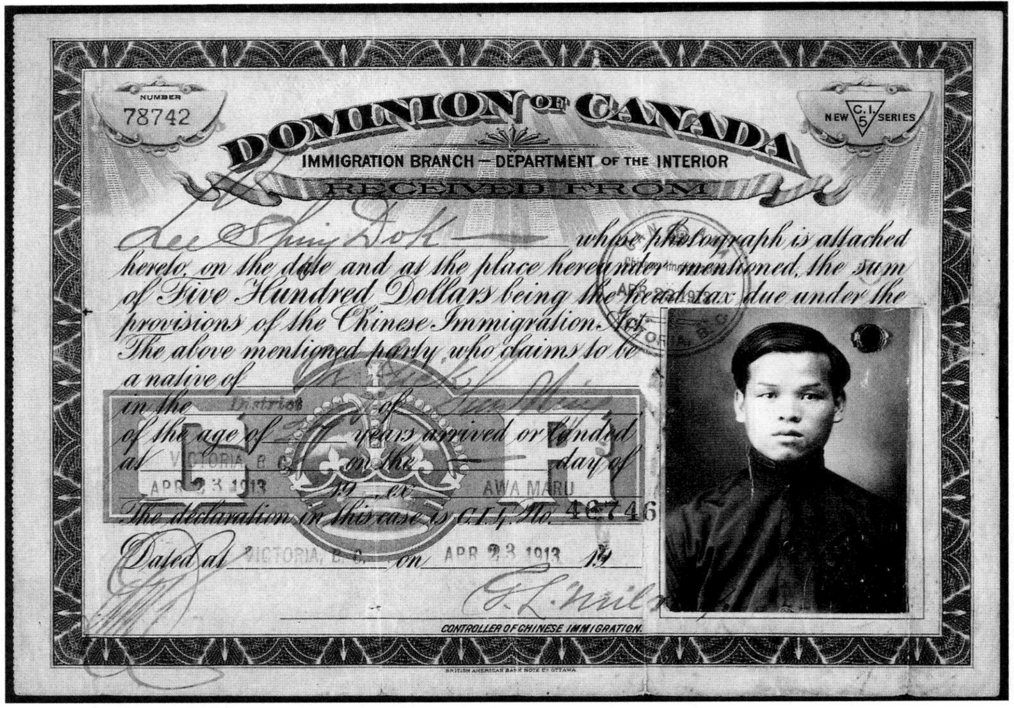

NUMBER 78742

DOMINION OF CANADA

NEW C.I. 5 SERIES

IMMIGRATION BRANCH — DEPARTMENT OF THE INTERIOR

RECEIVED FROM

whose photograph is attached hereto, on the date and at the place hereunder mentioned, the sum of Five Hundred Dollars being the head tax due under the provisions of the Chinese Immigration Act. The above mentioned party who claims to be a native of in the District of of the age of years arrived or landed at VICTORIA B.C. on the day of APR 23 1913 19 per AWA MARU. The declaration in this case is C.I. 4. No.

Dated at VICTORIA, B.C. on APR 23 1913 19

CONTROLLER OF CHINESE IMMIGRATION.

Head Tax Certificate: In another example of legislated racism, immigrants from China were required by law to pay a "head tax" to enter Canada between 1885 and 1923. The tax began as a fee of $50 and rose as high as $500.

With the introduction of the point system in 1967, nationality and race were removed as selection criteria from the Immigration Act. In 2005, the top four source countries were China, India, the Philippines, and Pakistan.

Underlying European-Canadian animosity against Asian immigration was a split labour market. The fact that Asian immigrants were willing to work for much lower wages than European Canadians fuelled deep resentment among European Canadians, especially when the labour market was flooded with far too many job seekers. European Canadians formed "exclusion leagues" to pressure the government to restrict Asian immigration, and on occasion they even staged anti-Asian riots. Such actions solidified racial identities among both the rioters and the victims of the riots and made assimilation impossible.

In sum, the theory of split labour markets, like the theory of internal colonialism, emphasizes the social-structural roots of race and ethnicity and helps overcome the main weakness of Park's ecological theory. The groups that have had most trouble assimilating into the British values and institutions that dominate Canadian society are those that were subjected to expulsion from their native lands, conquest, slavery, and split labour markets. These circumstances have left a legacy of racism that has created social-structural impediments to assimilation—such impediments as forced segregation in low-status jobs and low-income neighbourhoods. By focusing on factors like these, we arrive at a more realistic picture of the state of race and ethnic relations in Canada than is afforded by ecological theory alone.

# Some Advantages of Ethnicity

The theories of internal colonialism and split labour markets emphasize how social forces outside a racial or an ethnic group force its members together, preventing their assimilation into the dominant values and institutions of society. They focus on the disadvantages of race and ethnicity. Moreover, they deal only with the most disadvantaged minorities. The theories have less to say about the internal conditions that promote group cohesion and in particular about the value of group membership. They do not help us understand why some European Canadians of Greek or German or Irish origin continue to participate in the life of their ethnic communities, even if their families have been in the country for more than two or three generations.

High levels of immigration renew racial and ethnic communities by providing them with new members who are familiar with ancestral languages, customs, and so forth. Part of the reason that ethnic communities remain vibrant in Canada is that immigration continues at a rapid pace; only Australia and Israel have a

**Figure 7.3**
Percentage of Canada's Population Foreign-Born, 1901–2001

■ Source: Adapted from Statistics Canada (1997, 2003d).

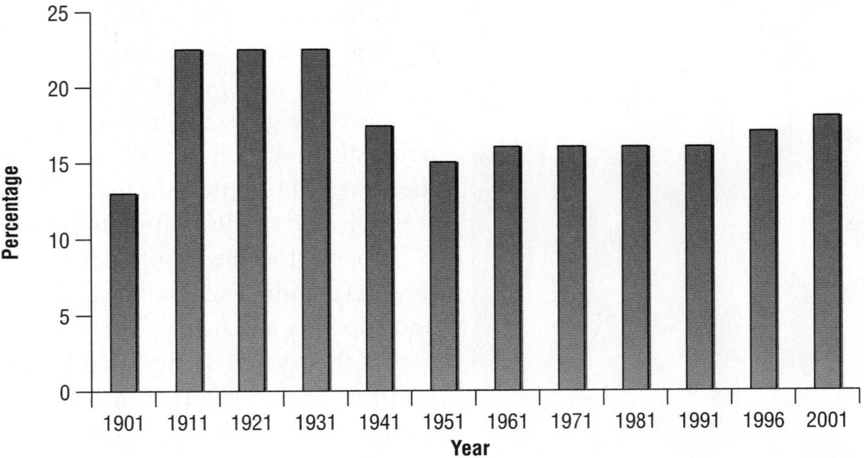


larger percentage of immigrants than Canada (see Figure 7.3). But as we have seen, little of Canada's current immigration is composed of white Europeans. Immigration levels do not explain the persistence of ethnic identity among members of some white ethnic groups of European origin.

Three main factors enhance the value of continued ethnic group membership:

1. Ethnic group membership can have economic advantages. *The economic advantages of ethnicity are most apparent for immigrants, who often lack extensive social contacts and fluency in English or French. They commonly rely on members of their ethnic group to help them find jobs and housing. In this way, immigrant communities become tightly knit. However, some economic advantages extend into the third generation and beyond. For example, community solidarity is an important resource for "ethnic entrepreneurs." These are businesspeople who operate largely within their ethnic community. They draw on their community for customers, suppliers, employees, and credit, and they may be linked economically to the homeland as importers and exporters. They often pass on their businesses to their children, who in turn can pass the businesses on to the next generation. In this way, strong economic incentives encourage some people to remain ethnic group members, even beyond the immigrant generation (Light, 1991; Portes and Manning, 1991).*
2. Ethnic group membership can be politically useful. *Consider, for instance, the way some Canadians reacted to the rise of separatism in Quebec in the 1960s. To bridge the growing divide between francophone Quebec and the rest of the country, the federal government under Pierre Trudeau's Liberals promoted a policy of bilingualism. French and English were made official languages. This policy meant that federal government services would be made available in both languages and instruction in French, including total immersion instruction, would be encouraged in English schools. Members of some ethnic groups, such as people of Ukrainian origin in Western Canada, felt neglected by this turn of events. They saw no reason why the French should be accorded special status and wanted a share of the resources available for promoting ethnic languages and cultures. As a result, the Trudeau government proclaimed a new policy of multiculturalism in 1971. Federal funds became available*

*for the promotion of Ukrainian and all other ethnic cultures in Canada. This entire episode of Canadian ethnic history bolstered Western support for the Liberal Party and softened Western opposition to bilingualism. Moreover, it helped to stimulate ethnic culture and ethnic identification throughout the country. We thus see that ethnicity can be a political tool for achieving increased access to resources.*

3. Ethnic group membership tends to persist because of the emotional support it provides. *Like economic benefits, the emotional advantages of ethnicity are most apparent in immigrant communities. Speaking the ethnic language and sharing other elements of our own native culture are valuable sources of comfort in an alien environment. Even beyond the second generation, however, ethnic group membership can perform significant emotional functions. For example, some ethnic groups have experienced unusually high levels of prejudice and discrimination involving expulsion or attempted genocide. For people who belong to such groups, the resulting trauma is so severe it can be transmitted for several generations. In such cases, ethnic group membership offers security in a world still seen as hostile long after the threat of territorial loss or annihilation has disappeared (Bar-On, 1999). Ethnic group membership also offers emotional support beyond the second generation by providing a sense of rootedness. Especially in a highly mobile, urbanized, technological, and bureaucratic society such as ours, ties to an ethnic community can be an important source of stability and security (Isajiw, 1978).*

Retaining ethnic ties beyond the second generation has never been easier. Inexpensive international communication and travel allow ethnic group members to maintain strong ties to their ancestral homeland in a way that was never possible in earlier times. Immigration used to involve cutting all or most ties to a country of origin because of the high costs of travel and of long-distance telephone rates. This lack of communication encouraged assimilation in people's newly adopted countries. Today, however, ties to the ancestral communities are often maintained in ways that sustain ethnic culture. For example, about 50 000 Jews have immigrated from the former Soviet Union to Canada since the early 1970s, settling mainly in Toronto. They frequently visit relatives in the former Soviet Union and Israel, speak with them on the phone,

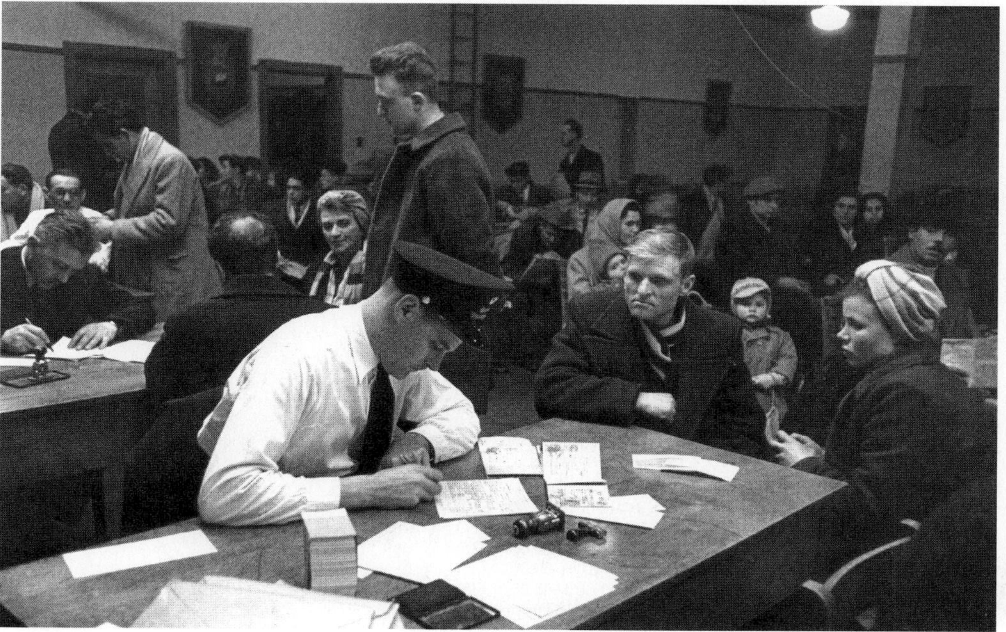

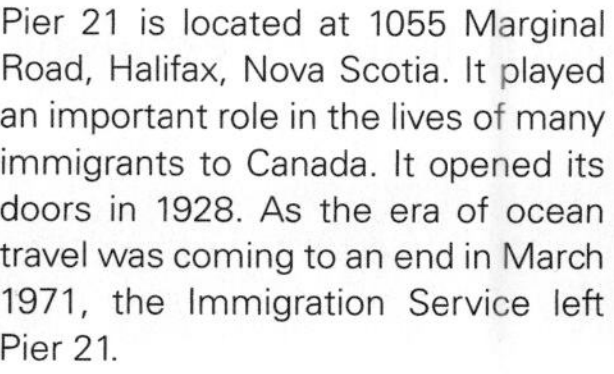

Pier 21 is located at 1055 Marginal Road, Halifax, Nova Scotia. It played an important role in the lives of many immigrants to Canada. It opened its doors in 1928. As the era of ocean travel was coming to an end in March 1971, the Immigration Service left Pier 21.

and use the Internet to exchange e-mail with them. They also receive Russian-language radio and TV broadcasts, act as conduits for foreign investment, and send money to relatives abroad (Brym, 2001; Brym with Ryvkina, 1994; Markowitz, 1993). This sort of intimate and ongoing connection with the motherland is typical of most recent immigrant communities in North America. Thanks to inexpensive international travel and communication, some ethnic groups have become **transnational communities** whose boundaries extend among countries.

In sum, ethnicity remains a vibrant force in Canadian society for a variety of reasons. Even some white Canadians whose families settled in this country more than two generations ago have reason to identify with their ethnic group. Bearing this in mind, what is the likely future of race and ethnic relations in Canada? We conclude by offering some tentative answers to that question.

# The Future of Race and Ethnicity in Canada

The world comprises more than 200 countries and more than 5000 ethnic and racial groups. As a result, no country is ethnically and racially homogeneous and in many countries, including Canada, the largest ethnic group forms less than half the population (see Figure 7.4 and Table 7.3). Canada's British roots remain important. Our parliamentary democracy is based on the British model; the Queen's representative, the governor general, is our head of state; we still celebrate May 24, Queen Victoria's birthday; and English is the country's predominant language, with more than 60 percent of Canadians claiming it as their mother tongue. Nonetheless, Canada is one of the most racially and ethnically heterogeneous societies in the world.

As racial and ethnic diversity has increased, Canadian ethnic and race relations have changed radically. Two hundred years ago, Canada was a society based on expulsion,

**Figure 7.4**
**Percentage of Population Accounted for by Largest Ethnic Group**

Sources: "Ethnic Groups" (1998); Central Intelligence Agency (2001).

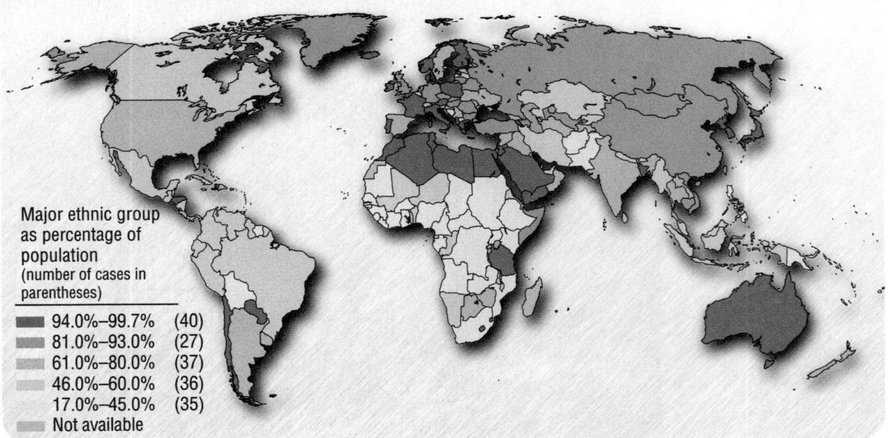

**Table 7.3**
Canada's Twenty Biggest Ethnic Groups, 2001

| Ethnic Origins | Total Responses[1] | Single Responses | Multiple Responses[2] |
|---|---|---|---|
| Canadian | 11 682 680 | 6 748 135 | 4 934 550 |
| English | 5 978 875 | 1 479 520 | 4 499 355 |
| French | 4 668 410 | 1 060 755 | 3 607 655 |
| Scottish | 4 157 210 | 607 235 | 3 549 975 |
| Irish | 3 822 660 | 496 865 | 3 325 800 |
| German | 2 742 765 | 705 595 | 2 037 170 |
| Italian | 1 270 370 | 726 275 | 544 090 |
| Chinese | 1 094 700 | 936 210 | 158 490 |
| Ukrainian | 1 071 060 | 326 200 | 744 860 |
| North American Indian | 1 000 890 | 455 805 | 545 085 |
| Dutch (Netherlands) | 923 310 | 316 220 | 607 090 |
| Polish | 817 085 | 260 415 | 556 670 |
| East Indian | 713 330 | 581 665 | 131 665 |
| Norwegian | 363 760 | 47 230 | 316 530 |
| Portuguese | 357 690 | 252 835 | 104 855 |
| Welsh | 350 365 | 28 445 | 321 925 |
| Jewish | 348 605 | 186 475 | 162 130 |
| Russian | 337 960 | 70 890 | 267 070 |
| Filipino | 327 545 | 266 140 | 61 410 |
| Métis | 307 845 | 72 210 | 235 635 |

Source: Statistics Canada (n.d.-3).

[1] Includes origins with total response counts of 15 000 or more for Canada.

[2] Respondents who reported multiple ethnic origins are counted more than once, as they are included in the multiple responses for each origin they reported. For example, a respondent who reported "English and Scottish" would be included in the multiple responses for English and for Scottish.

conquest, slavery, and segregation. Today, we are a society based on segregation, pluralism, and assimilation, with **pluralism** being understood as the retention of racial and ethnic culture combined with equal access to basic social resources. Thus, on a scale of tolerance, Canada has come a long way in the past 200 years (see Figure 7.5).

In comparison with most other countries, Canada is a relatively tolerant land. In the late twentieth and early twenty-first centuries, racial and ethnic tensions in some parts of the world erupted into wars of secession and attempted genocide. Conflict among Croats, Serbs, and other ethnic groups tore Yugoslavia apart. Russia fought a bloody war against its Chechen ethnic minority. In Rwanda, Hutu militia and soldiers massacred many thousands of Tutsi civilians. A few years later, Tutsi soldiers massacred many thousands of Hutu civilians. Comparing Canada with such poor countries may seem to stack the deck in favour of concluding that Canada is a relatively tolerant society. However, even when we compare Canada with other rich, stable, postindustrial countries, our society seems relatively tolerant by most measures. For example, a 2002 survey of 44 countries found that "only in Canada does a strong majority of the population (77 percent) have a positive view of immigrants." Far behind in second place came the United States, at 49 percent (Pew Research Center, 2002: 43; see also Figure 7.6).

Because of such factors as intermarriage and immigration, the growth of tolerance in Canada is taking place in the context of increasing ethnic and racial diversity. Given

**Figure 7.5**
**Six Degrees of Separation: Types of Ethnic and Racial Group Relations**

■ Source: Figure from p. 385 of *Sociology in a Changing World,* Fourth Edition by William Kornblum, copyright © 1997. Reprinted by permission of Wadsworth, a division of Thomson Learning: www.thomsonrights.com. Fax 800-730-2215.

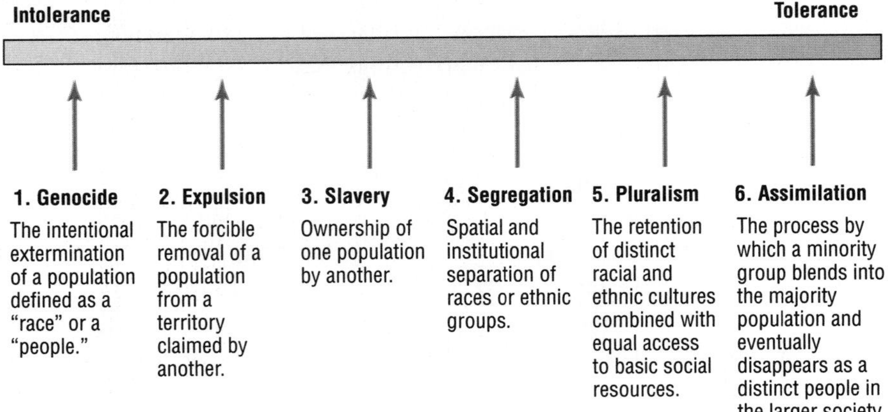


continuing migration in the coming decades, Canada will become even more of a racial and ethnic mosaic than it is now (Pendakur, 2000). If present trends continue, the racial and ethnic mosaic will continue to be stratified. That is, some groups, especially Aboriginal peoples, will be disproportionately clustered at the bottom of the socioeconomic hierarchy. Unless dramatic changes occur, they will continue to enjoy less wealth, income, education, good housing, health care, and other social rewards than other Canadians.

Intolerance
Tolerance
1. Genocide
The intentional extermination of a population defined as a "race" or a "people."
2. Expulsion
The forcible removal of a population from a territory claimed by another.
3. Slavery
Ownership of one population by another.
4. Segregation
Spatial and institutional separation of races or ethnic groups.
5. Pluralism
The retention of distinct racial and ethnic cultures combined with equal access to basic social resources.
6. Assimilation
The process by which a minority group blends into the majority population and eventually disappears as a distinct people in the larger society.

Political initiatives could decrease the verticality of the Canadian mosaic, speeding up the movement from segregation to pluralism and assimilation for the country's most disadvantaged groups. Such political initiatives include compensation for historical injustices (see Box 7.3), affirmative action or **employment equity** programs that encourage the hiring of qualified members of disadvantaged minorities, government-subsidized job training and child care, improvements in public education, and the creation of a system for efficiently upgrading credentials earned abroad to meet Canadian standards. All these initiatives would benefit disadvantaged Canadians the most.

**Figure 7.6**
**Influence of Immigrants**

■ Source: Reprinted by permission Pew Research Center For the People and The Press.

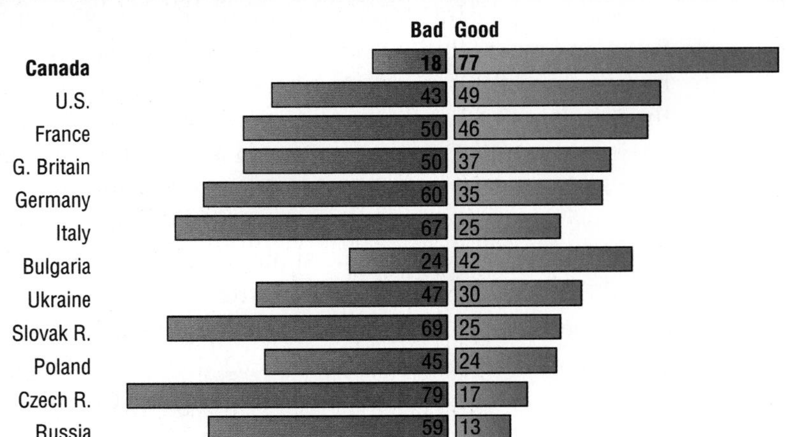

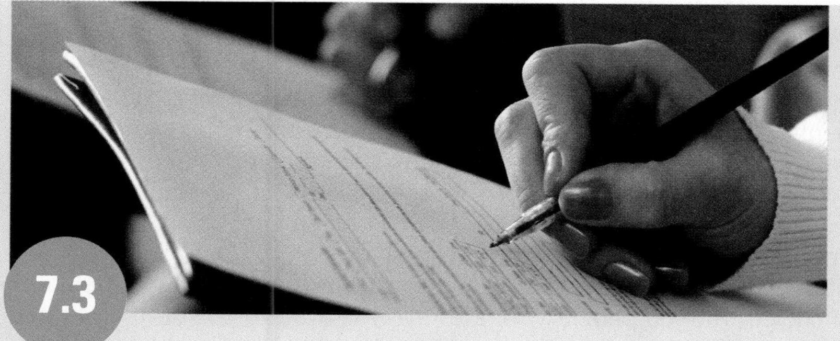

7.3

# SOCIAL POLICY: WHAT DO YOU THINK?

## Should We Pay the Price of Past Wrongs?

28 July 2001 was a hot, muggy day in Toronto and Randall Robinson added to the heat with his fiery oration to the African Canadian Legal Clinic (ACLC). "We're owed at least $11 trillion," he exhorted. "America must pay for slavery." The Harvard-educated Robinson was championing the cause of reparations for the descendants of American slaves—monetary compensation for past injustices. Black Americans, he argued, have been "bottom-stuck" since they were slaves. Their disadvantaged position today, he argued, is the legacy of slavery.

Although slavery was abolished in Canada more than 170 years ago, Robinson's arguments were endorsed by the ACLC and other Canadian groups that are not of African descent. Japanese Canadians, Chinese Canadians, Aboriginals, and Jewish Canadians all had representatives and gave advice at the meeting of the ACLC in July 2001:

- *Japanese Canadians. In 1942, three months after Japan attacked Pearl Harbor, the Canadian government invoked the War Measures Act. All people of Japanese origin residing within 160 kilometres of the Pacific Coast were removed from their homes. With about 24 hours' notice, almost 21 000 Japanese Canadians, 75 percent of them Canadian citizens, were moved to prisoner of war camps, work camps, and internment camps. Japanese Canadians have sought reparations for this historical injustice.*
- *Chinese Canadians. As noted above, the descendants of many Chinese Canadians were forced to pay a highly discriminatory head tax between 1885 and 1903. Chinese Canadians have requested compensation for this mistreatment.*
- *Aboriginal peoples. Many Aboriginal children were taken from their parents and placed in residential schools in the twentieth century. Many of them were physically and sexually abused in these schools. Aboriginal peoples also claim that much land was illegally taken from them. They, too, have sought a redress of grievances.*
- *Jewish Canadians. The Nazis enslaved and slaughtered European Jews by the millions during World War II. Jews were the first group in recent decades to seek reparations (from the German government) for the historical injustices they suffered.*

In the past, what was past was past. The vanquished were vanquished. The powerful wrote the history books and took no responsibility for what their ancestors had done. Today, things are different. Aggrieved groups in Canada and around the world are demanding reparations (Torpey, 2001). The recognition of fundamental human rights, signified first by the Human Rights Declaration of the United Nations in 1948, and the widespread delegitimization of racial and ethnic discrimination have provided fertile ground for this historical turn. The mobilization of shame has triggered a revolutionary change in how some people and governments view past injustices.

### CRITICAL THINKING QUESTIONS

- *Should you compensate black Canadians for slavery, Chinese Canadians for the head tax, Japanese Canadians for the internment camps, and Aboriginal peoples for residential schools and land? How responsible should you be for events that took place 50 or 200 years ago?*
- *In 1988 the Canadian government condemned the internment of Japanese Canadians during World War II, offered individual and community compensation to Japanese Canadians, and provided a $24 million endowment for the Canadian Race Relations Foundation. Does this seem fair to you? What about the far larger demands of Aboriginal peoples for self-government and land rights, given that they were pushed onto reserves to make way for exploration and resource development?*
- *In general, should Canada recognize its guilt and compensate those who have suffered? If not, why not? If so, should limits be placed on reparations? Why or why not?*

## The Points of the Compass

"All that is solid melts into the air," Marx wrote. He wasn't writing about ethnicity and race in the twenty-first century, but he could have been. One of the main lessons of this chapter is that although people's ethnic and racial identities seem fixed, they are, in fact, flexible to varying degrees. A variety of powerful social forces constrain people's freedom of ethnic and (especially) racial choice, but people have never been less constrained to remain a member of the ethnic or racial group into which they were born.

Significantly, opportunities for upward mobility are positively correlated with freedom of ethnic and racial choice. That is, people who are relatively free to decide their ethnic and racial identity tend to enjoy more opportunities for upward mobility, while those who are less free to decide their ethnic and racial identity have fewer opportunities for upward mobility. To paraphrase Orwell's *Animal Farm,* it is widely believed that everyone enjoys equal opportunity, but the reality is that members of some ethnic and especially racial groups enjoy less equal opportunity than others.

## Summary

### 1. *Is "race" a meaningful term?*

Some biologists suggest that race is not a useful term because biological differences that distinguish races do not predict differences in social behaviour. However, sociologists retain the term because *perceptions* of racial difference have important consequences for people's lives.

### 2. *What is the difference between race and ethnicity?*

A race is a category of people whose perceived *physical* markers are deemed socially significant. An ethnic group is a category of people whose perceived *cultural* markers are deemed socially significant. Just as physical distinctions don't cause differences in the behaviour of races, cultural distinctions are often not by themselves the major source of differences in the behaviour of various ethnic groups. *Social-structural* differences are typically the most important sources of differences in social behaviour.

### 3. *What is the main contribution of symbolic interactionism to the study of race and ethnicity?*

Symbolic interactionists emphasize that race and ethnicity are not fixed, and they are not inherent in people's biological makeup or cultural heritage. Rather, the way race and ethnicity are perceived and expressed depends on the history and character of race and ethnic relations in particular social contexts. These social contexts shape the way people construct their perceptions and expressions of race and ethnicity. Thus, racial and ethnic labels and identities change over time and place.

### 4. *What is the ecological theory of race and ethnic relations?*

The ecological theory of race and ethnic relations focuses on the way racial and ethnic groups struggle for territory and eventually blend into one another. Robert Park divides this struggle into five stages: (1) invasion, (2) resistance, (3) competition, (4) accommodation and cooperation, and (5) assimilation. The main problem with his theory is that some groups get "stuck" at stages 3 and 4, and Park offers no explanation for why this may happen.

### 5. *What are the theories of internal colonialism and split labour markets?*

These theories view the persistence of ethnic and racial identities as the result of social inequalities and social conflict. According to the theory of internal colonialism, immigrant settlers gain virtually complete control over a native population and change or destroy the native culture, then develop the racist belief that the natives are inherently inferior as they confine them to work they consider demeaning. This situation prevents assimilation by segregating the colonized in terms of jobs, housing, and social contacts ranging from friendship to marriage. According to split labour market theory, where low-wage workers of one race and high-wage workers of another race compete for the same jobs, high-wage workers are likely to resent the presence of low-wage competitors. Conflict is bound to result and racist attitudes develop or are reinforced.

6. ***Are Canadian ethnic and racial groups becoming less stratified over time?***

Since the early twentieth century, Canadian racial and ethnic groups have, on the whole, become less stratified, partly because tolerance for ethnic and racial differences has been on the rise and discrimination has been on the decline. Pluralism and assimilation have thus become more prominent features of Canadian society. However, these tendencies are weaker among members of some highly disadvantaged groups, notably Aboriginal Canadians and black people. That is because such groups remain highly segregated in jobs, housing, and social contacts. To a considerable degree, this is a historical legacy of internal colonialism and split labour markets.

7. ***Aside from the historical legacy of internal colonialism and split labour markets, do other reasons exist for the persistence of racial and ethnic identity, even among some white Canadians of European origin whose ancestors came to this country generations ago?***

Identifying with a racial or ethnic group can have economic, political, and emotional benefits.

8. ***How could the level of ethnic and racial stratification in Canada be lowered?***

The level of ethnic and racial stratification in Canada could be lowered by compensating disadvantaged groups for historical injustices, establishing employment equity programs that encourage the hiring of qualified members of disadvantaged minorities, subsidizing job training and child care, improving public education, and creating an efficient system for upgrading credentials earned abroad to meet Canadian standards.

# Key Terms

**assimilation (p. 209)**
**conquest (p. 213)**
**discrimination (p. 200)**
**ecological theory (p. 209)**
**employment equity (p. 224)**
**ethnic group (p. 202)**
**expulsion (p. 210)**
**genocide (p. 211)**
**institutional racism (p. 208)**
**internal colonialism (p. 210)**
**pluralism (p. 223)**
**prejudice (p. 200)**
**race (p. 202)**
**racism (p. 208)**
**scapegoat (p. 202)**
**segregation (p. 209)**
**slavery (p. 215)**
**split labour market (p. 217)**
**symbolic ethnicity (p. 207)**
**transnational communities (p. 222)**

# Questions to Consider

1. **How do you identify yourself in terms of your race or ethnicity? Do conventional ethnic and racial categories, such as black, white, Hispanic, and Asian, fit your sense of who you are? If so, why? If not, why not?**
2. **Do you think racism is becoming a more serious problem in Canada and worldwide? Why or why not? How do trends in racism compare with trends in other forms of prejudice, such as sexism? What accounts for similarities and differences in these trends?**

3. What are the costs and benefits of ethnic diversity in your college or university? Do you think it would be useful to adopt a policy of affirmative action or employment equity to make the student body and the faculty more ethnically and racially diverse? Why or why not?

# Web Resources

### Companion Web Site for This Book

http://www.pointsofthecompass.nelson.com

Begin by clicking on the Student Resources section of the Web site. Next, select the chapter you are currently studying from the pull-down menu. From the Student Resources page you will have easy access to InfoTrac® College Edition, MicroCase online exercises, and additional Weblinks. The Web site also has many useful tips to aid you in your study of sociology, including practice tests for each chapter.

### InfoTrac® Search Terms

These search terms are provided to assist you in beginning to conduct research on this topic by visiting http://www.infotrac-college.com:

**affirmative action**
**assimilation**
**discrimination**
**racism**
**transnational community**

### Recommended Web Sites

For information on the history and cultures of the people of Canada, visit Canadian Heritage at http://www.pch.gc.ca/index_e.cfm.

For a site that promotes cooperation between Aboriginal peoples and other Canadians, go to the Assembly of First Nations Web site at http://www.afn.ca.

For information about the United Nations human rights program, visit http://www.ohchr.org/english/.

# Note

1. Although sociologists commonly dispute a genetic basis of mean intelligence for races and ethnic groups, evidence suggests that *individual* differences in intelligence are partly genetically transmitted (Bouchard, Lykken, McGue, Segal, and Tellegen, 1990; Lewontin, 1991: 19–37; Scarr and Weinberg, 1978; Schiff and Lewontin, 1986).

# chapter 8

## sexuality and gender



### In this chapter, you will learn that

→ Although biology determines sex, social structure and culture largely determine gender, or the expression of culturally appropriate masculine and feminine roles.

→ The social construction of gender is evident in the way parents treat babies, teachers treat pupils, and the mass media portray ideal body images.

→ The social forces pushing people to assume conventionally masculine or feminine roles are compelling.

→ The social forces pushing people toward heterosexuality operate with even greater force.

→ The social distinction between men and women serves as an important basis of inequality in the family and in the workplace.

→ Male aggression against women is rooted in gender inequality.

# Sex versus Gender

## *Is It a Boy or a Girl?*

On 27 April 1966, what was supposed to be a routine circumcision of an eight-month-old twin at the St. Boniface Hospital in Winnipeg, Manitoba, went horribly wrong. Either because of mechanical malfunction or physician error, the infant's penis was burned off by the electric cauterizing machine. A parade of specialists informed the boy's distraught parents that their son's prognosis was grim. Medical technology of the time did not permit the reconstruction of a penis that would resemble a normal organ in appearance or sexual function. A psychiatric report prepared on the boy's projected future concluded that "he will be unable to live a normal sexual life from the time of adolescence . . . he will be unable to consummate marriage or have normal heterosexual relations, . . . he will have to recognize that he is incomplete, physically defective and . . . must live apart" (Colapinto, 2001: 16).

About 10 months after the accident, the child's parents experienced a glimmer of hope when they saw a TV interview of John Money, a psychologist at the renowned Johns Hopkins Hospital in Baltimore. Money was the driving force behind the creation of the world's first "sex change" clinic at Johns Hopkins (Bullough, 2000). He was well known for his research on **intersexed** infants, babies born with ambiguous genitals because of a hormone imbalance in the womb or some other cause. It was Money's opinion that infants with "unfinished genitals" should be *assigned* a sex by surgery and hormone treatments, and reared in accordance with their newly assigned sex (Money and Ehrhardt, 1972). According to Money, these strategies would lead to the child's eventual possession of a self-identity that was consistent with the assigned sex.

The Winnipeg couple wrote to Dr. Money, who urged them to bring their child to Baltimore immediately. After consultation with various physicians and with Money, the parents agreed to have their son's sex reassigned. In anticipation of what would follow, the boy's parents stopped cutting his hair, began dressing him in feminine clothes, and changed his name from Bruce to Brenda. Surgical castration was performed when the twin was 22 months old.

Early reports of the child's progress indicated success (Money and Ehrhardt, 1972). In contrast to her biologically identical brother, Brenda was said to disdain cars, gas pumps, and tools. She was supposedly fascinated by dolls, a dollhouse, and a doll carriage. Brenda's mother reported that, at the age of four and a half, Brenda preferred and took pleasure in her feminine clothing: "She is so feminine. I've never seen a little girl so neat and tidy . . . and yet my son is quite different. I can't wash his face for anything . . . She is very proud of herself, when she puts on a new dress, or I set her hair" (quoted in Money and Ehrhardt, 1972: 11).

The "twins case" generated worldwide attention. Textbooks in medicine and the social sciences were rewritten to incorporate Money's reports of the child's progress (Robertson, 1977: 316; Mackie, 1991: 69). However, later reports on the reassigned twin cast doubt on the accuracy of Dr. Money's report and on the apparent success of the transformation (Diamond and Sigmundson, 1999). Brenda insisted on urinating standing up, refused to undergo the further "feminizing" surgeries that had been planned for her, and, from age seven, daydreamed of her ideal future self "as a twenty-one-year-old male with a moustache, a sports car, and surrounded by admiring friends" (Colapinto, 2001: 93). She experienced academic failure and rejection and ridicule from her classmates, who dubbed her "Cavewoman" (Diamond, 1982). At age nine, Brenda had a nervous breakdown. At age 14, in a state of acute despair, she attempted suicide (Colapinto, 2001: 96, 262).

In 1980, Brenda learned the details of her sex reassignment from her father. At age 16, she decided to be reassigned once more and to live as a man rather than a woman. Advancements in medical technology made it possible for Brenda, who then adopted the name David, to have an artificial penis constructed. At age 25, David married a woman and adopted her three children, but that did not end his ordeal (Gorman, 1997). In May 2004, at the age of 38, David Reimer committed suicide.

## *Gender Identity and Gender Role*

The story of Bruce/Brenda/David introduces the first big question of this chapter. What makes us male or female? Of course, part of the answer is biological. Your **sex** depends on whether you are born with distinct male or female genitals and a genetic program that releases male or female hormones to stimulate the development of your reproductive system. However, the case of Bruce/Brenda/David also shows that more is involved in becoming male or female than biological sex differences.

Definitions of *male* and *female* traits vary across societies. For example, the ceremonial dress of male Wodaabe nomads in Niger may appear "feminine" by conventional North American standards.

Recalling his life as Brenda, David said: "Everyone is telling you that you're a girl. But you say to yourself, 'I don't *feel* like a girl.' You think girls are supposed to be delicate and *like* girl things—tea parties, things like that. But I like to *do* guy stuff. It doesn't match" (quoted in Colapinto, 1997: 66; our emphasis). As this quotation suggests, being male or female involves not just biology but also certain "masculine" and "feminine" feelings, attitudes, and behaviours. Accordingly, sociologists distinguish biological sex from sociological **gender.** Your gender comprises the feelings, attitudes, and behaviours typically associated with being male or female. **Gender identity** is your identification with, or sense of belonging to, a particular sex—biologically, psychologically, and socially. When you behave according to widely shared expectations about how males or females are supposed to act, you adopt a *gender role.*

### The Social Learning of Gender

Contrary to first impressions, the case of Bruce/Brenda/David suggests that, unlike sex, gender is not determined solely by biology. Research suggests that babies first develop a vague sense of being a boy or a girl at about the age of one. They develop a full-blown sense of gender identity between the ages of two and three (Blum, 1997). We can therefore be confident that baby Bruce already had a good idea he was a boy when he was assigned a female gender identity at the age of 22 months. He had seen boys behaving differently from girls on TV and in storybooks, and he lived with the role model of masculinity provided by his twin brother. Despite his parents' efforts to reinforce his identity as a girl, these early childhood lessons in masculinity were likely influential. Many researchers still believe that if gender reassignment occurs before the age of 18 months, it can be successful (Creighton and Mihto, 2001; Lightfoot-Klein, Chase, Hammond, and Goldman, 2000).

However, once the social learning of gender takes hold, as with baby Bruce, it is apparently very difficult to undo, even by means of reconstructive surgery, hormones, and parental and professional pressure. The main lesson we draw from this story is not that biology is destiny but that the social learning of gender begins very early in life.

The first half of this chapter helps you better understand what makes us male or female. We first outline two competing perspectives on gender differences. The first perspective argues that gender is inherent in our biological makeup and that society must reinforce those tendencies if it is to function smoothly. Functionalist theory is compatible with this argument. The second perspective argues that gender is constructed mainly by social influences and can be altered to benefit society's members. Conflict, feminist, and symbolic interactionist theories are compatible with the second perspective.

In the course of our discussion we examine how people learn gender roles during socialization in the family and at school. We show how everyday social interactions and advertising reinforce gender roles. We also discuss how members of society enforce **heterosexuality**—the preference for members of the opposite sex as sexual partners. For reasons that are still poorly understood, some people resist and even reject the gender roles that are assigned to them based on their biological sex. When this occurs, negative sanctions are often applied to get them to conform or to punish them for their deviance. Members of society are often eager to use emotional and physical violence to enforce conventional gender roles.

The second half of the chapter examines one of the chief consequences of people learning conventional gender roles. Gender, as currently constructed, creates and maintains social inequality. We illustrate this in two ways. We investigate why gender is associated with the earnings gap between women and men in the paid labour force. We also show how gender inequality encourages sexual harassment and rape. In concluding our discussion of sexuality and gender, we discuss some social policies that sociologists have recommended to decrease gender inequality and improve women's safety.

# Theories of Gender

Most arguments about the origins of gender differences in human behaviour adopt one of two perspectives. Some analysts see gender differences as a reflection of naturally evolved tendencies and argue that society must reinforce those tendencies if it is to function smoothly. Sociologists call this perspective **essentialism** (Weeks, 1986) because it views gender as part of the nature or "essence" of one's biological and social makeup. Other analysts see gender differences mainly as a reflection of the different social positions occupied by women and men. Sociologists call this perspective **social constructionism** because it views gender as "constructed" by social structure and culture. Conflict, feminist, and symbolic interactionist theories focus on various aspects of the social construction of gender.

## Essentialism

Sociobiologists and evolutionary psychologists have proposed one popular essentialist theory. They argue that humans instinctively try to ensure that their genes are passed on to future generations. However, they say, men and women develop different strategies for achieving that goal. A woman has a bigger investment than a man does in ensuring the survival of their offspring because she produces only a small number of eggs during her reproductive life. At most, she can give birth to about 20 children. It is therefore in a woman's best interest to maintain primary responsibility for her genetic children and to seek out the single mate who can best help support and protect them. In contrast, men can produce as many as a billion sperm per ejaculation and this feat can be replicated every day or two (Saxton, 1990: 94–95). To maximize their chance of passing on their genes to future generations, men must have many sexual partners.

According to sociobiologists and evolutionary psychologists, as men compete with other men for sexual access to many women, competitiveness and aggression emerge (DeSteno and Salovey, 2001). Women, says one evolutionary psychologist, are greedy for money, while men want casual sex with women, treat women's bodies as their property, and react violently to women who incite male sexual jealousy. These are supposedly "universal features of our evolved selves" that contribute to the survival of the human species (Buss, 2000). Thus, from the point of view of sociobiology and evolutionary psychology, gender differences in behaviour are based in biological differences between women and men.

## Functionalism and Essentialism

Functionalists reinforce the essentialist viewpoint when they claim that traditional gender roles help to integrate society (Parsons, 1942). In the family, wrote Talcott Parsons, women traditionally specialize in raising children and managing the household. Men traditionally work in the paid labour force. Each generation learns to perform these complementary roles by means of *gender role socialization.*

For boys, noted Parsons, the essence of masculinity is a series of "instrumental" traits, such as rationality, self-assuredness, and competitiveness. For girls, the essence of femininity is a series of "expressive" traits, such as nurturance and sensitivity to others. Boys and girls first learn their respective gender traits in the family as they see their parents going about their daily routines. The larger society also promotes *gender role conformity.* It instills in men the fear that they won't be attractive to women if they are too feminine, and it instills in women the fear that they won't be attractive to men if they are too masculine. In the functionalist view, then, learning the essential features of femininity and masculinity integrates society and allows it to function properly.

## A Critique of Essentialism from the Conflict and Feminist Perspectives

Conflict and feminist theorists disagree sharply with the essentialist account. They have lodged four main criticisms against it.

1. Essentialists ignore the historical and cultural variability of gender and sexuality. *Wide variations exist in what constitutes masculinity and femininity. Moreover, the level of gender inequality, the rate of male violence against women, the criteria used for mate selection, and other gender differences that appear universal to the essentialists vary widely*

*too. This variation deflates the idea that there are essential and universal behavioural differences between women and men. Three examples help illustrate the point:*

» In societies with low levels of gender inequality, the tendency decreases for women to stress the good provider role in selecting male partners, as does the tendency for men to stress women's domestic skills (Eagley and Wood, 1999).

» When women become corporate lawyers or police officers or take other jobs that involve competition or threat, their production of the hormone testosterone is stimulated, causing them to act more aggressively. Aggressiveness is partly role related (Blum, 1997: 158–88).

» Literally hundreds of studies conducted mainly in North America show that women are developing traits that were traditionally considered masculine. Women have become considerably more assertive, competitive, independent, and analytical in the last 35 years or so (Biegler, 1999; Nowell and Hedges, 1998).

*As these examples show, gender differences are not constants, and they are not inherent in men and women. They vary with social conditions.*

2. Essentialism tends to generalize from the average, ignoring variations within gender groups. *On average, women and men do differ in some respects. For example, one of the best-documented gender differences is that men are on average more verbally and physically aggressive than women. However, when sociobiologists and evolutionary psychologists say men are inherently more aggressive than women, they make it seem as if this is true of all men and all women. As Figure 8.1 shows, however, it is not. When trained researchers measure verbal or physical aggressiveness, scores vary widely within gender groups. Aggressiveness is distributed so that considerable overlap exists between women and men. Thus, many women are more aggressive than the average man and many men are less aggressive than the average woman.*

3. Little or no evidence directly supports the essentialists' major claims. *Sociobiologists and evolutionary psychologists have not identified any of the genes that, they claim, cause male jealousy, female nurturance, the unequal division of labour between men and women, and so forth.*

**Figure 8.1**
**The Distribution of Aggressiveness among Men and Women**

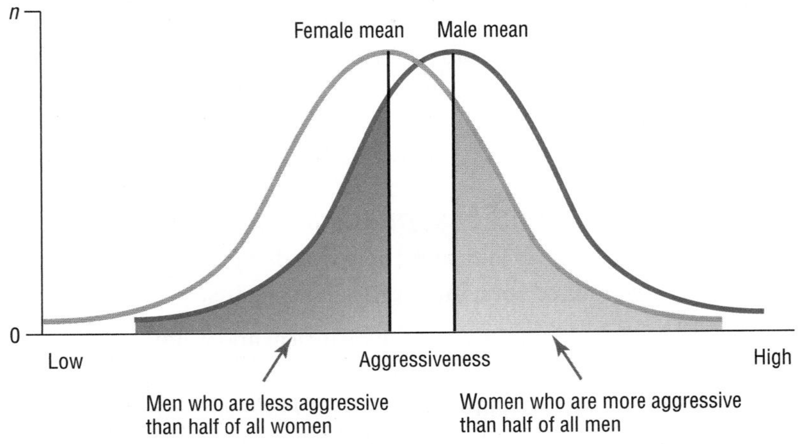

4. Essentialists' explanations for gender differences ignore the role of power. *Essentialists assume that existing behaviour patterns help ensure the survival of the species and the smooth functioning of society. However, as conflict and feminist theorists argue, their assumption overlooks the fact that men are usually in a position of greater power and authority than women.*

Conflict theorists dating back to Marx's collaborator, Friedrich Engels, have located the root of male domination in class inequality (Engels, 1970 [1884]). According to Engels, men gained substantial power over women when preliterate societies were first able to produce more than their members needed for their own subsistence. At that point, some men gained control over the economic surplus. They soon devised two means of ensuring that their offspring would inherit the surplus. First, they imposed the rule that only men could own property. Second, by means of socialization and force, they ensured that women remained sexually faithful to their husbands. As industrial capitalism developed, Engels wrote, male domination increased because industrial capitalism made men still wealthier and more powerful while it relegated women to subordinate, domestic roles.

Feminist theorists doubt that male domination is so closely linked to the development of industrial capitalism. For one thing, they note that gender inequality is greater in agrarian than in industrial capitalist societies. For another, male domination is evident in societies that call themselves socialist or communist. These observations lead many feminists to conclude that male domination is rooted less in industrial capitalism than in the patriarchal authority relations, family structures, and patterns of socialization and culture that exist in most societies (Lapidus, 1978: 7).

Despite this disagreement, conflict and feminist theorists concur that behavioural differences between women and men result less from any essential differences between them than from men being in a position to advance their interests over the interests of women. From the conflict and feminist viewpoints, functionalism, sociobiology, and evolutionary psychology can themselves be seen as examples of the exercise of male power, that is, as rationalizations for male domination and sexual aggression.

## *Social Constructionism and Symbolic Interactionism*

Essentialism is the view that masculinity and femininity are inherent and universal traits of men and women, whether because of biological or social necessity or some combination of the two. In contrast, social constructionism is the view that *apparently* natural or innate features of life, such as gender, are actually sustained by *social* processes that vary historically and culturally. As such, conflict and feminist theories can be regarded as types of social constructionism. So can symbolic interactionism. Symbolic interactionists, you will recall, focus on the way people attach meaning to things in the course of their everyday communication. One of the things to which people attach meaning is what it means to be a man or a woman. We illustrate the symbolic interactionist approach by first considering how boys and girls learn masculine and feminine roles in the family and at school. We then show how gender roles are maintained in the course of everyday social interaction and through advertising in the mass media.

### Gender Socialization

Barbie dolls have been around since 1959. Based on the creation of a German cartoonist, Barbie is the first modern doll modelled after an adult. (Lili, the German original, became a pornographic doll for men.) Some industry experts predicted mothers would

A Barbie doll

never buy their little girls a doll that had breasts. Were *they* wrong. Mattel now sells about 10 million Barbies and 20 million accompanying outfits annually. The Barbie trademark is worth US$1 billion.

What do girls learn when they play with Barbie? The author of a Web site devoted to Barbie undoubtedly speaks for many when she writes: "Barbie was more than a doll to me. She was a way of living: the Ideal Woman" (Elliott, 1995; see also Nicolaiedis, 1998; Turkel, 1998). One ideal that Barbie stimulates among many girls concerns body image. After all, Barbie is a scale model of a woman with a 40-18-32 figure (Hamilton, 1996: 197). Researchers who compared Barbie's gravity-defying proportions with the actual proportions of several representative groups of adult women concluded that the probability of this body shape was less than 1 in 100 000 (Norton, Olds, Olive, and Dank, 1996). (Ken's body shape is far more realistic at 1 in 50.) The closets of Barbie's pink house are jammed with outfits. Bathrooms, gyms, beauty parlours, and vanity sets feature prominently among the Barbie accessories available. Presumably, this quest for physical perfection is designed to attract Ken, Barbie's boyfriend. The message Barbie conveys to girls is that the ideal woman is defined primarily by her attractiveness to men.

A comparable story, with competition and aggression as its theme, could be told about how boys' toys, such as GI Joe, teach stereotypical male roles. True, a movement to market more gender-neutral toys arose in the 1960s and 1970s; there is now even a Presidential Barbie. However, a strong tendency remains to market toys based on gender. Typically, in the late 1990s, toy manufacturer Mattel produced a pink, flowered Barbie computer for girls with fewer educational programs than its blue Hot Wheels computer for boys (Mooney, Schacht, Knox, and Nelson, 2003: 232).

A movement to market more gender-neutral toys emerged in the 1960s and 1970s. However, it has now been overtaken by the resumption of a strong tendency to market toys based on gender.

Toys are only part of the story of gender socialization and hardly its first or final chapter. Research conducted in the early 1970s showed that from birth, infant boys and girls who are matched in length, weight, and general health are treated differently by parents—fathers in particular. Girls tend to be identified as delicate, weak, beautiful, and cute; boys as strong, alert, and well coordinated (Rubin, Provenzano, and Lurra, 1974). Recent research shows that although parents' gender-stereotyped perceptions of newborns have declined, especially among fathers, they have not disappeared (Fagot, Rodgers, and Leinbach, 2000; Gauvain, Fagot, Leve, and Kavanagh, 2002). One experiment found that when viewing a videotape of a nine-month-old infant, subjects tended to label its startled reaction to a stimulus as "anger" if the child had earlier been identified by the experimenters as a boy, and as "fear" if it had earlier been identified as a girl, *regardless of the infant's actual sex* (Condry and Condry, 1976).

Parents, and especially fathers, are more likely to encourage their sons to engage in boisterous and competitive play and discourage their daughters from doing likewise. In general, parents tend to encourage girls to engage in cooperative, role-playing games (Fagot et al., 2000; Gauvain et al., 2002; Parke, 2001, 2002). These different play patterns lead to the heightened development of verbal and emotional skills among girls and to more concern with winning and the establishment of hierarchy among boys (Tannen, 1990). Boys are more likely than girls to be praised for assertiveness. Girls are more likely than boys to be rewarded for compliance (Kerig, Cowan, and Cowan, 1993). Given this early socialization, it seems perfectly "natural" that boys' toys stress aggression, competition, spatial manipulation, and outdoor activities, while girls' toys stress nurturing, physical attractiveness, and indoor activities (Hughes, 1995). Still, what seems natural must be continuously socially reinforced. Presented with a choice between playing with a tool set and a dish set, preschool boys are about as likely to choose one as the other—unless the dish set is presented as a girl's toy and they think their fathers would view playing with it as "bad." Then, they tend to pick the tool set (Raag and Rackliff, 1998).

"Our own experience suggests that although traditional patterns of gender socialization weigh heavily on most men, they are not inescapable. For example, John Lie grew up in a patriarchal household. His father worked outside the home, and his mother stayed home to do nearly all the housework and child care. "I remember my grandfather telling me that a man should never be seen in the kitchen," recalls John, "and it is a lesson I learned well. In fact, everything about my upbringing—the division of labour in my family, the games I played, the TV programs I watched—prepared me for the life of a patriarch. I vaguely remember seeing members of the 'women's liberation movement' staging demonstrations on the TV news in the early 1970s. Although I was only about 11 or 12 years old, I recall dismissing them as slightly crazed, bra-burning man haters. Because of the way I grew up and what I read, heard, and saw, I assumed the existing gender division of labour was natural. Doctors, pilots, and professors should be men, I thought, and people in the 'caring' professions, such as nurses and teachers, should be women.

"But socialization is not destiny," John insists. "Entirely by chance, when I got to college I took some courses taught by female professors. It is embarrassing to say so now, but I was surprised that they seemed brighter, more animated, and more enlightening than my male high school teachers had been. In fact, I soon realized that many of my best professors were women. I think this is one reason why I decided to take the first general course in women's studies offered at my university. It was an eye opener. I soon became convinced that gender inequalities are about as natural and inevitable as racial inequalities. I also came to believe that gender equality could be as enriching for men as for women. Sociological reflection overturned what my socialization had taught me. Sociology promised—and delivered. I think many college-educated men have similar experiences today, and I hope I now contribute to their enlightenment.""

### Gender Segregation and Interaction

Only someone who has spent very little time in the company of children would think they are passive objects of socialization. They are not. Parents, teachers, and other authority figures typically try to impose their ideas of appropriate gender behaviour on children, but children creatively interpret, negotiate, resist, and self-impose these ideas all the time. Gender, we might say, is something that is done, not just given (Messner, 2000; West and Zimmerman, 1987).

Even children "do" gender. Consider the grade-four and grade-five classroom that sociologist Barrie Thorne (1993) observed. The teacher periodically asked the children to choose their own desks. With the exception of one girl, they always segregated *themselves* by gender. Similarly, when children played chasing games in the schoolyard, groups often *spontaneously* crystallized along gender lines. The teacher often reaffirmed such gender boundaries by pitting the boys against the girls in spelling and math contests. These contests were marked by cross-gender antagonism and expression of within-gender solidarity.

However, Thorne also observed many cases of boys and girls playing together. She also noticed quite a lot of "boundary crossing." Boundary crossing involves boys playing stereotypically girls' games and girls playing stereotypically boys' games. The most common form of boundary crossing involved girls who were skilled at specific sports that were central to the boys' world, such as soccer, baseball, and basketball. Boys and girls also interacted easily and without strong gender identities coming to the fore in activities requiring cooperation, such as a group project. Mixed-gender interaction was also more common in less public and crowded settings. Thus, boys and girls were more likely to play together and in a relaxed way in the relative privacy of their neighbourhoods. In contrast, in the schoolyard, where they were under the scrutiny of their peers, gender segregation and antagonism were more evident.

In sum, Thorne's research makes two important contributions to our understanding of gender socialization. First, children are actively engaged in the process of constructing gender roles. They are not merely passive recipients of adult demands. Second, while schoolchildren tend to segregate themselves by gender, boundaries between boys and girls are sometimes fluid and sometimes rigid, depending on social circumstances. In other words, the content of children's gendered activities is by no means fixed.

This is not to suggest that adults have no gender demands and expectations. They do, and their demands and expectations contribute importantly to gender socialization. For instance, many schoolteachers and guidance counsellors still expect boys to do better in sciences and math and girls to achieve higher marks in English (Lips, 1999). Parents

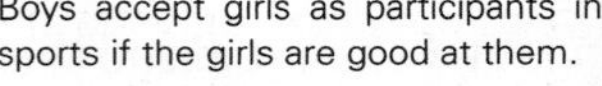

Boys accept girls as participants in sports if the girls are good at them.

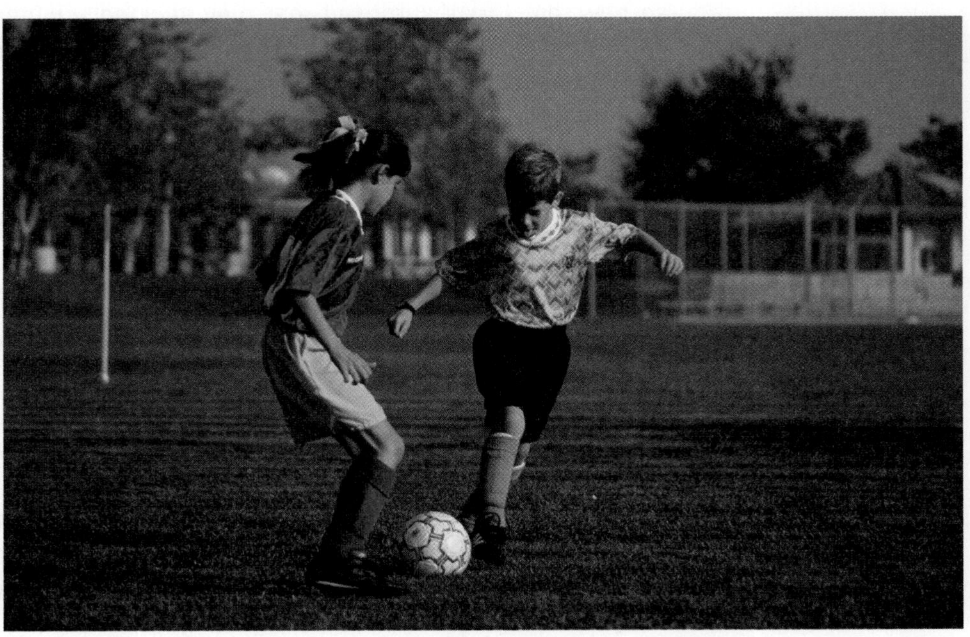

often reinforce these stereotypes in their evaluation of different activities (Eccles, Jacobs, and Harold, 1990). Although not all studies comparing mixed- and single-sex schools suggest that girls do much better in the latter (Bornholt, 2001; Jackson and Smith, 2000), most do. In single-sex schools, girls experience faster cognitive development; higher occupational aspirations and attainment; greater self-esteem and self-confidence; and more teacher attention, respect, and encouragement in the classroom. They also develop more egalitarian attitudes toward the role of women in society. Why? Because such schools place more emphasis on academic excellence and less on physical attractiveness and heterosexual popularity; they provide more successful same-sex role models, and they eliminate sex bias in teacher–student and student–student interaction because there are no boys around (Hesse-Biber and Carter, 2000: 99–100).

Adolescents must usually start choosing courses in school by the age of 14 or 15. By then, their **gender ideologies** are well formed. Gender ideologies are sets of interrelated ideas about what constitutes appropriate masculine and feminine roles and behaviour. One aspect of gender ideology becomes especially important around grades 9 and 10: adolescents' ideas about whether, as adults, they will focus mainly on the home, paid work outside the home, or a combination of the two. Adolescents usually make course choices with gender ideologies in mind. Boys are strongly inclined to consider only their careers in making course choices. Most girls are inclined to consider both home responsibilities and careers, although a minority considers only home responsibilities and another minority considers only careers. Consequently, boys tend to choose career-oriented courses, particularly in math and science, more often than do girls. In college and university, the pattern is accentuated. Young women tend to choose easier courses that lead to lower-paying jobs because they expect to devote a large part of their lives to child rearing and housework (Hochschild with Machung, 1989: 15–18). The top 10 fields of study for university and college graduates clearly indicate the continuing impact of gender ideologies on Canadian men and women (Table 8.1). We examine the wage gap between women and men in the second half of this chapter.

### *The Mass Media and Body Image*

If you systematically observe the roles played by women and men on TV programs and in ads one evening, you will probably discover a pattern noted by sociologists since the 1970s. Women will more frequently be seen cleaning house, taking care of children, modelling clothes, and acting as objects of male desire. Men will more frequently be seen in aggressive, action-oriented, and authoritative roles (Signorielli, 1998). The effect of these messages on viewers is much the same as that of the Disney movies and Harlequin romances we discussed in Chapter 3 (Socialization). They reinforce the normality of traditional gender roles. Many people even try to shape their bodies after the body images portrayed in the mass media (see Box 8.1).

Survey data show just how widespread dissatisfaction with our bodies is and how important a role the mass media play in generating our discomfort. One survey of North American university graduates showed that 56 percent of women and 43 percent of men were dissatisfied with their overall appearance (Garner, 1997). Only 3 percent of the dissatisfied women, but 22 percent of the dissatisfied men, wanted to "bulk up." This difference reflects the greater desire of men for muscular, stereotypically male physiques. Most of the dissatisfied men, and even more of the dissatisfied women (89 percent), wanted to lose weight. This fact reflects the general societal push toward slimness and its greater effect on women. Another survey shows that Canadian women are far more

**Table 8.1**
University and College Graduates' Top Ten Subjects of Study, by Sex, Canada, 2001

| **University Graduates**[1] | | | |
|---|---|---|---|
| **Men** | | **Women** | |
| Engineering | 15.38 | Elementary, secondary, pre-primary teaching | 20.08 |
| Business and commerce | 9.99 | Nursing | 6.49 |
| Elementary, secondary, pre-primary teaching | 8.22 | Business and commerce | 6.06 |
| Financial management | 7.16 | Financial management | 5.19 |
| Computer science and applied mathematics | 4.48 | Psychology | 4.83 |
| Economics | 3.49 | Medical-related subjects | 3.20 |
| Law and jurisprudence | 3.36 | English language and literature | 3.01 |
| Medicine | 2.98 | Social work and social services | 2.80 |
| Psychology | 2.16 | Sociology | 2.68 |
| History | 1.96 | Engineering | 2.36 |
| All other subjects | 40.84 | All other subjects | 43.30 |
| Total | 100.02 | Total | 100.00 |
| **College Graduates**[1] | | | |
| **Men** | | **Women** | |
| Electronic and electrical technologies | 10.03 | Office administration and secretarial sciences | 17.04 |
| Data processing and computer science technologies | 9.38 | Nursing | 13.35 |
| Mechanical engineering technologies | 8.70 | Financial management | 9.40 |
| Business and commerce | 7.28 | Business and commerce | 7.07 |
| Financial management | 6.66 | Elementary, secondary, pre-primary teaching | 5.84 |
| Building and construction technologies | 5.08 | Social work and social services | 4.52 |
| General and civil engineering technologies | 4.90 | Data processing and computer science technologies | 4.34 |
| Social work and social services | 4.55 | Nursing assistance | 3.93 |
| Industrial engineering technologies | 3.45 | Marketing, merchandising, retail trade, and sales | 2.61 |
| Marketing, merchandising, retail trade, and sales | 3.25 | Medical treatment technologies | 2.30 |
| All other subject areas | 36.71 | All other subject areas | 29.61 |
| Total | 99.99 | Total | 100.01 |

Source: Adapted from Statistics Canada (2003b).

Note: Totals may not add to 100 percent because of rounding.

[1] University and college graduates aged 25 to 64

likely than men to attempt losing weight, even if they fall within the range of healthy weights (Health Canada, 1999b: 118).

Figure 8.2 reveals gender differences in body ideals in a different way. It compares North American women's and men's attitudes toward their stomachs. It also compares women's attitudes toward their breasts with men's attitudes toward their chests. It

8.1

# MASS MEDIA AND SOCIETY

## Why Thinner?

The human body has always served as a sort of personal billboard that advertises gender. However, historian Joan Jacobs Brumberg (1997) makes a good case for the view that the importance of body image to our self-definition has grown over the past century. Just listen to the difference in emphasis on the body in the diary resolutions of two typical white, middle-class North American girls, separated by 90 years. From 1892: "Resolved, not to talk about myself or feelings. To think before speaking. To work seriously. To be self restrained in conversation and actions. Not to let my thoughts wander. To be dignified. Interest myself more in others." From 1982: "I will try to make myself better in any way I possibly can with the help of my budget and baby-sitting money. I will lose weight, get new lenses, already got new haircut, good makeup, new clothes and accessories" (quoted in Brumberg, 1997: xxi).

As body image became more important to a person's self-definition during the twentieth century, the ideal body image became thinner, especially for women. Thus, the first "glamour girl" was Mrs. Charles Dana Gibson, who was famous in advertising and society cartoons in the 1890s and 1900s as the "Gibson Girl." According to the Metropolitan Museum of Art's Costume Institute, "Every man in America wanted to win her" and "every woman in America wanted to be her. Women stood straight as poplars and tightened their corset strings to show off tiny waists" (Metropolitan Museum of Art, 2000). As featured in the *Ladies Home Journal* in 1905, the Gibson Girl measured 38-27-45 inches—certainly not slim by today's standards. During the twentieth century, however, the ideal female body type thinned out. The "White Rock Girl," featured on the logo of the White Rock Beverage Company, was 5 feet 4 inches and weighed 140 pounds (65 kilograms) in 1894. In 1947 she had slimmed down to 125 pounds (55 kilograms). By 1970 she was 5 feet 8 inches and 118 pounds (53 kilograms) (Peacock, 2000). Similarly, beauty pageant winners grew much thinner between 1922 and 1999 (Curran, 2000).

Why did body image become more important to people's self-definition during the twentieth century? Why was slimness stressed? Part of the answer to both questions is that more North Americans grew overweight as their lifestyles became more sedentary. As they became better educated, they became increasingly aware of the health problems associated with being overweight. The desire to slim down was, then, partly a reaction to bulking up. But that is not the whole story. The rake-thin models

The "White Rock Girl" in 1894 *(left)* and 1947 *(right)*.

who populate modern ads are not promoting good health. They are promoting an extreme body shape that is virtually unattainable for most people. They do so because it is good business. The fitness, diet, low-calorie-food, and cosmetic surgery industries do tens of billions of dollars of business every year (Hesse-Biber, 1996). Bankrolled by these industries, advertising in the mass media blankets us with images of slim bodies and makes these body types appealing. Once people become convinced that they need to develop bodies like the ones they see in ads, many of them are really in trouble; these body images are very difficult for most people to attain.

**CRITICAL THINKING QUESTIONS**

- *What is your ideal body image?*
- *What has influenced your ideal?*
- *Are you concerned about the impact of the mass media on your body image? Why or why not?*

shows, first, that women are more concerned about their stomachs than men are about their own. Second, it shows that men are more concerned about their chests than women are about their breasts. Clearly, then, people's body ideals are influenced by their gender. Note also that Figure 8.2 shows trends over time. North Americans' anxiety about their bodies increased substantially over the 25-year period covered by the survey.

Table 8.2 suggests that advertising is highly influential in creating anxiety and insecurity about appearance and particularly about body weight. We see that nearly 30 percent of North American women compared themselves with the fashion models they saw in advertisements, felt insecure about their own appearance, and wanted to lose weight as a result. Among women who were dissatisfied with their appearance, the percentages were much larger, with about 45 percent making comparisons with fashion models and two-thirds feeling insecure and wanting to lose weight.

**Figure 8.2**
**Body Dissatisfaction, North America (in percent, $n = 4000$)**

Note: The *n* of 4000 refers to the 1997 survey only. The number of respondents in the earlier surveys was not given.

Source: "The 1997 Body Image Results" by David M. Garner, *Psychology Today*, Vol. 30, No. 1, pp. 30–44. Reprinted with permission from Psychology Today Magazine. Copyright © 1997 Sussex Publishers, LLC.

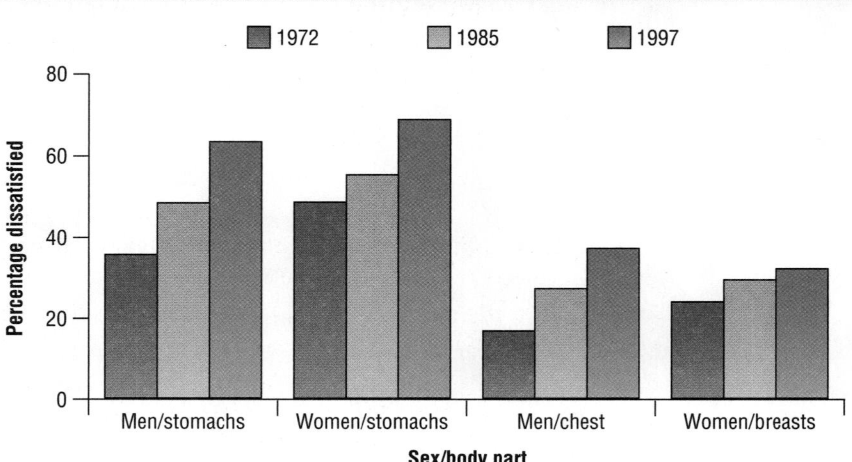

**Table 8.2**
The Influence of Fashion Models on Feelings about Appearance, North America ($n = 4000$)

| | Men (%) | Women (%) | Extremely Dissatisfied (%) |
|---|---|---|---|
| I always or often | | | |
| Compare myself with models in magazines | 12 | 27 | 43 |
| Carefully study the shape of models | 19 | 28 | 47 |
| Very thin or muscular models make me | | | |
| Feel insecure about my weight | 15 | 29 | 67 |
| Want to lose weight | 18 | 30 | 67 |

Source: Adapted from Garner (1997).

The diet-food and weight-loss industries promote an ideal of slimness that is often impossible to attain and that generates widespread body dissatisfaction.

Body dissatisfaction, in turn, motivates dieting. For many people, achieving their weight goals is a life or death issue: about a quarter of women and a sixth of men say they would willingly trade more than three years of their lives to achieve their weight goals (Garner, 1997).

Body dissatisfaction prompts some people to take dangerous and even life-threatening measures to reduce their weight. Smoking is often employed as a strategy to control and lose weight, especially among adolescent and young adult women (Boles and Johnson, 2001). In addition, between 1 percent and 5 percent of North American women suffer from anorexia nervosa (characterized by drastic weight loss, excessive exercise, food aversion, distorted body image, and an intense and irrational fear of body fat and weight gain). About the same percentage of North American female university students suffer from bulimia, characterized by cycles of binge eating and purging (through self-induced vomiting and the use of laxatives, purgatives, or diuretics). For university men, the prevalence of bulimia is between 0.2 percent and 1.5 percent (Averett and Korenman, 1996: 305–06).

## *Male–Female Interaction*

The gender roles children learn in their families, at school, and through the mass media form the basis of their social interaction as adults. For instance, by playing team sports, boys tend to learn that social interaction is most often about competition, conflict, self-sufficiency, and hierarchical relationships (leaders versus the led). They understand the importance of taking centre stage and boasting about their talents (Messner, 1995). Because many of the most popular video games for boys exclude female characters (*Game Boy* wasn't named *Game Boy* for nothing!), use women as sex objects, or involve violence against women, they reinforce some of the most unsavoury lessons of traditional gender socialization (Dietz, 1998). Conversely, by playing with dolls and baking sets, girls tend to learn that social interaction is most often about maintaining cordial relationships, avoiding conflict, and resolving differences of opinion through negotiation (Subrahmanyam and Greenfield, 1998). They are informed of the importance of giving advice and of not promoting themselves or being bossy.

Because of these early socialization patterns, misunderstandings between men and women are common. A stereotypical example: Harold is driving around lost. However, he refuses to ask for directions because doing so would amount to an admission of inadequacy and therefore a loss of status. Meanwhile, it seems perfectly "natural" to Sybil to want to share information, so she urges Harold to ask for directions. The result: conflict between Harold and Sybil (Tannen, 1990: 62).

Gender-specific interaction styles also have serious implications for who is heard and who gets credit at work. For instance, Deborah Tannen's research discovered the typical case of the female office manager who doesn't want to seem bossy or arrogant. Eager to preserve consensus among her coworkers, she spends much time soliciting their opinions before making an important decision. But her boss perceives her approach as indecisive and incompetent. He wants to recruit leaders for upper-management positions, so he overlooks the woman and selects an assertive man for a senior job that just opened up (Tannen, 1994a: 132).

The contrasting interaction style between male and female managers can lead to women not getting credit for competent performance. That is why they sometimes complain about a **glass ceiling,** a social barrier that makes it difficult for them to rise to the top level of management. As we will see soon, factors other than interaction styles—such as outright discrimination and women's generally greater commitment to family responsibilities—also restrict women's upward mobility. But gender differences in interaction styles also play a role in constraining women's career progress.

# Homosexuality

We have outlined some powerful social forces that push us to define ourselves as conventionally masculine or feminine in behaviour and appearance. For most people, gender socialization by the family, the school, and the mass media is compelling and sustained by daily interactions. A minority of people, however, resist conventional gender roles.

**Transgendered** people defy society's gender norms and blur widely accepted gender roles. About 1 in every 5000 to 10 000 people in North America is transgendered. Some transgendered people are **transsexuals.** Transsexuals are people who want to alter their gender by changing their appearance or resorting to medical intervention. Transsexuals believe they were born with the "wrong" body. They identify with, and want to live fully as, members of the opposite sex. They often take the lengthy and painful path to a sex-change operation. About 1 in every 30 000 people in North America is a transsexual (Nolen, 1999).

While **heterosexuals** are people who desire sexual partners of the other sex, **homosexuals** are people who prefer sexual partners of the same sex, and **bisexuals** are people who enjoy sexual partners of either sex. People usually call homosexual men *gays* and homosexual women *lesbians.* Some 1.8 percent of Canadian men and 1.5 percent of Canadian women think of themselves as homosexual or bisexual (see Table 8.3). In Toronto, the comparable figures are 6.1 percent and 1.5 percent, respectively. Because of widespread animosity toward homosexuals, however, some people who engage in same-sex acts or want to do so do not identify themselves as gay, lesbian, or bisexual

**Table 8.3**
Homosexuality in North America

| | Men (%) | Women (%) |
|---|---|---|
| Toronto: Identified themselves as homosexual or bisexual | 6.1 | 1.5 |
| Canada: Identified themselves as homosexual or bisexual | 1.8 | 1.5 |
| U.S.: Identified themselves as homosexual or bisexual | 2.8 | 1.4 |
| U.S.: Had sex with person of same sex in past 12 months | 3.4 | 0.6 |
| U.S.: Had sex with person of same sex at least once since puberty | 5.3 | 3.5 |
| U.S.: Felt desire for sex with person of same sex | 7.7 | 7.5 |
| U.S.: Had some same-sex desire or experience or identified themselves as homosexual or bisexual | 10.1 | 8.6 |

Sources: "Homosexuality and Bisexuality," (2000); Michael, Gagnon, Laumann, and Kolata (1994: 40); Statistics Canada (2004b).
Note: U.S. data are for 1992. Toronto data are for 1999. Canadian data are for 2003.

(Flowers and Buston, 2001; Herdt, 2001). Thus, some 10.1 percent of American men and 8.6 percent of American women think of themselves as homosexual or bisexual *or* have had some same-sex experience or desire.

Homosexuals were not identified as a distinct category of people until the 1860s, when the term *homosexuality* was coined. The term *lesbian* is of even more recent vintage. Nevertheless, homosexual behaviour has existed in every society. Some societies, such as ancient Greece, have encouraged it. More frequently, homosexual acts have been forbidden.

We do not yet understand well why some individuals develop homosexual orientations. Some scientists believe that the cause of homosexuality is mainly genetic, others think it is chiefly hormonal, while still others point to life experiences during early childhood as the most important factor. According to the American Psychological Association (1998), it "emerges for most people in early adolescence without any prior sexual experience.... [It] is not changeable."

In general, sociologists are less interested in the origins of homosexuality than in the way it is socially constructed, that is, in the wide variety of ways it is expressed and repressed (Foucault, 1990 [1978]; Plummer, 1995). Homosexuality has become less of a stigma over the past century. Two factors are chiefly responsible for this, one scientific, the other political. In the twentieth century, sexologists—psychologists and physicians who study sexual practices scientifically—first recognized and stressed the wide diversity of existing sexual practices. Alfred Kinsey was among the pioneers in this field. He and his colleagues interviewed thousands of men and women. In the 1940s, they concluded that homosexual practices were so widespread that homosexuality could hardly be considered an illness affecting a tiny minority (Kinsey, Pomeroy, and Martin, 1948; Kinsey, Pomeroy, Martin, and Gebhard, 1953).

If sexologists provided a scientific rationale for belief in the normality of sexual diversity, sexual minorities themselves provided the social and political energy needed to legitimize sexual diversity among a large section of the public. Especially since the middle of the twentieth century, gays and lesbians have built large communities and subcultures, particularly in major urban areas (Greenhill, 2001; Ingram, 2001). They have gone public with their lifestyles (Owen, 2001). They have organized demonstrations, parades, and political pressure groups to express their self-confidence and demand equal rights with the heterosexual majority (Goldie, 2001). These actions have done much to legitimize homosexuality and sexual diversity in general.

A Gay Pride Day parade

Nonetheless, opposition to people who don't conform to conventional gender roles remains strong at all stages of the life cycle (Box 8.2). When you were a child, did you ever poke fun at a sturdily built girl who was good at sports by calling her a "dike"? As an adolescent or young adult, have you ever attempted to insult a man by calling him a "fag"? If so, your behaviour was not unusual. Many children and young adults continue to express the belief that heterosexuality is superior to homosexuality (Bibby, 2001). "That's gay!" is a common expression of disapproval among teenagers.

Among adults, such opposition is also strong. What is your attitude today toward transgendered people, transsexuals, and homosexuals? Do you, for example, think relations between adults of the same sex are always, or almost always, wrong? If so, you are not that unusual. A 2000 survey of Canadians found that almost one in three Canadians believes same-sex relations are "always wrong"—admittedly about half the 1975 figure, but still a substantial number (Bricker and Greenspon, 2001; "Acceptable but Not Equal," 2002).

On April 1, 2001, the Netherlands became the first country to recognize full and equal marriage rights for homosexual couples. Within hours, Dutch citizens were taking advantage of the new law. The Dutch law is part of a worldwide trend to legally recognize long-term same-sex unions. On 20 July 2005 Canada became the fourth country to legalize homosexual marriage.

Antipathy to homosexuals is so strong among some people that they are prepared to back up their beliefs with force. A study of about 500 young adults in the San Francisco Bay area (probably the most sexually tolerant area in North America) found that 1 in 10 admitted physically attacking or threatening people they believed were homosexuals. Twenty-four percent reported engaging in anti-gay name-calling. Among male respondents, 18 percent reported acting in a violent or threatening way and 32 percent reported name-calling. In addition, a third of those who had *not* engaged in anti-gay aggression said they would do so if a homosexual flirted with or propositioned them (Franklin, 2000).

The consequences of **homophobia,** or fear of homosexuals, can be devastating. For example, when 14-year-old Christian Hernandez told his best friend that he was gay, the consequences proved disastrous. "He told me he couldn't accept it," recalls

8.2

## SOCIOLOGY AT THE MOVIES

Heath Ledger (left) and Jake Gyllenhaal in *Brokeback Mountain*

### *Brokeback Mountain* (2005)

It would not be an exaggeration to say that Westerns—often called "Cowboy and Indian" movies—shaped a generation of North Americans' expectations about gender and sexuality. John Wayne, Gary Cooper, Jimmy Stewart, and many others became role models for North American men and their idea of masculinity: silent but strong, gentle toward the weak (women and children) but ferocious toward the evil (often Aboriginals), community-minded but ultimately lone, rugged individualists. Even today, it's hard not to be stirred and engrossed by such classic Westerns as *The Man Who Shot Liberty Valence* and *High Noon.*

Westerns, however, have not been a popular genre since the 1970s. The Civil Rights movement questioned the racial ideology of many Westerns, which presumed the superiority of the white race against the native populations. The movement against the War in Vietnam challenged the vision of the world as a place that should be pacified and ruled by white Americans. The feminist movement criticized the patriarchal masculine viewpoint of Westerns. The few Westerns since the 1970s have therefore deviated from classical Westerns, often parodying them.

*Brokeback Mountain* (2005), nominated for the 2005 best picture Oscar, traces the romantic love between two cowboys. They fall in love in the early 1960s, when both are 19 years old, long before they had heard of gay culture or even the notion of homosexual identity. They lead seemingly conventional married lives. Yet they continue to love each other and carry on their affair for two decades, periodically telling their wives that they are going on fishing trips together but raising suspicions when they fail to bring any fish home. More than the passion, however, what the movie depicts is the high emotional cost of keeping sexual orientation and love a secret. Eventually, their marriages crumble, their social relationships suffer, and happiness and fulfilment prove elusive.

One of the reasons that Ennis (Heath Ledger, nominated for the 2005 best actor Oscar) cannot imagine the possibility of settling down with Jack (Jake Gyllenhaal, nominated for the 2005 best supporting actor Oscar) is a childhood experience. His father took him to see two men who were beaten to death, two "tough old birds" who happened to be "shacked up together." Fear of expressing his homosexuality was thus instilled early on. In fact, both men deny their homosexuality. After their first night together, Ennis says to Jack, "You know I ain't queer." To which Jack replies, "Me neither." Jack and Ennis's affair ends when Jack is beaten to death by homophobic men. Three grisly murders of gay men, then, provide the tragic backdrop to *Brokeback Mountain.*

**CRITICAL THINKING QUESTIONS**

- *How much have things changed since the 1960s, 1970s, and 1980s? Could Brokeback Mountain be set in 2007? Why or why not?*

Hernandez. "And he began to spread it around." For two years, the Niagara Falls student was teased and harassed almost daily. After school one day, a group of boys waited for him. Their leader told Hernandez that "he didn't accept faggots, that we brought AIDS into the world" and stabbed him in the neck with a knife. Hernandez required a week's hospitalization. When he told his parents what had happened, his father replied that he'd "rather have a dead son than a queer son" (Fisher, 1999).

Research suggests that some anti-gay crimes may result from repressed homosexual urges on the part of the aggressor (Adams, Wright, and Lohr, 1998). From this point of view, aggressors are homophobic because they cannot cope with their own, possibly subconscious, homosexual impulses. Their aggression is a way of acting out a denial of these impulses. Although this psychological explanation may account for some anti-gay violence, it seems inadequate when set alongside the finding that fully half of all young male adults admitted to some form of anti-gay aggression in the San Francisco study cited above. An analysis of the motivations of these San Franciscans showed that some of them did commit assaults to prove their toughness and heterosexuality. Others committed assaults just to alleviate boredom and have fun. Still others believed they were defending themselves from aggressive sexual propositions. A fourth group acted violently because they wanted to punish homosexuals for what they perceived as moral transgressions (Franklin, 1998). It seems clear, then, that anti-gay violence is not just a question of abnormal psychology but a broad cultural problem with several sources. Still, anecdotal evidence suggests that opposition to anti-gay violence is also growing (see Box 8.3).

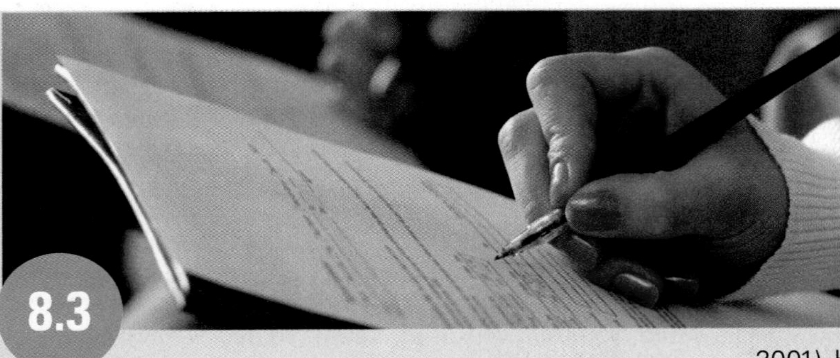

8.3

## SOCIAL POLICY: WHAT DO YOU THINK?

### Hate Crime Law and Homophobia

On 17 November 2001, Aaron Webster, a 42-year-old gay man, was beaten to death in a vicious attack in Vancouver. Tim Chisholm, Aaron's friend for 15 years, discovered Aaron's bloodied body, naked except for his hiking boots, in a parking lot in Stanley Park. Aaron had been bludgeoned with either a baseball bat or a pool cue by a group of three to four men. After phoning 911, Chisholm attempted CPR on his unconscious friend. It was no use. Aaron died in Chisholm's arms before help could arrive.

This brutal murder is believed to have been British Columbia's first fatal case of "gay bashing." At a memorial service for Webster that drew more than 1500 people, Vancouver Police Inspector Dave Jones identified Webster as the victim of "a hate crime, pure and simple" and pledged that the city's police department would "do everything in our power" to find the perpetrators and "bring them to justice" (Associated Press, 2001; Nagle, 2001).

One issue raised by Webster's death concerns the definition of hate crime (Wetzel, 2001). Hate crimes are criminal acts motivated by a victim's race, religion, ethnicity, or sexual orientation. Under section 718.2 of the Canadian Criminal Code, "evidence that [an offence] was motivated by bias, prejudice or hate based on race, national or ethnic origin, colour, religion, sex, age, mental or physical disability, sexual orientation or any other similar factor" is to be considered an aggravating circumstance in sentencing convicted offenders. Despite this provision in law, "gay-bashers are often able to rely on the discredited 'homosexual panic' defence, claiming they were justified in committing murder because the victim 'came on' to them" (EGALE, 2001).

**CRITICAL THINKING QUESTIONS**

- *Do you think crimes motivated by the victim's sexual orientation are the same as crimes motivated by the victim's race, religion, or ethnicity? If so, why? If not, why not?*
- *Do you think crimes motivated by the perceived sexual orientation of the victim should be included in the legal definition of hate crime? Why or why not?*

In sum, strong social and cultural forces lead us to distinguish men from women and heterosexuals from homosexuals. We learn these distinctions throughout the socialization process, and we continuously construct them anew in our daily interactions. Most people use positive and negative sanctions to ensure that others conform to conventional heterosexual gender roles. Some people resort to violence to enforce conformity and punish deviance.

Our presentation also suggests that the social construction of conventional gender roles helps create and maintain social inequality between women and men. In the remainder of this chapter, we examine some of the present-day consequences of gender inequality.

## Gender Inequality

### *The Earnings Gap*

You might think that gender inequality is a thing of the past. If so, you would be wrong. That fact is evident if we focus on the earnings gap between men and women, one of the most important expressions of gender inequality today.

When Canadian data on female and male earnings were first collected in 1967, the ratio of female to male earnings for full-year, full-time workers stood at about 58 percent. This means that women were earning 58 cents for every dollar men earned. By 1980, the ratio was 64 percent and it rose fairly steadily to about 71 percent in 1993 (Statistics Canada, 2003h). Since then, however, the ratio has fluctuated between about 68 percent and 72 percent. In 2004, the most recent year for which data are available as of this writing, women earned just less than 70 cents for every dollar men earned. At the 1980–2004 rate of improvement, women will achieve earnings equality with men in 2124 (see Figure 8.3).

**Figure 8.3**
**Ratio of Female to Male Earnings, Canada, 1980–2004**

Note: Data are for full-time workers expressed in 2004 dollars.

■ Source: Adapted from Statistics Canada (n.d.-4).

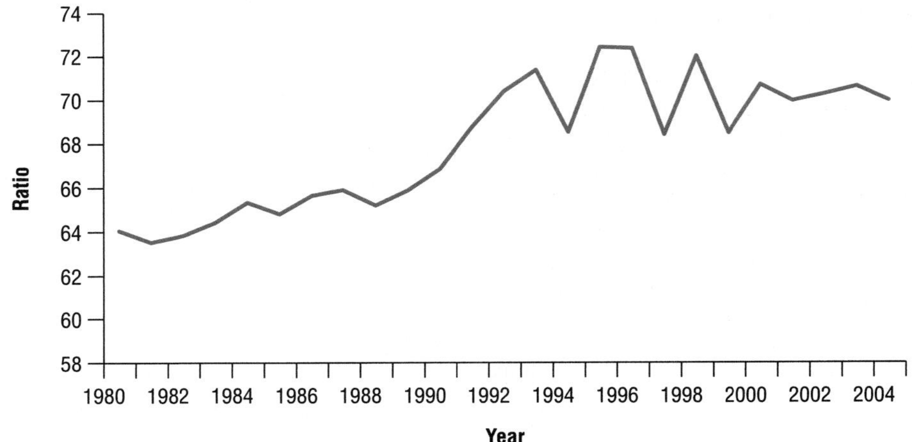

**Table 8.4**
Earnings of Men and of Women and Gender Composition in the Ten Best and Ten Worst Paid Occupations, Canada, 2000

| Occupation | Average Annual Earnings | Percentage Women | Female-to-Male Earnings Ratio |
|---|---|---|---|
| **Ten highest-earning occupations** | | | |
| Judges | $142 518 | 24.4 | 90.2 |
| Specialist physicians | 141 597 | 30.8 | 61.2 |
| Senior managers: Financial, communications carriers, and other business services | 130 802 | 21.5 | 63.9 |
| General practitioners and family physicians | 122 463 | 30.8 | 72.5 |
| Dentists | 118 350 | 22.9 | 63.7 |
| Senior managers: Goods production, utilities, transportation, and construction | 115 623 | 11.6 | 62.2 |
| Lawyers and Quebec notaries | 103 287 | 31.0 | 67.4 |
| Senior managers: Trade, broadcasting and other services, N.E.C | 101 176 | 17.8 | 61.8 |
| Securities agents, investment dealers, and traders | 98 919 | 36.8 | 44.5 |
| Petroleum engineers | 96 703 | 10.0 | 60.7 |
| **Ten lowest-earning occupations** | | | |
| Babysitters, nannies, and parents' helpers | 15 846 | 97.1 | 104.3 |
| Food and beverage servers | 18 319 | 77.1 | 75.1 |
| Service station attendants | 18 470 | 9.2 | 80.9 |
| Food counter attendants, kitchen helpers, and related occupations | 19 338 | 71.8 | 94.1 |
| Bartenders | 19 877 | 58.2 | 83.4 |
| Cashiers | 19 922 | 85.0 | 84.5 |
| Harvesting labourers | 20 158 | 48.8 | 83.0 |
| Tailors, dressmakers, furriers, and milliners | 20 499 | 81.6 | 68.2 |
| Sewing machine operators | 20 575 | 91.5 | 74.7 |
| Ironing, pressing, and finishing occupations | 20 663 | 63.9 | 83.8 |

Source: Adapted from Statistics Canada (2002a).
Note: Only full-time, full-year workers are included.

Table 8.4 shows the gender wage gap in the average earnings of people in the 10 highest-paying and 10 lowest-paying occupations in Canada. If the wage gap were due to universal gender differences, it would not vary across occupations. But it does vary considerably, suggesting that social conditions specific to given occupations account in part for the magnitude of the gender wage gap.

Four main factors contribute to the gender gap in earnings (Bianchi and Spain, 1996; England, 1992):

1. Gender discrimination. *In February 1985, when Microsoft already employed about 1000 people, it hired its first two female executives. According to a well-placed source involved in the hiring, both women got their jobs because Microsoft was trying to win*

Although women have entered many traditionally "male" occupations since the 1970s, they are still concentrated in lower-paying clerical and service occupations and underrepresented in higher-paying manual occupations.

*a U.S. Air Force contract. Under the government's guidelines, Microsoft didn't have enough women in top management positions to qualify. The source quotes then 29-year-old Bill Gates, president of Microsoft, as saying: "Well, let's hire two women because we can pay them half as much as we will have to pay a man, and we can give them all this other 'crap' work to do because they are women" (quoted in Wallace and Erickson, 1992: 291).*

*This incident is a clear illustration of* **gender discrimination,** *rewarding women and men differently for the same work. Discrimination on the basis of sex is against the law in Canada. Yet progress is slow; as noted earlier, the female-to-male earnings ratio has actually deteriorated since 1993.*

2. Women tend to be concentrated in low-wage occupations and industries. *The second factor leading to lower earnings for women is that the programs they select in high school and afterward tend to limit them to jobs in low-wage occupations and industries. The concentration of women in certain occupations and men in others is referred to as* **occupational sex segregation.** *Although women have made big strides since the 1970s in several fields, including management, business and financial professions, medicine, and law, they are still concentrated in lower-paying clerical and service occupations and the teaching profession, and underrepresented in higher-paying manual occupations (see Table 8.5). This pattern is particularly strong for women of colour, Aboriginal women, and women with disabilities (Chard, 2000: 229; Shain, 1995).*

3. Heavy domestic responsibilities reduce women's earnings. *In 2003, single women who had never been married earned 93 cents for every dollar earned by men. The comparable figure for all women was 70.5 cents. A substantial part of this 22.5-cent gap represents the economic cost to women of getting married and assuming disproportionately heavy domestic responsibilities. Of course, raising children can be one of the most emotionally satisfying experiences. That should not, however, blind us to the fact it is also work that decreases the time available for education, training, and paid work. Because women are disproportionately involved in child rearing, they suffer the brunt of this economic*

**Table 8.5**
Percentage Women by Occupational Category, Canada, 1987 and 2006

| | 1987 | 2006 |
|---|---|---|
| Managerial | 30.1 | 36.3 |
| Professional | 50.4 | 55.9 |
| Clerical and administrative | 73.9 | 75.0 |
| Sales and service | 55.2 | 56.8 |
| Primary industries (mining, farming, fishing, etc.) | 19.7 | 20.5 |
| Trades, transport, and construction | 5.2 | 6.5 |
| Processing, manufacturing, and utilities | 32.4 | 31.1 |

Source: Almey (2007).

*reality. They devote fewer hours to paid work than men do, experience more labour-force interruptions, and are more likely than men to take part-time jobs, which pay less per hour and offer fewer benefits than full-time work does (Waldfogel, 1997). Women also do considerably more housework and eldercare than men do (Sauve, 2002). Globally, women do between two-thirds and three-quarters of all unpaid child care, housework, and care for aging parents (Boyd, 1997: 55). Even when they work full time in the paid labour force, women continue to shoulder a disproportionate share of domestic responsibilities, working, in effect, a "double shift" (Chapter 9, Families).*

4. Work done by women is commonly considered less valuable than work done by men, because it is viewed as involving fewer skills. *Women tend to earn less than men because the skills involved in their work are often undervalued (Figart and Lapidus, 1996; Sorenson, 1994). For example, kindergarten teachers (nearly all of whom are women) earn less than office machine repair technicians (nearly all of whom are men). It is, however, questionable whether it takes less training and skill to teach a young child the basics of counting and cooperation than it takes to get a photocopier to collate paper properly. As this example suggests, we apply somewhat arbitrary standards to reward different occupational roles. In our society, these standards systematically undervalue the kinds of skills needed for jobs where women are concentrated.*

We thus see that the gender gap in earnings is based on several *social* circumstances rather than on any inherent difference between women and men. This means that people can reduce the gender gap if they want to. Later in the chapter, we discuss social policies that could create more equality between women and men. But first, to stress the urgency of such policies, we explain how the persistence of gender inequality encourages sexual harassment and rape.

## *Male Aggression against Women*

Serious acts of aggression between men and women are common. The great majority are committed by men against women. For example, in recent years, more than 25 000 sexual assaults have been reported to Canadian police annually. More than 8 out of 10 victims are women and nearly all of the accused perpetrators are men. Among young singles, the rate of sexual assault is higher than in the population as a whole (Integration Analysis Program, 1999: 272; Statistics Canada, 2003i; see Figure 8.4).

Consider research on **acquaintance rape**—sexual assaults committed by someone the victim knows (Meyer, 1984; Senn, Desmarais, Veryberg, and Wood, 2000). One Canadian study found that more than a fifth of female postsecondary students said they had given in to unwanted sexual intercourse because they had been overwhelmed by a man's continued arguments and pressure. Nearly 7 percent reported they had unwanted sexual intercourse because a man threatened or used some degree of physical force, and almost 14 percent claimed that a man had attempted unwanted sexual intercourse while they were either intoxicated or under the influence of drugs (DeKeseredy and Kelly, 1993). Although Canadian law requires that people take "reasonable steps to ascertain consent" before engaging another in any sexual act, interpretations of what is "reasonable" vary. Moreover, the courts have failed to provide explicit norms for what "reasonable steps" should be. Indeed, the biggest category of cases in which men accused of sexual assault successfully argue "reasonable steps" and win acquittals are cases in which women have been deliberately drugged or are unconscious because of excessive alcohol use at the time of the assault (Sheehy, 2003: 579).

**Figure 8.4**

**Percentage of University Students Who Severely Assaulted a Dating Partner in the Past Year, by Country, 2001–2005 ($n = 6700$)**

Note: Some of the American data were collected in 1998. "Severely assaulted" was defined as students who, in the year preceding the survey, used a knife or a gun on a partner, punched or hit a partner with something that could hurt, choked a partner, slammed a partner against a wall, beat up a partner, burned or scalded a partner, or kicked a partner.

Source: From International Dating Violence Study, tabulation courtesy of Murray A. Straus based on Douglas and Straus (2006).

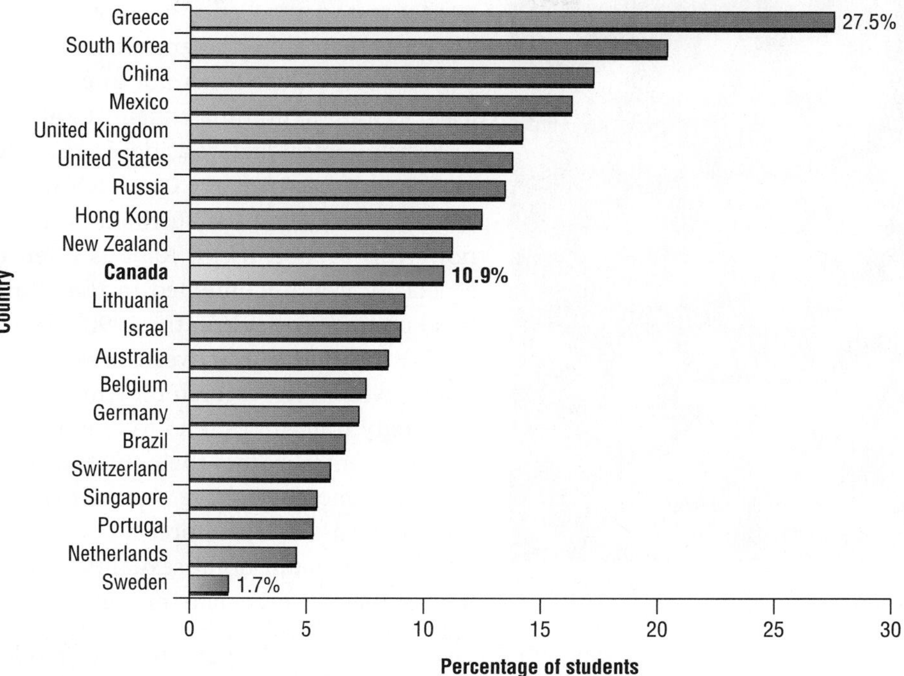


Why do men commit more frequent (and more harmful) acts of aggression against women than women commit against men? It is *not* because men on average are physically more powerful than women. Greater physical power is more likely to be used to commit acts of aggression only when norms justify male domination and men have much more *social* power than women. When women and men are more equal socially, and norms justify gender equality, the rate of male aggression against women is lower. This point is evident if we consider sexual assault and sexual harassment (see also the discussion of wife abuse in Chapter 9, Families).

## Sexual Assault

Some people think rapists are men who suffer a psychological disorder that compels them to achieve immediate sexual gratification even if violence is required. Others think rape occurs because of flawed communication. They believe some victims give mixed signals to their assailants by, for example, wearing revealing clothes or flirting.

Such explanations are not completely invalid. Interviews with victims and perpetrators show that some offenders do suffer from psychological disorders. Others misinterpret signals in what they regard as sexually ambiguous situations (Hannon, Hall, Kuntz, Laar, and Williams, 1995). But such cases account for only a small proportion of the total. Men who commit sexual assault rarely have a mental illness, and it is abundantly clear to most assailants that they are doing something their victims strongly oppose.

What then accounts for sexual assault being as common as it is? A sociological answer is suggested by the fact that sexual assault is sometimes not about sexual gratification at all. Some offenders cannot ejaculate or even achieve an erection. Significantly, however, all forms of sexual assault involve domination and humiliation as principal motives. It is

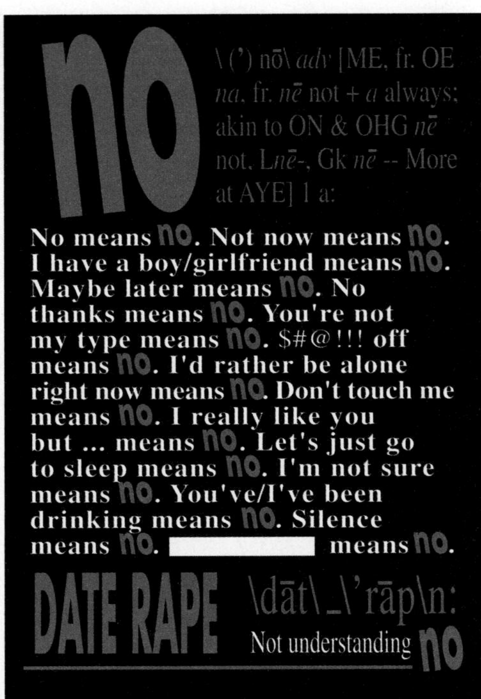
no
\ (') nō\ adv [ME, fr. OE na, fr. nē not + a always; akin to ON & OHG nē not, L nē-, Gk nē -- More at AYE] 1 a:
No means no. Not now means no. I have a boy/girlfriend means no. Maybe later means no. No thanks means no. You're not my type means no. $#@!!! off means no. I'd rather be alone right now means no. Don't touch me means no. I really like you but ... means no. Let's just go to sleep means no. I'm not sure means no. You've/I've been drinking means no. Silence means no. means no.
DATE RAPE \dāt_\'rāp\n:
Not understanding no
This poster suggests that men still need to be reminded that no means no.

not surprising, therefore, that some offenders were physically or sexually abused in their youth. They develop a deep need to feel powerful as psychological compensation for their early powerlessness. Others are men who, as children, saw their mothers as potentially hostile figures who needed to be controlled or as mere objects available for male gratification. They saw their fathers as emotionally cold and distant. Raised in such an atmosphere, rapists learn not to empathize with women. Instead, they learn to want to dominate them (Lisak, 1992).

Psychological factors aside, certain *social* situations also increase the rate of sexual aggression. One such situation is war. In war, conquering male soldiers often feel justified humiliating the vanquished, who are powerless to stop them. Rape is often used for this purpose, as was especially well documented in the ethnic wars that accompanied the breakup of Yugoslavia in the 1990s (Human Rights Watch, 1995).

The relationship between male dominance and sexual aggression is also evident in research on American fraternities. Many college and university fraternities tend to emphasize male dominance and aggression as a central part of their culture. Sociologists who have interviewed fraternity members have shown that most fraternities try to recruit members who can reinforce a macho image and avoid any suggestion of effeminacy and homosexuality. Research also shows that fraternity houses that are especially prone to sexual assault tend to sponsor parties that treat women in a particularly degrading way. By emphasizing a very narrow and aggressive form of masculinity, some fraternities tend to facilitate sexual assault on campuses (Boswell and Spade, 1996).

Another social circumstance that increases the likelihood of sexual assault is participation in athletics. Of course, the overwhelming majority of athletes are not rapists. However, there are proportionately more rapists among men who participate in athletics than among non-athletes (Welch, 1997). That is because many sports embody a particular vision of masculinity in North American culture: competitive, aggressive, and domineering. By recruiting men who display these characteristics and by encouraging the development of these characteristics in athletes, sports can contribute to off-field aggression, including sexual aggression. Furthermore, among male athletes, there is a distinct hierarchy of sexual aggression. Male athletes who engage in contact sports are more prone to be rapists than other athletes. There are proportionately even more rapists among athletes involved in collision and combative sports, notably football (Welch, 1997).

Sexual assault, we conclude, involves the use of sex to establish dominance. Its incidence is highest in situations in which early socialization experiences predispose men to want to control women, where norms justify the domination of women, and where a big power imbalance between men and women exists.

### Sexual Harassment

Sexual harassment comes in two forms. **Quid pro quo sexual harassment** takes place when sexual threats or bribery are made a condition of employment decisions. (The Latin phrase *quid pro quo* means "something for something.") **Hostile environment sexual harassment** involves sexual jokes, touching, and comments that interfere with work or create a hostile work environment. Research suggests that relatively powerless women are the most likely to be sexually harassed. Specifically, women who are young, unmarried, and employed in nonprofessional jobs are most likely to become objects of sexual harassment, particularly if they are temporary workers, if the ratio of women to men in the workplace is low, and if the organizational culture of the workplace tolerates sexual harassment (Sev'er, 1999; Welsh, 1999).

Ultimately then, male aggression against women, including sexual harassment and sexual assault, is encouraged by a lesson most of us still learn at home, in school, at work, through much of organized religion, and in the mass media: it is natural and right for men to dominate women. To be sure, recent decades have witnessed important changes in the way women's and men's roles are defined. Nevertheless, in the world of paid work, in the household, in government, and in all other spheres of life, men still tend to command substantially more power and authority than women. Daily patterns of gender domination, viewed as legitimate by most people, are built into our courtship, sexual, family, and work norms. From this point of view, male aggression against women is simply an expression of male authority by other means.

These facts do not mean that all men endorse the principle of male dominance, much less that all men are inclined to engage in sexual assault or other acts of aggression against women. Indeed, scholars increasingly speak of *masculinities* in the plural, rather than the singular, to acknowledge differences among men and to emphasize that "masculinity" is neither innate nor a fixed entity (Messerschmidt, 1993). Many men favour gender equality, and most men never abuse a woman. Nevertheless, the fact remains that many aspects of our culture legitimize male dominance, making it seem valid or proper. For example, pornography, jokes about "dumb blondes," and leering might seem examples of harmless play. At a subtler, sociological level, however, they are assertions of the appropriateness of women's submission to men. Such frequent and routine reinforcements of male authority increase the likelihood that some men will consider it their right to assault women physically or sexually if the opportunity to do so exists or can be created. "Just kidding" has a cost. For instance, researchers have found that university men who enjoy sexist jokes are most likely to report engaging in acts of sexual aggression against women (Ryan and Kanjorski, 1998).

We thus see that male aggression against women and gender inequality are not separate issues. Gender inequality is the foundation of aggression against women. In concluding this chapter, we consider how gender equality can be increased in the coming decades. As we proceed, you should bear in mind that gender equality is not just a matter of justice; it is also a matter of safety.

## *Toward 2124*

The twentieth century witnessed growing equality between women and men in many countries. In Canada, the decline of the family farm made children less economically useful and more costly to raise. As a result, women started having fewer children. The industrialization of Canada, and then the growth of the economy's service sector, increased demand for women in the paid labour force (see Figure 8.5). This demand gave women substantially more economic power and also encouraged them to have fewer children. The legalization and availability of contraception made it possible for women to exercise unprecedented control over their own bodies. The women's movement fought for, and won, increased rights for women on a number of economic, political, and legal fronts. All these forces brought about a massive cultural shift, a fundamental reorientation of thinking on the part of many Canadians about what women could and should do in society.

## Figure 8.5
## Percentage of Adults Ages 25 and Older in Paid Labour Force, Canada, 1946–2004

Sources: Adapted from Denton (1983); Statistics Canada (n.d.-5).

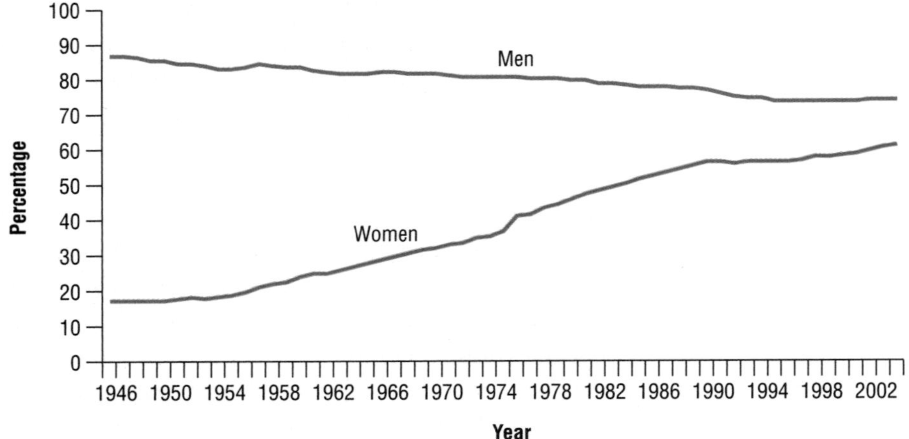


One indicator of the progress of women is the Gender Empowerment Measure (GEM). The GEM is computed by the United Nations. It takes into account women's share of seats in Parliament; women's share of administrative, managerial, professional, and technical jobs; and women's earning power. A score of 1.0 indicates equality with men on these three dimensions.

As Figure 8.6 shows, Norway, Sweden, Iceland, and Denmark were the four most gender-egalitarian countries among the 75 on which data were available in 2005. They had GEM scores ranging from 0.932 to 0.861. This means that women in these countries

## Figure 8.6
## Gender Empowerment Measure, Top 11 and Bottom 9 Countries, 2005

Note: Data are available for 75 countries.

Source: United Nations (2006: 367–69).

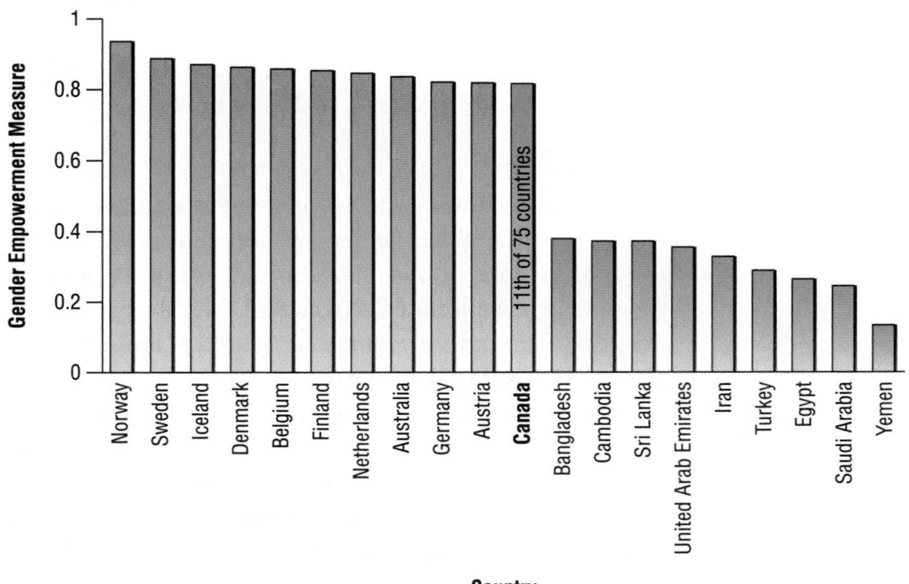

were between 86 percent and 93 percent of the way to equality with men on these three dimensions. Canada ranked 11th, with a GEM score of 0.81.

In general, more gender equality exists in rich than in poor countries. The top-ranked countries are all rich, suggesting that gender equality is a function of economic development. However, our analysis of the GEM data suggests that there are some exceptions to the general pattern. For example, the Bahamas and Barbados rank considerably higher on the GEM than the richer countries of Italy and Japan. This fact suggests that gender equality may also be a function of government policy. This impression is reinforced by the fact that, in some of the former communist countries of Eastern Europe—such as Poland, Slovakia, Slovenia, and the Czech Republic—gender equality is *higher* than we would expect given their level of economic development. Meanwhile, in some of the Islamic countries, gender inequality is *lower* than we would expect given their level of economic development (e.g., the United Arab Emirates). These anomalies exist because the former communist countries made gender equality a matter of public policy while many Islamic countries do just the opposite (Brym et al., 2005).

The GEM figures suggest that Canadian women still have a considerable way to go before they achieve equality with men. We have also seen that the gender gap in earnings is shrinking but will disappear only in 2124—and then only if it continues to diminish at the same rate as it did from 1980 to 2004. That is a big "if," because progress is never automatic.

Socializing children at home and in school to understand that women and men are equally adept at all jobs is important in motivating them to excel in non-traditional fields. Hiring more women to compensate for past discrimination in hiring, firing, promotion, and training is also important. However, without in any way minimizing the need for such initiatives, we should recognize that their impact will be muted if women continue to undertake disproportionate domestic responsibilities and if occupations with a high concentration of women continue to be undervalued in monetary terms.

Two main policy initiatives will probably be required in the coming decades to bridge the gender gap in earnings. One is the development of a better child-care system. The other is the development of a policy of pay equity. Let us briefly consider these issues.

## Child Care

High-quality, government-subsidized, affordable child care is widely available in most Western European countries. Sixty percent of children in the United Kingdom are in regulated child care as are 69 percent of children in France and 78 percent in Denmark. In contrast, a team from the Organisation for Economic Co-operation and Development (OECD) strongly faulted Canada's efforts as a patchwork that has been chronically underfunded. Only 20 percent of Canadian children under the age of seven are in regulated child care (OECD, 2004: 7). As a result, many Canadian women with small children are either unable to work outside the home or able to work outside the home only on a part-time basis.

A universal system of daycare was proposed in Canada as early as 1970 but little was done at the federal level or in most provinces and territories. Quebec is an exception. In 1997 that province introduced a comprehensive family policy that attempts to integrate family benefits, paid parental leave, child care, and kindergarten. Its child-care component heralded universally available, affordable child care. A rapid expansion in the number of spaces occurred, although waiting lists grew as well. By 2004, 40 percent of the regulated daycare spaces available in Canada were in Quebec. Unfortunately, that was in part because no new spaces had been added outside Quebec in the preceding decade.

The need exists. In 2001, 52 percent of Canadian preschoolers received some kind of care outside of the home, up from 42 percent just seven years earlier. But only 25 percent of these children were enrolled in daycare programs; a growing number were cared for by relatives: 14 percent, up from 8 percent in 1994 (Statistics Canada, 2005c.)

In 2004, affordable, high-quality, regulated daycare was a central electoral promise of the victorious Liberal Party. By mid-2005, the beginnings of a national system began to take shape when the federal government reached child-care agreements with Saskatchewan, Manitoba, Ontario, and Newfoundland and Labrador. The system, had it taken root across the country, would have paid for itself. One study estimated that a high-quality, affordable, universal system of child care and early child-care education would cost $7.9 billion annually, while the increased employment of mothers would be worth $6.2 billion and the improvement in child development would be worth $4.3 billion (Cleveland and Krashinsky, 1998). However, after his election in 2006, Prime Minister Stephen Harper scrapped the agreements in favour of taxable benefits of $1200 for every child under six. The amount and the targeting were widely criticized as failing to address the burdens of women who work for pay needed to support their families.

### Equal Pay for Work of Equal Value

On paper, Canadian women have had the right to equal pay for the same jobs done by men since the 1950s. Unfortunately, although early laws proclaimed lofty goals, they failed to result in fair wages.

In the 1980s, researchers found that women earn less than men partly because jobs in which women are concentrated are valued less than jobs in which men are concentrated. They therefore tried to establish gender-neutral standards by which they could judge the dollar value of work. These standards include such factors as the education and experience required to do a particular job and the level of responsibility, amount of stress, and working conditions associated with it. Researchers felt that, by using these criteria to compare jobs in which women and men are concentrated, they could identify pay inequities. The underpaid could then be compensated accordingly. In other words, women and men would receive equal pay for work of equal value, even if they did different jobs. During the mid-1980s, some governments amended the law to state that women should be paid equally for work of equal value. This amendment required employers to compare the rates of pay for women and men in dissimilar jobs that nevertheless involved the same level of skill, effort, and responsibility, and the same working conditions. In 1985, Manitoba became the first Canadian province to demand that its public sector be proactive and implement plans for equal pay for work of equal value—or **pay equity,** as it came to be called. Pay equity is now official policy in 10 of 13 Canadian jurisdictions (Alberta, Saskatchewan, and the Northwest Territories are the exceptions). However, provisions vary widely. Enforcement mechanisms are meagre and employers have found various ways to argue that unequal wages do not signify discrimination based on sex. Thus, although pay equity is undoubtedly a significant step toward achieving gender equality, inequity remains, as evidenced by the persistence of the wage gap between working men and women.

# The Women's Movement

Improved daycare and pay equity would do much to bridge the gender gap in earnings between women and men. However, improvements in the social standing of women do not depend just on the sympathy of government and business leaders. Progress on this front has always depended in part on the strength of the organized women's movement. That is likely to be true in the future, too. In concluding this chapter, it is therefore fitting to consider the state of the women's movement and its prospects.

The "first wave" of the women's movement emerged during the late nineteenth century and lasted into the early 1920s. The most important public achievements of this movement in Canada were the right to vote and the right to be considered *persons* under Canadian law (Nelson and Robinson, 2002). In 1916, women in Alberta, Manitoba, and Saskatchewan won the right to vote in provincial elections. Other provinces and territories followed: British Columbia (1917), Ontario (1917), Nova Scotia (1918), New Brunswick (1919), Yukon (1919), Prince Edward Island (1922), Newfoundland and Labrador (1925), Quebec (1940), and, finally, the Northwest Territories (1951). These rights were first granted to white women. Women from certain ethnic and racial groups did not receive the franchise until later (Nelson and Robinson, 2002).

In the mid-1960s, the "second wave" of the women's movement emerged. Second-wave feminists were inspired in part by the successes of the civil rights movement in the United States. They felt that women's concerns were largely ignored despite persistent and pervasive gender inequality. Like their counterparts more than a century earlier, they held demonstrations, lobbied politicians, and formed women's organizations to further

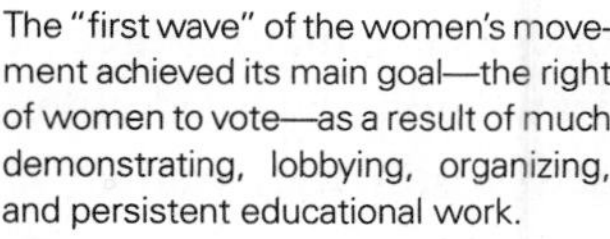

The "first wave" of the women's movement achieved its main goal—the right of women to vote—as a result of much demonstrating, lobbying, organizing, and persistent educational work.

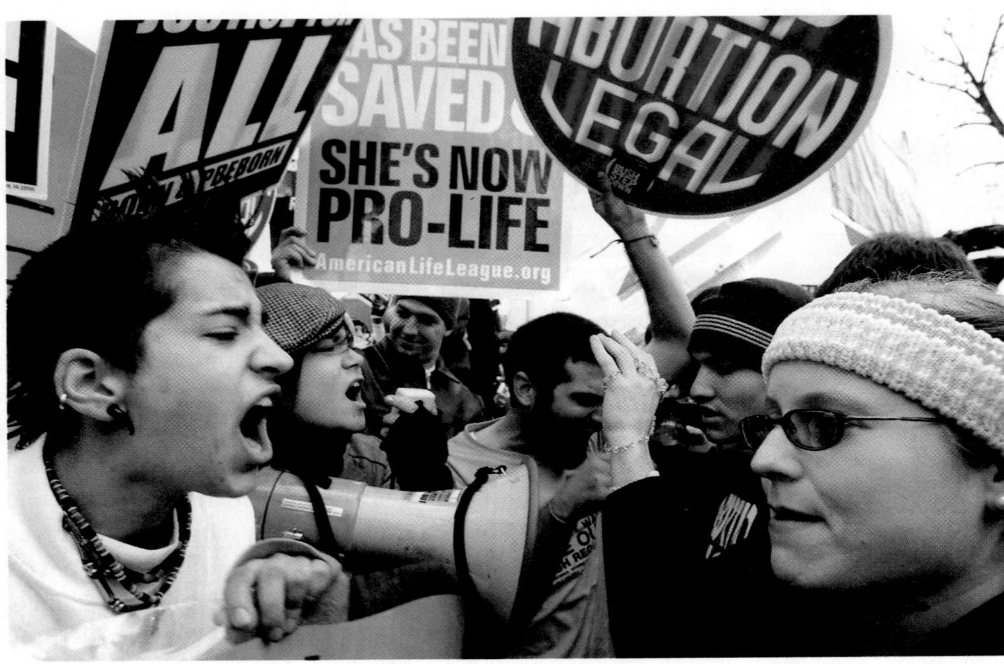


The "second wave" of the women's movement started to grow in the mid-1960s. Members of the movement advocated equal rights with men in education and employment, the elimination of sexual violence, and women's control over reproduction.

their cause. They demanded equal rights with men in education and employment, the elimination of sexual violence, and women's control over reproduction.

Currently, considerable intellectual diversity exists in the feminist movement concerning ultimate goals. Three main streams may be distinguished (Tong, 1989).

*Liberal feminism* is the most popular current in the women's movement today. Its advocates believe that the main sources of women's subordination are learned gender roles and the denial of opportunities to women. Liberal feminists advocate non-sexist methods of socialization and education, more sharing of domestic tasks between women and men, and extending to women all the educational, employment, and political rights and privileges that men enjoy.

*Socialist feminists* regard women's relationship to the economy as the main source of women's disadvantages. They believe that the traditional nuclear family emerged along with inequalities of wealth. In their opinion, once men possessed wealth, they wanted to ensure that their property would be transmitted to their children, particularly their sons. They accomplished this in two ways. First, men exercised complete economic control over their property, thus ensuring it would not be squandered and would remain theirs and theirs alone. Second, they enforced female monogamy, thus ensuring that their property would be transmitted only to *their* offspring. Thus, according to socialist feminists, the economic and sexual oppression of women has its roots in capitalism. Socialist feminists also assert that the reforms proposed by liberal feminists are inadequate because they can do little to help working-class women, who are too poor to take advantage of equal educational and work opportunities. Socialist feminists conclude that only the elimination of private property and the creation of economic equality can bring about an end to the oppression of all women.

*Radical feminists* find the reforms proposed by liberals and the revolution proposed by socialists inadequate. Patriarchy—male domination and norms justifying that domination—is more deeply rooted than capitalism, say the radical feminists. After all, patriarchy predates capitalism. Moreover, it is just as evident in self-proclaimed communist societies as it is in capitalist societies. Radical feminists conclude that the very idea of gender must be changed to bring an end to male domination. Some radical feminists argue that new reproductive technologies, such as in vitro fertilization, are bound to be helpful in this regard because they can break the link between women's bodies and child-bearing (see Chapter 9, Families). However, the revolution envisaged by radical feminists goes beyond the realm of reproduction to include all aspects of male sexual dominance. From their point of view, pornography, sexual harassment, restrictive contraception, sexual assault, incest, sterilization, and physical assault must be eliminated so that women can reconstruct their sexuality on their own terms.

This thumbnail sketch by no means exhausts the variety of streams of the contemporary women's movement. Indeed, some observers say the movement entered its "third wave" in the mid-1980s, characterized by *anti-racist* and *postmodernist* feminists criticizing liberal, socialist, and radical feminists for generalizing from the experience of white women and for failing to understand how women's lives are rooted in particular historical and racial experiences (Cassidy, Lord, and Mandell, 1998: 26; hooks, 1984). These new currents have done much to extend the relevance of feminism to previously marginalized groups.

Partly because of the political and intellectual vigour of the women's movement, some feminist ideas have gained widespread acceptance in Canadian society over the past three decades. For example, opposition to women in the paid labour force has declined and most Canadians now believe that both spouses should contribute to household income when possible (Ghalam, 1997). However, these values appear to conflict with other attitudes and beliefs. For example, one national survey reports that 46 percent of women and 44 percent of men agree or strongly agree with the statement that a "job is alright, but what most women really want is a home and children" (Ghalam, 1997: 16). It appears that the tapestry of our social lives is interwoven with threads of the new and the old.

## The Points of the Compass

The constraints on human sexuality and gender are both natural and social. People's sex organs and hormones strongly influence their sexual identity, preferences, and behaviour. Social forces—especially socialization patterns and power relations—generally reinforce biological predispositions. But strong influences and general reinforcements leave a lot of room for variation. For example, a person's sex organs may not "fit" his or her hormonal balance or sexual identity. Changing social requirements and conventions may allow or encourage departures from traditional gender roles. Such circumstances give those who are so inclined the freedom to escape the constraints imposed by tradition.

The sharper the distinction between masculine and feminine roles, the greater the inequality of income and opportunity between men and women. One society may regard femininity as centred on unpaid domestic work and masculinity as centred on work in the paid labour force. A second society may broaden the conventional view of femininity to include work in "helping" occupations: nurse, secretary, teacher, and the like. A third society may go still further and regard femininity as perfectly consistent with women holding the same kinds of jobs as men in the paid labour force. It may also regard the sharing of domestic responsibilities between men and women as highly desirable. As we move from the first society to the third, the distinction between masculine and feminine work roles becomes blurred and opportunities for women and men become more equal.

# Summary

**1.** ***Are sex and gender rooted in nature?***

While *sex* refers to certain anatomical and hormonal features of a person, *gender* refers to the culturally appropriate expression of masculinity and femininity. Sex is rooted largely in nature, although people can change their sex by undergoing a sex-change operation and hormone therapy. In contrast, social forces strongly influence gender. Sociologists study the way social conditions affect the expression of masculinity and femininity.

**2.** ***What are some of the major social forces that channel people into performing culturally appropriate gender roles?***

Various agents of socialization channel people into performing culturally approved gender roles. The family, the school, and the mass media are among the most important of these agents of socialization. Once the sex of children is known, parents and teachers tend to treat boys and girls differently in terms of the kind of play, dress, and learning they encourage. The mass media reinforce the learning of masculine and feminine roles by making different characteristics seem desirable in boys and girls, men and women.

**3.** ***Aside from agents of socialization, are there other social forces that influence the expression of masculinity and femininity?***

Yes. One of the most important non-socialization forces that influence the expression of masculinity and femininity is the level of social inequality between men and women. High levels of gender inequality encourage more traditional or conventional gender roles. There are fewer differences in gender roles when low levels of gender inequality prevail. Today, we can see the influence of gender inequality on gender roles by examining male aggression against women, which tends to be high when men are much more socially powerful than women and low when there is greater gender equality.

**4.** ***What is homosexuality and why does it exist?***

Homosexuals are people who prefer sexual partners of the same sex. We do not yet well understand the causes of homosexuality—whether it is genetic, hormonal, psychological, or some combination of the three. We do know that homosexuality does not appear to be a choice and that it emerges for most people in early adolescence, before they have any sexual experience. Sociologists are, in any case, more interested in the way homosexuality is expressed and repressed. For example, they have studied how, in the twentieth century, scientific research and political movements have made the open expression of homosexuality more acceptable. Sociologists have also studied the ways in which various aspects of society reinforce heterosexuality and treat homosexuality as a form of deviance subject to tight social control.

**5.** ***How does the existence of sharply defined gender roles influence men's and women's income?***

One important consequence of strict gender differentiation is the existence of a big earnings gap between women and men. The gender gap in earnings derives from outright discrimination against women, women's disproportionate domestic responsibilities, women's concentration in low-wage occupations and industries, and the undervaluation of work typically done by women.

**6.** ***How might the gender gap in earnings be reduced or eliminated?***

Among the major reforms that could help eliminate the gender gap in earnings and reduce the overall level and expression of gender inequality are (1) the development of an affordable, accessible system of high-quality daycare and (2) the remuneration of men and women on the basis of their work's actual worth.

## Key Terms

acquaintance rape (p. 252)
bisexuals (p. 244)
essentialism (p. 232)
gender (p. 231)
gender discrimination (p. 251)
gender identity (p. 231)
gender ideology (p. 239)
glass ceiling (p. 244)
heterosexuality (p. 232)
heterosexuals (p. 244)
homophobia (p. 246)
homosexuals (p. 244)
hostile environment sexual harassment (p. 254)
intersexed (p. 230)
occupational sex segregation (p. 251)
pay equity (p. 258)
quid pro quo sexual harassment (p. 254)
sex (p. 231)
social constructionism (p. 232)
transgendered (p. 244)
transsexuals (p. 244)

## Questions to Consider

1. By interviewing your family members and using your memory, compare the gender division of labour in (a) the households in which your parents (or someone from their generation) grew up, and (b) the household(s) in which you grew up. Then, imagine the gender division of labour you would like to see in the household you hope to live in about 10 years from now. What accounts for change over time in the gender division of labour in these households? Do you think your hopes are realistic? Why or why not?
2. In your own case, rank the relative importance of your family, your schools, and the mass media in your gender socialization. What criteria do you use to judge the importance of each socialization agent?
3. Systematically note the roles played by women and men on TV programs and ads one evening. Is there a gender division of labour on TV? If so, describe it.
4. Are you a feminist? If so, which of the types of feminism discussed in this chapter do you find most appealing? Why? If not, what do you find objectionable about feminism? In either case, what is the ideal form of gender relations in your opinion? Why do you think this form is ideal?

## Web Resources

### Companion Web Site for This Book

http://www.pointsofthecompass.nelson.com

Begin by clicking on the Student Resources section of the Web site. Next, select the chapter you are currently studying from the pull-down menu. From the Student Resources page you will have easy access to InfoTrac® College Edition, MicroCase online exercises, and additional Weblinks. The Web site also has many useful tips to aid you in your study of sociology, including practice tests for each chapter.

### InfoTrac® Search Terms

These search terms are provided to assist you in beginning to conduct research on this topic by visiting **http://www.infotrac-college.com**:

**gender**
**gender discrimination**
**gender role**
**glass ceiling**
**sexual harassment**

## Recommended Web Sites

Status of Women Canada is "the federal government agency which promotes gender equality, and the full participation of women in the economic, social, cultural and political life of the country." Its Web site is at **http://www.swc-cfc.gc.ca/index_e.html**.

For recent Canadian data on women in the paid labour force, visit Statistics Canada's *Women in Canada: Work Chapter Updates* at **http://www.statcan.ca/english/freepub/89F0133XIE/89F0133XIE2006000.htm**.

For information on gender roles and sex stereotyping in children's literature, see **http://www.indiana.edu/~reading/ieo/bibs/childgen.html**.

# PART 4 INSTITUTIONS

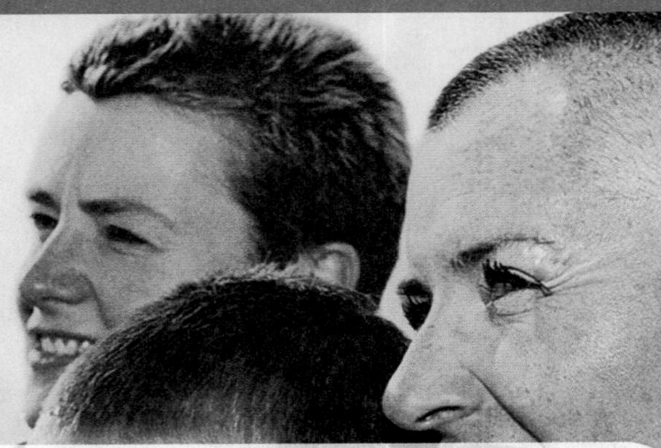

# chapter 9

## families



### In this chapter, you will learn that

→ The traditional nuclear family is less common than it used to be. Several new family forms are becoming more popular.

→ The frequency of one family form or another varies by class, ethnicity, sexual orientation, and region of the country.

→ Among the most important forces underlying the change from the traditional nuclear family are the entry of women into the paid labour force and the legalization of contraception. Doing paid work and having access to contraception increases women's ability to leave unhappy marriages and control whether and when they will have children.

→ Marital satisfaction increases (1) as people move up the class structure, (2) where divorce laws are liberal, (3) when teenage children leave the home, (4) in families where housework is shared equally, and (5) among spouses who enjoy satisfying sexual relations.

→ The worst effects of divorce on children can be eliminated if there is no parental conflict and the children's standard of living does not fall after divorce.

→ A more equal division of power between spouses leads to men contributing more to domestic labour and to a decline in domestic violence.

→ The decline of the traditional nuclear family is sometimes associated with a host of social problems, such as poverty, welfare dependency, and crime. However, policies have been adopted in some countries that reduce these problems.

# Introduction

One Saturday morning, the married couple who lived next door to Robert Brym and his family asked Robert for advice on new speakers they wanted to buy for their sound system. Robert volunteered to go shopping with them at a nearby mall. They told him they also wanted to buy two outdoor garbage cans at a hardware store. Robert told them he didn't mind waiting.

"After they made the purchases, we returned to their minivan in the mall's parking lot," says Robert. "The wife opened the trunk, cleared some space, and said to her husband, 'Let's put the garbage cans back here.'

"Meanwhile, the husband had opened the side door. He had already put the speakers on the back seat and was struggling to do the same with the second garbage can. 'It's okay,' he said, 'I've already got one of them partway in here.'

"'Oh,' laughed the wife, 'I can judge space better than you, and you'll never get that in there. Bring it back here.'

"'You know,' answered the husband, 'we don't always have to do things your way. I'm a perfectly intelligent person. I think there's room up here and that's where I'm going to put this thing. You can put yours back there or stick it anywhere else you like.'

"'Why are you yelling at me?' snapped the wife.

"'I'm not yelling,' shouted the husband. 'I'm just saying that I know as well as you what fits where. There's more than one way—your way—to do things.'

"So, the wife put one garbage can in the trunk, the husband put one in the back seat (it was, by the way, a tight squeeze) and we piled into the van for the drive home. The husband and the wife did not say a word to each other. When we got back to our neighbourhood, I said I was feeling tired and asked whether I could perhaps hook up their speakers on Sunday. Actually, I wasn't tired. I just had no desire to referee round two. I went home, full of wonder at the occasional inability of presumably mature adults to talk rationally about something as simple as how to pack garbage cans into a minivan.

"But trivializing the couple's argument in this way prevented me from thinking about it sociologically. If I had been thinking like a sociologist, I would have at least recognized that, for better or for worse, our most intense emotional experiences are bound up with our families—which is why family ties so often connect murderers with their victims (see Table 9.1). We love, hate, protect, hurt, express generosity toward, and envy nobody as much as our parents, siblings, children, and mates. Little wonder, then, that most people are passionately concerned with the rights and wrongs, the dos and don'ts, of family life. Little wonder that family issues lie close to the centre of political debate in this country. Little wonder that words, gestures, and actions that seem trivial to an outsider can hold deep meaning and significance for family members."

**Table 9.1**
Homicides by Accused-Victim Relationship, Canada, 2005

| Relationship | Percent |
|---|---|
| Family | 32.9% |
| Boyfriend/girlfriend (current or former) | 3.3 |
| Casual acquaintance | 18.1 |
| Close friend or neighbour | 12.8 |
| Criminal relationship | 12.2 |
| Business | 1.9 |
| Authority | 0.6 |
| Stranger | 18.1 |
| Total | 99.9 |

Source: Statistics Canada (2006f).
Note: Total does not equal 100 percent because of rounding. Data are for 475 solved homicides in which the accused was known.

# Is the Family in Decline?

Because families are emotional minefields, few subjects of sociological inquiry generate as much controversy. Much of the debate centres on a single question: Is the family in decline and, if so, what should be done about it? These questions are hardly new. John Laing, a Protestant minister in Ontario, wrote in 1878, "We may expect to see further disintegration until the family shall disappear. . . . In all things civil and sacred the tendency of the age is towards individualism . . . its plausible aphorisms and popular usages silently undermining the divine institution of the family." This alarm, or one much like it, is sounded whenever the family undergoes rapid change, and particularly when the divorce rate increases.

Today, when some people speak about the decline of the family, they are referring to the **nuclear family.** The nuclear family comprises a cohabiting man and woman who maintain a socially approved sexual relationship and have at least one child. Others are referring more narrowly to what we call the **traditional nuclear family.** The traditional nuclear family is a nuclear family in which the wife works in the home without pay while the husband works outside the home for money. This makes him the "primary provider and ultimate authority" (Popenoe, 1988: 1; see Box 9.1).

In the 1940s and 1950s, many sociologists and much of the Canadian public considered the traditional nuclear family to be the most widespread and ideal family form. However, for reasons we will examine below, only 42 percent of Canadian families in 2001 were nuclear families, compared with 55 percent in 1981 and 69 percent in 1901 (see Figure 9.1). Moreover, because about 80 percent of mothers with school-aged children are in the paid labour force, only a small minority of Canadian adults live in traditional nuclear families today (Canadian Council on Social Development, 2001). New family forms, including single-parent families, common-law families, and gay and lesbian families, have become increasingly prevalent in recent decades (see Table 9.2).

9.1

# SOCIOLOGY AT THE MOVIES

Joaquin Phoenix and Reese Witherspoon in *Walk the Line*

## *Walk the Line* (2005)

When legendary country singer Johnny Cash was 12, his older brother was killed in an accident and his father screamed that "God took the wrong son," assuming, unjustly and without evidence, that Johnny was to blame for the boy's death. Burdened by the loss of his beloved brother and his father's constant rejection, Johnny Cash becomes a deeply troubled adult. Fame didn't help. He drinks too much, pops amphetamine pills like they are Tic Tacs, neglects his children, ruins his marriage, and does time for trying to smuggle narcotics across the U.S. border from Mexico.

Redemption arrives in the form of fellow performer June Carter (Reese Witherspoon, who won the 2005 Best Actress Oscar for her performance). Cash (played by Joaquin Phoenix, nominated for the 2005 Best Actor Oscar) pursues her relentlessly for years, eventually resorting to a proposal in the middle of a performance in Toronto, which she accepts. From that moment, Cash's life changes. But it is not just June who rescues him with her love and support. It is the entire Carter family. The Carters display all the grace and generosity we would expect of a royal family, which is just about what they were in the country music scene. At a Thanksgiving dinner attended by the Carters and the Cashes at Johnny's new house, Johnny's father starts in on him with the usual putdowns. "So how do you like it?" Johnny asks his father, referring to the house. "Jack Benny's is bigger," snaps the father. But Mr. Carter springs to Johnny's defence, mildly rebuking Mr. Cash by asking, "Oh, have you been to Jack Benny's house?" Johnny is upset enough to leave the meal but Mrs. Carter encourages June to go after him and ease his pain. Later, Johnny's supplier arrives with a fresh bag of pills, but June's parents chase him away with a shotgun. They integrate Johnny into their family as the beloved son he always wanted and needed to be, and Johnny lives with June and their four girls from previous marriages happily ever after.

What is a family? A cohabiting man and woman who maintain a socially approved sexual relationship and perhaps have at least one child? By that standard definition, Johnny's parents and their children formed a family—but a pretty sorry one by any reasonable standard because their family failed to provide the emotional support that could have allowed Johnny to thrive and become a happy adult. The Carters were not part of Johnny's family according to the standard definition, but their generosity of spirit led them to treat him like a son anyway. Johnny eventually became part of their extended family, but only because they cared deeply for his welfare. The story of Johnny Cash suggests that the first definition of a family we presented may be too narrow. Perhaps it is appropriate to think of a **family** more broadly as a set of intimate social relationships that adults create to sh resources so as to ensure the welfare of themsel their dependents.

### CRITICAL THINKING QUESTIONS

- *What values are implicit in the two family offered above?*
- *Which definition of family do yo*

**Figure 9.1**
The Growing Diversity of Families, Canada, 1981–2001

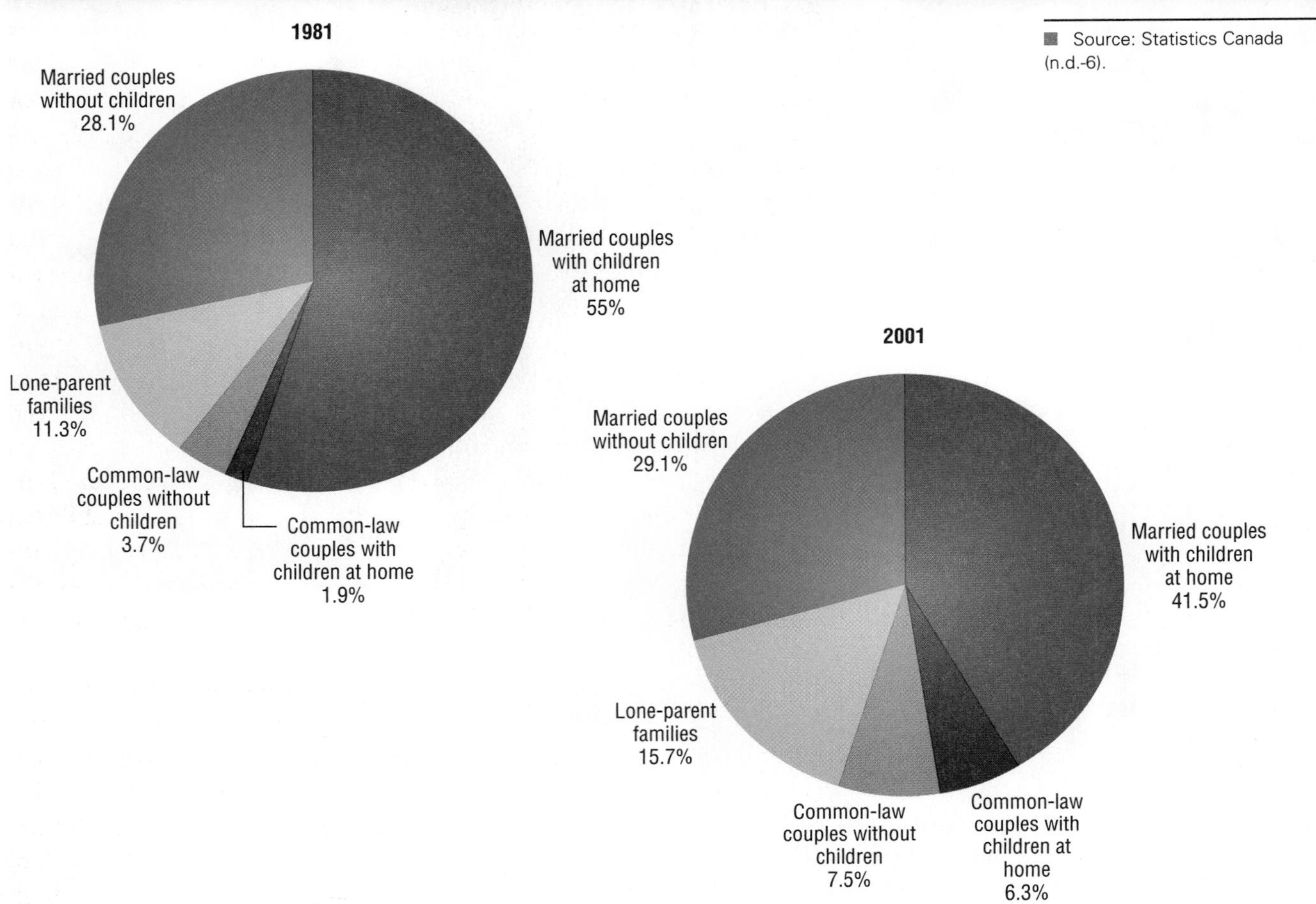


Source: Statistics Canada (n.d.-6).

**Table 9.2**
The Traditional Nuclear Family and New Alternatives

| Traditional Nuclear Family | New Alternatives |
|---|---|
| Legally married | Never-married singlehood, non-marital cohabitation |
| With children | Voluntary childlessness |
| Two-parent | Single-parent (never married or previously married) |
| Permanent | Divorce, remarriage (including binuclear family involving joint custody, stepfamily, or "blended" family) |
| Male primary provider, ultimate authority | Egalitarian marriage (including dual-career and commuter marriage) |
| Sexually exclusive | Extramarital relationships (including sexually open marriage, swinging, and intimate friendships) |
| Heterosexual | Same-sex intimate relationships or households |
| Two-adult household | Multi-adult households (including multiple spouses, communal living, affiliated families, and multigenerational families) |

Source: Adapted from Macklin (1980: 906).

Some sociologists, many of them functionalists, view the decreasing prevalence of the married-couple family and the rise of the "working mother" as an unmitigated disaster (Popenoe, 1996, 1998). In their view, rising rates of crime, illegal drug use, poverty, and welfare dependency (among other social ills) can be traced to the fact that so many children are not living in two-parent households with stay-at-home mothers. They call for various legal and cultural reforms to shore up the traditional nuclear family. For instance, they want to make it harder to get a divorce, and they want people to place less emphasis on individual happiness at the expense of family responsibility.

Other sociologists, influenced by conflict and feminist theories, disagree with the functionalist assessment (Coontz, 1992; Stacey, 1996). In the first place, they argue that it is inaccurate to talk about *the* family, as if this important social institution assumes or should assume only a single form. They emphasize that families have been structured in many ways and that the diversity of family forms is increasing as people accommodate the demands of new social pressures. Second, they argue that changing family forms do not necessarily represent deterioration in the quality of people's lives. In fact, such changes often represent *improvement* in the way people live. These sociologists believe that the decreasing prevalence of the traditional nuclear family and the proliferation of diverse family forms have benefited many men, women, and children and have not harmed other children as much as the functionalists think. They also believe that various economic and political reforms, such as the creation of an affordable nationwide daycare system, could eliminate most of the negative effects of single-parent households.

We first outline the functional theory of the family because the issues raised by functionalism are still a focus of sociological controversy (Mann, Grimes, Kemp, and Jenkins, 1997). Borrowing from the work of conflict theorists and feminists, we next show that the nuclear family has been in decline since the nineteenth century and is less prevalent than is often assumed. We then explain how change in the distribution of power between husbands and wives has affected mate selection, marital satisfaction, divorce, reproductive choice, domestic labour, and wife abuse. The discussion then turns to alternative family forms—how they are structured and how their frequency varies by class and sexual orientation. Finally, you will learn that although postindustrial families solve some problems, they are hardly an unqualified blessing. The chapter's concluding section considers the kinds of policies that might help alleviate some of the most serious concerns faced by families today. Let us first review the functionalist theory of the family.

## Functionalism and the Nuclear Ideal

### *Functional Theory*

For any society to survive, its members must cooperate economically. They must have babies. And they must raise offspring in an emotionally supportive environment so the offspring can learn the ways of the group and eventually operate as productive adults. Since the 1940s, functionalists have argued that the nuclear family is ideally suited to

The idealized North American family of the 1950s

meet these challenges. In their view, the nuclear family provides a basis for five main functions: regulated sexual activity, economic cooperation, reproduction, socialization, and emotional support (Murdock, 1949: 1–22; Parsons, 1955).

Functionalists cite the pervasiveness of the nuclear family as evidence of its ability to perform these functions. To be sure, other family forms exist. **Polygamy** expands the nuclear unit "horizontally" by adding one or more spouses (almost always wives) to the household. Polygamy is still legally permitted in many less industrialized countries in Africa and Asia. However, the overwhelming majority of families are monogamous, because they cannot afford to support several wives and many children. The **extended family** expands the nuclear family "vertically" by adding another generation—one or more of the spouses' parents—to the household. Extended families used to be common throughout the world. They still are in some places. However, according to the functionalists, the basic building block of the extended family (and of the polygamous family) is the nuclear unit.

George Murdock was a functionalist who conducted a famous study of 250 mainly preliterate societies in the 1940s. Murdock wrote, "Either as the sole prevailing form of the family or as the basic unit from which more complex familial forms are compounded, [the nuclear family] exists as a distinct and strongly functional group in every known society" (Murdock, 1949: 2). Moreover, the nuclear family, Murdock continued, is everywhere based on **marriage.** He defined marriage as a socially approved, presumably long-term, sexual and economic union between a man and a woman. It involves rights and obligations between spouses and between spouses and their children.

## *Functions of the Nuclear Family*

Let us consider the five main functions of marriage and the nuclear family in more detail.

1. Sexual regulation. *The nuclear family defines the boundaries within which legitimate sexual activity is permitted, thus making an orderly social life possible. Of course, sex is readily available outside of marriage. Murdock found that only 22 percent of 250 mainly preliterate societies forbade or disapproved of premarital sex between non-relatives, and in more than half the societies, a married man could legitimately have an extramarital affair with one or more female relatives (Murdock, 1949: 5–6). It is hardly news that premarital and extramarital sex are common in postindustrial societies (especially if you believe what you see in* Desperate Housewives*). So sex is not the primary motivation for marrying.*
2. Economic cooperation. *People marry also because "a man and a woman make an exceptionally efficient cooperating unit" (Murdock, 1949: 7). Historically, pregnancy and nursing have restricted women in their activities, whereas men possess superior strength. Therefore, women have traditionally performed lighter tasks close to home while men have specialized in lumbering, mining, quarrying, land clearing, house building, hunting, fishing, herding, and trade (Murdock, 1937). Thus, "marriage exists only when the economic and the sexual are united into one relationship, and this combination occurs only in marriage" (Murdock, 1949: 8).*
3. Reproduction. *Before the invention of modern contraception, sex often resulted in the birth of a baby. In pre-modern societies, children are an investment in the future. By the age of six or seven, children in such societies do some chores. Their economic value to the family increases as they mature. When children become adults, they often help support their aging parents. Thus, there is a big economic incentive to having children.*
4. Socialization. *The investment in children can be realized only if adults rear the young to maturity. This involves not only caring for them physically but also teaching them language, values, beliefs, skills, religion, and much else. Some functionalists regarded socialization as the "basic and irreducible" function of the family (Parsons, 1955: 16).*
5. Emotional support. *Functionalists note that the nuclear family universally gives its members love, affection, and companionship. In the nuclear family, it is mainly the mother who is responsible for ensuring the family's emotional well-being. It falls on the father to take on the role of earning a living outside the family (Parsons, 1955: 23). The fact that he is the "primary provider" makes him the ultimate authority.*

Does this functionalist account provide an accurate picture of family relations across history? To assess the adequacy of the theory, let us discuss the families in which the early functionalists themselves lived: families in urban and suburban middle-class North America in the 1950s.

### *The Canadian Middle-Class Family in the 1950s*

As a description of family patterns in the 15 years after World War II, functionalism has its merits. During the Great Depression (1929–39) and World War II (1939–45), Canadians were forced to postpone marriage because of widespread poverty, government-imposed austerity, and physical separation. After this long and dreadful ordeal, many Canadians just wanted to settle down, have children, and enjoy the peace, pleasure, and security that family life seemed to offer. Conditions could not have been better for doing just that. The immediate post-war era was one of unparalleled optimism and prosperity (Nelson and Robinson, 2002). Real per capita income rose, as did the percentage of Canadians who owned their own homes. Various laws passed during World War II to encourage women to join the paid labour force were rescinded. Things were now supposed to return to "normal," meaning that women were supposed to go back to being housewives and men to being breadwinners (Kingsbury and Scanzoni, 1993).

## Figure 9.2
Marriage Rate, Canada, 1921–2003

■ Source: Statistics Canada (1992, 1998b, 2004c, 2007d).

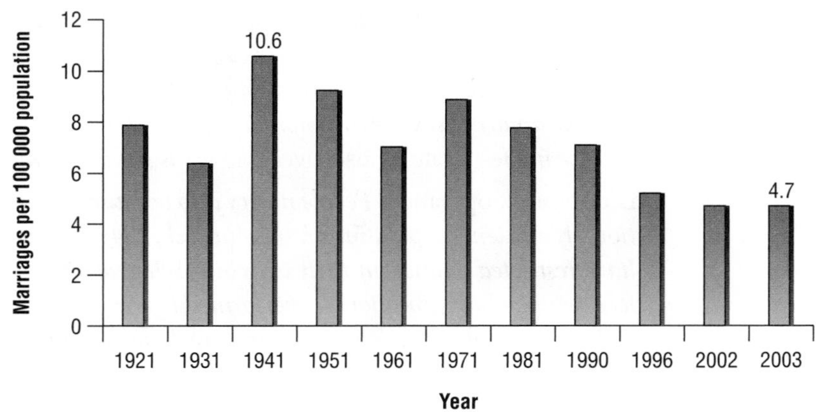


As a result of these conditions, Canadians experienced a marriage boom (see Figure 9.2). Increasingly, Canadians lived in married-couple families. The proportion of "never married" Canadians decreased and the average age at first marriage dropped for both women and men (McVey and Kalbach, 1995: 225; see Figure 9.3). As we might expect, the marriage boom soon gave way to a baby boom. The average Canadian family had four children; nearly all married women stayed home to raise their children (Nikiforuk, 1999). In 1951, 90.0 percent of married men but only 11.2 percent of married women worked in the paid labour force. Most women engaged in what has been called an "orgy of domesticity" in the post-war years, devoting increasing attention to child rearing and housework. They also became increasingly concerned with the emotional quality of family life as love and companionship became firmly established as the main motivation for marriage (Coontz, 1992: 23–41; Skolnick, 1991: 49–74).

## Figure 9.3
Average Age at First Marriage, 1921 to 2003

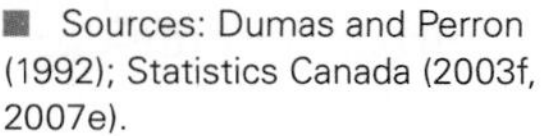

■ Sources: Dumas and Perron (1992); Statistics Canada (2003f, 2007e).

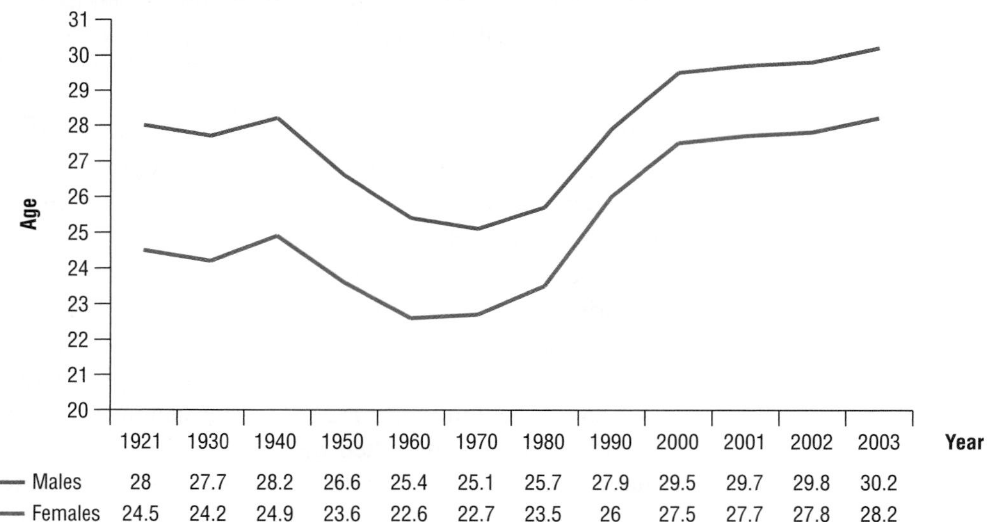


| Year | 1921 | 1930 | 1940 | 1950 | 1960 | 1970 | 1980 | 1990 | 2000 | 2001 | 2002 | 2003 |
|---|---|---|---|---|---|---|---|---|---|---|---|---|
| Males | 28 | 27.7 | 28.2 | 26.6 | 25.4 | 25.1 | 25.7 | 27.9 | 29.5 | 29.7 | 29.8 | 30.2 |
| Females | 24.5 | 24.2 | 24.9 | 23.6 | 22.6 | 22.7 | 23.5 | 26 | 27.5 | 27.7 | 27.8 | 28.2 |

**Figure 9.4**
**Total Fertility Rate, 1950–2005**

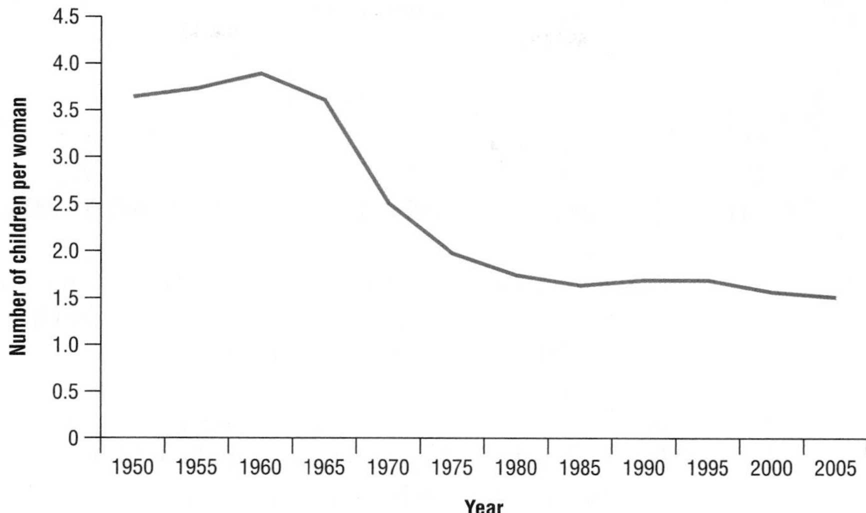


■ Source: United Nations Statistical Division Common Database.

Nevertheless, the immediate post-war period was in many respects a historical aberration (Cherlin, 1992: 6–30). Trends in divorce, marriage, and child-bearing show a gradual *weakening* of the nuclear family from the second half of the nineteenth century until the mid-1940s, and continued weakening after the 1950s. Specifically, throughout the nineteenth century, the divorce rate rose slowly. The **divorce rate** is the number of divorces that occur in a year for every 1000 people in the population. Meanwhile, the marriage rate fell. The **marriage rate** is the number of marriages that occur in a year for every 1000 people in the population. The total fertility rate also fell (see Figure 9.4). The **total fertility rate** is the average number of children that would be born to a woman over her lifetime if she had the same number of children as do women in each age cohort in a given year.

Canada's marriage rate started falling after 1946. The divorce rate started rising in the 1960s when the law was changed to make it easier to divorce. The total fertility started falling after 1961. Thus, by the early 1960s, the earlier trends had reasserted themselves. Only the peculiar historical circumstances of the post-war years, noted above, temporarily reversed them. The big picture from the nineteenth century until the present is that of a gradually weakening nuclear family. The early functionalists, it seems, generalized too hastily from the families they knew best—their own.

According to many modern-day functionalists, the nuclear family has become less prevalent since the nineteenth century largely because many of the traditional functions of the nuclear family have been eroded or partly taken over by other institutions. For example, the traditional division of labour, based on the physical capabilities and limitations of husband and wife, has weakened. That is because contraception and child-care services are now available, while demand for women to enter the paid labour force and pursue a higher education has increased. Women are no longer tied to the home in the way they once were. Children are not the economic asset they were in agricultural societies that lacked a social welfare system—quite the opposite: it is now expensive to raise children. Meanwhile, part of the task of socialization has been taken over by schools, the mass media, and peer groups, while reproduction outside the nuclear family is possible due to the introduction of in vitro fertilization and other reproductive technologies. Thus, contemporary functionalists argue that the traditional nuclear family has been in decline for more than a century because other institutions perform many of the economic, reproductive, and socialization functions that were formerly reserved for the nuclear family.

## Conflict and Feminist Theories

Other sociologists, influenced less by functionalism than by the conflict and feminist traditions, see the proliferation of non-nuclear families as a response to changes in power relations between women and men.

The idea that power relations between women and men explain the prevalence of different family forms was first suggested by Marx's close friend and coauthor, Friedrich Engels. Engels argued that the traditional nuclear family emerged along with inequalities of wealth. For once wealth was concentrated in the hands of a man, wrote Engels, he became concerned about how to transmit it to his children, particularly his sons. How could a man safely pass on an inheritance, asked Engels? Only by controlling his wife sexually and economically. Economic control ensured that the man's property would not be squandered and would remain his and his alone. Sexual control, in the form of enforced female monogamy, ensured that his property would be transmitted only to *his* offspring. Engels concluded that only the elimination of private property and the creation of economic equality—in a word, communism—could bring an end to gender inequality and the traditional nuclear family (Engels, 1970 [1884]: 138–39).

Engels was right to note the long history of male economic and sexual domination in the traditional nuclear family. A century ago, any money a wife earned typically belonged to her husband. As recently as the 1950s, a Canadian wife could not rent a car, take a loan, or sign a contract without her husband's permission. It was only in the 1980s that it became illegal in Canada for a husband to rape his wife.

However, Engels was wrong to think that communism would eliminate gender inequality in the family. Gender inequality has been as common in societies that call themselves communist as in those that call themselves capitalist. For example, the Soviet Union left "intact the fundamental family structures, authority relations, and socialization patterns crucial to personality formation and sex-role differentiation. Only a genuine sexual revolution [or, as we prefer to call it, a *gender revolution*] could have shattered these patterns and made possible the real emancipation of women" (Lapidus, 1978: 7).

Because gender inequality exists in non-capitalist (including pre-capitalist) societies, most feminists believe something other than, or in addition to, capitalism accounts for gender inequality and the persistence of the traditional nuclear family. In their view, *patriarchy*—male dominance and norms justifying that dominance—is more deeply rooted in the economic, military, and cultural history of humankind than the classical Marxist account allows. For them, only a "genuine gender revolution" can alter this state of affairs.

Just such a revolution in family structures, authority relations, and socialization patterns picked up steam in Canada and other rich industrialized countries about 50 years ago, although its roots extend back to the eighteenth century. As you will now see, the revolution is evident in the rise of romantic love and happiness as bases for marriage, the rising divorce rate, and women's increasing control over reproduction through their use of contraceptives, among other factors. We begin by considering the sociology of mate selection.

# Power and Families

## *Love and Mate Selection*

Most Canadians take for granted that marriage ought to be based on love. Our assumption is evident, for example, in the way most popular songs celebrate love as the sole basis of long-term intimacy and marriage. In contrast, most of us view marriage devoid of love as tragic.

Yet in most societies throughout human history, love has had little to do with marriage. Marriages were typically arranged by third parties, not by brides and grooms. The selection of marriage partners was based mainly on calculations intended to maximize their families' prestige, economic benefits, and political advantages.

The idea that love should be important in the choice of a marriage partner first gained currency in eighteenth-century England with the rise of liberalism and individualism, philosophies that stressed the freedom of the individual over community welfare (Stone, 1977). The intimate linkage between love and marriage that we know today emerged only in the early twentieth century, when Hollywood and the advertising industry began to promote self-gratification on a grand scale. For these new spinners of fantasy and desire, an important aspect of self-gratification was heterosexual romance leading to marriage (Rapp and Ross, 1986). Today, wherever individualism is highly prized, love has come to be defined as the essential basis for marriage. A survey of college undergraduates

Hollywood glamorized heterosexual romantic love and solidified the intimate linkage between love and marriage that we know today. Clark Gable and Vivien Leigh in *Gone with the Wind* (1939).

**Figure 9.5**
**Responses to Question: "If a man (woman) had all the other qualities you desired, would you marry this person if you were not in love with him (her)?"**

Note: Percentages may not add up to 100 because of rounding.

■ Source: Robert Levine, Suguru Sato, Tsukasa Hashimoto, and Jyoti Verma. *Journal of Cross-Cultural Psychology* 26, 5: 554–71. Copyright 1995 by Sage Publications. Reprinted with permission of Sage Publications, Inc.

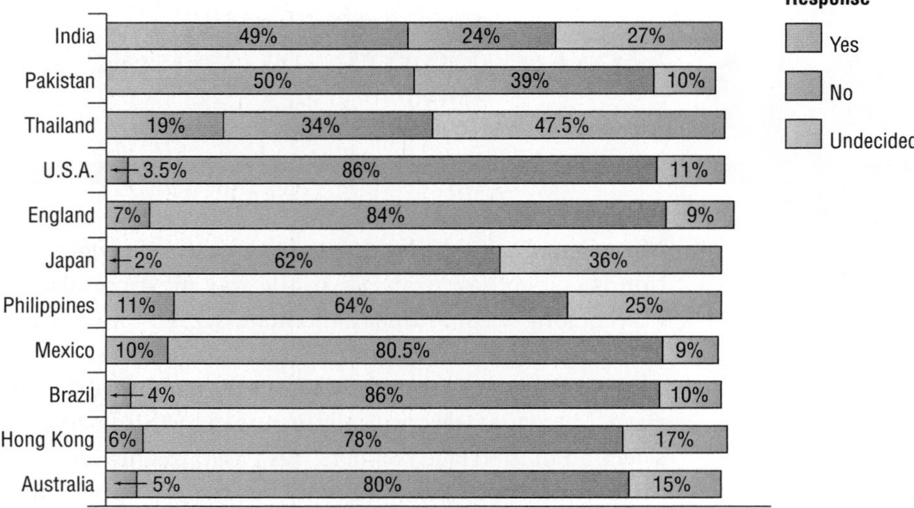


in 11 countries asked, "If a man (woman) had all the qualities you desired, would you marry this person if you were not in love with him (her)?" In the five rich countries plus Brazil, between 3 percent and 8 percent of students said they would marry someone they were not in love with if that person possessed all the qualities they were looking for in a partner. In the five developing countries, the comparable percentage ranged from 10 percent to 50 percent (Levine et al., 1995; see Figure 9.5).

Still, it would be a mistake to think that love alone determines mate selection in our society—far from it. Three sets of social forces influence whom you are likely to fall in love with and marry (Kalmijn, 1998: 398–404):

1. Marriage resources. *Potential spouses bring certain resources with them to the "marriage market." They use these resources to attract mates and compete against rivals. These resources include financial assets, status, values, tastes, and knowledge. Most people want to maximize the financial assets and status they gain from marriage, and they want a mate who has similar values, tastes, and knowledge. As a result, whom you fall in love with and choose to marry is determined partly by the assets you bring to the marriage market.*
2. Third parties. *A marriage between people from two groups can threaten the internal cohesion of one or both groups. Therefore, to varying degrees, families, neighbourhoods, communities, and religious institutions raise young people to identify with the groups they are members of and think of themselves as different from members of other groups. They may also apply sanctions to young people who threaten to marry outside the group. For example, although ethnic intermarriage has become increasingly common in Canada, parents often encourage their children to marry within their own ethnic group to preserve their unique culture (Kalbach, 2000; Kitano and Daniels, 1995). This is especially true*

*among immigrants who come to Canada from cultures in which arranged marriage has been the tradition (Dugger, 1996). As a result, whom you fall in love with and choose to marry is determined partly by the influence of third parties.*

3. Demographic and compositional factors. *The probability of marrying inside your group increases with the group's size and geographical concentration. If you are a member of a small group or a group that is dispersed geographically, you stand a greater chance of having to choose an appropriate mate from outside your group. There may simply be too few prospects in your group from which to choose (Brym, Gillespie, and Gillis, 1985). In addition, the ratio of men to women in a group influences the degree to which members of each sex marry inside or outside the group. For instance, war and imprisonment can eliminate many male group members as potential marriage partners and encourage female group members to marry outside the group or forgo marriage altogether. Finally, because people usually meet potential spouses in "local marriage markets"—schools, universities and colleges, places of work, neighbourhoods, bars, and clubs—the degree to which these settings are socially segregated influences mate selection. You are more likely to marry outside your group if local marriage markets are socially heterogeneous. As a result, whom you fall in love with and choose to marry is determined partly by the size, geographical dispersion, and sex ratio of the groups you belong to and the social composition of the local marriage markets you frequent.*

As a result of the operation of these three sets of social forces, the process of falling in love and choosing a mate is far from random. Most of us have selected or will select a partner of similar racial or ethnic background, age, and social class.

## *Marital Satisfaction*

Just as mate selection came to depend more on romantic love over the years, so marital stability came to depend more on having a happy rather than merely a useful marriage. This change occurred because women in Canada and many other societies have become more autonomous, especially over the past half century; that is, one aspect of the gender revolution women are experiencing is that they are freer than ever to leave marriages in which they are unhappy.

One factor that contributed to women's autonomy was the legalization of birth control measures in Canada in 1969. The birth control pill made it easier for women to delay childbirth and have fewer children. A second factor that contributed to women's autonomy was their increased participation in the paid labour force. Once women enjoyed a source of income independent of their husbands, they gained the means to decide the course of their own lives to a greater extent than ever before. A married woman with a job outside the home is less tied to her marriage by economic necessity than a woman who works only at home. If the woman who works is deeply dissatisfied with her marriage, she can more easily leave. In addition, beginning in the late 1960s, laws governing divorce were changed to make divorce easier.

### The Social Roots of Marital Satisfaction

If marital stability now depends largely on marital satisfaction, what are the main factors underlying marital satisfaction? The sociological literature emphasizes five sets of forces (Collins and Coltrane, 1991: 394–406, 454–64):

1. Economic forces. *Money issues are the most frequent subjects of family quarrels, and money issues loom larger when there isn't enough money to satisfy a family's needs and desires. Accordingly, marital satisfaction tends to fall and the divorce rate tends to rise*

*as you move down the socioeconomic hierarchy. The lower the social class and the lower the educational level of the spouses, the more likely it is that financial pressures will make them unhappy and the marriage unstable. Marital dissatisfaction and divorce are also more common among groups with high poverty rates. In contrast, the marital satisfaction of wives and, even more, of husbands, generally increases when wives enter the paid labour force (Hughes, Galinsky, and Morris, 1992; Lupri and Frideres, 1988). This increase is mainly due to the beneficial financial effects. However, if* either *spouse spends so much time on the job that he or she neglects the family, marital satisfaction falls.*

2. Divorce laws. *Many surveys show that, on average, married people are happier than unmarried people. Moreover, when people are free to end unhappy marriages and remarry, the average level of happiness increases among married people. Thus, the level of marital happiness has increased in Canada over the past few decades, especially for wives, partly because it has become easier to get a divorce. For the same reason, in countries where getting a divorce is more difficult (e.g., Italy and Spain), husbands and wives tend to be less happy than in countries where getting a divorce is easier (e.g., Canada and the United States; Stack and Eshleman, 1998).*
3. The family life cycle. *In Canada, the rate of divorce per 1000 population reaches a peak in the fifth year of marriage and then falls (Ambert, 1998: 5). For marriages that last, marital satisfaction generally starts high, falls when children are born (especially for wives), reaches a low point when children are in their teenage years, and rises again when children reach adulthood (Glenn, 1990; Rollins and Cannon, 1974). Couples without children and parents whose children have left home (so-called empty nesters) enjoy the highest level of marital satisfaction. Parents who are just starting families or who have adult children living at home enjoy intermediate levels of marital satisfaction. Marital satisfaction is lowest during the "establishment" years, when children are attending school. Although most people get married at least partly to have children, it turns out that children, and especially teenagers, usually put big emotional and financial strains on families. These strains result in relatively low marital satisfaction.*
4. Housework and child care. *Marital happiness is higher among couples who perceive an equitable distribution of housework and child care (Rosenbluth, Steil, and Whitcomb, 1998). The further couples are from an equitable sharing of domestic responsibilities, the more tension there is among all family members (Risman and Johnson-Sumerford, 1998). Research finds that equitable sharing tends to increase with education (Berk, 1985).*
5. Sex. *Having a good sex life is associated with marital satisfaction. Contrary to popular belief, surveys show that sex generally improves during a marriage. From these findings, some experts conclude that general marital happiness leads to sexual compatibility (Collins and Coltrane, 1991: 344). However, the reverse can also be true. Good sex can lead to a good marriage. After all, sexual preferences are deeply rooted in our psyches and our earliest experiences. They cannot be altered easily to suit our partners. If spouses are sexually incompatible, they may find it hard to change, even if they communicate well, argue little, and are generally happy on other grounds. However, if a husband and wife are sexually compatible, they may work hard to resolve other problems in the marriage for the sake of preserving their good sex life. Thus, the relationship between marital satisfaction and sexual compatibility is probably reciprocal. Each factor influences the other.*

Let us now see what happens when low marital satisfaction leads to divorce.

## *Divorce*

Before 1968, adultery was the only grounds for divorce in Canada, except in Nova Scotia, where cruelty was sufficient grounds even before Confederation (Morrison, 1987). The Divorce Act of 1968, the first federal divorce statute, expanded the grounds under which a divorce could be granted. With the amendment of Canada's Divorce Act in 1985, only one ground is available for divorce—marital breakdown, defined in three ways: (1) the spouses have lived apart for one year, (2) one of the spouses has committed an act of adultery, (3) one spouse has treated the other with mental or physical cruelty. Today, a spouse seeking divorce no longer has to prove grounds. Instead, a marriage is legally "dissolved" because the relationship is "irretrievably broken." Following these amendments, the divorce rate reached a historic high in 1987 but has since declined (Statistics Canada, 2000d). It is expected that about 38 percent of marriages taking place in recent years will end in divorce (Statistics Canada, 2002c).

### Economic Effects

Women's income usually falls after divorce, while men's generally rises (Finnie, 1993). That is because husbands tend to earn more than wives, children typically live with their mothers after divorce, and child-support payments are often inadequate.

In the past, Canadian laws regarding the division of marital assets on divorce and the awarding of alimony contributed to women's declining living standards after a divorce. For example, in the early 1970s, Irene Murdock, a farm wife, claimed that her labours over 15 years had earned her a share in the family farm. However, the Supreme Court of Canada ruled that her work was simply that of an "ordinary farm wife" and did not entitle Mrs. Murdock to share in the property that she and her husband had accumulated during their marriage (Steel, 1987: 159).

Although all Canadian provinces and territories have laws requiring spouses to share assets in the event of marital breakdown, the precise definition of what constitutes a family asset varies and creates inconsistencies across jurisdictions (Dranoff, 2001: 257). In addition, although the monetary value of tangible family assets (e.g., money in the bank, a house) can be calculated and shared, the valuable "new property" (Glendon, 1981) today is the earning power of a professional degree, highly paid employment, work experience, a skilled trade, or other "human capital." On divorce, the wife may receive an equal share of tangible property, but that does not usually result in her beginning post-divorce life on an equal footing with her former husband, especially if she retains physical custody of the couple's children and if she sacrificed her education and career so that he could earn a college or university degree.

**Child support** is money paid by the non-custodial parent to the custodial parent to support the children of a separated marital, cohabiting, or sexual relationship. Under the Divorce Act, either parent can be ordered to pay child support. However, because mothers retain custody in the great majority of cases—and because women are more likely to be economically disadvantaged in employment—those ordered to pay child support are usually fathers.

Every jurisdiction in Canada requires parents to support their children following separation or divorce. Court orders in themselves, however, do not always guarantee that child support will be paid. In practice, orders for child and spousal support have often been difficult to enforce, and default rates have been high. All Canadian provinces and territories now have their own programs to protect against non-payment of child support. Nonetheless, the problem of "deadbeat parents" remains serious (Families Against Deadbeats, 2000).

Some analysts argue that the principal reason for non-payment of child support is the unemployment or underemployment of the non-custodial parent (Meyer and Bartfield, 1996). If that is correct, "coercive child-support collection policies, such as automatic wage withholding, will have only limited success" and solving the problem "will be the old and unglamorous one, of solving un- and underemployment, both for the fathers and the mothers" (Braver, Fitzpatrick, and Bay, 1991: 184–85).

### Emotional Effects

Although divorce enables spouses to leave unhappy marriages, questions have been raised about the emotional consequences of divorce for children, particularly in the long term. Some scholars claim that divorcing parents are simply trading the well-being of their children for their own happiness. What does research say about this issue?

Research shows that children of divorced parents tend to develop behavioural problems and do less well in school than children in intact families (Demo, Fine, and Ganong, 2000). They are more likely to engage in delinquent acts and to abuse drugs and alcohol. They often experience an emotional crisis, particularly in the first two years after divorce. What is more, when children of divorced parents become adults, they are less likely than children of non-divorced parents to be happy. They are more likely to suffer health problems, depend on welfare, earn low incomes, and experience divorce themselves. In one study, almost half the children of divorced parents entered adulthood as worried, underachieving, self-deprecating, and sometimes angry young men and women (Wallerstein, Lewis, and Blakeslee, 2000). Clearly, divorce can have serious, long-term, negative consequences for children.

However, much of the research that seems to establish a link between divorce and long-term negative consequences for children is based on families who seek psychological counselling. Such families are a small and unrepresentative minority of the population. By definition, they have more serious emotional problems than the large majority, who do not need psychological counselling after divorce. We must be careful not to generalize from such studies. Another problem with much of this research is that some analysts fail to ask whether factors other than divorce might be responsible for the long-term distress experienced by many children of divorced parents.

### Factors Affecting the Well-Being of Children

Researchers who rely on representative samples and examine the separate effects of many factors on children's well-being provide the best evidence on the consequences of divorce for children. For example, a re-analysis of 92 relevant studies showed that, on average, the overall effect of divorce on children's well-being is not strong and is declining over time (Amato and Keith, 1991). This research also found that three factors account for much of the distress among children of divorce:

1. A high level of parental conflict. *A high level of parental conflict creates long-term distress among children (Jekielek, 1998). Divorce without parental conflict does children much less harm. In fact, children in divorced families have a higher level of well-being on average than children in high-conflict* intact *families. The effect of parental conflict on the long-term well-being of children is substantially greater than the effect of any other factor.*

2. A decline in living standards. *By itself, the economic disadvantage experienced by most children in divorced families exerts a small impact on their well-being. Nonetheless, it is clear that children of divorce who do not experience a decline in living standards suffer less harm.*

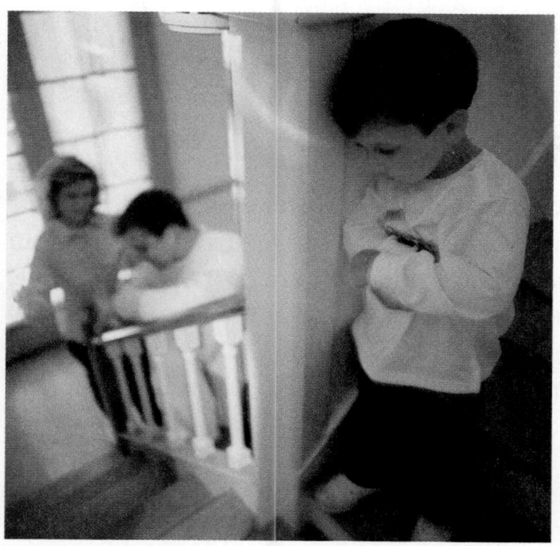

A high level of parental conflict creates long-term distress among children. Divorce without parental conflict does children much less harm. Children in divorced families have a higher level of well-being on average than children in high-conflict intact families.

3. The absence of a parent. *Children of divorce usually lose a parent as a role model and a source of emotional support, practical help, and supervision. By itself, this factor also has a small effect on children's well-being, even if the child has continued contact with the non-custodial parent (Resnick et al., 1997).*

Subsequent studies confirm these generalizations and add an important observation. Many of the behavioural and adjustment problems experienced by children of divorce existed before the divorce took place. We cannot therefore attribute them to the divorce itself (Nielsen, 1999; Pasley and Minton, 2001; Stewart, Copeland, Chester, Malley, and Barenbaum, 1997; Thompson and Amato, 1999).

In sum, claiming that divorcing parents selfishly trade the well-being of their children for their own happiness is an exaggeration. Although the heightened risk of poverty is real, high levels of parental conflict can also have serious negative consequences for children, even when they enter adulthood. In such high-conflict situations, divorce can benefit children. By itself, the absence of a parent has a small negative effect on children's well-being. But this effect is becoming smaller over time, perhaps in part because divorce is so common it is no longer a stigma.

### *Reproductive Choice*

We have seen that the power women gained from working in the paid labour force put them in a position to leave a marriage if it made them deeply unhappy. Another aspect of the gender revolution women are experiencing is that they are increasingly able to decide what happens in the marriage if they stay. For example, women now have more say over whether they will have children and, if so, when they will have them and how many they will have.

Children are increasingly expensive to raise. Children no longer give the family economic benefits, as they did, say, on the family farm. Most women want to work in the paid labour force, many of them to pursue a career. As a result, most women decide to have fewer children, to have them farther apart, and to have them at an older age. Some decide to have none at all (Dalphonse, 1997).

Women's reproductive decisions are carried out by means of contraception and abortion. Abortion was declared a criminal offence in Canada in 1892. In the 1960s, an abortion reform movement spearheaded by Dr. Henry Morgentaler urged the repeal of abortion laws that, in his words, "compelled the unwilling to bear the unwanted" (quoted in Dranoff, 2001: 16). The first such change occurred with the 1969 amendment that allowed for "therapeutic abortion" if performed by a physician in an accredited hospital and if a three-member committee certified that the continuation of the pregnancy would likely endanger the health of the mother. In 1988, the Supreme Court of Canada struck down the law on abortion on the grounds that it contravened a woman's right to control her own reproductive life and, as such, contravened her constitutionally protected guarantees to security of her person (under the equality rights provision of the Canadian Charter of Rights and Freedoms). In 1989, the Supreme Court also unanimously determined that the civil law in Quebec, the Quebec Charter, and the common law do not protect fetal life or interests. In 1993, the Supreme Court of Canada struck down legislation that banned abortion clinics. By 1995, abortion clinics outside hospitals operated throughout Canada with the exception of Prince Edward Island, Saskatchewan, and the territories.

In 2003, 103 768 Canadian women obtained abortions (Statistics Canada, 2006g). On a global scale, the abortion rate in Canada is low at about 15 per 1000 women between the ages of 15 and 44. The rate is 21 per 1000 women in the United States and 119 per 1000 women in Russia (Health Canada, 1999b; Statistics Canada, 2003j). Attitudes toward abortion are mixed. Surveys show that most Canadians agree that abortion should be legal only under certain circumstances. However, agreement with the statement that abortion should be legal under any circumstance fell from 35 percent in 1995 to 28 percent in 1999 (Tun, 2000). Moreover, attitudes toward abortion vary by age, with teens more likely than adults to approve of the availability of legal abortion for any reason (55 percent versus 43 percent, respectively) (Bibby, 2001: 250–51). Ninety percent of adults and 84 percent of teens support the availability of legal abortion when rape is involved.

Although Canadians are divided on the abortion issue, right-to-life versus pro-choice activists have been clashing since the 1970s. Right-to-life activists object to the decriminalization of abortion; pro-choice activists want the current situation preserved. Both groups have tried to influence public opinion and lawmakers to achieve their aims. A few extreme right-to-life activists (almost all men) have resorted to violence (Gegax and Clemetson, 1998; see Box 9.2).

As sociologists Randall Collins and Scott Coltrane (1995) note, it seems likely that the criminalization of abortion would likely return us to the situation that existed in the 1960s. Many abortions took place then, but because they were illegal, they were

9.2

## YOU AND THE SOCIAL WORLD

### The Abortion Issue

Many shades of opinion and ambiguities exist in people's attitudes toward the abortion issue. At the extremes, however, we can distinguish between right-to-life and pro-choice advocates. Right-to-life advocates argue that life begins at conception. Therefore, they say, abortion destroys human life and is morally indefensible. They advocate adoption instead of abortion. In their opinion, the pro-choice option is selfish, expressing greater concern for career advancement and sexual pleasure than moral responsibility. In contrast, pro-choice advocates argue that every woman has the right to choose what happens to her own body and that bearing an unwanted child can harm not only a woman's career but the child too. For example, unwanted children are more likely to be neglected or abused. They are more likely to get in trouble with the law because of inadequate adult supervision and discipline. Furthermore, according to pro-choice advocates, religious doctrines claiming that life begins at conception are arbitrary. In any case, they point out, such ideas have no place in law because they violate the principle of separation of church and state.

**WRITING ASSIGNMENT**

- *What are your views on abortion? To what degree are your views influenced by your social characteristics (family income, education, religiosity, etc.)? How do your views compare with those of people with social characteristics similar to yours? Table 9.3 shows some results from one survey on the abortion issue. Why do certain social characteristics influence public opinion on abortion in more or less predictable ways? What variables other than those listed in Table 9.3 might influence public opinion on the abortion issue? Answer these questions in about 500 words.*

**Table 9.3**
"Please tell me whether or not you think it should be possible for a pregnant woman to obtain a legal abortion if the woman wants it for any reason."

| | Yes | No | % | *N* |
|---|---|---|---|---|
| Gender | | | | |
| Male | 44 | 56 | 100 | 484 |
| Female | 41 | 59 | 100 | 416 |
| Highest year of schooling completed | | | | |
| 0–11 | 31 | 69 | 100 | 154 |
| 12 | 39 | 61 | 100 | 258 |
| 13+ | 49 | 51 | 100 | 485 |
| Age | | | | |
| 18–29 | 42 | 58 | 100 | 168 |
| 30–39 | 46 | 54 | 100 | 184 |
| 40–49 | 52 | 48 | 100 | 170 |
| 50–59 | 44 | 56 | 100 | 143 |
| 60–69 | 35 | 65 | 100 | 114 |
| 70+ | 34 | 64 | 100 | 125 |
| Total annual family income | | | | |
| $0–49 999 | 37 | 63 | 100 | 488 |
| $50 000+ | 53 | 47 | 100 | 317 |
| Attendance at religious services | | | | |
| Less than once a month | 55 | 45 | 100 | 495 |
| Once a month or more | 28 | 72 | 100 | 400 |

Source: National Opinion Research Center (2006). Data are from the 2002 U.S. General Social Survey.

expensive, hard to obtain, and posed dangers to women's health. If abortion laws were repealed, they predict that poor women and their unwanted children would suffer most. Taxpayers would wind up paying bigger bills for social assistance and medical care.

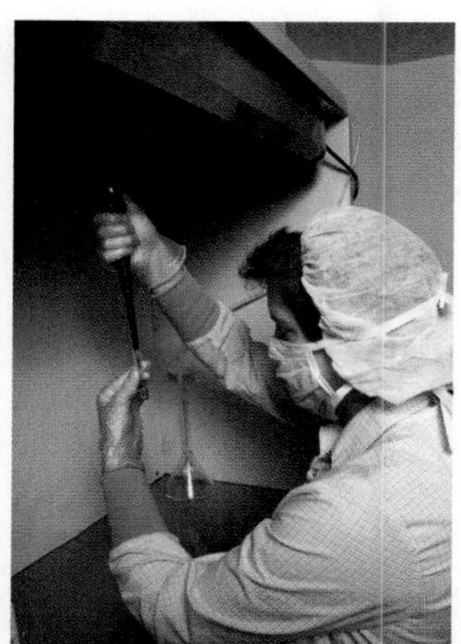
Fertilizing an egg in vitro

## *Reproductive Technologies*

For most women, exercising reproductive choice means being able to prevent pregnancy and birth by means of contraception and abortion. For some women, however, it means *facilitating* pregnancy and birth by means of reproductive technologies. As many as 15 percent of couples are infertile. With a declining number of so-called desirable children (i.e., healthy white newborns) available for adoption, and a persistent and strong desire by most people to have biologically related children, demand is strong for techniques to help infertile couples, some lesbian couples, and some single women have babies.

Four main reproductive technologies exist. In *artificial insemination*, a donor's sperm is inserted in a woman's vaginal canal or uterus during ovulation. In *surrogate motherhood*, a donor's sperm is used to artificially inseminate a woman who has signed a contract to surrender the child at birth in exchange for a fee. In *in vitro fertilization*, eggs are surgically removed from a woman and joined with sperm in a culture dish, and an embryo is then transferred to the woman's uterus. Finally, various screening techniques are used on sperm and fetuses to increase the chance of giving birth to a baby of the desired sex and end pregnancies deemed medically problematic.

These procedures raise several sociological and ethical issues. We mention two here (Achilles, 1993). The first problem is discrimination. Most reproductive technologies are expensive. Surrogate mothers charge $10 000 or more to carry a child. In vitro fertilization fees are in the range of $25 000. Obviously, poor and middle-income earners who happen to be infertile cannot afford these procedures. In addition, there is a strong tendency for members of the medical profession to deny single women and lesbian couples access to reproductive technologies. In other words, the medical community discriminates not just against those of modest means but also against those wanting to rear children in non-traditional families.

A second problem introduced by reproductive technologies is that they render the terms *mother* and *father* obsolete or at least vague. Is the mother the person who donates the egg, carries the child in her uterus, or raises the child? Is the father the person who donates the sperm or raises the child? As these questions suggest, a child conceived through a combination of reproductive technologies and raised by a heterosexual couple could have as many as three mothers and two fathers! This is not just a terminological problem. If it were, we could just introduce new distinctions such as *egg mother, uterine mother,* and *social mother* to reflect the new reality. The real problem is social and legal. The question of who has what rights and obligations to the child, and what rights and obligations the child has vis-à-vis each parent, is unclear. This lack of clarity has already caused anguished court battles over child custody (Franklin and Ragone, 1999).

Public debate on a wide scale is needed to decide who will control reproductive technologies and to what ends. On the one hand, reproductive technologies can bring the greatest joy to infertile people. They can also prevent the birth and suffering of children with chronic, progressive, and fatal diseases. On the other hand, reproductive technologies may continue to benefit mainly the well-to-do, reinforce traditional family forms that are no longer appropriate for many people, and cause endless legal wrangling and heartache.

## *Housework and Child Care*

As we have seen, women's increased participation in the paid labour force, their increased participation in the system of higher education, and their increased control over reproduction transformed several areas of family life. Despite this far-ranging gender revolution, however, one domain remains largely resistant to change: housework, child care, and senior care. This fact was first documented in detail by sociologist Arlie Hochschild. She showed that even women who work full time in the paid labour force usually begin a "second shift" when they return home. There, they prepare meals, help with homework, do laundry, and so forth (Hochschild with Machung, 1989).

Men do take a more active role in the day-to-day running of the household than they used to, but the change has been modest. For example, a study of household labour in 10 rich countries found that "women continue to be responsible for the majority of hours of unpaid labour" ranging from a low of 70 percent in Sweden to a high of 88 percent

**Table 9.4**
Persons Aged 15 and Over, by Number of Hours Doing Housework, Canada, 2001

| | Women (%) | Men (%) |
|---|---|---|
| No hours | 7.5 | 13.3 |
| Fewer than 5 Hours | 17.4 | 30.0 |
| 5 to 14 Hours | 29.7 | 33.5 |
| 15 to 29 Hours | 23.9 | 15.4 |
| 30 or more hours | 21.4 | 7.8 |
| Total | 99.9 | 100.0 |

Source: Adapted from Statistics Canada (2002b).
Note: Totals may not add to 100 percent because of rounding.

in Italy (Bittman and Wajcman, 2000: 173). In Canada, 21 percent of women—but only 8 percent of men—devoted 30 hours or more to unpaid household work during the week before the 2001 census. Men were also more likely than women to claim that they did not devote any hours during that week to such work (see Table 9.4).

Even these figures do not reveal the whole picture, however. Men tend to do low-stress chores that can often wait a day or a week. These jobs include mowing the lawn, repairing the car, and painting the fence. Although fathers of young children under the age of five may be happy to play with their children, they spend less time than mothers providing the more time-intensive forms of child care, such as feeding, washing, dressing, and medical care. In general, women tend to do the repetitive, higher stress chores that cannot wait. In short, the picture is hardly that of a revolution (Harvey, Marshall, and Frederick, 1991).

Two main factors shrink the gender gap in housework, child care, and senior care. First, the smaller the difference between the husband's and the wife's earnings, the more equal the division of household labour. Women who earn relatively high incomes use some of their money to pay outsiders to do domestic work. In addition, such women are able to translate earning power into domestic influence. Put bluntly, their increased financial status enables them to get their husbands to do more around the house.

Attitude is the second factor that shrinks the gender gap in domestic labour. The more the husband and wife agree that there *should* be equality in the household division of labour, the more equality there is. Seeing eye to eye on this issue is often linked to both spouses having a postsecondary education (Greenstein, 1996). Thus, if greater equality is going to exist between men and women in doing household chores, two things have to happen: (1) there must be greater equality between men and women in the paid labour force and (2) broader cultural acceptance of the need for gender equality must be achieved.

The double day

## Domestic Violence

The most comprehensive Canadian survey on domestic violence to date shows that 7 percent of Canadians in a marital or cohabiting relationship experienced some form of violence at the hands of their partner over the preceding five years. Although the five-year rates of violence were similar for women and men, women were three times more likely to suffer an injury, five times more likely to require medical attention, and five times more likely to report that the violence they experienced caused them to fear for their lives. Compared with men, women were more likely to report being beaten, choked, or threatened with a gun or knife, or having these weapons used against them. Women were also more likely than men to report multiple incidents of spousal violence. Compared with women, men were more likely to report being slapped, having something thrown at them, or being kicked, bit, or hit (Bunge, 2000).

Three main types of domestic violence exist (Johnson and Ferraro, 2000):

» *Common couple violence* occurs when partners have a specific argument and one partner lashes out physically at the other. For a couple that engages in this type of violence, violent acts are unlikely to occur often, escalate over time, or be severe. Both partners are about equally likely to engage in common couple violence, regardless of their gender.
» *Intimate terrorism* is part of a general desire of one partner to control the other. Where one partner engages in intimate terrorism, violent acts are likely to occur often, escalate over time, and be severe. Among heterosexual couples, the aggressor is usually the man.
» *Violent resistance* is the third main type of domestic violence. Among heterosexual couples, it typically involves a woman violently defending herself against a man who has engaged in intimate terrorism.

### Gender Inequality and Domestic Violence

For heterosexual couples, domestic violence is associated with the level of gender equality in the family and in the larger society. The higher the level of gender inequality, the greater the frequency of domestic violence. Thus, severe wife assault is more common in lower-class, less highly educated families in which gender inequality tends to be high and men are likely to believe that male domination is justified. Severe wife abuse is also more common among couples who witnessed their mothers being abused and who were themselves abused when they were children, although recent research suggests that these socialization factors are considerably less influential than was once believed (Gelles, 1997; Simons, Wu, Johnson, and Conger, 1995; M. Smith, 1990). Still, male domination in both childhood socialization and current family organization increases the likelihood of severe wife assault (see Box 9.3).

In addition, Straus (1994) has shown that wife assault is associated with gender inequality in the larger society. He first constructed a measure of wife assault for each U.S. state by using data from a national survey. The measure shows the percentage of couples in each state in which the wife was physically assaulted by her partner during the 12 months preceding the survey. He then used government data to measure gender inequality in each state. His measure of gender inequality tapped the economic, educational, political, and legal status of women. He found that as gender equality increases—as women and men become more equal in the larger society—wife assault declines. We conclude that for heterosexual couples, the incidence of domestic violence is highest where a big power imbalance between men and women exists, where norms justify the male domination of women, and, to a lesser extent, where early socialization experiences predispose men to behave aggressively toward women.

Summing up, we can say that conflict theorists and feminists have performed a valuable sociological service by emphasizing the importance of power relations in structuring family life. A substantial body of research shows that the gender revolution

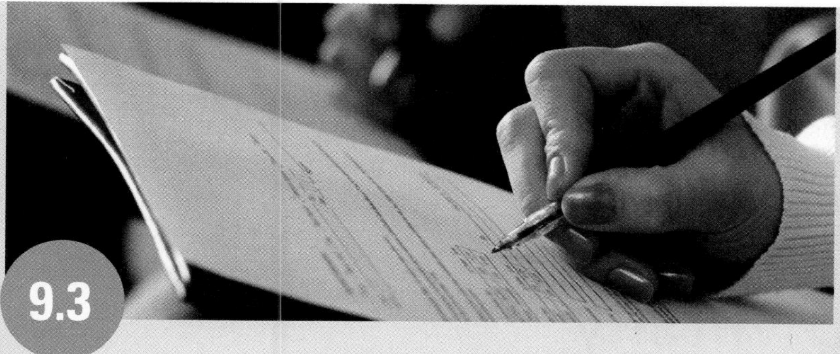

9.3

# SOCIAL POLICY: WHAT DO YOU THINK?

## Is Spanking Ever Appropriate?

In 2001, child welfare workers took seven children, aged 6 to 14, from their home in southern Ontario amid concerns that they were being spanked with paddles by their fundamentalist Christian parents. The children's parents, members of the Church of God, admitted that they used paddles to discipline their children. However, they noted that doing so was consistent with the teachings of their religion. A media statement released by the Church of God noted the group's belief that "the Word of God advocates corporal punishment under certain circumstances" (Church of God, 2001). According to the group's spiritual adviser, Daniel Layne, "The whole issue is spanking and discipline, and how we see in modern times that when parents don't discipline their children it leads to all kinds of social problems. . . . Switching is used as a last resort, but the Scriptures clearly call for it and we won't give it up" (quoted in Clairborne, 2001).

The children were returned to their home a few weeks later, after their parents agreed to abstain from the use of corporal punishment while the case was before the courts. Children's Aid Society (CAS) workers were given unannounced access to the children in their home and at school and allowed to discuss alternative methods of child discipline with the parents. However, more than 100 members of the Church of God fled Canada over fears that authorities would attempt to seize their children. In January 2002, the Ontario Court of Appeal found in favour of the children's parents and upheld the right of parents, teachers, and persons standing in place of parents to physically discipline their young charges (McCarten, 2002).

In Austria, Cyprus, Denmark, Finland, Italy, Norway, and Sweden, the law prohibits the use of corporal punishment against children. Since 1892, Canadian law has specifically allowed parents to use corporal punishment as a form of discipline. However, not all Canadians agree with the decision of the Ontario Court of Appeal in the Church of God case—or with other related decisions rendered in other Canadian courtrooms.

Is spanking ever appropriate? Experts themselves have conflicting opinions about this issue. Sociologist Murray Straus (1994) advises parents never to hit children of any age under any circumstances. There is considerable evidence to suggest that children who are spanked by their parents (including those who are otherwise loving) are more likely to cheat, lie, bully, be intentionally cruel to others, disobey in school, and misbehave in various ways (Stormshak, Bierman, McMahon, and Lengua, 2000). Research has also linked being spanked to depression and suicide in childhood, alcohol or drug abuse in adolescence, and, during adulthood, a heightened likelihood of abusing one's own children and engaging in spousal violence (Garvey, 1999). Spanking apparently teaches children that it is acceptable to hit someone and that those who love you can hit you with impunity. This message confuses love and violence—and sets the stage for subsequent abusive acts directed against intimate partners (Straus and Yodanis, 1996).

In contrast, other researchers contend that Straus and others may be overstating and oversimplifying the situation (Gilbert, 1997). One review of the literature on non-abusive and customary physical punishment by parents reports that the observed consequences of such punishment vary by method employed, the child's personality, and other factors (Larzelere, 2000). Some studies find that non-abusive spanking as an occasional backup form of child discipline had such beneficial outcomes as reduced noncompliance and less fighting among two- to six-year-olds.

### CRITICAL THINKING QUESTIONS

- *Do you agree with the decision of the Ontario Court of Appeal in the Church of God case?*
- *Is corporal punishment an appropriate form of child discipline? Is corporal punishment child abuse?*
- *Should Canada repeal the law that allows corporal punishment? Is spanking a training ground for violence against intimate partners in later life?*

that has been taking place for nearly half a century has influenced the way we select mates, our reasons for being satisfied or dissatisfied with marriage, our propensity to divorce, the reproductive choices women make, the distribution of housework and child care, variations in the rate of severe domestic violence—in short, all aspects of family life. As you will now learn, the gender revolution has also created a much greater diversity of family forms.

# Family Diversity

## *Heterosexual Cohabitation*

Although Canada has always been a highly "married society," with about 90 percent of each age cohort marrying at least once, evidence suggests that the importance of marriage is waning for some Canadians. Even in 1995, when asked, "In order for you to be happy in life, is it very important, important, not very important, or not at all important to be married?" just two-thirds of Canadian women rated marriage as important or very important. Younger Canadians were less likely than older Canadians to consider marriage important or very important. Those living in Quebec were markedly less likely to do so: 53 percent of women and 59 percent of men in Quebec considered marriage important or very important (Wu, 2000: 65–66). Although living in a common-law relationship may be a prelude to marriage for some people, for others it has become an alternative to legal marriage.

Since the Canadian census first began to collect information on cohabitation in 1981, the number of cohabiting people 15 years of age and older has increased dramatically. The 2001 census recorded 1 158 410 common-law families in Canada. Cohabiting unions (also known as common-law unions) grew from 6 percent to 14 percent of all unions between 1981 and 2001. In Quebec, the 2001 figure was 25 percent. Most Canadian women aged 18 to 49 approve of both premarital sex and non-marital cohabitation when couples intend to marry at some point in the future. In addition, 55 percent of women outside Quebec and 73 percent of women in Quebec believe it is acceptable for couples to live together when they have no intention of making a long-term commitment and are simply sexually attracted to each other. In both cases, younger women and women in Quebec are particularly likely to voice such approval (Statistics Canada, 2004a; Wu, 2000: 59).

## *Same-Sex Marriage and Civil Unions*

In 2001, the Netherlands became the first country in the world to legalize same-sex marriage. Belgium and Spain soon followed suit. Canada did so in 2005.

Seven other countries allow homosexuals to register their partnerships under the law in so-called civil unions. Civil unions recognize the partnerships as having some or all of the legal rights of marriage. These countries include Denmark (along with its dependency, Greenland), Hungary, Norway, Sweden, France, Iceland, and Germany. In the United States, there is more opposition to registered partnerships and same-sex marriages than in these other countries. In fact, 38 states have passed laws opposing such unions. A 2004 poll showed that 53 percent of Americans oppose same-sex marriages and 41 percent oppose civil unions for same-sex partners (Gallup Organization,

2004). Yet, despite continuing opposition to same-sex marriage, the ultimate direction of change in many parts of the world is clear. Amid sharp controversy, the legal and social definition of "family" is being broadened to include cohabiting, same-sex partners in long-term relationships.

Research shows that most homosexuals, like most heterosexuals, want a long-term, intimate relationship with one other adult (Chauncey, 2005). In fact, in Denmark, where homosexual couples can register partnerships under the law, the divorce rate for registered homosexual couples is lower than for heterosexual married couples (Ontario Consultants on Religious Tolerance, 2000). We estimate that about 75 000 gay men and 75 000 gay women are living together in Canada and that about half of these people are raising children who (1) were the offspring of previous, heterosexual marriages, (2) were adopted, or (3) resulted from artificial insemination.

### Raising Children in Homosexual Families

Many people believe that children brought up in homosexual families will develop a confused sexual identity, exhibit a tendency to become homosexuals themselves, and suffer discrimination from children and adults in the "straight" community. Unfortunately, there is little research in this area. Much of the research is based on small, unrepresentative samples. Nevertheless, the research findings are consistent. They suggest that children who grow up in homosexual families are much like children who grow up in heterosexual families. For example, a 14-year study assessed 25 young adults who were the offspring of lesbian families and 21 young adults who were the offspring of heterosexual families (Tasker and Golombok, 1997). The researchers found that the two groups were equally well adjusted and displayed little difference in sexual orientation. Two respondents from the lesbian families considered themselves lesbians, whereas all of the respondents from the heterosexual families considered themselves heterosexual. Even violence between same-sex partners occurs at approximately the same rate as it does in heterosexual relationships (Chesley, MacAulay, and Ristock, 1991).

Homosexual and heterosexual families do differ in some respects. Lesbian couples with children record higher satisfaction with their partnerships than lesbian couples without children. In contrast, among heterosexual couples, it is the childless who record higher marital satisfaction (Koepke, Hare, and Moran, 1992). On average, the partners of lesbian mothers spend more time caring for children than the husbands of heterosexual mothers. Because children usually benefit from adult attention, this must be considered a plus. Homosexual couples also tend to be more egalitarian than heterosexual couples, sharing most decision making and household duties equally (Rosenbluth, 1997). That is because they tend to reject traditional marriage patterns. The fact that they tend to have the same gender socialization and earn about the same income also encourages equality (Kurdek, 1996; Reimann, 1997). In sum, available research suggests that raising children in lesbian families has no apparent negative consequences for the children. Indeed, there may be some benefits for all family members.

## *Lone-Parent Families*

During the first half of the twentieth century, lone-parent families were generally the result of the death of one parent (Oderkirk and Lochhead, 1992). Today, solo parenting is usually the product of marital dissolution (separation or divorce), after which child custody is typically granted to mothers. In 2001, 16 percent of Canadian families were headed by a lone parent and 81 percent of those were headed by women (Statistics

In 2002, in a precedent-setting move hailed by gay-right activists as the first of its kind in the world, full parental rights were extended to homosexual couples in Quebec. In addition, same-sex couples were granted the same status and obligations as heterosexual married couples when they entered into a civil union. Here, lesbians react as the Quebec legislature passes the law.

Canada, 2002d, 2004a). Poverty is far more prevalent among female-headed single-parent families than among any other type of family. The poverty rate in female-headed single-parent families is more than four times the level for all Canadians (National Council of Welfare, 2002: 5).

Low levels of social support, family dysfunction, and parental depression all have significant negative effects on children and are more common in low-income households (National Council of Welfare, 1999b). Child poverty is related to school failure,

Divorce is responsible for the majority of lone-parent families in Canada today. Female-headed lone-parent families are far more common than male-headed lone-parent families.

negative involvement with parents, stunted growth, reduced cognitive abilities, limited emotional development, and a high likelihood of dropping out of school (Duncan, Yeung, Brooks-Gunn, and Smith, 1998; Fields and Smith, 1998).

### *Zero-Child Families*

In Canada, what we prefer to call "zero-child families" are increasingly common. Our admittedly clumsy term seems necessary because the alternatives are so value laden: a "childless family" implies that a family without children lacks something it should have, while the more recent "child-free family" suggests that a family without a child is unencumbered and that a child is therefore a burden. To maintain neutrality, we resort to clumsiness.

Roughly a fifth of women between the ages of 40 and 44 had never given birth (Lamanna and Riedmann, 2003: 369). To explain this fact we must first recognize that not having a child may be the result of circumstances beyond a couple's control. For example, one or both partners may be infertile, and some evidence suggests that infertility is a growing issue, perhaps because of chemical pollutants in the air and water. It seems that not having a child is more often a matter of choice, however, and the main reasons for the increasing prevalence of zero-child families are the rising cost of raising a child and the growth of attractive alternatives.

Just how expensive are children? In 2004, the cost of raising a child in Manitoba to the age of 18 was about $167 000 (Canadian Council on Social Development, 2007). Add the cost of college or university and that is a lot of money that could be spent on investments, the couple's own education, and other desirable things. Mothers bear most of the cost of lost economic opportunities. Usually, they are the ones whose careers are disrupted when they decide to stay home to raise children and who lose income, pension, and pension benefits in the process. Couples also incur non-economic costs when they have a child, the most important of which is stress. The birth of a child requires that couples do more work in the home, give up free time and time alone together, develop an efficient daily routine, and divide responsibilities. All this adds sources of disagreement and tension to daily life, so it is little wonder that marital satisfaction declines with a child in the house, as noted earlier.

Alternative attractions decrease the desire of some couples to have a child. People with high income, high education, and professional and managerial occupations are most likely to have zero-child families. Such people tend to place an especially high value on mobility, careers, and leisure-time pursuits. Usually, they are neither frustrated nor unhappy that they do not have a child. Despite their tendency to feel negatively stereotyped as "selfish," they tend to be more satisfied with their marriage than couples with a child (Lamanna and Riedmann, 2003: 380).

## Family Policy

Having discussed several aspects of the decline of the traditional nuclear family and the proliferation of diverse family forms, we can now return to the big question posed at the beginning of this chapter: Is the decline of the nuclear family a bad thing for society? Said differently, do two-parent families—particularly those with stay-at-home moms—provide the kind of discipline, role models, help, and middle-class lifestyle that children need to stay out of trouble with the law and grow up to become well-adjusted, productive members of society? Conversely, are family forms other than the traditional nuclear family the main source of teenage crime, poverty, welfare dependency, and other social ills?

The answer suggested by research is clear: yes and no (Houseknecht and Sastry, 1996; Popenoe, 1996; Sandqvist and Andersson, 1992). Yes, the decline of the traditional nuclear family can be a source of many social problems. No, it doesn't have to be that way.

The United States is a good example of how social problems can emerge from nuclear family decline. Sweden is a good example of how such problems can be averted. Table 9.5 illustrates this. On almost all indicators of nuclear family decline, Sweden leads the United States. In Sweden, a smaller percentage of people get married. People usually get married at a later age than in the United States. The proportion of births outside of marriage is twice as high as in the United States. A much larger proportion of Swedish than American women with children under the age of three work in the paid labour force. Significantly, however, on almost all measures of children's well-being, Sweden also leads the United States. Thus, in Sweden, children enjoy higher average reading test scores than children in the United States. The poverty rate in two-parent families is only 1/10 the U.S. rate, while the poverty rate in single-parent families is only 1/12 as high. The rate of infant abuse is 1/11th the U.S. rate. Overall, then, the decline of the traditional nuclear family has gone further in Sweden than in the United States, but children are much better off on average (Houseknecht and Sastry, 1996). How is this possible?

One explanation is that Sweden has something the United States lacks: a substantial family support policy. When a child is born in Sweden, a parent is entitled to a

**Table 9.5**
The "Decline" of the Nuclear Family and the Well-Being of Children: The United States and Sweden Compared

| Indicators of Nuclear Family "Decline" | United States | Sweden | #1 "Decline" |
|---|---|---|---|
| Median age at first marriage | | | |
| Men | 26.5 | 29.4 | Sweden |
| Women | 24.4 | 27.1 | Sweden |
| Percentage of 45–49 population never married | | | |
| Men | 5.7 | 15.4 | Sweden |
| Women | 5.1 | 9.1 | Sweden |
| Non-marital birth rate | 25.7 | 50.9 | Sweden |
| One-parent households with children < 15 as % of all households with children < 15 | 25.0 | 18.0 | U.S.A. |
| % of mothers in labour force with children < 3 | 51.0 | 84.0 | Sweden |
| Total fertility rate | 2.0 | 2.0 | Tie |
| Average household size | 2.7 | 2.2 | Sweden |
| **Indicators of Child Well-Being** | **United States** | **Sweden** | **#1 Well-Being** |
| Mean reading performance score at 14 | 5.14 | 5.29 | Sweden |
| % of children in poverty | | | |
| Single-mother households | 59.5 | 5.2 | Sweden |
| Two-parent households | 11.1 | 2.2 | Sweden |
| Death rate of infants from abuse | 9.8 | 0.9 | Sweden |
| Suicide rate for children 15–19 (per 100 000) | 11.1 | 6.2 | Sweden |
| Juvenile delinquency rate (per 100 000) | 11.6 | 12.0 | U.S.A. |
| Juvenile drug offence rate (per 100 000) | 558.0 | 241.0 | Sweden |

Source: Adapted from Houseknecht and Sastry (1996).

year of parental leave at 80 percent of his or her salary and an additional 90 days at a flat rate. Fathers can take 10 days of leave with pay when the baby is born. Parents are entitled to free consultations at "well baby clinics." Like all citizens of Sweden, they receive free health care from the state-run system. Temporary parental benefits are available for parents with a sick child under the age of 12. One parent can take up to 60 days off per sick child per year at 80 percent of salary. All parents can send their children to heavily government-subsidized, high-quality daycare. Finally, Sweden offers its citizens generous direct cash payments based on the number of children in each family.[1]

Among industrialized countries, the United States stands at the other extreme. Since 1993, a parent has been entitled to 12 weeks of *unpaid* parental leave. About 44 million citizens have no health care coverage. Health care is at a low standard for many millions more. There is no system of state daycare and no direct cash payments to families based on the number of children they have. The value of the dependent deduction on income tax has fallen nearly 50 percent in current dollars since the 1940s. Thus, when an unwed Swedish woman has a baby, she knows she can rely on state institutions to maintain her standard of living and help give her child an enriching social and educational environment. When an unwed American woman has a baby, she is pretty much on her own. She stands a good chance of sinking into poverty, with all the negative consequences that has for her and her child.

In a recent study of 33 countries, Canada was tied for fifth place on the number of weeks it allows new parents to take off work, but stood in 15th place in terms of the generosity of its maternity leave payments (Smyth, 2003). Canada thus stands between the United States and Sweden, and much of the debate surrounding family policy in Canada concerns whether we should move in the direction of the American or the Swedish model.

In Canada, three criticisms are commonly raised against generous family support policies. First, some people say these policies encourage long-term dependence on welfare, illegitimate births, and the breakup of two-parent families. However, research shows that the divorce rate and the rate of births to unmarried mothers are not higher when welfare payments are more generous (Albelda and Tilley, 1997). Moreover, not all people who prefer to work are able to find full-time, secure employment, and part-time jobs offer little in the way of job security, decent wages, or benefits. Some provinces, such as Ontario, have incorporated "workfare" in their welfare systems. Workfare requires able-bodied people to do specific jobs as a condition of receiving welfare. However, most workfare jobs are menial dead-end jobs that are unlikely to lead to permanent employment. Finally, it is surely absurd to believe that living on welfare represents a preferred lifestyle. For the overwhelming majority of welfare recipients, it indicates the loss of a job, spouse, or health—personal tragedies to which none of us is immune (National Council of Welfare, 1999b: 68).

A second criticism of generous family support policies focuses on child care. Some critics say that non-family child care is bad for children under the age of three. In their view, only parents can provide the love, interaction, and intellectual stimulation infants and toddlers need for proper social, cognitive, and moral development. However, when studies compare family care and daycare involving a strong curriculum, a stimulating environment, plenty of caregiver warmth, low turnover of well-trained staff, and a low ratio of caregivers to children, they find that daycare has no negative consequences for children over the age of one (Clarke-Stewart, Gruber, and Fitzgerald, 1994; Harvey, 1999). Research also shows that daycare has some benefits, notably enhancing a child's ability to make friends. The benefits of high-quality daycare are even more evident in low-income families, which often cannot provide the kind of stimulating environment offered by high-quality daycare.

Painting class in a state-subsidized daycare facility in Stockholm, Sweden

The third criticism lodged against generous family support policies is that they are expensive and have to be paid for by high taxes. That is true. Swedes are more highly taxed than the citizens of any other country. They have made the political decision to pay high taxes, partly to avoid the social problems and associated costs that sometimes emerge when the traditional nuclear family is replaced with other family forms and no institutions are available to help family members in need. The Swedish experience teaches us, then, that there is a clear trade-off between expensive family support policies and low taxes. It is impossible to have both, and the degree to which any country favours one or the other is a political choice.

## The Points of the Compass

Do certain functional requirements of society constrain the variety of family forms and the nature of gender roles that are performed in families? Functionalists think so. In their view, sexual regulation, economic cooperation, reproduction, socialization, and emotional support are necessary for social equilibrium. Because the nuclear family is ideally suited to perform these functions, it predominates. Moreover, when women focus on providing emotional support and men focus on playing the breadwinner role, the efficiency of the family in performing its functions is supposedly maximized. Hence the gendered division of labour in the nuclear family.

Where functionalism goes wrong is in neglecting power relations between women and men in the family and the larger society. A gender revolution has mobilized many millions of women, especially since the 1960s. In most societies, women are now more economically independent and more in control of their own bodies than ever before. These and other social changes have enabled a variety of family forms to proliferate and the gendered division of labour in the family to be relaxed. Social constraints on family life have not, of course, been entirely removed. But people are now freer to constitute families and gender roles in ways that suit their individual preferences. To be sure, social problems sometimes accompany this increased freedom, but people are also free to deal creatively and responsibly with them.

## Summary

1. *What is the traditional nuclear family, and what other family forms have proliferated in recent decades?*

The traditional nuclear family consists of a father-provider, mother-homemaker, and at least one child. Many other family forms have proliferated in recent decades, including cohabiting couples (with or without children), same-sex couples (with or without children), single-parent families, and zero-child families.

2. *What is the functionalist theory of the family, and how accurate is it?*

The functionalist theory holds that the nuclear family is a distinct and universal family form because it performs five important functions in society: sexual regulation, economic cooperation, reproduction, socialization, and emotional support. The theory is most accurate in depicting families in rich countries in the two decades after World War II. Families today and in other historical periods depart from the functional model in important respects.

3. *What are the emphases of Marxist and feminist theories of families?*

Marxists stress how families are tied to the system of capitalist ownership. They argue that only the elimination of capitalism can end gender inequality in families. Feminists note that gender inequality existed before capitalism and in communist societies. They stress how the patriarchal division of power and patriarchal norms reproduce gender inequality.

4. *What consequences does the entry of women into the paid labour force have?*

The entry of women into the paid labour force increases their power to leave unhappy marriages and control whether and when to have children. However, it does not have a big effect on the sexual division of labour in families.

5. *What accounts for variation in marital satisfaction?*

Marital satisfaction is lower at the bottom of the class structure, where divorce laws are strict, when children reach their teenage years, in families where housework is not shared equally, and among couples who do not have a good sexual relationship.

6. *Under what circumstances are the effects of divorce on children worst?*

The effects of divorce on children are worst if there is a high level of parental conflict and the children's standard of living drops.

7. *Under what social circumstances is domestic violence among heterosexual couples most frequent?*

Domestic violence is most frequent among heterosexual couples where a big power imbalance between men and women exists, where norms justify the male domination of women, and, to a lesser extent, where early socialization experiences predispose men to behave aggressively toward women.

8. *Does growing up in a household with lesbian parents have any known negative effects on children?*

Growing up in a household with lesbian parents has no known negative effects on children.

9. *Are various social problems a result of the decline of the traditional nuclear family?*

People sometimes blame the decline of the traditional nuclear family for increasing poverty, welfare dependence, and crime. However, some countries have adopted policies that largely prevent these problems. Therefore, the social problems are in a sense a political choice.

# Key Terms

**child support (p. 281)**
**divorce rate (p. 275)**
**extended family (p. 272)**
**family (p. 269)**
**marriage (p. 272)**
**marriage rate (p. 275)**
**nuclear family (p. 268)**
**polygamy (p. 272)**
**total fertility rate (p. 275)**
**traditional nuclear family (p. 268)**

# Questions to Consider

1. Do you agree with the functionalist view that the traditional nuclear family is the ideal family form for Canada today? Why or why not?
2. Ask your grandparents and parents (or people from their generations) how many people lived in their households when they were your age. Ask them to identify the role of each household member (mother, brother, sister, grandfather, boarder, etc.) and to describe the work done by each member inside and outside the household. Compare the size, composition, and division of labour of your household with that of your grandparents' and parents'. How have the size, composition, and division of labour of your household changed over three generations? Why have these changes occurred?

# Web Resources

## Companion Web Site for This Book

http://www.pointsofthecompass.nelson.com

Begin by clicking on the Student Resources section of the Web site. Next, select the chapter you are currently studying from the pull-down menu. From the Student Resources page you will have easy access to InfoTrac® College Edition, MicroCase online exercises, and additional Weblinks. The Web site also has many useful tips to aid you in your study of sociology, including practice tests for each chapter.

## InfoTrac® Search Terms

These search terms are provided to assist you in beginning to conduct research on this topic by visiting **http://www.infotrac-college.com**:

**divorce**
**extended family**
**family values**
**marriage**
**nuclear family**

### Recommended Web Sites

"Marriage and Family Processes" at **http://www.trinity.edu/mkearl/family.html** contains a wide range of valuable resources on family sociology.

For Canadian resources on families, visit the Web site of the Vanier Institute of the Family at **http://www.vifamily.ca**.

On same-sex marriage and civil unions, see **http://www.religioustolerance.org/hom_marr.htm**.

For Canadian statistics on domestic violence, visit **http://www.phac-aspc.gc.ca/ncfv-cnivf/familyviolence/**.

## Note

1. **We are grateful to Gregg Olsen, Department of Sociology, University of Manitoba, for some of this information.**

# chapter 10

## religion and education



### In this chapter, you will learn that

→ The structure of society and a person's place in it influence a person's religious beliefs and practices.

→ Under some circumstances religion creates societal cohesion, while under others it promotes social conflict. When religion creates societal cohesion, it also reinforces social inequality.

→ Religion governs fewer aspects of most people's lives than in the past. However, a religious revival has taken place in many parts of the world in recent decades, and many people still adhere to religious beliefs and practices.

→ Adults who were brought up in religious families attend religious services more frequently than adults who were brought up in non-religious families. Attendance also increases with age.

→ Secular schools have substantially replaced the church and religious schools as educational institutions. Today, the educational system is second in importance only to the family as an agent of socialization.

→ The educational system often creates social cohesion. In the process, it also reinforces existing inequalities in relation to class, race, and ethnicity.

# Religion

In 1902, psychologist William James observed that religion is the common human response to the fact that we all stand at the edge of an abyss. It helps us to cope with the terrifying fact that we must die (James, 1976 [1902]: 116). It offers us immortality, the promise of better times to come, and the security of benevolent spirits who watch over us. It provides meaning and purpose in a world that might otherwise seem cruel and senseless.

The motivation for religion may be psychological, as James argued. However, the content and intensity of our religious beliefs, and the form and frequency of our religious practices, are influenced by the structure of society and our place in it. Why does one religion predominate here, another there? Why is religious belief more fervent at one time than at another? Under what circumstances does religion act as a source of social stability, and under what circumstances does it act as a force for social change? Are we becoming more or less religious? These are all questions that have occupied the sociologists of religion, and we will touch on all of them here. Note that we will not have anything to say about the truth of religion in general or the value of any religious belief or practice in particular. These are questions of faith, not science. They lie outside the province of sociology.

The cover of *Time* magazine once proclaimed that "God is dead." As a sociological observation, the assertion is preposterous. In a nationwide Canadian survey, 81 percent of adults and 71 percent of teenagers agreed with the statement "God or a higher power cares about you" (Bibby, 2001: 252). By this measure (and by other measures we will examine below), God is still very much alive in Canada. Nonetheless, as we will show, the scope of religious authority has declined in Canada and many other parts of the world. That is, religion governs fewer aspects of life than it used to. Some Canadians still look to religion to deal with all of life's problems. But increasingly more Canadians expect that religion can help them deal with only a restricted range of spiritual issues. Other institutions—medicine, psychiatry, criminal justice, education, and so forth—have grown in importance as the scope of religious authority has declined.

Foremost among these other institutions is the system of education. Organized religion used to be the main purveyor of formal knowledge and the most important agent of socialization apart from the family. Today, the education system is the main purveyor of formal knowledge and the most important agent of socialization apart from the family. It is the partial displacement of religion by the educational system that justifies our analyzing religion and education side by side in a single chapter.

Although Canadians hold a strong belief in the importance of education, we have only a moderate level of confidence in our public education system. Just 44 percent of Canadians are satisfied with the educational system and most Canadians think it is in worse shape now than it was 25 years ago. Our chief concerns are low academic performance, lack of discipline and respect, the future employability of students, and equality of opportunity (Bricker and Greenspon, 2001: 162–65). We will address these issues below, paying particular attention to the way they are related to the larger problem of social inequality.

By taking this approach, we follow tradition. Sociologists of education have long been interested in the relationship between education and inequality. Some say that education promotes upward mobility. Others argue that education reproduces inequality generation after generation. As you will see, the evidence offers stronger support for the second argument. Plenty of scope thus remains for educational reform. Before tackling these issues, however, we first examine the influence of society on religion and the influence of religion on society.

# Classical Approaches in the Sociology of Religion

## *Durkheim: A Functionalist Approach*

More than one person has said that hockey is Canada's "national religion." Do you agree with that opinion? Before making up your mind, consider the following facts. In February 2002, more than 3 million Canadians gathered in front of their TVs to watch the Canadian men's hockey team begin their pursuit of a gold medal at the Winter Olympics. During the 1998 Winter Olympics, the Canada–Czech Republic game drew more than 2.5 million viewers—even though it was broadcast at 3:30 a.m. And, of course, when Canada's hockey team came from behind to defeat the Soviets in 1972, the nation virtually came to a standstill.

Few events attract the attention and enthusiasm of Canadians as much as the annual Stanley Cup finals. Apart from drawing a huge audience, the Stanley Cup playoffs generate a sense of what Durkheim would have called "collective effervescence." That is, the Stanley Cup finals excite us by making us feel part of something larger than us: the Montreal Canadiens, the Edmonton Oilers, the Toronto Maple Leafs, the Vancouver Canucks, the Calgary Flames, the Ottawa Senators, the institution of Canadian hockey, the spirit of Canada itself. As celebrated Canadian writer Roch Carrier (1979: 77) wrote in his famous short story, "The Hockey Sweater": "School was . . . a quiet place where we could prepare for the next hockey game, lay out our next strategies. As for church . . . there we forgot school and dreamed about the next hockey game. Through our daydreams it might happen that we would recite a prayer: we would ask God to help us play as well as Maurice Richard." For many hours each year, hockey enthusiasts transcend their everyday lives and experience intense enjoyment by sharing the sentiments and values of a larger collective. In their fervour, they banish thoughts of their own mortality. They gain a glimpse of eternity as they immerse themselves in institutions that will outlast them and athletic feats that people will remember for generations to come.

So, do you think the Stanley Cup playoffs are a religious event? There is no god of the Stanley Cup (although the nickname of Canadian hockey legend Wayne Gretzky—The Great One—certainly suggests that he transcended the status of a mere mortal). Nonetheless, the Stanley Cup playoffs may meet Durkheim's definition of a religious experience. Durkheim said that when people live together, they come to

From a Durkheimian point of view, the Stanley Cup Finals can be considered a religious holiday.

share common sentiments and values. These common sentiments and values form a **collective conscience** that is larger than any individual. On occasion, we experience the collective conscience directly. This causes us to distinguish the secular everyday world of the **profane** from the religious, transcendent world of the **sacred.** We designate certain objects as symbolizing the sacred. Durkheim called these objects **totems.** We invent certain public practices to connect us with the sacred. Durkheim referred to these practices as **rituals.**

The effect (or function) of rituals and of religion as a whole is to reinforce social solidarity, said Durkheim. The ritual heightens our experience of belonging to certain groups, increases our respect for certain institutions, and strengthens our belief in certain ideas. Thus, the game is a sacred event, in Durkheim's terms. It cements society in the way Durkheim said all religions do (Durkheim, 1976 [1915/1912]). Durkheim would have found support for his theory in research showing that the suicide rate dips during the two days preceding Super Bowl Sunday and on Super Bowl Sunday itself,

Religious rituals are public practices that help unite people into a moral community.

just as it does for the last day of the World Series, Christmas Day, and other collective celebrations (Curtis, Loy, and Karnilowicz, 1986). He would have found additional support in the finding that in Quebec, the suicide rate among young men is higher when the Montreal Canadiens are not in the Stanley Cup playoffs than when they are (Trovato, 1998). These patterns are consistent with Durkheim's theory of suicide, which predicts a lower suicide rate when social solidarity increases (see Chapter 1, A Sociological Compass).

## *Religion, Conflict Theory, and Feminist Theory*

Durkheim's theory of religion is a functionalist account. It offers useful insights into the role of religion in society. Yet conflict and feminist theorists lodge two main criticisms against it. First, it overemphasizes religion's role in maintaining social cohesion. In reality, religion often incites social conflict. Second, it ignores the fact that when religion does increase social cohesion, it often reinforces social inequality.

### Religion and Social Inequality

Consider first the role of major world religions and social inequality (Figure 10.1 and Table 10.1). Little historical evidence helps us understand the social conditions that gave rise to the first world religions, Judaism and Hinduism, 3800 to 4000 years ago. But we know enough about the rise of Buddhism, Christianity, and Islam between 2700 and 1500 years ago to say that the impulse to find a better world is often encouraged by adversity in this one. We also know that Moses, Jesus, Muhammad, and Buddha all had egalitarian and emancipatory messages, claiming to stand for equality and freedom. Finally, we know that over generations, the charismatic leadership of the world religions became "routinized." The **routinization of charisma** is Weber's term

**Figure 10.1**
**The World's Predominant Religions**

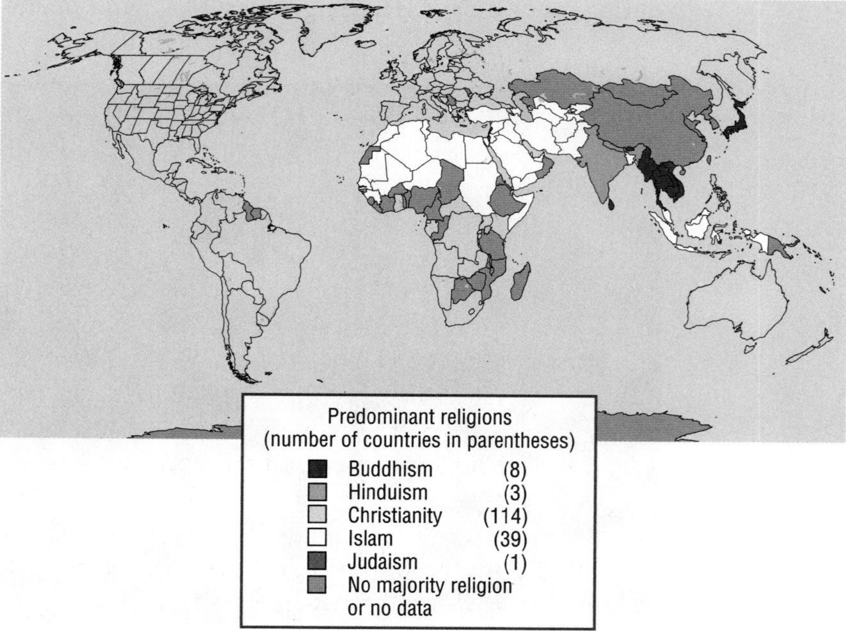


This map shows the predominant religion in each of the world's countries, defined as the religion to which more than 50 percent of a country's population adheres.

Source: Adherents.com (2001).

for the transformation of divine enlightenment into a permanent feature of everyday life. It involves turning religious inspiration into a stable social institution with defined roles, such as interpreters of the divine message, teachers, dues-paying laypeople, and so forth. The routinization of charisma typically makes religion less responsive to the needs of ordinary people, and it often supports social inequalities and injustices.

### Religion and the Subordination of Women

It was Marx who first stressed how religion often tranquillizes the underprivileged into accepting their lot in life. He called religion "the opium of the people" (Marx, 1970 [1843]: 131). We can draw evidence for Marx's interpretation from many times, places, and institutions. For example, all the major world religions have traditionally placed women in a subordinate position. Catholic priests and Muslim mullahs must be men, as must Jewish rabbis in the Conservative and Orthodox denominations. Women have been allowed to serve as Protestant ministers only since the mid-nineteenth century and as rabbis in the more liberal branches of Judaism since the 1970s. There are also many scriptural examples of the subordination of women:

- Corinthians in the New Testament emphasizes that "women should keep silence in the churches. For they are not permitted to speak, but should be subordinate, as even the law says. If there is anything they desire to know, let them ask their husbands at home. For it is shameful for a woman to speak in church."
- The Sidur, the Jewish prayer book, includes this morning prayer: "Blessed are you, Lord our God, King of the Universe, who did not make me a woman."
- The Koran, the holy book of Islam, contains a Book of Women in which it is written that "righteous women are devoutly obedient.... As to those women on whose part you fear disloyalty and ill-conduct, admonish them, refuse to share their beds, beat them."

### Religion and Class Inequality

If religion has traditionally supported gender inequality, it has also traditionally supported class inequality once religion became routinized. In medieval and early modern Europe, Christianity promoted the view that the Almighty ordains class inequality, promising rewards to the lowly in the afterlife ("the meek shall inherit the earth"). The Hindu scriptures say that the highest caste sprang from the lips of the supreme creator, the next highest caste from his shoulders, the next highest from his thighs, and the lowest, "polluted" caste from his feet. They warn that if people attempt to achieve upward mobility, they will be reincarnated as animals. And the Koran says that social inequality is due to the will of Allah (Ossowski, 1963: 19–20).

### Religion and Social Conflict

We can also find plenty of examples to illustrate religion's role in promoting conflict. One example is the role played by black churches during the 1950s and 1960s in spearheading the American civil rights movement. Black churches were the breeding ground of the civil rights movement (Morris, 1984). Their impact was both organizational and inspirational. Organizationally, they supplied the ministers who formed the leadership of the civil rights movement and the congregations within which marches, boycotts, sit-ins, and other forms of protest were coordinated. In addition, ideas from Christian doctrine inspired the protesters. Among the most powerful of these was the notion that blacks, like the Jews in Egypt, were slaves who would be freed. (It was, after all, Michael—regarded by Christians as the patron saint of the Jews—who rowed the boat

**Table 10.1**

**The Five World Religions: Origins, Beliefs, and Divisions**

| | Origins | Beliefs | Divisions |
|---|---|---|---|
| **Judaism** | Judaism originated about 4000 years ago in what is now Iraq, when Abraham first asserted the existence of just one God. About 800 years later, Moses led the Jews out of Egyptian bondage. The emancipation of the Jews from slavery was a defining moment in the history of Judaism. | The central teachings rest on belief in one God (*Yahweh*) and on the idea that God sanctions freedom and equality. The 613 divine commandments (*mitzvot*) mentioned in the Five Books of Moses (Torah) form the core of orthodox Jewish practice. The *mitzvot* include prescriptions for justice, righteousness, and observance: rest and pray on the Sabbath, honour the old and the wise, do not wrong a stranger in buying or selling, do not seek revenge or hold a grudge, and so on. The Torah forms part of the Old Testament. | In seventeenth-century Eastern Europe, ecstatic *Chasidic* sects broke away from the bookish Judaism of the time. In nineteenth-century Germany, the Reform movement allowed prayer in German, the integration of women in worship, and so on. Orthodox Judaism was a reaction against the liberalizing tendencies of Reform and involved a return to traditional observance. Conservative Judaism crystallized in Britain and the United States in the nineteenth century to reconcile what its practitioners regarded as the positive elements in Orthodoxy with the dynamism of Reform. Reconstructionism is a liberal twentieth-century movement known for its social activism and gender-egalitarianism. |
| **Christianity** | Christianity originated about 35 C.E. in what is now Israel. Jesus, a poor Jew, criticized the Judaism of his time for its external conformity to tradition and ritual at the expense of developing a true relationship to God as demanded by the prophets. | Believe in God and love him; love your neighbour—these are the two main lessons of Jesus. These teachings were novel because they demanded that people match outward performance with inner conviction. It was not enough not to murder; people should not even hate. Nor was it enough not to commit adultery; no one should even lust after a neighbour's wife (Matthew V, 21–30). These teachings made Jesus anti-authoritarian and even revolutionary. Admonishing people to love their neighbours impressed on them the need to emancipate slaves and women. Christians retained the Jewish Bible as the Old Testament, adding the gospels and letters of the apostles as the New Testament. | In 312 C.E., the Roman Emperor converted to Christianity and turned Christianity into a state religion, after which the Church became the dominant institution in Europe. In the sixteenth century, Martin Luther, a German priest, challenged the Christian establishment by seeking to establish a more personal relationship between the faithful and God. His ideas quickly captured the imagination of half of Europe and led to the split of Christianity into Catholicism and Protestantism. In the Middle Ages, Christianity had split into Western and Eastern halves, the former centred in Rome, the latter in Constantinople (now Istanbul, Turkey). Various Orthodox churches today derive from the Eastern tradition. Protestantism has been especially prone to splintering because it emphasizes the individual's relationship to God rather than a central authority. Today, there are hundreds of different Protestant churches. |
| **Islam** | Islam originated about 600 C.E. in what is now Saudi Arabia. The powerful merchants of Mecca had become greedy and corrupt, impoverishing and enslaving many people. Also, fear grew that the Persian and Roman Empires might soon fall, bringing the end of the world. Into this crisis stepped Muhammad, who claimed to have visions from God. | People who profess Islam have five duties. At least once in their life they must recite the Muslim creed aloud, correctly, with full understanding, and with heartfelt belief. (The creed is: "There is no god but Allah and Muhammad is his prophet.") Five times a day they must worship in a religious service. They must fast from sunrise to sunset every day during the ninth month of the lunar calendar (Ramadan). They must give charity to the poor. And at least once in their life they must make a pilgrimage to the holy city of Mecca. Muhammad's teachings were written down in the Koran. | A dispute broke out over how the followers of Muhammad could identify his successor. The Sunni argued that the successor should be an elected member of a certain Meccan tribe. The Shia claimed that the successor should be Muhammad's direct descendant. Today, most Muslims are Sunni. The Shia, concentrated in Iran and southern Iraq, are generally more conservative and fundamentalist. Islam spread rapidly in the Middle East, Africa, and parts of Europe. It began a great cultural flowering and considerable religious tolerance. Wahabbism, a Sunni fundamentalist movement, originated in the eighteenth century and became the state religion of what is now Saudi Arabia. Shia subgroups include the "Twelvers" (about 80 percent of the Shia) and the Ismailis. Sufism is a mystical sect within Islam. |

| | | | |
|---|---|---|---|
| **Hinduism** ॐ | Hinduism originated about 2000 C.E. in India in unknown circumstances. It had no single founder. | Hinduism has many gods, all of them thought to be aspects of the one true God. The major texts are epic poems, such as the *Bhagavad Gita*. Only the body dies in Hindu belief. The soul returns in a new form after death. The form in which it returns depends on how the person lived his or her life. Hindus believe that people who live in a way that is appropriate to their position in society will live better future lives. People can reach a state of spiritual perfection (*nirvana*) that allows the soul to escape the cycle of birth and rebirth, and reunite with God. But people who do not live in a way that is appropriate to their position in society supposedly live an inferior life when they are reincarnated. These ideas made vertical social mobility nearly impossible because, according to Hindu belief, striving to move out of your station in life ensures reincarnation in a lower form. | Unlike the Western religions, Hinduism assimilates rather than excludes other religious beliefs and practices. Traditionally, Western religions rejected non-believers unless they converted. God tells Moses on Mount Sinai: "You shall have no other gods before me." In contrast, in the *Bhagavad Gita*, Krishna says that "whatever god a man worships, it is I who answer the prayer." This attitude of acceptance helped Hinduism absorb many of the ancient religions of the peoples of the Indian subcontinent. It also explains why there are such wide regional and class variations in Hindu beliefs and practices. Hinduism as it is practised bears the stamp of many other religions. |
| **Buddhism** | About 600 B.C.E., Gautama Buddha objected to the stale ritualism of Hinduism and sought to achieve a direct relationship with God. He rejected Hindu ideas of caste and reincarnation, and offered a new way for everyone to achieve spiritual enlightenment, promising salvation to everyone. | Buddha promoted the "Four Noble Truths": (1) Life is suffering. Moments of joy are overshadowed by sorrow. (2) All suffering derives from desire. We suffer when we fail to achieve what we want. (3) Suffering ceases by training ourselves to eliminate desire. (4) We can eliminate desire by behaving morally, focusing intently on our feelings and thoughts, meditating, and achieving wisdom. Buddhism does not presume the existence of one true God. Rather, it holds out the possibility of everyone becoming a god of sorts. Similarly, it does not have a central church or text, such as the Bible. | Buddhism is notable for the diversity of its beliefs and practices. Buddhism spread rapidly across Asia after India's ruler adopted it as his own religion in the third century B.C.E. He sent missionaries to convert people in Tibet, Cambodia (Kampuchea), Nepal, Sri Lanka (formerly Ceylon), Myanmar (formerly Burma), China, Korea, and Japan. The influence of Buddhism in the land of its birth started to die out after the fifth century C.E. and is negligible in India today. One of the reasons for the popularity of Buddhism in East and Southeast Asia is that Buddhism is able to coexist with local religious practices. Unlike Western religions, Buddhism does not insist on holding a monopoly on religious truth. |

Sources: Brown (1996); Flood (1996); Gombrich (1996); Gottwald (1979); Hodgson (1974); Lapidus (2002); Lopez (2001); McManners (1990); Robinson and Johnson (1997); Rodinson (1996); Roth (1961); Schwartz (2003).

ashore.) Some white segregationists reacted strongly against efforts at integration, often meeting the peaceful protesters with deadly violence. But the American South was never the same again. Religion had helped promote the conflict needed to make the South a more egalitarian and racially integrated place.

Closer to home, it is worth remembering the important role played in the creation of our medicare system and our social welfare network by the "radical Christianity" of the early twentieth-century Social Gospel movement. The Social Gospel emphasized that Christians should be as concerned with improving the here and now as with life in the hereafter. The efforts of Tommy Douglas, a Baptist minister, the leader of the Co-operative Commonwealth Federation (precursor of the New Democratic Party), and the "father of socialized medicine," exemplify the Social Gospel concern with social justice issues. More recently, the Social Affairs Commission of the Canadian Conference of Catholic Bishops has called on the Canadian government to base its economic and social policy "on the principle of a 'preferential option for the poor, the afflicted and the oppressed' as well as the notion that 'labour, not capital, must be given priority in the development of an economy based on justice'" (Dawson, 1993: 323). And the United Church of Canada has ignited conflict by declaring that "all persons, regardless of their sexual orientation, are welcome to become full members of the church and are eligible for ordination as ministers" (in Dawson, 1993: 323). These Canadian cases illustrate how religion can sometimes promote conflict and change.

In sum, religion can maintain social order under some circumstances, as Durkheim said. When it does so, however, it often reinforces social inequality. Moreover, under other circumstances religion can promote social conflict.

### *Weber and the Problem of Social Change: A Symbolic Interactionist Interpretation*

If Durkheim highlighted the way religion contributes to social order, Max Weber stressed the way religion can contribute to social change. Weber captured the core of his argument in a memorable image: if history is like a train, pushed along its tracks by economic and political interests, then religious ideas are like railroad switches, determining exactly which tracks the train will follow (Weber, 1946: 280).

Weber's most famous illustration of his thesis is his short book *The Protestant Ethic and Spirit of Capitalism*. Like Marx, Weber was interested in explaining the rise of modern capitalism. Again like Marx, he was prepared to recognize the "fundamental importance of the economic factor" in his explanation (Weber, 1958 [1904–05]: 26). But Weber was also bent on proving the one-sidedness of any exclusively economic interpretation. He did so by offering what we would today call a symbolic interactionist interpretation of religion. True, the term "symbolic interactionism" was not introduced into sociology until more than half a century after Weber wrote *The Protestant Ethic*. Yet Weber's focus on the worldly significance of the *meanings* people attach to religious ideas makes him a forerunner of the symbolic interactionist tradition.

For specifically religious reasons, wrote Weber, followers of the Protestant theologian John Calvin stressed the need to engage in intense worldly activity and to display industry, punctuality, and frugality in their everyday life. In the view of men like John Wesley and Benjamin Franklin, people could reduce their religious doubts and ensure a state of grace by working diligently and living simply. Many Protestants took up this idea. Weber called it the Protestant ethic (Weber, 1958 [1904–05]: 183). According to

Weber, the Protestant ethic had wholly unexpected economic consequences. Where it took root, and where economic conditions were favourable, early capitalist enterprise grew most robustly.

Subsequent research showed that the correlation between the Protestant ethic and the strength of capitalist development is weaker than Weber thought. In some places, Catholicism has coexisted with vigorous capitalist growth and Protestantism with relative economic stagnation (Samuelsson, 1961 [1957]). Nonetheless, Weber's treatment of the religious factor underlying social change is a useful corrective to Durkheim's emphasis on religion as a source of social stability. Along with Durkheim's work, Weber's contribution stands as one of the most important insights into the influence of religion on society.

## The Rise, Decline, and Partial Revival of Religion

### *Secularization*

In 1651, the British political philosopher Thomas Hobbes described life as "poore, nasty, brutish, and short" (Hobbes, 1968 [1651]: 150). The standard of living in medieval and early modern Europe was abysmally low. On average, a person lived only about 35 years. The forces of nature and human affairs seemed entirely unpredictable. In this context, magic was popular. It offered easy answers to mysterious, painful, and capricious events.

As material conditions improved, popular belief in magic, astrology, and witchcraft gradually lost ground (Thomas, 1971). Christianity substantially replaced them. The better and more predictable times made Europeans more open to the teachings of

The persecution of witches in the early modern era was partly an effort to eliminate competition and establish a Christian monopoly over spiritual life. *Burning of Witches by Inquisition in a German Marketplace.* After a drawing by H. Grobert.

organized religion. In addition, the Church campaigned vigorously to stamp out opposing belief systems and practices. The persecution of witches in this era was partly an effort to eliminate competition and establish a Christian monopoly over spiritual life.

The Church succeeded in its efforts. In medieval and early modern Europe, Christianity became a powerful presence in religious affairs, music, art, architecture, literature, and philosophy. Popes and saints were the rock musicians and movie stars of their day. The Church was the centre of life in both its spiritual and its worldly dimensions. Church authority was supreme in marriage, education, morality, economic affairs, politics, and so forth. European countries proclaimed official state religions. They persecuted members of religious minorities.

In contrast, a few hundred years later, Max Weber remarked on how the world had become thoroughly "disenchanted." By the turn of the twentieth century, he said, scientific and other forms of rationalism were replacing religious authority. His observations formed the basis of what came to be known as the **secularization thesis,** undoubtedly the most widely accepted argument in the sociology of religion until the 1990s. According to the secularization thesis, religious institutions, actions, and consciousness are unlikely to disappear, but they are certainly on the decline worldwide (Tschannen, 1991).

### *Religious Revival and Religious Fundamentalism*

Despite the consensus about secularization that was evident in the 1980s, many sociologists modified their judgments in the 1990s. One reason for the change was that accumulated survey evidence showed that religion was not in an advanced state of decay. Actually, in many places, such as the United States, it was in robust health (see Figure 10.2). In Canada, just one-fifth of Canadians said they attended religious services weekly in 2001, down from two-thirds in the 1940s (Clark, 2003: 2). Yet 81 percent of Canadians said they believed in God, 70 percent said that spirituality was important to them, 76 percent said religious groups have a role to play in Canadian lives, and 84 percent identified with a religious group (Bibby, 2002: 140, 179, 184).

**Figure 10.2**
**Percentage of People Who Think Religion Is Very Important, 44 Countries, 2002**

This figure is derived from a survey of 38 000 people in 44 countries. (Poland is a former communist country and the UN ranks it 37th in its list of 53 countries in the "high human development" group. It is classified here as a former communist country.)

■ Sources: Pew Research Center (2002); United Nations (2002).

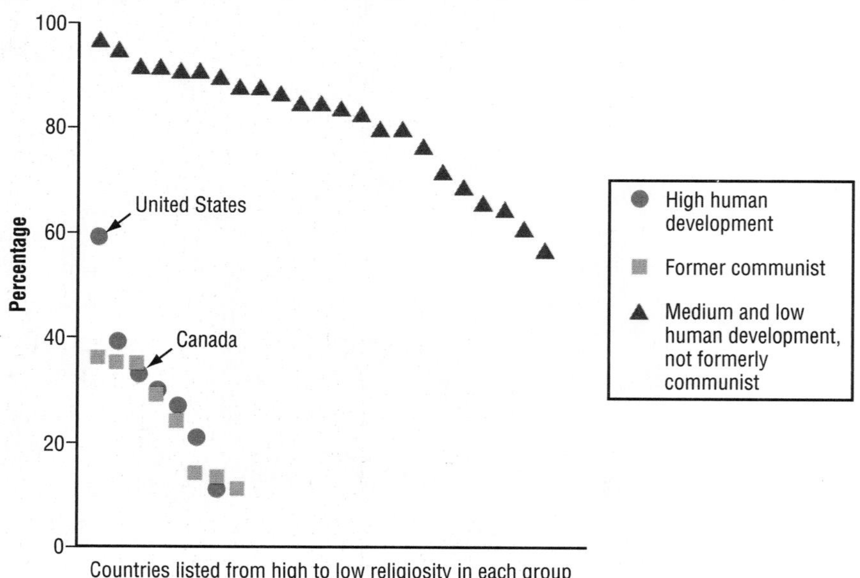

The second reason many sociologists have modified their views about secularization is that an intensification of religious belief and practice has taken place among some people in recent decades. For example, since the 1960s, fundamentalist religious organizations have increased their membership, especially among Protestants (Finke and Starke, 1992). **Fundamentalists** interpret their scriptures literally, seek to establish a direct, personal relationship with the higher being(s) they worship, and are relatively intolerant of non-fundamentalists (Hunter, 1991). Fundamentalists often support conservative social and political issues (Bruce, 1988; see Box 10.1).

During the same period, religious movements became dominant forces in many other countries. Hindu nationalists formed the government in India from 1998 to 2004. Jewish fundamentalists were always important players in Israeli political life, often holding the balance of power in Israeli governments, but they have become even more influential in recent years (Kimmerling, 2001: 173–207). A revival of Muslim fundamentalism began in Iran in the 1970s. Muslim fundamentalism then swept much of the Middle East, Africa, and parts of Asia. In Iran, Afghanistan, and Sudan, Muslim fundamentalists took power. Other predominantly Muslim countries' governments have begun to introduce elements of Islamic religious law (*shari'a*), either from conviction or as a precaution against restive populations (Lewis, 2002: 106). Religious fundamentalism has thus become a worldwide political phenomenon. In not a few cases it has taken extreme forms and involved violence as a means of establishing fundamentalist ideas and institutions (Juergensmeyer, 2000). At the same time, the Catholic Church played a critically important role in undermining communism in Poland, and Catholic "liberation theology" animated the successful fight against right-wing governments in Latin America (Kepel, 1994 [1991]; Smith, 1991). All these developments amount to a religious revival that was quite unexpected in, say, 1970.

## *Fundamentalism and Extremist Politics in the Muslim World*

In 1972, Robert Brym was finishing his B.A. at the Hebrew University of Jerusalem. One May morning he switched on the radio to discover that a massacre had taken place at Lod (now Ben Gurion) International Airport outside Tel Aviv, just 42 kilometres from his apartment. Three Japanese men dressed in business suits had arrived on Air France flight 132 from Paris. They were members of the Japanese Red Army, a small, shadowy terrorist group with links to the General Command of the Popular Front for the Liberation of Palestine. Both groups wanted to help wrest Israel from Jewish rule.

After they picked up their bags, the three men pulled out automatic rifles and started firing indiscriminately. Before pausing to slip in fresh clips, they lobbed hand grenades into the crowd at the ticket counters. One man ran onto the tarmac, shot some disembarking passengers, and then blew himself up. This was the first suicide attack in modern Middle East history. Security guards shot a second terrorist and arrested the third, Kozo Okamoto. When the firing stopped, 26 people lay dead. Half were non-Jews. In addition to the two terrorists, 11 Catholics were murdered. They were Puerto Rican tourists who had just arrived on a pilgrimage to the Holy Land.

10.1

# SOCIOLOGY AT THE MOVIES

*Harry Potter and the Goblet of Fire* (2005)

The first Harry Potter movie introduced us to Harry Potter (played by Daniel Radcliffe), who was orphaned when the evil wizard Lord Voldemort murdered Harry's parents and tried to kill Harry. The infant Harry, who bears a scar on his forehead in the shape of a lightning bolt as the result of Lord Voldemort's attack, is deposited by the gentle giant Hagrid on the doorstep of his unwelcoming relatives, the Dursleys. He lives a miserable, lonely existence.

Shortly before his 11th birthday, Harry's life is turned upside down. He is summoned to Hogwarts School of Witchcraft and Wizardry. At Hogwarts, Harry learns that he is a witch. He makes friends, but danger lurks. For Voldemort stalks Harry, determined that he will yet accomplish what he earlier failed to do—kill the young wizard.

Harry's battles with Voldemort continue through all the Harry Potter movies but we see the Evil One in full for the first time only in *Harry Potter and the Goblet of Fire*. Together with his legion of Death Eaters, Voldemort now threatens to destroy Harry and his world. To survive, Harry and his friends must overcome fire-breathing dragons, rescue people trapped in a lagoon, and enter an enormous, complex maze where Voldemort hides, waiting for his prey.

Daniel Radcliffe as Harry Potter in *Harry Potter and the Goblet of Fire*

Every Harry Potter movie has enjoyed enormous box-office success. Children, many of them outfitted as if for Halloween, are prominent in the ticket lines. Some of the children are there on organized field trips after studying the books at school. Although most people view the Harry Potter movies as harmless, others see things differently. They have denounced the films and the books on which they are based as "demonic." Many of the critics are conservative Protestants who claim that the book glorifies witchcraft, makes "evil look innocent," and subtly draws "children into an unhealthy interest in a darker world that is occultic and dangerous to physical, psychological and spiritual well-being" (Shaw, 2001). According to one Christian fundamentalist ministry, "the effect of [the movie] is undoubtedly to raise curiosity about magic and wizardry. And any curiosity raised on this front presents a danger that the world will satisfy it with falsehood before the church or the family can satisfy it with truth" (Ontario Consultants on Religious Tolerance, 2002). Scenes from the Harry Potter movies have been scrutinized for possible demonic messages. A similarity has been proclaimed between the lightning bolt that appears on Harry Potter's forehead and the symbol adopted by Hitler's SS. Harry Potter books have been banned from some schools.

### CRITICAL THINKING QUESTIONS

- *Do you agree with the decision to ban the Harry Potter books and condemn the movie?*
- *In general, should religious organizations be allowed to influence schools to censor, or should censoring by religious organizations be banned?*
- *Do you draw the line at some types of influence? Would it be acceptable if a white religious organization got a predominantly white school to ban the works of Toni Morrison and Maya Angelou because they say derogatory things about whites? Would it be acceptable if a Jewish religious organization got a predominantly Jewish school to ban Shakespeare's* The Merchant of Venice *because it portrays Jews in an unflattering way? Would it be acceptable if a religious organization strongly influenced by feminism convinced authorities in an all-girls school to ban the works of Ernest Hemingway ("too sexist") or if an anti-feminist religious organization convinced authorities in an all-boys school to ban the writings of Margaret Atwood ("too anti-male")?*

Both the Japanese Red Army and the General Command of the Popular Front for the Liberation of Palestine were strictly non-religious organizations. Their members were atheists who quoted Bakunin and Trotsky, not Jesus or Muhammad. Yet something unexpected happened to Kozo Okamoto, the sole surviving terrorist of the Lod massacre. Israel sentenced him to life in prison but freed him in 1985 in a prisoner exchange with Palestinian forces. Okamoto wound up living in Lebanon's Beka'a Valley, the main base of the Iranian-backed Hezbollah fundamentalist organization. A revival of Islamic fundamentalism was sweeping the Middle East, and in 2000, he converted to Islam.

Kozo Okamoto's life tells us something important and not at all obvious about religious fundamentalism and politics in the Middle East and elsewhere. Okamoto was involved in extremist politics first and came to religion later. Religious fundamentalism became a useful way for him to articulate and implement his political views. This is quite common. Religious fundamentalism often provides a convenient vehicle for framing political extremism, enhancing its appeal, legitimizing it, and providing a foundation for the solidarity of political groups (Pape, 2003; Sherkat and Ellison, 1999: 370).

Many people regard Islamic fundamentalism as an independent variable and extremist politics as a dependent variable. In this view, some people happen to become religious fanatics and then their fanaticism commands them to go out and kill their opponents. But Islamic fundamentalism has political sources (Brym, 2008). For example, Al-Qaeda is strongly antagonistic to American foreign policy in the Middle East. It despises U.S. support for repressive and non-democratic Arab governments like those of Kuwait and Saudi Arabia, which fail to distribute the benefits of oil wealth to the largely impoverished Arab people. It is also virulently opposed to the American position on the Israeli–Palestinian conflict, which it regards as too pro-Israeli and insufficiently supportive of Palestinian interests (to put it mildly). These political complaints are the breeding ground of support for Al-Qaeda in the Arab world. Thus, recent public opinion polls show that Arabs in the Middle East hold largely favourable attitudes toward American culture, democracy, and the American people, but extremely negative attitudes toward precisely those elements of American Middle East policy that Al-Qaeda opposes (Zogby International, 2001). Al-Qaeda and other extremist organizations in the Middle East gain in strength to the degree that these political issues are not addressed in a meaningful way. As Zbigniew Brzezinski, national security adviser to President Jimmy Carter, wrote: "To win the war on terrorism, one must . . . set two goals: first, to destroy the terrorists and, second, to begin a political effort that focuses on the conditions that brought about their emergence" (Brzezinski, 2002; Hunter, 1998). These are wise words. They are based on the sociological understanding that fundamentalism, like other forms of religion, is powerfully influenced by the social context in which it emerges.

## *The Revised Secularization Thesis*

The spread of fundamentalist religion and the resilience and relative importance of religion in some highly developed countries, especially the United States, led some sociologists to revise the secularization thesis in the 1990s. The revisionists acknowledge that religion has become increasingly influential in the lives of some individuals and groups over the past 30 years. They insist, however, that the scope of religious authority has continued to decline in most people's lives. That is, for most people, religion has less and less to say about education, family issues, politics, and economic affairs even though it may continue to be an important source of spiritual belief and practice. In this sense, secularization continues (Chaves, 1994; Yamane, 1997).

According to the **revised secularization thesis,** in most countries, worldly institutions have broken off (or "differentiated") from the institution of religion over time. One such worldly institution is the education system. Religious bodies used to run schools and institutions of higher learning that are now run almost exclusively by non-religious authorities. Moreover, like other specialized institutions that separated from the institution of religion, the educational system is generally concerned with worldly affairs rather than spiritual matters. The overall effect of the differentiation of secular institutions has been to make religion applicable only to the spiritual part of most people's lives. Because the scope of religious authority has been restricted, people look to religion for moral guidance in everyday life less often than they used to. Moreover, most people have turned religion into a personal and private matter rather than one imposed by a powerful, authoritative institution. Said differently, people feel increasingly free to combine beliefs and practices from various sources and traditions to suit their own tastes. As supermodel Cindy Crawford said in a *Redbook* interview in 1992: "I'm religious but in my own personal way. I always say that I have a Cindy Crawford religion—it's my own" (quoted in Yamane, 1997: 116). No statement could more adequately capture the decline of religion as an authoritative institution suffusing all aspects of life.

# Religion in Canada

## *Church, Sect, and Cult*

Sociologists generally divide religious groups into just three types: churches, sects, and cults (Troeltsch, 1931 [1923]; Stark and Bainbridge, 1979; see Table 10.2).

In the sociological sense of the term, a **church** is any bureaucratic religious organization that has accommodated itself to mainstream society and culture. Because of this accommodation, it may endure for many hundreds if not thousands of years. The bureaucratic nature of a church is evident in the formal training of its leaders, its

**Table 10.2**
Church, Sect, and Cult Compared

| | Church | Sect | Cult |
|---|---|---|---|
| Integration into society | High | Medium | Low |
| Bureaucratization | High | Low | Low |
| Longevity | High | Low | Low |
| Leaders | Formally trained | Charismatic | Charismatic |
| Class base | Mixed | Low | Various but segregated |

strict hierarchy of roles, and its clearly drawn rules and regulations. Its integration into mainstream society is evident in its teachings, which are generally abstract and do not challenge worldly authority. In addition, churches integrate themselves into the mainstream by recruiting members from all classes of society.

Churches take two main forms. First are **ecclesia,** or state-supported churches. For example, Christianity became the state religion in the Roman Empire in the fourth century, and Islam is the state religion in Iran and Sudan today. State religions impose advantages on members and disadvantages on non-members. Tolerance of other religions is low in societies with ecclesia.

Alternatively, churches can be pluralistic, allowing diversity within the church and expressing tolerance of non-members. Pluralism allows churches to increase their appeal by allowing various streams of belief and practice to coexist under their overarching authority. These subgroups are called **denominations.** For example, United Church, Anglican, Baptist, Lutheran, and Presbyterian are the major Protestant denominations in Canada today.

**Sects** typically form by breaking away from churches because of disagreement about church doctrine. Sometimes, sect members choose to separate themselves geographically, as the Hutterites do in their some 200 colonies, mostly in the Western provinces. However, even in urban settings, strictly enforced rules concerning dress, diet, prayer, and intimate contact with outsiders can separate sect members from the larger society. Hasidic Jews in Toronto and Montreal prove the viability of this isolation strategy. Sects are less integrated into society and less bureaucratized than churches. They are often led by **charismatic** leaders, men and women who claim to be inspired by supernatural powers and whose followers believe them to be so inspired. These leaders tend to be relatively intolerant of religious opinions other than their own. They tend to recruit like-minded members mainly from lower classes and marginal groups. Worship in sects tends to be highly emotional and based less on abstract principles than immediate personal experience (Stark, 1985: 314). In general, sectlike groups tend to appeal to the less affluent and churchlike groups to the more affluent. Many sects are short-lived, but those that do persist tend to bureaucratize and turn into churches. If religious organizations are to enjoy a long life, they require rules, regulations, and a clearly defined hierarchy of roles.

Although major Muslim subgroups are sometimes called denominations by non-Muslims, they are in some respects more appropriately seen as sects. That is because they often do not recognize one another as Muslim and sometimes come into violent conflict with one another, like the Sunni and Shia in Iraq today.

**Cults** are small groups of people deeply committed to a religious vision that rejects mainstream culture and society. Cults are generally led by charismatic individuals. They tend to be class-segregated groups, recruiting members from only one segment of the stratification system: high, middle, or low. For example, many North American cults today recruit nearly all their members from among the university educated. Some of these cults seek converts almost exclusively on university and college campuses (Kosmin, 1991). Because they propose a radically new way of life, cults tend to recruit few members and soon disappear. There are, however, exceptions—and some extremely important ones at that. Jesus and Muhammad were both charismatic leaders of cults. They were so compelling that they and their teachings were able to inspire a large number of followers, including rulers of states. Their cults were thus transformed into churches.

Even in urban settings, strictly enforced rules concerning dress, diet, prayer, and intimate contact with outsiders can separate sect members from the larger society.

In spite of the common perception that the recent waves of immigrants have lessened the Christian domination of Canada, little, in fact, has changed. Catholics and Protestants composed 72 percent of Canada's population in the most recent census, and most recent immigrants are Christian (see Table 10.3 and Figure 10.3). In the 1990s, Muslims composed 15 percent of immigrants; Hindus, 7 percent; Buddhists, 5 percent;

**Table 10.3**
Religious Groups, Canada, 2001

| Group | Percentage |
|---|---|
| Roman Catholic | 43.2 |
| Protestant | 29.2 |
| United Church | 9.6 |
| Anglican | 6.9 |
| Baptist | 2.5 |
| Lutheran | 2.0 |
| Presbyterian | 1.4 |
| Other Protestant | 6.8 |
| Christian Orthodox | 1.6 |
| Other Christian | 2.6 |
| Muslim | 2.0 |
| Jewish | 1.1 |
| Buddhist | 1.0 |
| Hindu | 1.0 |
| Sikh | 0.9 |
| Other | 1.2 |
| No religion | 16.2 |
| Total | 100.0 |

Source: Adapted from Statistics Canada (2003g).

**Figure 10.3**
**Religious Affiliations, Canada, 1871–2001**

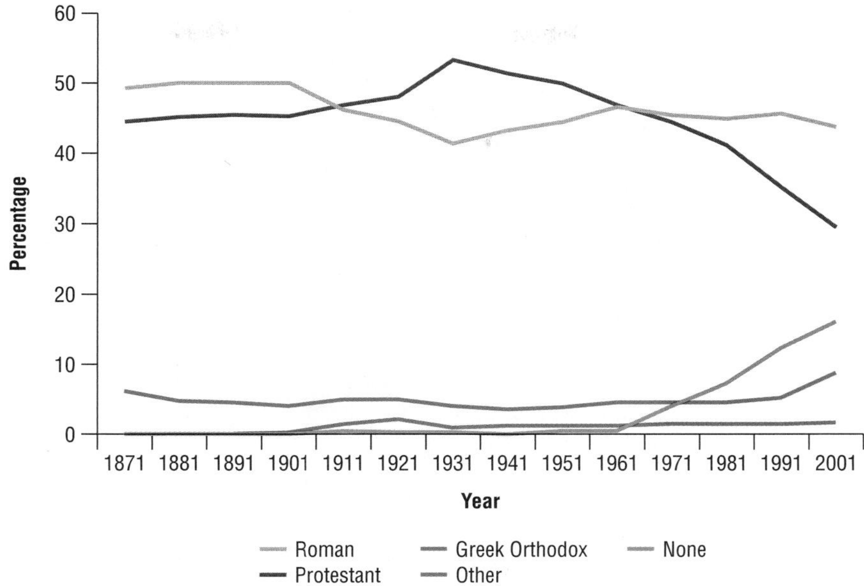


Sources: 1871–1971 from Statistics Canada (1999a); 1981 from Ontario Consultants on Religious Tolerance (2005); 1991 and 2001 from Statistics Canada (2003f).

and Sikhs, 5 percent (Statistics Canada, 2003g: 8). To be sure, Canada's changing immigration patterns have resulted in large gains for some religious groups. For example, the number of Muslims more than doubled between 1991 and 2001, reaching nearly 600 000, about 2 percent of the population. Hindus, Sikhs, and Buddhists each represent about 1 percent of the population.

# Religiosity

We have reviewed the major classical theories of religion and society, the modern debate about secularization, and the major types of religious organizations. It is now time to consider some social factors that determine how important religion is to people, that is, their **religiosity.**

We can measure religiosity in various ways. Strength of belief, emotional attachment to a religion, knowledge about a religion, frequency of performing rituals, and frequency of applying religious principles in daily life all indicate how religious a person is (Glock, 1962). Ideally, we ought to examine many measures to get a fully rounded and reliable picture of the social distribution of religiosity. For simplicity's sake, however, we focus on just one measure here. In a Canada-wide survey, respondents were asked to indicate whether their level of involvement in religious activities at various points in their lives was "high," "moderate," "low," or "none." Figure 10.4 summarizes the results.

## Figure 10.4
## Religious Involvement over Time by Group

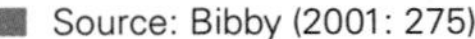

Source: Bibby (2001: 275).

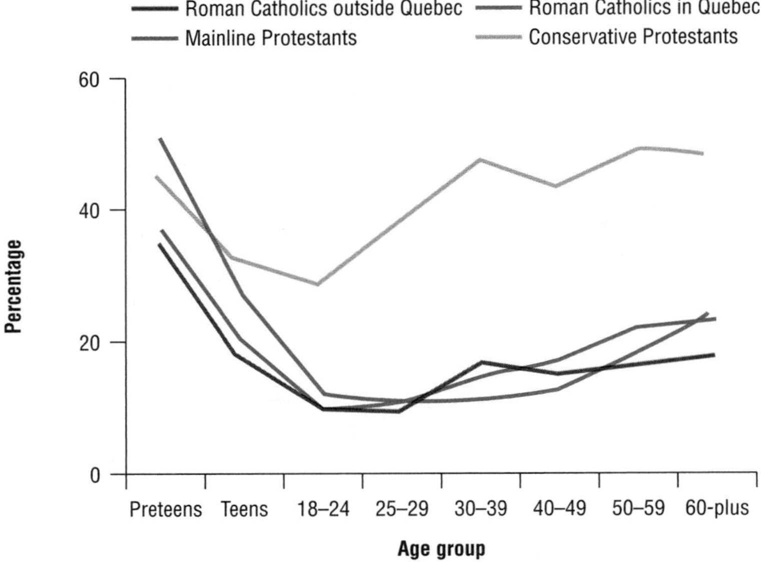


Some fascinating patterns emerge from the data. First, the people most heavily involved in religious activities are preteens and seniors. As a result, involvement forms a U-shaped curve, falling among teenagers and young adults and then beginning to rise steadily after the age of about 24.

How can we explain this pattern? Preteens have little say over whether they attend Sunday school, Hebrew school, confirmation classes, and the like. For many preteens, religious involvement is high because it is required of them, even if their parents do not always follow suit. Seniors have more time and more need for religion. Because they are not usually in school, employed in the paid labour force, or busy raising a family, they have more opportunity than young people to attend religious services. Moreover, because seniors are generally closer to illness and death than are young people, they are more likely to require the solace of religion. To a degree, then, involvement in religious activities is a life-cycle issue. That is, children are relatively actively involved in religious activities because they are required to be and seniors are relatively actively involved because they feel greater need for religious involvement and are in a position to act on that need.

But another issue is at stake here, too. Different age groups live through different times, and today's seniors reached maturity when religion was a more authoritative force in society. A person's current religious involvement depends partly on whether he or she grew up in more religious times. Thus, although young people are likely to become more religiously involved as they age, they are unlikely ever to become as involved as seniors are today.

Second, the region of the country in which you live is also correlated with the likelihood that you will attend religious services weekly. Newfoundland and Labrador, Prince Edward Island, and New Brunswick have the highest rates of monthly attendance; Quebec, Alberta, and British Columbia have the lowest. However, Figure 10.5 shows pockets of high attendance in Cape Breton, Gaspé, and parts of southwestern Ontario, southern Manitoba, Saskatchewan, and Alberta (Clark, 2003: 3).

**Figure 10.5**
**Canada, Monthly Religious Attendance**

■ Source: *Time*. 1999. "A Changing People." Canadian Edition 31 May: 30–34. © 1999 TIME Inc. Reprinted by permission.

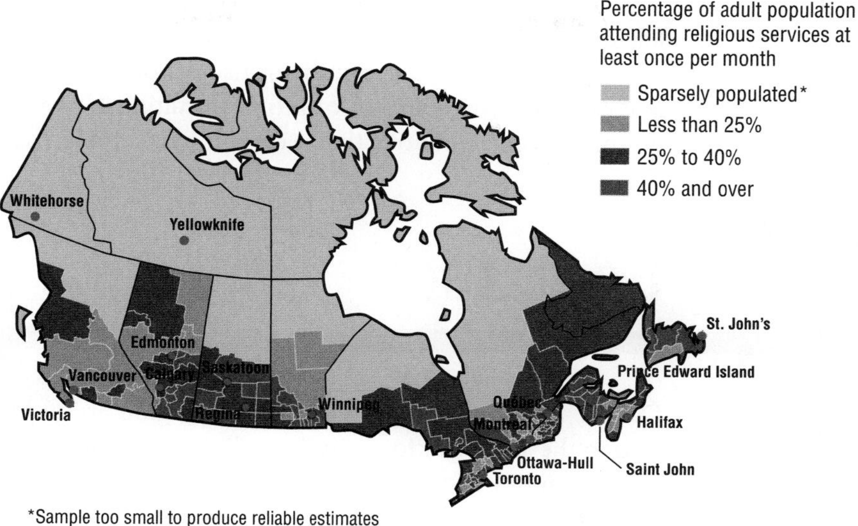

Religiosity is partly a learned behaviour. Whether parents give a child a religious upbringing is likely to have a lasting impact on the child.

Third, respondents whose parents attended religious services frequently are more likely to do so themselves (Jones, 2000). Religiosity is partly a learned behaviour. Whether parents give a child a religious upbringing is likely to have a lasting impact on the child.

This is by no means an exhaustive list of the factors that determine the frequency of attending religious services. For example, research also indicates that social inequality can promote religiosity. Thus, rich countries with the lowest levels of social inequality, such as Denmark, tend to have the lowest levels of church attendance. Rich countries with the highest levels of social inequality, such as the United States, tend to have the highest levels of church attendance. However, even this brief overview suggests that religiosity depends on obligation, opportunity, need, and learning. The people who attend religious services most frequently are those who must, those who were taught to be religious as children, those who need organized religion most because of their advanced age, and those who have the most time to go to services.

## *The Future of Religion*

Secularization is one of the dominant trends influencing religion throughout the world. We can detect secularization in survey data that track religious attitudes and practices over time and also in the growing percentage of people who indicate in succeeding censuses that they have no religious affiliation (see Figure 10.3). We also know that various secular institutions are taking over some of the functions formerly performed by religion, thus robbing it of its once pervasive authority over all aspects of life. It is an exaggeration to claim, as Max Weber did, that the whole world is gradually becoming "disenchanted." But certainly part of it is.

However, we also know that even as secularization grips many people, many others have been caught up by a religious revival of vast proportions. Religious belief and practice are intensifying for these people, in part because religion serves as a useful vehicle for political expression. The fact that this revival was quite unexpected just a few decades ago should warn us not to be overly bold in our forecasts. It seems to us, however, that the two contradictory social processes of secularization and revival are likely to persist for some time to come, resulting in a world that is neither more religious nor more secular, but one that is certainly more polarized.

# Education

Despite the continuing significance of religion around the world, the revised secularization thesis is right to claim that religion does not dominate life and thought as it did even a century ago. For example, it is not religion but education that is now the dominant institution of socialization outside the family. Almost everyone goes to school, a large minority goes to college or university, and many people continue their education in middle age. Beyond its importance as an agent of socialization, education is also a central determinant of opportunities for upward mobility. We care deeply about education not just because it shapes us but also because it influences how well we do.

# Macrosociological Processes

## *The Functions of Education*

Many Canadians believe that we enjoy equal access to basic schooling. They think schools identify and sort students based on merit and effort. They regard the education system as an avenue of upward mobility. From their point of view, the brightest students are bound to succeed, whatever their economic, ethnic, racial, or religious background. In their view, **educational attainment** is largely an outcome of individual talent and hard work. Educational attainment refers to number of years of school completed. **Educational achievement** refers to how much students actually learn.

The view that the Canadian education system is responsible for *sorting* students based on talent and effort is a central component of the functional theory of education. The functional theory also stresses the *training* role of schools. That is, in schools, most people learn how to read, write, count, calculate, and perform other tasks essential to the workings of a modern industrial society. A third function of the education system involves the *socialization* of the young (Durkheim, 1956, 1961 [1925]). Schools teach the young to view their nation with pride, respect the law, think of democracy as the best form of government, and value capitalism. Finally, schools *transmit culture* from generation to generation, fostering a common identity and social cohesion in the process. Schools have played a particularly important role in assimilating the disadvantaged, minorities, and immigrants into Canadian society, although in recent decades our common identity has been based increasingly on respect for cultural diversity.

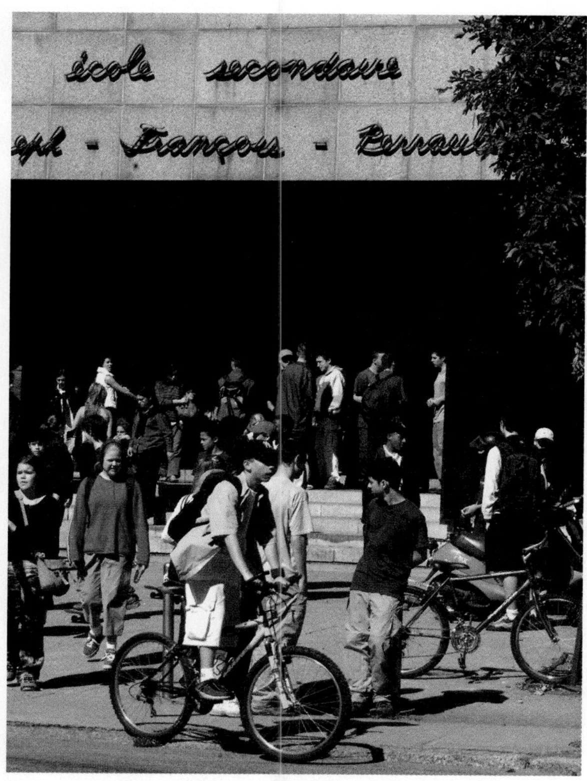


Schools encourage the development of a separate youth culture that often conflicts with parents' values.

Durkheim emphasized the role of schools in socializing the young and in promoting social integration. Human beings, he said, are torn between egoistic needs and moral impulses. Like religion in an earlier era, educational institutions must ensure that the moral side predominates. By instilling a sense of authority, discipline, and morality in children, schools make society cohesive (Durkheim, 1956, 1961 [1925]).

Sorting, training, socializing, and transmitting culture are *manifest* functions, or positive goals that schools accomplish intentionally. But schools also perform certain *latent,* or unintended, functions too. For example, schools encourage the development of a separate youth culture that often conflicts with parents' values (Coleman, Campbell, and Hobson, 1966). Especially at the college and university levels, educational institutions bring potential mates together, thus serving as a "marriage market." Schools perform a useful custodial service by keeping children under surveillance for much of the day and freeing parents to work in the paid labour force. By keeping millions of young people temporarily out of the full-time paid labour force, colleges and universities restrict job competition and support wage levels (Bowles and Gintis, 1976). Finally, because they can encourage critical, independent thinking, educational institutions sometimes become "schools of dissent" that challenge authoritarian regimes and promote social change (Brower, 1975; Freire, 1972).

### *The Effect of Economic Inequality from the Conflict Perspective*

From the conflict perspective, the chief problem with the functionalist view is that it exaggerates the degree to which schools sort students by ability and thereby ensure that the most talented students eventually get the most rewarding jobs. Conflict theorists argue that, in fact, schools distribute the benefits of education unequally, allocating most of the benefits to children from upper classes and higher-status racial and ethnic groups. Because amount and type of formal education are strongly correlated with earning power (see Figure 10.6), schools tend to reproduce the stratification system generation after generation (Jencks et al., 1972; Lucas, 1999).

Much evidence supports the conflict perspective. For instance, the green columns in Figure 10.7 show that Canadians from high-income families are 61 percent as likely as those from low-income families to be enrolled in university at the age of 19. (Here, "high-income" families are those in the top 25 percent of family income and "low-income" families are those in the bottom 25 percent.) Research also shows that about 60 percent of 25- to 34-year-old Canadians whose fathers are professionals or managers attend university. The figure falls to 35 percent for those whose fathers are supervisory workers and to less than 30 percent for those whose fathers are skilled workers. Among those whose fathers are unskilled workers, fewer than 20 percent attend university, and for those whose fathers are farmers, the figure is around 10 percent (Guppy and Davies, 1998). We conclude that class strongly influences whether a person gets to university.

**Figure 10.6**
**Earnings by Amount of Education, Canada, 2001**

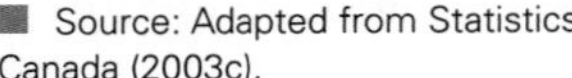

Source: Adapted from Statistics Canada (2003c).

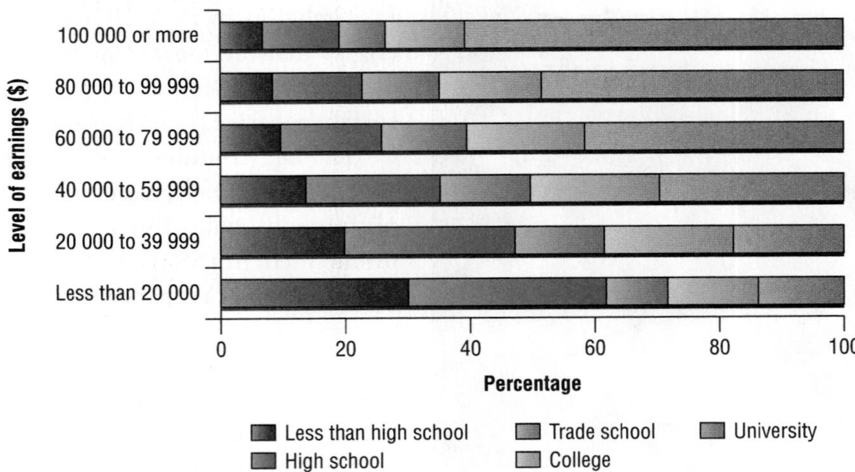


But exactly how does class exert an effect on university attendance? The sociological literature emphasizes four class mechanisms that operate in conjunction with the school system to reproduce inequality:

1. Financial constraint. *Some people do not attend university because they feel they can't afford it, even if they work part time and take advantage of student loans. More than twice as many 19-year-olds from low-income families feel this way compared with 19-year-olds from high-income families (see the yellow columns in Figure 10.7).*
2. One-parent households. *Low-income parents are more likely than high-income parents to experience the kinds of financial problems that can make marriage difficult and contribute to divorce. In turn, children from one-parent households are usually unable*

**Figure 10.7**
**The Effects of Parents' Social Class on the Education of 19-Year-Old Canadians**

Source: Frenette (2007).

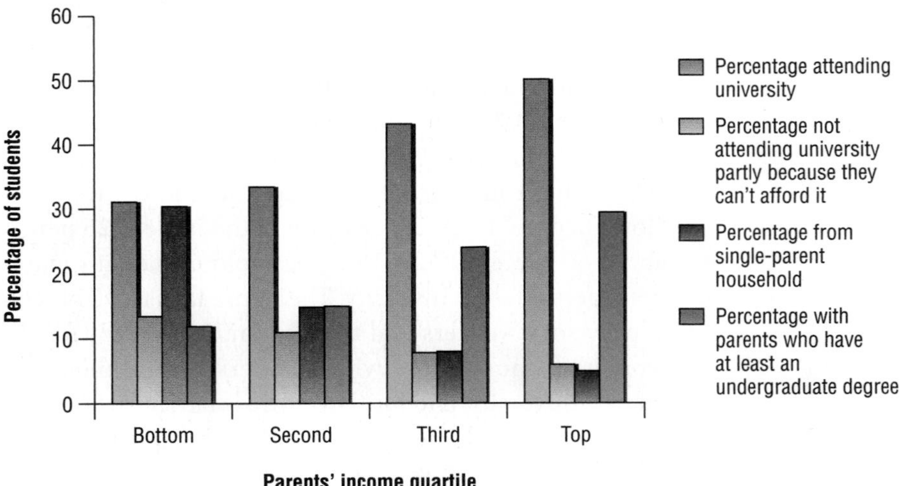

*to rely on adults for tutoring, emotional support and encouragement, supervision, and role modelling to the same degree as children from two-parent households can. This puts children from one-parent households at a big disadvantage. Significantly, the red columns in Figure 10.7 show that 19-year-olds from low-income families are six times as likely as 19-year-olds from high-income families to have been raised in a one-parent household.*

3. Lack of cultural capital. *High-income parents are two-and-a-half times as likely as low-income parents to have earned undergraduate degrees (see the blue columns in Figure 10.7). This fact is important because university education gives people cultural capital that they can transmit to their children, thus improving their chance of financial success. Cultural capital refers to "widely shared, high status cultural signals (attitudes, preferences, formal knowledge, behaviors, goals, and credentials) used for social and cultural exclusion" (Lamont and Lareau, 1988: 156). For example, if you own a lot of cultural capital, you are more likely to have "highbrow" tastes in literature, music, art, dance, and sports, and behave according to established rules of etiquette. You are likely to create a household environment that promotes refined taste, provides formal lessons to help instill such taste in your children, and thus increases their chance of success in school and, eventually, in the paid labour force (Bourdieu and Passeron, 1990 [1977]; DiMaggio, 1982; Kingston, 2001).*

4. Streaming. *The more intelligent you are, the more likely you are to do well in school and to achieve economic success later in life. IQ and other standardized tests are employed to sort students by intelligence; test scores are used to channel them into high-ability ("enriched"), middle-ability, and low-ability ("basic" or "special education") classrooms. The trouble is that IQ and other standardized tests can only measure acquired proficiency in a given cultural system. The quantity and quality of a person's exposure to whatever is counted as proper or correct plays a large role here; even the most able Anglo-Canadian children would perform abysmally if tested in Mongolian. The results of IQ and other standardized tests thus depend on two factors: (1) how effectively an individual absorbs what his or her environment offers and (2) how closely his or her environment reflects what the test includes. As a result, members of underprivileged groups tend to score low on IQ and other standardized tests—not because they are on average less intelligent than members of privileged groups but because they do not have the training and the cultural background needed to score high (Fischer et al., 1996). Still, educators persist in using IQ and other standardized tests to sort students into different types of classes (Samuda, Crawford, Philip, and Tinglen, 1980). The result: streaming reproduces class differences, determines who goes to university and who doesn't, and influences who enters which social class in the larger society (see Box 10.2).*

## *Case Study: Functionalist versus Conflict Theories of the Community College*

We can more fully illustrate how sociologists of education use functionalist and conflict theories by applying them to the case of the community college system, with its more than 400 000 full-time students in Canada. Aside from Canada's general population increase, two social forces contributed most heavily to the rise of the community college system. First, the country needed skilled workers in industry and services. Second, the belief grew that higher education would contribute to upward mobility and greater equality. The accuracy of that belief has become a point of contention among sociologists.

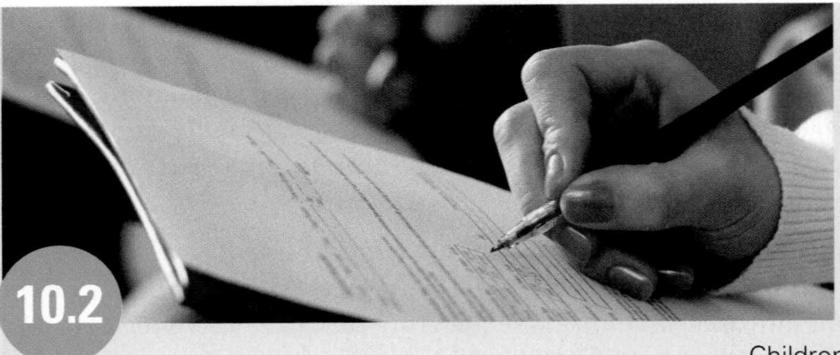

10.2

# SOCIAL POLICY: WHAT DO YOU THINK?

## Is School Enough?

Sociologists began to understand how little schools could do on their own to encourage upward mobility and end poverty in the 1960s, when sociologist James Coleman conducted a monumental study of academic performance and schools in the United States (Coleman et al., 1966). He found that differences in the quality of schools—measured by assessment of such factors as school facilities and curriculum—accounted at most for about a third of the variation in students' academic performance. At least two-thirds of the variation in academic performance was due to inequalities imposed on children by their homes, neighbourhoods, and peers. Almost four decades later, little research contradicts Coleman's finding.

Various social commentators have argued that if we are to improve the success of disadvantaged students, we must develop policies that are aimed at improving the social environment of young, disadvantaged children before they enter the formal education system (Hertzman, 2000). Compensatory education programs for preschool children were largely developed in the United States and attempt to meet the needs of children who are socially and economically disadvantaged. In Canada, such programs have also been aimed at children believed to face a heightened risk of poor academic performance or social adjustment. Although the traditional focus of early childhood education has been on children's social and emotional development, at least some of these programs focus on children's intellectual development.

The biggest survey of Canadian children found that household income was associated with school readiness, an important indicator of maturity and future success at school (Health Canada, 1999a: 73; Doherty, 1997). In addition, as family income decreases, the likelihood increases that children will experience a host of other problems that will negatively influence their school performance. For example, poor health, hyperactivity, and delayed vocabulary development are higher among children in low-income families than among children in middle- and high-income families (Ross, 1998). Children who score low on school readiness are also more likely to have mothers with a low level of education and live in neighbourhoods that their mothers characterize as unsafe or lacking in social cohesiveness (Health Canada, 1999a: 79).

Early developmental programs can decrease the chance of developmental problems arising among children and enhance their performance in school. For example, Headstart programs are based on the belief that, to assist children, the entire family must be helped. Evaluations of Headstart programs in Canada report such benefits as "more students completing school and with better grades; fewer young people needing mental health services; fewer parents abusing alcohol with concurrent reductions of alcohol's impact on children; a reduction in family violence; [and] fewer students with preventable disabilities and reduced demand for medical services" (Government of Canada, 2001). Such programs have been identified as particularly important in increasing the educational success of Aboriginal students. However, it is estimated that existing programs reach only about 5 percent of the Aboriginal children who could potentially benefit from them (George, 1998).

The cost of early childhood intervention programs is substantial. However, investments made in the critical early years of a child's life not only benefit Canada's children but also our economy. One study reports that "every dollar spent in early intervention can save seven dollars in future expenditures in health and social spending" (Health Canada, 1999a: 88).

### CRITICAL THINKING QUESTIONS

- *Do you believe that early childhood intervention programs would be useful in improving the educational success of children? If not, why not?*
- *If so, do you feel that attendance should be compulsory? Should parents who refuse to send their children to such programs be penalized for their decision?*
- *What background factors do you feel should be used to select children and their families for inclusion in such programs?*

*Functionalists* examine the social composition of the student body in community colleges and find a somewhat disproportionate number of students from lower socioeconomic strata and minority ethnic groups. Many community colleges are located close to the neighbourhoods of disadvantaged students, allowing them to live at home while studying. Community college tuition fees are generally lower than in four-year colleges and universities. Graduates of community colleges are usually able to find relatively good jobs and steady employment. These facts seem to confirm the functionalist view that the community college system creates new opportunities for disadvantaged youth who might otherwise have less rewarding jobs.

*Conflict theorists* deny that the growth of community colleges increases upward mobility and equality. In the long run, they argue, it is the entire stratification system that is upwardly mobile. That is, the quality of nearly *all* jobs improves but the *relative* position of community college graduates versus graduates of four-year institutions remains the same. In fact, conflict theorists argue that community colleges reinforce prevailing patterns of social and class inequality by directing students from disadvantaged backgrounds away from four-year institutions and thus decreasing the probability that they will earn a four-year degree and a high-status position in society (Karabel, 1986: 18).

Functionalists and conflict theorists both have a point. Community colleges do create opportunities for individual upward mobility that some students would otherwise not have. Community colleges do not, however, change the overall pattern of inequality in Canadian society. In fact, expecting community colleges or, for that matter, any part of the institution of education to change the stratification system as a whole is probably naive. Decreasing the level of inequality in society requires comprehensive preschool programs to help disadvantaged children and laws that change people's entitlements and the rewards they receive for doing different kinds of work, not just increasing educational opportunities.

We conclude that functionalists paint a somewhat idealized picture of the education system. Although usefully identifying the manifest and latent functions of education, they fail to emphasize sufficiently the far-reaching effects of stratified home environments on student achievement and placement. A similar conclusion is warranted if we examine the effects of gender on education.

## *Gender and Education: The Feminist Contribution*

In some respects, women are doing better than men in the Canadian education system. Women in colleges and universities have higher grade point averages than men and they complete their degrees faster. The number of women enrolled as college and university undergraduates has exceeded the number of men for decades, and more women than men are enrolled in some graduate and professional programs, such as medicine and law. The enrolment gap between women and men is growing—not just in Canada but also in the United States, the UK, France, Germany, and Australia (Berliner, 2004; see Table 10.4).

The facts just listed represent considerable improvement over time in the position of women in the education system. Yet feminists who have looked closely at the situation have established that women are still at a disadvantage. Consider field of study. A disproportionately large number of men earn Ph.D.s and professional degrees in engineering, computer science, dentistry, and specialized areas of medicine—all

**Table 10.4**
University Degrees Awarded by Degree, Selected Program, and Gender, Canada, 2003

| | Men (%) | Women (%) | Total (%) |
|---|---|---|---|
| Degree | | | |
| Bachelor's | 38.5 | 61.5 | 100.0 |
| Master's | 47.9 | 52.1 | 100.0 |
| Doctorate | 56.4 | 43.6 | 100.0 |
| Selected Program | | | |
| Education | 24.5 | 75.5 | 100.0 |
| Social and behavioural sciences and law | 33.3 | 66.7 | 100.0 |
| Physical and life sciences and technologies | 41.9 | 58.1 | 100.0 |
| Business, management, public administration | 44.9 | 55.1 | 100.0 |
| Architecture, engineering and related | 74.0 | 26.0 | 100.0 |

Source: Statistics Canada (2005b).

relatively high-paying fields, most requiring a strong math and science background. A disproportionately large number of women earn Ph.D.s and professional degrees in education, English, foreign languages, and other relatively low-paying fields requiring little background in math and science. Parents and teachers are partly responsible for these choices because they tend to direct boys and girls toward what they regard as masculine and feminine fields of study. Gender segregation in the labour market also influences choice of field of study. University students know women are more likely to get jobs in certain fields than others and they make career choices accordingly (Spade, 2001). Like class and race, gender structures the educational experience and its consequences.

## Microsociological Processes

### *The Stereotype Threat: A Symbolic Interactionist Perspective*

Macrosociological issues, such as the functions of education and the influence of class and gender on educational achievement, do not exhaust the interests of sociologists of education. They have also contributed much to our understanding of the face-to-face interaction processes that influence the educational process. Consider this finding from American research: when black and white children begin school, their achievement test scores are similar. Yet the longer they stay in school, the more black students fall behind. By grade 6, blacks in many school districts are two full grades behind whites in achievement. Clearly, something happens in school to increase the gap between black and white students. Symbolic interactionists suggest that this something is the self-fulfilling prophecy, an expectation that helps bring about what it predicts.

We encountered examples of self-fulfilling prophecies in educational settings in Chapter 4 (From Social Interaction to Social Organizations). For instance, we discussed one famous experiment in which, at the beginning of a school year, researchers randomly identified students as high or low achievers to their teachers. At the end of the school year, they found that the students arbitrarily singled out as high achievers scored higher on an IQ test than those arbitrarily singled out as low achievers. The researchers concluded that teachers' expectations influenced students' performance (Rosenthal and Jacobson, 1968; Weinstein, 2002).

In general, many teachers expect members of lower classes and some visible minority groups to do poorly in school. Rather than being treated as young people with good prospects, such students are often under suspicion of intellectual inferiority and often feel rejected by teachers, white middle-class classmates, and the curriculum. This expectation, sometimes called a **stereotype threat,** has a negative impact on the school performance of disadvantaged groups (Massey, Charles, Lundy, and Fischer, 2003; Steele, 1997).

Minority-group students often cluster together because they feel alienated from dominant groups in their school or college or perhaps even from the institution itself. Too often, such alienation turns into resentment and defiance of authority. Many students from minority groups reject academic achievement as a goal because they see it as a goal of the dominant culture. Discipline problems, ranging from apathy to disruptive and illegal behaviour, can result. The corollary of identifying your race or ethnicity with poor academic performance is thinking of good academic performance as "selling out" to the dominant culture (Ogbu, 2003; Willis, 1984). Consistent with this argument, Aboriginal and black students in Canada have higher-than-average school dropout rates (Livingstone, 1999: 743; Toronto Board of Education, 1993). In contrast, research shows that challenging lower-class and minority students, giving them emotional support and encouragement, giving greater recognition in the curriculum to the accomplishments of the groups from which they originate, creating an environment in which they can relax and achieve—all these strategies explode the self-fulfilling prophecy and improve academic performance (Steele, 1992). Anecdotal evidence supporting this argument can be found in the compelling 1988 movie *Stand and Deliver,* based on the true-life story of

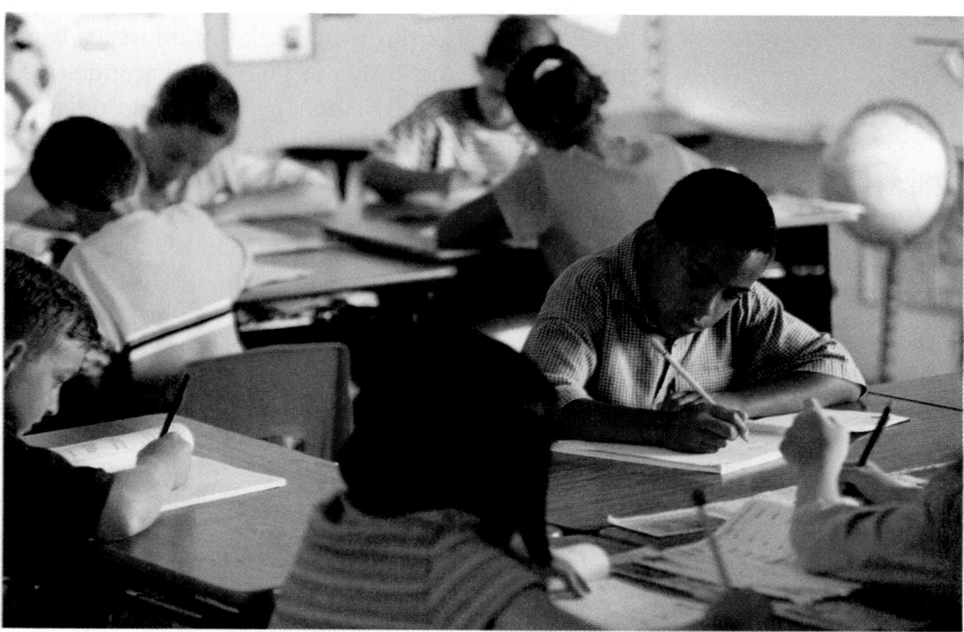

Although the composition of Canada's student population is becoming increasingly multicultural, this is less true of Canada's teachers. An ongoing debate in Canada is whether students at all levels would be better served by a faculty whose composition reflects the diversity of our population and who offer a more inclusive curriculum.

high school math teacher Jaime Escalante. Escalante refused to write off his failing East Los Angeles Chicano pupils as "losers" and inspired them to remarkable achievements as they registered the best performance in the Advanced Placement Calculus Exam in the southern California school system.

In sum, the stereotype threat at the microsociological level combines with the macrosociological processes described earlier to help reproduce the stratification system. These social mechanisms increase the chance that those who are socially marginal and already disadvantaged will earn low grades and wind up with jobs closer to the bottom than to the top of the occupational structure.

# Education and Globalization

In Europe 300 years ago, the nobility and the wealthy usually hired personal tutors to teach their children to read and write; learn basic history, geography, and foreign languages; and study how to dress properly, conduct themselves in public, greet status superiors, and so on. Few people went to college. Only a few professions, such as theology and law, required extensive schooling. The great majority of Europeans were illiterate. As late as the 1860s, more than 80 percent of Spaniards and more than 30 percent of the French could not read (Vincent, 2000). Even as recently as a century ago, most people in the world had never attended even a day of school. As late as 1950 only about 10 percent of the world's countries boasted systems of compulsory mass education (Meyer, Ramirez, and Soysal, 1992).

Today the situation is different. Compulsory mass education had become a universal feature of European and North American life by the early twentieth century, and nearly universal literacy was achieved by the middle of the twentieth century (Curtis, 1988; Vincent, 2000). Today, every country in the world has a system of mass schooling. Mass education is part of globalization. Many of the conditions that contributed to mass education in the West now exist in the world's less developed countries. Religious authority is growing weaker, democracy is growing stronger, and new governments require the loyalty of their citizens and see education as necessary for economic development (McMahon, 1999). In addition, transnational corporations require a more literate and highly educated world population to do business, and transnational organizations, such as the United Nations, promote literacy and schooling. Still, this high moral principle remains a far-off goal. More than 860 million adults in the world are illiterate, two-thirds of them women. In sub-Saharan Africa, 40 percent of primary-school-age children do not attend school (UNESCO, 2002). Although mass education has been globalized, global inequality in educational attainment is profound.

## *Canadian School Standards in International Perspective*

Canadians are among the most highly educated people in the world. In 2001, 41 percent of Canada's population aged 25 to 64 had either a college or university education, compared with 37 percent in the United States, 36 percent in Ireland, and 34 percent in Japan (Statistics Canada, 2003b: 10). Still, many Canadians believe that our public school system has turned soft if not rotten. They argue that the youth of Japan and South Korea spend long hours concentrating on the basics of math,

Many Canadians feel that the youth of Japan and South Korea spend long hours concentrating on the basics of math, science, and language, while Canadian students spend fewer hours in school and study more non-basic subjects that are of little practical value.

science, and language, while Canadian students spend fewer hours in school and study more non-basic subjects (e.g., art, music, drama, physical education) that are of little practical value. If students do not spend more school time on subjects that "really" matter, they warn, Canada will suffer declining economic competitiveness in the twenty-first century. Many Canadians—8 in 10 according to one poll—want province-wide standardized tests for students and teachers because they presumably allow school performance to be objectively assessed (Bricker and Greenspon, 2001: 165–66). Because of the perceived decline in school standards, an increasingly large number of parents who can afford to do so—about 5 percent of all Canadian parents—are sending their children to private school and a small number are schooling their children at home.

In reality, international comparisons show that Canadians perform well in standardized math, science, and literacy tests. In particular, students from Alberta, Quebec, and British Columbia rank among the best in the world (see Figure 10.8). Canada is also among the top six countries in terms of providing good education to students from all socioeconomic classes (the others are Finland, Iceland, Japan, Korea, and Sweden; Sokoloff, 2001).

## *School Reform*

Despite the encouraging results of the international studies cited above, the quality of Canada's public schools may erode in coming decades. Hundreds of millions of dollars have been removed from education budgets since the early 1990s. As a result, schools are closing and non-core programs in art, music, drama, physical education, and special education are being cut. Parents are being asked to dig deeper into their pockets to pay for more books and supplies. Many teachers and staff members are required to work longer hours for salaries that do not keep pace with inflation. Demoralization follows. More teachers and staff members are going on strike more often, while fewer young people are being attracted to the teaching profession. Statistics Canada

## Figure 10.8
## Results from PISA International Literacy Test, 2003

■ Source: PISA Canada (2003). Reproduced with the permission of the Minister of Public Works and Government Services Canada, 2006.

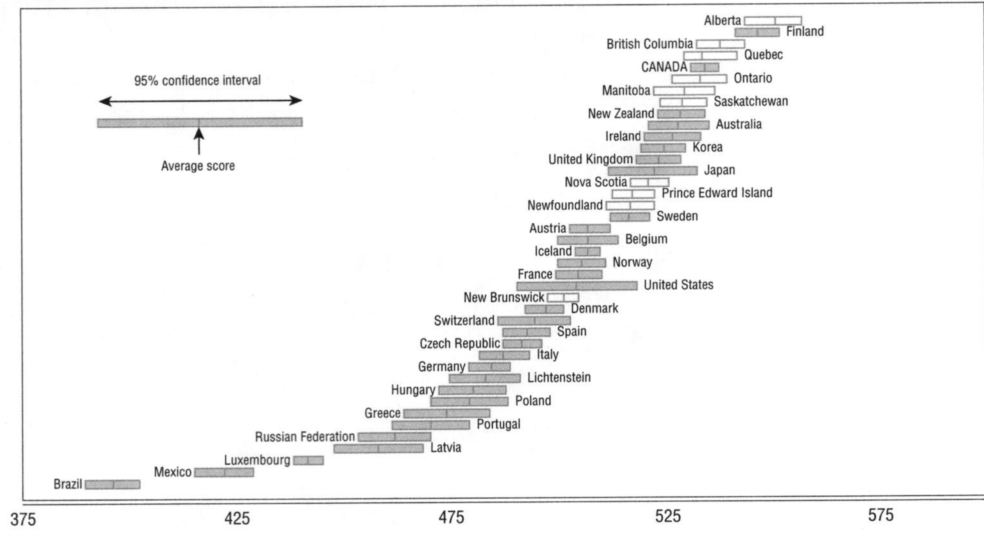


estimates a shortfall of 20 000 teachers nationwide. Meanwhile, at the postsecondary level, tuition fees are increasing annually, making it more difficult for working-class and even middle-class families to send their adolescent children to college or university.

Budget cuts are not the only change the Canadian school system has experienced since the early 1990s. In addition, provincial governments, particularly in Ontario, have centralized control of schools by imposing standardized testing and new curricula while reducing the power of school boards. Their stated aim is to do more with less, improving

Recent surveys suggest that Canadians have only a moderate level of confidence in the job being done by the public education sector.

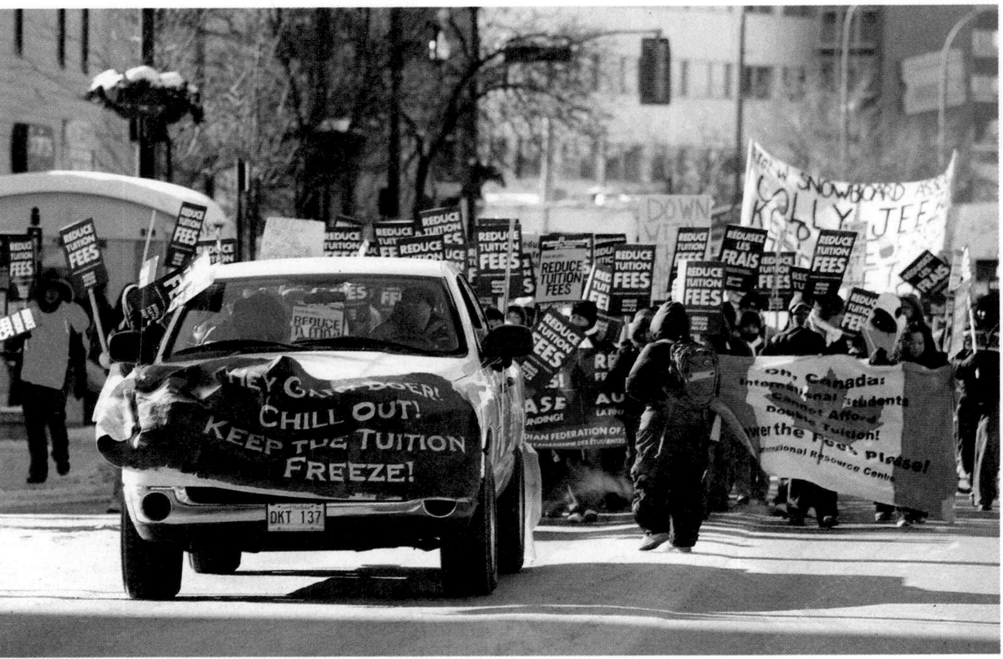

school standards while removing resources from the educational system. In theory, this helps provincial governments balance their budgets and borrow less money while taxpayers enjoy tax cuts. This presumably stimulates economic growth.

Nobody can reasonably object to the goals of stimulating economic growth and improving school standards. However, the way in which provincial governments have gone about the task of achieving these goals cuts two ways. For one thing, taking money out of the school system decreases the number of jobs available for principals, teachers, and support staff while keeping a lid on the purchasing power of the people who remain employed in the education sector. This decreases demand for goods and services and thus puts a damper on economic growth. In addition, taking money out of the school system increases educational inequality by decreasing opportunities for children from poor and modest economic backgrounds. With fewer teachers, impoverished curricula, and increasing costs being shouldered by families rather than the state, the prospects of children from lower socioeconomic strata have not looked so dim since World War II (Johnston, 2002).

Canadians can ponder two models of educational reform as they consider what to do with their public school system. One model is American; the other is British.

In the United States, decades of cutbacks in public education have created a school system in which a third of the schools are merely "okay" and another third are in "terrible shape" (Bracey, 1998). The great majority of mediocre and bad schools are in the cores of big cities, which are disproportionately populated by racial minorities. On an average day in Chicago, teachers are unavailable for 57 000 downtown students. Many schools lack adequate furniture and books. Meanwhile, in an upper-middle-class Chicago suburb, spending per pupil is 78 percent higher than in downtown. Schools offer college-level courses and boast the latest audiovisual, computer, photographic, and sporting equipment (Kozol, 1991). A third of the schools in the United States are "world class," but only the well-to-do can attend them (Bracey, 1998). The American model, then, drains resources from the public school system, creating excellence for the few and mediocrity and demoralization for the majority.

The United Kingdom has taken a diametrically opposed approach. Since 1997, education spending has been on the increase. Professional development is strongly emphasized. For example, nearly all of England's elementary teachers have been retrained so they can teach reading, writing, and math more effectively. A new National College for School Leadership has been created to develop top principals. Standardized testing has become more widespread so that educators can pinpoint areas of weakness and improve them. Teachers' salaries are linked to performance. The results of these initiatives are impressive. In 1997, 56 percent of 11-year-olds scored in the top two levels of the national literacy test. By 2001, the figure stood at 75 percent. Similar improvements have been registered in math. Areas of the country that in 1997 were below the national average in literacy and numeracy are now above the national average (Schofield, 2001).

Recent British educational reforms do not involve simply throwing more money at the school system. Rather, they involve establishing nationwide standards and then providing the resources necessary to meet those standards by creating "meaningful learning communities." The British reforms are based on the ideas of Michael Fullan of the Ontario Institute for Studies in Education (OISE) at the University of Toronto (Fullan, 2001; Hammonds, 2002).

In Fullan's use of the term, a meaningful learning community is a social setting in which all participants engage in education because it brings them substantial moral benefits. Students learn well when they feel they are actively engaged in achieving mastery of subjects that are relevant to their lives. Their opinions, needs, and backgrounds must therefore be taken into account in formulating curricula. Teachers teach well when they feel they are making a positive difference in the lives of their students. They require autonomy, resources, the support of their colleagues, and ongoing training or professional development to do so. Principals lead well when they feel they are creating a new school culture that facilitates beneficial social change. To achieve this they must forge consensus, encourage professional collaboration, ensure that top-quality instructional tools are readily available, and set expectations for students and teachers that are high, clear, and consistent. All this is a recipe for excellence based on high standards gauged by nationwide testing. As Fullan (1998) notes, "student achievement increases substantially in schools with collaborative work cultures that foster a professional learning community among teachers and others, focus continuously on improving instructional practices in light of student performance data, and link to external standards and staff development support."

Admittedly, most Canadians are in no mood to pay higher taxes in the short term. But we need to consider the long term, too. In a world in which economic growth depends increasingly on the availability of a flexible, highly skilled, and well-educated labour force, do we want to provide most of our students with an inferior education? Do we want to live in a society whose educational system is a mechanism for increasing the distance between the affluent and the less well-to-do? In thinking about how we should deal with the public school system, these are surely questions worth pondering.

## The Points of the Compass

Much of the sociological study of education turns on the "opportunity" axis of the sociological compass we introduced in Chapter 1. The education system is supposed to function as a great leveller, ensuring that all children are able to realize their full potential and rise to a level of accomplishment that maximizes their rewards once they reach the job market. Opportunities are not supposed to be limited by such background factors as class, race, and gender. But they are. True, the education system affords opportunities for upward mobility; many bright children from humble origins "make it." Yet many do not. And while some children from privileged families do poorly in school, their background typically buffers them from the threat of steep plunges down the social hierarchy. The education system remains far from the equal opportunity ideal.

Much of the sociological study of religion turns on the "freedom" axis of our sociological compass. We enjoy increased choice of religious beliefs and practices, partly because monolithic religious authority no longer exists in much of the world and also because globalization has exposed us to more options. Amid this growing freedom of choice, however, a quite remarkable constraint imposes itself. Just four decades ago, most observers thought that religion was a weakening force. Now, in the midst of religious revivals in much of the world, they have changed or at least qualified their assessment. Religion, while by no means compulsory, is widely considered an important part of life in many countries and has therefore proven to be more resilient than was once thought.

# Summary

1. *What is Durkheim's theory of religion and what are the main criticisms that have been lodged against it?*

Durkheim argued that the main function of religion is to increase social cohesion by providing ritualized opportunities for people to experience the collective conscience. Critics note that Durkheim ignored the ways in which religion can incite social conflict and reinforce social inequality.

2. *What is Weber's theory of religion and what are the main criticisms that have been lodged against it?*

Weber argued that religion acts like a railroad switch, determining the tracks along which history will be pushed by the force of political and economic interest. Protestantism, for example, invigorated capitalist development. Critics note that the correlation between economic development and the predominance of Protestantism is not as strong as Weber thought.

3. *What is the secularization thesis and what are the main criticisms that have been lodged against it?*

The secularization thesis holds that religious institutions, actions, and consciousness are on the decline worldwide. Critics of the secularization thesis point out that a religious revival has occurred in the United States and elsewhere over the past 35 years or so.

4. *What is the revised secularization thesis?*

The revised secularization thesis recognizes the religious revival and the resilience of religion but still maintains that the scope of religious authority has declined over time. The revisionists say that religion is increasingly restricted to the realm of the spiritual; it governs fewer aspects of people's lives and is more a matter of personal choice than it used to be.

5. *What determines the frequency with which people attend religious services?*

Among other factors, the frequency of attending religious services is determined by opportunity (how much time people have available for attending), need (whether people are in a social position that increases their desire for spiritual answers to life's problems), and learning (whether people were brought up in a religious household).

6. *What are the functions of education?*

Sorting, training, socializing, and transmitting culture are *manifest* functions, or goals that schools accomplish intentionally. Schools perform certain *latent,* or unintended, functions too, including the development of a separate youth culture, marriage market, custodial service, and tradition of dissent.

7. *How does the stratification system influence the education system and how does the educational system help to reproduce the stratification system?*

The stratification system imposes financial constraints on students from less well-to-do families, preventing some of them from pursuing a higher education. It also causes more marital instability in lower-class families, which limits the amount of tutoring, emotional support and encouragement, supervision, and role modelling that children from these families enjoy. Parents from lower-class families possess little cultural capital that they can pass on to their children to assist them in educational and occupational attainment. For their part, schools employ standardized tests to stream students into classes that reflect class and other inequalities in the larger society.

8. *Does gender influence educational outcomes?*

Women are ahead of men in college and university enrolments, speed of completion of degrees, and grade point average. Still, they lag behind men substantially when it comes to the prestige and earning potential of their fields of study.

9. *How does the stereotype threat work in the education system?*

Teachers' expectations that certain students will do poorly in school often result in poor student performance. Teachers' expectations that certain students will do well in school often result in good student performance. These expectations reinforce the effects of background factors and, like background factors, help to reproduce existing patterns of inequality.

10. *What are the dominant American and British models of educational reform?*

In the United States, money has been drained from the public school system and invested in various privatization schemes on the assumption that schools that are responsive to market forces will perform better. This has resulted in a highly stratified educational system. In the UK, high national standards have been set and enforced, while more money has been pumped into the public school system so that standards can be met. As a result, student performance in standardized tests has improved.

## Key Terms

**charismatic (p. 315)**
**church (p. 314)**
**collective conscience (p. 303)**
**cults (p. 315)**
**denominations (p. 315)**
**ecclesia (p. 315)**
**educational achievement (p. 320)**
**educational attainment (p. 320)**
**fundamentalists (p. 311)**
**profane (p. 303)**
**religiosity (p. 317)**
**revised secularization thesis (p. 314)**
**rituals (p. 303)**
**routinization of charisma (p. 304)**
**sacred (p. 303)**
**sects (p. 315)**
**secularization thesis (p. 310)**
**stereotype threat (p. 327)**
**totems (p. 303)**

## Questions to Consider

1. Does the sociological study of religion undermine a person's religious faith, make a person's religious faith stronger, or have no necessary implications for a person's religious faith? On what do you base your opinion? What does your opinion imply about the connection between religion and science in general?
2. In your opinion, how meritocratic were the schools you attended? Did the most talented students tend to perform best? Did material advantages and parental support help the best students? Did material disadvantages and lack of parental support hinder the achievements of weaker students?
3. How would you try to solve the problem of unequal access to education? What do you think of the solutions to the education crisis discussed at the end of this chapter? Do you have some suggestions of your own?

# Web Resources

## Companion Web Site for This Book

**http://www.pointsofthecompass.nelson.com**

Begin by clicking on the Student Resources section of the Web site. Next, select the chapter you are currently studying from the pull-down menu. From the Student Resources page you will have easy access to InfoTrac® College Edition, MicroCase online exercises, and additional Weblinks. The Web site also has many useful tips to aid you in your study of sociology, including practice tests for each chapter.

## InfoTrac® Search Terms

These search terms are provided to assist you in beginning to conduct research on this topic by visiting **http://www.infotrac-college.com**:

**cult**
**educational achievement**
**educational attainment**
**fundamentalism**
**secularization**

## Recommended Web Sites

Ontario Consultants on Religious Tolerance is an excellent Web site that provides basic, unbiased information on dozens of religions, religious tolerance and intolerance, religion and science, abortion and religion, and so forth. Visit **http://www.religioustolerance.org**.

Statistics on education in Canada are available from Statistics Canada at **http://cansim2.statcan.ca/cgi-win/cnsmcgi.pgm?Lang=E&SP_Action=Theme&SP_ID=1821**.

The Canadian Federation of Students represents close to half a million students at colleges and universities across Canada through a cooperative alliance of more than 60 students' unions. This site is particularly helpful for those seeking information on issues that affect postsecondary students in Canada. Visit **http://www.cfs-fcee.ca/html/english/home/index.php**.

# PART 5 SOCIAL CHANGE

# chapter 11

## technology, the environment, and social movements

# chapter 11

## technology, the environment, and social movements



**In this chapter, you will learn that**

→ Technology transforms society and history, but human need, increasingly influenced by multinational corporations and the military establishments of the major world powers, shapes technological growth.

→ Technological development has degraded the environment, but environmental issues do not become social problems until policy-oriented scientists, the environmental movement, the mass media, and respected organizations discover and promote environmental issues, and the public connects the information learned from these groups to real-life events.

→ Economically disadvantaged groups experience more environmental risks than economically advantaged groups.

→ Some people have created social movements to influence governments and corporations to act on environmental issues, but few people are prepared to pay the price of creating a safe environment until repeated environmental catastrophes compel them to do so.

→ People are more inclined to rebel against existing conditions and form a social movement when strong social ties bind them to many other people who feel similarly wronged; when they have the time, money, and other resources needed to protest; and when political structures and processes give them opportunities to express discontent.

→ For social movements to grow, members must make the activities, goals, and ideology of the movement consistent with the interests, beliefs, and values of potential recruits.

# Technology: Saviour or Frankenstein?

On 6 August 1945, the United States Air Force dropped an atomic bomb on Hiroshima. The bomb killed about 200 000 Japanese, almost all of them civilians. It hastened the end of the World War II, thus making it unnecessary for American troops to suffer heavy losses in a land invasion of Japan.

Scholars interested in the relationship between technology and society recognize that Hiroshima divided the twentieth century into two distinct periods. We can call the period before Hiroshima the era of naive optimism. During that time, technology could do no wrong, or so it seemed to nearly all observers. **Technology** was widely defined as the application of scientific principles to the *improvement* of human life. It seemed to be driving humanity down a one-way street named progress, picking up speed with every passing year thanks to successively more powerful engines: steam, turbine, internal combustion, electric, jet, rocket, and nuclear. Technology produced tangible benefits. Its detailed workings rested on scientific principles that were mysterious to all but those with advanced science degrees. Therefore, most people regarded technologists with reverence and awe. They were viewed as a sort of priesthood whose objectivity allowed them to stand outside the everyday world and perform near-magical acts.

With Hiroshima, the blush was off the rose. Growing pessimism was, in fact, evident three weeks earlier, when the world's first nuclear bomb exploded at the Alamogordo Bombing Range in New Mexico. The bomb was the child of J. Robert Oppenheimer, appointed head of the top-secret Manhattan Project just 28 months earlier. After recruiting what General Leslie Groves called "the greatest collection of eggheads ever," including three past and seven future Nobel Prize winners, Oppenheimer organized the largest and most sophisticated technological project in human history up to that time. As an undergraduate at Harvard, Oppenheimer had studied Indian philosophy, among other subjects. On the morning of 16 July 1945, as the flash of intense white light faded and the purplish fireball rose, sucking desert sand and debris into a mushroom cloud more than 12 kilometres high, Oppenheimer quoted from Hindu scripture: "I am become Death, the shatterer of worlds" (quoted in Parshall, 1998).

J. Robert Oppenheimer, the "father" of the atomic bomb

Overall, North Americans value science and technology highly. Still, in the post-war years a growing number of people have come to share Oppenheimer's doubts about the bomb. Indeed, they have extended those doubts not just to the peaceful use of nuclear energy but also to technology in general. Increasingly, people are beginning to think of technology as a monster run amok, a Frankenstein rather than a saviour.

In the 1970s and 1980s, a series of horrific disasters alerted many people (including some sociologists) to the fact that technological advance is not always beneficial, not even always benign. A gas leak at a poorly maintained Union Carbide pesticide plant in Bhopal, India, killed about 4000 people in 1984 and injured 30 000, a third of whom died excruciating deaths in the following years. In 1986, the No. 4 reactor at Chernobyl,

The world's first major nuclear reactor accident occurred in December 1952 at the Chalk River nuclear facility about 125 kilometres northwest of Ottawa. A partial meltdown of the reactor's uranium fuel core caused the 4-tonne lid to blow off the reactor, spurting radioactive water and creating lethal radiation levels. Some analysts consider the Chalk River Nuclear Laboratories one of the most contaminated pieces of real estate in Canada, with toxic radioactive pollution seeping from several nuclear waste dumps into aquifers, bogs, streams, and lakes, and ultimately into the Ottawa River.

Ukraine, exploded, releasing 30 to 40 times as much radioactivity as the blast at Hiroshima. It resulted in mass evacuations, more than 10 000 deaths, countless human and animal mutations, and hundreds of square kilometres of unusable cropland. In 1989, the *Exxon Valdez* ran aground in Prince William Sound, Alaska, spilling 42 million litres of crude oil, producing a dangerous slick more than 1600 kilometres long, causing billions of dollars of damage, and killing hundreds of thousands of animals.

By the mid-1980s, sociologist Charles Perrow was referring to such events as "normal accidents." The term **normal accident** recognizes that the very complexity of modern technologies ensures they will *inevitably* fail, though in unpredictable ways (Perrow, 1984). For example, a large computer program contains many thousands of conditional statements. They take the form if $x = y$, do $z$; if $a = b$, do $c$. When in use, the program activates many billions of *combinations* of conditional statements. As a result, complex programs cannot be tested for all possible eventualities. Therefore, when rare combinations of conditions occur, they have unforeseen consequences that are usually minor, occasionally amusing, sometimes expensive, and too often dangerous. You experience normal accidents when your home computer crashes or hangs.

German sociologist Ulrich Beck also coined a term that stuck when he said we live in a risk society. A **risk society** is a society in which technology distributes danger among all categories of the population. Some categories, however, are more exposed to technological danger than others. Moreover, in a risk society, danger does not result from technological accidents alone. In addition, increased risk is due to mounting *environmental* threats that are more widespread, chronic, and ambiguous than technological accidents—and therefore more stressful (Beck, 1992 [1986]; Freudenburg, 1997). New and frightening terms—greenhouse effect, global warming, acid rain, ozone depletion, endangered species—have entered our vocabulary. To many people, technology seems to be spinning out of control. From their point of view, it enables the production of ever more goods and services, but at the cost of breathable air, drinkable water, safe sunlight, plant and animal diversity, and normal weather patterns.

These considerations raise four tough questions. We tackle each of them below. First, is technology *the* great driving force of historical and social change? This is the opinion of both cheerleaders and naysayers, those who view technology as our saviour and those who fear it as a Frankenstein. In contrast, we argue that technology is able to transform society only when it is coupled with a powerful social need. People control technology as much as technology transforms people. Second, if some people do control technology, then exactly who are they? We argue against the view that scientific and engineering wizards are in control. The military and big corporations now decide the direction of most technological research and its application. Third, what are the most dangerous spinoffs of technology and how is risk distributed among various social groups? We focus on global warming and "genetic pollution." We show that although these dangers put all of humanity at risk, the degree of danger varies by class, race, and country. In brief, the socially and economically disadvantaged are most at risk. Fourth, how can we overcome the dangers of environmental degradation? We argue that market and technological solutions are insufficient by themselves. In addition, much self-sacrifice, cooperation, and political activism will be required.

## *Technology* and *People Make History*

Russian economist Nikolai Kondratiev was the first social scientist to notice that technologies are invented in clusters. As Table 11.1 shows, a new group of major inventions has cropped up every 40 to 60 years since the Industrial Revolution. Kondratiev argued that these flurries of creativity cause major economic growth spurts beginning 10 to 20 years later and lasting 25 to 35 years each. Thus, Kondratiev subscribed to a form of **technological determinism,** the belief that technology is the major force shaping human society and history (Ellul, 1964 [1954]).

**Table 11.1**
"Kondratiev Waves" of Modern Technological Innovation and Economic Growth

| Wave | Invention Dates | New Technologies | Base | Economic Growth Spurt |
|---|---|---|---|---|
| 1 | 1760s–70s | Steam engine, textile manufacturing, chemistry, civil engineering | Britain | 1780–1815 |
| 2 | 1820s | Railways, mechanical engineering | Britain, Continental Western Europe | 1840–70 |
| 3 | 1870s–80s | Chemistry, electricity, internal combustion engine | Germany, United States | 1890–1914 |
| 4 | 1930s–40s | Electronics, aerospace, chemistry | United States | 1945–70 |
| 5 | 1970s | Microelectronics, biotechnology | United States, Japan | 1985–? |

Source: Adapted from Pacey (1983: 32).

Is it true that technology helps shape society and history? Of course it is. James Watt invented the steam engine in Britain in 1766. It was the main driving force in the mines, mills, factories, and railways of the Industrial Revolution. Gottlieb Daimler invented the internal combustion engine in Germany in 1883. It was the foundation stone of two of the world's biggest industries: automobiles and petroleum. John Atanasoff was among the first people to invent the computer in 1939 at Iowa State College (now University). It utterly transformed the way we work, study, and entertain ourselves. It also put the spurs to one of the most sustained economic booms ever. We could easily cite many more examples of how technology shapes history and transforms society.

However, if we probe a little deeper into almost any technology, we notice a pattern: they did not become engines of economic growth until *social* conditions allowed them to do so. The original steam engine, for instance, was invented by Hero of Alexandria in the first century C.E. He used it as an amusing way of opening a door. People then promptly forgot the steam engine. Some 1700 years later, when the Industrial Revolution began, factories were first set up near rivers and streams, where water power was available. That was several years before Watt patented his steam engine. Watt's invention was all the rage once its potential became evident. But it did not cause the Industrial Revolution and it was adopted on a wide scale only after the social need for it emerged (Pool, 1997: 126–27).

Similarly, Atanasoff stopped work on the computer soon after the outbreak of World War II. But once the military potential of the computer became evident, its development resumed. The British computer, Colossus, helped decipher secret German codes in the last two years of the war and played an important role in the Allied victory. The University of Illinois delivered one of the earliest computers, the ORDVAC, to the Ballistic Research Laboratory at the Aberdeen Proving Ground of the U.S. Army. Again we see how a new technology becomes a major force in society and history only after it is coupled with an urgent social need. We conclude that technology and society influence each other. Scientific discoveries, once adopted on a wide scale, often transform societies. But scientific discoveries are turned into useful technologies only when social need demands it.

ORDVAC, an early computer developed at the University of Illinois, was delivered to the Ballistic Research Laboratory at the Aberdeen Proving Ground of the United States Army. Technology typically advances when it is coupled with an urgent social need.

### *How High Tech Became Big Tech*

Enjoying a technological advantage usually translates into big profits for businesses and military superiority for countries. In the nineteenth century, gaining technological advantage was still inexpensive. It took only modest capital investment, a little knowledge about the best way to organize work, and a handful of highly trained workers to build a shop to manufacture stirrups or even steam engines. In contrast, mass-producing cars, sending people to outer space, and performing other feats of twentieth- and twenty-first century technology requires enormous capital investment, detailed attention to the way work is organized, and legions of technical experts. Add to this the intensely competitive business and geopolitical environment of the twentieth and twenty-first centuries, and you can readily understand why ever-larger sums have been invested in research and development over the past hundred years.

It was, in fact, already clear in the last quarter of the nineteenth century that turning scientific principles into technological innovations was going to require not just genius but also substantial resources, especially money and organization. Thus, Thomas Edison established the first "invention factory" at Menlo Park, New Jersey, in the late 1870s. Historian of science Robert Pool notes:

> *The most important factor in Edison's success—outside of his genius for invention—was the organization he had set up to assist him. By 1878, Edison had assembled at Menlo Park a staff of thirty scientists, metalworkers, glassblowers, draftsmen, and others working under his close direction and supervision. With such support, Edison boasted that he could turn out "a minor invention every ten days and a big thing every six months or so." (Pool, 1997: 22)*

The phonograph and the electric light bulb were two such "big things." Edison inspired both. Both, however, were also expensive team efforts, motivated by vast commercial possibilities. (Edison founded General Electric, the most profitable company in the world and the second most valuable based on market capitalization.)

At the beginning of the twentieth century, the scientific or engineering genius operating in isolation was only rarely able to contribute much to technological innovation. By mid-century, most technological innovation was organized along industrial lines. Entire armies of experts and vast sums of capital were required to run the new invention factories. The prototype of today's invention factory was the Manhattan Project, which built the nuclear bomb in the last years of World War II. By the time of Hiroshima, the manufacturing complex of the U.S. nuclear industry was about the same size as that of the U.S. automobile industry. The era of big science and big technology had arrived. Only governments and, increasingly, giant multinational corporations could afford to sustain the research effort of the second half of the twentieth century.

As the twentieth century ended, there seemed to be no limit to the amount that could be spent on research and development. During the twentieth century, the number of research scientists in North America increased a hundredfold. In the last 40 years of the century, research and development spending tripled, taking inflation into account. In that same period, industry's share of spending rose from one-third to two-thirds of the total while government's share dropped proportionately (Hobsbawm, 1994: 523; U.S. Department of Commerce, 1998: 609; Woodrow Federal Reserve Bank of Minneapolis, 2000; see Figure 11.1).

As a result of these developments, it should come as no surprise that military and profit-making considerations now govern the direction of most research and development. A reporter once asked bank robber Willie Sutton why he robbed banks. Sutton answered: "Because that's where the money is." This is hardly the only motivation prompting scientists and engineers to research particular topics. Personal interests, individual creativity, and the state of a field's intellectual development still influence the direction of inquiry. This is especially true for theoretical work done in universities, as opposed to applied research funded by governments and private industry. It would, however, be naive to think that practicality doesn't also enter the scientist's calculation of what he or she ought to study. Many researchers—even many of those who do theoretically driven research in universities—are pulled in particular directions by large research grants, well-paying jobs, access to expensive state-of-the-art equipment, and the possibility of winning patents and achieving commercial success. For example, many leading molecular biologists in North America have established genetic engineering companies, serve on their boards of directors, or receive research funding from them.

**Figure 11.1**
**Market Penetration by Years since Invention**

Because large multinational corporations now routinely invest astronomical sums in research and development to increase their chance of being the first to bring innovations to market, the time lag between new scientific discoveries and their technological application is continually shrinking.

■ Source: "The Silent Boom" (1998). Reprinted by permission of Forbes Magazine © 2006 Forbes Inc.

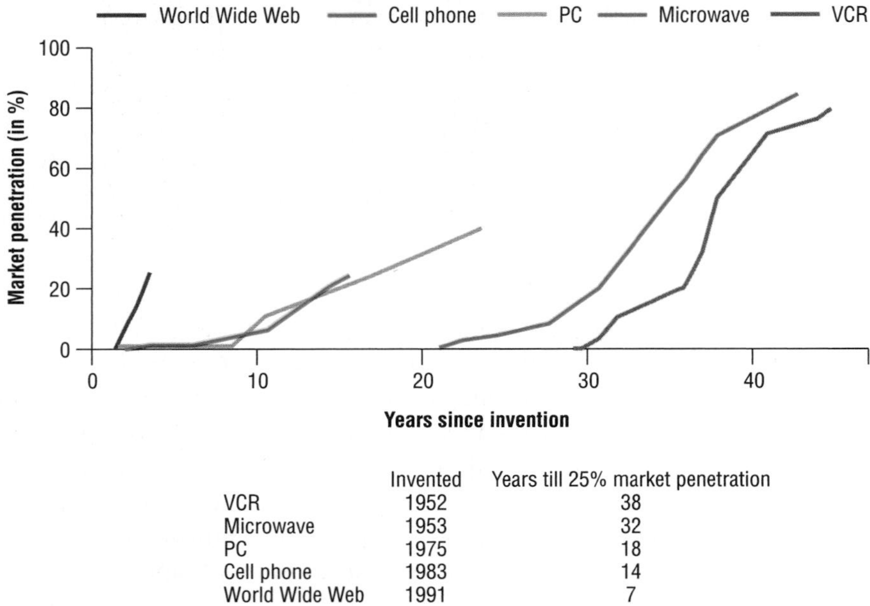


| | Invented | Years till 25% market penetration |
|---|---|---|
| VCR | 1952 | 38 |
| Microwave | 1953 | 32 |
| PC | 1975 | 18 |
| Cell phone | 1983 | 14 |
| World Wide Web | 1991 | 7 |

In not a few cases, major pharmaceutical and agrochemical corporations have bought out these companies because they see their vast profit potential (Rural Advancement Foundation International, 1999). Close to a majority of leading biotechnology scientists have industry affiliations (Rifkin, 1998: 56).

Economic lures, increasingly provided by the military and big corporations, have generated moral and political qualms among some researchers. Some scientists and engineers wonder whether work on particular topics achieves optimum benefits for

Research in biotechnology is big business. Close to a majority of leading biotechnology scientists have industry affiliations.

humanity. Certain researchers are troubled by the possibility that some scientific inquiries may be harmful to humankind. However, a growing number of scientists and engineers recognize that to do cutting-edge research, they must still any residual misgivings, hop on the bandwagon, and adhere to military and industrial requirements and priorities. That, after all, is where the money is.

## *Global Warming*

The side effect of technology that has given people the most serious cause for concern is environmental degradation, two aspects of which we now consider: global warming and genetic pollution.

Since the Industrial Revolution, humans have been burning increasing quantities of fossil fuels (coal, oil, gasoline, natural gas, etc.) to drive their cars, furnaces, and factories. Burning these fuels releases carbon dioxide into the atmosphere. The accumulation of carbon dioxide allows more solar radiation to enter the atmosphere and less heat to escape. This process contributes to **global warming,** a gradual increase in the world's average surface temperature. Figure 11.2 graphs the world's annual average surface air temperature and the concentration of carbon dioxide in the atmosphere from 1866 to 2004. The graph shows a warming trend that mirrors the increased concentration of carbon dioxide in the atmosphere. It also shows that the warming trend intensified sharply in the last third of the twentieth century. In the century between 1866 and 1965, average surface air temperature fluctuated from year to year but was almost the same at the end of the 100-year period as at the beginning. From 1966 to 2004, average surface air temperature rose at a rate of 1.76 degrees Celsius per century.

Most scientists believe global warming is already producing serious climatic change. As temperatures rise, more water evaporates. This causes more rainfall and bigger storms, which leads to more flooding and soil erosion, which in turn leads to less cultivable land. People suffer and die all along the causal chain.

Figure 11.3 graphs the worldwide dollar cost of damage because of "natural" disasters from 1970 to 2004. ("Natural" is in quotation marks because, as we have just seen, an increasingly large number of meteorological events are rendered extreme by human action.) Clearly, the damage caused by extreme meteorological events is on the upswing. This, however, may be only the beginning. It seems that global warming

**Figure 11.2**
**Average Air Temperature and Carbon Dioxide Level, 1866–2004**

Sources: Goddard Institute for Space Studies (2003, 2005); Karl and Trenberth (1999: 102); Quaschning (2003).

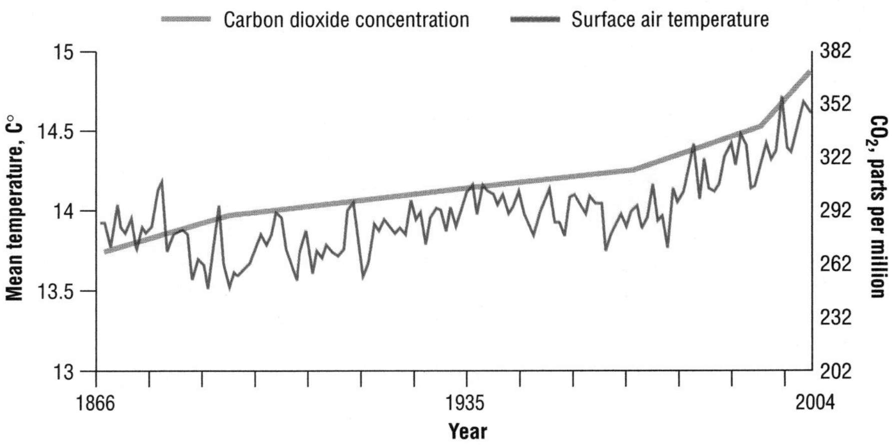

Because of global warming, glaciers are melting, the sea level is rising, and extreme weather events are becoming more frequent.

is causing the oceans to rise. That is partly because warmer water expands and partly because the partial melting of the polar ice caps puts more water in the oceans. In the twenty-first century, this may result in the flooding of some heavily populated coastal regions throughout the world. For instance, just a one-metre rise in the sea level would flood about 12 percent of the surface area of heavily populated Egypt and Bangladesh (Kennedy, 1993: 110).

### *Genetic Pollution*

**Genetic pollution** is the second main form of environmental degradation that we consider here. It refers to the health and ecological dangers that may result from artificially splicing genes together (Rifkin, 1998).

**Figure 11.3**
Worldwide Insured Losses Due to Natural and Human Catastrophes, 1970–2006 (in 2005 $US billions)

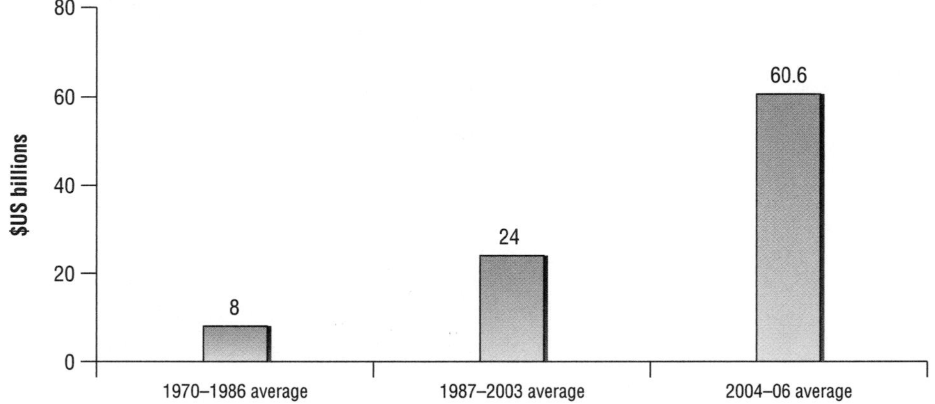


Sources: Swiss Re (2003: 8; 2004: 7; 2005: 5; 2007: 7); U.S. Department of Labor (2005).

Artificially splicing genes together may yield benefits as well as dangers. Woody Allen in *Sleeper* (1973).

The genetic information of all living things is coded in a chemical called DNA. When members of a species reproduce, the characteristics of the mates are naturally transmitted to their offspring through DNA. **Recombinant DNA,** in contrast, is a technique developed by molecular biologists in the last few decades. It involves removing a segment of DNA from a gene or splicing together segments of DNA from different living things, thus effectively creating a new life form. For example, scientists inserted the gene that makes fireflies sparkle at night into a tobacco plant. The offspring of the plant had leaves that glowed in the dark. Researchers inserted human growth hormone into a mouse embryo. This created mice that grew twice as big and twice as fast as ordinary mice. Biologists combined embryo cells from a sheep and a goat and placed them in the womb of a surrogate animal. The surrogate animal then gave birth to an entirely new species, half sheep, half goat.

These wonders of molecular biology were performed in the mid-1980s and helped to dramatize and publicize the potential of recombinant DNA. Since 1990, governments and corporations have been engaged in a multibillion-dollar international effort to create a complete genetic map of humans and various plants, micro-organisms, and animal species. With human and other genetic maps in hand, and by using recombinant DNA and related techniques, it is possible to design what some people regard as more useful animals and plants and superior humans. By 2000, scientists had identified the location and chemical structure of every one of the approximately 40 000 human genes. This will presumably enable them to understand the function of each gene. They can then detect and eliminate hereditary propensities to a wide range of diseases. Recombinant DNA will also enable farmers to grow disease- and frost-resistant crops with higher yields. It will allow miners to pour ore-eating microbes into mines, pump the microbes above ground after they have had their fill, and then separate out the ore. This will greatly reduce the cost and danger of mining. Recombinant DNA will allow companies to grow plants that produce cheap biodegradable plastic and micro-organisms that consume oil spills and absorb radioactivity. The potential health and economic benefits to humankind of these and many other applications of recombinant DNA are truly startling.

But so are the dangers that genetic pollution poses to human health and the stability of ecosystems (Rifkin, 1998: 67–115). For example, when a non-native organism enters a new environment, it usually adapts without a problem. Sometimes, however, it unexpectedly wreaks havoc. Now, however, the potential for ecological catastrophe has multiplied, because scientists are regularly testing genetically altered plants (effectively, non-native organisms) in the field. Some have gone commercial, and many more will soon be grown on a wide scale. These plants are resistant to insects, disease, and frost. However, once their pollen and seeds escape into the environment, weeds, insects, and micro-organisms will eventually build up resistance to the genes that resist herbicides, pests, and viruses. Thus, superbugs, superweeds, and superviruses will be born. We cannot predict the exact environmental consequences of these developments. That is why the insurance industry refuses to insure genetically engineered crops against the possibility of their causing catastrophic ecological damage.

Global warming and genetic pollution threaten everyone. However, as you will now see, the degree to which they are perceived as threatening depends on certain social conditions being met. Moreover, the threats are not evenly distributed in society.

# The Social Construction of Environmental Problems

Environmental problems do not become social issues spontaneously. Before they can enter the public consciousness, policy-oriented scientists, the environmental movement, the mass media, and respected organizations must discover and promote them. People have to connect real-life events to the information learned from these groups. Because some scientists, industrial interests, and politicians dispute the existence of environmental threats, the public can begin to question whether environmental issues are, in fact, social problems that require human intervention. We must not, then, think that environmental issues will inevitably be perceived as problematic. Rather, they are contested phenomena. They can be socially constructed by proponents, and they can be socially demolished by opponents (Hannigan, 1995).

The controversy over global warming is a good example of how people create and contest definitions of environmental problems (Gelbspan, 1999; Ungar, 1992, 1999). The theory of global warming was first proposed about a century ago but an elite group of scientists began serious research on the subject only in the late 1950s. They attracted no public attention until the 1970s, when the environmental movement emerged and gave new legitimacy and momentum to the scientific research and helped secure public funds for it. Respected and influential scientists now began to promote the issue of global warming. The mass media, always thirsting for sensational stories, were highly receptive to these efforts. Newspaper and television reports about the problem began to appear in the late 1970s and proliferated in the mid- to late 1980s.

The summer of 1988 brought the worst drought in half a century to North America. Respected organizations outside the scientific community, the mass media, and the environmental movement began expressing concern about the effects of global warming. By the early 1990s, public opinion polls showed that most North Americans with an opinion on the subject thought that using coal, oil, and gas contributes to global warming.

However, some industrialists, politicians, and scientists began to question whether global warming was, in fact, taking place. This group included Western coal and oil companies, the member states of the Organization of the Petroleum Exporting Countries (OPEC), other coal- and oil-exporting nations, and right-wing think-tanks, such as Canada's Fraser Institute in Vancouver, which is subsidized in part by major oil companies operating in Canada. "Bad scientific reporting, bad economics and bad judgement" is how the Fraser Institute summarized the analyses of those who regarded global warming as a serious issue requiring immediate action (Jones, 1997). Largely as a result of this onslaught, public concern about global warming began to falter.

Yet the evidence that global warming was substantial, dangerous, and caused by human activity continued to accumulate. In Canada, for example, ordinary people experienced firsthand ongoing drought on the Prairies, falling water levels in the Great Lakes, the melting of glaciers in the North, and the collapse of fish stocks on the east coast. In 2007, a large blue-ribbon panel of international climate experts issued a definitive report showing that global warming was real, dangerous, and stoppable through human intervention (Intergovernmental Panel on Climate Change, 2007). The public mood shifted again, and all of the country's political parties adopted "green" platforms that promised swift and effective action. We conclude that environmental issues become social problems only when social, political, and scientific circumstances allow them to be defined as such.

As you will now see, in addition to being socially defined, environmental problems are socially distributed. That is, environmental risks are greater for some groups than for others.

## *The Social Distribution of Risk*

You may have noticed that after a minor twister touches down on some unlucky community, TV reporters often rush to interview the surviving residents of trailer parks. The survivors stand amid the rubble that was their lives. They heroically remark on the generosity of their neighbours, their good fortune in still having their family intact, and our inability to fight nature's destructive forces. Why trailer parks? Small twisters aren't particularly attracted to them, but reporters are. That is because trailers are pretty flimsy in the face of a small tornado. They often suffer a lot of damage from twisters and therefore make a more sensational story than the minor damage typically inflicted on upper-middle-class homes with firmly shingled roofs and solid foundations. This is a general pattern. Whenever disaster strikes, economically and politically disadvantaged people almost always suffer most. That is because their circumstances render them most vulnerable. In fact, the advantaged often consciously put the disadvantaged in harm's way to avoid risk themselves. This is what is known as **environmental racism,** the tendency to heap environmental dangers on the disadvantaged and especially on disadvantaged racial minorities.

### The Canadian Case

Environmental racism is evident in Canada. For example, the uranium used to construct the atom bombs that were dropped on Hiroshima and Nagasaki came from Port Radium in the Northwest Territories, the world's first uranium mine. More than 30 Dene hunters and trappers were recruited from the nearby village of Deline to haul and barge 45-kilogram burlap sacks of the raw ore along a 2100 kilometre route to Fort McMurray, Alberta, for $3 a day. The American and Canadian governments had known about the dangers of exposure to uranium at least since 1931 (McClelland, 1931). Yet they withheld this information from the workers, who were completely unprotected from the ore's deadly radiation. In the surrounding community, the Dene ate fish from contaminated dredging ponds and hunted and camped in contaminated areas. Dene children played with ore dust at docks and landings. Dene women sewed tents from used uranium sacks. Until recent decades, cancer was unknown in the community. Elders often lived into their 90s. By 1998, however, nearly half the uranium workers had died of cancer while still in their 60s and 70s. Cancer and lung disease are alarmingly widespread in the community. Deline is known locally as "The Village of the Widows." Neither the workers nor their families have received any compensation from the government, not even an apology (Nikiforuk, 1998).

Broadly similar stories of environmental racism are legion. There is a disturbing association in Canada between level of contamination and the concentration of Aboriginal populations. Figure 11.4 illustrates this association. Using a broad measure of airborne pollution, it shows that where Aboriginal Canadians form a larger proportion of the population, the per capita weight of particulates in the air is heaviest.

Class also structures exposure to environmental risk in Canada. For example, Sydney, Nova Scotia, is a poor, working-class town with the highest rate of cancer of any city in Canada. The people who live around Frederick Street, the poorest part of Sydney, have the highest neighbourhood cancer rate in town. Skin ailments, birth defects, respiratory problems, diseases of the nervous system, and other medical conditions are also unusually common around Frederick Street. The main reason? Sydney was home to a large steel mill for a century. Waste from the mill poured into the so-called tar ponds, a 50-hectare site polluted to a depth of 24 metres with cancer-causing chemicals. Frederick Street borders the tar ponds. Sludge oozes into people's basements, pervades their vegetable gardens, and runs in open streams where children play. Billions of federal and provincial tax dollars have been spent subsidizing the steel mill that is the source of the problem. Yet neither government nor private industry has ever done anything to clean up the scandalous mess (Barlow and May, 2000: 144).

**Figure 11.4**
**Environmental Racism in Canada**

Note: The data are for 1995.

■ Sources: Statistics Canada (2000a, 2000b); U.S. Environmental Protection Agency, Office of Air Quality Planning and Standards (2000).

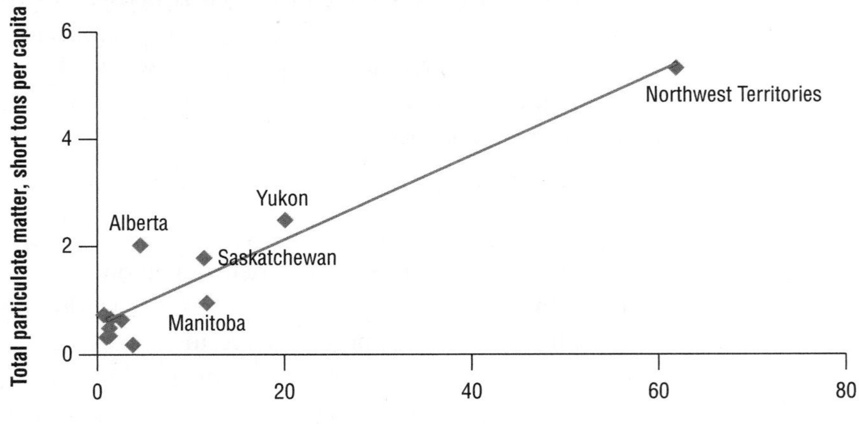

Canada's biggest toxic dump is in Sydney, Nova Scotia, where waste from 100 years of nearly unregulated steel production has created the infamous Sydney tar ponds. Containing 700 000 tonnes of toxic sludge in close proximity to residential neighbourhoods, the Sydney tar ponds are widely regarded as the second-worst toxic site in North America.

## The Less Developed Countries

What is true for disadvantaged classes and racial groups in North America also holds for the less developed countries. The underprivileged face more environmental dangers than the privileged (Kennedy, 1993: 95–121). Mexico, Brazil, China, India, and other southern countries are industrializing rapidly. That puts tremendous strain on their natural resources. Rising demand for water, electricity, fossil fuels, and consumer products is creating more polluted rivers, dead lakes, and industrial waste sites. At a quickening pace, rain forests, grazing land, cropland, and wetlands are giving way to factories, roads, airports, and housing complexes. Smog-blanketed megacities continue to sprawl. Eighteen of the world's 21 biggest cities are in less developed countries.

Given the picture sketched above, it should be unsurprising that, on average, people in less developed countries are more concerned about the environment than people in rich countries are (Brechin and Kempton, 1994). However, the developing countries cannot afford much in the way of pollution control, so anti-pollution regulations are lax by North American, Western European, and Japanese standards. This state of affairs is an incentive for some multinational corporations to situate some of their foulest operations in the Southern Hemisphere. It is also the reason that the industrialization of the less developed countries is proving so punishing to the environment. When car ownership grows from, say, 5 percent to 20 percent of the population in China, and when 50 million or 75 million Indians with motor scooters upgrade to cars, the result will be a choking mess. China and India have few regulations phasing in the use of technologies that save energy and pollute less.

For the time being, however, the rich countries do most of the world's environmental damage. That is because their inhabitants earn and consume more than the inhabitants of less developed countries. How much more? The richest fifth of humanity earns about 80 times as much as the poorest fifth (up from 30 times as much in 1950). In the past half-century, the richest fifth doubled its per capita consumption of energy, meat, timber, steel, and copper, and quadrupled its car ownership. In that same period, the per capita consumption of the poorest fifth hardly changed. The United States has only 4.5 percent of the world's population, but it uses about 25 percent of the Earth's resources. And it produces more than 20 percent of global emissions of carbon dioxide, the pollutant responsible for about half of global warming. Thus, the inhabitants of the Northern Hemisphere cause a disproportionately large share of the world's environmental problems, enjoy a disproportionate share of the benefits of technology, and live with fewer environmental risks than people in the Southern Hemisphere.

### Inequality and Biotechnology

Social inequalities are also apparent in the field of biotechnology. For instance, the large multinational companies that dominate the pharmaceutical, seed, and agrochemical industries now routinely send anthropologists, biologists, and agronomists to all corners of the world. There they take samples of wild plants, the crops people grow, and human blood. They hope to find genetic material with commercial value in agriculture and medicine. If they discover genes with commercial value, the company they work for patents the discovery. This gives them the exclusive legal right to manufacture and sell the genetic material without compensating the donors. Thus, Indian farmers and then scientists worked for a hundred generations discovering, skillfully selecting, cultivating, and developing techniques for processing the neem tree, which has powerful antibacterial and pesticidal properties. However, a giant corporation based in the United States (W. R. Grace) became the sole commercial beneficiary of their labour. Monsanto (U.S.), Novartis (Switzerland), GlaxoSmithKline (UK), and other prominent companies in the life sciences call this "protection of intellectual property." Indigenous people and their advocates throughout the world call it "biopiracy" (Rifkin, 1998: 37–66).

Finally, consider the possible consequences of people having their babies genetically engineered. This should be possible on a wide scale in 10 or 20 years. Free of inherited diseases and physical abnormalities, and perhaps genetically programmed to enjoy superior intellectual and athletic potential, these children would, in effect, speed up and improve the slow and imperfect process of natural evolution. That, at least, is the rosy picture sketched by proponents of the technology. In practice, because only the well-to-do are likely to be able to afford fully genetically engineered babies, the new technology could introduce an era of increased social inequality and low social mobility. Only the economically underprivileged would bear a substantial risk of genetic inferiority.

## What Is to Be Done?

### *The Market and High-Tech Solutions*

Some people believe the environmental crisis will resolve itself. More precisely, they think we already have two weapons that will work together to end the crisis: the market and high technology. The case of oil illustrates how these weapons can combine forces. If oil reserves drop or oil is withheld from the market for political reasons, the price of oil goes up. This makes it worthwhile for oil exploration companies to develop new technologies to recover more oil. When they discover more oil and bring it to market, prices fall back to where they were. Generalizing these experiences and projecting them into the future, optimists believe global warming, industrial pollution, and other

forms of environmental degradation will be dealt with similarly. In their view, human inventiveness and the profit motive will combine to create the new technologies we need to survive and prosper.

Some evidence supports this optimistic scenario. For example, following the oil shocks of 1973 (when prices tripled) and 1978–79 (when prices tripled again), new discoveries were made and new efficiencies were implemented so oil reserves grew and prices fell. In recent years, we have adopted new technologies to combat some of the worst excesses of environmental degradation. For example, we have replaced brain-damaging leaded gas with unleaded gas. We have developed environmentally friendly refrigerants and stopped the production of ozone-destroying CFCs. In a model of international cooperation, rich countries have even subsidized the cost of replacing CFCs in the developing countries. Efficient windmills and solar panels are now common. More factories are equipped with high-tech pollution-control devices, preventing dangerous chemicals from seeping into the air and water. We have introduced cost-effective ways to recycle metal, plastic, paper, and glass. New methods are being developed for eliminating carbon dioxide emissions from the burning of fossil fuels. We can now buy hybrid cars.

However, three factors suggest market forces cannot solve environmental problems on their own:

1. Imperfect price signals. *The price of many commodities does not reflect their actual cost to society. Gasoline costs about a dollar a litre at the time of this writing. But the social cost, including the cost of repairing the environmental damage caused by burning the gas, is four times that. Because of many such price distortions, the market often fails to send signals that might result in the speedy adoption of technological and policy fixes.*
2. The slow pace of change. *Our efforts so far to deal with the environmental consequences of rapid technological change are just not good enough. For example, global warming continues to accelerate, partly because automobile use is increasing as public transportation ridership declines and standards on automobile emissions remain weak. All of the world's renewable resources are in decline (see Figure 11.5).*

**Figure 11.5**
**Renewable Resources, World, Percentage Change, 1990–2010 (projected)**

Source: Postel (1994: 11).

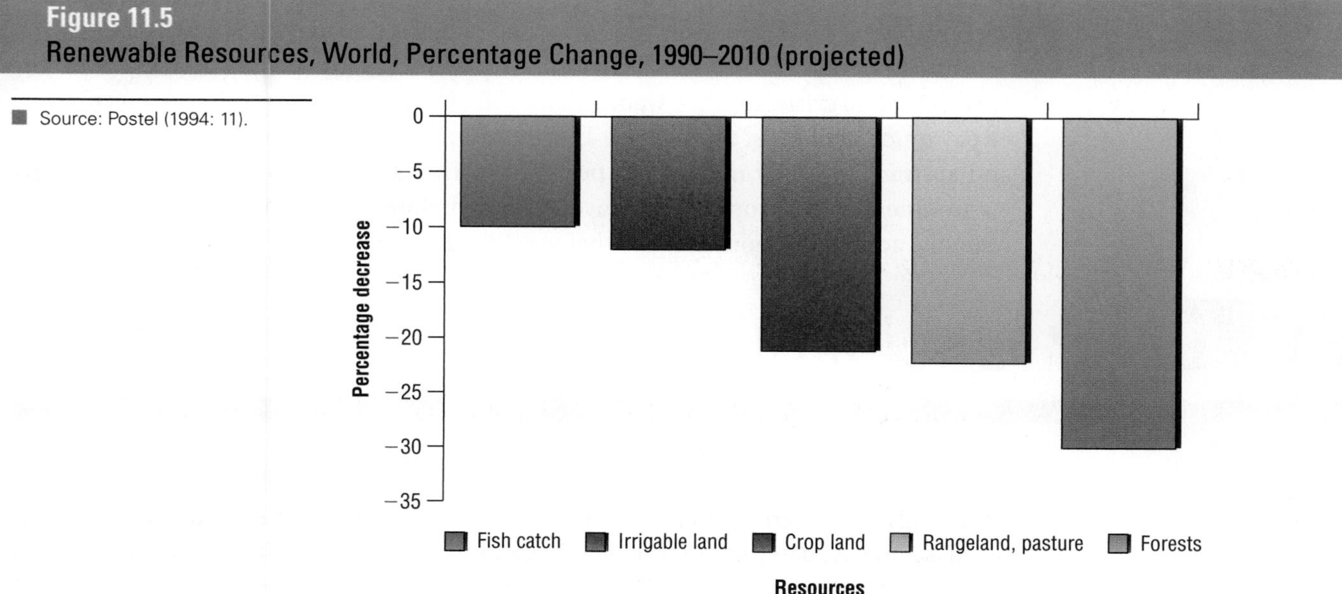

3. **The importance of political pressure.** *Political pressure exerted by environmental activists, community groups, and public opinion is often necessary to motivate corporate and government action on environmental issues. For instance, organizations like Greenpeace have successfully challenged the practices of logging companies, whalers, the nuclear industry, and other groups engaged in environmentally dangerous practices. Without the efforts of such organizations, it is doubtful many environmental issues would be defined as social problems by corporations and governments.*

### The Cooperative Alternative

The alternative to the market and high-tech approach involves people cooperating to reduce greatly their overconsumption of just about everything. This strategy includes investing heavily in energy-saving technologies, environmental cleanup, and subsidized, environmentally friendly industrialization in the developing countries. It would require renewed commitment to voluntary efforts, new laws and enforcement bodies to ensure compliance, increased environmentally related research and development by industry and government, more environmentally directed foreign aid, and new taxes (Livernash and Rodenburg, 1998). In addition, a cooperative strategy entails careful assessment of all the risks associated with biotechnology projects and consultation with the public before such projects are allowed to go forward. Profits from genetic engineering would also have to be shared equitably with donors of genetic material.

Is the solution realistic? Not in the short term. It would be political suicide for anyone in the rich countries to propose the drastic measures listed above. Not too many Canadian drivers would be happy paying $4 a litre for gas, for example. For the solution to be politically acceptable, the broad public in North America, Western Europe, and Japan must be aware of the gravity of the environmental problem and be willing to make substantial economic sacrifices to get the job done.

Survey data suggest that nearly all Canadians are aware of the environmental problem and are doing something about it. For instance, in 2006, sorting and recycling programs for glass, cans, plastic, and paper were available to about 90 percent of Canadians, 95 percent of whom used them. However, it seems that we are in general prepared to act only when it doesn't inconvenience us much. When asked to indicate their main ways of getting to work, 81 percent of Canadians said they usually go by motor vehicle and 17 percent said they usually take public transit, cycle, or walk (Statistics Canada, 2006h: 52, 62).

Other surveys reveal much the same pattern. Many people know about the environmental crisis, say they want it dealt with, but are unwilling to be inconvenienced or pay much of the cost themselves. They regard environmental problems as too remote and abstract to justify making big personal sacrifices. It follows that more and bigger environmental catastrophes may have to occur before more people are willing to take remedial action. The good news is that we still have time to act.

## Social Movements

We noted above that governments and corporations are inclined to act on environmental issues only if they are pressured to do so by the public. But under what circumstances do many individuals engage in **collective action,** working in unison to bring about or resist social, political, and economic change by means of demonstrations, strikes, riots, and the like? And under what circumstances is collective action turned into a **social movement,** an enduring collective attempt to change or resist change to part or all of society by establishing organizations, lobbies, unions, and political parties?

Answers to these questions are unclear, as Robert Brym learned in grade 11: "One day in chemistry class I learned that water combined with sulphur dioxide produces sulphurous acid. The news shocked me. To understand why, you have to know that I lived in Saint John, New Brunswick, about 100 metres downwind of one of the largest pulp and paper mills in Canada. Waves of sulphur dioxide billowed from the mill's smokestacks day and night. The town's pervasive rotten-egg smell was a long-standing complaint in the area. But, for me, disgust turned to upset when I realized the fumes were toxic. Suddenly it was clear why many people I knew—especially people living near the mill—woke up in the morning with a kind of 'smoker's cough.' Through the simple act of breathing we were causing the gas to mix with the moisture in our bodies and form an acid that our lungs tried to expunge, with only partial success.

"Twenty years later, I read the results of a medical research report showing that area residents suffered from rates of lung disease, including emphysema and lung cancer, significantly above the North American average. But even in 1968 it was evident my hometown had a serious problem. I therefore hatched a plan. Our high school was about to hold its annual model parliament. The event was notoriously boring, partly because, year in year out, virtually everyone voted for the same party, the Conservatives. But here was an issue, I thought, that could turn things around. A local man, K. C. Irving, owned the pulp and paper mill. *Forbes* magazine ranked him as one of the richest men in the world. I figured that when I told my fellow students what I had discovered, they would quickly demand the closure of the mill until Irving guaranteed a clean operation.

"Was *I* naive. As head of the tiny Liberal Party, I had to address the entire student body during assembly on election day to outline the party platform and rally votes. When I got to the part of my speech that explained why Irving was our enemy, the murmuring in the audience, which had been growing like the sound of a hungry animal about to pounce on its prey, erupted into loud "boos." A couple of students rushed the stage. The principal suddenly appeared from the wings and commanded the student body to settle down. He then took me by the arm and informed me that, for my own safety, my speech was finished. So, I discovered on election day, was our high school's Liberal Party. And so, it emerged, was my high-school political career.

"This incident troubled me for years, partly because of the embarrassment it caused, partly because of the puzzles it presented. Why didn't my fellow students rebel in the way I thought they would? Why did they continue to support an arrangement that was enriching one man at the cost of a community's health? Couldn't they see the injustice? I didn't know it at the time, but to answer such questions, it is necessary to turn to the literature on social movements."

### *Breakdown Theory: A Functionalist Account*

Until about 1970, most sociologists believed that two conditions must be met for social movements to form:

1. Social marginality. *The early leaders of social movements and their first recruits must be poorly integrated in society. Without such socially marginal people, social movements supposedly cannot form.*

**Figure 11.6**
**Relative Deprivation Theory**

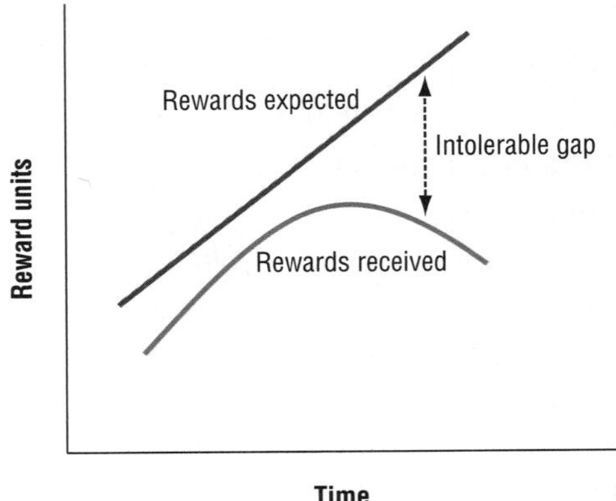


2. Strain. *People's norms must be strained or disrupted. For example, one of the most popular variants of breakdown theory is relative deprivation theory.* ***Relative deprivation*** *refers to the growth of an intolerable gap between the social rewards people expect to receive and those they actually receive. (Social rewards are widely valued goods, such as money, education, security, prestige, and so forth.) Supposedly, people are most likely to form social movements when the gap between rising expectations (brought on by, say, rapid economic growth and migration) and the receipt of social rewards (sometimes lowered by economic recession or war) becomes intolerable (Davies, 1969; Gurr, 1970; see Figure 11.6)*

Following sociologist Charles Tilly and his associates, we can group these two conditions together as the **breakdown theory** of collective action. That is because both conditions assume that social movements result from the disruption or breakdown of previously integrative social structures and norms (Tilly, Tilly, and Tilly, 1975: 4–6). At a more abstract level, breakdown theory can be seen as a variant of functionalism because it regards collective action as a form of social imbalance that results from the improper functioning of social institutions.

Can breakdown theory adequately account for the crystallization of social movements? The short answer is no. Since 1970, sociologists have uncovered two main flaws in the theory. First, research shows that in most cases, leaders and early joiners of social movements are well-integrated members of their community, not socially marginal outsiders (Brym, 1980; Lipset, 1971). Second, researchers have found that high levels of relative deprivation are generally not associated with the crystallization of social movements. That is because certain social conditions can prevent people from translating their discontent into an enduring social movement with a more or less stable membership, hired office personnel, a publicity bureau, a regularly published newsletter, and the like (McPhail, 1994; Tilly et al., 1975; Torrance, 1986: 115–45). We now consider those social conditions.

## *Solidarity Theory: A Conflict Approach*

**Solidarity theory** is a type of conflict theory that focuses on the social conditions that allow people to turn their discontent into a unified (or "solidary") political force. It identifies three such social conditions: adequate resource mobilization, sufficient political opportunity, and weak or inconsistent social control.

## Resource Mobilization

Most collective action is part of a power struggle. The struggle usually intensifies as groups whose members feel disadvantaged become more powerful relative to other groups. How do disadvantaged groups become more powerful? By gaining new members, becoming better organized, and increasing their access to scarce resources, such as money, jobs, and means of communication (Bierstedt, 1974). **Resource mobilization** is the process by which groups engage in more collective action as their power increases because of their growing size and increasing organizational, material, and other resources (Jenkins, 1983; Zald and McCarthy, 1979).

Consider the effect of resource mobilization on the frequency of strikes in Canada. Research shows that in Canada between the mid-1940s and the mid-1970s, strike frequency was high when (1) unemployment was low, (2) union membership was high, and (3) governments were generous in their provision of social welfare benefits. *Low unemployment* indicates a strong economy. Workers are inclined to strike when business activity is robust because in such conditions they accumulate healthy strike funds, enjoy many alternative job opportunities, and know that employers and governments can afford to make concessions (employers make bigger profits and governments collect more taxes during economic booms). *A high level of unionization* is conducive to more strike activity because unions provide workers with leadership, strike funds, and coordination. Finally, *generous government benefits* give workers an economic buffer and thus increase their readiness to strike. Thus, as resource mobilization theory suggests, strong social ties among workers (as indicated by a high level of unionization) and access to jobs and money (as indicated by a booming economy and generous government benefits) increase challenges to authority (as indicated by strikes).

Figure 11.7 shows the pattern of strike activity in Canada between 1946 and 2000. It adds substance to the resource mobilization approach. Until 1974, the trend in strike activity was upward. This was a period of growing prosperity, low unemployment, expanding state benefits, and increasing unionization. With access to increasing organizational and material resources, workers challenged authority increasingly more often in the three decades after World War II. In 1973, however, economic crisis struck. As a result of war and revolution in the Middle East, oil prices tripled, and then tripled again

**Figure 11.7**
**Weighted Frequency of Strikes, Canada, 1946–2000**

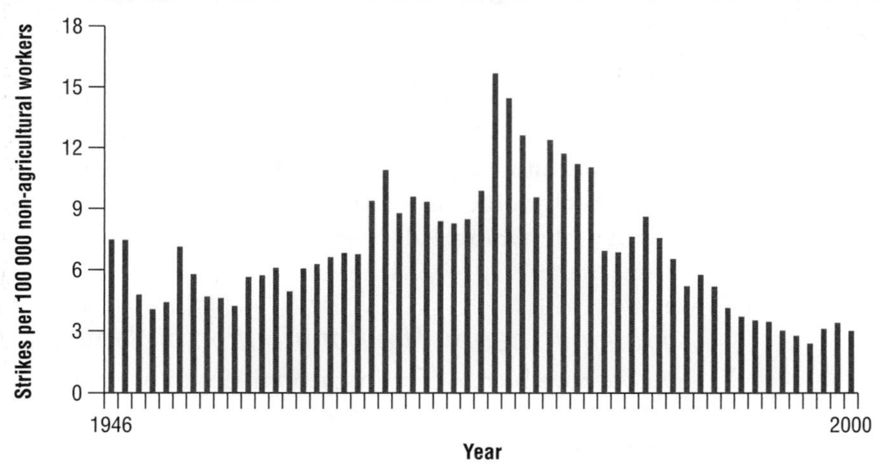


■ Sources: "Chronological Perspective on Work Stoppage in Canada" (1999, 2001); "Chronological Perspective on Work Stoppages in Canada (Work Stoppages Involving One or More Workers), 1976–2000" (2001); *Labour Organizations in Canada 1972* (1973: xxii–xxiii); *1994–1995 Directory of Labour Organizations in Canada* (1995: xiii); *1998 Directory of Labour Organizations in Canada* (1998: 15); *Strikes and Lockouts in Canada 1968* (1970: 12–13); *Strikes and Lockouts in Canada 1985* (1985: 9); Workplace Information Directorate (1996).

at the end of the decade. Inflation increased and unemployment rose. Soon, the government was strapped for funds and had to borrow heavily to maintain social welfare programs. Eventually, the debt burden was so heavy the government felt obliged to cut various social welfare programs. At the same time, federal and provincial governments introduced laws and regulations limiting the right of some workers to strike and putting a cap on the wage gains that workers could demand. The percentage of Canadian workers who belonged to unions began to decline. Strike action was made even more difficult when Canada signed free trade deals with the United States in 1988 and Mexico in 1994. It was now possible for employers to threaten to relocate in the United States or Mexico in the face of protracted strikes. Thus, in the post-1973 climate, the organizational and material resources of workers fell. As a result, strike activity plummeted. In 2000, the frequency of strikes per 100 000 Canadian non-agricultural workers was less than 20 percent that of 1974 (Brym, 2003).

### Political Opportunities

A second social condition that allows mass discontent to be translated into social movement formation involves the emergence of new **political opportunities** (McAdam, 1982; Piven and Cloward, 1977; Tarrow, 1994). Specifically, chances for protest and social movement formation emerge when influential allies offer support, when ruling political alignments become unstable, when elite groups are divided and come into conflict with one another, and when election campaigns provide a focus for discontent and a chance to put new representatives with new policies in positions of authority (Tarrow, 1994: 86–9; Useem, 1998). Said differently, collective action takes place and social movements crystallize not just when disadvantaged groups become more powerful but also when privileged groups and the institutions they control are divided and therefore become weaker. As economist John Kenneth Galbraith once said about the weakness of the Russian ruling class at the time of the 1917 revolution, if someone manages to kick in a rotting door, some credit has to be given to the door.

### Social Control

The third main lesson of solidarity theory is that government reactions to protests influence subsequent protests (see Box 11.1). Specifically, governments can try to lower the frequency and intensity of protest by taking various *social control* measures (Oberschall, 1973: 242–83). These measures include making concessions to protesters, co-opting the most troublesome leaders (for example, by appointing them advisers), and violently repressing collective action. Note, however, that social control measures do not always have the desired effect. If grievances are very deeply felt, and yielding to protesters' demands greatly increases their hopes, resources, and political opportunities, government concessions may encourage protesters to press their claims further. And although the firm and decisive use of force usually stops protest, using force moderately or inconsistently often backfires. That is because unrest typically intensifies when protesters are led to believe that the government is weak or indecisive (Piven and Cloward, 1977: 27–36; Tilly et al., 1975: 244).

## *Framing Theory: The Contribution of Symbolic Interactionism*

As we have seen, solidarity theory helps to overcome the flaws in breakdown theory. Still, the rise of a social movement sometimes takes strict solidarity theorists by surprise. So does the failure of an aggrieved group to press its claims by means of collective

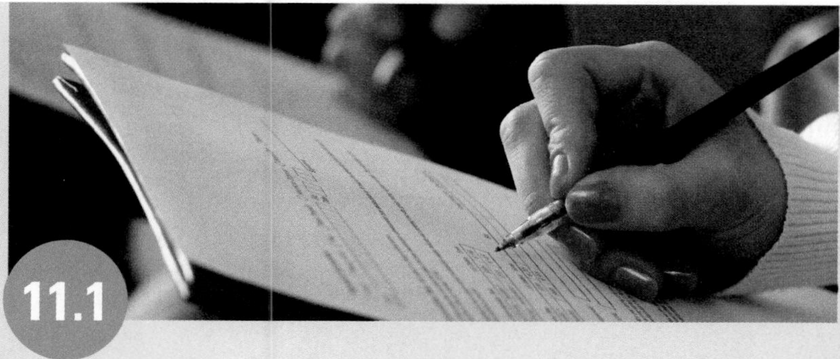

11.1

# SOCIAL POLICY: WHAT DO YOU THINK?

## State Surveillance of Demonstrations

On 15 June 2000, members of the Ontario Coalition Against Poverty (OCAP) organized a demonstration of about 1000 people in front of the provincial legislature at Queen's Park to protest the policies of Mike Harris's Progressive Conservative government toward the poor and homeless. It didn't take long before a violent confrontation developed between protesters and the police. Gary Morton, one of the demonstrators, described the events as follows:

> An angry crowd of protesters, most of them wearing clothing to protect them from chemical attack by police, marches across the city to the legislature at Queen's Park. They make noise, bang drums and chant. When they arrive, huge numbers of riot police meet them. . . . The protesters send a delegation to the barricades at the front. Their demand—that they be allowed to address the legislature on homeless issues. The response is that no such thing will be allowed and no representative of the Harris Government will be speaking to them. The delegation informs the crowd of this and they surge forward to [the] barricades. . . . The people at the front grab the barricades and walk backward with them, opening a hole for the crowd to get through. Then all hell breaks loose. Gas smoke rolls and police charge out swinging batons. Some protesters struggle with them and others throw a few things like small water bottles. Horseback cops follow up, riding in from the north to force the crowd back and then swinging back in from the south. Between the horse sweeps the riot cops charge out and then get pushed back in. The police slowly gain ground. People are being picked off and beaten and cops begin to charge viciously into the larger body of peaceful protesters. At this point many people, myself included, begin to throw anything they can at the police. Bottles of water, mud and stones from the garden, picket signs. Brutality increases; anarchists tear apart a sidewalk and throw the chunks of stone at police. Horse charges swing in through the grassy area of the park and as the fight continues for some time we get forced out on the road, which we block. . . . The police are now saying that they are going to review their videos frame by frame. (Morton, 2000)

The videos to which Morton refers came from seven cameras police set up to record the demonstration. In addition, police had a still photographer and several plainclothes officers with disposable cameras on duty. Two cameras belonging to Queen's Park security officers were also rolling during the melee. Finally, after the demonstration, the police seized film and videotape of the demonstration from television networks and newspapers.

What effect might police surveillance of demonstrations have on collective action? In the first place, if journalists fear their film and videos might be seized, they may be less likely to produce objective news reports. For example, a journalist might be disinclined to film a demonstrator being beaten by the police knowing that the film could be edited and used to identify and prosecute the demonstrator (Canadian Journalists for Free Expression, 2000). Moreover, according to sociologist Gary Marx, surveillance systems can be "used against those with the 'wrong' political beliefs; against racial, ethnic, or religious minorities; and against those with lifestyles that offend the majority" (quoted in Boal, 1998). One journalist comments: "Social psychologists say that taping political events can affect a participant's self-image, since being surveilled is unconsciously associated with criminality. Ordinary citizens shy away from politics when they see activists subjected to scrutiny. As this footage is splayed across the nightly news, everyone gets the meta-message: hang with dissenters and you'll end up in a police video" (Boal, 1998). In short, police surveillance of demonstrations can limit dissent and the free expression of political opinion.

### CRITICAL THINKING QUESTIONS

- *In the interest of maintaining law and order, should the police be entirely free to record demonstrations by using cameras? Should they be allowed to seize film and videos from journalists?*
- *Do such actions infringe the fundamental democratic rights of both the media and the citizenry?*

action. It seems, therefore, that something lies between (1) the capacity of disadvantaged people to mobilize resources for collective action, and (2) the recruitment of a substantial number of movement members. That "something" is **frame alignment** (Benford, 1997; Goffman, 1974; Snow, Rochford Jr., Worden, and Benford, 1986). Frame alignment is the process by which social movement leaders make their activities, ideas, and goals congruent with the interests, beliefs, and values of potential new recruits to their movement—or fail to do so. Thanks to the efforts of scholars operating mainly in the symbolic interactionist tradition, frame alignment has recently become the subject of sustained sociological investigation.

## Types of Frame Alignment

Frame alignment can be encouraged in several ways:

1. *Social movement leaders can reach out to other organizations that, they believe, contain people who may be sympathetic to their movement's cause. Thus, leaders of an anti-nuclear movement may use the mass media, telephone campaigns, and direct mail to appeal to feminist, anti-racist, and environmental organizations. In doing so, they assume these organizations are likely to have members who would agree, at least in general terms, with the anti-nuclear platform.*
2. *Movement activists can stress popular values that have so far not featured prominently in the thinking of potential recruits. They can also elevate the importance of positive beliefs about the movement and what it stands for. For instance, in trying to win new recruits, movement members might emphasize the seriousness of the social movement's purpose. They might analyze the causes of the problem the movement is trying to solve in a clear and convincing way. Or they might stress the likelihood of the movement's success. By doing so, they can increase the movement's appeal to potential recruits and perhaps win them over to the cause.*

The Live 8 concert in Barrie, Ontario, July 2005, featured Bruce Cockburn, Kevin Hearn of the Barenaked Ladies, Neil Young, Gordon Lightfoot, and many other Canadian rock stars. When bands play at protest rallies or festivals, it is not just for entertainment and not just because the music is relevant to the social movement's goals. The bands also attract non-members to the movement. This is one way of framing a social movement's goals to make them appealing to non-members.

and the level of unionization were among the lowest of any state or province in North America. The unemployment rate was among the highest. In contrast, K. C. Irving, who owned the pulp and paper mill, was so powerful that most people in the region could not even conceive of the need to rebel against the conditions of life he created for them. He owned most of the industrial establishments in the province. Every daily newspaper, most of the weeklies, all of the TV stations, and most of the radio stations were his, too. Little wonder anyone rarely heard a critical word about his operations. Many people believed that Irving could make or break local governments single-handedly. Should we therefore be surprised that mere high-school students refused to take him on? In their reluctance, Robert's fellow students were only mimicking their parents, who, on the whole, were as powerless as Irving was mighty (Brym, 1979).

Second, many of Robert's classmates did not share his sense of injustice. Most of them regarded Irving as the great provider. They thought his pulp and paper mill, as well as his myriad other industrial establishments, gave many people jobs. They regarded that fact as more important for their lives and the lives of their families than the pollution problem Robert raised. Frame alignment theory suggests Robert needed to figure out ways to build bridges between their understanding and his. He did not. Therefore, he received an unsympathetic hearing (see Box 11.3).

11.3

## YOU AND THE SOCIAL WORLD

### Organizing for Change

Try applying solidarity and frame alignment theories to times when *you* felt a deep sense of injustice against an institution, such as a school, an organization, a company, or a government.

**CRITICAL THINKING QUESTIONS**

- *Did you do anything about your upset? If not, why not? If so, what did you do? Why were you able to act in the way you did?*
- *Did you try to get other people to join you in your action? If not, why not? If so, how did you manage to recruit them? Did you reach the goal you set out to achieve? If not, why not? If so, what enabled you to succeed?*
- *Write a 500-word essay answering these questions. If you've never been involved in collective action to correct a perceived injustice, analyze a movie about collective action by using insights gleaned from solidarity and frame alignment theories. Classics include* Norma Rae *(1979), in which Sally Field plays a textile worker who helps a labour organizer unionize her mill; and* Matewan *(1987), which shows how employers prevented workers from organizing in the 1920s by fomenting racial and ethnic conflict among them. Alternatively, see* North Country *(2005), starring Charlize Theron, which tells the true story of Lois Jenson, a mineworker who, against much resistance, lodged a successful sexual harassment suit against Eveleth Mines.*

# New Social Movements

We can now turn to this chapter's final goal: sketching the prospects of social movements in broad, rapid strokes.

Between 1700 and the 1950s, social movements became larger and generally less violent, and they extended their focus from local to national issues. Often, they struggled to expand the rights of citizens, fighting at first for the right to free speech, freedom of religion, and justice before the law; next for the right to vote and run for office; and then, in the twentieth century, for the right to a certain minimum level of economic security and full participation in social life (Marshall, 1965; Tilly, 1979a, 1979b). In the 1960s, so-called "new social movements" set still broader goals, attracted new kinds of participants, and became global in scope (Melucci, 1980, 1995). Let us consider each of these issues in turn.

## Goals

Some new social movements promote the rights not of specific groups but of humanity as a whole to peace, security, and a clean environment. Such movements include the peace movement, the environmental movement, and the human rights movement. Other

In medieval Europe, social movements were small, localized, and violent. This painting depicts a spontaneous uprising against the nobility in the Beauvais region of France in the mid-fourteenth century.

new social movements, such as the women's movement and the gay rights movement, promote the rights of particular groups that have been excluded from full social participation. Accordingly, gay rights groups have fought for laws that eliminate all forms of discrimination based on sexual orientation. They have also fought for the repeal of laws that discriminate on the basis of sexual orientation, such as anti-sodomy laws and laws that negatively affect parental custody of children (Adam, Duyvendak, and Krouwel, 1999). Since the 1960s, the women's movement has succeeded in getting admission practices altered in professional schools, winning more freedom of reproductive choice for women, and opening up opportunities for women in the political, religious, military, educational, medical, and business systems (Adamson, Briskin, and McPhail, 1988). The emergence of the peace, environmental, human rights, gay rights, and women's movements involves the extension of citizenship rights to all adult members of society and to society as a whole (Roche, 1995; Turner, 1986: 85–105).

### Membership

New social movements are also novel in that they attract a disproportionately large number of highly educated, relatively well-to-do people from the social, educational, and cultural fields. Such people include teachers, professors, journalists, social workers, artists, actors, writers, and student apprentices to these occupations. For several reasons, people in these occupations are more likely to participate in new social movements than are people in other occupations. Their higher education exposes them to radical ideas and makes those ideas appealing. They tend to hold jobs outside the business community, which often opposes their values. And they often become personally involved in the problems of their clients and audiences, sometimes even becoming their advocates (Brint, 1984; Rootes, 1995).

### Globalization Potential

Finally, new social movements increase the scope of protest beyond the national level. For example, members of the peace movement viewed federal laws banning nuclear weapons as necessary. Environmentalists felt the same way about federal laws protecting the environment. However, environmentalists also recognized that the condition of the Brazilian rain forest affects climatic conditions worldwide. Similarly, peace activists understood that the spread of weapons of mass destruction could destroy all of humanity. Therefore, members of the peace and environmental movements pressed for *international* agreements binding all countries to protect the environment and stop the spread of nuclear weapons. Social movements went global.

Since 1994, protests have been staged wherever major international trade talks have been held. For example, when the Summit of the Americas took place in Quebec City in April 2001, more than 20 000 protesters took to the streets. They catapulted teddy bears, smoke bombs, and rocks at riot police and at one point breached the chain-link security fence surrounding the summit. Police responded with tear gas, water cannons, rubber bullets, and arrests.

Inexpensive international travel and communication facilitate the globalization of social movements. New technologies make it easier for people in various national movements to work with like-minded activists in other countries. In the age of CNN, inexpensive jet transportation, fax machines, Web sites, and e-mail, it is possible not only to see the connection between apparently local problems and their global sources but also to act both locally and globally (see Box 11.4).

Consider the case of Greenpeace. Greenpeace is a highly successful environmental movement that originated in Vancouver in the mid-1970s. It now has offices in 41 countries, with its international office in Amsterdam. Among many other initiatives, it has mounted a campaign to eliminate the international transportation and dumping of toxic wastes. Its representatives visited local environmental groups in African and other developing countries. They supplied the Africans with organizing kits to help them tie their local concerns to global political efforts. They also published a newsletter to keep activists up to date on legal issues. Thus, Greenpeace coordinated a global campaign that enabled weak environmental organizations in developing countries to act more effectively. Their campaign also raised the costs of continuing the international trade in toxic waste.

11.4

## MASS MEDIA AND SOCIETY

Subcomandante Marcos

### The First Postmodern Revolution

An example of a social movement using modern technology to go global involves the peasants of Chiapas, a southern Mexican province. They participated in the 1910 Mexican Revolution and in a more globalized uprising against the Mexican government in 1994. Oppressed by Europeans and their descendants for nearly 500 years, the poor, indigenous people of southern Mexico were now facing a government edict preventing them from gaining access to farmland. They wanted the land for subsistence agriculture. But the government wanted to make sure the land stayed in the hands of large, Hispanic ranchers and farmers, who could earn foreign revenue by exporting goods to the United States and Canada under the terms of the new North American Free Trade Agreement. The peasants seized a large number of ranches and farms. A mysterious masked man known simply as Subcomandante Marcos was their leader. Effectively using the Internet and the international mass media as his secret weapon against the Mexican government, Marcos led what the *New York Times* called "the first postmodern revolution," combining a peasant uprising with the World Wide Web, short-wave radio, and photo spreads in *Marie Claire*. Ingeniously keeping the movement in the international public eye by using modern technologies of communication, Marcos mobilized support abroad and limited the retaliatory actions of the Mexican government (*A Place Called Chiapas,* 1998; Jones, 1999).

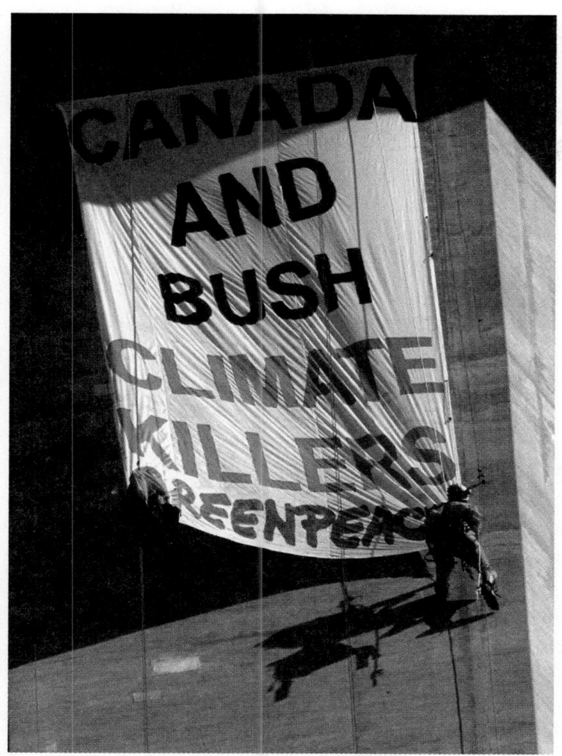


Greenpeace is a highly successful global environmental movement that originated in Vancouver in the mid-1970s and now has offices in 41 countries.

Greenpeace is hardly alone in its efforts to go global. In 1953, 110 international social movement organizations spanned the globe. By 1993, there were 631. About a quarter were human rights organizations and about a seventh were environmental organizations. The latter are by far the fastest-growing organizational type (Smith, 1998: 97).

The globalization of social movements can be further illustrated by coming full circle and returning to the anecdote with which we began this chapter. In 1991, Robert Brym visited his hometown. He hadn't been back in years. As he entered the city he vaguely sensed that something was different. "I wasn't able to identify the change until I reached the pulp and paper mill," says Robert. "Suddenly, it was obvious. The rotten-egg smell was virtually gone. I discovered that in the 1970s a local woman whose son developed a serious case of asthma took legal action against the mill and eventually won. The mill owner was forced by law to install a 'scrubber' in the main smokestack to remove most of the sulphur dioxide emissions. Soon, the federal government was putting pressure on the mill owner to purify the polluted water that poured out of the plant and into the local river system." Apparently, local citizens and the environmental movement had caused a deep change in the climate of opinion. This influenced the government to force the mill owner to spend millions of dollars to clean up his operation. It took decades, but what was political heresy in 1968 became established practice by 1991. That is because environmental concerns had been amplified by the voice of a movement that had grown to global proportions. In general, as this case illustrates, globalization helps ensure that many new social movements transcend local and national boundaries and promote universalistic goals.

## The Points of the Compass

For many thousands of years, humans have done well on this planet. That is because we have created cultural practices, including technologies, that allowed us to adapt to and thrive in our environment. Nonetheless, there have been some failures along the way. Many tribes and civilizations are extinct. And our success to date as a species is no warrant for the future. If we persist in using technologies that create an inhospitable environment, nature will deal with us in the same way it always deals with species that cannot adapt.

Broadly speaking, we have two survival strategies to cope with the challenges that lie ahead: competition and cooperation. Charles Darwin wrote famously about competition in *The Origin of Species* (1859). He observed that members of each species struggle against one another and against other species in their struggle to survive. Most of the quickest, the strongest, the best camouflaged, and the smartest live long enough to bear offspring. Most of the rest are killed off. Thus, the traits passed on to offspring are those most valuable for survival. Ruthless competition, it turns out, is a key survival strategy of all species, including humans.

In *The Descent of Man,* Darwin mentioned our second important survival strategy: cooperation. In some species mutual assistance is common. The species members that flourish are those that best learn to help one another (Darwin, 1871:163). The Russian geographer and naturalist Petr Kropotkin (1908 [1902]) elaborated this idea. After spending five years studying animal life in Siberia, he concluded that "mutual aid" is at least as important a survival strategy as competition. Competition takes place when members of the same species compete for limited resources, said Kropotkin. Cooperation occurs when species members struggle against adverse environmental circumstances. According to Kropotkin, survival in the face of environmental threat is best assured if species members help one another. Kropotkin also showed that the most advanced species in any group—ants among insects, mammals among vertebrates, humans among mammals—are the most cooperative. Many evolutionary biologists now accept Kropotkin's ideas (Gould, 1988; Nowak, May, and Sigmund, 1995: 81).

As we have seen, a strictly competitive approach to dealing with the environmental crisis—relying on the market alone to solve our problems—now seems inadequate. Instead, it appears we require more cooperation and self-sacrifice. This involves substantially reducing consumption, paying higher taxes for environmental cleanup and energy-efficient industrial processes, subsidizing the developing countries to industrialize in an environmentally friendly way, and so forth. Previously, we outlined some grave consequences of relying too little on a cooperative survival strategy at this historical juncture. But which strategy you emphasize in your own life is, of course, your choice.

Similarly, throughout this book—when we discussed families, gender inequality, crime, race, population, and many other topics—we raised social issues lying at the intersection of history, social structure, and biography. We arrayed these issues on our sociological compass, set out alternative courses of action, and outlined their consequences. We thus followed our disciplinary mandate: helping people make informed choices based on sound sociological knowledge (Wilensky, 1997). In the context of the present chapter, however, we can make an even bolder claim for the discipline. Conceived at its broadest, sociology promises to help in the rational and equitable evolution of humankind.

# Summary

### 1. *Does technology shape society?*

New technologies routinely transform societies, but this does not mean that technology is beyond human control. Human control is evident in the fact that new technologies are adopted only when there is a widespread social need for them. It is also evident in the fact that, since the last third of the nineteenth century, technological development has increasingly come under the control of multinational corporations and the military establishments of the major world powers.

### 2. *Why are a growing number of people skeptical about the benefits of technology?*

Skepticism about the benefits of technology derives from the fact that new technologies have unintended, negative consequences. These negative consequences include "normal accidents" (the inevitable but unpredictable failure of complex technologies) and growing environmental risks.

### 3. *Who is most exposed to the risks associated with environmental degradation?*

The people most exposed to the risks associated with the various forms of environmental degradation include members of racial minorities, lower classes, and less developed societies.

### 4. *How do environmental issues become social problems?*

Environmental issues become social problems when policy-oriented scientists, the environmental movement, the mass media, and respected organizations discover and promote environmental issues, and the public connects the information learned from these groups to real-life events.

5. *Are market and high-tech solutions capable of dealing with the problem of environmental degradation?*

Market and high-tech solutions can help solve many environmental problems, but they are insufficient by themselves because price signals do not always mirror market conditions, political pressure is often needed to motivate governments and corporations to take action on environmental issues, and the pace of change is too slow under present conditions.

6. *What needs to be done to solve the problem of environmental degradation?*

Increased cooperation among citizens, governments, and corporations is required to solve the environmental crisis. This cooperative strategy involves renewed commitment to voluntary efforts, new laws and enforcement bodies to ensure compliance, increased investment in energy-saving research and development by industry and government, more environmentally directed foreign aid, and new taxes to help pay for some if it. Many people are unwilling to undergo the personal sacrifices and changes in lifestyle required to deal with the problem of environmental degradation, while some interest groups with a deep stake in things as they are resist change. However, repeated environmental catastrophes could change the context of politics in a way that would make the cooperative strategy more popular.

7. *Is the formation of social movements associated with the experience of relative deprivation?*

Relative deprivation is generally not associated with social-movement formation because a number of social conditions can prevent discontent from being turned into collective action.

8. *What social conditions facilitate rebellion against the status quo?*

People are more inclined to rebel against the status quo when social ties bind them to many other people who feel similarly wronged and when they have the time, money, organization, and other resources needed to protest. In addition, collective action and social-movement formation are more likely to occur when political opportunities allow them. Political opportunities emerge because of elections, increased support by influential allies, the instability of ruling political alignments, and divisions among elite groups.

9. *How do authorities try to control unrest?*

Authorities try to control unrest by offering concessions to insurgents, co-opting leaders, and employing coercion.

10. *What is* framing?

For social movements to grow, members must make the activities, goals, and ideology of the movement congruent with the interests, beliefs, and values of potential new recruits. Doing so is known as *framing*.

11. *How have social movements changed in the past three centuries?*

In 1700, social movements were typically small, localized, and violent. By the mid-twentieth century, social movements had become typically large, national, and less violent. In the late twentieth century, new social movements developed broader goals, recruited more highly educated people, and developed global potential for growth.

# Key Terms

**breakdown theory (p. 356)**
**collective action (p. 354)**
**environmental racism (p. 349)**
**frame alignment (p. 360)**
**genetic pollution (p. 346)**
**global warming (p. 345)**
**normal accidents (p. 340)**
**political opportunities (p. 358)**
**recombinant DNA (p. 347)**
**relative deprivation (p. 356)**
**resource mobilization (p. 357)**
**risk society (p. 340)**
**social movements (p. 355)**
**solidarity theory (p. 356)**
**technological determinism (p. 341)**
**technology (p. 339)**

## Questions to Consider

1. What are the main environmental problems in your community? How are they connected to global environmental issues? (See Web Resources, below, for useful leads.)
2. Take an inventory of your environmentally friendly and environmentally dangerous habits. In what ways can you act in a more environmentally friendly manner?
3. How would you achieve a political goal? Map out a detailed strategy for reaching a clearly defined aim, such as a reduction in income tax or an increase in government funding of colleges. Whom would you try to recruit to help you achieve your goal? Why? What collective actions do you think would be most successful? Why? To whose attention would these actions be directed? Why? Write a manifesto that frames your argument in a way that is culturally appealing to potential recruits.

## Web Resources

### Companion Web Site for This Book

http://www.pointsofthecompass.nelson.com

Begin by clicking on the Student Resources section of the Web site. Next, select the chapter you are currently studying from the pull-down menu. From the Student Resources page you will have easy access to InfoTrac® College Edition, MicroCase online exercises, and additional Weblinks. The Web site also has many useful tips to aid you in your study of sociology, including practice tests for each chapter.

### InfoTrac® Search Terms

These search terms are provided to assist you in beginning to conduct research on this topic by visiting **http://www.infotrac-college.com**:

**environmental problems**
**environmental racism**
**frame alignment**
**global warming**
**resource mobilization**
**social movements**
**technology**

### Recommended Web Sites

For the federal government's view of environmental issues in Canada, visit the Environment Canada Web site at **http://www.ec.gc.ca**.

Greenpeace is perhaps the most successful environmental movement in the world. Founded in Vancouver in the mid-1970s, it now has offices in 41 countries. Its Web site is at **http://www.greenpeace.org/international/**.

Since 1910, March 8 has been celebrated as International Women's Day. For information about the demonstrations and other activities that take place around the world (including in Canada) on March 8, go to **http://www.internationalwomensday.com**.

The Canadian Labour Congress (CLC) is the country's biggest umbrella labour organization, with more than 2.3 million members. To learn about the CLC's current projects, campaigns, and boycotts, visit the CLC Web site at **http://canadianlabour.ca**.

**Abstraction** is the human capacity to create general ideas or ways of thinking that are not linked to particular instances. For example, languages, mathematical notations, and signs allow us to classify experience and generalize from it.

An **achievement**-based stratification system is one in which the allocation of rank depends on a person's accomplishments.

**Acquaintance rape** is a sexual assault committed by someone the victim knows.

**Altruistic suicide** occurs in settings that exhibit very high levels of social solidarity, according to Durkheim. In other words, altruistic suicide results from norms very tightly governing behaviour.

The **analysis of existing documents and official statistics** is a non-reactive research method that involves the analysis of diaries, newspapers, published historical works, and statistics produced by government agencies, all of which are created by people other than the researcher for purposes other than sociological research.

**Anomic suicide** occurs in settings that exhibit low levels of social solidarity, according to Durkheim. Anomic suicide results from vaguely defined norms governing behaviour.

**Anticipatory socialization** involves beginning to take on the norms and behaviours of the roles to which one aspires.

An **ascription**-based stratification system is one in which the allocation of rank depends on the features with which a person is born (ascribed characteristics).

**Assimilation** is the process by which a minority group blends into the majority population and eventually disappears as a distinct group.

An **association** exists between two variables if the value of one variable changes with the value of the other.

**Bisexuals** are people who enjoy sexual partners of either sex.

The **bourgeoisie** are owners of the means of production, including factories, tools, and land, according to Marx. They do not do any physical labour. Their income derives from profits.

**Breakdown theory** suggests that social movements emerge when traditional norms and patterns of social organization are disrupted.

A **bureaucracy** is a large, impersonal organization composed of many clearly defined positions arranged in a hierarchy.

**Charismatic** leaders are men and women who claim to be inspired by supernatural powers and whose followers believe them to be so inspired.

**Child support** involves money paid by the non-custodial parent to the custodial parent for the purpose of supporting the children of a separated marital, cohabiting, or sexual relationship.

A **church** is a bureaucratic religious organization that has accommodated itself to mainstream society and culture.

A **class** in Marx's sense of the term is determined by one's relationship to the means of production. In Weber's usage, class position is determined by his or her "market situation," including the possession of goods, opportunities for income, level of education, and level of technical skill.

**Class conflict** is the struggle between classes to resist and overcome the opposition of other classes.

**Class consciousness** is awareness of belonging to the social class of which one is a member.

A **closed-ended question** in a survey is a type of question that provides the respondent with a list of permitted answers. Each answer is given a numerical code so that the data can later be easily input into a computer for statistical analysis.

**Collective action** occurs when people act in unison to bring about or resist social, political, and economic change. Some collective actions are routine; others are non-routine. Routine collective actions are typically nonviolent and follow established patterns of behaviour in existing social structures. Non-routine collective actions take place when usual conventions cease to guide social action and people transcend, bypass, or subvert established institutional patterns and structures.

The **collective conscience** comprises the common sentiments and values that people share as a result of living together.

**Competition** is a mode of interaction in which power is unequally distributed but the degree of inequality is less than in systems of domination. Envy is an important emotion in competitive interactions.

**Conflict theories of social interaction** emphasize that when people interact, their statuses are often arranged in a hierarchy. Those on top enjoy more power than those on the bottom. The degree of inequality strongly affects the character of social interaction between the interacting parties.

**Conflict theory** generally focuses on large, macrolevel structures, such as the relations among classes. It shows how major patterns of inequality in society produce social stability in some circumstances and social change in others. It stresses how members of privileged groups try to maintain their advantages while subordinate groups struggle to acquire theirs. And it typically leads to the suggestion that eliminating privilege will lower the level of conflict and increase the sum total of human welfare.

**Conquest** is the forcible capture of land and the economic and political domination of its inhabitants.

**Constraint theories** identify the social factors that impose deviance and crime (or conventional behaviour) on people.

**Consumerism** is the tendency to define ourselves in terms of the goods and services we purchase.

A **control group** in an experiment is the group that is not exposed to the independent variable.

**Control theory** holds that the rewards of deviance and crime are ample. Therefore, nearly everyone would engage in deviance and crime if they could get away with it. The degree to which people are prevented from violating norms and laws accounts for variations in the level of deviance and crime.

**Cooperation,** the human capacity to create a complex social life, is a basis for social interaction in which power is more or less equally distributed between people of different status. The dominant emotion in cooperative interaction is trust.

**Core** capitalist countries are the world's major sources of capital and technology (the United States, Japan, and Germany).

**Countercultures** are subversive subcultures. Countercultures oppose dominant values and seek to replace them.

**Crime** is deviance that is against the law.

The **crude death rate** is the annual number of deaths per 1000 people in a population.

**Cults** are small groups of people deeply committed to a religious vision that rejects mainstream culture and society.

**Cultural capital** refers to the widely shared, high-status cultural signals (attitudes, preferences, formal knowledge, behaviours, goals, and credentials) used for social and cultural exclusion.

**Cultural relativism** is the belief that all cultures have equal value.

**Culture** is the sum of practices, languages, symbols, beliefs, values, ideologies, and material objects that people create to deal with real-life problems.

**Denominations** are the various streams of belief and practice that some churches allow to coexist under their overarching authority.

**Dependency theory** holds that global inequality is the result of patterns of domination and submission between rich and poor countries. From this point of view, rich countries have impoverished poor countries in order to enrich themselves.

A **dependent variable** is the presumed effect in a cause-and-effect relationship.

**Detached observation** is a type of field research that involves classifying and counting the behaviour of interest according to a predetermined scheme.

**Deviance** occurs when someone departs from a norm and evokes a negative reaction from others

**Differential association** theory holds that people learn to value deviant or non-deviant lifestyles depending on whether their social environment leads them to associate more with deviants or non-deviants.

**Discrimination** is unfair treatment of people due to their group membership.

The **divorce rate** is the number of divorces that occur in a year for every 1000 people in the population.

**Domination** is a mode of interaction in which nearly all power is concentrated in the hands of people with similar status. Fear is the dominant emotion in systems of interaction based on domination.

**Dramaturgical analysis** views social interaction as a sort of play in which people present themselves so that they appear in the best possible light.

A **dyad** is a social relationship between two nodes, or social units (e.g., people, firms, organizations, countries).

**Dysfunctions** are effects of social structures that create social instability.

**Ecclesia** are state-supported churches.

The **ecological theory** of race and ethnic relations focuses on the way racial and ethnic groups struggle for territory and eventually blend into one another.

**Educational achievement** refers to how much students actually learn.

**Educational attainment** refers to the number of years of school that students complete.

The **ego,** according to Freud, is a psychological mechanism that balances the conflicting needs of the pleasure-seeking id and the restraining superego.

**Egoistic suicide** results from the poor integration of people into society because of weak social ties to others, according to Durkheim.

**Emotion labour** is emotion management that many people do as part of their job and for which they are paid.

**Emotion management** involves people obeying "feeling rules" and responding appropriately to the situations in which they find themselves.

**Employment equity** is a policy that gives preference to minority group members if equally qualified people are available for a position.

**Environmental racism** is the tendency to heap environmental dangers on the disadvantaged, and especially on disadvantaged racial minorities.

**Essentialism** is a school of thought that views gender differences as a reflection of biological differences between women and men.

An **ethnic group** comprises people whose perceived cultural markers are deemed socially significant. Ethnic groups differ from one another in terms of language, religion, customs, values, ancestors, and the like.

**Ethnocentrism** is the tendency to judge other cultures exclusively by the standards of your own.

**Ethnomethodology** is the study of how people make sense of what others do and say by adhering to pre-existing norms.

**Exchange theory** holds that social interaction involves trade in valued resources.

An **experiment** is a carefully controlled artificial situation that allows researchers to isolate hypothesized causes and measure their effects precisely.

An **experimental group** in an experiment is the group that is exposed to the independent variable.

**Expulsion** is the forcible removal of a population from a territory claimed by another population.

The **extended family** expands the nuclear family "vertically" by adding another generation—one or more of the spouses' parents—to the household.

A **family** is a set of intimate social relationships that adults create to share resources so as to ensure the welfare of themselves and their dependents.

**Feminist theory** claims that patriarchy is at least as important as class inequality in determining a person's opportunities in life. It holds that male domination and female subordination are determined not by biological necessity but by structures of power and social convention. It examines the operation of patriarchy in both micro and macro settings. And it contends that existing patterns of gender inequality can and should be changed for the benefit of all members of society.

**Field research** is the systematic observation of people in their natural settings.

**Folkways** are the least important norms—the norms that evoke the least severe punishment.

**Formal organizations** are secondary groups designed to achieve specific and explicit objectives.

**Formal punishment** takes place when the judicial system penalizes someone for breaking a law.

**Frame alignment** is the process by which individual interests, beliefs, and values become congruent and complementary with the activities, goals, and ideology of a social movement.

The **functional theory of stratification** argues that (1) some jobs are more important than others, (2) people must make sacrifices to train for important jobs, and (3) inequality is required to motivate people to undergo these sacrifices.

**Functionalism** stresses that human behaviour is governed by relatively stable social structures. It underlines how social structures maintain or undermine social stability. It emphasizes that social structures are based mainly on shared values or preferences. And it suggests that re-establishing equilibrium can best solve most social problems.

**Fundamentalists** interpret their scriptures literally, seek to establish a direct, personal relationship with the higher being(s) they worship, and are relatively intolerant of non-fundamentalists.

Your **gender** is your sense of being male or female and your playing masculine and feminine roles in ways defined as appropriate by your culture and society.

**Gender discrimination** involves rewarding men and women differently for the same work.

**Gender identity** is a person's identification with, or sense of belonging to, a particular sex—biologically, psychologically, and socially.

A **gender ideology** is a set of ideas about what constitutes appropriate masculine and feminine roles and behaviour.

A **gender role** is the set of behaviours associated with widely shared expectations about how males or females are supposed to act.

The **generalized other,** according to Mead, is a person's image of cultural standards and how they apply to him or her.

**Genetic pollution** refers to the potential dangers of mixing the genes of one species with those of another.

**Genocide** is the intentional extermination of an entire population defined as a "race" or a "people."

The **glass ceiling** is a social barrier that makes it difficult for women to rise to the top level of management.

**Global structures** are patterns of social relations that lie outside and above the national level. They include international organizations, patterns of worldwide travel and communication, and the economic relations among countries.

**Global warming** is the gradual worldwide increase in average surface temperature.

**Globalization** is the process by which formerly separate economies, nation-states, and cultures are becoming tied together and people are becoming increasingly aware of their growing interdependence.

**Groupthink** refers to group pressure to conform despite individual misgivings.

**Heterosexuals** are people who prefer members of the opposite sex as sexual partners.

A **hidden curriculum** teaches students what will be expected of them as conventionally good citizens once they leave school.

**High culture** is culture consumed mainly by upper classes.

**Homophobia** is fear of homosexuals.

**Homosexuals** are people who prefer sexual partners of the same sex. People usually call homosexual men *gay* and homosexual women *lesbians*.

**Hostile environment sexual harassment** involves sexual jokes, touching, and comments that interfere with work or create an unfriendly work environment.

**Human capital** is investment in education and training. Just as productivity increases by upgrading manufacturing plants and introducing new technology, productivity gains can also result from investment in the skills and abilities of people.

The **I,** according to Mead, is the subjective and impulsive aspect of the self that is present from birth.

The **id,** according to Freud, is the part of the self that demands immediate gratification.

An **independent variable** is the presumed cause in a cause-and-effect relationship.

The **Industrial Revolution,** often regarded as the most important event in world history since the development of agriculture and cities, refers to the rapid economic transformation that began in Britain in the 1780s. It involved the large-scale application of science and technology to industrial processes, the creation of factories, and the formation of a working class.

**Informal punishment** involves a mild sanction that is imposed during face-to-face interaction, rather than by the judicial system.

An **in-group** comprises people who belong to a group.

An **initiation rite** is a ritual that signifies the transition of the individual from one group to another and helps to ensure his or her loyalty to the new group.

**Institutional racism** is bias that is inherent in social institutions and is often not noticed by members of the majority group.

**Intergenerational mobility** is social mobility that occurs between generations.

**Internal colonialism** involves one race or ethnic group subjugating another in the same country. It prevents assimilation by segregating the subordinate group in terms of jobs, housing, and social contacts.

**Intersexed** infants are babies born with ambiguous genitals because of a hormone imbalance in the womb or some other cause.

**Intragenerational mobility** is social mobility that occurs within a single generation.

**Labelling theory** holds that deviance results not so much from the actions of the deviant as from the response of others, who label the rule breaker a deviant.

A **language** is a system of symbols strung together to communicate thought.

**Latent functions** are the invisible and unintended effects of social structures.

A **law** is a norm stipulated and enforced by government bodies.

The **looking-glass self** is Cooley's description of the way our feelings about who we are depend largely on how we see ourselves evaluated by others.

**Macrostructures** are overarching patterns of social relations that lie outside and above your circle of intimates and acquaintances. Macrostructures include classes, bureaucracies, and power systems such as patriarchy.

**Manifest functions** are visible and intended effects of social structures.

**Marriage,** traditionally defined, is a socially approved, presumably long-term sexual and economic union between a man and a woman. It involves reciprocal rights and obligations between spouses and between parents and children.

The **marriage rate** is the number of marriages that occur in a year for every 1000 people in the population.

**Mass culture** (See *popular culture*).

**Material culture** comprises the tools and techniques that enable people to accomplish tasks.

The **me,** according to Mead, is the objective component of the self that emerges as people communicate symbolically and learn to take the role of the other.

The **medicalization of deviance** is the process of medical definitions of deviant behaviour becoming more prevalent.

**Mesostructures** are mid-level social structures, such as groups, networks, and bureaucracies, that shape human behaviour.

**Microstructures** are the patterns of relatively intimate social relations formed during face-to-face interaction. Families, friendship circles, and work associations are all examples of microstructures.

**Modernization theory** holds that global inequality results from various dysfunctional characteristics of poor societies: lack of investment capital, Western-style business techniques, stable Western-style governments, and a Western mentality.

A **moral panic** occurs when many people fervently believe that some form of deviance or crime poses a profound threat to society's well-being.

**Mores** are core norms that most people believe are essential for the survival of their group or their society.

**Motivational theories** identify the social factors that drive people to commit deviant and criminal acts.

**Multiculturalism** reflects Canada's ethnic and racial diversity in the past and its growing ethnic and racial diversity today.

**Non-material culture** is composed of symbols, norms, and other non-tangible elements of culture.

**Normal accidents** are accidents that occur inevitably though unpredictably because of the very complexity of modern technologies.

**Norms** are generally accepted ways of doing things.

A **nuclear family** consists of a cohabiting man and woman who maintain a socially approved sexual relationship and have at least one child.

**Occupational sex segregation** is the concentration of women in certain occupations and men in others.

An **open-ended question,** in a survey, is a type of question that allows respondents to answer in their own words.

An **out-group** comprises people who are excluded from the in-group.

**Participant observation** involves carefully observing people's face-to-face interaction and actually participating in their lives over a long period, thus achieving a deep and sympathetic understanding of what motivates them to act in the way they do.

**Parties,** in Weber's usage, are organizations that seek to impose their will on others.

**Patriarchy** is the traditional system of economic and political inequality between women and men.

**Pay equity** is equal pay for work of equal value, or the equal dollar value of different jobs. It is established in gender-neutral terms by comparing jobs in terms of the education and experience needed to do them and the stress, responsibility, and working conditions associated with them.

A person's **peer group** comprises people who are about the same age and of similar status as that person. The peer group acts as an agent of socialization.

**Peripheral** countries are the world's major sources of raw materials and cheap labour (the former colonies).

**Pluralism** is the retention of racial and ethnic culture combined with equal access to basic social resources.

**Political opportunities** for collective action and social movement growth occur during election campaigns, when influential allies offer insurgents support, when ruling political alignments become unstable, and when elite groups become divided and conflict with one another.

**Polygamy** expands the nuclear family "horizontally" by adding one or more spouses (usually women) to the household.

**Popular culture** (or **mass culture**) is culture consumed by all classes.

A **population** is the entire group about which the researcher wants to generalize.

The **Postindustrial Revolution** refers to the technology-driven shift from manufacturing to service industries and the consequences of that shift for virtually all human activities.

**Postmodernism** is characterized by an eclectic mix of cultural elements from different times and places, the erosion of authority, and the decline of consensus around core values.

**Poverty** lacks an agreed-on definition. Analysts disagree whether poverty should be defined in absolute or relative terms and whether it should be based on income or consumption. Canada does not have an official poverty line. Statistics Canada reports low income cut-off that marks "the income level at which a family may be in straitened circumstances because it has to spend a greater proportion of its income on necessities than the average family of similar size."

**Power** is the probability that one actor in a social relationship will be in a position to carry out his or her own will despite resistance.

**Prejudice** is an attitude that judges a person on his or her group's real or imagined characteristics.

**Primary groups** are social groups in which norms, roles, and statuses are agreed upon but are not put in writing. Social interaction leads to strong emotional ties. It extends over a long period and involves a wide range of activities. It results in group members knowing one another well.

**Primary socialization** is the process of acquiring the basic skills needed to function in society during childhood. Primary socialization usually takes place in the family.

In a **probability sample,** the units have a known and non-zero chance of being selected.

**Production** is the human capacity to make and use tools. It improves our ability to take what we want from nature.

The **profane** refers to the secular, everyday world.

The **proletariat** is the term Marx gave to the working class. Members of the proletariat perform physical labour but do not own means of production. They are thus in a position to earn wages.

The **Protestant ethic** is the sixteenth- and seventeenth-century Protestant belief that religious doubts can be reduced, and a state of grace assured, if people work diligently and live ascetically. According to Weber, the Protestant work ethic had the unintended effect of increasing savings and investment and thus stimulating capitalist growth.

**Quid pro quo sexual harassment** takes place when sexual threats or bribery are made a condition of employment decisions.

**Race** is a social construct used to distinguish people in terms of one or more physical markers, usually with profound effects on their lives.

**Racism** is the belief that a visible characteristic of a group, such as skin colour, indicates group inferiority and justifies discrimination.

**Randomization** in an experiment involves assigning individuals to groups by chance processes.

**Rational choice theory** focuses on the way interacting people weigh the benefits and costs of interaction. According to rational choice theory, interacting people always try to maximize benefits and minimize costs.

**Rationalization** is the application of the most efficient means to achieve given goals and the unintended, negative consequences of doing so.

**Reactivity** is the tendency of people who are observed by a researcher to react to the presence of the researcher by concealing certain things or acting artificially to impress the researcher.

**Recidivism rates** tell us what proportion of people are re-arrested after an initial arrest.

**Recombinant DNA** involves removing a segment of DNA from a gene or splicing together segments of DNA from different living things, thus effectively creating a new life form.

A **reference group** is a group of people against whom an individual evaluates his or her situation or conduct.

**Relative deprivation** is an intolerable gap between the social rewards people feel they deserve and the social rewards they expect to receive.

**Reliability** is the degree to which a measurement procedure yields consistent results.

**Religiosity** refers to how important religion is to people.

**Research** is the process of systematically observing reality to assess the validity of a theory.

**Resocialization** occurs when powerful socializing agents deliberately cause rapid change in a person's values, roles, and self-conception, sometimes against that person's will.

**Resource mobilization** refers to the process by which social movements crystallize because of the increasing organizational, material, and other resources of movement members.

A **respondent** is a person who answers a researcher's questions.

The **revised secularization thesis** holds that worldly institutions break off from the institution of religion over time. As a result, religion governs an ever-smaller part of most people's lives and has become largely a matter of personal choice.

The **rights revolution** is the process by which socially excluded groups have struggled to win equal rights under the law and in practice.

A **risk society** is a society in which technology distributes environmental dangers among all categories of the population, albeit to varying degrees.

**Rites of passage** are cultural ceremonies that mark the transition from one stage of life to another (e.g., baptisms, confirmations, weddings) or from life to death (e.g., funerals).

**Rituals** are public practices designed to connect people to the sacred.

A **role** is a set of expected behaviours, or the behaviour expected of a person occupying a particular position in society.

**Role distancing** involves giving the impression that we are just going through the motions and that we lack serious commitment to a role.

A **role set** is a cluster of roles attached to a single status.

**Role strain** occurs when incompatible role demands are placed on a single person in a single status.

The **routinization of charisma** is Weber's term for the transformation of the unique gift of divine enlightenment into a permanent feature of everyday life. It involves turning religious inspiration into a stable social institution with defined roles (interpreters of the divine message, teachers, dues-paying laypeople, and so forth).

The **sacred** refers to the religious, transcendent world.

A **sample** is the part of the population of interest that is selected for analysis.

A **sampling frame** is a list of all the people in the population of interest.

**Sanctions** are rewards and punishments intended to ensure conformity to cultural guidelines.

The **Sapir-Whorf thesis** holds that we experience certain things in our environment and form concepts about those things. We then develop language to express our concepts. Finally, language itself influences how we see the world.

A **scapegoat** is a disadvantaged person or category of people whom others blame for their own problems.

**Secondary groups** are social groups that are larger and more impersonal than primary groups. Compared with primary groups, social interaction in secondary groups creates weaker emotional ties. It extends over a shorter period, and it involves a narrow range of activities. It results in most group members having at most a passing acquaintance with one another.

**Secondary socialization** is socialization outside the family after childhood.

**Sects** usually form by breaking away from churches because of disagreement about church doctrine. Sects are less integrated into society and less bureaucratized than churches. They are often led by charismatic leaders, who tend to be relatively intolerant of religious opinions other than their own.

The **secularization thesis** says that religious institutions, actions, and consciousness are on the decline worldwide.

**Segregation** involves the spatial and institutional separation of racial or ethnic groups.

The **self** is a set of ideas and attitudes about who one is as an independent being.

A **self-fulfilling prophecy** is an expectation that helps bring about what it predicts.

In **self-report surveys**, respondents are asked to report their involvement in criminal activities, either as perpetrators or as victims.

**Self-socialization** involves choosing socialization influences from the wide variety of mass media offerings.

**Semiperipheral** countries are former colonies that are making considerable headway in their attempt to become prosperous.

Your **sex** depends on whether you were born with distinct male or female genitals and a genetic program that released either male or female hormones to stimulate the development of your reproductive system.

**Significant others** are the people who play important roles in the early socialization experiences of children.

**Slavery** is the ownership and control of people.

**Social capital** refers to the networks or connections that individuals possess.

A **social category** is composed of people who share similar status but do not identify with one another.

**Social constructionism** is a school of thought that views gender differences as a reflection of the different social positions occupied by women and men.

**Social control** refers to methods of ensuring conformity.

A **social group** is composed of one or more networks of people who identify with one another and adhere to defined norms, roles, and statuses.

**Social interaction** involves people communicating face-to-face, acting and reacting in relation to other people. It is structured around norms, roles, and statuses.

**Social mobility** refers to movement up or down the stratification system.

**Social movements** are collective attempts to change all or part of the political or social order by means of rioting, petitioning, striking, demonstrating, and establishing pressure groups, unions, and political parties.

A **social network** is a bounded set of individuals who are linked by the exchange of material or emotional resources.

**Social solidarity** refers to (1) the degree to which group members share beliefs and values, and (2) the intensity and frequency of their interaction.

**Social stratification** refers to the way society is organized in layers or strata.

**Social structures** are relatively stable patterns of social relations.

**Socialization** is the process by which people learn their culture. They do so by (1) entering into and disengaging from a succession of roles and (2) becoming aware of themselves as they interact with others.

A **society** is a number of people who interact, usually in a defined territory, and share a culture.

The **sociological imagination** is the quality of mind that enables one to see the connection between personal troubles and social structures.

**Sociology** is the systematic study of human behaviour in social context.

**Solidarity theory** holds that social movements are social organizations that emerge when potential members can mobilize resources, take advantage of new political opportunities, and avoid high levels of social control by authorities.

A **split labour market** exists where low-wage workers of one race and high-wage workers of another race compete for the same jobs. In that situation, high-wage workers are likely to resent the presence of low-wage competitors. Conflict is bound to result and racist attitudes to develop or become reinforced.

**Status** refers to a recognized social position that an individual can occupy.

**Status cues** are visual indicators of a person's social position.

**Status groups** differ from one another in terms of the prestige or social honour they enjoy and in terms of their style of life.

A **status set** is the entire ensemble of statuses occupied by an individual.

The **stereotype threat** is the impact of negative stereotypes on the school performance of disadvantaged groups.

**Stereotypes** are rigid views of how members of various groups act, regardless of whether individual group members really behave that way.

People who are **stigmatized** are negatively evaluated because of a marker that distinguishes them from others.

**Strain theory** holds that people may turn to deviance when they experience strain. Strain results when a culture teaches people the value of material success and society fails to provide enough legitimate opportunities for everyone to succeed.

**Street crimes** include arson, break and enter, assault, and other illegal acts disproportionately committed by people from lower classes.

**Subcultural theory** argues that gangs are a collective adaptation to social conditions. Distinct norms and values that reject the legitimate world crystallize in gangs.

A **subculture** is a set of distinctive values, norms, and practices within a larger culture.

The **superego**, according to Freud, is the part of the self that acts as a repository of cultural standards.

In a **survey**, people are asked questions about their knowledge, attitudes, or behaviour, either in a face-to-face or telephone interview or in a paper-and-pencil format.

A **symbol** is anything that carries a particular meaning, including the components of language, mathematical notations, and signs. Symbols allow us to classify experience and generalize from it.

**Symbolic ethnicity** is a nostalgic allegiance to the culture of the immigrant generation, or that of the old country, that is not usually incorporated in everyday behaviour.

**Symbolic interactionism** focuses on face-to-face communication, or interaction in microlevel social settings. It emphasizes that an adequate explanation of social behaviour requires understanding the subjective meanings people attach to their social circumstances. It stresses that people help to create their social circumstances rather than merely react to them. And by underscoring the subjective meanings people create in small social settings, it validates unpopular and unofficial viewpoints. This validation increases our understanding and tolerance of people who may be different from us.

The **system of social control** is the sum of sanctions in society by means of which conformity to cultural guidelines is ensured.

**Taboos** are the strongest norms. When someone violates a taboo, it causes revulsion in the community and punishment is severe.

**Techniques of neutralization** are the rationalizations that deviants and criminals use to justify their activities. Techniques of neutralization make deviance and crime seem normal, at least to the deviants and criminals themselves.

**Technological determinism** is the belief that technology is the main factor shaping human history.

**Technology** is the practical application of scientific principles.

A **theory** is a tentative explanation of some aspect of social life that states how and why certain facts are related.

The **Thomas theorem** states: "Situations we define as real become real in their consequences."

The **total fertility rate** is the average number of children that would be born to a woman over her lifetime if she had the same number of children as do women in each age cohort in a given year.

**Total institutions** are settings in which people are isolated from the larger society and under the strict control and constant supervision of a specialized staff.

**Totems** are objects that symbolize the sacred.

A **traditional nuclear family** is a nuclear family in which the husband works outside the home for money and the wife works without pay in the home.

**Transgendered** people break society's gender norms by defying the rigid distinction between male and female. They may be heterosexual or homosexual.

**Transnational communities** are communities whose boundaries extend among countries.

**Transsexuals** are people who want to alter their gender by changing their appearance or resorting to medical intervention. Transsexuals believe they were born with the "wrong" body. They identify with, and want to live fully as, members of the opposite sex.

A **triad** is a social relationship among three nodes, or social units (e.g., people, firms, organizations, countries).

The **unconscious**, according to Freud, is the part of the self that contains repressed memories that we are not normally aware of.

**Validity** is the degree to which a measure actually measures what it is intended to measure.

**Values** are ideas about what is right and wrong, good and bad, beautiful and ugly.

A **variable** is a concept that can take on more than one value.

**Victimization surveys** are surveys in which people are asked whether they have been victims of crime.

**Victimless crimes** involve violations of the law in which no victim has stepped forward and been identified.

A **virtual community** is an association of people, scattered across the city or around the world, who communicate via computer and modem about a subject of common interest.

**White-collar crime** refers to an illegal act committed by a respectable, high-status person in the course of work.

# REFERENCES


"A Changing People." 1999. *Time* (Canadian Edition), 31 May: 30–34.

"Acceptable but Not Equal." 2002. *Maclean's* 3 June: 12.

Achilles, Rhona. 1993. "Desperately Seeking Babies: New Technologies of Hope and Despair." Pp. 214–29 in Bonnie J. Fox, ed. *Family Patterns, Gender Relations*. Toronto: Oxford University Press.

Adam, Barry, Jan Willem Duyvendak, and Andre Krouwel. 1999. *The Global Emergence of Gay and Lesbian Politics*. Philadelphia: Temple University Press.

"Adams Mine." 2000. On the World Wide Web at http://server1.nt.net/customers/13/tpc/www/togarbag.htm#Anchor-First-14210 (8 October 2000).

Adams, Henry E., Lester W. Wright, Jr., and Bethany A. Lohr. 1998. "Is Homophobia Associated with Homosexual Arousal?" *Journal of Abnormal Psychology* 105: 440–45.

Adams, Michael. 1997. *Sex in the Snow: Canadian Social Values at the End of the Millennium*. Toronto: Penguin.

Adamson, Nancy, Linda Briskin, and Margaret McPhail. 1988. *Feminist Organizing for Change: The Contemporary Women's Movement in Canada*. Toronto: Oxford University Press.

Adherents.com. 2001. "Religion Statistics: Predominant Religions." On the World Wide Web at http://www.adherents.com/adh_predom.html (30 November 2001).

Adler, Patricia A. and Peter Adler. 1998. *Peer Power: Preadolescent Culture and Identity*. New Brunswick, NJ: Rutgers University Press.

Agenda Inc. "American Bandstand 2005." On the World Wide Web at http://www.agendainc.com/brandstand05.pdf (26 March 2005).

Ahmad, Imad-ad-Dean. 2000. "Female Genital Mutilation: An Islamic Perspective." On the World Wide Web at http://www.minaret.org/fgm-pamphlet.htm (20 January 2003).

Akin, David. 2002. "Kevin Warwick Is a Borg." *Globe and Mail* 1 June: F7.

Albas, Daniel and Cheryl Albas. 1989. "Modern Magic: The Case of Examinations." *The Sociological Quarterly* 30: 603–13.

Albelda, Randy and Chris Tilly. 1997. *Glass Ceilings and Bottomless Pits: Women's Work, Women's Poverty*. Boston, MA: South End Press.

Almey, Marcia. 2007. "Women in Canada: Work Chapter Updates." On the World Wide Web at http://www.statcan.ca/english/freepub/89F0133XIE/89F0133XIE2006000.htm#10 (21 April 2007).

Amato, Paul R. and Bruce Keith. 1991. "Parental Divorce and the Well-Being of Children: A Meta-Analysis." *Psychological Bulletin* 110: 26–46.

Ambert, Anne-Marie. 1998. "Divorce: Facts, Figures and Consequences." Vanier Institute of the Family. On the World Wide Web at http://www.vifamily.ca/cft/divorce/divorcer.htm (17 February 2000).

American Psychological Association. 1998. "Answers to Your Questions About Sexual Orientation and Homosexuality." On the World Wide Web at http://www.apa.org/pubinfo/orient.html (14 June 2000).

American Society of Plastic Surgeons. 2007. "2000/2005/2006 National Plastic Surgery Statistics." On the World Wide Web at http://www.plasticsurgery.org/media/statistics/loader.cfm?url=/commonspot/security/getfile.cfm&PageID=23628 (25 March 2007).

American Sociological Association. 1999. *Code of Ethics and Policies and Procedures of the ASA Committee on Professional Ethics*. Washington, DC: Author.

Anderson, Benedict O. 1991. *The Imagined Community*, rev. ed. London: Verso.

Anderson, Craig and Brad J. Bushman. 2002. "The Effects of Media Violence on Society." *Science* 295, 5564: 2377–79.

Anderson, Michael. 2003. "Reading Violence in Boys' Writing." *Language Arts* 80, 3: 223–31.

Arace, Michael. 2000. "Oft-injured Forward Feels OK." *Columbus Dispatch* 17 September. On the World Wide Web at http://www.dispatch.com/news/sports00/sept00/424238.html (22 July 2002).

Ariès, Phillipe. 1962 [1960]. *Centuries of Childhood: A Social History of Family Life*, Robert Baldick, trans. New York: Knopf.

Arnett, Jeffrey Jensen. 1995. "Adolescents' Uses of Media for Self-Socialization." *Journal of Youth and Adolescence* 24: 519–33.

Asch, Solomon. 1955. "Opinion and Social Pressure." *Scientific American* July: 31–35.

Associated Press. 2001. "Vancouver Gay Man Beaten to Death: Police Suspect Hate Crime." On the World Wide Web at http://www.planetqnews.com/0812/11.shtml (17 February 2002).

Averett, Susan and Sanders Korenman. 1996. "The Economic Reality of The Beauty Myth." *Journal of Human Resources* 31: 304–30.

Baer, Doug. 1999. "Educational Credentials and the Changing Occupational Structure." Pp. 92–106 in James Curtis, Edward Grabb, and Neil Guppy, eds. *Social Inequality in Canada: Patterns, Problems, Policies*, 3rd ed. Scarborough, ON: Prentice Hall Allyn and Bacon Canada.

Baran, Paul A. 1957. *The Political Economy of Growth*. New York: Monthly Review Press.

Barlow, Maude and Elizabeth May. 2000. *Frederick Street: Life and Death on Canada's Love Canal*. Toronto: HarperCollins.

Bar-On, Dan. 1999. *The Indescribable and the Undiscussable: Reconstructing Human Discourse after Trauma*. Ithaca, NY: Cornell University Press.

Barth, Fredrik, ed. 1969. *Ethnic Groups and Boundaries: The Social Organization of Cultural Difference*. Boston: Little, Brown.

Baudrillard, Jean. 1988 [1986]. *America,* Chris Turner, trans. London: Verso.

Bauman, Zygmunt. 1989. *Modernity and the Holocaust.* Ithaca, NY: Cornell University Press.

Beaupré, Pascale, Pierre Turcotte, and Anne Milan. 2007. "When Is Junior Moving Out? Transitions from the Parental Home to Independence." *Canadian Social Trends* 82: 9–15. Catalogue no. 11-008-XPE. On the World Wide Web at http://www.statcan.ca/english/freepub/11-008-XIE/2006002/pdf/11-008-XIE20060029274.pdf (26 March 2007).

Beck, Ulrich. 1992 [1986]. *Risk Society: Towards a New Modernity,* Mark Ritter, trans. London, UK: Sage.

Becker, Howard S. 1963. *Outsiders: Studies in the Sociology of Deviance.* New York: Free Press.

Bell, Daniel. 1973. *The Coming of Post-Industrial Society: A Venture in Social Forecasting.* New York: Basic Books.

Benford, Robert D. 1997. "An Insider's Critique of the Social Movement Framing Perspective." *Sociological Inquiry* 67: 409–39.

Berger, Peter L. and Thomas Luckmann. 1966. *The Social Construction of Reality: A Treatise in the Sociology of Knowledge.* Garden City, NY: Doubleday.

Berk, Sarah Fenstermaker. 1985. *The Gender Factory: The Apportionment of Work in American Households.* New York: Plenum.

Berliner, Wendy. 2004. "Where Have All the Young Men Gone?" *Manchester Guardian* 18 May: 8.

Besserer, Sandra. 2002. "Criminal Victimization: An International Perspective: Results of the 2000 International Crime Victimization Survey." *Juristat* 22, 4 (May). Catalogue no. 85-002-XPE. Ottawa: Canadian Centre for Justice Statistics and Statistics Canada.

Betcherman, Gordon and Graham Lowe. 1997. *The Future of Work in Canada: A Synthesis Report.* Ottawa: Canadian Policy Research Networks Inc.

Bianchi, Suzanne M. and Daphne Spain. 1996. "Women, Work, and Family in America." *Population Bulletin* 51, 3: 2–48.

Bibby, Reginald W. 1987. *Fragmented Gods: The Poverty and Potential of Religion in Canada.* Toronto: Irwin.

______. 2001. *Canada's Teens: Today, Yesterday, and Tomorrow.* Toronto: Stoddart.

______. 2002. *Restless Gods: The Renaissance of Religion in Canada.* Toronto: Stoddart.

______. 2007. "Religion." Pp. 334–62 in Robert J. Brym, ed. *New Society*, 5th ed. Toronto: Nelson.

Biegler, Rebecca S. 1999. "Psychological Interventions Designed to Counter Sexism in Children: Empirical Limitations and Theoretical Foundations." Pp. 129–52 in William B. Swann, Jr., Judith H. Langlois, and Lucia A. Gilbert, eds. *Sexism and Stereotypes in Modern Society: The Gender Science of Janet Taylor Spence.* Washington, DC: American Psychological Association.

Bierstedt, Robert. 1963. *The Social Order.* New York: McGraw-Hill.

______. 1974. "An Analysis of Social Power." Pp. 220–41 in *Power and Progress: Essays in Sociological Theory.* New York: McGraw-Hill.

Bittman, Michael and Judy Wajcman. 2000. "The Rush Hour: The Character of Leisure Time and Gender Equity." *Social Forces* 79: 165–89.

Blau, Peter M. 1964. *Exchange and Power in Social Life.* New York: Wiley.

Blauner, Robert. 1972. *Racial Oppression in America.* New York: Harper & Row.

Blazer, Dan G., Ronald C. Kessler, Katherine A. McGonagle, and Marvin S. Swartz. 1994. "The Prevalence and Distribution of Major Depression in a National Community Sample: The National Comorbidity Survey." *American Journal of Psychiatry* 151: 979–86.

Blossfeld, Hans-Peter and Yossi Shavit, eds. 1993. *Persistent Inequality: Changing Educational Attainment in Thirteen Countries.* Boulder, CO: Westview Press.

Blum, Deborah. 1997. *Sex on the Brain: The Biological Differences Between Men and Women.* New York: Penguin.

Blumer, Herbert. 1969. *Symbolic Interactionism: Perspective and Method.* Englewood Cliffs, NJ: Prentice-Hall.

Boal, Mark. 1998. "Spycam City." *The Village Voice* (30 September–6 October). On the World Wide Web at http://www.villagevoice.com/issues/9840/boal.shtml (26 March 2001).

Boles, Sharon and Patrick Johnson. 2001. "Gender, Weight Concerns and Adolescent Smoking." *Journal of Addictive Diseases* 20, 2: 5–14.

Bonacich, Edna. 1972. "A Theory of Ethnic Antagonism: The Split Labor Market." *American Sociological Review* 37: 547–59.

Bornholt, Laurel. 2001. "Self-Concepts, Usefulness and Behavioural Intentions on the Social Context of Schooling." *Educational Psychology* 21, 1 (March): 67–78.

Boswell, A. Ayres and Joan Z. Spade. 1996. "Fraternities and Collegiate Rape Culture: Why Are Some Fraternities More Dangerous Places for Women?" *Gender and Society* 10: 133–47.

Bouchard, Thomas J., Jr., David T. Lykken, Matthew McGue, Nancy L. Segal, and Auke Tellegen. 1990. "Sources of Human Psychological Differences: The Minnesota Study of Twins Reared Apart." *Science* 250, 4978: 223–26.

Bourdieu, Pierre. 1977 [1972]. *Outline of a Theory of Practice,* Richard Nice, trans. Cambridge, UK: Cambridge University Press.

______. 1984 [1979]. *Distinction: A Social Critique of the Judgment of Taste*, R. Nice, trans. Cambridge, MA: Harvard University Press.

Bourdieu, Pierre, and Jean-Claude Passeron. 1990. *Reproduction in Education, Society and Culture,* 2nd ed., Richard Nice, trans. London: Sage.

Bowles, Samuel and Herbert Gintis. 1976. *Schooling in Capitalist America: Educational Reform and the Contradictions of Economic Life.* New York: Basic Books.

Boyd, Monica. 1997. "Feminizing Paid Work." *Current Sociology* 45, 2 (April): 49–73.

______. 1999. "Canadian, Eh? Ethnic Origin Shifts in the Canadian Census." *Canadian Ethnic Studies* 31, 3: 1–19.

Boyd, Monica and Doug Norris. 2001. "Who Are the 'Canadians'? Changing Census Responses, 1986–1996." *Canadian Ethnic Studies* 33, 1: 1–25.

Bracey, Gerald W. 1998. "Are U.S. Students Behind?" *The American Prospect* 37, March–April: 54–70. On the World Wide Web at http://www.prospect.org/archives/37/37bracfs.html (1 May 2000).

Braithwaite, John. 1981. "The Myth of Social Class and Criminality Revisited." *American Sociological Review* 46: 36–57.

———. 1989. *Crime, Shame and Reintegration*. New York: Cambridge University Press.

Braver, Sanford L., Pamela J. Fitzpatrick, and R. Curtis Bay. 1991. "Noncustodial Parent's Report of Child Support Payments." *Family Relations* 40, 2 (April): 180–85.

Brechin, Steven R. and Willett Kempton. 1994. "Global Environmentalism: A Challenge to the Postmaterialism Thesis." *Social Science Quarterly* 75: 245–69.

Bricker, Darrell and Edward Greenspon. 2001. *Searching for Certainty: Inside the New Canadian Mindset*. Toronto: Doubleday Canada.

Brint, Stephen. 1984. "New Class and Cumulative Trend Explanations of the Liberal Political Attitudes of Professionals." *American Journal of Sociology* 90: 30–71.

Brower, David. 1975. *Training the Nihilists: Education and Radicalism in Tsarist Russia*. Ithaca, NY: Cornell University Press.

Brown, Lyn Mikel and Carol Gilligan. 1992. *Meeting at the Crossroads: Women's Psychology and Girls' Development*. Cambridge, MA: Harvard University Press.

Brown, Peter. 1996. *The Rise of Western Christendom: Triumph and Diversity, A.D. 200–1000*. Oxford: Blackwell.

Browne, Kevin D. and Catherine Hamilton-Giachritsis. 2005. "The Influence of Violent Media on Children and Adolescents: A Public-Health Approach." *The Lancet* 365, 9460: 702–10.

Browning, Christopher R. 1992. *Ordinary Men: Reserve Police Battalion 101 and the Final Solution in Poland*. New York: HarperCollins.

Bruce, Steve. 1988. *The Rise and Fall of the New Christian Right: Conservative Protestant Politics in America 1978–1988*. Oxford, UK: Clarendon Press.

Brumberg, Joan Jacobs. 1997. *The Body Project: An Intimate History of American Girls*. New York: Random House.

Bryant, Marian E. 1999. "Sentencing Aboriginal Offenders." *Law Now*, October/November: 20–21.

Brym, Robert J. 1979. "Political Conservatism in Atlantic Canada." Pp. 59–79 in Robert J. Brym and R. James Sacouman, eds. *Underdevelopment and Social Movements in Atlantic Canada*. Toronto: New Hogtown Press.

———. 1980. *Intellectuals and Politics*. London, UK: George Allen and Unwin.

———. 1989. "Canada." Pp. 177–206 in Tom Bottomore and Robert J. Brym, eds. *The Capitalist Class: An International Study*. New York: New York University Press.

———. 2001. "Jewish Immigrants from the Former Soviet Union in Canada, 1996." *East European Jewish Affairs* 31: 36–43.

———. 2003. "Affluence, Strikes, and Power in Canada, 1973–2000." In James Curtis, Edward Grabb, and Neil Guppy, eds. *Social Inequality in Canada: Patterns, Problems, Policies*, 4th ed. Scarborough, ON: Prentice-Hall.

———. 2006. "How High School Drama Helped Me to Become a Sociologist: An Essay in the Sociology of Autobiography." *Canadian Journal of Sociology* 31: 245–57.

———. 2007a. "Hip Hop from Caps to Bling." Pp. 13–31 in *Sociology as a Life or Death Issue*. Toronto: Penguin.

———. 2007b. "The Six Lessons of Suicide Bombers." *Contexts* 6, 4: 37–43.

———. 2008. "Religion, Politics, and Suicide Bombing: An Interpretative Essay." *Canadian Journal of Sociology* 33. On the World Wide Web at http://ejournals.library.ualberta.ca/index.php/CJS/ (31 January 2008).

Brym, Robert J. et al. 2005. "In Faint Praise of the World Bank's Gender Development Policy." *Canadian Journal of Sociology* 30: 95–111.

Brym, Robert J. and Bader Araj. 2006. "Suicide Bombing as Strategy and Interaction: The Case of the Second *Inifada*." *Social Forces* 84: 165–82.

Brym, Robert J. and Rhonda Lenton. 2001. *Love Online: A Report on Digital Dating in Canada*. Toronto: MSN.CA. On the World Wide Web at http://www.nelson.com/nelson/harcourt/sociology/newsociety3e/loveonline.pdf (20 December 2001).

Brym, Robert J. with the assistance of Rozalina Ryvkina. 1994. *The Jews of Moscow, Kiev and Minsk: Identity, Antisemitism, Emigration*. New York: New York University Press.

Brym, Robert J., Michael Gillespie, and A. Ron Gillis. 1985. "Anomie, Opportunity, and the Density of Ethnic Ties: Another View of Jewish Outmarriage in Canada." *Canadian Review of Sociology and Anthropology* 22: 102–12.

Brym, Robert J., William Shaffir, and Morton Weinfeld, eds. 1993. *The Jews in Canada*. Toronto: Oxford University Press.

Brzezinski, Zbigniew. 2002. "Confronting Anti-American Grievances." *New York Times* 1 September. On the World Wide Web at http://www.nytimes.com (1 September 2002).

Bullough, Vern L. 2000. "Transgenderism and the Concept of Gender." *International Journal of Transgenderism*, Special Issue 4, 3 (July–Sept).

Bunge, Valerie Pottie. 2000. "Spousal Violence." Pp. 11–21 in Statistics Canada. *Family Violence in Canada: A Statistical Profile 2000*. Catalogue no. 85-224-XIE. Ottawa: Minister of Industry.

Burns, Tom and George M. Stalker. 1961. *The Management of Innovation*. London, UK: Tavistock.

"Business of Touch, The." 2006. On the World Wide Web at http://www.businessoftouch.com/index2.html (7 April 2006).

Buss, David M. 2000. *Dangerous Passion: Why Jealousy Is As Necessary As Love and Sex*. New York: Free Press.

Campbell, Donald and Julian Stanley. 1963. *Experimental and Quasi-experimental Designs for Research*. Chicago: Rand McNally.

Campbell, Frances A. and Craig T. Ramey. 1994. "Effects of Early Intervention on Intellectual and Academic Achievement: A Follow-up Study of Children from Low-income Families." *Child Development* 65: 684–99.

Canadian Council on Social Development. 2001. *The Progress of Canada's Children 2001—Highlights*. On the World Wide Web at http://www.ccsd.ca/pubs/2-1/pcc2001.hl.htm (17 February 2002).

———. 2007. "Families: A Canadian Profile." On the World Wide Web at http://www.ccsd.ca/factsheets/family/ (24 April 2007).

Canadian Journalists for Free Expression. 2000. "CJFE Disappointed at Ontario Superior Court Ruling Against Media Freedom." On the World Wide Web at http://www.cjfe.org/releases/2000/seizures.html (22 March 2001).

Cancio, A. Silvia, T. David Evans, and David J. Maume. 1996. "Reconsidering the Declining Significance of Race: Racial Differences in Early Career Wages." *American Sociological Review* 61: 541–56.

Cardinal, Harold. 1977. *The Rebirth of Canada's Indians*. Edmonton: Hurtig Publishers.

Cardoso, Fernando Henrique, and Enzo Faletto. 1979. *Dependency and Development in Latin America,* Marjory Mattingly Urquidi, trans. Berkeley: University of California Press.

Caron, Roger. 1979. *Go-Boy! The True Story of a Life Behind Bars*. London, UK: Arrow Books Limited.

Carrier, Roch. 1979. *The Hockey Sweater and Other Stories,* Sheila Fischman, trans. Toronto: Anansi.

Cassidy, Barbara, Robina Lord, and Nancy Mandell. 1998. "Silenced and Forgotten Women: Race, Poverty and Disability." Pp. 26–54 in Nancy Mandell, ed. *Race, Class and Sexuality,* 2nd ed. Scarborough: Prentice-Hall Allyn and Bacon.

Cavalli-Sforza, L. Luca, Paola Menozzi, and Alberto Piazza. 1994. *The History and Geography of Human Genes*. Princeton, NJ: Princeton University Press.

CBC News. 2006. "How Do We Measure Poverty?" On the World Wide Web at http://www.cbc.ca/news/background/economy/poverty-line.html (4 April 2007).

Central Intelligence Agency. 2001. *The World Factbook 2001*. On the World Wide Web at http://www.cia.gov/cia/publications/factbook/ (January 10, 2002).

———. 2002. *The World Factbook 2002*. On the World Wide Web at http://www.cia.gov/cia/publications/factbook (6 February 2003).

Chagnon, Napoleon. 1992. *Yanomamö: The Last Days of Eden*. New York: Harcourt, Brace Yovanovich.

Chambliss, William J. 1989. "State-Organized Crime." *Criminology* 27: 183–208.

Chard, Jennifer. 2000. "Women in a Visible Minority." Pp. 219–44 in *Women in Canada, 2000: A Gender-Based Statistical Report*. Ottawa: Statistics Canada.

Chauncey, George. 2005. *Why Marriage? The History Shaping Today's Debate over Gay Equality*. New York: Basic Books.

Chaves, Mark. 1994. "Secularization as Declining Religious Authority." *Social Forces* 72: 749–74.

Cherlin, Andrew J. 1992. *Marriage, Divorce, Remarriage*, revised and enlarged ed. Cambridge, MA: Harvard University Press.

Chesley, Laurie, Donna MacAulay, and Janice L. Ristock. 1991. *Abuse in Lesbian Relationships: A Handbook of Information and Resources*. Toronto: Counselling Centre for Lesbians and Gays.

"Chronological Perspective on Work Stoppages in Canada (Work Stoppages Involving One or More Workers), 1976–2000." 2001. Human Resources Development Canada. On the World Wide Web at http://labour-travail.hrdc-drhc.gc.ca/doc/wid-dimt/eng/ws-at/table.cfm (27 March 2001).

"Chronological Perspective on Work Stoppages in Canada." 1999. Human Resources Development Canada. On the World Wide Web at http://labour.hrdc-drhc.gc.ca/doc/wid-dimt/eng/ws-at/table.cfm (30 June 2003).

"Chronological Perspective on Work Stoppages in Canada." 2001. Human Resources Development Canada. On the World Wide Web at http://labour.hrdc-drhc.gc.ca/doc/wid-dimt/eng/ws-at/table.cfm (22 March 2003).

Church of God. 2001. On the World Wide Web at http://www.childrentaken.com/mediastatement.html (1 October 2002).

Cicourel, Aaron. 1968. *The Social Organization of Juvenile Justice*. New York: Wiley.

Citizenship and Immigration Canada. 2005. *Annual Report to Parliament on Immigration 2005*. Ottawa. On the World Wide Web at http://www.cic.gc.ca/english/pdf/pub/immigration2005_e.pdf (22 March 2007).

———. 2006. "Annual Report to Parliament on Immigration, 2006." On the World Wide Web at http://www.cic.gc.ca/english/pdf/pub/immigration2006_e.pdf (13 April 2007).

Clairborne, William. 2001. "Canadians from Sect Flee to U.S. over Right to Spank." On the World Wide Web at http://www. nospank.net/n-i27.htm (1 October 2003).

Clairmont, Donald H. and Dennis W. Magill. 1999. *Africville: The Life and Death of a Canadian Black Community,* 3rd ed. Toronto: Canadian Scholars' Press.

Clark, Warren. 2003. "Pockets of Belief: Religious Attendance Patterns in Canada." *Canadian Social Trends* 68 (Spring): 2–5. Catalogue no. 11-008-XPE.

Clarke, Harold D., Jane Jenson, Lawrence LeDuc, and Jon H. Pammett. 1996. *Absolute Mandate: Canadian Electoral Politics in an Era of Restructuring*, 3rd ed. Toronto: Gage.

Clarke-Stewart, K. Alison, Christian P. Gruber, and Linda May Fitzgerald. 1994. *Children at Home and in Day Care*. Hillsdale, NJ: Lawrence Erlbaum.

Clement, Wallace H. P. 1897. *The History of the Dominion of Canada*. Toronto: William Briggs.

Cleveland, Gordon and Michael Krashinsky. 1998. *The Benefits and Costs of Good Child Care: The Economic Rationale for Public Investment in Young Children*. Toronto: University of Toronto.

Cloward, Richard A. and Lloyd E. Ohlin. 1960. *Delinquency and Opportunity: A Theory of Delinquent Gangs*. New York: Free Press.

Cohen, Albert. 1955. *Delinquent Boys: The Subculture of a Gang*. New York: Free Press.

Cohen, Lynne. 1999. "Suing the Alternative Health-Care Provider." *Canadian Lawyer* November/December: 47–51.

Cohen, Stanley. 1972. *Folk Devils and Moral Panics: The Creation of the Mods and Rockers*. London: MacGibbon and Kee.

Colapinto, John. 1997. "The True Story of John/Joan." *Rolling Stone* 11 December: 54–73, 92–97.

———. 2001. *As Nature Made Him: The Boy Who Was Raised as a Girl*. Toronto: HarperCollins.

Cole, Michael. 1995. *Cultural Psychology*. Cambridge, MA: Harvard University Press.

Coleman, J. 1988. "Social Capital in the Creation of Human Capital." *American Journal of Sociology* 94: 95–120.

Coleman, James S. 1961. *The Adolescent Society*. New York: Free Press.

______. 1990. *Foundations of Social Theory*. Cambridge, MA: Harvard University Press.

Coleman, James, Ernest Q. Campbell, and Carol J. Hobson. 1966. *Equality of Educational Opportunity*. Washington, DC: United States Department of Health, Education, and Welfare, Office of Education.

Collins, Randall. 1979. *The Credential Society: An Historical Sociology of Education*. New York: Academic Press.

______. 1982. *Sociological Insight: An Introduction to Nonobvious Sociology*. New York: Oxford University Press.

Collins, Randall and Scott Coltrane. 1991. *Sociology of Marriage and the Family: Gender, Love, and Property*, 3rd ed. Chicago: Nelson-Hall.

Commins, Patricia. 1997. "Foreign Sales Prop Up McDonald's." *Globe and Mail* 26 August: B8.

Comte, Auguste. 1975. *Auguste Comte: The Foundation of Sociology*, Kenneth Thompson, ed. New York: Wiley.

Condry, John and Sandra Condry. 1976. "Sex Differences: A Study of The Eye of the Beholder." *Child Development* 47: 812–19.

Converse, Jean M. and Stanley Presser. 1986. *Survey Questions: Handcrafting the Standardized Questionnaire*. Newbury Park, CA: Sage.

Cooley, Charles Horton. 1902. *Human Nature and the Social Order*. New York: Scribner's.

Coontz, Stephanie. 1992. *The Way We Never Were: American Families and the Nostalgia Trap*. New York: Basic Books.

Correctional Service of Canada. 2001. "Basic Facts About Federal Corrections." On the World Wide Web at http://www.csc-scc.gc.ca/text/faits/facts07-content02_e.shtml (1 October 2003).

Coser, Rose Laub. 1960. "Laughter among Colleagues: A Study of the Functions of Humor among the Staff of a Mental Hospital." *Psychiatry* 23: 81–95.

Costanzo, Mark. 1997. *Just Revenge: Costs and Consequences of the Death Penalty*. New York: St. Martin's Press.

Creedon, Jeremiah. 1998. "God with a Million Faces." *Utne Reader* July–August: 42–48.

Creighton, Sarah and Catherine Mihto. 2001. "Managing Intersex." *BMJ: British Medical Journal* 323, 7324 (December): 1264–65.

Crozier, Michel. 1964. *The Bureaucratic Phenomenon*. Chicago: University of Chicago Press.

Culver, John H. 1992. "Capital Punishment, 1997–1998: Characteristics of the 143 Executed." *Sociology and Social Research* 76, 2 (January): 59–61.

Curran, John. 2000. "Thinner Miss Americas: Study: Some Contestants Undernourished." ABCNEWS.com. On the Internet at wysiwyg://7/http://abcnews.go.com/sections/living/DailyNews/missamerica000322.htmk (1 October 2003).

Curtis, Bruce. 1988. *Building the Educational State: Canada West, 1836–1871*. London, ON: Althouse Press.

Curtis, James, John Loy, and Wally Karnilowicz. 1986. "A Comparison of Suicide-Dip Effects of Major Sport Events and Civil Holidays." *Sociology of Sport Journal* 3: 1–14.

CyberPress. 2001. "The Recidivist Roger Caron Stopped Once Again" (translated from the French), 14 October. On the World Wide Web at http://216.239.37.120/transl (1 October 2003).

Dalphonse, Sherri. 1997. "Childfree by Choice." *The Washingtonian* 32, 5: 48–57.

Darwin, Charles. 1859. *On the Origin of Species by Means of Natural Selection*. London: John Murray.

______. 1871. *The Descent of Man*. London: John Murray.

Dauvergne, Mia. 2002. "Homicide in Canada, 2001." *Juristat* 22, 7 (September). Catalogue no. 85-002-XPE. Ottawa: Canadian Centre for Justice Statistics and Statistics Canada.

Davies, James B. 1999. "Distribution of Wealth and Economic Inequality." Pp. 138–50 in James Curtis, Edward Grabb, and Neil Guppy, eds. *Social Inequality in Canada: Patterns, Problems, Policies*, 3rd ed. Scarborough, ON: Prentice Hall Allyn and Bacon Canada.

Davies, James C. 1969. "Toward a Theory of Revolution." Pp. 85–108 in Barry McLaughlin, ed. *Studies in Social Movements: A Social Psychological Perspective*. New York: Free Press.

Davies, Mark and Denise B. Kandel. 1981. "Parental and Peer Influences on Adolescents' Educational Plans: Some Further Evidence." *American Journal of Sociology* 87: 363–87.

Davis, Fred. 1992. *Fashion, Culture, and Identity*. Chicago: University of Chicago Press.

Davis, Kingsley and Wilbert E. Moore. 1945. "Some Principles of Stratification." *American Sociological Review* 10: 242–49.

Dawson, Carl A. 1936. *Group Settlement: Ethnic Communities in Western Canada*. Toronto: Macmillan Company of Canada.

Dawson, Lorne. 1993. "Religion and Legitimacy." Pp. 311–27 in Peter S. Li and B. Singh Bolaria, eds. *Contemporary Sociology: Critical Perspectives*. Toronto: Copp Clark Pitman.

DeKeseredy, Walter S. and Katherine Kelly. 1993. "The Incidence and Prevalence of Woman Abuse in Canadian University and College Dating Relationships." *Canadian Journal of Sociology* 18: 137–59.

Demo, David H., Mark A. Fine, and Lawrence H. Ganong. 2000. "Divorce as a Family Stressor." Pp. 279–302 in P. C. McKenry and S. J. Price, eds. *Families & Change: Coping with Stressful Events and Transitions*, 2nd ed. Thousand Oaks, CA: Sage Publications.

Denton, Frank T. 1983. "Section D: The Labour Force." *Historical Statistics of Canada*. Catalogue 11-516, Series D160-174. On the World Wide Web at http://www.statcan.ca/english/freepub/11-516-XIE/sectiond/sectiond.htm (23 August 2007).

Denzin, Norman K. 1992. *Symbolic Interactionism and Cultural Studies: The Politics of Interpretation*. Oxford, UK: Blackwell.

Derber, Charles. 1979. *The Pursuit of Attention: Power and Individualism in Everyday Life*. New York: Oxford University Press.

DeSteno, David and Peter Salovey. 2001. "Evolutionary Origins of Sex Differences in Jealousy: Questioning the 'Fitness' of the Model." Pp. 150–56 in W. Gerrod Parrott, ed. *Emotions in Social Psychology: Essential Readings*. Philadelphia: Psychology Press.

Diamond, Milton. 1982. "Sexual Identity: Monozygotic Twins Reared in Discordant Sex Roles and a BBC Follow-up." *Archives of Sexual Behavior* 11: 181–86.

Diamond, Milton and H. Keith Sigmundson. 1999. "Sex Reassignment at Birth." Pp. 55–75 in Stephen J. Ceci and Wendy W. Williams, eds. *The Nature–Nurture Debate: The Essential Readings*. Maldan, MA: Blackwell.

Dickens, Charles. *A Tale of Two Cities*. 2004 [1859]. On the World Wide Web at http://www.literature.org/authors/dickens-charles/two-cities/ (4 July 2005).

Dietz, Tracy L. 1998. "An Examination of Violence and Gender Role Portrayals in Video Games: Implications for Gender Socialization and Aggressive Behavior." *Sex Roles* 38: 425–42.

"Digital Dilemmas." 2003. *The Economist* 25 January: 3–26. On the World Wide Web at http://www.economist.com/displayStory.cfm?Story_id 1534303 (29 May 2003).

DiMaggio, Paul. 1982. "Cultural Capital and School Success: The Impact of Status Culture Participation on the Grades of U.S. High School Students." *American Sociological Review* 47: 189–201.

Doherty, Gillian. 1997. *Zero to Six: The Basis for School Readiness*. Ottawa: Applied Research Branch, Human Resources Development Canada (#R-97-8E).

Donahue III, John J., and Steven D. Levitt. 2001. "The Impact of Legalized Abortion on Crime." *Quarterly Journal of Economics* 116: 379–420.

Douglas, Emily M. and Murray A. Straus. 2006. "Assault and Injury of Dating Partners by University Students in 19 Nations and Its Relation to Corporal Punishment Experienced as a Child." *European Journal of Criminology* 3: 293–318.

Doyle, Aaron, Brian Elliott, and David Tindall. 1997. "Framing the Forests: Corporations, the B.C. Forest Alliance, and the Media." Pp. 240–68 in William Carroll, ed. *Organizing Dissent: Contemporary Social Movements in Theory and Practice,* 2nd ed. Toronto: Garamond Press.

Dranoff, Linda Silver. 2001. *Everyone's Guide to the Law*. Toronto: HarperCollins.

Dugger, Karen. 1996. "Social Location and Gender-Role Attitudes: A Comparison of Black and White Women." Pp. 32–51 in Esther Ngan-Ling Chow, Doris Wilkinson, and Maxine Baca Zinn, eds. *Race, Class, and Gender*. Newbury Park, CA: Sage.

Dumas, Jean and Yves Perron. 1992. *Current Demographic Analysis: Marriage and Conjugal Life in Canada*. Catalogue no. 91-534. Ottawa: Statistics Canada.

Duncan, Greg, W. Jean Yeung, Jeanne Brooks-Gunn, and Judith Smith. 1998. "How Much Does Childhood Poverty Affect the Life Chance of Children?" *American Sociological Review* 63: 402–23.

Durkheim, Émile. 1938 [1895]. *The Rules of Sociological Method,* G.E.G. Catlin, ed., Solovay and J. Mueller, trans. Chicago: University of Chicago Press.

______. 1951 [1897]. *Suicide: A Study in Sociology,* G. Simpson, ed., J. Spaulding and G. Simpson, trans. New York: Free Press.

______. 1956. *Education and Sociology,* Sherwood D. Fox, trans. New York: Free Press.

______. 1961 [1925]. *Moral Education: A Study in the Theory and Application of the Sociology of Education,* Everett K. Wilson and Herman Schnurer, trans. New York: Free Press.

______. 1973 [1899–1900]. "Two Laws of Penal Evolution." *Economy and Society* 2: 285–308.

______. 1976 [1915/1912]. *The Elementary Forms of the Religious Life,* Joseph Ward Swain, trans. New York: Free Press.

______. 1997 [1893]. *The Division of Labor in Society.* New York: Free Press.

Dutton, Judy. 2000. "Detect His Lies Every Time." *Cosmopolitan* April: 126.

e.Harlequin.com. 2006. "About eHarlequin.com." On the World Wide Web at http://www.eharlequin.com/articlepage.html;jsessionid=88F358D3D78BC869CC43E64EDA5987F8?articleId=36& chapter=0 (24 August 2007).

Eagley, Alice H. and Wendy Wood. 1999. "The Origins of Sex Differences in Human Behaviour: Evolved Dispositions versus Social Roles." *American Psychologist* 54: 408–23.

Eccles, Jacquelynne S., Janis E. Jacobs, and Rena D. Harold. 1990. "Gender Role Stereotypes, Expectancy Effects and Parents' Socialization of Gender Differences." *Journal of Social Issues* 46: 183–201.

"Echoes of the Columbine Massacre." 2000. *Maclean's* 1 May: 20.

Edmundson, Mark. 2003. "How Teachers Can Stop Cheaters." *New York Times* 9 September. On the World Wide Web at http://www.nytimes.com (9 September 2003).

EGALE. 2001. "Svend Robinson Introduces Bill, EGALE Renews Call for Hate Crimes Protection in Wake of Murder of Gay Man in Vancouver." Press release, 22 November. On the World Wide Web at http://www.egale.ca/pressrel/011122.htm (9 September 2003).

Eichler, Margrit. 1987. *Nonsexist Research Methods*. Boston: Allen and Unwin.

______. 1988. *Families in Canada Today,* 2nd ed. Toronto: Gage.

Ekman, Paul. 1978. *Facial Action Coding System*. New York: Consulting Psychologists Press.

Elias, Norbert. 1994 [1939]. *The Civilizing Process,* Edmund Jephcott, trans. Oxford: Blackwell.

Elliott, H. L. 1995. "Living Vicariously Through Barbie." On the World Wide Web at http://ziris.syr.edu/path/public_html/barbie/main.html (19 November 1998).

Ellul, Jacques. 1964 [1954]. *The Technological Society,* John Wilkinson, trans. New York: Vintage.

Engels, Frederick. 1970 [1884]. *The Origins of the Family, Private Property and the State,* Eleanor Burke Leacock, ed., Alec West, trans. New York: International Publishers.

England, Paula. 1992. *Comparable Worth: Theories and Evidence*. Hawthorne, NY: Aldine de Gruyter.

Entine, J. 2000. *Taboo: Why Black Athletes Dominate Sports and Why We Are Afraid to Talk about It*. New York: Public Affairs.

Estrich, Susan. 1987. *Real Rape*. Cambridge, MA: Harvard University Press.

"Ethnic Groups in the World." 1998. *Scientific American*. On the World Wide Web at http://www.sciam.com/1998/0998issue/0998numbers.html (4 December 2001).

"Face of the Web Study Pegs Global Internet Population at More than 300 Million." 2000. On the World Wide Web at http://www.angusreid.com/media/content/displaypr.cfm?idto_view=1001 (2 October 2000).

Fagot, Berly I., Caire S. Rodgers, and Mary D. Leinbach. 2000. "Theories of Gender Socialization." Pp. 65–89 in Thomas Eckes, ed. *The Developmental Social Psychology of Gender*. Mahwah, NJ: Lawrence Erlbaum Associates.

Families Against Deadbeats. 2000. On the World Wide Web at http://www.wantedposters.com (9 September 2003).

Farrell, Colin. n.d. "The Canadian Prison Strap." On the World Wide Web at http://www.corpun.com/canada2.html (9 September 2003).

Fattah, Ezzat A. 1991. *Understanding Criminal Victimization: An Introduction to Theoretical Victimology*. Scarborough, ON: Prentice Hall.

Fekete, John. 1994. *Moral Panics: Biopolitics Rising*. Toronto: Robert Davies.

Fellegi, Ivan. 2000. "On Poverty and Low Income." In Statistics Canada. *Income in Canada 1998*. Ottawa: Ministry of Industry.

Felson, Richard B. 1996. "Mass Media Effects on Violent Behavior." *Annual Review of Sociology* 22: 103–28.

Fernandez-Dols, Jose-Miguel, Flor Sanchez, Pilar Carrera, and Maria-Angeles Ruiz-Belda. 1997. "Are Spontaneous Expressions and Emotions Linked? An Experimental Test of Coherence." *Journal of Nonverbal Behavior* 21: 163–77.

Fields, Jason and Kristin Smith. 1998. "Poverty, Family Structure, and Child Well-Being." Population Division. Washington, DC: U.S. Bureau of Census.

"50 Largest (Population) Countries in the World." 2003. *GeoHive*. On the World Wide Web at http://www .geohive.com/global/c_p_pop50.php (24 May 2003).

Figart, Deborah M. and June Lapidus. 1996. "The Impact of Comparable Worth on Earnings Inequality." *Work and Occupations* 23: 297–318.

Finke, Roger and Rodney Starke. 1992. *The Churching of America, 1776–1990: Winners and Losers in Our Religious Economy*. New Brunswick, NJ: Rutgers University Press.

Finnie, Ross. 1993. "Women, Men and the Economic Consequences of Divorce: Evidence from Canadian Longitudinal Data." *Canadian Review of Sociology and Anthropology* 30, 2: 205–41.

Fischer, Claude S., Michael Hout, Martín Sánchez Jankowski, Samuel R. Lucas, Ann Swidler, and Kim Voss. 1996. *Inequality by Design: Cracking the Bell Curve Myth*. Princeton, NJ: Princeton University Press.

Fisher, John. 1999. *A Report on Lesbian, Gay and Bisexual Youth*. Ottawa: EGALE.

Flood, Gavin D. 1996. *An Introduction to Hinduism*. Cambridge: Cambridge University Press.

Flowers, Paul and Katie Buston. 2001. "'I Was Terrified of Being Different': Exploring Gay Men's Accounts of Growing-Up in a Heterosexist Society." *Journal of Adolescence, Special Issue: Gay, Lesbian, and Bisexual Youth* 24, 1 (February): 51–65.

Forbes.com. 2007. "The World's Billionaires." On the World Wide Web at http://www.forbes.com/lists/2007/10/07billionaires_The-Worlds-Billionaires-North-America_6Rank.html (3 April 2007).

Förster, Michael and Michele Pellizzari. 2000. *Trends and Driving Factors in Income Distribution and Poverty in the OECD Area*. Labour Market and Social Policy Occasional Papers No. 42. Paris: OECD.

Foucault, Michel. 1977 [1975]. *Discipline and Punish: The Birth of the Prison,* Alan Sheridan, trans. New York: Pantheon.

———. 1990 [1978]. *The History of Sexuality: An Introduction,* vol. 1. Robert Hurley, trans. New York: Vintage.

Frank Porter Graham Child Development Center. 1999. "Early Learning, Later Success: The Abecedarian Study." On the World Wide Web at http://www.fpg.unc.edu/~abc/abcedarianWeb/index.htm (10 August 2000).

Frank, Robert H. 1988. *Passions within Reason: The Strategic Role of the Emotions*. New York: Norton.

Frank, Thomas and Matt Weiland, eds. 1997. *Commodify Your Dissent: Salvos from the Baffler*. New York: W. W. Norton.

Franklin, Karen. 1998. "Psychosocial Motivations of Hate Crime Perpetrators." Paper presented at the annual meetings of the American Psychological Association (San Francisco: 16 August).

———. 2000. "Antigay Behaviors Among Young Adults." *Journal of Interpersonal Violence,* 15, 4: 339–62.

Franklin, Sara and Helen Ragone, eds. 1999. *Reproducing Reproduction*. Philadelphia: University of Pennsylvania Press.

Freedman, Jonathan L. 2002. *Media Violence and Its Effect on Aggression: Assessing the Scientific Evidence*. Toronto: University of Toronto Press.

Freire, Paolo. 1972. *The Pedagogy of the Oppressed*. New York: Herder and Herder.

Frenette, Marc. 2007. "Why Are Youth from Lower-Income Families Less Likely to Attend University? Evidence from Academic Abilities, Parental Influences, and Financial Constraints." Catalogue no. 11F0019MIE. Ottawa: Statistics Canada. On the World Wide Web at http://www.statcan.ca/english/research/11F0019MIE/11F0019MIE2007295.pdf (26 April 2007).

Freud, Sigmund. 1962 [1930]. *Civilization and Its Discontents,* James Strachey, trans. New York: W. W. Norton.

———. 1973 [1915–17]. *Introductory Lectures on Psychoanalysis,* James Strachey, trans., James Strachey and Angela Richards, eds. Harmondsworth, UK: Penguin.

Freudenburg, William R. 1997. "Contamination, Corrosion and the Social Order: An Overview." *Current Sociology* 45, 3: 19–39.

Friedenberg, Edgar Z. 1959. *The Vanishing Adolescent*. Boston: Beacon Press.

Fullan, Michael. 1998. "Leadership for the 21st Century: Breaking the Bonds of Dependency." *Educational Leadership* 55, 7. On the World Wide Web at http://ascd.org/readingroom/edlead/9804/full.html (29 September 2000).

———. 2001. *The New Meaning of Educational Change,* 3rd ed. New York: Teachers College Press.

Gabor, Thomas. 1994. *Everybody Does It: Crime by the Public.* Toronto: University of Toronto Press.

Gado, Mark. 2003. "A Cry in the Night: The Kitty Genovese Murder." *Court TV's Crime Library.* On the World Wide Web at http://www.crimelibrary.com/serial_killers/predators/kitty_genovese/1.html (23 July 2003).

Gallup Organization. 2004. "American Public Opinion about Gay and Lesbian Marriages." On the World Wide Web at http://www.gallup.com/poll/focus/sr040127.asp (5 March 2004).

Galper, Joseph. 1998. "Schooling for Society." *American Demographics* 20, 3: 33–34.

Gamson, William A., Bruce Fireman, and Steven Rytina. 1982. *Encounters with Unjust Authority.* Homewood, IL: Dorsey Press.

Gans, Herbert. 1991. "Symbolic Ethnicity: The Future of Ethnic Groups and Cultures in America." Pp. 430–43 in Norman R. Yetman, ed. *Majority and Minority: The Dynamics of Race and Ethnicity in American Life,* 5th ed. Boston, MA: Allyn and Bacon.

Garfinkel, Harold. 1967. *Studies in Ethnomethodology.* Englewood Cliffs, NJ: Prentice-Hall.

Garland, David. 1990. *Punishment and Modern Society: A Study in Social Theory.* Chicago: University of Chicago Press.

Garner, David M. 1997. "The 1997 Body Image Survey Results." *Psychology Today* 30, 1: 30–44.

Garvey, Christine Ann. 1999. "The Intergenerational Transmission of Discipline." *Dissertation Abstracts International, Section A: The Sciences and Engineering* 60, 3-B (September): 1027.

Gaskell, Jane, Arlene McLaren, and Myra Novogrodsky. 1995. "What's Worth Knowing? Defining the Feminist Curriculum." Pp. 100–18 in Adie D. Nelson and Barrie W. Robinson, eds. *Gender in the 1990s: Images, Realities, and Issues.* Scarborough: Nelson Canada.

Gauvain, Mary, Beverly I. Fagot, Craig Leve, and Kate Kavanagh. 2002. "Instruction by Mothers and Fathers During Problem Solving with Their Young Children." *Journal of Family Psychology* 6, 1 (March): 81–90.

Gegax, T. Trent and Lynette Clemetson. 1998. "The Abortion Wars Come Home." *Newsweek* 9 November: 34–35.

Geis, Gilbert. 1994. "Corporate Crime: 'Three Strikes You're Out?'" *Multinational Monitor* 15, 6 (June): 30–31.

Gelbspan, Ross. 1999. "Trading Away Our Chances to End Global Warming." *Boston Globe* 16 May: E2.

Gelles, Richard J. 1997. *Intimate Violence in Families,* 3rd ed. Thousand Oaks, CA: Sage.

George, Jane. 1998. "Kuujjuaq Daycare Thrives on Federal Head Start Program." *Nunatsiaq News* 29 October. On the World Wide Web at http://www.nunatsiaq.com/archives/nunavut981031/nvt81030_13.html (19 September 2000).

Ghalam, Nancy Z. 1997. "Attitudes Towards Women, Work and Family." *Canadian Social Trends* 46: 13–17. Catalogue no. 11-008-XPE.

Giddens, Anthony. 1987. *Sociology: A Brief but Critical Introduction,* 2nd ed. New York: Harcourt Brace Jovanovich.

______. 1990. *The Consequences of Modernity.* Stanford, CA: Stanford University Press.

Gilbert, Susan. 1997. "2 Spanking Studies Indicate Parents Should Be Cautious." *New York Times* 20 August.

Gilman, Sander L. 1991. *The Jew's Body.* New York: Routledge.

Gleick, James. 2000. *Faster: The Acceleration of Just About Everything.* New York: Vintage.

Glendon, Mary Ann. 1981. *The New Family and the New Property.* Toronto: Butterworths.

Glenn, Norval D. 1990. "Quantitative Research on Marital Quality in the 1980s: A Critical Review." *Journal of Marriage and the Family* 52 (November): 818–31.

Global Reach. 2001. "Global Internet Statistics (by Language)." On the World Wide Web at http://www.glreach.com/globstats/index.php3 (23 September 2001).

______. 2004. "Global Internet Statistics (by Language)." On the World Wide Web at http://www.glreach.com/globstats/ (27 January 2005).

Glock, Charles Y. 1962. "On the Study of Religious Commitment." *Religious Education* 62, 4: 98–110.

Goddard Institute for Space Studies. 2003. "Annual Mean Temperature Anomalies in .01 C: Selected Zonal Means." On the World Wide Web at http://www.giss.nasa.gov/data/update/gistemp/zonann.ts.txt (29 July 2003).

Goffman, Erving. 1959. *The Presentation of Self in Everyday Life,* reprinted ed. Garden City, NY: Anchor.

______. 1961. *Asylums: Essays on the Social Situation of Mental Patients and Other Inmates.* Garden City, NY: Anchor Books.

______. 1963. *Stigma: Notes on the Management of Spoiled Identity.* Englewood Cliffs, NJ: Prentice-Hall.

______. 1974. *Frame Analysis.* Cambridge, MA: Harvard University Press.

Goldie, Terry. 2001. *In a Queer Country: Gay & Lesbian Studies in the Canadian Context.* Vancouver: Arsenal Pulp Press.

Gombrich, Richard Francis. 1996. *How Buddhism Began: The Conditioned Genesis of the Early Teachings.* London: Athlone.

Goode, Erich and Nachman Ben-Yehuda. 1994. *Moral Panics: The Social Construction of Deviance.* Cambridge, MA: Blackwell.

Gordon, Sarah. 1984. *Hitler, Germans, and the Jewish Question.* Princeton, NJ: Princeton University Press.

Gorman, Christine. 1997. "A Boy without a Penis." *Time* 24 March: 83.

Gottfredson, Michael and Travis Hirschi. 1990. *A General Theory of Crime.* Stanford, CA: Stanford University Press.

Gottwald, Norman K. 1979. *The Tribes of Yahweh: A Sociology of the Religion of Liberated Israel, 1250–1050 B.C.E.* Maryknoll, NY: Orbis.

Gould, Stephen J. 1988. "Kropotkin Was No Crackpot." *Natural History* 97, 7: 12–18.

______. 1996. *The Mismeasure of Man,* rev. ed. New York: W. W. Norton.

Government of Canada. 2001. *Job Futures.* On the World Wide Web at http://www.11hrdc-drhc.gc.ca/doc/jf/index.shtml (2 March 2001).

———. 2002. "Study Released on Firearms in Canada." On the World Wide Web at http://www .cfc-ccaf.gc.ca/media/news_releases/2002/ survey-08202002_e.asp (29 December 2005).

Grange, Michael. 2000. "Recreational Hockey Not All Fun and Games." *Globe and Mail* 26 February: S1, S5.

Granovetter, Mark. 1973. "The Strength of Weak Ties." *American Sociological Review* 78: 1360–80.

Greenhill, Pauline. 2001. "Can You See the Difference: Queerying the Nation, Ethnicity, Festival, and Culture in Winnipeg." Pp. 103–21 in Terry Goldie, ed. *In a Queer Country: Gay & Lesbian Studies in the Canadian Context.* Vancouver: Arsenal Pulp Press.

Greenstein, Theodore. 1996. "Husbands' Participation in Domestic Labor: Interactive Effects of Wives' and Husbands' Gender Ideologies." *Journal of Marriage and the Family* 58: 585–95.

Grimes, Craig. 1997. "Adult Criminal Court Statistics, 1995–96." *Juristat* 17, 6 (May). Catalogue no. 85-002-XPE. Ottawa: Canadian Centre for Justice Statistics and Statistics Canada. On the World Wide Web at http://dsp-psd.pwgsc.gc.ca/Collection-R/Statcan/85-002-XIE/0069785-002-XIE.pdf (23 August 2007).

Guillén, Mauro F. 2001. "Is Globalization Civilizing, Destructive or Feeble? A Critique of Five Key Debates in the Social Science Literature." *Annual Review of Sociology* 27. On the World Wide Web at http://knowledge.wharton.upenn.edu/PDFs/938.pdf (6 February 2003).

Gundersen, Edna, Bill Keveney, and Ann Oldenburg. 2002. "The Osbournes Find a Home in America's Living Rooms." *USA Today* 19 April: 1A–2A.

Guppy, Neil and Scott Davies. 1998. *Education in Canada: Recent Trends and Future Challenges.* Ottawa: Ministry of Industry.

Gurr, Ted Robert. 1970. *Why Men Rebel.* Princeton, NJ: Princeton University Press.

Haas, Jack and William Shaffir. 1987. *Becoming Doctors: The Adoption of a Cloak of Competence.* Greenwich, CT: JAI Press.

Hagan, John. 1994. *Crime and Disrepute.* Thousand Oaks, CA: Pine Forge Press.

———. 2000. "White-Collar and Corporate Crime." Pp. 459–82 in Rick Linden, ed. *Criminology: A Canadian Perspective,* 4th ed. Toronto: Harcourt Canada.

Hagan, John, John Simpson, and A. R. Gillis. 1987. "Class in the Household: A Power-Control Theory of Gender and Delinquency." *American Journal of Sociology* 92: 788–816.

Haines, Herbert H. 1996. *Against Capital Punishment: The Anti-Death Penalty Movement in America, 1972–1994.* New York: Oxford University Press.

Hall, Edward. 1959. *The Silent Language.* New York: Doubleday.

———. 1966. *The Hidden Dimension.* New York: Doubleday.

Hamachek, D. 1995. "Self-concept and School Achievement: Interaction Dynamics and a Tool for Assessing the Self-concept Component." *Journal of Counseling and Development* 73: 419–25.

Hamilton, Roberta. 1996. *Gendering the Vertical Mosaic: Feminist Perspectives on Canadian Society.* Toronto: Copp-Clark.

Hammonds, Bruce. 2002. "The Latest Ideas on School Reform by Michael Fullan." *Leading and Learning for the 21st C* 1, 3. On the World Wide Web at http://www.leading-learning.co.nz/newsletters/vol101-no03-2002.html (29 June 2002).

Hampton, Keith N. and Barry Wellman. 1999. "Netville On-Line and Off-Line: Observing and Surveying a Wired Suburb." *American Behavioral Scientist* 43: 475–92.

Hancock, Lynnell. 1994. "In Defiance of Darwin: How a Public School in the Bronx Turns Dropouts into Scholars." *Newsweek* 24 October: 61.

Haney, Craig, W. Curtis Banks, and Philip G. Zimbardo. 1973. "Interpersonal Dynamics in a Simulated Prison." *International Journal of Criminology and Penology* 1: 69–97.

Hanke, Robert. 1998. "'Yo Quiero Mi MTV!' Making Music Television for Latin America." Pp. 219–45 in Thomas Swiss, Andrew Herman, and John M. Sloop, eds. *Mapping the Beat: Popular Music and Contemporary Theory.* Oxford, UK: Blackwell.

Hannigan, John. 1995. "The Postmodern City: A New Urbanization?" *Current Sociology* 43, 1: 151–217.

Hannon, Roseann, David S. Hall, Todd Kuntz, Van Laar, and Jennifer Williams. 1995. "Dating Characteristics Leading to Unwanted vs. Wanted Sexual Behavior." *Sex Roles* 33: 767–83.

Harding, David J., Cybelle Fox, and Jal D. Mehta. 2002. "Studying Rare Events through Qualitative Case Studies: Lessons from a Study of Rampage School Shootings." *Sociological Methods and Research* 31, 2: 174–217.

Harris, Marvin. 1974. *Cows, Pigs, Wars and Witches: The Riddles of Culture.* New York: Random House.

Hartnagel, Timothy F. 2000. "Correlates of Criminal Behaviour." Pp. 94–136 in Rick Linden, ed. *Criminology: A Canadian Perspective,* 4th ed. Toronto: Harcourt Canada.

Harvey, Andrew S., Katherine Marshall, and Judith A. Frederick. 1991. *Where Does the Time Go?* Ottawa: Statistics Canada.

Harvey, Elizabeth. 1999. "Short-Term and Long-Term Effects of Early Parental Employment on Children of the National Longitudinal Survey of Youth." *Developmental Psychology* 35: 445–49.

Haythornwaite, Caroline, and Barry Wellman. 2002. "The Internet in Everyday Life: An Introduction." Pp. 3–41 in Caroline Haythornwaite and Barry Wellman, eds. *The Internet in Everyday Life.* Oxford: Blackwell.

Health Canada. 1999a. *Statistical Report on the Health of Canadians.* Available on the World Wide Web at http://www.hc-sc.gc.ca/hppb/phdd/report/state/englover.html (25 December 1999).

———. 1999b. *Toward a Healthy Future: Second Report on the Health of Canadians.* Prepared by the Federal, Provincial, and Territorial Advisory Committee on Population Health for the Meeting of Ministers of Health, Charlottetown, PEI. September. On the World Wide Web at http://www.hc-sc.gc.ca (4 April 2000).

Hechter, Michael. 1974. *Internal Colonialism: The Celtic Fringe in British National Development, 1536–1966.* Berkeley, CA: University of California Press.

———. 1987. *Principles of Group Solidarity.* Berkeley, CA: University of California Press.

Hendrick, Dianne. 1997. "Youth Court Statistics Highlights, 1995–96." *Juristat* 17, 10 (October). Catalogue no. 85-002-XPE. Ottawa: Canadian Centre for Justice Statistics and Statistics Canada. On the World Wide Web at http://dsp-psd.pwgsc.gc.ca/Collection-R/Statcan/85-002-XIE/0109785-002-XIE.pdf (23 August 2007).

Hendrick, Dianne and Lee Farmer. 2002. "Adult Correctional Services in Canada, 2000/01." *Juristat* 22, 10 (October). Catalogue no. 85-002-XPE. Ottawa: Canadian Centre for Justice Statistics and Statistics Canada.

Henry, Frances, Carol Tator, Winston Mattis, and Tim Rees. 2001. "The Victimization of Racial Minorities in Canada." Pp. 145–60 in Robert J. Brym, ed. *Society in Question: Sociological Readings for the 21st Century,* 3rd ed. Toronto: Harcourt Canada.

Herdt, Gilbert. 2001. "Social Change, Sexual Diversity, and Tolerance for Bisexuality in the United States." Pp. 267–83 in Anthony R. D'Augelli and Charlotte J. Patterson, eds. *Lesbian, Gay, and Bisexual Identities and Youth: Psychological Perspectives.* New York: Oxford University Press.

Herman, Edward S. and Gerry O'Sullivan. 1989. *The "Terrorism" Industry: The Experts and Institutions That Shape Our View of Terror.* New York: Pantheon.

Herrnstein, Richard J. and Charles Murray. 1994. *The Bell Curve: Intelligence and Class Structure in American Life.* New York: Free Press.

Hersch, Patricia. 1998. *A Tribe Apart: A Journey into the Heart of American Adolescence.* New York: Ballantine Books.

Hertzman, Clyde, 2000. "The Case for Early Childhood Development Strategy." *Isuma: Canadian Journal of Policy Research* 1, 2: 11–18.

Hesse-Biber, Sharlene. 1996. *Am I Thin Enough Yet? The Cult of Thinness and the Commercialization of Identity.* New York: Oxford University Press.

Hesse-Biber, Sharlene and Gregg Lee Carter. 2000. *Working Women in America: Split Dreams.* New York: Oxford University Press.

Hirschi, Travis. 1969. *Causes of Delinquency.* Berkeley, CA: University of California Press.

Hirschman, Albert O. 1970. *Exit, Voice, and Loyalty: Responses to Decline in Firms, Organizations, and States.* Cambridge, MA: Harvard University Press.

Hobbes, Thomas. 1968 [1651]. *Leviathan.* Middlesex, UK: Penguin.

Hoberman, John. 1997. *Darwin's Athletes: How Sport Has Damaged Black America and Preserved the Myth of Race.* Boston: Houghton Mifflin.

Hobsbawm, Eric. 1994. *Age of Extremes: The Short Twentieth Century, 1914–1991.* London: Abacus.

Hochschild, Arlie Russell. 1979. "Emotion Work, Feeling Rules, and Social Structure." *American Journal of Sociology* 85: 551–75.

______. 1983. *The Managed Heart: Commercialization of Human Feeling.* Berkeley: University of California Press.

Hochschild, Arlie Russell with Anne Machung. 1989. *The Second Shift: Working Parents and the Revolution at Home.* New York: Viking.

Hodgson, Marshall G. S. 1974. *The Venture of Islam: Conscience and History in a World Civilization,* 3 vols. Chicago: University of Chicago Press.

Homans, George Caspar. 1950. *The Human Group.* New York: Harcourt, Brace.

______. 1961. *Social Behavior: Its Elementary Forms.* New York: Harcourt, Brace and World.

"Homosexuality and Bisexuality." 2000. *Report #5 to the Toronto Sun on the Third Annual Sun/COMPAS Sex Survey.* On the World Wide Web at http://www.compas.ca/html/archivesdocument.asp?compasSection=Sun+Media+Sex+Poll&GO=GO&compasID=61 (9 August 2002).

hooks, bell. 1984. *Feminist Theory: From Margin to Center.* Boston: South End Press.

Houpt, Simon. 2004. "Pass the Popcorn, Save the World." *Globe and Mail* 29 May: R1, R13.

Houseknecht, Sharon K., and Jaya Sastry. 1996. "Family 'Decline' and Child Well-Being: A Comparative Assessment." *Journal of Marriage and the Family* 58: 726–39.

"How to Tell Your Friends from the Japs." 1941. *Time* 22 December: 33.

Huesmann, L. Rowell, Jessica Moise-Titus, Cheryl-Lynn Podolski, and Leonard D. Eron. 2003. "Longitudinal Relations between Children's Exposure to TV Violence and their Aggressive and Violent Behavior in Young Adulthood: 1977–1992." *Developmental Psychology* 39, 2: 201–21.

Hughes, Diane, Ellen Galinsky, and Anne Morris. 1992. "The Effects of Job Characteristics on Marital Quality: Specifying Linking Mechanisms." *Journal of Marriage and the Family* 54, 1 (February): 31–42.

Hughes, Everett C. 1943. *French Canada in Transition.* Chicago: University of Chicago Press.

Hughes, Fergus P. 1995. *Children, Play and Development,* 2nd ed. Boston: Allyn and Bacon.

Human Resources and Social Development Canada. 2006. "Database on Minimum Wages." On the World Wide Web at http://srv116.services.gc.ca/wid-dimt/mwa/menu.aspx (1 April 2007).

Human Rights Watch. 1995. *The Human Rights Watch Global Report on Women's Human Rights.* New York: Human Rights Watch.

Hunter, James Davison. 1991. *Culture Wars: The Struggle to Define America.* New York: Basic Books.

Hunter, Shireen T. 1998. *The Future of Islam and the West: Clash of Civilizations or Peaceful Coexistence?* Westport, CT: Praeger.

Ignatieff, Michael. 2000. *The Rights Revolution.* Toronto: Anansi.

Ignatiev, Noel. 1995. *How the Irish Became White.* New York: Routledge.

Infocom. 2003. "Bureaucracy." On the World Wide Web at http://infocom.elsewhere.org/gallery/bureaucracy.bureaucracy.html (14 March 2003).

InfoPlease. 2005. "Democratic Republic of the Congo." On the World Wide Web at http://www.infoplease.com/ipa/A0198161.html (18 July 2005).

Ingram, Gordon Brent. 2001. "Redesigning Wreck: Beach Meets Forest as Location of Male Homoerotic Culture in Placemaking in Pacific Canada." Pp. 188–208 in Terry Goldie, ed. *In a Queer Country: Gay & Lesbian Studies in the Canadian Context.* Vancouver: Arsenal Pulp Press.

Inkeles, Alex and David H. Smith. 1976. *Becoming Modern: Individual Change in Six Developing Countries.* Cambridge, MA: Harvard University Press.

Integration Analysis Program. 1999. "Sex Offenders." Pp. 267–81 in Canadian Centre for Justice Statistics. *The Juristat Reader: A Statistical Overview of the Canadian Criminal Justice System*. Toronto: Thompson Educational Publishing.

Intergovernmental Panel on Climate Change. 2007. On the World Wide Web at http://www.ipcc.ch/ (2 May 2007).

"Internet Growth." 2000. On the World Wide Web at http://citywideguide.com/InternetGrowth.html (29 April 2000).

Isajiw, Wsevolod W. 1978. "Olga in Wonderland: Ethnicity in a Technological Society." Pp. 29–39 in L. Driedger, ed. *The Canadian Ethnic Mosaic: A Quest for Identity*. Toronto: McClelland & Stewart.

Jackson, Carolyn and Ian David Smith. 2000. "Poles Apart? An Exploration of Single-Sex and Mixed-Sex Educational Environments in Australia and England." *Educational Studies* 26, 4 (December): 409–22.

James, Carl E. 2003. *Seeing Ourselves: Exploring Race, Ethnicity and Culture,* 3rd ed. Toronto: Thompson Educational Publishing, Inc.

James, William. 1976 [1902]. *The Varieties of Religious Experience: A Study in Human Nature*. New York: Collier Books.

Janis, Irving. 1972. *Victims of Groupthink*. Boston: Houghton Mifflin.

Jekielek, Susan M. 1998. "Parental Conflict, Marital Disruption and Children's Emotional Well-Being." *Social Forces* 76: 905–35.

Jencks, Christopher, Marshall Smith, Henry Acland, Mary Jo Bane, David Cohen, Herbert Gintis, Barbara Heyns, and Stephan Michelson. 1972. *Inequality: A Reassessment of the Effect of Family and Schooling in America*. New York: Basic Books.

Jenkins, J. Craig. 1983. "Resource Mobilization Theory and the Study of Social Movements." *Annual Review of Sociology* 9: 527–53.

John Howard Society. 1999b. *Fact Sheet: Population Trends and Crime*. Toronto: John Howard Society of Ontario.

Johnson, Jeffrey G., Patricia Cohen, Elizbaeth M. Smailes, Stephanie Kasen, and Judith S. Brook. 2002. "Television Viewing and Aggressive Behavior during Adolescence and Adulthood." *Science* 295, 5564: 2468–71.

Johnson, Michael P. and Kathleeen J. Ferraro. 2000. "Research on Domestic Violence in the 1990s: Making Distinctions." *Journal of Marriage and the Family* 62: 948–63.

Johnson, Sara. 2004. "Adult Correctional Services in Canada, 2002/03." *Juristat* 24, 10: 16. Catalogue no. 85-002-XPE. Ottawa: Canadian Centre for Justice Statistics and Statistics Canada. On the World Wide Web at http://www.statcan.ca/bsolc/english/bsolc?catno=85-002-X20040108409 (8 May 2005).

Johnston, William A. 2002. "Class and Politics in the Era of the Global Economy." Pp. 288–306 in Douglas Baer, ed. *Political Sociology: Canadian Perspectives*. Toronto: Oxford University Press.

Jones, Christopher. 1999. "Chiapas' Well-Connected Rebels." *Wired News* 1 February. On the World Wide Web at http://www.wired.com/news/print/0,1294,17633,00.html (30 July 2000).

Jones, Frank. 2000. "Are Children Going to Religious Services?" Pp. 202–25 in *Canadian Social Trends* 54 (Fall): 3–13. Catalogue no. 11-008-XPE.

Jones, Laura. 1997. "Global Warming Is All the Rage These Days . . . Which Enrages Many Doubting Scientists." The Fraser Institute. On the World Wide Web at http://oldfraser.lexi.net/media/media_releases/1997/19971201a.html (5 May 2002).

Joyce, Terrence and Lloyd Keigwin. 2004. "Abrupt Climate Change: Are We on the Brink of a New Little Ice Age?" Ocean and Climate Change Institute, Woods Hole Oceanographic Institution. On the World Wide Web at http://www.whoi.edu/institutes/occi/currenttopics/abruptclimate_joyce_keigwin.html (29 May 2004).

Juergensmeyer, Mark. 2000. *Terror in the Mind of God: The Global Rise of Religious Violence*. Berkeley, CA: University of California Press.

Kalbach, Madeline A. 2000. "Ethnicity and the Altar." Pp. 111–21 in Madeline A. Kalbach and Warren E. Kalbach, eds. *Perspectives on Ethnicity in Canada: A Reader*. Toronto: Harcourt Canada.

Kalbach, Madeline A. and Warren E. Kalbach. 1998. "Becoming Canadian: Problems of an Emerging Identity." *Canadian Ethnic Studies* 31, 2: 1–17.

Kalmijn, Matthijs. 1998. "Intermarriage and Homogamy: Causes, Patterns, Trends." *Annual Review of Sociology* 24: 395–421.

Kanter, Rosabeth Moss. 1989. *When Giants Learn to Dance: Mastering the Challenges of Strategy, Management, and Careers in the 1990s*. New York: Simon and Schuster.

Karabel, Jerome. 1986. "Community Colleges and Social Stratification in the 1980s." In L. S. Zwerling, ed. *The Community College and Its Critics*. San Francisco: Jossey-Bass.

Karl, Thomas R. and Kevin E. Trenberth. 1999. "The Human Impact on Climate." *Scientific American* 281, 6: September: 100–05.

Kay, Fiona and John Hagan. 1998. "Raising the Bar: The Gender Stratification of Law Firm Capitalization." *American Sociological Review* 63: 728–43.

Kennedy, Paul. 1993. *Preparing for the Twenty-First Century*. New York: HarperCollins.

Kepel, Gilles. 1991 [1994]. *The Revenge of God: The Resurgence of Islam, Christianity and Judaism in the Modern World,* Alan Braley, trans. University Park, PA: Pennsylvania State University Press.

Kerig, Patricia K., Philip A. Cowan, and Carolyn Pape Cowan. 1993. "Marital Quality and Gender Differences in Parent–Child Interaction." *Developmental Psychology* 29: 931–39.

Kimmerling, Baruch. 2001. *The Invention and Decline of Israeliness: State, Society, and the Military*. Berkeley, CA: University of California Press.

King, Martin Luther. 1967. *Conscience for Change*. Toronto: CBC Learning Systems.

Kingsbury, Nancy and John Scanzoni. 1993. "Structural-Functionalism." Pp. 195–217 in Pauline G. Boss, William J. Doherty, Ralph LaRossa, Walter R. Schumm, and Suzanne K. Steinmetz, eds. *Sourcebook of Family Theories and Methods: A Contextual Approach*. New York: Plenum.

Kingston, Paul W. 2001. "The Unfulfilled Promise of Cultural Capital Theory." *Sociology of Education* Supplement: 88–91.

Kinsey, Alfred C., Wardell B. Pomeroy, and Clyde E. Martin. 1948. *Sexual Behavior in the Human Male*. Philadelphia: W. B. Saunders.

Kinsey, Alfred, Wardell Pomeroy, Clyde Martin, and Paul Gebhard. 1953. *Sexual Behavior in the Human Female*. Philadelphia: W. B. Saunders.

Kitano, Harry and Roger Daniels. 1995. *Asian Americans: Emerging Minorities,* 2nd ed. Englewood Cliffs, NJ: Prentice-Hall.

Kling, Kristen C., Janet Shibley Hyde, Carolin J. Showers, and Brenda N. Buswell. 1999. "Gender Differences in Self-Esteem: A Meta-Analysis." *Psychological Bulletin* 125, 4: 470–500.

Koepke, Leslie, Jan Hare, and Patricia B. Moran. 1992. "Relationship Quality in a Sample of Lesbian Couples with Children and Child-Free Lesbian Couples." *Family Relations* 41: 224–29.

Kohlberg, Lawrence. 1981. *The Psychology of Moral Development: The Nature and Validity of Moral Stages.* New York: Harper and Row.

Kong, Rebecca. 1997. "Canadian Crime Statistics, 1996." *Juristat* 17, 8 (July). Catalogue no. 85-002-XPE. Ottawa: Canadian Centre for Justice Statistics and Statistics Canada. On the World Wide Web at http://dsp-psd.pwgsc.gc.ca/Collection-R/Statcan/85-002-XIE/0089785-002-XIE.pdf (23 August 2007).

Kornblum, William. 1997. *Sociology in a Changing World,* 4th ed. Fort Worth, TX: Harcourt Brace & Company.

Kosmin, Barry A. 1991. *Research Report of the National Survey of Religious Identification.* New York: CUNY Graduate Center.

Kozol, Jonathan. 1991. *Savage Inequalities: Children in America's Schools.* New York: Crown.

Kropotkin, Petr. 1908 [1902]. *Mutual Aid: A Factor of Evolution,* rev. ed. London: W. Heinemann.

Kurdek, Lawrence A. 1996. "The Deterioration of Relationship Quality for Gay and Lesbian Cohabiting Couples: A Five-Year Prospective Longitudinal Study." *Personal Relationships* 3: 417–42.

Kurzweil, Ray. 1999. *The Age of Spiritual Machines: When Computers Exceed Human Intelligence.* New York: Viking Penguin.

*Labour Organizations in Canada 1972.* 1973. Ottawa: Economics and Research Branch, Canada Department of Labour. Cat. No. L2-2-1972.

LaFeber, Walter. 1993. *Inevitable Revolutions: The United States in Central America,* 2nd ed. New York: W. W. Norton.

Lamanna, Mary Ann and Agnes Riedmann. 2003. *Marriages and Families: Making Choices in a Diverse Society,* 8th ed. Belmont, CA: Wadsworth.

Lamont, Michele and Annette Lareau. 1988. "Cultural Capital: Allusions, Gaps, and Glissandos in Recent Theoretical Developments." *Sociological Theory* 6: 153–68.

Lapchick, Richard. 2004. *2004 Racial and Gender Report Card.* Orlando, FL: University of Central Florida. On the World Wide Web at http://www.bus.ucf.edu/sport/public/downloads/2004_Racial_Gender_Report_Card.pdf (29 April 2006).

Lapidus, Gail Warshofsky. 1978. *Women in Soviet Society: Equality, Development, and Social Change.* Berkeley, CA: University of California Press.

Lapidus, Ira M. 2002. *A History of Islamic Societies,* 2nd ed. Cambridge: Cambridge University Press.

Larzelere, Robert E. 2000. "Child Outcomes of Nonabusive and Customary Physical Punishment by Parents: An Updated Literature Review." *Clinical Child & Family Psychology Review* 3, 4 (December): 199–221.

Lautard, Hugh and Neil Guppy. 2008. "Multiculturalism or Vertical Mosaic? Occupational Stratification among Canadian Ethnic Groups." Pp. 120–29 in Robert J. Brym, ed. *Society in Question,* 5th ed. Toronto: Nelson.

Lazare, Daniel. 1999. "Your Constitution Is Killing You: A Reconsideration of the Right to Bear Arms." *Harper's* 299, 1793 (October): 57–65.

Lefkowitz, Bernard. 1997a. "Boys Town: Did Glen Ridge Raise Its Sons to Be Rapists?" *Salon* 13 August. On the World Wide Web at http://www.salon.com/aug97/mothers/(13 January 2000).

______. 1997b. *Our Guys: The Glen Ridge Rape and the Secret Life of the Perfect Suburb.* Berkeley: University of California Press.

Leidner, Robin. 1993. *Fast Food, Fast Talk: Service Work and the Routinization of Everyday Life.* Berkeley, CA: University of California Press.

Lenton, Rhonda L. 1989. "Homicide in Canada and the U.S.A." *Canadian Journal of Sociology* 14: 163–78.

Levine, R. A. and D. T. Campbell. 1972. *Ethnocentrism: Theories of Conflict, Ethnic Attitudes, and Group Behavior.* New York: Wiley.

Levine, Robert, Suguru Sato, Tsukasa Hashimoto, and Jyoti Verma. 1995. "Love and Marriage in Eleven Cultures." *Journal of Cross-Cultural Psychology* 26, 5: 554–71.

Lewis, Bernard. 2002. *What Went Wrong? Western Impact and Middle Eastern Response.* New York: Oxford University Press.

Lewontin, Richard C. 1991. *Biology as Ideology: The Doctrine of DNA.* New York: HarperCollins.

Li, Peter. 1995. "Racial Supremacism under Social Democracy." *Canadian Ethnic Studies* 27, 1: 1–17.

______. 1998. *The Chinese in Canada,* 2nd ed. Toronto: Oxford University Press.

Lian, Jason Z. and David R. Matthews. 1998. "Does the Vertical Mosaic Still Exist? Ethnicity and Income in Canada, 1991." *Canadian Review of Sociology and Anthropology* 35: 461–81.

Lie, John. 1998. *Han Unbound: The Political Economy of South Korea.* Stanford, CA: Stanford University Press.

______. 2001. *Multiethnic Japan.* Cambridge, MA: Harvard University Press.

Light, Ivan. 1991. "Immigrant and Ethnic Enterprise in North America." Pp. 307–18 in Norman R. Yetman, ed. *Majority and Minority: The Dynamics of Race and Ethnicity in American Life,* 5th ed. Boston: Allyn and Bacon.

Lightfoot-Klein, Hanny, Cheryl Chase, Tim Hammond, and Ronald Goldman. 2000. "Genital Surgery on Children Below the Age of Consent." Pp. 440–79 in Lenore T. Szuchman and Frank Muscarella, eds. *Psychological Perspectives on Human Sexuality.* New York: John Wiley & Sons.

Lips, Hilary M. 1999. *A New Psychology of Women: Gender, Culture and Ethnicity.* Mountain View, CA: Mayfield Publishing Company.

Lipset, Seymour Martin. 1963. "Value Differences, Absolute or Relative: The English-Speaking Democracies." Pp. 248–73 in *The First New Nation: The United States in Historical Perspective.* New York: Basic Books.

———. 1971. *Agrarian Socialism: The Cooperative Commonwealth Federation in Saskatchewan,* rev. ed. Berkeley: University of California Press.

Lipset, Seymour Martin, Martin A. Trow, and James S. Coleman. 1956. *Union Democracy: The Internal Politics of the International Typographical Union.* Glencoe, IL: Free Press.

Lisak, David. 1992. "Sexual Aggression, Masculinity, and Fathers." *Signs* 16: 238–62.

Livernash, Robert and Eric Rodenburg. 1998. "Population Change, Resources, and the Environment." *Population Bulletin* 53, 1. On the World Wide Web at http://www.prb.org/pubs/population_bulletin/bu53-1.htm (25 August 2000).

Livingstone, David W. 1999. *The Education-Jobs Gap: Underemployment or Economic Democracy.* Toronto: Garamond Press.

Lofland, John and Lyn H. Lofland. 1995. *Analyzing Social Settings: A Guide to Qualitative Observation and Analysis,* 3rd ed. Belmont, CA: Wadsworth.

Lofland, Lyn. H. 1985. "The Social Shaping of Emotion: Grief in Historical Perspective." Symbolic Interaction 8: 171–90.

Logan, Ron. 2001. "Crime Statistics in Canada, 2000." *Juristat* 21, 8 (July). Catalogue no. 85-002-XPE. Ottawa: Canadian Centre for Justice Statistics and Statistics Canada.

Lopez, Donald S. 2001. *The Story of Buddhism: A Concise Guide to Its History and Teachings.* San Francisco: Harper.

Lowman, John, Robert T. Menzies, and Ted S. Palys. 1987. *Transcarceration: Essays in the Sociology of Social Control.* Aldershot, ON: Gower.

Lucas, Samuel Roundfield. 1999. *Tracking Inequality: Stratification and Mobility in American High Schools.* New York: Teachers College Press.

Lupri, Eugen and James Frideres. 1988. "Marital Satisfaction over the Life Cycle." Pp. 436–48 in Lorne Tepperman and James Curtis, eds. *Readings in Sociology: An Introduction.* Toronto: McGraw-Hill Ryerson.

Lurie, Alison. 1981. *The Language of Clothes.* New York: Random House.

Lynch, Michael and David Bogen. 1997. "Sociology's Asociological 'Core': An Examination of Textbook Sociology in Light of the Sociology of Scientific Knowledge." *American Sociological Review* 62: 481–93.

Lyon, David and Elia Zureik, eds. 1996. *Computers, Surveillance, and Privacy.* Minneapolis: University of Minnesota Press.

Mackie, Marlene. 1991. *Gender Relations in Canada: Further Explorations.* Toronto: Butterworths.

MacKinnon, Catharine A. 1979. *Sexual Harassment of Working Women.* New Haven, CT: Yale University Press.

Macklin, Eleanor D. 1980. "Nontraditional Family Forms: A Decade of Research." *Journal of Marriage and the Family* 42: 905–22.

MacLennan, Hugh. 1945. *Two Solitudes.* Toronto: Collins.

"Mad about Hockey: Superstitions." 2002. On the World Wide Web at http://www.mcg.org/societe/hockey/pages/aasuperstitions_2.html (20 June 2002).

Mann, Susan A., Michael D. Grimes, Alice Abel Kemp, and Pamela J. Jenkins. 1997. "Paradigm Shifts in Family Sociology? Evidence from Three Decades of Family Textbooks." *Journal of Family Issues* 18: 315–49.

Markowitz, Fran. 1993. *A Community in Spite of Itself: Soviet Jewish Émigrés in New York.* Washington, DC: Smithsonian Institute Press.

Marshall, S. L. A. 1947. *Men Against Fire: The Problem of Battle Command in Future War.* New York: Morrow.

Marshall, Thomas H. 1965. "Citizenship and Social Class." Pp. 71–134 in Thomas H. Marshall, ed. *Class, Citizenship, and Social Development: Essays by T. H. Marshall.* Garden City, NY: Anchor.

Martineau, Harriet. 1985. *Harriet Martineau on Women,* Gayle Graham Yates, ed. New Brunswick, NJ: Rutgers University Press.

Marx, Karl. 1904 [1859]. *A Contribution to the Critique of Political Economy,* N. Stone, trans. Chicago: Charles H. Kerr.

———. 1967 [1867–94]. *Capital,* 3 vols. New York: International Publishers.

———. 1970 [1843]. *Critique of Hegel's "Philosophy of Right,"* Annette Jolin and Joseph O'Malley, trans. Cambridge, MA: Harvard University Press.

Marx, Karl and Friedrich Engels. 1972 [1848]. "Manifesto of the Communist Party." Pp. 331–62 in R. Tucker, ed. *The Marx-Engels Reader.* New York: Norton.

Massey, Douglas S., Camille Z. Charles, Garvey F. Lundy, and Mary J. Fischer. 2003. *The Source of the River: The Social Origins of Freshman at America's Selective Colleges and Universities.* Princeton, NJ: Princeton University Press.

Matsueda, Ross L. 1988. "The Current State of Differential Association Theory." *Crime and Delinquency* 34: 277–306.

———. 1992. "Reflected Appraisals, Parental Labeling, and Delinquency: Specifying a Symbolic Interactionist Theory." *American Journal of Sociology* 97: 1577–611.

McAdam, Doug. 1982. *Political Process and the Development of Black Insurgency, 1930–1970.* Chicago: University of Chicago Press.

McCarten, James. 2002. "Child Spanking Law Upheld by Ontario Court: Childs' Rights Group Ponders Taking Case to Supreme Court." On the World Wide Web at http://www.oacas.org/Whatsnew/newsstories/jan02news/spankinglawupheld.pdf.

McClelland, W. R. 1931. "Precautions for Workers in the Treating of Radium Ores." *Investigations in Ore Dressing and Metallurgy.* Ottawa: Bureau of Mines. On the World Wide Web at http://www.ccnr.org/radium_warning.html (8 October 2000).

McCormick, Chris, ed. 1999. *The Westray Chronicles: A Case Study in Corporate Crime.* Halifax: Fernwood.

McCrum, Robert, William Cran, and Robert MacNeil. 1992. *The Story of English,* new and rev. ed. London: Faber and Faber.

McLaren, Angus. 1990. *Our Own Master Race: Eugenics in Canada, 1885–1945.* Toronto: McClelland & Stewart.

McLuhan, Marshall. 1964. *Understanding Media: The Extensions of Man.* New York: McGraw-Hill.

McMahon, Maeve W. 1992. *The Persistent Prison? Rethinking Decarceration and Penal Reform.* Toronto: University of Toronto Press.

McMahon, Walter W. 1999. *Education and Development: Measuring the Social Benefits*. Oxford, UK: Oxford University Press.

McManners, John, ed. 1990. *Oxford Illustrated History of Christianity*. Oxford: Oxford University Press.

McPhail, Clark. 1994. "The Dark Side of Purpose: Individual and Collective Violence in Riots." *The Sociological Quarterly* 35: 1–32.

McRoberts, Kenneth. 1988. *Quebec: Social Change and Political Crisis*, 3rd ed. Toronto: McClelland & Stewart.

McVey, Wayne W., Jr. and Warren E. Kalbach. 1995. *Canadian Population*. Scarborough, ON: Nelson.

Mead, George H. 1934. *Mind, Self and Society*. Chicago: University of Chicago Press.

Melton, J. Gordon. 1996. *Encyclopedia of American Religions*, 5th ed. Detroit: Gale.

Melucci, Alberto. 1980. "The New Social Movements: A Theoretical Approach." *Social Science Information* 19: 199–226.

______. 1995. "The New Social Movements Revisited: Reflections on a Sociological Misunderstanding." Pp. 107–19 in Louis Maheu, ed. *Social Classes and Social Movements: The Future of Collective Action*. London, UK: Sage.

Merton, Robert K. 1938. "Social Structure and Anomie." *American Sociological Review* 3: 672–82.

______. 1968 [1949]. *Social Theory and Social Structure*, enlarged ed. New York: Free Press.

______. 1985 [1956]. *On the Shoulders of Giants: A Shandean Postscript*. New York: Harcourt Brace Jovanovitch.

Messerschmidt, James W. 1993. *Masculinities and Crime: Critique and Reconceptualization of Theory*. Lanham, MD: Roman and Littlefield.

Messner, Michael. 1995. "Boyhood, Organized Sports, and the Construction of Masculinities." Pp. 102–14 in Michael S. Kimmel and Michael A. Messner. *Men's Lives*, 3rd ed. Boston: Allyn and Bacon.

______. 2000. "Barbie Girls versus Sea Monsters: Children Constructing Gender." *Gender & Society, Special Issue* 14, 6 (December): 765–84.

Metropolitan Museum of Art. 2000. "Mrs. Charles Dana Gibson (1873–1956)." On the World Wide Web at http://costumeinstitute.org/gibson.htm (13 June 2000).

Meyer, David R. and Judi Bartfield. 1996. "Compliance with Child Support Orders in Divorce Cases." *Journal of Marriage and the Family* 58, 1: 201–12.

Meyer, John W., Francisco O. Ramirez, and Yasemin Nuhoglu Soysal. 1992. "World Expansion of Mass Education, 1870–1980." *Sociology of Education* 65: 128–49.

Meyer, Thomas. 1984. "'Date Rape': A Serious Campus Problem that Few Talk About." *Chronicle of Higher Education* 5 December: 1, 12.

Michael, Robert T., John H. Gagnon, Edward O. Laumann, and Gina Kolata. 1994. *Sex in America: A Definitive Survey*. Boston: Little, Brown and Company.

Milanovic, Branko. 2005. *Worlds Apart: Measuring International and Global Inequality*. Princeton, NJ: Princeton University Press.

Milem, Jeffrey F. 1998. "Attitude Change in College Students: Examining the Effect of College Peer Groups and Faculty Normative Groups." *The Journal of Higher Education* 69: 117–40.

Miles, Robert. 1989. *Racism*. London: Routledge.

Milgram, Stanley. 1974. *Obedience to Authority: An Experimental View*. New York: Harper.

Miller, Ted R. and Mark A. Cohen. 1997. "Costs of Gunshot and Cut/Stab Wounds in the United States, with Some Canadian Comparisons." *Accident Analysis and Prevention* 29: 329–41.

Milloy, John S. 1999. *A National Crime: The Canadian Government and the Residential School System, 1879 to 1986*. Winnipeg: University of Manitoba Press.

Mills, C. Wright. 1959. *The Sociological Imagination*. New York: Oxford University Press.

Minkel, J. R. 2002. "A Way with Words." *Scientific American* 25 March. On the World Wide Web at http://www.mit.edu/~lera/sciam (21 January 2003).

Mohr, Johann W. and Keith Spencer. 1999. "Crime." Pp. 587–89 in James H. Marsh, ed. *The Canadian Encyclopedia*, Year 2000 Edition. Toronto: McClelland & Stewart.

Money, John and Anke Ehrhardt. 1972. *Man and Woman, Boy and Girl*. Boston: Little Brown.

Montgomery, Malcolm. 1965. "The Six Nations and the Macdonald Franchise." *Ontario History* 57: 13.

Mooney, Linda A., David Knox, Caroline Schacht, and Adie Nelson. 2001. *Understanding Social Problems*. Toronto: Nelson Thomson Learning.

Mooney, Linda, Caroline Schacht, David Knox, and Adie Nelson. 2003. *Understanding Social Problems*, 2nd ed. Toronto: Nelson Thomson Learning.

Morris, Aldon D. 1984. *The Origins of the Civil Rights Movement: Black Communities Organizing for Change*. New York: Free Press.

Morris, Norval and David J. Rothman, eds. 1995. *The Oxford History of the Prison: The Practice of Punishment in Western Society*. New York: Oxford University Press.

Morrison, Nancy. 1987. "Separation and Divorce." Pp. 125–43 in M. J. Dymond, ed. *The Canadian Woman's Legal Guide*. Toronto: Doubleday.

Mortimer, Jeylan T. and Roberta G. Simmons. 1978. "Adult Socialization." *Annual Review of Sociology* 4: 421–54.

Morton, Gary. 2000. "Showdown at Queen's Park." On the World Wide Web at http://www.tao.ca/earth/toronto/archive/1999/toronto01278.html (22 March 2001).

Mundell, Helen. 1993. "How the Color Mafia Chooses Your Clothes." *American Demographics* November. On the World Wide Web at http://www.demographics.com/publications/ad/93_ad/9311_ad/ad281.htm (2 May 2000).

Murdock, George Peter. 1937. "Comparative Data on the Division of Labor by Sex." *Social Forces* 15: 551–53.

______. 1949. *Social Structure*. New York: Macmillan.

Nagle, Matt. 2001. "Gay Man Murdered in Vancouver's Stanley Park." *Seattle Gay News* 23 November. On the World Wide Web at http://www.sgn.org/2001/11/23 (29 April 2004).

National Council of Welfare. 1999a. "A New Poverty Line: New, No or Maybe?" On the World Wide Web at http://www.ncwcnbes.net/htmdocument/reportnewpovline/newpovline.html (9 April 2000).

———. 1999b. *Children First: A Pre-Budget Report by the National Council of Welfare.* On the World Wide Web at http://www.ncwcnbes.net.htmdocument/reportchildfirst.htm (9 April 2000).

———. 2002. *Poverty Profile, 1999.* On the World Wide Web at http://www.ncwcnbes.net/htmdocument/reportwelfinc02/welfare2002.htm (9 April 2004).

———. 2004. *Poverty Profile 2001.* Catalogue no. SD25-1/2001E. Ottawa: Minister of Public Works and Government Services Canada.

National Opinion Research Center. 2006. *General Social Survey, 1972–2004.* Chicago: University of Chicago. Machine readable file.

National Rifle Association. 2005. "Guns, Gun Ownership, & RTC at All-Time Highs, Less 'Gun Control,' and Violent Crime at 30-Year Low." On the World Wide Web at http://www.nraila.org/Issues/FactSheets/Read.aspx?ID=126 (29 December 2005).

Nelson, Adie and Barrie W. Robinson. 2002. *Gender in Canada,* 2nd ed. Toronto: Prentice Hall.

Nevitte, Neil. 1996. *The Decline of Deference.* Peterborough, ON: Broadview Press.

"New York Knicks History." 2000. On the World Wide Web at http://www.nba.com/knicks/news/00400499.html?nav=ArticleList#2 (9 May 2000).

Nicolaiedis, Nicos. 1998. "Pierre Marty's 'Doll' and Today's Barbies." *Revue française de psychanalyse, Special Issue: Psychosomatique et pulsionnalité* 62, 5 (Nov/Dec): 1579–81.

Nielsen, Linda. 1999. "College Aged Students with Divorced Parents: Facts and Fiction." *College Student Journal* 33: 543–72.

Nikiforuk, Andrew. 1998. "Echoes of the Atomic Age: Cancer Kills Fourteen Aboriginal Uranium Workers." *Calgary Herald* 14 March: A1, A4. On the World Wide Web at http://www.ccnr.org/deline_deaths.html (8 October 2000).

———. 1999. "A Question of Style." *Time* 31 May: 58–59.

*1994–1995 Directory of Labour Organizations in Canada.* 1995. Catalogue no. L2-2-1995. Ottawa: Minister of Supply and Services Canada.

*1998 Directory of Labour Organizations in Canada.* 1998. Ottawa: Workplace Information Directorate.

Nisbett, Richard E., Kaiping Peng, Incheol Choi, and Ara Norenzayan. 2001. "Culture and Systems of Thought: Holistic versus Analytic Cognition." *Psychological Review* 108: 291–310.

Nolen, Stephanie. 1999. "Gender: The Third Way." *Globe and Mail* 25 September: D1, D4.

Norton, Kevin I., Timothy S. Olds, Scott Olive, and Stephen Dank. 1996. "Ken and Barbie at Life Size." *Sex Roles* 34, 3–4 (February): 287–94.

Nowak, Martin A., Robert M. May, and Karl Sigmund. 1995. "The Arithmetics of Mutual Help." *Scientific American* 272, 6: 76–81.

Nowell, Amy and Larry V. Hedges. 1998. "Trends in Gender Differences in Academic Achievement from 1960 to 1994: An Analysis of Differences in Mean, Variance, and Extreme Scores." *Sex Roles* 39: 21–43.

Oates, Joyce Carol. 1999. "The Mystery of JonBenét Ramsey." *New York Review of Books* 24 (June): 31–37.

Oberschall, Anthony. 1973. *Social Conflict and Social Movements.* Englewood Cliffs, NJ: Prentice-Hall.

Oderkirk, Jillian and Clarence Lochhead. 1992. "Lone Parenthood: Gender Differences." *Canadian Social Trends* 27, Spring: 16–19. Catalogue no. 11-008-XPE.

OECD (Organisation for Economic Co-operation and Development). 2004. "Statistical Annex." *OECD Employment Outlook 2004.* On the World Wide Web at http://www.oecd.org/dataoecd/42/55/32494755.pdf (1 December 2005).

Ogbu, John U. 2003. *Black American Students in an Affluent Suburb: A Study of Academic Disengagement.* Mahwah, NJ: L. Erlbaum Associates.

Omi, Michael and Howard Winant. 1986. *Racial Formation in the United States.* New York: Routledge.

Ontario Consultants on Religious Tolerance. 2000. "Homosexual (Same-Sex) Marriages." On the World Wide Web at http://www.religioustolerance.org/hom_marr.htm (20 August 2000).

———. 2002. "The Harry Potter Books: Efforts to Ban Books." On the World Wide Web at http://www.religioustolerance.org/potter3.htm (15 January 2005).

———. 2005. "Information about Religion in Canada." On the World Wide Web at http://www.religioustolerance.org/can_rel.htm (14 November 2005).

Organization of African Unity. 2000. *Rwanda: the Preventable Genocide.* New York. On the World Wide Web at http://www.visiontv.ca/RememberRwanda/Report.pdf (15 January 2005).

Ornstein, Michael D. 1998. "Survey Research." *Current Sociology* 46, 4: 1–87.

Ossowski, Stanislaw. 1963. *Class Structure in the Social Consciousness,* S. Patterson, trans. London: Routledge and Kegan Paul.

Owen, Michelle K. 2001. "'Family' as a Site of Contestation: Queering the Normal or Normalizing the Queer?" Pp. 86–102 in Terry Goldie, ed. *In a Queer Country: Gay and Lesbian Studies in the Canadian Context.* Vancouver: Arsenal Pulp Press.

Pacey, Arnold. 1983. *The Culture of Technology.* Cambridge, MA: MIT Press.

Pammett, Jon H. 1997. "Getting Ahead Around the World." Pp. 67–86 in Alan Frizzell and Jon H. Pammett, eds. *Social Inequality in Canada.* Ottawa: Carleton University Press.

Pape, Robert A. 2003. "The Strategic Logic of Suicide Terrorism." *American Political Science Review* 97: 343–61.

———. 2005. *Dying to Win: The Strategic Logic of Suicide Terrorism.* New York: Random House.

Park, Robert E. 1950 [1914]. *Race and Culture,* Everett C. Hughes, ed. New York: Free Press.

Park, Robert Ezra, Ernest W. Burgess, and Roderick D. McKenzie. 1967 [1925]. *The City,* reprinted ed. Chicago: University of Chicago Press.

Parke, Ross D. 2001. "Paternal Involvement in Infancy: The Role of Maternal and Paternal Attitudes." *Journal of Family Psychology* 15, 4 (December): 555–58.

______. 2002. "Parenting in the New Millennium: Prospects, Promises and Pitfalls." Pp. 65–93 in James P. McHale and Wendy S. Grolnick, eds. *Retrospect and Prospect in the Psychological Study of Families*. Mahwah, NJ: Lawrence Erlbaum Associates, Inc.

Parshall, Gerald. 1998. "Brotherhood of the Bomb." *US News and World Report* 125, 7 (17–24 August): 64–68.

Parsons, Talcott. 1942. "Age and Sex in the Social Structure of the United States." *American Sociological Review* 7: 04–616.

______. 1951. *The Social System*. New York: Free Press.

______. 1955. "The American Family: Its Relation to Personality and to the Social Structure." Pp. 3–33 in Talcott Parsons and Robert F. Bales, eds. *Family, Socialization and Interaction Process*. New York: Free Press.

Pascual, Brian. 2002. "Avril Lavigne Hates Britney Spears." *ChartAttack* 19 April. On the World Wide Web at http://www.chartattack.com/damn/2002/04/1901.cfm (15 January 2003).

Pasley, Kay and Carmelle Minton. 2001. "Generative Fathering After Divorce and Remarriage: Beyond the 'Disappearing Dad.'" Pp. 239–48 in Theodore F. Cohen, ed. *Men and Masculinity: A Text Reader*. Belmont, CA: Wadsworth.

Peacock, Mary. 2000. "The Cult of Thinness." On the World Wide Web at http://www.womenswire.com/image/toothin.html (13 June 2000).

Pendakur, Krishna and Ravi Pendakur. 1998. "The Colour of Money: Earnings Differentials among Ethnic Groups in Canada." *Canadian Journal of Economics* 31: 518–48.

Pendakur, R. 2000. *Immigrants and the Labour Force: Policy, Regulation and Impact*. Montreal: McGill-Queen's University Press.

Peritz, Ingrid. 2006. "Spreading the (English) Word." *Globe and Mail* 11 February 2006: A1, A7.

Perrow, Charles B. 1984. *Normal Accidents*. New York: Basic Books.

Peters, John F. 1994. "Gender Socialization of Adolescents in the Home: Research and Discussion." *Adolescence* 29: 913–34.

Pew Research Center. 2002. *The Pew Global Attitudes Project: How Global Publics View Their Lives, Their Countries, the World, America*. On the World Wide Web at http://www. people-press.org (12 April 2003).

Piaget, Jean and Bärbel Inhelder. 1969. *The Psychology of the Child*, Helen Weaver, trans. New York: Basic Books.

PISA Canada. 2003. "Measuring Up: The Performance of Canada's Youth in Reading, Mathematics and Science." *International Literacy Test*. Program for International Student Assessment. Ottawa: Human Resources Development Canada, Statistics Canada, and Council of Ministers of Education, Canada. On the World Wide Web at http://www.pisa.gc.ca/pisa/brochure_e.shtml (23 August 2007).

Piven, Frances Fox and Richard A. Cloward. 1977. *Poor People's Movements: Why They Succeed, How They Fail*. New York: Vintage.

*Place Called Chiapas*. 1998. Vancouver: Canada Wild Productions. (Movie).

Plummer, Kenneth. 1995. *Telling Sexual Stories: Power, Change and Social Worlds*. London, UK: Routledge.

Pool, Robert. 1997. *Beyond Engineering: How Society Shapes Technology*. New York: Oxford University Press.

Popenoe, David. 1988. *Disturbing the Nest: Family Change and Decline in Modern Societies*. New York: Aldine de Gruyter.

______. 1996. *Life without Father: Compelling New Evidence that Fatherhood and Marriage Are Indispensable for the Good of Children and Society*. New York: Martin Kessler Books.

______. 1998. "The Decline of Marriage and Fatherhood." Pp. 312–19 in John J. Macionis and Nijole V. Benokraitis, eds. *Seeing Ourselves: Classic, Contemporary and Cross-Cultural Readings in Sociology*, 4th ed. Upper Saddle River, NJ: Prentice Hall.

"Population Explosion!" 2003. *Cyberatlas*. On the World Wide Web at http://cyberatlas.internet.com/big_picture/geographics/article/0,1323,5911_151151,00.html (23 May 2003).

Porter, John. 1965. *The Vertical Mosaic: An Analysis of Social Class and Power in Canada*. Toronto: University of Toronto Press.

______. 1979. *The Measure of Canadian Society: Education, Equality, and Opportunity*. Toronto: Gage.

Portes, Alejandro and Robert D. Manning. 1991. "The Immigrant Enclave: Theory and Empirical Examples." Pp. 319–32 in Norman R. Yetman, ed. *Majority and Minority: The Dynamics of Race and Ethnicity in American Life*, 5th ed. Boston: Allyn and Bacon.

Postel, Sandra. 1994. "Carrying Capacity: Earth's Bottom Line." Pp. 3–21 in Linda Starke, ed. *State of the World 1994*. New York: W. W. Norton.

Postman, Neil. 1982. *The Disappearance of Childhood*. New York: Delacorte.

Poulantzas, Nicos. 1975 [1968]. *Political Power and Social Classes*, T. O'Hagan, trans. London: New Left Books.

Poverty Mapping. 2005. "The Poverty Lines: Population Living with Less Than 2 Dollars and Less Than 1 Dollar a Day." On the World Wide Web at http://www.povertymap.net/mapsgraphics/index.cfm?data_id=23417&theme= (1 December 2005).

Provine, Robert R. 2000. *Laughter: A Scientific Investigation*. New York: Penguin.

Quaschning, Volker. 2003. "Development of Global Carbon Dioxide Emissions and Concentration in Atmosphere." On the World Wide Web at http://www.volker-quaschning.de/datserv/CO2/index_e.html (2 March 2005).

Raag, Tarja and Christine L. Rackliff. 1998. "Preschoolers' Awareness of Social Expectations of Gender: Relationships to Toy Choices." *Sex Roles* 38: 685–700.

Rapp, Rayna and Ellen Ross. 1986. "The 1920s: Feminism, Consumerism and Political Backlash in the United States." Pp. 52–62 in J. Friedlander, B. Cook, A. Kessler-Harris, and C. Smith-Rosenberg, eds. *Women in Culture and Politics*. Bloomington, IN: Indiana University Press.

Reimann, Renate. 1997. "Does Biology Matter? Lesbian Couples' Transition to Parenthood and Their Division of Labor." *Qualitative Sociology* 20, 2: 153–85.

Reiter, Ester. 1991. *Making Fast Food: From the Frying Pan into the Fryer*. Montreal: McGill-Queen's University Press.

Reitz, Jeffrey G. 2008. "Tapping Immigrants' Skills." Pp. 130–40 in Robert J. Brym, ed. *Society in Question*, 5th ed. Toronto: Nelson.

Resnick, Michael, Peter S. Bearman, Robert W. Blum, Karl E. Bauman, Kathleen M. Harris, Jo Jones, Joyce Tabor, Trish Beubring, Renee E. Sieving, Marcia Shew, Marjoie Ireland, Linda H. Beringer, and J. Richard Udry. 1997. "Protecting Adolescents from Harm." *Journal of the American Medical Association* 278: 823–32.

Rifkin, Jeremy. 1998. *The Biotech Century: Harnessing the Gene and Remaking the World.* New York: Jeremy P. Tarcher/Putnam.

Risman, Barbara J. and Danette Johnson-Sumerford. 1998. "Doing It Fairly: A Study of Postgender Marriages." *Journal of Marriage and the Family* 60: 23–40.

Ritzer, George. 1993. *The McDonaldization of Society.* Thousand Oaks, CA: Pine Forge Press.

———. 1996. "The McDonaldization Thesis: Is Expansion Inevitable?" *International Sociology* 11: 291–307.

Roberts, Julian and Thomas Gabor. 1990. "Race and Crime: A Critique." *Canadian Journal of Criminology* 92, 2 (April): 291–313.

Robertson, Ian. 1977. *Sociology.* New York: Worth Publishing.

Robinson, Richard H. and Willard L. Johnson. 1997. *The Buddhist Religion: A Historical Introduction,* 4th ed. Belmont, CA: Wadsworth.

Roche, Maurice. 1995. "Rethinking Citizenship and Social Movements: Themes in Contemporary Sociology and Neoconservative Ideology." Pp. 186–219 in Louis Maheu, ed. *Social Classes and Social Movements: The Future of Collective Action.* London, UK: Sage.

Rodinson, Maxime. 1996. *Muhammad,* 2nd ed. Anne Carter, trans. London: Penguin.

Roediger, David R. 1991. *The Wages of Whiteness: Race and the Making of the American Working Class.* London: Verso.

Rogan, Mary. 2001. "An Epidemic of Gas Sniffing Decimates Arctic Indian Tribe." *New York Times on the Web.* On the World Wide Web at http://www.uwec.edu/Academic/Curric/majstos/p390/Articles/030301gas-sniffing-Indians.htm (4 March).

Rollins, Boyd C. and Kenneth L. Cannon. 1974. "Marital Satisfaction over the Family Life Cycle." *Journal of Marriage and the Family* 36: 271–84.

Romaniuc, Anatole. 1984. "Fertility in Canada: From Baby-Boom to Baby-Bust." *Current Demographic Analysis.* Ottawa: Statistics Canada.

Rootes, Chris. 1995. "A New Class? The Higher Educated and the New Politics." Pp. 220–35 in Louis Maheu, ed. *Social Classes and Social Movements: The Future of Collective Action.* London, UK: Sage.

Rose, Michael S. 2001. "The Facts Behind the Massacre." *Catholic World News* 17 October. On the World Wide Web at http://www.cwnews.com/news/viewstory.cfm?recnum=20654 (15 January 2005).

Rosenbluth, Susan C. 1997. "Is Sexual Orientation a Matter of Choice?" *Psychology of Women Quarterly* 21: 595–610.

Rosenbluth, Susan C., Janice M. Steil, and Juliet H. Whitcomb. 1998. "Marital Equality: What Does It Mean?" *Journal of Family Issues* 19, 3: 227–44.

Rosenthal, Robert and Lenore Jacobson. 1968. *Pygmalion in the Classroom: Teacher Expectation and Pupils' Intellectual Development.* New York: Holt, Rinehart, and Winston.

Ross, David. 1998. "Rethinking Child Poverty." *Insight, Perception* 22, 1: 9–11.

Rostow, Walt W. 1960. *The Stages of Economic Growth: A Non-Communist Manifesto.* New York: Cambridge University Press.

Roth, Cecil. 1961. *A History of the Jews.* New York: Schocken.

Rothman, David J. 1998. "The International Organ Traffic." *New York Review of Books* 45, 5: 14–17.

Rubin, Jeffrey Z., Frank J. Provenzano, and Zella Lurra. 1974. "The Eye of the Beholder: Parents' Views on Sex of Newborns." *American Journal of Orthopsychiatry* 44: 512–19.

Rural Advancement Foundation International. 1999. "The Gene Giants." On the World Wide Web at http://www.rafi.org/web/allpub-one.shtml?dfl=allpub.db&tfl=allpub-one-frag.ptml&operation=display&ro1=recNo&rf1=34&rt1=34&usebrs=true (2 May 2000).

Russett, Cynthia Eagle. 1966. *The Concept of Equilibrium in American Social Thought.* New Haven, CT: Yale University Press.

Ryan, Kathryn M. and Jeanne Kanjorski. 1998. "The Enjoyment of Sexist Humor, Rape Attitudes, and Relationship Aggression in College Students." *Sex Roles* 38: 743–56.

Sampson, Robert and John H. Laub. 1993. *Crime in the Making: Pathways and Turning Points through Life.* Cambridge, MA: Harvard University Press.

Samson, Colin, James Wilson, and Jonathan Mazower. 1999. *Canada's Tibet: The Killing of the Innu.* London UK: Survival. On the World Wide Web at http://www.survival.org.uk/pdf/Innureport.pdf (1 May 2001).

Samuda, R. J., D. Crawford, C. Philip, and W. Tinglen. 1980. *Testing, Assessment, and Counselling of Minority Students: Current Methods in Ontario.* Toronto: Ontario Ministry of Education.

Samuelsson, Kurt. 1961 [1957]. *Religion and Economic Action,* E. French, trans. Stockholm: Scandinavian University Books.

Sandqvist, Karin and Bengt-Erik Andersson. 1992. "Thriving Families in the Swedish Welfare State." *Public Interest* 109: 114–16.

Sarlo, Christopher. 2001. *Measuring Poverty in Canada.* Vancouver: The Fraser Institute.

Sartre, Jean-Paul. 1965 [1948]. *Anti-Semite and Jew,* George. J. Becker, trans. New York: Schocken.

Sauve, Roger. 2002. "Job, Family and Stress among Husbands, Wives and Lone-Parents 15–64 from 1990 to 2000." On the World Wide Web at http://www.vifamily.ca/cft/connect.htm (3 March 2003).

Savoie, Josée. 2002. "Crime Statistics in Canada, 2001." *Juristat* 22, 6. Catalogue no. 85-002-XPE. Ottawa: Canadian Centre for Justice Statistics and Statistics Canada.

Saxton, Lloyd. 1990. *The Individual, Marriage, and the Family,* 9th ed. Belmont, CA: Wadsworth.

Scarr, Sandra and Richard A. Weinberg. 1978. "The Influence of 'Family Background' on Intellectual Attainment." *American Sociological Review* 43: 674–92.

Schiff, Michel and Richard Lewontin. 1986. *Education and Class: The Irrelevance of IQ Genetic Studies.* Oxford, UK: Clarendon Press.

Schippers, Mimi. 2002. *Rockin' Out of the Box: Gender Maneuvering in Alternative Hard Rock.* New Brunswick, NJ: Rutgers University Press.

Schneider, Barbara and David Stevenson. 1999. *The Ambitious Generation: America's Teenagers: Motivated but Directionless.* New Haven, CT: Yale University Press.

Schofield, John. 2001. "Saving Our Schools." *Maclean's* 14 May.

Schor, Juliet B. 1992. *The Overworked American: The Unexpected Decline of Leisure.* New York: Basic Books.

______. 1999. *The Overspent American: Why We Want What We Don't Need.* New York: Harper.

Schwartz, Stephen. 2003. *The Two Faces of Islam: The House of Sa'ud from Tradition to Terror.* New York: Doubleday.

Scott, James C. 1998. *Seeing Like a State: How Certain Schemes to Improve the Human Condition Have Failed.* New Haven, CT: Yale University Press.

Scott, Peter Dale and Jonathan Marshall. 1991. *Cocaine Politics: Drugs, Armies, and the CIA in Central America.* Berkeley, CA: University of California Press.

Scott, Wilbur J. 1990. "PTSD in *DSM-III*: A Case in the Politics of Diagnosis and Disease." *Social Problems* 37: 294–310.

Scully, Diana. 1990. *Understanding Sexual Violence: A Study of Convicted Rapists.* Boston: Unwin Hyman.

Senn, Charlene Y., Serge Desmarais, Norine Veryberg, and Eileen Wood. 2000. "Predicting Coercive Sexual Behavior Across the Lifespan in a Random Sample of Canadian Men." *Journal of Social and Personal Relationships* 17, 1 (February): 95–113.

Sentencing Project. 2001. "News & Updates." August. On the World Wide Web at http://www.sentencingproject.org/news/news.html#newpop (22 July 2002).

______. 2006. "New Incarceration Figures." On the World Wide Web at http://www.sentencingproject.org/Admin%5CDocuments%5Cpublications%5Cinc_newfigures.pdf (30 March 2007).

Sev'er, Aysan. 1999. "Sexual Harassment: Where We Were, Where We Are and Prospects for the New Millennium." *Canadian Review of Sociology and Anthropology* 36, 4: 460–97.

Sewell, William H. 1958. "Infant Training and the Personality of the Child." *American Journal of Sociology* 64: 150–59.

Shain, A. 1995. "Employment of People with Disabilities." *Canadian Social Trends* 38: 8–13. Catalogue no. 11-008-XPE.

Shakur, Sanyika (a.k.a. Monster Kody Scott). 1993. *Monster: The Autobiography of an L.A. Gang Member.* New York: Penguin.

Shattuck, Roger. 1980. *The Forbidden Experiment: The Story of the Wild Boy of Aveyron.* New York: Farrar, Straus, and Giroux.

Shaw, Karen. 2001. "Harry Potter Books: My Concerns." On the World Wide Web at http://www.reachouttrust.org/regulars/articles/occult/hpotter2.htm (13 November 2003).

Shea, Sarah E., Kevin Gordon, Ann Hawkins, Janet Kawchuk, and Donna Smith. 2000. "Pathology in the Hundred Acre Wood: A Neurodevelopmental Perspective on A. A. Milne." *Canadian Medical Association Journal* 163, 12: 1557–59. On the World Wide Web at http://www.cma.ca/cmaj/vol-163/issue-12/1557.htm (12 December 2000).

Sheehy, Elizabeth. 2003. "From Women's Duty to Resist to Men's Duty to Ask: How Far Have We Come?" Pp. 576–81 in T. Brettel Dawson, ed. *Women, Law and Social Change: Core Readings and Current Issues,* 4th ed. Concord, ON: Captus Press.

Sherif, Muzafer, L. J. Harvey, B. Jack White, William R. Hood, and Carolyn W. Sherif. 1988. *The Robber's Cave Experiment: Intergroup Conflict and Cooperation,* reprinted ed. Middletown, CT: Wesleyan University Press.

Sherkat, Darren E. and Christopher G. Ellison. 1999. "Recent Developments and Current Controversies in the Sociology of Religion." *Annual Review of Sociology* 25: 363–94.

Shorter, Edward. 1997. *A History of Psychiatry: From the Era of the Asylum to the Age of Prozac.* New York: John Wiley and Sons.

Signorielli, Nancy. 1998. "Reflections of Girls in the Media: A Content Analysis Across Six Media Overview." On the World Wide Web at http://childrennow.org/media/mc97/ReflectSummary.html (2 May 2000).

Silberman, Steve. 2000. "Talking to Strangers." *Wired* 8, 5: 225–33, 288–96. On the World Wide Web at http://www.wired.com/wired/archive/8.05/translation.html (23 May 2002).

"Silent Boom." 1998. *Fortune* 7 July: 170–71.

Simmel, Georg. 1950. *The Sociology of Georg Simmel,* Kurt H. Wolff, trans. and ed. New York: Free Press.

Simon, Jonathan. 1993. *Poor Discipline: Parole and the Social Control of the Underclass, 1890–1990.* Chicago: University of Chicago Press.

Simons, Ronald L., Chyi-In Wu, Christine Johnson, and Rand D. Conger. 1995. "A Test of Various Perspectives on the Intergenerational Transmission of Domestic Violence." *Criminology* 33: 141–60.

Sissing, T. W. 1996. "Some Missing Pages: The Black Community in the History of Québec and Canada." On the World Wide Web at http://www.qesnrecit.qc.ca/mpages/title.htm (14 June 2002).

Skolnick, Arlene. 1991. *Embattled Paradise: The American Family in an Age of Uncertainty.* New York: Basic Books.

Smith, Christian. 1991. *The Emergence of Liberation Theology: Radical Religion and Social Movement Theory.* Chicago: University of Chicago Press.

Smith, Jackie. 1998. "Global Civil Society? Transnational Social Movement Organizations and Social Capital." *American Behavioral Scientist* 42: 93–107.

Smith, Michael. 1990. "Patriarchal Ideology and Wife Beating: A Test of a Feminist Hypothesis." *Violence and Victims* 5: 257–73.

Smyth, Julie. 2003. "Sweden Ranked as Best Place to Have a Baby: Canada Places Fifth on Maternity Leave, 15th for Benefits." *National Post* 17 January. On the World Wide Web at http://www.childcarecanada.org/ccin/2003/ccin1_17_03.html (27 June 2004).

Snider, Laureen. 1999. "White-Collar Crime." P. 2504 in James H. Marsh, ed. *The Canadian Encyclopedia,* Year 2000 Edition. Toronto: McClelland & Stewart.

Snow, David A., E. Burke Rochford, Jr., Steven K. Worden, and Robert D. Benford. 1986. "Frame Alignment Processes, Micromobilization, and Movement Participation." *American Sociological Review* 51: 464–81.

Sofsky, Wolfgang. 1997 [1993]. *The Order of Terror: The Concentration Camp,* William Templer, trans. Princeton, NJ: Princeton University Press.

Sokoloff, Heather. 2001. "Wealth Affects Test Scores." *National Post* 5 December: A17.

Solicitor General Canada. 2002a. "Factsheets." On the World Wide Web at http://www.sgc.ca/Efact/emyths.htm (22 January 2004).

Sorenson, Elaine. 1994. *Comparable Worth: Is It a Worthy Policy?* Princeton, NJ: Princeton University Press.

Spade, Joan Z. 2001. "Gender and Education in the United States." Pp. 270–78 in Jeanne H. Ballantine and Joan Z. Spade, eds. *Schools and Society: A Sociological Approach to Education.* Belmont, CA: Wadsworth.

Spitz, René A. 1945. "Hospitalism: An Inquiry into the Genesis of Psychiatric Conditions in Early Childhood." Pp. 53–74 in *The Psychoanalytic Study of the Child,* vol. 1. New York: International Universities Press.

———. 1962. "Autoerotism Re-examined: The Role of Early Sexual Behavior Patterns in Personality Formation." Pp. 283–315 in *The Psychoanalytic Study of the Child,* vol. 17. New York: International Universities Press.

Spitzer, Steven. 1980. "Toward a Marxian Theory of Deviance." Pp. 175–91 in Delos H. Kelly, ed. *Criminal Behavior: Readings in Criminology.* New York: St. Martin's Press.

Stacey, Judith. 1996. *Brave New Families: Stories of Domestic Upheaval in Late Twentieth Century America.* New York: Basic Books.

Stack, Stephen and J. Ross Eshleman. 1998. "Marital Status and Happiness: A 17-Nation Study." *Journal of Marriage and the Family* 60: 527–36.

Stark, Rodney. 1985. *Sociology.* Belmont, CA: Wadsworth.

Stark, Rodney and William Sims Bainbridge. 1979. "Of Churches, Sects, and Cults: Preliminary Concepts for a Theory of Religious Movements." *Journal for the Scientific Study of Religion* 18: 117–31.

Starr, Paul. 1992/1994. *The Logic of Health Care Reform: Why and How the President's Plan Will Work,* rev. ed. New York: Penguin.

Statistics Canada. n.d.-1. CANSIM (database). "Table 202-0701: Market, Total and After-Tax Income, by Economic Family Type and Income Quintiles, 2005 Constant Dollars, Annual." Version updated April 30, 2007. On the World Wide Web at http://cansim2.statcan.ca (23 August 2007).

———. n.d.-2. CANSIM (database). Using CHASS (distributor). Version updated August 16, 2005. http://dc1.chass.utoronto.ca.myaccess.library.utoronto.ca/census/mainmicro.html.

———. n.d.-3. "Selected Ethnic Origins, for Canada, Provinces and Territories, 20% Sample Data (table)." *Ethnocultural Portrait of Canada: Highlight Tables, 2001 Census.* Catalogue no. 97F0024XIE2001013. Ottawa: Minister of Industry. On the World Wide Web at http://www12.statcan.ca/english/census01/products/highlight/ETO/Table1.cfm?Lang=E&T=501&GV=1&GID=0 (14 April 2007).

———. n.d.-4. CANSIM (database). "Table 202-0104: Female-to-Male Earnings Ratios, by Selected Characteristics, Annual (Percent)." Version updated April 30, 2007. On the World Wide Web at http://cansim2.statcan.ca (23 August 2007).

———. n.d.-5. CANSIM (database). "Table: 282-0002: Labour Force Survey Estimates (LFS), by Sex and Detailed Age Group, Annual (Persons Unless Otherwise Noted)." Using E-STAT (distributor). Version updated January 3, 2007. On the World Wide Web at http://estat.statcan.ca (23 August 2007).

———. n.d.-6. "Census Families: Time Series." *Profile of the Canadian Population by Age and Sex.* Catalogue no. 96F0030XIE2001002. Ottawa: Minister of Industry. Analysis Series, 2001 Census. On the World Wide Web at http://www12.statcan.ca/english/census01/products/analytic/companion/fam/family.cfm (22 April 2007).

———. 1992. *Selected Marriage Statistics 1921–1990.* Catalogue No. 82-552. Ottawa: Ministry of Industry.

———. 1997. *Profile of the Canadian Population by Age and Sex: Canada Ages.* Statistics Canada Catalogue no. 96F0030XIE2001002. Ottawa. December 19. Analysis Series, 1996 Census. On the World Wide Web at http://www12.statcan.ca/english/census01/info/census96.cfm (accessed 23 April 2007).

———. 1998a. *Canada Yearbook 1999.* Catalogue no. 11-402-XPE. Ottawa: Minister of Industry.

———. 1998b. "Marriages and Divorces, 1996." *The Daily* 29 January. On the World Wide Web at http://www.statcan.ca/Daily/English/980129/d980129.htm#ART1 (26 May 2006).

———. 1999a. "National Longitudinal Survey of Children and Youth: Transition into Adolescence 1996/97." *The Daily* 6 July. On the World Wide Web at http://www.statcan.ca/Daily/English/990706/d990706a.htm (10 May 2001).

———. 2000a. "Population by Aboriginal Group, 1996 Census." On the World Wide Web at http://www.statcan.ca/english/Pgdb/People/Population/demo39a.htm (7 October 2000).

———. 2000b. "Household Environmental Practices." On the World Wide Web at http://www.statcan.ca/english/ Pgdb/Land/Environment/envir01a.htm (7 October 2000).

———. 2000c. *Income in Canada 1998.* Ottawa: Ministry of Industry.

———. 2000d. "Divorces, 1998." *The Daily* 28 September. On the World Wide Web at http://www.statcan.ca/Daily/English/000928/d000926.htm (10 May 2001).

———. 2001a. "Television Viewing: Fall 1999." *The Daily* 25 January. On the World Wide Web at http://www.statcan.ca/Daily/English/010125/d010125a.htm (23 July 2002).

———. 2002a. *Profile of the Canadian Population by Age and Sex: Canada Ages.* Catalogue no. 96F0030XIE2001002. Ottawa: Minister of Industry. Analysis Series, 2001 Census. On the World Wide Web at http://www12.statcan.ca/english/census01/Products/Analytic/Index.cfm (23 August 2007).

———. 2002b. "Hours Spent Doing Unpaid Housework (7), Age Groups (7) and Sex (3) for Population 15 Years and Over, for Canada, Provinces, Territories, Census Metropolitan Areas and Census Agglomerations, 1996 and 2001 Censuses, 20% Sample Data (table)." *Topic-Based Tabulations: Canada's Workforce: Unpaid Work.* Catalogue no. 97F0013. On the World Wide Web at http://www12.statcan.ca/english/census01/Products/standard/themes/DataProducts.cfm?S=1&T=47&ALEVEL=2&FREE=0 (23 August 2007).

______. 2002c. "Divorces, 1999 and 2000." *The Daily* 2 December. On the World Wide Web at http://www. statcan.ca/Daily/English/021202/d021202f.htm (4 July 2003).

______. 2002d. "2001 Census: Marital Status, Common-Law Status, Families, Dwellings and Households." *The Daily* 22 October. On the World Wide Web at http://www.statcan.ca/Daily/English/021022/td021022.htm (4 July 2003).

______. 2003a. "Census of Population: Immigration, Birthplace and Birthplace of Parents, Citizenship, Ethnic Origin, Visible Minorities and Aboriginal Peoples." *The Daily* 21 January. On the World Wide Web at http://www.statcan.ca/Daily/English/030121/d030121a.htm (15 September 2004).

______. 2003b. "Education in Canada: Raising the Standard." Catalogue no. 96F0030XIE2001012. On the World Wide Web at http://www12.statcan.ca/english/census01/products/Analytic/companion/educ/contents.cfm (15 September 2004).

______. 2003c. *Earnings of Canadians: Making a Living in the New Economy*. Catalogue no. 96F0030XIE2001014. On the World Wide Web at http://www.statcan.ca/census01/products/analytic/companion/earn/contents.cfm (15 September 2004).

______. 2003d. *Canada's Ethnocultural Portrait: The Changing Mosaic.* Catalogue no. 96F0030XIE2001008. Ottawa: Minister of Industry. On the World Wide Web at http://www.statcan.ca/english/IPS/Data/96F0030XIE2001008.htm (27 August 2007).

______. 2003e. "Marriages, 2000." *The Daily* 2 June. On the World Wide Web at http://www.statcan.ca/Daily/English/030602/d030602a.htm (15 September 2004).

______. 2003f. "Marriages, 1999." *The Daily* 6 February. On the World Wide Web at http://www.statcan.ca/Daily/English/030206/d030206c.htm (15 September 2004).

______. 2003g. *Religions in Canada.* Catalogue no. 96F0030XIE2001015. Ottawa: Minister of Industry. http://www12.statcan.ca/english/census01/Products/Analytic/companion/rel/canada.cfm (24 January 2004).

______. 2003h. "Non-Wage Job Benefits, 2000." *The Daily* 21 May. On the World Wide Web at http://www.statcan.ca/Daily/English/030521/d030521c.htm (15 September 2004).

______. 2003i. "Sexual Offences." *The Daily* 23 July. On the World Wide Web at http://www.statcan.ca/Daily/English/030725/d030725a.htm (26 July 2005).

______. 2003j. "Induced (Therapeutic) Abortions, 2000." *The Daily* 28 March. On the World Wide Web at http://www.statcan.ca/Daily/English/030328/d030328e.htm (15 September 2004).

______. 2004a. "Census Families in Private Households by Family Structure and Presence of Children, Provinces and Territories." On the World Wide Web at http://www.statcan.ca/english/Pgdb/famil54b.htm (25 January 2004).

______. 2004b. "Canadian Community Health Survey, 2003." On the World Wide Web at http://www.statcan.ca/Daily/English/040615/d040615b.htm (21 April 2007).

______. 2004c. "Marriages, 2002." *The Daily* 21 December. On the World Wide Web at http://www.statcan.ca/Daily/English/041221/d041221d.htm (26 May 2006).

______. 2004d. *Research Paper: Low Income Research Series. Low Income Cutoffs from 1994 to 2003 and Low Income Measures from 1992 to 2001.* Catalogue no. 75F0002MIE. Ottawa: Income Statistics Division. On the World Wide Web at http://www.statcan.ca/english/research/75F0002MIE/75F0002MIE2004002.pdf (13 May 2006).

______. 2005a. "Television Viewing: Data Tables." On the World Wide Web at http://www.statcan.ca/english/freepub/87F0006XIE/2005001/data.htm (25 March 2007).

______. 2005b. "University Degrees, Diplomas and Certificates." *The Daily* 11 October. On the World Wide Web at http://www.statcan.ca/Daily/English/051011/d051011d.htm (26 April 2007).

______. 2005c. "Child Care, 1994/95 and 2000/01." *The Daily* 7 February. On the World Wide Web at http://www.statcan.ca/Daily/English/050207/d050207b.htm (14 March 2006).

______. 2006a. "Suicides and Suicide Rate, by Sex and by Age Group (Females)." On the World Wide Web at http://www40.statcan.ca/l01/cst01/perhlth66c.htm (16 March 2006).

______. 2006b. "Suicides and Suicide Rate, by Sex and by Age Group (Males)." On the World Wide Web at http://www40.statcan.ca/l01/cst01/perhlth66b.htm (16 March 2006).

______. 2006c. "Crime Statistics." *The Daily* 20 July. On the World Wide Web at http://www.statcan.ca/Daily/English/060720/d060720b.htm (29 March 2007).

______. 2006d. "Study: Inequality in Wealth." *The Daily* 13 December. On the World Wide Web at http://www.statcan.ca/Daily/English/061213/d061213c.htm (3 April 2007).

______. 2006e. "Low Income Cut-Offs for 2005 and Low Income Measures for 2004." On the World Wide Web at http://www.statcan.ca/bsolc/english/bsolc?catno=75F0002MIE2006004 (4 April 2007).

______. 2006f. "Homicides." *The Daily* 8 November. On the World Wide Web at http://www.statcan.ca/Daily/English/061108/d061108b.htm (22 April 2007).

______. 2006g. "Induced Abortion Statistics 2003." On the World Wide Web at http://www.statcan.ca/english/freepub/82-223-XIE/82-223-XIE2006000.pdf (24 April 2007).

______. 2006h. "Households and the Environment 2006." On the World Wide Web at http://www.statcan.ca/english/freepub/11-526-XIE/11-526-XIE2007001.pdf (22 September 2007).

______. 2007a. "Lates Release from the Labour Force Survey." On the World Wide Web at http://www.statcan.ca/english/Subjects/Labour/LFS/lfs-en.htm (16 March 2007).

______. 2007b. "Average Hourly Wages of Employees by Selected Characteristics and Profession, Unadjusted Data, by Province (Monthly) (Canada)." On the World Wide Web at http://www40.statcan.ca/l01/cst01/labr69a.htm (4 April 2007).

______. 2007c. "Consumer Price Index, Historical Summary, by Province or Territory." On the World Wide Web at http://www40.statcan.ca/l01/cst01/econ46a.htm (1 April 2007).

______. 2007d. "Marriages, 2003." *The Daily* 17 January. On the World Wide Web at http://www.statcan.ca/Daily/English/070117/d070117a.htm (22 April 2007).

______. 2007e. CANSIM (database). "Table 101-1002: Mean Age and Median Age of Males and Females, by Type of Marriage and Marital Status, Canada, Provinces and Territories, Annual." Version updated April 4, 2007. On the World Wide Web at http://cansim2.statcan.ca/cgi-win/cnsmcgi.exe?Lang=E&RootDir=CII/&ResultTemplate=CII/CII___&Array_Pick=1&ArrayId=1011002 (22 April 2007).

Steel, Freda M. 1987. "Alimony and Maintenance Orders." Pp. 155–67 in Sheilah L. Martin and Kathleen E. Mahoney, eds. *Equality and Judicial Neutrality*. Toronto: Carswell.

Steele, Claude M. 1992. "Race and the Schooling of Black Americans." *The Atlantic Monthly* April. On the World Wide Web at http://www.theatlantic.com/unbound/flashbks/blacked/steele.htm (2 May 2000).

———. 1997. "A Threat in the Air: How Stereotypes Shape the Intellectual Identities and Performance of Women and African-Americans." *American Psychologist* 52: 613–29.

Sternberg, Robert J. 1998. *In Search of the Human Mind*, 2nd ed. Fort Worth, TX: Harcourt Brace.

Stewart, Abigail, Anne P. Copeland, Nia Lane Chester, Janet E. Malley, and Nicole B. Barenbaum. 1997. *Separating Together: How Divorce Transforms Families*. New York: The Guilford Press.

Stone, Lawrence. 1977. *The Family, Sex and Marriage in England, 1500–1800*. New York: Harper and Row.

Stormshak, Elizabeth A., Karen L. Bierman, Robert J. McMahon, and Liliana J. Lengua. 2000. "Parenting Practices and Child Disruptive Behavior Problems in Early Elementary School." *Journal of Clinical Child Psychology* 29, 1 (March): 17–29.

Stouffer, Samuel A. et al. 1949. *The American Soldier*, 4 vols. Princeton, NJ: Princeton University Press.

Straus, Murray A. 1994. *Beating the Devil Out of Them: Corporal Punishment in American Families*. New York: Lexington Books.

Straus, Murray A. and Carrie L. Yodanis. 1996. "Corporal Punishment in Adolescence and Physical Assaults on Spouses Later in Life: What Accounts for the Link?" *Journal of Marriage and the Family* 58, 4: 825–924.

Strauss, Anselm L. 1993. *Continual Permutations of Action*. New York: Aldine de Gruyter.

*Strikes and Lockouts in Canada 1968*. 1970. Catalogue no. L2-1/1968. Ottawa: Economic and Research Branch, Canada Department of Labour.

*Strikes and Lockouts in Canada 1985*. 1985. Catalogue no. L160-2999/85B. Ottawa: Minister of Supply and Services Canada.

Subrahmanyam, Kaveri and Patricia M. Greenfield. 1998. "Computer Games for Girls: What Makes Them Play?" Pp. 46–71 in Justine Cassell and Henry Jenkins, eds. *From Barbie to Mortal Kombat: Gender and Computer Games*. Cambridge, MA: MIT Press.

Sullivan, Mercer L. 2002. "Exploring Layers: Extended Case Method as a Tool for Multilevel Analysis of School Violence." *Sociological Methods and Research* 31, 2: 255–85.

Sutherland, Edwin H. 1939. *Principles of Criminology*. Philadelphia: Lippincott.

———. 1949. *White Collar Crime*. New York: Dryden.

Swiss Re. 2007. "Natural Catastrophes and Man-Made Disasters in 2006." On the World Wide Web at http://www.swissre.com/internet/pwswpspr.nsf/fmBookMarkFrameSet?ReadForm&BM=../vwAllbyIDKeyLu/mpdl-6z2krc?OpenDocument (30 April 2007).

Sykes, Gresham and David Matza. 1957. "Techniques of Neutralization: A Theory of Delinquency." *American Sociological Review* 22: 664–70.

Tajfel, Henri. 1981. *Human Groups and Social Categories: Studies in Social Psychology*. Cambridge, UK: Cambridge University Press.

Tannen, Deborah. 1990. *You Just Don't Understand Me: Women and Men in Conversation*. New York: William Morrow.

———. 1994a. *Talking from 9 to 5: How Women's and Men's Conversational Styles Affect Who Gets Heard, Who Gets Credit, and What Gets Done at Work*. New York: William Morrow.

———. 1994b. *Gender and Discourse*. New York: Oxford University Press.

Tarrow, Sidney. 1994. *Power in Movement: Social Movements, Collective Action and Politics*. Cambridge, UK: Cambridge University Press.

Tasker, Fiona L. and Susan Golombok. 1997. *Growing Up in a Lesbian Family: Effects on Child Development*. New York: The Guilford Press.

Tec, Nechama. 1986. *When Light Pierced the Darkness: Christian Rescue of Jews in Nazi-Occupied Poland*. New York: Oxford University Press.

Thoits, Peggy A. 1989. "The Sociology of Emotions." *Annual Review of Sociology* 15: 317–42.

Thomas, Keith. 1971. *Religion and the Decline of Magic*. London: Weidenfeld and Nicolson.

Thomas, Mikhail. 2002. "Adult Criminal Court Statistics, 2000/01." *Juristat* 22, 2 (March). Catalogue no. 85-002-XPE. Ottawa: Canadian Centre for Justice Statistics and Statistics Canada.

———. 2004. "Adult Criminal Court Statistics, 2003–04." *Juristat* 24, 12. Catalogue no. 85-002-XPE. Ottawa: Canadian Centre for Justice Statistics and Statistics Canada.

Thomas, William Isaac. 1966 [1931]. "The Relation of Research to the Social Process." Pp. 289–305 in Morris Janowitz, ed. *W.I. Thomas on Social Organization and Social Personality*. Chicago: University of Chicago Press.

Thompson, E. P. 1967. "Time, Work Discipline, and Industrial Capitalism." *Past and Present* 38: 59–67.

Thompson, Ross A. and Paul R. Amato. 1999. "The Postdivorce Family: An Introduction to the Issues." Pp. xi–xxiii in Ross A. Thompson and Paul R. Amato, eds. *The Postdivorce Family: Children, Parenting and Society*. Thousand Oaks, CA: Sage Publications.

Thorne, Barrie. 1993. *Gender Play: Girls and Boys in School*. New Brunswick, NJ: Rutgers University Press.

Tilly, Charles. 1979a. "Collective Violence in European Perspective." Pp. 83–118 in H. Graham and T. Gurr, eds. *Violence in America: Historical and Comparative Perspective*, 2nd ed. Beverly Hills: Sage.

———. 1979b. "Repertoires of Contention in America and Britain, 1750–1830." Pp. 126–55 in Mayer N. Zald and John D. McCarthy, eds. *The Dynamics of Social Movements: Resource Mobilization, Social Control, and Tactics*. Cambridge, MA: Winthrop Publishers.

Tilly, Charles, Louise Tilly, and Richard Tilly. 1975. *The Rebellious Century, 1830–1930*. Cambridge, MA: Harvard University Press.

Tkacik, Maureen. 2002. "The Return of Grunge." *Wall Street Journal* 11 December: B1, B10.

Toffler, Alvin. 1990. *Powershift: Knowledge, Wealth, and Violence at the Edge of the 21st Century*. New York: Bantam.

Tong, Rosemarie. 1989. *Feminist Thought: A Comprehensive Introduction*. Boulder, CO: Westview.

Tönnies, Ferdinand. 1988 [1887]. *Community and Society (Gemeinschaft und Gesselschaft)*. New Brunswick, NJ: Transaction.

Toronto Board of Education. 1993. *The 1991 Every Secondary Student Survey. Part II: Detailed Profiles of Toronto's Secondary School Students*. Toronto: Toronto Board of Education Research Services.

Torpey, J. 2001. "Making Whole What Has Been Smashed: Reflections on Reparations." *The Journal of Modern History* 73: 333–58.

Torrance, Judy M. 1986. *Public Violence in Canada*. Toronto: University of Toronto Press.

Troeltsch, Ernst. 1931 [1923]. *The Social Teaching of the Christian Churches,* Olive Wyon, trans. 2 vols. London, UK: George Allen and Unwin.

Trovato, Frank. 1998. "The Stanley Cup of Hockey and Suicide in Quebec, 1951–1992." *Social Forces* 77, 1 (September): 105–27.

Tschannen, Olivier. 1991. "The Secularization Paradigm: A Systematization." *Journal for the Scientific Study of Religion* 30: 395–415.

Tufts, Jennifer. 2000. "Public Attitudes Toward the Criminal Justice System." *Juristat* 20, 12 (December). Catalogue no. 85-002-XPE. Ottawa: Canadian Centre for Justice Statistics and Statistics Canada.

Tumin, M. 1953. "Some Principles of Stratification: A Critical Analysis." *American Sociological Review* 18: 387–94.

Tun, Paul. 2000. "Polls Show Canadians Not Settled on Abortion." *The Interim* August. On the World Wide Web at http://www.lifesite.net/interim/2000/aug/09pollsshow.html (10 February 2001).

Turcotte, Martin. 2007. "Time Spent with Family During a Typical Workday, 1986 to 2005." *Canadian Social Trends* 82: 2–11. Catalogue no. 11-008-XPE. On the World Wide Web at http://www.statcan.ca/english/freepub/11-008-XIE/2006007/pdf/11-008-XIE20060079574.pdf (26 March 2007).

Turkel, Ann Ruth. 1998. "All About Barbie: Distortions of a Transitional Object." *Journal of the American Academy of Psychoanalysis* 26, 1 (Spring): 165–77.

Turkle, Sherry. 1995. *Life on the Screen: Identity in the Age of the Internet*. New York: Simon & Schuster.

Turner, Bryan S. 1986. *Citizenship and Capitalism: The Debate over Reformism*. London, UK: Allen and Unwin.

U.S. Department of Commerce. 1998. "Statistical Abstract of the United States: 1998." On the World Wide Web at http://www.census.gov/prod/3/98pubs/98statab/sasec1.pdf (8 October 2000).

U.S. Environmental Protection Agency, Office of Air Quality Planning and Standards. 2000. *National Air Pollutant Emission Trends, 1900–1998*. On the World Wide Web at http://www.epa.gov/ttn/chief/trends98/emtrnd.html (3 August 2000).

Ungar, Sheldon. 1992. "The Rise and (Relative) Decline of Global Warming as a Social Problem." *Sociological Quarterly* 33: 483–501.

______. 1999. "Is Strange Weather in the Air? A Study of U.S. National Network News Coverage of Extreme Weather Events." *Climatic Change* 41: 133–50.

United Nations. 1998a. "Universal Declaration of Human Rights." On the World Wide Web at http://www.un.org/Overview/rights.html (25 January 2003).

______. 1998b. "World Population Growth from Year 0 to 2050." On the World Wide Web at http://www.popin.org/pop1998/4.htm (3 July 1999).

______. 2002. *Human Development Report 2002.* New York: Oxford University Press. On the World Wide Web at http://hdr.undp.org/reports/global/2002/en (16 April 2003).

______. 2004. "Human Development Report 2004." On the World Wide Web at http://hdr.undp.org/reports/global/2004/ (1 February 2005).

______. 2006. "Human Development Report 2006." On the World Wide Web at http://hdr.undp.org/hdr2006/pdfs/report/HDR06-complete.pdf (21 April 2007).

United Nations Educational, Scientific, and Cultural Organization (UNESCO). 2002. "Education Goals Remain Elusive in More Than 70 Countries." On the World Wide Web at http://www.unesco.org/bpi/eng/unescopress/2002/02-93e.shtml (6 February 2003).

Useem, Bert. 1998. "Breakdown Theories of Collective Action." *Annual Review of Sociology* 24: 215–38.

Vago, Stephen and Adie Nelson. 2003. *Law and Society*. Don Mills, ON: Pearson Educational Publishing.

Veblen, T. 1899. *The Theory of the Leisure Class*. On the World Wide Web at http://socserv2.socsci.mcmaster.ca/~econ/ugcm/3ll3/veblen/leisure/index.html (29 April 2000).

Vincent, David. 2000. *The Rise of Mass Literacy: Reading and Writing in Modern Europe*. Cambridge, England: Polity Press.

Vygotsky, Lev S. 1987. *The Collected Works of L. S. Vygotsky*, vol. 1, N. Minick, trans. New York: Plenum.

Wald, Matthew L. and John Schwartz. 2003. "Alerts Were Lacking, NASA Shuttle Manager Says." *New York Times* 23 July. On the World Wide Web at http://www.nytimes.com (23 July 2003).

Waldfogel, Jane. 1997. "The Effect of Children on Women's Wages." *American Sociological Review* 62: 209–17.

Wallace, James and Jim Erickson. 1992. *Hard Drive: Bill Gates and the Making of the Microsoft Empire*. New York: John Wiley.

Wallace, M. 2004. "Crime Statistics in Canada, 2003." *Juristat* 24, 6 (July). Catalogue no. 85-002-XPE. Ottawa: Canadian Centre for Justice Statistics and Statistics Canada. On the World Wide Web at http://dsp-psd.pwgsc.gc.ca/Collection-R/Statcan/85-002-XIE/0060485-002-XIE.pdf (8 May 2005).

Wallerstein, Immanuel. 1974–89. *The Modern World-System*, 3 vols. New York: Academic Press.

Wallerstein, Judith S., Julia Lewis, and Sandra Blakeslee. 2000. *The Unexpected Legacy of Divorce: A 25 Year Landmark Study*. New York: Hyperion.

Wanner, R. 1999. "Expansion and Ascription: Trends in Educational Opportunity in Canada, 1920–1994." *Canadian Review of Sociology and Anthropology* 36 (August): 409–42.

Wasserman, Stanley and Katherine Faust. 1994. *Social Network Analysis: Methods and Applications.* Cambridge: Cambridge University Press.

Webb, Eugene J., Donald T. Campbell, Richard D. Schwartz, and Lee Sechrest. 1966. *Unobtrusive Measures: Nonreactive Research in the Social Sciences*. Chicago: Rand McNally.

Weber, Max. 1946. *From Max Weber: Essays in Sociology*, rev. ed., H. Gerth and C. W. Mills, eds. and trans. New York: Oxford University Press.

———. 1947. *The Theory of Social and Economic Organization,* T. Parsons, ed., A. M. Henderson and T. Parsons, trans. New York: Free Press.

———. 1958 [1904–05]. *The Protestant Ethic and the Spirit of Capitalism*. New York: Scribner.

———. 1968 [1914]. *Economy and Society,* Guenther Roth and Claus Wittich, eds. Berkeley, CA: University of California Press.

Weeks, Jeffrey. 1986. *Sexuality.* London: Routledge.

Weinstein, Rhona S. 2002. *Reaching Higher: The Power of Expectations in Schooling.* Cambridge, MA: Harvard University Press.

Weis, Joseph G. 1987. "Class and Crime." Pp. 71–90 in Michael Gottfredson and Travis Hirschi, eds. *Positive Criminology*. Beverly Hills, CA: Sage.

Welch, Michael. 1997. "Violence Against Women by Professional Football Players: A Gender Analysis of Hypermasculinity, Positional Status, Narcissism, and Entitlement." *Journal of Sport and Social Issues* 21: 392–411.

Wellman, Barry and Stephen Berkowitz, eds. 1997. *Social Structures: A Network Approach*, updated ed. Greenwich, CT: JAI Press.

Wellman, Barry, Peter J. Carrington, and Alan Hall. 1997. "Networks as Personal Communities." Pp. 130–84 in Barry Wellman and Stephen D. Berkowitz, eds., *Social Structures: A Network Approach,* updated ed. Greenwich, CT: JAI Press.

Welsh, Sandy. 1999. "Gender and Sexual Harassment." *Annual Review of Sociology* 25: 169–90.

West, Candace and Don Zimmerman. 1987. "Doing Gender." *Gender and Society* 1: 125–51.

Wetzel, Janice Wood. 2001. "Human Rights in the 20th Century: Weren't Gays and Lesbians Human?" Pp. 15–31 in Mary E. Swigonski and Robin S. Mama, eds. *From Hate Crimes to Human Rights: A Tribute to Matthew Shepard*. New York: Haworth Press.

Wheeler, Stanton. 1961. "Socialization in Correctional Communities." *American Sociological Review* 26: 697–712.

Whitaker, Reg. 1987. *Double Standard*. Toronto: Lester and Orpen Dennys.

Whorf, Benjamin Lee. 1956. *Language, Thought, and Reality,* John B. Carroll, ed. Cambridge, MA: MIT Press.

"Why Britney Spears Matters." 2001. *The Laughing Medusa.* On the World Wide Web at http://www.gwu.edu/~medusa/2001/britney.html (18 April 2006).

Whyte, William F. 1981. *Street Corner Society: The Social Structure of an Italian Slum*, 3rd ed. Chicago: University of Chicago Press.

Wilensky, Harold L. 1967. *Organizational Intelligence: Knowledge and Policy in Government and Industry*. New York: Basic Books.

———. 1997. "Social Science and the Public Agenda: Reflections on the Relation of Knowledge to Policy in the United States and Abroad." *Journal of Health Politics, Policy and Law* 22: 1241–65.

Willardt, Kenneth. 2000. "The Gaze He'll Go Gaga For." *Cosmopolitan* April: 232–37.

Willis, Paul. 1984. *Learning to Labour: How Working-Class Kids Get Working-Class Jobs,* reprinted ed. New York: Columbia University Press.

Wolf, Naomi. 1997. *Promiscuities: The Secret Struggle for Womanhood.* New York: Vintage.

Wong, Lloyd and Michele Ng. 1998. "Chinese Immigrant Entrepreneurs in Vancouver: A Case Study of Ethnic Business Development." *Canadian Ethnic Studies* 30: 64–85.

Wood, Julia. 1999. *Everyday Encounters: An Introduction to Interpersonal Communication,* 2nd ed. Belmont, CA: Wadsworth.

Woodbury, Anthony. 2003. "Endangered Languages." *Linguistic Society of America.* On the World Wide Web at http://www.lsadc.org/web2/endangeredlgs.htm (19 July 2003).

Woodrow Federal Reserve Bank of Minneapolis. 2000. "What's a Dollar Worth?" On the World Wide Web at http://woodrow.mpls.frb.fed.us/economy/calc/cpihome.html (8 October 2000).

Workplace Information Directorate. 1996. *Special Tabulation of Strikes Statistics for 1986–95.* Ottawa: Human Resources Development Canada.

World Health Organization. 2001. *World Health Report 2001.* On the World Wide Web at http://www.who.int (11 March 2002).

———. 2002a. "World Report on Violence and Health." Pp. 186–87. On the World Wide Web at http://www.who.int/violence_injury_prevention/violence/world_report/en/full_en.pdf (22 April 2005).

*World Values Survey*. 2003. Machine readable data set. On the World Wide Web at http://www.worldvaluessurvey.org (1 May 2004).

Wortley, Scot, David Brownfield, and John Hagan. 1996. "The Usual Suspects: Race, Age and Gender Differences in Police Contact." Paper presented at the 48th Annual Conference of the American Society of Criminology, Chicago: November.

Wu, Zheng. 2000. *Cohabitation: An Alternative Form of Family Living.* Don Mills, ON: Oxford University Press.

X, Malcolm. 1965. *The Autobiography of Malcolm X.* New York: Grove.

Yancey, William L., Eugene P. Ericksen, and George H. Leon. 1979. "Emergent Ethnicity: A Review and Reformulation." *American Sociological Review* 41: 391–403.

Zald, Meyer N. and John D. McCarthy. 1979. *The Dynamics of Social Movements*. Cambridge, MA: Winthrop.

Zimbardo, Philip G. 1972. "Pathology of Imprisonment." *Society* 9, 6: 4–8.

Zimring, Franklin E. and Gordon Hawkins. 1995. *Incapacitation: Penal Confinement and the Restraint of Crime.* New York: Oxford University Press.

Zogby International. 2001. "Arab American Institute Polls Results: Arab Americans Are Strong Advocates of War Against Terrorism; Overwhelmingly Endorse President Bush's Actions; Significant Numbers Have Experienced Discrimination since Sept. 11." On the World Wide Web at http://www.zogby.com/news/ReadNews.dbm?ID487 (21 December 2002).

## C

## D



## E

## F



## G

## H



## I

## J



## K



## L



## M

## N



## O



## P

## Q



## R

## S

## T

## U



## V



## W

## Y



## Z

# PHOTO CREDITS

### Boxes

**Mass Media and Society:** Shutterstock/Tebenkova Svetlana.

**You and the Social World:** Shutterstock/Losevsky Pavel.

**Social Policy: What Do You Think?:** Shutterstock/Petro Feketa.

**Sociology at the Movies:** Shutterstock/Lou Oates.

### Chapter 1

**2:** Getty Images/Stone/Windsor & Wiehahn. **3:** Lisa M. Ripperton. **6, top:** Courtesy of A.C. Fine Art. Nova Scotia. Photographer: James Chambers. **6, bottom:** Getty Images/Photodisc. **8:** CP Picture Archive/Ryan Remiorz. **11:** CP Picture Archive/20th Century Fox & DreamWorks LLC. **13:** © Musee du Louvre, Paris/Giraudon, Paris/Superstock. **14, top:** © Bettmann/Corbis. **14, bottom:** Courtesy of Columbia University. **15, top:** © The Art Archive/Corbis. **15, bottom:** Brown Brothers. **16:** Carleton University Archives. **17, top:** The Granger Collection, New York. **17, bottom:** American Sociological Association. **18:** Margrit Eichler. **22, left:** Reuters NewMedia Inc./Corbis. **22, right:** David Bergman/Corbis. **25:** © Siegfried Kuttig/Alamy. **28:** Alamy Images/Peter Olive. **30:** Shutterstock/Oleg Kozlov, Sophy Kozlova.

### Chapter 2

**40:** Canadian Press Picture Archives/Kevin Frayer. **41:** CP Picture Archive/Ron Frehm. **43:** Toronto Star/Dick Loek. **46:** TM & © 20th Century Fox. All rights reserved. Courtesy Everett Collection. **47:** © Dinodia/V.H. Mishra. **50:** CP Photo Archives/Steve White. **53:** Courtesy of Kelloggs. **56:** © Owen Franklin/Corbis/Magma. **60:** The Everett Collection. **62:** SuperStock. **64:** CP Picture Archive/Nick Ut. **65:** Getty Images/Rob Loud.

### Chapter 3

**68:** First Light/Tannis Toohey. **70:** Corbis/Magma. **72:** CP Picture Archive/Mike Ridewood. **74:** Index Stock/Key Color. **76, top:** © moodboard/Corbis. **76, bottom:** Courtesy of Carol Gilligan. Photo by Jerry Bauer. **78:** Corbis/David P. Hall. **80:** Getty Images/© Photodisc. **83:** Getty Images/Catherine Ledner. **85:** Getty Images/Digital Vision. **87:** Warner Bros./Getty Images. **90:** ©New Line/Courtesy Everett Collection.

### Chapter 4

**96:** CP Photo Archive/Paul Chiasson. **97:** Photos.com. **100:** SuperStock. **105:** Everett Collection/Magma. **108, all:** Courtesy of Robert J. Brym. **114:** The Everett Collection. **118:** The Everett Collection. **120:** Photos.com. **123:** CP Photo Archive/Adrian Wyld.

### Chapter 5

**132:** image 100/Corbis. **133:** CP Picture Archive/Frank Gunn. **134:** ©WarnerBros/Everett Collection. **136:** National Library of Medicine, Washington, DC. **137:** CP Picture Archive/AP/Ed Betz. **147:** CP Picture Archive/©HBO/Courtesy Everett Collection. **153:** Ted Streshinsky/Corbis/Magma. **154:** CP Picture Archive/Fred Chartrand. **155:** New York Public Library. **156:** CP Picture Archive/Frank Gunn.

### Chapter 6

**164:** Getty Images/Bruce Ayers. **166:** TM & Copyright © 20th Century Fox Film Corp. All rights reserved. **167:** CP Picture Archive/Tibor Kolley. **176:** Getty Images/Stone/Bushnell/Soifer. **180, left:** Agriculture and Agri-Food Canada. **180, right:** BSIP Agency/Index Stock Imagery. **182:** © Walt Disney/Courtesy Everett Collection. **185, left:** CP Picture Archive/Stan Behal. **185, right:** CP Picture Archive/Hans Deryk. **189:** Photo by Miro Cernetig, *Globe and Mail,* Toronto. Reprinted with permission from *The Globe and Mail.* **192:** Weidenfeld and Nicolson Archives. **194:** Brand X Pictures/Jupiter Images.

### Chapter 7

**198:** CP Photo Archive/AP Photo/David Zalubowski. **200:** CP Picture Archive/Andrew Vaughan. **201:** "How to Tell Your Friends From the Japs," 1941, *Time* Magazine, Dec. 22, p. 33. Copyright TIME INC. Reprinted by permission. TIME is a registered trademark of Time Inc. All rights reserved. **206:** © Eyewire/Getty Images. **208, top:** Globe & Mail/Tibor Kolley. **208, bottom:** Bettmann/Corbis. **211, all:** Saskatchewan Archives

Board, R-82239[1] and R-82239[2]. **212:** United Artists/ Courtesy Everett Collection. **215, top:** Upper Canada Gazette, February 10, 1806. **215, bottom:** The Phillips Collection, Washington DC. **218:** National Archives of Canada/C149236. **219:** Canadian Pacific Airlines/ National Archives of Canada/C-45080. **221:** Courtesy of the Pier 21 Society.

### Chapter 8

**229:** Getty Images/Image Source Pink. **231:** © Bernard and Catherine Desjeux/Corbis/Magma. **236, bottom:** Getty Images/Sandy Huffaker. **238:** Myrleen Cate/ IndexStock. **241, all:** Courtesy of the White Rock Beverage Company. **246, top:** CP Picture Archive/ David Lucas. **246, bottom:** © Michael Kooren/Archive Photos, NY. **247:** Focus Features/The Kobal Collection. **251:** Getty Images/Dex Image. **254:** Courtesy of the Canadian Federation of Students. **259:** © SuperStock. **260:** Getty Images/Alex Wong.

### Chapter 9

**266:** Digital Vision/Getty Images. **269:** 20th Century Fox/Courtesy Everett Collection. **272:** Getty Images/ The Image Bank/Tim Bieber. **277:** The Everett Collection. **283:** Jupiter Images/ABStudio. **285:** © Jacques M. Chenet/Corbis/Magma. **287:** © Michael Newman/ PhotoEdit. **292, top:** CP Picture Archive/Clement Allard. **292, bottom:** Jupiter Images/BananaStock. **296:** © Jonathan Blair/Corbis/Magma.

### Chapter 10

**300:** Charles O'Rear/Corbis. **303, top:** CP Photo Archive/Ian Jackson. **303, bottom:** Getty Images/ Angelo Cavalli. **309:** © Bettmann/Corbis/Magma. **312:** Warner Bros./ZUMA/Corbis. **316:** Nathan Benn/ Corbis. **319:** © Omni Photo Communications/Index Stock Imagery. **321:** CP Picture Archive/Jacques Boissinot. **327:** Getty Images/Photodisc. **329:** © The Purcell Team/Corbis/Magma. **330:** CP Photo Archive/ Winnipeg Free Press/Marc Gallant.

### Chapter 11

**338:** Rex Features/The Canadian Press (Jon Santa Cruz). **339:** Bettmann/Corbis. **340:** CP Archives/Toronto Star Syndicate [2003] All Rights Reserved. **342:** U.S. Army Photos. **344:** Shutterstock. **346:** Shutterstock/Armin Rose. **347:** The Everett Collection. **351:** CP Photo Archive/Lee Brown. **360:** CP Photo/Adrian Wyld. **362:** 20th Century Fox/Courtesy Everett Collection. **364:** Bibliotheque Nationale de France. **365, left:** CP Picture Archive/Ryan Remiorz. **365, right:** CP Picture Archive/ Fred Chartrand. **366:** Corbis/Reuters. **367:** CP Picture Archive/Frank Gunn.